CORE MEDIA COLLECTION
FOR ELEMENTARY SCHOOLS

CORE MEDIA COLLECTION FOR ELEMENTARY SCHOOLS

Lucy Gregor Brown

Assisted by

Betty McDavid,
Technical Librarian,
Mt. Diablo Unified School District

R. R. Bowker Company
New York & London, 1978

Published by R. R. Bowker Company
1180 Avenue of the Americas, New York, N.Y. 10036
Copyright © 1978 by Lucy Gregor Brown
All rights reserved.
Printed and bound in the United States of America

Library of Congress Cataloging in Publication Data

Brown, Lucy Gregor.
    Core media collection for elementary schools.

    Includes indexes.
    1. Audio-visual materials—Catalogs. I. Title.
LB1043.Z9B75   016.3731'33   78-11674
ISBN 0-8352-1096-0

CONTENTS

PREFACE

The purpose of *Core Media Collection for Elementary Schools* is to provide a qualitative selection guide to nonprint media titles. The majority of the titles in this book are for sound or captioned filmstrips, kits, recordings, and some 16mm films; however, study prints, art prints, 8mm loops, slides, and transparencies are also listed. They cover a wide variety of subject and ability levels.

In many instances, only the series or set title has been listed as a "main" entry, but parts of the set or series are available separately and should be considered by checking the Contents under the "main" entry. Including these separate items, over 3,000 titles are listed. Although not listed separately, these titles are readily accessible through the expanded use of subject headings. All titles, as sets, series, or individually, should be considered for purchase based on needs and budget requirements.

This collection was developed with the school curriculum needs of students in grades K–6 in mind, but it is expected that librarians working with children in public libraries also will find the recommendations and ordering information helpful in developing their collections. School librarians and teachers will find media noted as appropriate for grade levels as well as suitable for various subjects.

Materials included have been favorably reviewed, are award winners, or have been evaluated for their authenticity, technical quality, appropriateness for the subjects being considered, student level, interest and motivation, accuracy in content, and validity in treatment. It is recognized that not all the titles included are in the award-winning class, just as all entries in print collections are not "classics." However, all entries have generally met the criteria stated and have proven to be of interest to students as well as being directly pertinent to the elementary curriculum.

This list is not intended to replace the selection process by an individual librarian or media specialist. The variables considered in selecting books for a particular library collection apply equally to selecting nonprint material and eliminate the possibility of developing a collection applicable to all schools. Individuals will want to apply their own selection criteria, responsive to local conditions of curriculum design, budget, student interest, nonprint materials currently owned, facilities, and equipment. This guide, featuring selections based on authoritative sources, author experience, and widely accepted criteria, will provide a substantial reduction in time investment in the evaluation process for the acquisition of a viable and accountable collection.

Only a few titles produced before 1973 are listed, since many titles are by nature subject to rapid obsolescence through advances in technological fields, and because of frequent changes in topical areas. Such materials were closely examined before inclusion. Some older materials in such areas as literature, art, and music are included since their date of production is more irrelevant. Some older but excellent materials are not included because they have been withdrawn by producers, or have become impossible to locate with the changes in acquisitions of companies over the past few years. The new "owners" of material are making a mistake when they make it impossible to locate known good materials. New titles released before and even after the cut-off date for this book—February, 1978—have been included prior to the appearance of reviews if they were known and evaluated by the author and met the other prescribed criteria or were known spring award winners.

Inclusion of all other materials in the list was based on favorable reviews in professional review journals and authoritative content area publications such as *Reading Teacher*, *Book-*

list, and *The Instructor*, and/or award winners in major festivals. The 38 librarians and interested and knowledgeable teachers who have been involved in reviewing nonprint materials for a number of major producers over the past six years and have had these reviews published by the Mt. Diablo Unified School District have been included as a source. Finally, some materials have been included based on the author's experience derived from many years working with nonprint materials as a school librarian, as a program administrator of library services in both small and large public school districts, and as an instructor of courses on the evaluation and selection of nonprint materials for the University of California, Berkeley, and San Jose State University.

American Library Association standards, informal discussions at professional meetings with librarians who manage effective media libraries, plus reports from producer/distributor representatives were instrumental in determining the quantities of each of the various medium formats included. Since this list is intended to be a *practical* guide and resource for elementary school librarians and media specialists, it intentionally deviates from the numbers recommended in standards. The limited number of 16mm films, for example, is a reflection of the number of schools that actually purchase few, if any, films. Those included in this book are primarily short films (due to budget considerations) or longer films if there is a lack of less expensive recommended material available. More expensive films are expected to be available from a district, county, regional, or rental source. This is not to be taken as a recommendation against purchasing this valuable medium if possible, but information available about actual school practice indicates that such films are the exceptional purchase, not the norm.

It also may be noted that few 8mm single-concept loop films are included. Lack of review recommendations, as well as the discontinuance of these loops by a number of producer/distributors, is a major reason for the limited number. However, the delight and interest shown this medium by elementary children requires their inclusion. The "attention time span," as well as the ease of handling, makes this a particularly attractive format for young children. Recognition of this valuable teaching tool perhaps has not been fully recognized. If the old adage, "a picture is worth a thousand words" has merit, then a four-minute *moving* picture is well worth the current price, if the need for "motion" is applicable to the concept being presented.

The number of musical recordings included is not indicative of the percentage of recordings that most media libraries should and do purchase. Selections in this medium are so vast and so influenced by the school curriculum, ever-changing student interests, and local budgets, that only some basic music recordings are noted. Reviews for recorded music for elementary schools are sketchy and often incomplete.

My professional background and experience provides me with an understanding of the problems a librarian faces in setting up a new media library or in updating an older print collection. It is the intent of this book to provide reliable titles to make the selection task easier and to provide cataloging information to make the nonprint media compatible with the print collection.

A special thanks for the cooperation of the many people who supported the compilation of this book. Librarians were generous with their time, assistance, and sharing of evaluations. Producers and distributors were responsive in supplying information requested promptly and completely. The editorial staff at Bowker was helpful and understanding. Betty McDavid did a very professional job in the descriptive cataloging and Chris P. Williams, who programmed the computer (and almost became a librarian in the process), both are deserving of recognition. Most of all, my thanks to my husband, Tom, who worked with Chris and the computer and did the final editing before sending the manuscript to Bowker. And, of course, my family, who allowed me the time and gave their support to complete this project, also have my appreciation. Last but not least, Estelle Rash, my typist, with all her library clerk experience kept the project on schedule. From all of us who made this book possible, to all of you who will use it, take the time to read the section on How to Use This Book so you may get the most from it and save the time that we have put in for you.

Lucy Gregor Brown
Program Administrator
Library Services
Mt. Diablo Unified School District

HOW TO USE THIS BOOK

It is extremely important for the reader to examine the Preface of this book to understand completely the purpose and scope of the titles included in this collection. The organization of entries under a subject index and a title index will be explained here as well as some suggestions on how most effectively to use this core media collection of recommended titles. Librarians and media specialists are usually looking for titles in a subject area to meet their nonprint needs rather than looking for specific titles. Therefore, information for selecting, ordering, and cataloging will be found in the main part of the book, "Media Indexed by Subject." However, indications of the correct subject heading in the "Media Indexed by Title" section will enable the person looking for a particular title to locate it readily.

ORGANIZATION OF ENTRIES

Titles are annotated under subjects, with headings based on the *Sears List of Subject Headings* (11th edition). The main entry from each title is listed under its appropriate subject heading, except in cases where the whole of a title is attributable to a single author, composer, artist, or performer. The main entry contains adequate information to be used as both a selection guide and ordering source. The inclusion of the Dewey Decimal number in the main subject entry will assist in the cataloging process for those so involved. Additional subject headings may be necessary for specific school situations, however.

Many main entry titles represent a set or series that includes several individual titles. Usually these individual titles have not been listed separately, but full bibliographic information is given under the set or series title. Most of these individual titles are available from the producer/distributor separately, and if only one or two titles are desired from a set or series, they should be purchased this way. These individual titles will show up in the entry as "Contents." Each main entry is arranged as follows:

TITLE (Medium)
Producer/Distributor, Release Date, Series title, Collation, Order Number (Price). Grade Level, Recommending Sources, Dewey Classification, Contents and Annotation.

The title is followed by its format, spelled out in full. Terms used to designate media are those advocated by the Anglo-American Cataloging Rules. The producer/distributor is in abbreviated form; full names and addresses are given in the Producer/Distributor Directory. The addresses of some producers were not available. The order number is given if the producer uses one or it was available, and the prices are the most current prior to the printing of this book or that could be located. The prices are "list" and do not reflect discounts for quantity orders or prompt payment providing the producers/distributors give such discounts. Price variables due to different formats (phonodiscs or cassettes) are indicated. No black and white 16mm films have been included, although they may be available on request and would be lower in price. Note: Probable general price increases after January 1, 1979.

Production and/or release dates on nonprint materials are often unavailable or unreliable. Every effort has been made to make these as accurate as possible, or they have not been given. The collation includes sufficient physical description to indicate what the type of hardware required may be, in addition to the shelving and circulation requirements.

The recommended range of grade levels is usually K–6, the lowest and highest levels of comprehension or interest for each title. These should not be taken as absolutes, for some materials have no real grade limitations.

Code letters refer to the recommending sources for each title as well as its known awards.

Only three codes have been listed as a maximum even though some have received more. A list of the codes along with the names and addresses of the sources follows these explanatory notes. Some new recommendations have been given to titles since they were originally included in this book, but it has been impossible to update all the completed listings as work progressed. It has been rewarding to see the same titles receive additional recommendations, but in the interest of time they have not been shown.

Following the codes in each entry, a Dewey Decimal classification is given without specifying the media designation. We recommend spelling out the name of the medium rather than using codes, which act as a barrier for the user in locating the needed information, not to mention the lack of consistency in the use of codes available. Additional information about cataloging will be found later in this section.

Supplementary notes, containing such information as the names of performers and the individual titles within a series or set, may follow the Dewey Decimal classification. A brief annotation is included for explanation of the content or treatment of the material, but is omitted infrequently if it is absolutely not valuable.

DESCRIPTIVE CATALOGING AND CLASSIFICATION

Cataloging for items included in this volume is based on the theory and application of rules as found in: *Anglo-American Cataloging Rules* (1967), *Dewey Decimal Classification and Relative Index* (18th edition), *Sears List of Subject Headings* (11th edition), *Nonbook Materials: The Organization of Integrated Collections* (1973), and *ALA Rules for Filing Catalog Cards* (2nd edition). However, the author sometimes departs from these sources for very practical reasons, the most important being service to the ultimate user of library materials: the student, the teacher, the parent volunteer, and others who may not be familiar with library procedure. Of course, librarians, audiovisual specialists, and library technicians are understood to be potential users of the book as well. But for generations library staff members have communicated with one another through esoteric cataloging rules, tending to leave the patron outside the conversation. It is our conviction that simplified, clear cataloging will greatly aid *all* users of library materials.

All library materials (print and nonprint) must be made available to the users through that library index—The Catalog—whether in card form, book style, microfiche, or other format. A pox on the person who believes all materials on the Civil War will be found on the shelf in the 973.7 section! Reference to the catalog must be encouraged. Straightforward, practical cataloging will enhance catalogs and thus the learning environment. Cataloging that has as one of its basic rationales the curriculum of the school will be most useful. Better accountability will be realized and cost effectiveness improved if all items in a multimedia collection can be quickly and accurately located by every user.

Classification and cataloging rationale for this book is discussed below in several parts: Main entry, Added entry, Classification, Subject cataloging, Cross-references.

Main Entry. All entries are by title. The main entry containing all information describing each item will be found under its "main" subject. Other references to each title will refer back to the "main" subject.

Added Entry. Relevant entries are made for author, artist, composer, etc. Some added title entries are made in order to analyze series, where the individual titles are unique and there may be need for recall by the user.

Classification. The Dewey Decimal system was chosen because it is so frequently used by school and public libraries in this country and abroad. Accession numbers are still used by some nonprint libraries as a classifying device. They lack the flexibility inherent in the expandable Dewey system, however. Shelving materials by accession numbers is very rigid, and when materials are not clustered in relative subject areas (as in Dewey) the advantages of user browsing are lost. Serendipity, that great boon to library work, cannot operate as well in the accession number system as it does under Dewey. Interfiling of print and nonprint materials can be accomplished only when the same classifying scheme is used. Where interfiling can be achieved, the best use of all materials will take place.

Through the maintenance of an authority file, the author has been able to be consistent in the use of the Dewey numbers with subject heading choices. It will be noted that abridged numbers are not always chosen even though these materials are being recommended for elementary school library use. It has been our experience that children respond well to the Dewey system when properly instructed. It is often the grown-ups in the learning situation who are concerned about the length of the classification numbers. When all users remember that the decimal in the Dewey system is less an arithmetic concept and more a notation form, eager and accurate use can be made by any child who can count.

Some special uses have been adopted for this book. All fiction is classified using the three letters Fic. This classification includes the so-called picture or easy media. It is felt that this type of material has a far wider use than with primary age students. By classifying it along with other more difficult (in the sense of comprehension) items, this type of material will be acceptable to older youngsters who may need it for remedial work or for sheer enjoyment. The Dewey classification 920 has been adopted for all collected biographies, while 921 has been used for all individual biographies.

Subject Cataloging. Sears Subject Headings were chosen partly for their universality, but also because of their compatibility with curriculum areas. Many nonprint libraries still use lists of curriculum headings as subjects for cataloging. These are judged by the author to be too easily outdated and too limiting in their scope, since they are, by necessity, very general.

Subject headings have been given to all items listed in this book, including fiction, poetry, drama, etc. This practice increases the usefulness of all materials in the curriculum. The authors urge librarians to carry through with this idea to the local card catalog. Sometimes both specific and general headings are given for an item, contrary to the instructions in Sears. It is felt that there is a need to show as complete a picture of the library holdings as possible to the user, who may not be ready to research all possible specifics nor have the patience to do so. Therefore, an item about eagles may be cataloged under that heading, and also under BIRDS, or perhaps under BIRDS OF PREY. Sears is a very flexible system and allows for the free addition of many specific topics not covered in its chosen list. The author has added such cataloger-prepared headings. The authority file keeps usage consistent. Other additions have been made to give access to items that do not fit under the standard headings. It is hoped that the terminology chosen will allow persons to discover these items easily. Representative of such headings are: METAMORPHOSIS, STRING ART, and COMPARISONS.

The "form" headings in Sears are advocated for application to items about the literary form, such as books and software describing fiction, essays, poetry. Many teachers are interested in these materials on form, but they are equally interested in examples of the form to be used in classroom presentations and for individual study by young people. FICTION, of course, is no problem to locate. But AUTOBIOGRAPHIES is a different matter! And so the author has bent the rules a little to allow retrieval of materials through the use of form headings to meet a definite curriculum need.

Because this book has been prepared by computer filing and printing, certain adaptations of the basic library filing rules have had to be made. Machines cannot make the same kind of intellectual decisions that the human mind can make during manual filing. It has been useful to us to refer to Hines and Harris's *Computer Filing of Index, Bibliographic, and Catalog Entries* (Bro-Dart Foundation, 1966). The most noticeable application will be found by the reader in the filing of headings indicating a chronology. Here we have put the dates first before the descriptive words, e.g., U.S.—HISTORY—1775–1783—REVOLUTION. The computer then knows that the Revolution came before the Civil War, and should be filed accordingly. This practice also can aid manual filing and searching, and can be recommended for all catalog preparation.

Cross-References. Three types of cross-references will be found in this book. There are two "See" references. One occurs when the reader has looked under a term that has not been chosen as a subject heading. In that case, the reader will be referred to the proper term; for instance, GANGS. *See* Juvenile Delinquency.

The other "See" reference occurs when a title, but not full information, is given under a subject heading. The reader will be referred to the subject heading where the full (main) information is listed; e.g., TROUT. *See* FISHES.

There is a "See also" reference. It occurs when the reader has looked under a preferred term and finds other related subjects are also suggested; such as ANIMALS. *See also* names of individual types, e.g., BEARS.

The 1970s witnessed a real revolution in the learning resources area. The book remains a basic tool, but has been joined by a myriad of other media. The ranks are ever growing. At the same time the traditional three Rs are being re-emphasized, with more attention to a variety of instructional designs that require a great many materials. The school library in its multimedia form is needed more today than ever before.

The fourth R looms great on the horizon. It cannot be stressed enough. Its name is Retrieval of Information, and it is a skill that must be emphasized early in a student's training. Cataloging of the materials for school media libraries needs to partake more freely of new information science techniques. There must be more points of entry to the cataloging system, even at the risk of redundancy, which has been formerly eschewed by catalogers for economy and a certain intellectual discipline.

Newer technology makes it possible to duplicate catalog cards, store data electronically, and share cataloging information efficiently. There is no longer the need to be parsimonious with catalog information because every character on a card was made by the expensive key stroke of a manual typewriter. Our responsibility to today's student is to increase access to all forms of information. The professional cataloger must be flexible, sensitive, and responsive to the needs of users in order to meet the challenge of today's multimedia world.

RECOMMENDING SOURCES

AAS American Association for the Advancement of Science. 1515 Massachusetts Avenue, N.W., Washington, DC 20005.

AAW *Academy Award Winner.* Academy of Motion Picture Arts and Sciences, 9038 Melrose Avenue, Los Angeles, CA 90069.

ABT *American Biology Teacher.* National Association of Biology Teachers, 11250 Roger Bacon Drive, Reston, VA 22090.

ACI American Council on Consumer Interests, 238 Stanley Hall, University of Missouri, Columbia, MO 65201.

AFF *American Film Festival Award.* Educational Film Library Association, 17 West 60 Street, New York, NY 10023.

AIF Atlanta International Film Festival, Drawer 13258K, Atlanta, GA 30324.

ALR *Annotated List of Recordings in Language Arts.* Schreiber, Morris, NCTE (*see* NCT), 1111 Kenyon Road, Urbana, IL 61801.

ARA *Arts and Activities.* Publishers Development Corporation, 8150 Central Park Avenue, Skokie, IL 60076.

ATE *Arithmetic Teacher.* National Council of Teachers of Mathematics, 1906 Association Drive, Reston, VA 22091.

AUR *Author's Recommendation.* Brown, Lucille Gregor, P. O. Box 615, Alamo, CA 94507.

AVI *A V Instruction.* Association for Educational Communication & Technology, 1201 16 Street, N.W., Washington, DC 20036.

BKL *The Booklist.* American Library Association, 50 East Huron Street, Chicago, IL 60611.

CCI Council on Consumer Interests (*see* ACI).

CFF *Columbus Film Festival.* Chamber of Commerce, Kresge Building, Room 408, 83 South High Street, Columbus, OH 43215.

CGE *CINE Golden Eagle.* Council of International Nontheatrical Events, 1201 16 Street, N.W., Washington, DC 20036.

CHH Children's House. P. O. Box 111, Caldwell, NJ 07006.

CHT *Children Today.* U.S. Government Printing Office, c/o Superintendent of Documents, Washington, DC 20402.

CIF *Chicago International Film Festival.* Chicago Film Board, 415 North Dearborn Street, Chicago, IL 60610.

CPR *Curriculum Product Review.* McGraw-Hill Inc., 230 West Monroe Street, Suite 1100, Chicago, IL 60606.

CRA *Chris Award.* Film Council of Greater Columbus, 8 East Broad Street, Suite 706, Columbus, OH 43215.

EFL *Educational Film Library Association Evaluations.* Educational Film Library Association, 17 West 60 Street, New York, NY 10023.

EGT *English Journal.* National Council of Teachers of English, 1111 Kenyon Road, Urbana, IL 61801.

ELE	*Elementary English (see* LAM).
ESL	*The Elementary School Library Collection.* Bro-Dart Foundation, 1609 Memorial Avenue, Williamsport, PA 17701.
EYR	*Early Years.* 11 Hale Lane, Box 1223, Darien, CT 06820.
FLI	*Film Information Communication Commission.* National Council of Churches, 475 Riverside Drive, Room 853, New York, NY 10027.
FLN	*Film News.* Film News Company, 250 West 57 Street, New York, NY 10019.
FLQ	*Film Library Quarterly.* University of California Press, Berkeley, CA 94720.
GCA	*Gold Camera Award.* U.S. Industrial Film Festival, 161 East Grand Avenue, Suite 216, Chicago, IL 60611.
GGF	*Golden Gate Film Festival.* San Francisco International Film Festival, 425 California Street, San Francisco, CA 94104.
GRT	*Grade Teacher.* Macmillan Professional Magazines, Inc., One Fawcett Place, Greenwich, CT 06830.
HOB	*The Horn Book.* The Horn Book, Inc., 585 Boylston Street, Boston, MA 02116.
IAF	International Animation Film Festival. 45 West 47 Street, New York, NY 10036.
IFF	International Film Festival *(see* IFT).
IFP	Information Film Producers of America Film Festival. P. O. Box 1470, Hollywood, CA 90028.
IFT	*International Film and TV Award.* International FTF Corporation, 251 West 57 Street, New York, NY 10019.
INS	*The Instructor.* Instructor Publications, Inc., 7 Bank Street, Dansville, NY 14437.
JEH	*Journal of Environmental Health.* 1600 Pennsylvania, Denver, CO 80203.
JLD	*Journal of Learning Disabilities.* 101 East Ontario Street, Chicago, IL 60611.
JOR	*Journal of Reading.* International Reading Association, 800 Barksdale Road, Newark, DE 19711.
LAM	*Language Arts Magazine.* National Council of Teachers of English, 1111 Kenyon Road, Urbana, IL 61801.
LBJ	*Library Journal.* R. R. Bowker Company, 1180 Avenue of the Americas, New York, NY 10036.
LFR	*Landers Film Reviews.* Lander's Associates, Box 6970, Los Angeles, CA 90069.
LGB	*Learning Magazine, "Best of the Year."* Education Today Co., Inc., 530 University Avenue, Palo Alto, CA 94301.
LNG	*Learning Magazine.* Education Today Co., Inc., 530 University Avenue, Palo Alto, CA 94301.
LTP	*Listening Post.* Bro-Dart Inc., 1236 South Hatcher, La Puente, CA 91748.
M&M	*Media and Method.* North American Publishing Co., 401 Broad Street, Philadelphia, PA 19108.
MDU	*Validated Nonprint Review List.* Library Media Services Division, Mt. Diablo Unified S.D., 1936 Carlotta Drive, Concord, CA 94519.
MEJ	*Music Educator's Journal.* Music Educator's National Conference, 1902 Association Drive, Reston, VA 22091.
MER	*Media Review.* University of Chicago Laboratory Schools, 1362 East 59 Street, Chicago, IL 60637.
MMT	*K-Eight.* North American Publishing Co., 134 North 13 Street, Philadelphia, PA 19107.
MTE	*Mathematics Teacher.* National Council of Teachers of Mathematics, 1906 Association Drive, Reston, VA 22091.
NCT	National Council of Teachers of English. 1111 Kenyon Road, Urbana, IL 61801.
NEF	National Educational Film Festival. 5555 Ascot Drive, Oakland, CA 94611.

NST   National Science Teachers Association. 1742 Connecticut Avenue, N.W., Washington, DC 20009.

NYF   New York Film and TV Festival. 1865 Broadway, New York, NY 10023.

NYR   *Recordings for Children*. New York Library Association, Box 521, Woodside, NY 11377.

NYT   *New York Times*. 229 West 43 Street, New York, NY 10036.

PRV   *Previews*. R. R. Bowker Company, 1180 Avenue of the Americas, New York, NY 10036.

PVB   *Previews "Best of the Year."* R. R. Bowker Company, 1180 Avenue of the Americas, New York, NY 10036.

RTE   *Reading Teacher*. International Reading Association, 800 Barksdale, Newark, DE 19711.

SAC   *Science and Children*. 1742 Connecticut Avenue, N.W., Washington, DC 20009.

SAM   *Scientific American*. 415 Madison Avenue, New York, NY 10017.

SLJ   *School Library Journal*. R. R. Bowker Company, 1180 Avenue of the Americas, New York, NY 10036.

STE   *Scholastic Teacher*. Scholastic Magazines, Inc., 50 West 44 Street, New York, NY 10036.

TEA   *Teacher (Magazine)*. Beauvais, Paul, publisher, One Fawcett Place, Greenwich, CT 06830.

WLB   *Wilson Library Journal*. 950 University Avenue, Bronx, NY 10452.

MEDIA INDEXED BY SUBJECT

AARDEMA, VERNA

WHY MOSQUITOES BUZZ IN PEOPLE'S EARS (Kit). *See* Animals—Fiction

ACCIDENTS

YOUR INVISIBLE ARMY (Filmstrip—Sound). Filmstrip House/United Learning, 1976. 4 color, sound filmstrips, av. 37–45 fr. ea.; 4 cassettes or discs, av. 6–8 min. ea.; Teacher's Guide. Cassettes #90202 ($60), Discs #90201 ($60). Gr. 2–5. PRV (3/77), PVB (4/78). 614.8

Contents: 1. Peter's Fall and an Enemy Invasion. 2. On Parade. 3. Into Battle. 4. How the Invisible Army Patches Up Peter.

Geared for young school-age children and designed to allay their fears when they have slight accidents that cause pain and bleeding.

ACTING

CHAPLIN—A CHARACTER IS BORN (Motion Picture—16mm—Sound). *See* Chaplin, Charles Spencer

ADOLESCENCE—FICTION

SADDLE UP! (Kit). *See* Horses—Fiction

TEN TALES OF MYSTERY AND TERROR (Cassette). *See* Literature—Collections

TWO FOR ADVENTURE (Kit). *See* Animals—Fiction

ADVENTURE AND ADVENTURERS— FICTION

HUCKLEBERRY FINN (Cassette). *See* U.S.—Social Life and Customs

NO SUCH THING. . . ? (Kit). *See* Mystery and Detective Stories

READING FOR THE FUN OF IT—ADVENTURE (Filmstrip—Sound). *See* Literature—Study and Teaching

THE SEA WOLF MYSTERIES (Kit). *See* Mystery and Detective Stories

STORIES OF ADVENTURE AND HEROISM (Filmstrip—Sound). *See* Reading Materials

SWISS FAMILY ROBINSON (Phonodisc or Cassette). Caedmon Records, 1975. 1 cassette or disc. Cassette #CDL51485 ($7.95), Disc #TC1485 ($6.98). Gr. 4–8. PRV (4/76). Fic

An abridgement of Johann Wyss's famous novel is presented by Anthony Quayle. This is the story of a family washed up on an island and forced to utilize their imagination and knowledge for survival.

ADVERTISING

SOOPERGOOP (Motion Picture—16mm—Sound). Churchill Films, 1975. 16mm, color, sound, animated film, 13 min.; Study Guide. ($205). Gr. 1–A. PRV (10/76). 659.1

A fast, animated story in which 2 irreverent characters concoct a TV commercial for a sweee-e-t cereal. Reveals selling techniques and commercialism behind the fun.

AERONAUTICS

AIRCRAFT: THEIR POWER AND CONTROL (Filmstrip—Sound). Prentice-Hall Media, 1973. 6 color, sound filmstrips; 6 cassettes or discs; 12 Activity Cards; Teacher's Guide. Cassettes #HAC5960 ($108), Discs #HAR5060 ($108). Gr. 4–8. STE (9/73). 629.13

Contents: 1. Lift and Thrust. 2. Controlling an Airplane. 3. How Helicopters Fly. 4. Jet Power. 5. Jet Flight 923. 6. Rocket Power.

An introduction to basic principles of flight and explanation of how various types of aircraft are controlled and propelled.

AESOP

AN AESOP ANTHOLOGY (Filmstrip—Sound). *See* Fables

AESOP (cont.)

THE PONY ENGINE AND OTHER STORIES
FOR CHILDREN (Phonodisc or Cassette).
See Short Stories

AESTHETICS. *See* Esthetics

AFRICA

AFRICA: PORTRAIT OF A CONTINENT
(Filmstrip—Sound). Educational Enrichment Materials, 1976. 6 color, sound filmstrips, av. 56–75 fr.; 6 cassettes or discs 13–
18 min.; 5 Wall Charts; 6 Spirit Duplicating
Masters; 1 Paperback Book. Teacher's Guide.
#51003 ($127). Gr. 4–9. BKL (1977),
LGB (1977). 916
Contents: 1. The Land and Its Resources.
2. The History of a Continent. 3. Religion
and Culture. 4. The Tribal Way of Life. 5.
The New Society. 6. Problems and Pros-
pects.
An excellent overview of the continent of
Africa. Well-written scripts are objective and
show a respect for the people and their culture. The fine visual photos of art objects
are unusually clear. This very informative
kit will hold the attention of the individual
viewer or classroom audience.

AFRICAN CLIFF DWELLERS: THE DOGON
PEOPLE OF MALI, PART ONE (Kit). EMC,
1970. 1 color, sound filmstrip, 74 fr.; 1 cas-
sette, 14 min.; 3 Charts; Teacher's Guide.
#SS-20400 ($50). Gr. 4–9. BKL (10/72),
INS (2/72), M&M (10/70). 916
Contents: 1. Home, Masks and Ancestors:
Village Life.
This program takes a close look at people
who live in total harmony with their envi-
ronment.

AFRICAN CLIFF DWELLERS: THE DOGON
PEOPLE OF MALI, PART TWO (Kit). EMC,
1970. 1 color, sound filmstrip, 67 fr.; 1 cassette, 12 min.; 3 Charts; Teacher's Guide.
#SS-20400 ($50). Gr. 4–9. BKL (10/72),
INS (2/72), M&M (10/70). 916
Contents: 1. Crafts, Culture and the Environment: The Dry Season.
As in Part I, a close look at people who live
in total harmony with their environment.

MODERN AFRICA: LAND/PEOPLE/ART
(Filmstrip—Sound). Educational Dimensions Group, 1976. 2 color, sound filmstrips, 60 fr.; 2 cassettes, 10 min.; 1 Guide.
#821 ($29.50). Gr. 5–6. BKL (5/1/77).
916
Scenic photographs, portraits, models, and
drawings are used to support the narrative
on basic information.

AFRICA, WEST

FAMILIES OF WEST AFRICA: FARMERS
AND FISHERMEN (Filmstrip—Sound).

EBEC, 1974. 4 color, sound filmstrips, av.
79 fr.; 4 cassettes av. 14 min. ea.; Teacher's
Guide. Discs #6498 ($57.95), Cassettes
#6498K ($57.95). Gr. 3–9. ESL (1977),
PRV (5/76). 916.6
Contents: 1. Cocoa Farmer of Ghana. 2.
Farmer of Mali. 3. Fisherman of Liberia. 4.
Rural Medic of the Ivory Coast.
Rural families in 4 West African countries
meet the challenges of survival, using meth-
ods dictated by their individual climates and
geography.

WEST AFRICAN ARTISTS AND THEIR ART
(Filmstrip—Sound). *See* Art, African

AGRICULTURE

FARMING (Film Loop—8mm—Captioned).
See Frontier and Pioneer Life

LIVING ON A FARM (Filmstrip—Sound).
See Farm Life

AIR

LEARNING ABOUT AIR (Motion Picture—
16mm—Sound). ACI Media/Paramount
Communications, 1976. (Learning about
Science). 16mm color, sound film, 11 min.;
Teacher's Guide. #7145 ($190). Gr. K–6.
BKL (1/15/77), EFL (1976), LFR (1/2/77).
551.5
Balloons, sailboats, and windmills all use air
for a purpose. Children learn the properties
of air and enjoy games that are really demonstrations of what air and wind can do.

AIR LINES

AIR TRAVEL TODAY (Filmstrip—Sound).
Society for Visual Education, 1972. 4 color,
sound filmstrips, 59–66 fr.; 2 cassettes or
discs, 10–11 min.; 4 Guides. Discs #223-
SAR ($54), Cassettes #223-SATC ($54).
Gr. 3–6. BKL (6/73), PRV (12/74). 387.7
Contents: 1. Let's Take an Airplane Trip. 2.
The Flight Crew and the Controllers. 3. Preparing a Plane for Flight. 4. Keeping the
Airport Running.
Presents full-color photographs of Chicago's
O'Hare Airport and Washington's National
Airport as well as inflight air travel. Students
share a family's flight experiences and see
how airline employees make a trip enjoyable
and comfortable. They visit behind the
scenes and observe the duties of the person-
nel who keep the big planes in the air, the
maintenance crew that prepares the plane
for flight, and the workers who keep the giant airports functioning.

AIRPLANES—MODELS

MODEL AIRPLANES (Kit). Children's Press,
1976. (Ready, Get-Set, Go). 1 cassette; 1
hardback book; Teacher's Guide. #07558-

6 ($11.95). Gr. 1–8. PRV (9/15/77). 629.122

Students enjoy the photographs and understand the instructions that explain how to choose, build, and fly a model airplane in this high interest, low reading ability set.

ALA NOTABLE CHILDREN'S BOOKS

AS I WAS CROSSING BOSTON COMMON (Filmstrip–Sound/Captioned). *See* Animals–Fiction

THE EMPEROR AND THE KITE (Filmstrip–Sound/Captioned). *See* China–Fiction

ROSIE'S WALK (Motion Picture–16mm–Sound). *See* Animals–Fiction

THE SECRET HIDING PLACE (Filmstrip–Sound or Captioned). *See* Hippopotamus–Fiction

ALASKA

ALASKA: THE BIG LAND AND ITS PEOPLE (Filmstrip–Sound). EBEC, 1975. 5 color, sound filmstrips, av. 100 fr. ea.; 5 discs or cassettes, 12 min. ea.; Teacher's Guide. Discs #6906 ($72.50), Cassettes #6906K ($72.50). Gr. 4–8. BKL (10/75), ESL (1977), PRV (9/75, 76). 917.98

Contents: 1. Alaska: The Big Land. 2. Alaska's Economy: Development or Exploitation? 3. The Core Area: Anchorage and Fairbanks. 4. The Life of the Eskimo: Hooper Bay, Alaska. 5. The Life of the Indian: Arctic Village, Alaska.

This series explores the cultures of the Eskimo and the Alaskan Indian–2 groups who live their lives poised between the old ways and the new, and find that neither life-style solves all their problems. It shows Alaska's problems as well as its promise as it traces the history of the 49th state to its place in the current American scene.

SEEING ALASKA (Filmstrip–Sound). Coronet Instructional Media, 1973. 4 color, sound filmstrips, 50–53 fr.; 2 discs or 4 cassettes, 8–13 min.; Teacher's Guide. #S246 ($65), #M246 ($65). Gr. 4–8. PRV (5/74). 917.98

Contents: 1. Land and Resources. 2. Fishing, Hunting, and Farming. 3. Industry and Commerce. 4. History and People.

In a land with abundant natural resources but rapid population growth, there is controversy between conservationists and the business interests concerning transportation and oil development. This set explores the issues involved.

ALCOHOL

ALCOHOL AND ALCOHOLISM (Filmstrip–Sound). *See* Alcoholism

ALCOHOL AND ALCOHOLISM: THE DRUG AND THE DISEASE (Filmstrip–Sound). *See* Alcoholism

WHAT ARE YOU GOING TO DO ABOUT ALCOHOL (Filmstrip–Sound). Guidance Associates, 1975. 2 color, sound filmstrips, av. 68 fr. ea.; 2 discs or cassettes, av. 8 min. ea.; Teacher's Guide. Discs #9A-301-182 ($52.50), Cassettes #9A-301-190 ($52.50). Gr. 5–8. PRV (4/76). 301.47

In Part I, basic facts of the physical and psychological effects of alcohol are presented and factors motivating alcohol use are explored. Part II consists of dramatized vignettes about peer pressure, advertising, parental models, and drunk driving as they relate to alcohol use.

ALCOHOLISM

ALCOHOL AND ALCOHOLISM (Filmstrip–Sound). Imperial Educational Resources, 1977. 4 color, sound filmstrips, av. 70–76 fr.; 4 discs or cassettes, av. 10–13 min. Cassettes #3KG-68300 ($62), Discs #RG-68300 ($56). Gr. 5–12. BKL (12/15/77). 616.861

Contents: 1. What Is Alcohol? 2. Why People Drink. 3. Teenagers and Drinking. 4. The Counterattack on Despair.

Diagrams, ancient artwork, and photos depict the tradition of the pleasures and problems of drinking alcohol.

ALCOHOL AND ALCOHOLISM: THE DRUG AND THE DISEASE (Filmstrip–Sound). University Films/McGraw-Hill Films, 1975. 4 color, sound filmstrips, av. 66 fr.; 4 cassettes or discs, 12 min.; Teacher's Guide. ($72). Gr. 5–12. ABT (5/77), NST (9/76), PRV (3/77). 616.861

Contents: 1. Alcohol and the Human Body. 2. Alcohol Abuse and Society. 3. Alcoholism and Youth. 4. Alcoholism: Danger Signals.

A comprehensive look at America's most widely used and abused drug. Each filmstrip probes a particular aspect of the problem of student drinking, to create a thought-provoking forum for discussion and to give young people the information they need to formulate healthy personal attitudes toward the use of alcohol.

ALCOTT, LOUISA MAY

CHILDHOOD OF FAMOUS WOMEN. VOLUME THREE (Cassette). *See* Women–Biography

LITTLE WOMEN (Phonodisc or Cassette). *See* Family Life-Fiction

ALEXANDER, LLOYD

LLOYD ALEXANDER (Filmstrip–Sound). *See* Authors

ALGEBRA

SIGNED NUMBERS (Filmstrip—Sound).
See Arithmetic

ALGERIA

ALGIERS: A STEP INTO THE FUTURE, A
STEP INTO THE PAST (Filmstrip—Sound).
National Film Board of Canada/Donars Productions, 1976. 1 color, sound filmstrip,
108 fr.; 1 cassette, 13 min.; 1 Guide. ($25).
Gr. 5-8. BKL (7/1/77). 916.5
Helps promote a better understanding of Algeria. Homes, food, leisure activities, jobs,
religion, education, culture, and history are
discussed.

ALIKI

THRESHOLD FILMSTRIPS, SERIES C (Kit).
See Children's Literature—Collections

ALLEN, ROACH VAN

LANGUAGE EXPERIENCES IN READING:
LEVEL 1 (Kit). *See* English Language—
Study and Teaching

LANGUAGE EXPERIENCES IN READING:
LEVEL 2 (Kit). *See* English Language—
Study and Teaching

LANGUAGE EXPERIENCES IN READING:
LEVEL 3 (Kit). *See* English Language—
Study and Teaching

ALLIGATORS

ALLIGATOR—BIRTH AND SURVIVAL
(Film Loop—8mm—Silent). Walt Disney
Educational Media, 1966. 8mm color, silent
film loop, approx. 4 min. #62-5053L ($30).
Gr. K-12. MDU (1978). 598.14
Baby alligators are viewed as they hatch and
head for water. They are shown running
into danger from an adult alligator and a
hungry raccoon.

BIG GATOR OF THE EVERGLADES (Kit).
Classroom Complements/EBEC, 1976. (Animal Life Stories). 1 color, sound filmstrip;
1 cassette; 5 identical Storybooks; Teacher's
Guide. #6970 ($27.95). Gr. K-6. TEA
(11/77). 598.14
Young readers can learn how alligators move,
build homes, and fight for food and survival,
as this scientifically accurate story describes
the lives of alligators in their natural habitat.
A storybook reproduces all the narration and
full-color art from the filmstrip.

ALPHABET

BRIAN WILDSMITH FROM A-Z (Study
Print). Franklin Watts. 26 posterweight
stock cardboard, 10 in. X 12 in. unmounted
color prints. Text on reverse side of each
print. #2686-8 ($9.95). Gr. K-3. PRV
(12/75). 411
Each letter of the alphabet is given on a
brightly illustrated card, with upper and
lower case letters. Some are illustrated
with animals, others with familiar objects.

LET'S LEARN THE ALPHABET (Filmstrip—
Sound). Troll Associates, 1973. 8 color,
sound filmstrips, av. 47 fr. ea.; 4 cassettes,
av. 7 min. ea.; Teacher's Guide. ($96). Gr.
K-1. BKL (11/1/73), PRV (10/74). 411
Contents: 1. Capital A-H. 2. Capital I-Q.
3. Capital R-Z. 4. Numerals 0-10. 5. Small
a-i. 6. Small j-r. 7. Small s-z. 8. Capital
and Small Letters Together.
Alphabet sounds and shapes introduced,
with recognition of upper and lower case letters stressed, and similar letters contrasted
and compared. Also introduces numerals
0-10.

LET'S WRITE THE ALPHABET (Filmstrip—
Sound). Troll Associates, 1973. 8 color,
sound filmstrips, av. 52 fr. ea.; 4 cassette
tapes, av. 11 min. ea.; Teacher's Guide.
($96). Gr. 2-4. BKL (11/73), PRV (10/
74). 411
Contents: 1. Transition: Recognizing Cursive Capitals. 2. Making Cursive Capitals A-
H. 3. Making Cursive Capitals I-Q. 4. Making Cursive Capitals R-Z. 5. Transition:
Recognizing Cursive Small Letters. 6. Making Cursive Small a-i. 7. Making Cursive
Small j-r. 8. Making Cursive Small s-z.
Introduces and reinforces cursive writing
techniques, and helps young children make
the transition from manuscript printing.

TROLL TALKING PICTURE DICTIONARY
(Kit). *See* English Language—Dictionaries

ALPHABET BOOKS

AS I WAS CROSSING BOSTON COMMON
(Filmstrip—Sound/Captioned). *See* Animals—Fiction

MARY POPPINS FROM A TO Z (Phonodisc
or Cassette). Caedmon Records. 1 cassette
or disc, approx. 60 min. Disc #TC1254
($6.98), Cassette #CDL51254 ($7.95). Gr.
K-3. LBJ, NYR. Fic
The purpose of this record is to teach children recognition of consonant and vowel
sounds by means of 26 Mary Poppins Happenings created around each letter of the alphabet. Robert Stephens reads the stories.
Music is composed and conducted by Leslie
Pearson.

AMBRUS, VICTOR G.

THE THREE POOR TAILORS (Filmstrip—
Sound). *See* Folklore—Hungary

AMERICA—ANTIQUITIES

DIGGING UP AMERICA'S PAST (Filmstrip—Sound). National Geographic, 1977. 5 color, sound filmstrips, 42–50 fr.; 5 cassettes or discs, 11–14 min.; Teacher's Guide. Cassettes #03240 ($74.50), Disc #03239 ($74.50). Gr. 5–12. PRV (3/78), PVB (4/78). 970.01

Contents: 1. North America before Columbus. 2. Middle America before Cortes. 3. South America before Pizarro. 4. The First Europeans in the Americas. 5. Colonization and After.

Covers archeological techniques and discoveries in the Americas.

AMERICA—EXPLORATION

DIGGING UP AMERICA'S PAST (Filmstrip—Sound). *See* America—Antiquities

AMERICAN FAMILIES

FAMILIAS NORTEAMERICANAS—AMERICAN FAMILIES (Filmstrip—Sound). *See* Family Life

AMERICAN POETRY

AMERICAN POETRY TO 1900 (Phonodiscs). Lexington Recording Company. 2 discs. ($16.95). Gr. 4–12. ALR. 808.81

Read by Nancy Marchand and others, poems by 20 American authors from Ann Bradstreet to Walt Whitman.

PAUL REVERE'S RIDE AND HIS OWN STORY (Cassette). Children's Classics on Tape, 1974. 1 cassette; Teacher's Guide. #130 ($9.50). Gr. 4–8. PRV (5/74). 811

Longfellow's poem *Paul Revere's Ride* is read, followed by Revere's own story of the famous night, as told 30 years later in a letter to a friend.

AMISH

THE AMISH: A PEOPLE OF PRESERVATION (Motion Picture—16mm—Sound). Heritage Productions/EBEC, 1976. 16mm color, sound film, 28 min. #3399 ($380). Gr. 4–A. BKL (2/77), CGE (7/76), M&M (12/77). 289.7

This documentary captures the sensitivity and humility of the Amish people, while examining their religious beliefs, closeness to nature, and strong sense of community. Viewers get an intimate look at a people who differ from most of society in fundamental ways, while proudly preserving their own values.

AMPHIBIANS

AMPHIBIANS (Filmstrip—Sound). Educational Development, 1973. 4 color, sound filmstrips, av. 42 fr.; 4 cassettes or discs, 11–13 min. Discs #401-R ($48), Cassettes #L01-C ($51.80). Gr. 5–8. BKL (7/1/74). 597.6

Contents: 1. Amphibians of North America. 2. Frogs and Toads. 3. Salamanders. 4. Catching and Caring for Amphibians.

This set gives a simple definition of vertebrates, explains in what ways amphibians differ from vertebrates, points out the habits and characteristics of frogs and toads, examines the life cycle of a typical amphibian, and describes putting an aquarium and a terrarium together. Photographs and drawings are used as illustrations.

ANATOMY

THE HUMAN BODY (Filmstrip—Sound). Clearvue, 1976. 6 color, sound filmstrips, 52–58 fr.; 6 cassettes or discs, 8–8:31 min.; 1 Guide. Cassettes #CL443-C ($81.50), Discs #CL443-R ($81.50). Gr. 3–6. BKL (9/15/77), TEA. 611

Contents: 1. Blood, Blood Vessels, and the Heart. 2. The Digestive System. 3. The Respiratory System. 4. The Nervous System. 5. Bones and Muscles. 6. Eyes and Ears.

Sam, the Invisible Man, is a leading character and the major attraction of the doctor-narrator's discussions of the human body. Sam can graphically display the basics of human anatomy and the internal structure.

HUMAN BODY AND HOW IT WORKS (Filmstrip—Sound). Troll Associates, 1974. 6 color, sound filmstrips av. 45 fr. ea.; 3 cassettes av. 16 min. ea.; Teacher's Guide. ($78). Gr. 6–9. PRV (4/75). 611

Contents: 1. Respiratory System. 2 Circulatory System. 3. Muscle and Skeletal System. 4. Nervous System. 5. Digestive System. 6. Reproductive System.

Introduces the basic functions of the human body, using diagrams with photographs. The material is in a precise, logical, easy-to-understand format. (Note: The strip on reproduction is tastefully and scientifically done, but careful previewing may be needed before use in some communities.)

THE HUMAN BODY, SET ONE (Filmstrip—Sound). University Films/McGraw-Hill Films, 1975. 4 color, sound filmstrips, av. 59 fr. ea.; 4 cassettes or discs, 11 min. ea.; Teacher's Guide. Cassettes #102579-0 ($72), Discs #103964-3 ($72). Gr. 4–8. BKL (11/1/76), SAC (1/77). 611

Contents: 1. The Teeth. 2. The Skin, Hair, and Nails. 3. The Eyes. 4. The Ears.

An introduction to human physiology from the outside in. The filmstrips view anatomical structure and function as they relate to the countless activities we do every day. The physiological answers are concise and are visualized in ways students can easily

ANATOMY (cont.)

relate to and remember. Specially designed transparency illustrations build anatomical structures layer by layer to clarify relationships.

THE HUMAN BODY, SET TWO (Filmstrip— Sound). University Films/McGraw-Hill Films, 1975. 5 color, sound filmstrips, av. 59 fr. ea.; 5 cassettes or discs, 11 min. ea.; Teacher's Guide. Cassettes #102584-7 ($90), Discs #103973-2 ($90). Gr. 4–8. ABT (5/77). 611

Contents: 1. The Respiratory System. 2. The Nervous System. 3. The Digestive System. 4. The Circulatory System. 5. The Muscular and Skeletal System.

The filmstrips view anatomical structure and function as they relate to the countless activities we do every day. The physiological answers are concise and are visualized in ways students can easily relate to and remember. Specially designed transparency illustrations build anatomical structures layer by layer to clarify relationships.

ANATOMY, COMPARATIVE

AN INSIDE LOOK AT ANIMALS (Study Print). Kenneth E. Clouse, 1974. 14 heavy stock cardboard, unmounted prints, 11 in. X 14 in. ($16). Gr. 5–9. PRV (11/75). 591.4

These are x-ray photographs with color added to enhance interest and highlight details of the skeletal structure. Included are such things as the top and side view of a frog, the bat (which shows the fingers on its wings), the remnants of a pelvic girdle on a snake, and eggs inside a turtle's body. On the reverse side of each print is a black-and-white photo of the animal, a labeled diagram pointing out all the details revealed by the x-ray, a list of key vocabulary words, and a 400-word text that explains the x-ray, the animal's group, and other facts about the animal.

ANDERSEN, HANS CHRISTIAN

ANDERSEN'S FAIRY TALES (Filmstrip— Sound). See Fairy Tales

THE EMPEROR'S NEW CLOTHES AND OTHER TALES (Phonodisc or Cassette). See Fairy Tales

HANS CHRISTIAN ANDERSEN CASSETTE-BOOKS (Kit). See Fairy Tales

LIBRARY 5 (Cassette). See Literature— Collections

THE LITTLE MATCH GIRL AND OTHER TALES (Phonodisc or Cassette). See Fairy Tales

THE LITTLE MERMAID (Phonodisc or Cassette). See Fairy Tales

THE PIED PIPER AND OTHER STORIES (Phonodisc or Cassette). See Fairy Tales

SNOW QUEEN (Phonodisc or Cassette). See Fairy Tales

THE SNOW QUEEN (Cassette). See Fairy Tales

TALES OF HANS CHRISTIAN ANDERSEN (Filmstrip—Sound). See Fairy Tales

THE UGLY DUCKLING AND THE STORY OF HANS CHRISTIAN ANDERSEN (Cassette). See Fairy Tales

ANGLO-SAXON LITERATURE

BEOWULF AND THE MONSTERS (Cassette). See Beowulf

ANIMALS

ANIMAL KINGDOM, SET ONE (Filmstrip— Sound). Random House, 1977. 2 color, sound filmstrips, 52–60 fr.; 2 discs or cassettes, 10–11 min.; Teacher's Guide. Cassettes #5071-1 ($39), Discs #5070-3 ($39). Gr. 4–8. LGB (1977), PRV (1/78). 591.5

Contents: 1. Sharks. 2. Lions.

This set was produced in collaboration with the New York Zoological Society and the New York Aquarium. The sets are brief and interesting. Photographs and drawings are used to present factual information in cooperation with a clearly narrated script.

ANIMALS AND HOW THEY GROW (Filmstrip—Sound). National Geographic, 1976. 5 color, sound filmstrips, av. 45–50 fr. ea.; 5 phonodiscs or cassettes, av. 11–14 min. ea.; 2 Teacher's Guides. Disc #03776 ($74.50), Cassette #03777 ($74.50). Gr. K–4. PRV (1/77). 591.3

Contents: 1. Mammals. 2. Fish. 3. Birds. 4. Amphibians and Reptiles. 5. Insects.

Each sound filmstrip contains several examples of the class of animal it is examining. The many similarities of the examples and changes in the growth of young animals are observed.

BACKYARD SCIENCE SERIES TWO: SPIDERS, SNAILS, FISH, REPTILES (Filmstrip—Sound). See Natural History

BEAR COUNTRY AND BEAVER VALLEY (Filmstrip—Sound). See Natural History

ENDANGERED SPECIES: MAMMALS (Study Print). See Rare Animals

JAGUAR: MOTHER AND CUBS (Film Loop —8mm—Silent). See Jaguars

OUR ANIMAL TREE (Filmstrip—Sound). Coronet Instructional Media, 1974. 4 color, sound filmstrips, av. 53 fr.; 2 discs or 4 cassettes, av. 10 min. Discs #S306 ($65), Cassettes #M306 ($65). Gr. K–3. BKL

(9/15/75); INS (8/9/76), PVB (1975–76). 591.5

Contents: 1. Backyard Neighbors. 2. Hopscotches, the Robin. 3. Rippletail, the Squirrel. 4. Red Cap, the Woodpecker.

Squirrels and various kinds of birds that frequent the northern residential areas are presented. Photography is clear and colorful. The narrator explains the bird calls and sounds and the habits of the backyard neighbors.

POUCHED ANIMALS AND THEIR YOUNG (Film Loop—8mm—Silent). Walt Disney Educational Media, 1966. 8mm color, silent film loop, approx. 4 min. #62-5253L ($30). Gr. K–12. MDU (1978). 599.2

Shows the childbearing habits of these animals. Closeups of a baby wombat struggling to enter its mother's pouch. A phalanger climbs in a tree, the young clinging to its back.

WILDLIFE STORIES (Filmstrip—Sound). Society for Visual Education, 1974. 6 color, sound filmstrips, 58–61 fr.; 3 discs or cassettes, av. 16 min. Discs #402-SAR ($83), Cassettes #402-SATC ($83). Gr. 4–7. BKL (7/1/75), PRV (4/76). 591

Contents: 1. Curly and Simba: Twin African Lions. 2. Beishung: The Giant Panda. 3. Buffy: The Sea Otter. 4. Coco and Chacha: The Coatis. 5. Windy: The Snow Goose. 6. Koolah: The White Koala.

These stories explore the lives, behavior, and natural environments of animals in the wild. Each sound filmstrip teaches natural science facts examining social relationships, survival techniques, feeding and breeding habits, and communications systems.

See also Names of orders and classes of animals, i.e., Mammals; and also names of individual animals, i.e., Bears, Lions, etc.

ANIMALS—AFRICA

ANIMALS OF AFRICA (Motion Picture—16mm—Sound). Coronet Instructional Media, 1977. 16mm color, sound film, 13 min.; Teacher's Guide. #3751 ($195). Gr. K–4. INS (12/77). 591.96

Roaming their natural habitat, the great national parks of Africa, rhinoceroses, leopards, lions, and zebras illustrate many science insights. Their speed, grace, ferocity, or gentleness will trigger many language arts activities.

ANIMALS—ANTARCTIC

CREATURES OF THE ANTARCTICA (Filmstrip—Sound). *See* Antarctic Regions

ANIMALS—FICTION

AS I WAS CROSSING BOSTON COMMON (Filmstrip—Sound/Captioned). Listening Library, 1976 (Look, Listen & Read).

Color, captioned filmstrip w/sound on cassette; 36 fr., 35mm; 11 min. cassette with manual and automatic advance; Teacher's Guide. ($14.95). Gr. 1–4. BKL (2/1/78), LGB (1977). Fic

Narration as well as illustrations are taken directly from the book by Arnold Lobel. A pedestrian encounters a variety of strange and exotic animals that really exist in distant lands.

THE CAT THAT WALKED BY HIMSELF AND OTHER JUST SO STORIES (Phonodisc or Cassette). Caedmon Records, 1965. 1 cassette or disc. Disc #TC1139 ($6.98), Cassette #CDL51139 ($7.95). Gr. K–6. AUR (1978), ESL, NCT. Fic

Contents: 1. The Cat That Walked by Himself. 2. The Butterfly That Stamped. 3. How the First Letter Was Written.

Humorous, whimsical, and suspense-filled stories by Rudyard Kipling, performed by Boris Karloff.

DOCTOR DOLITTLE (Filmstrip—Sound). Films, 1976. 2 color, sound filmstrips, approx. 200 fr.; 2 cassettes, 20 min.; Teacher's Guide. ($49). Gr. 3–6. MDU (4/77). Fic

Contents: 1. Part I. 2. Part II.

The film version of the famous doctor and his animals transferred to a sound filmstrip presentation.

FARMER PALMER'S WAGON RIDE (Filmstrip—Sound). Miller-Brody Productions, 1974 (Famous Author/Illustrator Filmstrips). 2 color, sound filmstrips; 2 cassettes or discs. Cassettes ($32), Discs ($32). Gr. K–3. BKL (10/1/77). Fic

The comedy of William Steig's book reproduced through his illustrations, low-key narration, and fitting background music.

JUST SO STORIES AND OTHER TALES (Phonodisc or Cassette). Caedmon Records, 1956. 1 cassette or disc, approx. 55 min. Disc #TC1028 ($6.98), Cassette #CDL51038 ($7.95). Gr. K–6. ESL, NCT, NYR. Fic

Contents: 1. How the Whale Got His Throat. 2. How the Camel Got His Hump. 3. How the Rhinoceros Got His Skin. 4. The Jungle Book: Mowgli's Brothers (Abridged).

This reading by Boris Karloff of tales by Kipling includes many old favorites.

JUST SO STORIES BY RUDYARD KIPLING (Filmstrip—Sound). Spoken Arts/Eye Gate Media, 1974. 4 color, sound filmstrips, 40–45 fr.; 4 cassettes or discs, av. 8 min.; Teacher's Guide. Cassettes #TA2036 ($79.95), Discs #DA2026 ($79.95). Gr. 1–4. PRV (9/75), PVB (4/76). Fic

Contents: 1. How the Whale Got His Throat. 2. How the Camel Got His Hump. 3. How the Rhinoceros Got His Skin. 4. The Sing Song of Old Man Kangaroo.

ANIMALS—FICTION (cont.)

Go on a fanciful flight with a collection of animals that offers absurd explanations of the origins of some of the species's characteristics—and some keen insights into human behavior. The stories are the classic versions and the illustrations are well done.

A KISS FOR LITTLE BEAR (Filmstrip—Sound). *See* Bears—Fiction

MOWGLI AND THE WOLVES (Cassette). Children's Classics on Tape, 1975. 1 cassette (2 parts), 45 min.; Study Guide. #CCT-102,142,144. ($10.95). Gr. K-8. PRV (1/75). Fic

Mowgli is adopted by a family of wolves. He is befriended by Baloo the Bear and Bagheera the Black Panther. When Mowgli grows up, he must confront his old enemy, Shere Khan the Tiger.

THE MULE WHO REFUSED TO BUDGE (Filmstrip—Sound/Captioned). *See* Cooperation—Fiction

RED DOG BY RUDYARD KIPLING (Phonodisc or Cassette). Caedmon Records, 1975. 1 cassette or disc. Disc #TC1482 ($6.98), Cassette #CDL51482 ($7.95). Gr. 3-6. AUR (1978). Fic

The stories of Mowgli and the animals of the Indian jungle have always had a particular attraction. Anthony Quayle reads this story.

RIKKI TIKKI TAVI AND WEE WILLIE WINKIE (Phonodisc or Cassette). Caedmon Records. 1 cassette or disc, approx. 55 min. Disc #TC1257 ($6.98), Cassette #CDL51257 ($7.95). Gr. K-6. SLJ. Fic

Contents: 1. Rikki-Tikki-Tavi. 2. Wee Willie Winkie.

Rudyard Kipling's story of Rikki-Tikki-Tavi involves the defeat of 2 cobras by a pet mongoose. This is a story found in numerous cultures, sometimes with a less happy ending. Wee Willie Winkie deals not with animals, but with a 6-year-old boy who becomes a hero.

ROSIE'S WALK (Motion Picture—16mm—Sound). Weston Woods Studios, 1970. 16mm color, sound, animated film, 5 min. ($120). Gr. K-6. AFF (1971), BKL (6/15/71), CGE (1972). Fic

Adapted from the book *Rosie's Walk* by Pat Hutchins. What Rosie doesn't know and the graphic illustrations reveal is that a fox stalks close behind the proud little hen. To the tune of "Turkey in the Straw," Rosie struts across the barnyard, keeping her country cool and unwittingly leading the fox into one disaster after another. The book on which the film is based was recommended by the American Library Association as a notable title in 1968.

RUDYARD KIPLING STORIES (Filmstrip—Sound). Xerox Educational Publications, 1976. 6 color, sound filmstrips; 6 cassettes; 3 Teaching Guides. #SC02700 ($110). Gr. K-8. CGE (1976), LGB (12/77). Fic

Contents: 1. The White Seal. 2. Rikki-Tikki-Tavi. 3. Mowgli's Brothers.

Adapted from the film version of the award-winning Kipling films.

THE SECRET HIDING PLACE (Filmstrip—Sound or Captioned). *See* Hippopotamus—Fiction

SQUAWK TO THE MOON, LITTLE GOOSE (Filmstrip—Sound). Viking Press, 1975. 1 color, sound filmstrip, 40 fr.; 1 cassette, 6:48 min.; 1 Guide. #670-90532-1 ($13.95). Gr. K-3. BKL (11/1/74), PRV (3/76), PVB (4/77). Fic

Barbara Cooney's watercolor illustrations from the book of the same title are used to unfold the tale of a disobedient gosling.

THE SURPRISE PARTY (Filmstrip—Sound). Weston Woods Studios, 1973. 1 color, sound filmstrip, 30 fr.; 1 cassette, 6 min. #SF139C ($12.75). Gr. K-3. PRV (12/73). Fic

Based on Pat Hutchin's charming story of Rabbit who is having a party tomorrow. "It's a surprise," he tells his friend Owl. Following the lines of the old game of "gossip," Owl tells Squirrel a modified story of what he was told by Rabbit. This friend, in turn, tells someone else . . . and so it goes with many conflicting stories as to what Rabbit is really going to do.

TREASURY OF BEATRIX POTTER STORIES (Filmstrip—Sound). Spoken Arts/Eye Gate Media, 1974. 4 color, sound filmstrips, 38-51 fr.; 4 discs or cassettes, 7:30-11:30 min.; Spirit Master; Teacher's Guide. Discs #SA2025 ($60), Cassettes #SAC2025 ($66). Gr. K-4. BKL (2/15/75), PRV (2/75), PVB (5/75). Fic

Contents: 1. The Tale of Peter Rabbit. 2. The Tale of Benjamin Bunny. 3. The Tale of Squirrel Nutkin. 4. The Tale of Mr. Jeremy Fisher.

This representation of 4 Potter tales is typical of her work, and perhaps these choices best introduce the wonderful Potter Land. The text is unaltered and the original illustrations are used, supplemented by a few present-day ones.

TWO FOR ADVENTURE (Kit). EMC, 1976. 2 color, sound filmstrips, 66-68 fr.; 2 cassettes, 2 paperback books; Activities and Duplicating Masters; Teacher's Guide. #EL-235000 ($63). Gr. 5-12. PRV (11/76). Fic

Contents: 1. The Incredible Journey. 2. Gifts of an Eagle.

A sound filmstrip accompanies each book but does not tell the story. Rather, the background of the story is presented as motivation to read the books. A dramatic reading cassette, in which parts of each book are read by a narrator, accompanies each book.

THE VOYAGES OF DOCTOR DOLITTLE (Filmstrip—Sound). Miller-Brody Productions, 1976 (Newbery Award). 2 color, sound filmstrips, av. 119 fr.; 2 cassettes or discs, av. 23 min.; 1 Guide. Cassettes #NSF-3069C ($32), Discs #NSF-3069 ($32). Gr. 2–5. BKL (5/15/77), LGB (1977). Fic
The exotic adventures of the unusual, round little man, John Dolittle, portrayed in Hugh Lofting's 1923 Newbery Award book, have been adapted to the sound filmstrip format in this presentation.

WHY MOSQUITOES BUZZ IN PEOPLE'S EARS (Kit). Society for Visual Education, 1976. 1 hardbound book; 1 cassette, 12 min.; 1 poster; 2 hand puppets; 1 Teacher's Guide. #MK-3000 ($35). Gr. K–3. BKL (5/15/77). 398.2
This kit, based on the 1976 Caldecott Medal book written by Verna Aardema and illustrated by Leo and Diane Dillon, focuses on value judgments.

THE WIND IN THE WILLOWS (Phonodisc or Cassette). Listening Library, 1974. 4 discs, 33-1/3 rpm with paperback book; 4 cassettes with paperback book, 185 min. Discs #AA-3392/94 ($22.95), Cassettes #CS392/4 ($22.95). Gr. 3–6. ESL (1977), LTP (5/75), PRV (4/75). 828.8
Mole, Rat, and Badger are kept busy trying to keep Toad out of trouble, and Toad has a series of exciting if not harrowing adventures before all ends well.

WINNIE THE POOH (Phonodiscs). Argo Records, 1975. 3 discs. #ZSW537-539 ($20.94). Gr. K–6. PRV (11/76). Fic
The album is a reading of the 10 stories from Winnie the Pooh. The narrator is British actor Norman Shelley, who created "Winnie the Pooh" for BBC.

THE WORLD OF JUNGLE BOOKS, SET ONE (Kit). Spoken Arts, 1976. 4 cassettes, 22–28 min.; 40 books (4 titles); 1 Guide. #SAC-6505 ($59.95). Gr. 5–A. BKL (9/15/77). Fic
Contents: 1. Mowgli's Brothers. 2. Rikki-Tikki-Tavi. 3. Tiger! Tiger! 4. Toomai of the Elephants.
This cassette-paperback set effectively presents Rudyard Kipling's characters in these high adventure stories.

THE WORLD OF JUST SO STORIES, SET ONE (Kit). Spoken Arts, 1976. 4 cassettes, av. 7–9 min.; 40 books (4 titles); 1 Guide. #SAC-6503 ($59.95). Gr. K–12. BKL (10/15/77). Fic
Contents: 1. How the Whale Got His

Throat. 2. The Sing Song of Old Man Kangaroo. 3. How the Camel Got His Hump. 4. How the Rhinoceros Got His Skin.
This production recounts how several jungle animals gained their special characteristics as told in Kipling's tales recording the oral folk traditions of India.

ANIMALS—HABITATIONS

INSECT COMMUNITIES (Film Loop—8mm—Silent). *See* Insects

WHY ANIMALS LIVE WHERE THEY DO (Filmstrip—Sound). Random House, 1973. 3 color, sound filmstrips; 3 discs or cassettes. Discs #12600-7 ($60), Cassettes #12600-9 ($60). Gr. K–3. PRV (12/73), PVB (5/74). 591.5
Contents: 1. Land Animals. 2. Ocean Animals. 3. Freshwater Animals.
Each filmstrip depicts how different climates create different environments, which in turn support particular kinds of animal life.

ANIMALS—HABITS AND BEHAVIOR

ANIMALS, ANIMALS (Filmstrip—Sound). Society for Visual Education, 1976. 6 color, sound filmstrips, av. 66 fr. ea.; 6 cassettes or phonodiscs, av. 9-1/4 min. ea.; Teacher's Guide. A442-SATC ($95), A442-SAR ($95). Gr. 5–12. BKL (2/15/76). 591.5
Contents: 1. Animal Societies. 2. How Animals Build. 3. How Animals Protect Themselves. 4. How Animals Migrate. 5. How Animals Communicate. 6. How Animals Feed Themselves.
Designed to help children develop the ability to observe the characteristics of animals at close range in order to recognize similarities among certain groupings. Students can then conclude that adaptations enable some animals to survive and thrive in well-defined habitats. While developing an appreciation for the wild animals of the world, children also will be developing skills in identifying and classifying animals more readily.

ANIMALS AROUND YOU (Filmstrip—Sound). National Geographic, 1977. 5 color, sound filmstrips; 5 discs or cassettes, 11–13 min. ea.; 2 Teacher's Guides. Discs #3245 ($74.50), Cassettes #3246 ($74.50). Gr. K–4. CPR (1/78). 591.5
Contents: 1. Cats and Dogs. 2. Birds, Fish, and Other Pets. 3. Farm Animals. 4. Zoo Animals. 5. Animals Near Your Home.
Insights into animal needs and behavior gained by keeping a cat, dog, or other pet. Covered are: both familiar and unusual pets; how to choose a pet and care for it; how farm animals help people and require human care; special diets and homes devised for zoo

ANIMALS–HABITS AND BEHAVIOR (cont.)

animals; and learning about the small creatures that live in parks, lawns, and gardens. Adapted from the books of the same name as contents.

ANIMALS IN DIFFERENT COMMUNITIES (Filmstrip–Sound/Captioned). Small World Productions, 1976. 4 color, sound, captioned filmstrips, av. 53–66 fr. ea.; 4 cassettes, av. 9–10 min. ea. #C119 ($52.50). Gr. 3–7. BKL (12/1/77). 591.5

Contents: 1. In a Desert: The Roadrunner. 2. In a Field: The Honeybee. 3. In the Ground: The Ant. 4. On a Seashore: The Crab.

The unhurried narrator tells of each animal's unique way of life, including its food, enemies, and housing. The script appears as captions to each frame so viewers can read along as they view.

ANIMALS WE SEE AROUND US (Filmstrip –Captioned). EBEC, 1976 (Developing Language Skills). 5 color, captioned filmstrips, 58–62 fr. Teacher's Guide. #13420 ($41). Gr. K–3. BKL (4/15/77), LAM (10/77), PRV (9/76). 591.5

Contents: 1. All Kinds of Dogs. 2. All Kinds of Cats. 3. All Kinds of Birds. 4. All Kinds of Fish. 5. All Kinds of Small Furry Animals.

An opportunity to observe, compare, and talk about familiar animals as general characteristics of each animal group are shown.

BEAVER (Film Loop–8mm–Silent). *See* Beavers

BEAVER DAM AND LODGE (Film Loop– 8mm–Silent). *See* Beavers

BIRTH OF A COLT (Film Loop–8mm– Silent). *See* Horses

THE CHEETAHS OF THE SERENGETI PLAIN (Kit). *See* Cheetahs

DAIRY COWS (Film Loop–8mm–Silent). *See* Cattle

DAIRY GOATS (Film Loop–8mm–Silent). *See* Goats

ELEMENTARY NATURAL SCIENCE– SMALL PREDATORY MAMMAL (Motion Picture–16mm–Sound). *See* Mammals

FIRST IDEAS ABOUT ANIMALS (Filmstrip –Sound). BFA Educational Media, 1974. 4 color, sound filmstrips; 4 cassettes or discs. Cassettes #VEF000 ($81), Discs #VEE000 ($81). Gr. 4–6. BKL (4/15/75). 591.5

Contents: 1. Variety among Animals. 2. Adaptations. 3. Interaction. 4. Animals Change.

Introduces students to the fascinating world of animals and to 4 great ideas–diversity, adaptation, interaction, change–which pro-vide the conceptual framework for much of our understanding of animal life.

FUR, FINS, TEETH AND TAILS (Filmstrip– Sound). Adrian Vance Productions, 1977. 6 color, sound filmstrips, av. 52–75 fr.; 6 cassettes, av. 7–10 min. ($90). Gr. 5–9. BKL (11/1/77). 591.5

Contents: 1. Animal Clothes. 2. Animal Motion. 3. Animal Teeth. 4. Animal Tails. 5. Animals in Balance. 6. Classification.

Natural sounds add to this introduction to biology. Consideration is given to the adaptation and variation of several physical characteristics–skin, teeth, tails, and loco-motion–throughout the animal kingdom.

THE GREAT TIGERS OF INDIA (Kit). *See* Tigers

HABITAT (Filmstrip–Captioned). BFA Educational Media, 1971. 5 color, captioned filmstrips. #VK2000 ($40). Gr. K–3. BKL (2/15/72). 591.5

Contents: 1. Where Do Animals Live? 2. Why Do Animals Live Together? 3. Why Do Animals Hide? 4. What Do Animals Eat? 5. What Does Change Do to Animals?

Controlled-vocabulary captions are used with these filmstrips to provide students with reading experiences as well as introducing some basic ideas in biology.

HOW I LIVE IN MY WORLD (Filmstrip). BFA Educational Media, 1973. 4 color filmstrips, av. 10–15 fr.; Teacher's Guide. ($32). Gr. K–1. BKL (4/1/74). 591

Contents: 1. Where I Sleep. 2. What I Eat. 3. What I Wear. 4. Things That Go.

Leads the child through participatory exercises including role playing, dialog, and games into understanding the material world that fulfills needs for shelter, sustenance, protection, comfort, and movement of animals and people.

IMPRINTING IN DUCKLINGS (Film Loop– 8mm–Silent). *See* Ducks

KANGAROO (Film Loop–8mm–Silent). *See* Kangaroos

KOALA BEAR (Film Loop–8mm–Silent). *See* Koala Bears

LIFE CYCLE (Filmstrip–Sound). National Geographic, 1974. 5 color, sound filmstrips, 60–72 fr.; 5 discs or cassettes, 12–14 min.; Teacher's Guide. Discs #3760 ($74.50), Cassettes #3761 ($74.50). Gr. 4–12. PRV, PVB (5/75). 591.5

Contents: 1. Mammals. 2. Fishes. 3. Birds. 4. Amphibians and Reptiles. 5. Insects.

Dramatic biographies of various animal species–from birth to death. Describes the dominant and distinguishing characteristics of each.

LIFE CYCLE OF COMMON ANIMALS, GROUP 2 (Filmstrip–Sound). *See* Sheep

THE LIFE OF ANIMALS (Filmstrip—Sound).
National Geographic, 1976. 5 color, sound
filmstrips, 43–51 fr.; 5 discs or cassettes,
11–14 min.; 2 sets Teacher's Guide. Discs
#3780 ($74.50), Cassettes #3781 ($74.50).
Gr. K-6. PRV (4/77), PVB (4/78). 591.5
Contents: 1. Ways Animals Get Food. 2.
Animals Homes. 3. Ways Animals Move
About. 4. Ways Animals Protect Them-
selves. 5. Animals and Their Families.
An introduction to the behavior of animals,
adapted from the book.

LION (Motion Picture—16mm—Sound). *See*
Lions

LION: MOTHER AND CUBS (Film Loop—
8mm—Silent). *See* Lions

THE MOUNTAIN GORILLA (Kit). *See*
Gorillas

NATURE ALL AROUND US: A CLOSE-UP
VIEW (Filmstrip—Sound). *See* Nature
Study

PET STORIES (Filmstrip—Sound). *See* Pets

PIGS (Film Loop—8mm—Silent). *See* Pigs

PLAYING IT SAFE WITH ANIMALS (Filmstrip—Sound). Marshfilm, 1976 (Safety). 1
color, sound filmstrip, 50 fr.; 1 cassette or
disc, 15 min.; Teacher's Guide. ($21). Gr.
K-A. INS (1/78), NYF (1976). 591.5
This filmstrip deals with what may happen
when wild animals such as raccoons, coyotes,
or possums are kept as pets; describes reactions and behavior of sick or injured animals;
presents first aid treatment for animal, snake,
and spider bites and wasp and bee stings.

POLAR BEAR: MOTHER AND CUBS (Film
Loop—8mm—Silent). *See* Bears

THE POLAR BEARS AND THE SEALS (Kit).
See Mammals

PRIDE OF LIONS (Film Loop—8mm—Silent).
See Lions

SHEEP (Film Loop—8mm—Silent). *See* Sheep

STORIES OF ANIMALS WHICH SHARE AN
ENVIRONMENT (Filmstrip—Sound). *See*
Ecology

WE LOVE ANIMALS (Kit). *See* Pets

ZIGGY, THE ELEPHANT (Kit). *See* Elephants

ANIMALS—IDENTIFICATION

ADVENTURES OF WILD ANIMALS (Filmstrip—Sound). *See* Zoology

ANIMALS AND THEIR WORLD (Filmstrip—
Sound). *See* Zoology

FUR, FINS, TEETH AND TAILS (Filmstrip—
Sound). *See* Animals—Habits and Behavior

ANIMALS—INFANCY

MAMMALS (Film Loop—8mm—Captioned).
BFA Educational Media, 1973 (Animal Behavior). 8mm color, captioned film loop,
approx. 4 min. #41821 ($30). Gr. 4-9.
BKL (5/1/76). 591.3
Demonstrates experiments, behavior, and
characteristics of mammals.

ANIMALS—TREATMENT

WORKING WITH ANIMALS (Filmstrip—
Sound). Troll Associates, 1975. 6 color,
sound filmstrips, av. 41 fr. ea.; 6 cassettes,
av. 7 min. ea.; Teacher's Guide. ($84). Gr.
2-5. BKL (11/15/75). 626.092
Contents: 1. Animal Careers for You. 2.
Canine Control Officer and Kennel Worker.
3. Pet Shop Worker and Dog Groomer. 4.
Veterinarian and Aides and Zoo Helper. 5.
Park Naturalist and Conservation Officer. 6.
Humane Educator and Obedience Trainer.
The skills, duties, and environment of each
career are explained for the many students
who are interested in the care and training
of animals.

ANIMALS—TREATMENT—FICTION

BLACK BEAUTY (Filmstrip—Sound). *See*
Horses—Fiction

ANIMATION. *See* Motion Pictures, Animated

ANTARCTIC REGIONS

ANTARCTICA: THE WHITE CONTINENT
(Filmstrip—Sound). Lyceum/Mook & Blanchard, 1974. 2 color, sound filmstrips, 44–
48 fr.; 2 cassettes or discs, 7–10 min.; Teacher's Guide. Cassettes #LY35673C ($46),
Discs #LY35673R ($37). Gr. 5-A. FLN (4/
5/74), PRV (10/74), PVB (7/75). 919.8
Contents: 1. Challenge of the Antarctic. 2.
Antarctica Today.
Helps to understand the Antarctic environment and the reasons for exploration and
research.

CREATURES OF THE ANTARCTICA (Filmstrip—Sound). Lyceum/Mook & Blanchard,
1974. 1 color, sound filmstrip, 46 fr.; 1 cassette or disc, 8-1/2 min.; Teachers Guide.
Cassette #LY35174C ($25), Disc
#LY35174R ($19). Gr. 5-A. FLN (9/74),
INS (2/75), PRV (2/74). 919.8
The filmstrip helps students understand and
appreciate Antarctic animal and marine life.
Photographs and little-known facts describe
the inhabitants of the area. Penguins, seals,
and other marine life stimulate scientific
research.

ARABS

THE ARAB WORLD (Kit). EMC, 1974. 4
color, sound filmstrips, 116–153 fr.; 4 discs

ARABS (cont).

or cassettes, 10–12 min.; 3 Paperback Books; Political Map; Student Activities; Teacher's Guide. #SS-212000 ($89). Gr. 4–6. BKL (4/75), FLN (9/74), INS (3/76). 953

Contents: 1. The Land and the Heritage. 2. Oil and Water: Keys to the Future. 3. Nomads, Villagers, City Dwellers. 4. A Time of Change.

This set highlights the comparison between these diverse but unified nations. The environment, history, and unifying culture are explored as traditional and changing lifestyles are presented.

ARCHEOLOGY

ART OF PERSEPOLIS (Slides). *See* Iran–Antiquities

THE BIG DIG (Motion Picture–16mm–Sound). *See* Israel–Antiquities

DIGGING UP AMERICA'S PAST (Filmstrip–Sound). *See* America–Antiquities

ARDIZZONE, EDWARD

POPULAR PICTURE BOOKS FILMSTRIPS: SET THREE (Filmstrip–Sound). *See* Reading Materials

ARITHMETIC

ARITHME-TOONS, UNITS ONE AND TWO (Kit). Imperial International Learning. 6 cassettes; 18 "funsheets." ($49.50). Gr. 3–6. TEA (2/78). 513

Contents: 1. Unit One–Addition with Bugs Bunny. 2. Unit Two–Subtraction with Road Runner.

Features the familiar voices, music, and sound effects from the popular animated cartoons. Each tape unfolds a comical tale along with the narrator's lesson. Pauses are programmed to allow students to complete the designated fun sheets. Answers are supplied by the narrator for instant evaluation by the children.

THE CARETAKER'S DILEMMA (Motion Picture–16mm–Sound). EBEC, 1975 (Math That Counts). 16mm color, sound film, 10 min. #3462 ($150). Gr. K–5. ATE (4/77), LFR (1/2/77), TEA (3/76). 513

This filmed fantasy introduces children to the convenience and efficiency of our number system by creating a make-believe time when each number had a name like "Marion" or "George." Because the names lacked system or sequence, people couldn't keep their numbers in order. The clever caretaker then invented 10 symbols, plus an ingenious place-value system, making the expression of any number possible and greatly simplifying addition.

DECIMAL NUMERATION SYSTEM (Filmstrip–Sound). Viewlex Educational Media, 1973. 3 color, sound filmstrips, 25–57 fr.; 3 discs or cassettes, 13–18 min.; Teacher's Guide; Worksheet Pads. #5507-9 ($48). Gr. 6–9. PRV (10/74), PVB (5/75). 513.2

Contents: 1. Development of Our Number System. 2. Decimal System. 3. Decimal Fractions.

Each filmstrip presents a lesson on a single topic related to the Decimal System of Numeration. Concepts are introduced in sequences. Line drawings and diagrams in colors stand out against a black background.

LINTOLA (Motion Picture–16mm–Sound). EBEC, 1975 (Math That Counts). 16mm color, sound film, 9 min. #3465 ($135). Gr. K–4. ATE (4/77), LFR (11/12/77), TEA (3/19/76). 513

The theory behind 2-digit addition with carrying is visualized in this tale set in outer space.

MAGIC RECTANGLE (Motion Picture–16mm–Sound). EBEC, 1976 (Math That Counts). 16mm color, sound film, 11 min. #3466 ($170). Gr. 3–6. ATE (4/77), LFR (11/12/77). 513

Three little pigs sally forth to seek their fortunes, each armed with 8 meters of magic rope. With it, they can form 2 sides of a rectangle. The area inside (visualized by arrays of square meters) will be wolf-proof. By comparing the different arrays of square meters that can be formed by the rope, the pig learns how to create the maximum protective area.

MONEY AND TIME: ADVENTURES OF THE LOLLIPOP DRAGON (Filmstrip–Sound). Society for Visual Education, 1976. 6 color, sound filmstrips, 48 fr.; 6 cassettes or discs, av. 11-1/2 min. ea.; Teacher's Guide; 24 Activity Sheets. Discs #106-SFR ($99), Cassettes #106-SFTC ($99). Gr. K–3. ATE (12/77). 513

Contents: 1. Value in Cents: Raindrops to Rainbows. 2. Coin Collections: Hubert's Kite. 3. Dollars and Cents: Alicia Blooms. 4. Time in Hours: Lollipop's Time Line. 5. Time in Minutes: Half Past Three! 6. Time Notation: Circus in the Sky.

Six interesting learning adventures are led by the gentle Lollipop Dragon, Prince Hubert, and Princess Gwendolyn as they explore the world of money and time.

SIGNED NUMBERS (Filmstrip–Sound). Educational Activities, 1976. 4 color, sound filmstrips; 4 cassettes; Guide. #FSC474 ($56). Gr. 3–6. MTE (11/77). 513.12

Contents: 1. Introduction to Signed Numbers. 2. Addition. 3. Subtraction. 4. Multiplication.

This program presents the concepts of, and operations with, signed numbers in a fashion certain to bring understanding.

SITUATIONAL MATH LEVEL TWO (Filmstrip—Sound). Knowledge Aid/United Learning, 1973. 5 color, sound filmstrips, av. 60–65 fr. ea.; 5 cassettes, av. 15–20 min. ea.; Teacher's Guide; Student Activities; Scope and Sequence Chart. Module I #6205 ($75), Module II #6225 ($75). Gr. 3–7. PRV (9/74), PVB (5/75). 513

Contents: 1. Module I—Whole Numbers and Fractions. 2. Module II—Fractions, Decimals & Percentages.

Using cartoon characters, these sound filmstrips contain problem-solving situations. The last story situation is always open-ended and requires the student to state the problem.

TREE OF TRUTH (Motion Picture—16mm—Sound). EBEC, 1975 (Math That Counts). 16mm color, sound film, 9 min. #3463 ($135). Gr. K–6. ATE (4/77), LFR (11/12/77), TEA (3/76). 513

The story of a greedy king teaches young mathematicians a very basic fact: addition and subtraction may be 2 ways of viewing the same problem.

UNDERSTANDING AND USING DECIMALS (Filmstrip—Sound). Pathescope Educational Media, 1976. 10 color, sound filmstrips; 10 cassettes; 68 Spirit Masters; Teacher's Manual. #441 ($225). Gr. 4–8. MTE (1/77). 513.2

Contents: 1. Reading and Writing Decimals. 2. Comparing Decimals. 3. Adding Decimals. 4. Subtracting Decimals. 5. Multiplying Decimals—Part 1. 6. Multiplying Decimals—Part 2. 7. Rounding Decimals. 8. Dividing Decimals by a Whole Number. 9. Dividing Decimals by a Decimal. 10. Changing Fractions to Decimals.

Aimed at giving students a thorough understanding of decimals and mastery of their use in real-life situations.

UNDERSTANDING AND USING PERCENT (Filmstrip—Sound). Pathescope Educational Media, 1976. 10 color, sound filmstrips; 10 cassettes; 68 Spirit Masters; Teacher's Guide. #442 ($225). Gr. 4–8. MTE (5/77). 513.2

Contents: 1. The Meaning of Percent. 2. Changing Percent to Fractions. 3. Changing Percent to Decimals. 4. Changing Decimals to Percent. 5. Changing Fractions to Percent. 6. Finding Percentage: Commission. 7. Finding Percentage: Discount. 8. Finding Percentage: Interest. 9. Finding the Rate of Percent. 10. Finding the Base.

Based on the concept that "percent means hundredths," this set is aimed at giving students a thorough understanding and mastery of percentage.

ARITHMETIC—STUDY AND TEACHING

STUMBLING BLOCKS IN ARITHMETIC (Filmstrip—Sound). Pathescope Educational Media, 1973. 3 color, sound filmstrips; 3 cassettes; Teacher's Manual. #304 ($55). Gr. 4–8. MTE (1/74). 372.7

Contents: 1. Regrouping in Subtraction. 2. The Two-Place Multiplier. 3. The Two-Place Divisor.

Covers 3 major areas of difficulty and makes mathematical abstractions real and understandable. Good questions are raised and answered. Each concept is presented at the concrete level first, then at the representational level, and finally at the abstract level. Live photography and cartoons are used with a story approach and touches of humor.

STUMBLING BLOCKS IN FRACTIONS (Filmstrip—Sound). Pathescope Educational Media, 1973. 4 color, sound filmstrips; 4 cassettes; Teacher's Manual. #305 ($70). Gr. 4–8. MTE (1/74). 372.7

Contents: 1. The Language of Fractions. 2. Equivalent Fractions. 3. Addition and Subtraction of Fractions. 4. Multiplication and Division of Fractions.

Four major problems in dealing with fractions are covered in this set. The students learn to understand the problems and then solve them with the aid of live photography and cartoon characters.

ARMSTRONG, WILLIAM

WILLIAM H. ARMSTRONG (Filmstrip—Sound). Miller-Brody Productions, 1977 (Meet the Newbery Author). 1 color, sound filmstrip, 87 fr.; 1 cassette or disc, 9 min. Cassette #MNA1011C ($32), Disc #MNA1011 ($32). Gr. 4–8. BKL (1/1/78). 921

The quietly busy life of author William H. Armstrong is depicted in this filmstrip that catches the man in his many roles as teacher, writer, shepherd, gardener, cabinetmaker, and real estate agent. Photos, family snapshots, and book illustrations add another dimension to the few remarks on Armstrong's childhood, education, and Connecticut home built by his own hands.

ART, AFRICAN

WEST AFRICAN ARTISTS AND THEIR ART (Filmstrip—Sound). EBEC, 1973. 7 color, sound filmstrips, av. 75 fr. ea.; 7 discs or cassettes, 8 min. ea.; Teacher's Guide. Discs #6464 ($101.50), Cassette #6464K ($101.50). Gr. 4–8. BKL (7/15/73), PRV (11/73). 709.6

Contents: 1. Kumasi Brass Caster. 2. Dschang Woodcarver. 3. Ghana Dancer. 4. Mali Mask Carver. 5. Cameroon Blacksmith. 6. Gambian Weaver. 7. Fumban Sculptors.

Vivid documentaries of artists and craftspeople at work transport students to many parts of West Africa.

ART, AMERICAN

AMERICA IN ART: THE AMERICAN RE-
VOLUTION (Filmstrip—Sound). *See* U.S.—
History—1775-1783—Revolution

ART AND NATURE

ENVIRONMENTAL AWARENESS (Filmstrip—Sound). *See* Natural History

ART APPRECIATION

THE ART OF SEEING (Filmstrip—Sound).
Warren Schloat Productions/Prentice-Hall
Media, 1968. 6 color, sound filmstrips; 6
cassettes or discs; Teacher's Guide. Cassettes #KAC 250 ($126), Discs #KAR 250
($126). Gr. 4-12. AFF, EFL, SLJ. 701.8
Contents: 1. How to Use Your Eyes, Part I.
2. How to Use Your Eyes, Part II. 3. Lines.
4. Shapes. 5. Colors. 6. Space.
This program explores the artist's visual
vocabulary.

OUR VISUAL WORLD (Filmstrip—Sound).
ACI Media/Paramount Communications,
1974. 4 color, sound filmstrips, av. 70 fr.;
4 cassettes, 8-10 min.; Teacher's Guide.
#9119 ($78). Gr. 4-12. PRV (5/75),
PVB (4/76). 701.8
Contents: 1. Line, Surface and Volume. 2.
Shape. 3. Light and Color. 4. Pattern and
Texture.
This set stimulates visual awareness to the
world around us. It helps to see things as if
for the first time. Students are led to consideration of the artistic process and the ways
in which works of art can alter the way we
see the world.

PICTURES ARE FUN TO LOOK AT (Art
Prints). Shorewood Reproductions. 12 paper stock, cardboard mounted or unmounted
22-1/2 in. X 28-1/2 in. color prints; Teacher's Guide. Unmounted #5005 ($45),
Mounted #5005 ($60). Gr. K-5. PRV (9/
75). 701.1
Artists Chagall, Foujita, Homer, Kirchner,
Klee, Lindner, Moillet, Pickett, Picasso,
Renoir, Rousseau, and Vasarely are presented. A variety of subjects and styles are
included in this introduction to painting.

ART—COLLECTIONS

EARLY TRANSPORTATION (Study Print).
See Transportation in Literature and Art

THE FAMILY (Art Prints). *See* Family in
Literature and Art

ART, DECORATIVE

EDIBLE ART (Filmstrip—Sound). *See*
Cookery

ART, JAPANESE

THE ARTS OF JAPAN—SLIDE SET (Slides).
Educational Dimensions Group, 1973. 20
cardboard mounted, color slides in plastic
storage page; Teacher's Guide. #926 ($25).
Gr. 6-A. BKL (5/75), PRV (1/75), PVB
(5/75). 709.52
Designed to provide a chronological view of
Japanese art, this set of slides includes sculpture, architecture, painting, and the crafts of
each major historical period.

ART—STUDY AND TEACHING

BAUHAUS (Filmstrip—Silent). International
Film Bureau. 2 color, silent filmstrips, 28-
31 fr.; 2 Guides. ($15). Gr. 6-A. MDU
(1974). 701
Contents: 1. Learning Through Doing. 2.
The World as a Total Work of Art.
These silent filmstrips present the overall
view of the Bauhaus School of Art. Probably more useful for teachers than students.

ART—TECHNIQUE

PAINTING FROM NATURE (Motion Picture
—16mm—Sound). Acorn Films. 16mm
color, sound film, 20 min. ($250). Gr. 6-A.
PRV (9/75). 751
Environmentalist Dennis Puleston shows
how a painting is developed from sketches
and photos, and helps students learn to
draw from nature.

WATCHING ARTISTS AT WORK (Filmstrip
—Sound). Imperial Educational Resources,
1972. 4 color, sound filmstrips, 49-53 fr.;
4 discs or cassettes. Discs #3RG32500
($56), Cassettes #3KG32500 ($62). Gr.
4-12. BKL (2/1/73). 702.8
Contents: 1. Creating an Abstract Watercolor. 2. Creating a Realistic Oil. 3. Creating a Ceramic Sculpture. 4. Creating a
Contemporary Print.
These filmstrips show the creation of 4
original works of art in different media.
The artists explain methods and procedures
and discuss their thoughts and feelings
about their work.

ARTHUR, KING

FAMOUS STORIES OF GREAT COURAGE
(Filmstrip—Sound). *See* Heroes and
Heroines

ARUEGO, JOSE

THRESHOLD FILMSTRIPS, SERIES C (Kit).
See Children's Literature—Collections

WHOSE MOUSE ARE YOU? (Filmstrip—
Sound). *See* Mice—Fiction

ASIA

FAMILIES OF ASIA (Filmstrip–Sound).
EBEC, 1975, 6 color, sound filmstrips,
av. 75 fr. ea.; 6 discs or cassettes, 8 min. ea.;
Teacher's Guide. Discs #6910 ($86.95),
Cassettes #6910K ($86.95). Gr. 1-8. BKL
(11/75), ESL (1977), PRV (9/75, 76). 915

Contents: 1. The Families of Hong Kong.
2. Family of Bangladesh. 3. Family of
India. 4. Family of Japan. 5. Family of
Java. 6. Family of Thailand.

Diverse ways of life in Asia are often too
large, too foreign for western students to
grasp. But when approached through a
single family with children, the life-styles of
Bangladesh, Hong Kong, and many other
Asian nations become more comprehensible.
Colorful, on-location photographs and
natural sounds depict everyday life in 6
different countries.

SOUTH ASIA: REGION IN TRANSITION
(Filmstrip–Sound). EBEC, 1976. 5 color,
sound filmstrips, av. 76 fr. ea.; 5 cassettes
or discs, 10 min. ea.; Teacher's Guide. Discs
#6924 ($72.50), Cassettes #6924K
($72.50). Gr. 5-9. BKL (10/1/77), MDU
(4/77). 915

Contents: 1. The Winning of Independence.
2. Religion and Change. 3. An Indian Village: Model for Change. 4. The Urban
Workers. 5. South Asia: Key Decisions.

This is an assessment of how India, Pakistan,
and the other countries of the Indian subcontinent are meeting economic change.
The filmstrips examine the changing urban
scene, inspect a model farming community,
and portray the struggle against a 3-pronged
threat; poverty, over population, and lack
of technology.

ASIA, SOUTHEAST

SOUTHEAST ASIA (Filmstrip–Sound).
Educational Design, 1976 (Global Culture
Series). 4 color, sound filmstrips, av. 75
fr.; 2 cassettes, av. 12:37 min.; 1 Guide.
#EDI-460 ($79). Gr. 5-9. BKL
(10/15/77). 915.9

Contents: 1. Many Ways of Life. 2. Beliefs
and Bread. 3. Fun and the Future. 4. The
Factors in Common.

Presents basic geographical, historical, economic, and cultural information of these
nations, revealing unusual and uncommon
insights into the people's lives.

ASTRONOMY

BEGINNING SCIENCE: EARTH AND
UNIVERSE (Kit). Society for Visual Education, 1976. 5 color, sound filmstrips;
5 cassettes; 48 Activity Cards; 48 Spirit
Masters; Poster with press-on plastic cut-
outs; 144 crayons; Teacher's Guide. #CM-
46 ($120). Gr. 2-4. BKL (5/15/77),
PRV (4/78). 523

Contents: 1. Earth: Planet in Space. 2.
Sun: Keeping Earth Warm. 3. Moon: Phases
and Facts. 4. Solar System: Family of
Planets. 5. Stars: Beyond the Solar System.

This kit is designed to supplement basic
earth science and astronomy concepts. The
basic concepts are presented in 5 stories set
in the year 2016.

JUNIOR ASTRONOMER (Filmstrip–Sound).
Filmstrip House/United Learning, 1974.
4 color, sound filmstrips, av. 47 fr. ea.; 2
cassettes or discs, av. 12 min. ea.; Script/
Guide. Cassettes #65702 ($55), Discs
#65701 ($55). Gr. 3-6. PRV (1/76).
523

Contents: 1. The Sky Above. 2. Seasons,
Day and Night. 3. The Family of Planets.
4. The Moon.

Informal lessons on the rotation and revolution of planets and their effect on light,
dark, and the seasons are provided by
Marie's dramatized visits to the observatory
where her aunt, an astronomer, works.

WHAT'S OUT THERE? (Filmstrip–Sound/
Captioned). Jam Handy/Prentice-Hall
Media, 1971. 7 color, captioned filmstrips,
51-62 fr.; 7 cassettes. #KAC3440 ($120).
Gr. 4-8. PRV (9/72), PVB (5/73). 523

Contents: 1. Looking at the Universe. 2.
The Solar System. 3. Earth, Venus and
Mercury. 4. Mars. 5. The Outer Planets. 6.
Our Satellite. 7. Beyond the Solar System.

A study of the changing explanations of the
universe as it has been observed through the
ages. Emphasis is placed on how theories
have been developed, tested, and proved or
discarded. The tools used, past and present,
are examined.

ATHLETES

BLACK AMERICAN ATHLETES (Kit).
EMC. 4 paperback books; 4 read-along
cassettes; Student Activities; Teacher's
Guide. #ELC-234000 ($55). Gr. 4-12.
BKL (7/76), SLJ (9/76). 920

Contents: 1. Lee Elder: The Daring Dream.
2. Julius Erving: Dr. J. and Julius W. 3.
Madeline Manning Jackson. 4. Arthur Ashe:
Alone in the Crowd.

Four black athletes who have reached superstar status—sometimes against great odds.
They stress the importance of effort and
discipline to reach the top.

HOCKEY HEROES (Kit). EMC, 1974.
4 paperback books; 4 read-along cassettes;
Teacher's Guide; Student Activities. #ELC-
217000 ($55). Gr. 4-12. SLJ (12/74). 920

Contents: 1. Stan Mikita: Tough Kid Who
Grew Up. 2. Bobby Hull: Superstar. 3. Gil
Perreault: Makes It Happen. 4. Frank
Mahovlich: The Big M.

ATHLETES (cont.)

Behind-the-scenes stories of 4 noted hockey favorites. These high-interest books demonstrate the patience, courage, and perseverance needed to succeed in this competitive sport.

SPORTS CLOSE-UPS 1 (Kit). EMC, 1973. 5 paperback books; 5 read-along cassettes, approx. 35 min.; Student Activities; Teacher's Guide. #ELC-212000 ($71.50). Gr. 3–8. BKL (7/73). 920

Contents: 1. Willie Mays: Most Valuable Player. 2. Johnny Unitas and the Long Pass. 3. Mickey Mantle Slugs It Out. 4. Hank Aaron: Home Run Superstar. 5. Jim Brown Runs with the Ball.

High interest reading materials for young sports buffs.

SPORTS CLOSE-UPS 3 (Kit). EMC, 1973. 5 paperback books; 5 read-along cassettes; Teacher's Guide; Student Activities. #ELC-212000 ($71.50). Gr. 4–12. BKL (6/75). 920

Contents: 1. O. J. Simpson: Juice on the Gridiron. 2. Bobby Hull: Hockey's Golden Jet. 3. Lee Trevino: The Golf Explosion. 4. Billie Jean King: Tennis Champion. 5. Roy Campanella: Brave Man of Baseball.

A best-selling series of photo-illustrated biographies, with read-along cassettes, examines the lives and careers of these outstanding athletes.

SPORTS CLOSE-UPS 4 (Kit). EMC, 1974. 7 paperback books; 7 Read-along cassettes; Teacher's Guide; Student Activities. #ELC228000 ($94). Gr. 4–12. BKL (5/76). 920

Contents: 1. Evonne Goolagong: Smasher from Australia. 2. Frank Robinson: Slugging Toward Glory. 3. Evel Knievel: Daredevil Stuntman. 4. Phil Esposito: The Big Bruin. 5. Joe Namath: High-Flying Quarterback. 6. Muhammad Ali: Boxing Superstar. 7. Vince Lombardi: The Immortal Coach.

The lives and careers of 7 outstanding athletes show the talent and competitive drive that brought them to stardom.

WOMEN WHO WIN, SET 1 (Kit). EMC, 1974. 4 paperback books; 4 read-along cassettes, 29–31 min.; Student Activities; Teacher's Guide. #ELC-221000 ($55). Gr. 4–12. BKL (9/74), INS (11/75), SLJ (11/74). 920

Contents: 1. Olga Korbut: Tears and Triumphs. 2. Shane Gould: Olympic Swimmer. 3. Janet Lynn: Sunshine on Ice. 4. Chris Evert: Tennis Pro.

There are 4 biographies in this set, introducing outstanding young women who have set their own goals, performed, competed, and reached the top of their chosen fields.

WOMEN WHO WIN, SET 2 (Kit). EMC, 1974. 4 read-along cassettes; 4 paperback books; Student Activities; Teacher's Guide. #ELC-125000 ($55). Gr. 4–12. BKL (5/1/75). 920

Contents: 1. Evonne Goolagong: Smiles and Smashes. 2. Laura Baugh: Golf's Golden Girl. 3. Wilma Rudolph: Run for Glory. 4. Cathy Rigby: On the Beam.

Four women superstars; biographies of top headliners who have generated drama and excitement in the sport's world.

WOMEN WHO WIN, SET 3 (Kit). EMC, 1975. 4 read-along books; 4 paperback books; Teacher's Guide; Student Activities. #ELC-126000 ($55). Gr. 4–12. PRV (2/76). 920

Contents: 1. Mary Dickie: Speed Records and Spaghetti. 2. Annemarie Proell: Queen of the Mountain. 3. Joan Moore Rice: The Olympic Dream. 4. Rosemary Casals: The Rebel Rosebud.

Young readers will thrill to the stories of these superb athletes from a wide world of sports.

WOMEN WHO WIN, SET 4 (Kit). EMC, 1975. 4 paperback books; 4 read-along cassettes; Students Activities; Teacher's Guide. #ELC-232000 ($55). Gr. 4–12. BKL (5/75), INS (11/75). 920

Contents: 1. Martina Navratilova: Tennis Fury. 2. Robyn Smith: In Silks. 3. Cindy Nelson: North Country Skier. 4. Robin Campbell: Joy in the Morning.

Stories of 4 superb athletes involved in a variety of sports. Young women who have reached the top in their chosen fields through discipline, practice, and commitment.

ATLANTIC STATES

SEEING THE MIDDLE ATLANTIC STATES (Filmstrip–Sound). Coronet Instructional Media, 1974. 6 color, sound filmstrips, av. 57 fr.; 6 cassettes or 3 discs, av. 11-1/2 min. Cassettes #M272 ($95). Discs #S272 ($95). Gr. 4–6. BKL (10/15/74), PRV, TEA. 917.4

Contents: 1. Land and Climate. 2. Natural Resources. 3. Agriculture and Fishing. 4. Industry. 5. Transportation and Commerce. 6. History and People.

The immediate problems of high population and limited energy sources of the Middle Atlantic States are explored.

ATOMS

MATTER (Filmstrip–Sound). *See* Nuclear Physics

ATTITUDE (PSYCHOLOGY)

ATTITUDES UNIT (Motion Picture–16mm–Sound). Sutherland Learning Associates/EBEC, 1972 (Most Important Person). 6

16mm color, sound films. Also avail. 8mm
film; 6 posters; 1 record; 4 Song Cards;
Teacher's Guide. #6731 ($345.60). Gr.
K–3. BKL (7/1/74), CHT (9/10/74), CPR
(1/76). 152.4

Contents: 1. Oops, I Made a Mistake! 2.
I'm Lonely. 3. Why Not Try? 4. We Can
Do It! 5. It's Not Much Fun Being Angry.
6. Nothing Ever Seems to Work Out for Me.
How can children cope with situations that
are discouraging? The unit suggests some
positive approaches.

ATTUCKS, CRISPUS

FAMOUS PATRIOTS OF THE AMERICAN
REVOLUTION (Filmstrip–Sound). *See*
U.S.–History–Biography

ATWOOD, ANN

THE GODS WERE TALL AND GREEN
(Filmstrip–Sound). *See* Forests and
Forestry

HAIKU: THE HIDDEN GLIMMERING
(Filmstrip–Sound). *See* Haiku

HAIKU: THE MOOD OF EARTH (Filmstrip
–Sound). *See* Haiku

THE LITTLE CIRCLE (Filmstrip–Sound).
See Fantasy

MY FORTY YEARS WITH BEAVERS
(Filmstrip–Sound). *See* Beavers

SAMMY THE CROW (Filmstrip–Sound).
See Crows

SEA, SAND AND SHORE (Filmstrip–
Sound). *See* Ocean

THE WILD YOUNG DESERT SERIES
(Filmstrip–Sound). *See* Deserts

AUDIO-VISUAL MATERIALS

MEDIA: RESOURCES FOR DISCOVERY
(Filmstrip–Sound). EBEC, 1974. 8 color,
sound filmstrips, av. 95 fr. ea.; 8 discs or
cassettes, 11 min. ea.; Teacher's Guide.
English/Spanish Edition available. Discs
#6902 ($132.95), Cassettes #6902K
($132.95). Gr. 4–8. BKL (6/1/75), CPR
(11/75), LFR (12/75). 028.7
Contents: 1. The World of Media. 2. Media
Organization: Fiction. 3. Media Organization: Nonfiction. 4. Indexes to Media. 5.
The Encyclopedia in the World of Media.
6. Resources for Reference. 7. Choosing
the Medium. 8. One Search, One Report.
Designed to make students self-sufficient
and at ease in the modern library media
center, this series demonstrates what a
media center is and how to use it.

AUDUBON, JOHN JAMES

AUDUBON'S SHORE BIRDS (Motion Picture
–16mm–Sound). *See* Water Birds

AUSTRALIA

AUSTRALIA AND NEW ZEALAND
(Filmstrip–Sound). EBEC, 1972. 6 color,
sound, sound filmstrips, av. 81 fr. ea.; 6
discs or cassettes, 13 min. ea.; Teacher's
Guide. Discs #6456 ($86.95), Cassettes
#6456 ($86.95). Gr. 4–8. BKL
(10/15/73), LFR (10/73), PRV (4/73).
919.4

Contents: 1. The Agricultural Achievement.
2. Toward Industrialization. 3. Australia:
The Island Continent. 4. New Zealand:
Land of the Long White Cloud. 5. The
Australians. 6. The New Zealanders.
Life "Down Under" has a flavor all its own.
From bustling coastal cities to lonely sheep
stations in the sun-scorched outback,
Australians are seen to mingle their British
heritage with the pioneer's independence
and zest for life. In New Zealand, the Poly-
nesian Maoris and their European-descended
neighbors share in the country's development–an outstanding example of racial
harmony and equality.

AUTHORS

CAROL RYRIE BRINK (Filmstrip–Sound).
See Brink, Carol Ryrie

ELEANOR ESTES (Filmstrip–Sound).
Miller-Brody Productions, 1974 (Meet the
Newbery Authors). 1 color, sound filmstrip, approx. 96 fr.; 1 cassette or disc,
approx. 17 min. Discs #8MNA1001C
($32), Cassettes #8MNA1001 ($32). Gr.
4–9. PRV (2/75), PVB (5/75). 921
In this on-screen interview, Estes captures
moments in her childhood and talks about
influences on her writings.

ELIZABETH YATES (Filmstrip–Sound).
See Yates, Elizabeth

FIRST CHOICE AUTHORS AND BOOKS
(Filmstrip–Sound). Pied Piper Productions,
1975. 8 units with 1 color, sound filmstrip,
av. 69–93 fr.; 2 discs or cassettes ea. unit,
11–16 min.; Teacher's Guide. 4 titles in
unit ($68), Individual titles ($19). Gr. 4–7.
BKL (7/15/76), LGB (12/76), PRV (5/77).
920
Contents: 1. The Mouse and the Motor-
cycle, Beverly Cleary. 2. White Bird, Clyde
Bulla. 3. Brighty of the Grand Canyon,
Marguerite Henry. 4. Jack and the Robbers,
Richard Chase's Jack Tales. 5. The Cay,
Theodore Taylor. 6. The Cat and Mrs.
Carey, Doris Gates. 7. By the Great Horn
Spoon, Sid Fleischman. 8. Black and Blue
Magic, Zilpha Snyder.

AUTHORS (cont).

Each of the strips presents an interview with the author and a story example of his or her work.

ISAAC BASHEVIS SINGER (Filmstrip–Sound). *See* Singer, Isaac Bashevis

JEAN CRAIGHEAD GEORGE (Filmstrip–Sound). Miller-Brody Productions, 1974 (Meet the Newbery Authors). 1 color, sound filmstrip, approx. 100 fr.; 1 cassette or disc, approx. 19 min. Disc #8-MNA1003 ($32), Cassette #8-MNA1003C ($32). Gr. 4–9. PRV (2/75), PVB (5/75). 921

Her passion for nature—from spiders to the beauty of a single leaf—is made clear in this filmstrip.

LAURA: LITTLE HOUSE, BIG PRAIRIE (Filmstrip–Sound). *See* Wilder, Laura Ingalls

LLOYD ALEXANDER (Filmstrip–Sound). Miller-Brody Productions, 1974 (Meet the Newbery Authors). 1 color, sound filmstrip, 98 fr.; 1 cassette or disc, approx. 18 min. Disc #8-MNA1002 ($32), Cassette #8-MNA1002C ($32). Gr. 4–9. PRV (2/75), PVB (5/75). 921

Besides his agonies over writing, the author's love of Mozart, cats, the epic hero, and more are discussed.

VIRGINIA HAMILTON (Filmstrip–Sound). *See* Hamilton, Virginia

WILLIAM H. ARMSTRONG (Filmstrip–Sound). *See* Armstrong, William

AUTOBIOGRAPHIES

A MISERABLE MERRY CHRISTMAS (Motion Picture–16mm–Sound). *See* Christmas

AUTOMOBILE RACING

AUTO RACING: SOMETHING FOR EVERYONE (Kit). Walt Disney Educational Media, 1976. 6 color, sound filmstrips, av. 72–91 fr.; 6 discs or cassettes, av. 8–10 min.; 6 Reading Books. Teacher's Guide. #63-8040 ($129), Individual Sound Filmstrip ($25). Gr. 6–12. BKL (12/15/77). 796.7

Contents: 1. It All Started with a Road Race. 2. The "Indy" Story. 3. Made in U.S.A.: Stock Car and Drag Racing. 4. Safety in Racing. 5. Off Road Racing. 6. Careers in Racing.

The filmstrips and books provide information on the various kinds of racing. In addition, they detail the development of standard accessories originally intended for racing and alert the viewer to occupations related to car racing. The illustrated text offers expanded information, including additional data on careers.

DRAGSTRIP CHALLENGE (Kit). Insight Media Programs, 1974. 1 color, sound filmstrip, 110 fr.; 1 disc or cassette, 13 min.; 1 book (also available with 6 paperback books). Disc ($23.45), Cassette ($25.45). Gr. 4–9. PRV (4/75), PVB (5/75). 796.7

Two real dragstrip racers introduce readers to the sport. A word-for-word reading of the first 2 chapters of the book is on the reverse of each disc or cassette for those with reading difficulties. There is also a glossary of racing terminology.

THE MIGHTY MIDGETS (Kit). Bowmar Publishing, 1967. 1 color, sound filmstrip, 37 fr.; 1 cassette or disc; 7 Student Readers and Reading Program; Teacher's Guide. Disc #4536 ($38.95), Cassette #4537 ($38.95). Gr. 3–12. MDU, SLJ. 629.22

A high interest level, easy readability unit on midget racers.

RACING NUMBERS (Kit). Children's Press, 1976 (Ready, Get-Set, Go). 1 cassette; 1 hardback book; Teacher's Guide. #07557-8 ($11.95). Gr. 1–8. PRV (9/15/77). 796.7

Color photographs of soap box racers, antique cars, motorcycles, and other racing machines combine with a simple text to help youngsters learn number recognition in this high interest, low reading ability kit.

AUTOMOBILES–FICTION

CHITTY CHITTY BANG BANG (Phonodisc or Cassette). Caedmon Records, 1973. 1 cassette or disc, 68: 43 min.; Jacket Notes. Disc #TC1390 ($6.98), Cassette #CDL51390 ($7.95). Gr. K–6. BKL (2/15/74), PRV (4/74). Fic

The book by the same name is a favorite, and the recording is superbly narrated by Hermione Gingold. Its author, Ian Fleming, delights all children with this story of the Potts family and their remarkable car.

AUTUMN

AUTUMN IN THE FOREST (Filmstrip–Sound). AIDS, 1973. 4 color, sound filmstrips, av. 42–50 fr. ea.; 4 discs or cassettes; Teacher's Guide. Disc #88901 ($72), Cassettes #88902 ($72). Gr. 2–6. PRV (12/74). 525

Contents: 1. Beech, Birch, and Sugar Maple. 2. The Hardwood Forest of the Northeast. 3. Pines and Hemlocks. 4. The Red Maple Swamp.

Presents a plea for environmental concern and awareness of our forests. You journey through the forest and discover our need for trees to care for the physical quality of our air, to fluff up the soil, recycle its minerals, and provide habitats for wildlife and plants.

FALL BRINGS CHANGES, SECOND EDITION (Motion Picture–16mm–Sound). Churchill Films, 1976. 16mm color, sound film, 12 min.; Study Guide. ($170). Gr. K–3. PRV (4/77). 525

Comments and activities of children are woven into this delightful experience of fall. Halloween, Thanksgiving, the changes that colder weather brings to plants, to birds, to animals, and to children are shown.

AZTECS

MARKET PLACE IN MEXICO (Motion Picture–16mm–Sound). *See* Mexico

BABOONS

BABOONS AND THEIR YOUNG (Film Loop–8mm–Silent). Walt Disney Educational Media, 1966. 8mm color, silent film loop, approx. 4 min. #62-5219L ($30). Gr. K–12. MDU (1974). 599.8

The maternal behavior of the baboon is illustrated in a variety of sequences, both on the ground and in trees. Both parents are shown caring for their young.

BADGERS–FICTION

FRANCES (Phonodisc or Cassette). Caedmon Records, 1977. 1 cassette or disc, approx. 45 min. Disc #TC15461 ($6.98), Cassette #CDL515461 ($7.95). Gr. K–3. AUR (1978). Fic

Contents: 1. Bedtime for Frances. 2. A Baby Sister for Frances. 3. Bread and Jam for Frances. 4. A Birthday for Frances.

Russell Hoban long has been delighting children with stories about Frances. Glynis Johns's performance of these stories is just right.

BAEZ, JOAN

FOLK SONGS IN AMERICAN HISTORY, SET ONE: 1700–1864 (Filmstrip–Sound). *See* Folk Songs–U.S.

FOLK SONGS IN AMERICAN HISTORY, SET TWO: 1865–1967 (Filmstrip–Sound). *See* Folk Songs–U.S.

BALLADS, AMERICAN

AMERICAN HISTORY: IN BALLAD AND SONG, VOLUME ONE (Phonodiscs). Folkways Records, 1954. 1 disc, 12 in. 33-1/3 rpm; Guide. #5801 ($6.98). Gr. 3–12. MDU (1978). 784.75

Pete Seeger, Woody Guthrie, and others sing about American history in song.

AMERICAN HISTORY: IN BALLAD AND SONG, VOLUME TWO (Phonodiscs). Folkways Records, 1963. 1 disc, 12 in 33-1/3 rpm; Guide. #5802 ($6.98). Gr. 3–12. MDU (1978). 784.75

Pete Seeger, Woody Guthrie, and others sing about American history in song.

BARLING, BOB

PETROGLYPHS: ANCIENT ART OF THE MOJAVE (Filmstrip–Sound). *See* Indians of North America–Art

BARLING, TILLY

PETROGLYPHS: ANCIENT ART OF THE MOJAVE (Filmstrip–Sound). *See* Indians of North America–Art

BARNHART, ROBERT

THE DICTIONARY (Filmstrip–Sound). *See* English Language–Dictionaries

BARRY, ROBERT

STORIES OF LATIN AMERICA, SET TWO (Filmstrip–Sound). *See* Latin America–Fiction

BARTON, BYRON

THRESHOLD FILMSTRIPS, SERIES C (Kit). *See* Children's Literature–Collections

BASKET MAKING

MOON BASKET: AN INDIAN LEGEND (Filmstrip–Sound). *See* Indians of North America–Legends

BASKETBALL

BASIC DRIBBLE/CONTROL DRIBBLE/ SPEED (Film Loop–8mm–Silent). Athletic Institute (Basketball–Women's). 8mm, color, silent film loop, approx. 4 min.; Guide. #TRWB-1 ($22.95). Gr. 3–12. AUR (1978). 796.323

A single-concept loop demonstrating the basic technique.

CHEST PASS/BOUNCE PASS (Film Loop– 8mm–Silent). Athletic Institute (Basketball–Women's). 8mm color, silent film loop, approx. 4 min.; Guide. #WB-4 ($22.95). Gr. 3–12. AUR (1978). 796.323

A single-concept loop demonstrating the basic technique.

CHEST PASS/OVERHEAD PASS (Film Loop–8mm–Silent). Athletic Institute (Basketball). 8mm color, silent film loop, approx. 4 min.; Guide. #M-4 ($22.95). Gr. 3–12. AUR (1978). 796.323

A single-concept loop demonstrating the basic technique.

BASKETBALL (cont.)

CROSSOVER CHANGE/REVERSE PIVOT CHANGE (Film Loop—8mm—Silent). Athletic Institute (Basketball). 8mm color, silent film loop, approx. 4 min.; Guide. #M-2 ($22.95). Gr. 3–12. AUR (1978). 796.323

A single-concept loop demonstrating the basic technique.

CROSSOVER DRIBBLE/REVERSE DRIBBLE (Film Loop—8mm—Silent). Athletic Institute (Basketball—Women's). 8mm color, silent film loop, approx. 4 min.; Guide. #WB-2 ($22.95). Gr. 3–12. AUR (1978). 796.323

A single-concept loop demonstrating the basic technique.

DRIVE/CROSSOVER DRIVE (Film Loop—8mm—Silent). Athletic Institute (Basketball). 8mm color, silent film loop, approx. 4 min.; Guide. #M-3 ($22.95). Gr. 3–12. AUR (1978). 796.323

A single-concept loop demonstrating the basic technique.

INSIDE POWER SHOT (Film Loop—8mm—Silent). Athletic Institute (Basketball). 8mm color, silent film loop, approx. 4 min.; Guide. #M-6 ($22.95). Gr. 3–12. AUR (1978). 796.323

A single-concept loop demonstrating the basic technique.

JUMP SHOT (Film Loop—8mm—Silent). Athletic Institute (Basketball). 8mm color, silent film loop, approx. 4 min.; Guide. #M-7 ($22.95). Gr. 3–12. AUR (1978). 796.323

A single-concept loop demonstrating the basic technique.

JUMP SHOT/ONE HAND SET SHOT/TURN-AROUND JUMP SHOT (Film Loop—8mm—Silent). Athletic Institute (Basketball—Women's). 8mm color, silent film loop, approx. 4 min.; Guide. #WB-7 ($22.95). Gr. 3–12. AUR (1978). 796.323

A single-concept loop demonstrating the basic technique.

LAY UP SHOT (Film Loop—8mm—Silent). Athletic Institute (Basketball—Women's). 8mm color, silent film loop, approx. 4 min.; Guide. #WB-6 ($22.95). Gr. 3–12. AUR (1978). 796.323

A single-concept loop demonstrating the basic technique.

ONE-ON-ONE DRIVE (Film Loop—8mm—Silent). Athletic Institute (Basketball—Women's). 8mm color, silent film loop, approx. 4 min.; Guide. #WB-3 ($22.95). Gr. 3–12. AUR (1978). 796.323

A single-concept loop demonstrating the basic technique.

OVERARM PASS/OVERHEAD PASS/UNDERHAND PASS (Film Loop—8mm—Si-

lent). Athletic Institute (Basketball—Women's). 8mm color, silent film loop, approx. 4 min.; Guide. #WB-5 ($22.95). Gr. 3–12. AUR (1978). 796.323

A single-concept loop demonstrating the basic technique.

REBOUNDING (Film Loop—8mm—Silent). Athletic Institute (Basketball). 8mm color, silent film loop, approx. 4 min.; Guide. #M-9 ($22.95). Gr. 3–12. AUR (1978). 796.323

A single-concept loop demonstrating the basic technique.

REBOUNDING/BLOCKING OUT (Film Loop—8mm—Silent). Athletic Institute (Basketball—Women's). 8mm, color, silent film loop, approx. 4 min.; Guide. #WB-8 ($22.95). Gr. 3–12. AUR (1978). 796.323

A single-concept loop demonstrating the basic technique.

SPEED DRIBBLE/CONTROL DRIBBLE (Film Loop—8mm—Silent). Athletic Institute (Basketball). 8mm color, silent film loop, approx. 4 min.; Guide. #TRM-1 ($22.95). Gr. 3–12 AUR (1978). 796.323

A single-concept loop demonstrating the basic technique.

TURN AROUND JUMP SHOT (Film Loop—8mm—Silent). Athletic Institute (Basketball). 8mm, color, silent film loop, approx. 4 min.; Guide. #M-8 ($22.95). Gr. 3–12. AUR (1978). 796.323

A single-concept loop demonstrating the basic technique.

BATIK

CREATIVE BATIK (Filmstrip—Sound). Warner Educational Productions, 1974 (Art Craft Teaching Films). 2 color, sound filmstrips; 1 cassette, 15 min.; Teacher's Guide. ($39.50). Gr. 6–A. BKL (1/15/75). 746.6

Demonstrates the technique of this art with close-up photographs of step-by-step procedures.

BATS

BATS (Film Loop—8mm—Silent). Walt Disney Educational Media, 1966. 8mm color, silent film loop, approx. 4 min. #62-51076 ($30). Gr. K–12. AUR (1974). 599.4

Millions of bats are seen awakening in a cave. Shows a close-up view of a bat hanging upside down. A hawk is shown trying to catch one of the bats as they fly off into the evening sky.

BAUM, LYMAN FRANK

QUEEN ZIXI OF IX, OR THE STORY OF THE MAGIC CLOAK (Phonodisc or Cassette). *See* Fantasy—Fiction

WIZARD OF OZ (Cassette). *See* Fantasy—
Fiction

BAUM, WILLI

BIRDS OF A FEATHER (Motion Picture—
16mm—Sound). *See* Birds—Fiction

BEARS

PANDAS: A GIFT FROM CHINA (Motion
Picture—16mm—Sound). *See* Pandas

PLAYFUL PANDAS (Motion Picture—
16mm—Sound). *See* Pandas

POLAR BEAR: MOTHER AND CUBS (Film
Loop—8mm—Silent). Walt Disney Educational Media, 1966. 8mm color, silent film
loop, approx. 4 min. #62-5355L ($30). Gr.
K–12. MDU (1974). 599.7
Arctic life of mother polar bear and her
cubs is viewed from within a snow cave, including close-ups of cubs nursing. Mother
follows young bears outside and observes as
they play on a snowslide.

THE POLAR BEARS AND THE SEALS (Kit).
See Mammals

BEARS—FICTION

THE GRIZZLY (Kit). Insight Media Programs, 1976. 1 color, sound filmstrip, 80
fr.; 1 disc or cassette, 15 min.; Teacher's
Guide; 8 paperback books. ($41.95). Gr.
5–9. BKL (11/15/76). Fic
Student copies of Annabel and Edgar Johnson's novel are included with the filmstrip
adaptation of a boy reunited with his father
after a 5-year separation. Their trout fishing
experience in a remote area ends with an encounter with a bear that injures the father.
The son finds his valor and develops self-
reliance, thereby earning his father's respect.
Father-son interdependency and communication are stressed.

A KISS FOR LITTLE BEAR (Filmstrip—
Sound). Weston Woods Studios, 1973. 1
color, sound filmstrip, 35 fr.; 1 cassette, 4
min. #SF141C ($12.75). Gr. K–3. PRV
(12/73). Fic
Little Bear draws a picture of a wild thing
and sends it to his grandmother, who sends
a kiss back to him, relayed via a hen, a cat, a
frog, and a skunk. This story is based on the
book with the same name by Else Holmelund
Minarik and illustrated by Maurice Sendak.

BEAVERS

BEAVER (Film Loop—8mm—Silent). Walt
Disney Educational Media, 1966. 8mm
color, silent film loop, approx. 4 min. #62-
5009L ($30). Gr. K–12. MDU (1974).
599.3
The beaver is seen swimming and shown in-

side its lodge with muskrats, which share its
home. A beaver choosing its life mate is
shown.

BEAVER DAM AND LODGE (Film Loop—
8mm—Silent). Walt Disney Educational
Media, 1966. 8mm color, silent film loop,
approx. 4 min. #62-5010L ($30). Gr. K–
12. MDU (1974). 599.3
A beaver is studied as it constructs its dam
and lodge. Pictures the beaver gnawing down
a tree, the inside of the completed lodge,
and its cleaning and grooming habits.

MY FORTY YEARS WITH BEAVERS (Filmstrip—Sound). Lyceum/Mook &Blanchard,
1975. 2 color, sound filmstrips, 60–65 fr.;
2 cassettes or discs, 14 min. Cassettes
#LY35374SC ($46), Discs #LY35374SR
($37). Gr. 3–A. BKL (12/15/75), LNG
(11/75). 599.3
Contents: 1. A Kinship with Wild Beavers.
2. A Houseful of Beavers.

Introduces students to the patient observation and study of nature as they follow the
unique experience of Dorothy Richards as
she studies and becomes friends with a pair
of beavers. Sensitive photographs are by
Ann Atwood.

BECKETT, SHEILAH

SIGHTS AND SOUNDS FILMSTRIPS, SET
3 (Filmstrip—Sound). *See* Reading—Study
and Teaching

BEES

THE HONEY BEE (Film Loop—8mm—Captioned). BFA Educational Media, 1973
(Animal Behavior). 8mm color, captioned
film loop, approx. 4 min. #481414 ($30).
Gr. 4–9. BKL (5/1/76). 595.79
Demonstrates experiments, behavior, and
characteristics of the honey bees.

LIFE OF A WORKER BEE (Film Loop—
8mm—Silent). BFA Educational Media,
1973 (Animal Behavior). 8mm color, silent film loop, approx. 4 min. #481415
($30). Gr. 4–9. BKL (5/1/76). 595.79
Demonstrates experiments, behavior, and
characteristics of the worker bees.

BEETHOVEN, LUDWIG VAN

SYMPHONIC MOVEMENTS NO. 2 (Phonodiscs). *See* Symphonies

BEHAVIOR. *See* Animals—Habits and Behavior; Human Behavior

BELPRE, PURA

CHIQUITIN AND THE DEVIL: A PUERTO
RICAN FOLKTALE (Filmstrip—Sound).
See Folklore—Puerto Rico

BEMELMANS, LUDWIG

MADELINE AND THE GYPSIES AND
OTHER STORIES (Phonodisc or Cassette).
See France—Stories

BENNETT, RAINEY

THE SECRET HIDING PLACE (Filmstrip—
Sound or Captioned). *See* Hippopotamus—
Fiction

BEOWULF

BEOWULF AND THE MONSTERS (Cassette). Children's Classics on Tape, 1973.
1 cassette, 45 min.; detailed Study Guide.
($10.95). Gr. 4–9. BKL (7/15/74), ESL
(10/77), PRV (1/75). 829.3
Contents: 1. Story of Beowulf. 2. History
of the Anglo-Saxons and Original Beowulf.
Beowulf goes to the great hall of King Hroth-
gar to kill the monster Grendel, who has ter-
rorized the kingdom. Beowulf battles the
Water Witch and a fire-breathing dragon.
Relates the history of the Anglo-Saxons and
the Beowulf story, telling of the original
Beowulf MS and how it survived. Story and
historical narrative by Ruth Lind.

BERENSTAIN, JAN

THE BEAR'S NATURE GUIDE (Kit). *See*
Nature Study—Fiction

BEGINNER BOOKS FILMSTRIPS, SET 2
(Filmstrip—Sound). *See* Reading—Study
and Teaching

BEGINNER BOOKS FILMSTRIPS, SET 3
(Filmstrip—Sound). *See* Reading—Study
and Teaching

BERENSTAIN, STAN

THE BEAR'S NATURE GUIDE (Kit). *See*
Nature Study—Fiction

BEGINNER BOOKS FILMSTRIPS, SET 2
(Filmstrip—Sound). *See* Reading—Study
and Teaching

BEGINNER BOOKS FILMSTRIPS, SET 3
(Filmstrip—Sound). *See* Reading—Study
and Teaching

BERNSTEIN, LEONARD

FUN AND FANTASY SERIES (Cassette).
See Literature—Collections

BERSON, HAROLD

THE MULE WHO REFUSED TO BUDGE
(Filmstrip—Sound/Captioned). *See* Cooperation—Fiction

NEW PATCHES FOR OLD (Filmstrip—
Sound). *See* Folklore—Turkey

BEUERMAN, LEO

LEO BEUERMAN (Motion Picture—16mm—
Sound). Centron Films, 1969. 16mm color,
sound film, 13 min.; Leader's Guide. ($205).
Gr. 4–A. AFF, BKL (12/1/70), M&M (2/74).
921
Documents the life of Leo Beuerman, an
unusual man physically handicapped since
birth, describing his outlook on life and his
attitudes toward life and people.

BIBLE STORIES

WHY NOAH CHOSE THE DOVE (Filmstrip—
Sound). Miller-Brody Productions, 1975.
(Famous Author/Illustrator Filmstrips). 1
color, sound filmstrip; 1 cassette or disc;
Teacher's Guide. Cassette ($16), Disc ($16).
Gr. K–3. PRV (3/77). 220.9
Based on a story by Isaac Bashevis Singer,
this is a particularly creative way of portray-
ing the biblical story and underscoring the
value of humility.

BICULTURALISM

THE MANY AMERICANS, UNIT ONE (Filmstrip—Sound). Learning Corporation of
America, 1976. 4 color, sound filmstrips, av.
150 fr.; 4 cassettes, 10–13 min.; Teacher's
Guide. #76-730197 ($94). Gr. 4–8. M&M
(4/77), PRV (12/77), PVB (4/78). 301.45
Contents: 1. Geronimo Jones. 2. Felipa:
North of the Border. 3. Todd: Growing Up
in Appalachia. 4. Matthew Aliuk: Eskimo
in Two Worlds.
These sets reveal the customs, attitudes, and
social problems of bicultural groups in America. Each presents the moving story of a
conflict in the life of an ethnic minority
child who seeks to assimilate 2 worlds (based
on films).

THE MANY AMERICANS, UNIT TWO
(Filmstrip—Sound). Learning Corporation
of America, 1976. 4 color, sound filmstrips,
av. 150 fr.; 4 cassettes, 10–13 min.; Teacher's
Guide. #76-730198 ($94). Gr. 4–8. M&M
(4/77), PRV (12/77), PVB (4/78). 301.45
Contents: 1. Lee Suzuki: Home in Hawaii.
2. Miguel: Up from Puerto Rico. 3. Siu Mei
Wong: Who Shall I Be? 4. William: From
Georgia to Harlem.
Each filmstrip presents the story of conflict of an ethnic minority child who seeks
to assimilate 2 worlds (based on films).

BICYCLES AND BICYCLING

BASIC BICYCLING SERIES (Filmstrip—
Sound). BFA Educational Media, 1976. 4
color, sound filmstrips, 55–69 fr.; 4 cassettes or discs, 5–5:17 min.; 1 Guide. Disc

#VGJ000 ($70), Cassettes #VGK000 ($70).
Gr. 4-6. BKL (12/1/76). 796.6

Contents: 1. Bicycle History. 2. Bicycle
Safety. 3. Bicycle Maintenance. 4. Bicycle
Theft Prevention.

A good bike in good condition is a first re-
quirement. This series helps young bike drivers learn to keep the bike in proper condition, to insure its safety from theft, and to
learn correct driving procedures.

BICYCLE SAFELY (Motion Picture—16mm—
Sound). FilmFair Communications, 1974.
16mm color, sound film, 12 min. #D257
($150). Gr. 3-12. BKL (6/74), LFR (9/74),
PRV (6/74). 614.8
This film shows the major causes of bicycle
accidents and establishes the safety practices
that can avoid them.

BICYCLING ON THE SAFE SIDE (Motion
Picture—16mm—Sound). Ramsgate Films,
1974. 16mm color, sound film, 16 min.;
Study Guide. ($225). Gr. 4-A. BKL (10/
15/74), LGB (1974-75), PRV (2/75). 796.6
This film utilizes the popular 10-speed bike
to illustrate principles of bicycle safety, as
well as rider comfort and efficiency.

BIKE SAFETY: MAKING THE RIGHT
MOVES (Motion Picture—16mm—Sound).
See Safety Education

SAFETY ON TWO WHEELS (Filmstrip—
Sound). Learning Tree Filmstrips, 1977. 2
color, sound filmstrips, 57–65 fr.; 2 cassettes or discs; Teacher's Guide. Set #LT761
($29), Individual Strip ($17). Gr. 1-6.
PRV (1/78), PVB (4/78). 614.8
Contents: 1. Getting Started. 2. Rules of
the Road.

The first strip (A) shows Janet with her
father as she buys and learns to operate her
first 2-wheeler safely. The second strip (B)
shows an experienced tourer who helps with
the rules of cycling. Potential hazards are
examined.

SAFETY ON WHEELS (Filmstrip—Sound).
January Productions, 1975. 2 color, sound
filmstrips, av. 46 fr. ea.; 2 cassettes, av. 7
min. ea.; Teacher's Guide. Set ($29), Strip
($14.95). Gr. K-4. PRV (10/76). 614.8
Contents: 1. Wheel It Right. 2. Graduation
Day.

Presents dangers that exist and what can be
done by drivers, passengers, and pedestrians
to make each situation safer.

BICYCLES AND BICYCLING—FICTION

THE BEAR'S BICYCLE (Filmstrip—Sound).
Viking Press, 1977. 1 color, sound filmstrip, 37 fr.; 1 cassette, 4 1/2 min. #0-670-
90540-2 ($14.95). Gr. 3-6. PRV (2/78),
PVB (4/78). Fic
A popular rendering of the book by the
same name written by Emilie Warren

McLeod. Basically it is a straightforward bicycle safety lesson, but when David Mac-
Pail's bear gets in the act to show what
should not be done, it becomes a comedy.

BILINGUALISM. See Education, Bilingual

BIOGRAPHY

THE DIARY OF ANNE FRANK (Filmstrip—Sound). Films. 3 color, sound filmstrips; 3 cassettes, 20 min. ea.; Plot Synop-
sis; 2 Theme Strips. ($69). Gr. 4–8. M&M
(4/76). 921
Adapted from the film directed by George
Stevens, this condensation of the original
soundtrack preserves the integrity of the
story.

BIOGRAPHY—COLLECTIONS

BLACK AMERICAN ATHLETES (Kit). See
Athletes

CONTINENTAL SOLDIERS: HEROES OF
THE AMERICAN REVOLUTION, SET
ONE (Filmstrip—Sound). See U.S.—His-
tory—1775-1783—Revolution

CONTINENTAL SOLDIERS: HEROES OF
THE AMERICAN REVOLUTION, SET
TWO (Filmstrip—Sound). See U.S.—His-
tory—1775-1783—Revolution

FAMOUS STORIES OF GREAT COURAGE
(Filmstrip—Sound). See Heroes and Heroines

HISPANIC HEROES OF THE U.S.A. (Kit).
EMC, 1976. 4 paperback books; 4 read-
along cassettes; Teacher's Guide; Student
Activities. #ELC-236000 ($55). Gr. 4-12.
BKL (7/76). 920
Contents: Book I—1. Raul H. Castro: Adver-
sity Is My Angel. 2. Tommy Nunez: NBA
Ref. 3. Presenting: Vikki Carr, Book II—
1. Henry B. Gonzalez: Greater Justice for
All. 2. Trini Lopez: The Latin Sound. 3.
Edward Roybal: Awaken the Sleeping Gi-
ant. Book III—1. Carmen Rose Maymi:
To Serve American Women. 2. Robert
Clemente: Death of a Proud Man. 3. Jose
Feliciano: One Voice, One Guitar. Book
IV—1. Tony Perez: The Silent Superstar.
2. Lee Trevino: Supermex. 3. Jim Plunk-
ett: He Didn't Drop Out.
Inspiring biographies of 12 famous Americans of Hispanic heritage, grouped 3 to a
book, representing the broad contributions
of Spanish-speaking Americans to the culture
of this country.

HOCKEY HEROES (Kit). See Athletes

LEADERS, DREAMERS AND HEROES
(Cassette). Troll Associates, 1972. 7 cassettes, approx. 10 min. ea. ($38.50). Gr. 4-
8. BKL (7/15/74). 920

BIOGRAPHY—COLLECTIONS (cont.)

Contents: 1. Daniel Boone. 2. Davy Crockett. 3. Francis Marion. 4. Lewis and Clark. 5. Kit Carson. 6. Buffalo Bill. 7. John Paul Jones.

A series of brief biographies of American heroes who emerged in the late Colonial period and during the westward expansion.

SPORTS CLOSE-UPS 1 (Kit). *See* Athletes

SPORTS CLOSE-UPS 3 (Kit). *See* Athletes

SPORTS CLOSE-UPS 4 (Kit). *See* Athletes

TRAILBLAZERS OF INVENTION (Filmstrip—Sound). *See* Inventors

BIOLOGY

FIRST IDEAS ABOUT ANIMALS (Filmstrip—Sound). *See* Animals—Habits and Behavior

BIRDS

ANTARCTIC PENGUINS (Film Loop—8mm—Silent). *See* Penguins

BIRDS FEEDING THEIR YOUNG (Film Loop—8mm—Silent). Walt Disney Educational Media, 1966. 8mm color, silent film loop, approx. 4 min. #62-5918L ($30). Gr. K–12. MDU (1974). 598.2

The grosbeak, woodpecker, hummingbird, and waxwing are closely studied as they gather food and feed their young. Close-up shots show parents feeding worms and caterpillars to their young.

CHUPAROSAS: THE HUMMINGBIRD TWINS (Filmstrip—Sound). *See* Hummingbirds

ELEMENTARY NATURAL SCIENCE—SONGBIRDS (Motion Picture—16mm—Sound). Centron Films, 1974 (Elementary Natural Science). 16mm color, sound film, 13 min.; Leader's Guide. ($205). Gr. K–8. LFR (12/74), LGB (1975). 598.2

Uses close-up photography of well-known songbirds of the United States to illustrate nesting and grooming habits, physical adaptation, and caring for young.

ENDANGERED SPECIES: BIRDS (Study Print). *See* Rare Birds

FASCINATING BIRDS (Filmstrip—Sound). Marshfilm, 1970 (Ecology). 1 color, sound filmstrip, 97 fr.; 1 cassette or disc, 30 min.; Teacher's Guide. #1007 ($31). Gr. K–6. BKL (1/1/71), SLJ (10/15/71), 598.2

Presenting habitat, feeding, courtship, and nesting behavior of many unusual birds of North America.

INVESTIGATING BIRDS (Filmstrip—Sound). Coronet Instructional Media, 1975. 6 color, sound filmstrips, av. 59 fr.; 3 discs or 6 cassettes, av. 11 min. Discs #S255 ($95), Cassettes #M255 ($95). Gr. 4–9. BKL (12/75), INS (1975), PVB (1975–76). 598.2

Contents: 1. Birds of the Forest. 2. Birds of the Meadow. 3. Birds of the Sea. 4. Birds of the Southern Swamps and Marshes. 5. Birds of Ponds and Lakes. 6. Birds Near Your Home.

The adaptations, characteristics, and behavior of birds. Authentic bird calls accompany the natural photographs.

OUR ANIMAL TREE (Filmstrip—Sound). *See* Animals

PELICANS (Film Loop—8mm—Silent). *See* Pelicans

SAMMY THE CROW (Filmstrip—Sound). *See* Crows

See also names of birds such as Chickens, Eagles, etc., and classes of birds such as Birds of Prey, Water Birds; etc.

BIRDS—FICTION

BIRDS OF A FEATHER (Motion Picture—16mm—Sound). Bosustow Productions, 1972. 16mm color, sound, animated film, 6-1/2 min.; Leader's Guide. ($125). Gr. 2–A. CGE (1973), LBJ (1973), NEF (1973). Fic

A plain little bird is attracted by plumes in the hat of a passer-by. He plucks them and proudly attaches them, greatly enhancing his natural plumage. A bird catcher swoops him up and places him in a cage with similarly adorned exotic birds. They know he is an imposter and remove his glorious feathers. Seeing he is just an ordinary little fellow, the bird catcher lets him go. But once he has been reunited with his flock, he immediately begins the next scheme of mischievous fun. Based on the book by Willi Baum.

THE HAPPY OWLS (Motion Picture—16mm—Sound). *See* Happiness—Fiction

THE HOARDER (Motion Picture—16mm—Sound). *See* Fables

BIRDS OF PREY

BIRDS OF PREY (Filmstrip—Sound). Coronet Instructional Media, 1976. 4 color, sound filmstrips, 47–55 fr.; 4 cassettes or discs, 10–12 min.; 1 Guide. Cassettes #M257 ($65), Discs #S257 ($65). Gr. 4–10. BKL (5/15/77). 598.9

Contents: 1. Their Characteristics. 2. Hawks, Eagles, and Vultures. 3. Owls. 4. Their Survival.

Firsthand observation of the physical characteristics and behavior of the great birds and the study of the destructive effects of human behavior on bird species.

THE GOLDEN EAGLES (Kit). *See* Eagles

BISON

BISON AND THEIR YOUNG (Film Loop—
8mm—Silent). Walt Disney Educational
Media, 1966. 8mm color, silent film loop,
approx. 4 min. #62-5152L ($30). Gr. K-
12. MDU (1974). 599.7
Bison and their young are seen feeding on a
plain. Adults are shown as well as newborn
calves trying to stand and nurse.

BLACKS—FICTION

GOGGLES (Filmstrip—Sound). *See* Boys—
Fiction

PHILIP HALL LIKES ME: I RECKON
MAYBE (Phonodisc or Cassette). *See*
Friendship—Fiction

BLAKE, QUENTIN

PATRICK (Motion Picture—16mm—Sound).
See Music—Fiction

SOUND FILMSTRIP SET 35 (Filmstrip—
Sound). *See* Children's Literature—Collections

BLOOM, CLAIRE

CINDERELLA AND OTHER FAIRY
TALES (Phonodisc or Cassette). *See*
Fairy Tales

THE SECRET GARDEN (Phonodisc or Cassette). *See* Fantasy—Fiction

BLUE RIDGE MOUNTAINS

THE BLUE RIDGE: AMERICA'S FIRST
FRONTIER (Filmstrip—Sound). Lyceum/
Mook & Blanchard, 1973 (Lyceum). 1
color, sound filmstrip, 64 fr.; 1 cassette or
disc, 10-3/4 min. Cassette #LT35273C
($25), Disc #LY35273R ($19.50). Gr. 4-
A. BKL (7/1/73), INS (12/73), PRV (12/
75). 917.55
Dramatic photographs and almost poetic
commentary describe the terrain, plants,
and wildlife of the Blue Ridge area. It traces
the historical exploration and development
of the region and shows the use of the land
and development of crafts using the natural
environment.

BOLGER, RAY

QUEEN ZIXI OF IX, OR THE STORY OF
THE MAGIC CLOAK (Phonodisc or Cassette). *See* Fantasy—Fiction

BOLLIGER-SAVELLI, ANTONELLA

THRESHOLD FILMSTRIPS, SERIES C (Kit).
See Children's Literature—Collections

BONES

AN INSIDE LOOK AT ANIMALS (Study
Print). *See* Anatomy, Comparative

BONSALL, CROSBY

MYSTERY STORY (Filmstrip—Sound). *See*
Mystery and Detective Stories

BOOKS

BOOKS TALK BACK (Filmstrip—Sound).
Library Filmstrip Center, 1974. 1 color,
sound filmstrip, 48 fr.; 1 cassette or disc,
9:13 min. ($26). Gr. K-3. AFF (1975).
025.84
A little red book character tells his story.
He traces the process of bookmaking and
gives the do's and dont's in using and caring
for books

HOW A PICTURE BOOK IS MADE (Filmstrip—Sound). Weston Woods Studios, 1976.
1 color, sound filmstrip, 66 fr.; 1 cassette,
9:30 min.; 1 Guide. #SF451C ($25). Gr.
K-A. BKL (1/15/77). 686
Author-illustrator Steven Kellogg describes
the steps involved in creating "The Island
of the Skog," a picture book relating the adventures of a group of mice on a faraway island. He begins with the idea and follows
the book's development through writing and
rewriting to reworking after consulting with
his editor. He explains the creation of the
illustrations, the characters, and the dummy
for the book. He follows the steps to the
final printing and binding.

BOTANY

BEGINNING SCIENCE: PLANTS LEARN-
ING MODULE (Kit). Society for Visual
Education, 1976. 4 color, sound filmstrips,
45 fr.; 4 cassettes or discs, av. 8-1/4 min.;
Teacher's Guide; 45 Activity Cards and
Sheets, 2 Posters, 144 Crayons; 2 Class-
room Management Guides. ($99.50). Gr.
1-3. BKL (5/15/77). 581
Contents: 1. Plant Parts and How They
Work. 2. How Plants Make Food. 3. Seed
Magic: Life Story of a Bean. 4. Plant Vari-
ety: The Plant Zoo.

The filmstrips and the activities that accompany them are designed to show the parts of
plants and their functions, the food-making
ability of plants, the life cycle of plants, and
their diversity.

DEBBIE GREENTHUMB (Filmstrip—Sound).
See Horticulture

BOTANY—EXPERIMENTS

ISOLATION AND FUNCTION OF AUXIN
(Film Loop—8mm—Silent). *See* Phototropism

BOTANY—EXPERIMENTS (cont.)

MECHANICS OF PHOTOTROPISM (Film Loop–8mm–Captioned). *See* Phototropism

THE NATURE OF PHOTOTROPISM (Film Loop–8mm–Captioned). *See* Phototropism

BOXING

BOXING (Kit). Educational Activities, 1973. 1 color, sound filmstrip, 32 fr.; 1 disc or cassette, 12 min.; 10 student books; Teacher's Guide. Disc #450 ($35), Cassette #450 ($36). Gr. 4–9. PRV (11/74), PVB (5/75) 796.83

A professional tells and illustrates the whys and wherefores of boxing. A mix of "vocabulary" extension, picture-reading practice, and improvement of comprehension as students are motivated by this high interest, low vocabulary kit. Action photography and interesting, informative narration add to its value.

BOYS—FICTION

GOGGLES (Filmstrip–Sound). Weston Woods Studios, 1974. 1 color, sound filmstrip; 1 cassette; Text Booklet. #152 ($12.75). Gr. K–6. RTE (1/76). Fic

This strip is based on the book by the same name. It describes some black boys' adventure with a gang of older boys.

BRADBURY, RAY

THE FOG HORN (Filmstrip–Sound). *See* Science Fiction

THE ILLUSTRATED MAN (Filmstrip–Sound). *See* Science Fiction

THE MARTIAN CHRONICLES (Phonodiscs). *See* Science Fiction

THE VELDT (Filmstrip–Sound). *See* Science Fiction

BRANDENBERG, FRANZ

THRESHOLD FILMSTRIPS, SERIES C (Kit). *See* Children's Literature—Collections

BRAZIL

BRAZIL (Filmstrip–Sound). EBEC, 1973. 6 color, sound filmstrips, av. 92 fr. ea.; 6 discs or cassettes, 12 min. ea.; Teacher's Guide. Discs #6466 ($86.95), Cassettes #6466K ($86.95). Gr. 4–8. CPR (4/74), INS (2/75), PRV (11/74, 75). 918.1

Contents: 1. The People of Brazil. 2. The Land of Brazil. 3. The Amazon Basin. 4. Flight to the Cities. 5. Coffee Fazenda in Brazil. 6. Two Brazilian Cities (Salvador and São Paulo).

Viewers are transported to semidesert backlands and prosperous coffee fazendas, to Amazon fishing villages and highly industrialized cities. They meet people of every race and discover that in Brazil racial democracy is a reality. There are intriguing glimpses of festivals and soccer games and searching looks at the problems that this advancing nation has yet to solve.

BRINK, CAROL RYRIE

CAROL RYRIE BRINK (Filmstrip–Sound). Miller-Brody Productions, 1973 (Meet the Newbery Author). 1 color, sound filmstrip, 86 fr.; 1 disc or cassette, 15 min. ($32). Gr. 3–8. CHH (9/77). 921

Carol Brink, author of *Caddie Woodlawn*, describes how and why she writes; she also talks about the stories her grandmother told her and shows old photographs of the areas she writes about. A segment from the book is illustrated.

BRONZES

THE BRONZE ZOO (Motion Picture–16mm–Sound). *See* Sculpture

BROWN, MARCIA

THE CRYSTAL CAVERN (Filmstrip–Sound). *See* Caves

BROWNING, ROBERT

LIBRARY 5 (Cassette). *See* Literature—Collections

BRUBECK, DAVE

ART OF DAVE BRUBECK: THE FANTASY YEARS (Phonodiscs). *See* Jazz Music

BUDBERG, MAURA

RUSSIAN FAIRY TALES (Phonodisc or Cassette). *See* Folklore—Russia

BUFFALO. *See* Bison

BUILDING

MEET THE BUILDERS (Filmstrip–Sound). Educational Dimensions Group, 1975. 6 color, sound filmstrips, av. 40 fr.; 6 cassettes, 7 min.; 1 Guide. #817 ($99). Gr. 3–5. BKL (1/15/77). 690.023

Contents: 1. Part 1: The Planners. 2. Part 2: Operating Engineers and Bricklayers. 3. Part 3: The Carpenters. 4. Part 4: The Electricians. 5. Part 5: Plumbers and Pipefitters. 6. Part 6: Glaziers, Decorators, and Artists.

A survey of the building trades and the co-operation and planning among all the trades necessary to build all types of buildings. Career information is inherent in the discussion and puts meaningful perspective to the description of numerous jobs.

BULLA, CLYDE

FIRST CHOICE AUTHORS AND BOOKS (Filmstrip—Sound). *See* Authors

BUNYAN, PAUL

JOHNNY APPLESEED AND PAUL BUNYAN (Phonodisc or Cassette). *See* Folklore—U.S.

THE LEGEND OF PAUL BUNYAN (Motion Picture—16mm—Sound). *See* Folklore—U.S.

PAUL BUNYAN IN STORY AND SONG (Phonodisc or Cassette). *See* Folklore—U.S.

BURGESS, GELETT

THE GOOPS: A MANUAL OF MANNERS FOR MOPPETS (Filmstrip—Sound/Captioned). *See* Etiquette

BURNETT, FRANCES HODGSON

THE SECRET GARDEN (Phonodisc or Cassette). *See* Fantasy—Fiction

BURNFORD, SHEILA

TWO FOR ADVENTURE (Kit). *See* Animals—Fiction

BURNINGHAM, JOHN

SOUND FILMSTRIP SET 35 (Filmstrip—Sound). *See* Children's Literature—Collections

BURTON, VIRGINIA LEE

THE LITTLE HOUSE (Filmstrip—Sound). *See* Houses—Fiction

BUSINESS

PARTNERS, UNIT 3 (Motion Picture—16mm—Sound). *See* Occupations

BUTTERFLIES

BUTTERFLY: THE MONARCH'S LIFE CYCLE (Motion Picture—16mm—Sound). International Film Bureau, 1975. 16mm color, sound film, 10-1/2 min.; Teacher's Guide. #1IFB 652 ($145). Gr. 4–8. PRV (11/76). 595.78
Good photographic close-ups of the egg; the young caterpillar emerging from the egg and passing through the repeated stages of eating, growing, and molting; building the button with which to attach itself for the pupa

stage; shedding the last skin and changing within the chrysalis; and finally the adult emerging to dry its wings before flight.

DON'T (Motion Picture—16mm—Sound). Phoenix Films, 1974. 16mm color, sound film, 19 min. #2072 ($275). Gr. 7–A. AAW (1975), FLI (2/76). 595.78
The lyric passage of a Monarch butterfly, beginning with its birth, through its delicate metamorphosis from caterpillar to butterfly and on its journey from country to city.

LIFE CYCLE OF COMMON ANIMALS, GROUP 3 (Filmstrip—Sound). Imperial Educational Resources, 1973. 2 color, sound filmstrips, 36–39 fr.; 2 cassettes or discs, 9:40–10:34 min. Discs #3RG 40300 ($30), Cassettes #3KG 40300 ($33). Gr. 4–9. PRV (2/74), PVB (5/74), STE (4/5/74). 595.78
Contents: 1. The Monarch Butterfly, Part One. 2. The Monarch Butterfly, Part Two.
Portrays the significant events in the life history of the Monarch butterfly.

METAMORPHOSIS (Motion Picture—16mm—Sound). Texture Films, 1977. 16mm color, sound film, 10 min. ($175). Gr. 2–8. BKL (1/15/78), CGE (1977). 595.78
A young people's science film about a girl watching the wonderful transformation of a caterpillar into a butterfly.

MONARCH: STORY OF A BUTTERFLY (Film Loop—8mm—Silent). Troll Associates. 3 8mm color, silent film loops, approx. 4 min. ($74.85). Gr. 1–8. AUR (1978). 595.78
Contents: 1. Monarch: Eggs to Caterpillar. 2. Monarch: Caterpillar to Pupa. 3. Chrysalis to Butterfly.
These loops document in close-up detail the life cycle of the Monarch butterfly.

BYARS, BETSY

THE LACE SNAIL (Filmstrip—Sound). *See* Snails—Fiction

CACTUS

CACTUS: PROFILE OF A PLANT (Motion Picture—16mm—Sound). EBEC, 1973. 16mm color, sound film, 11 min. #3174 ($150). Gr. K–3. NST (9/75), PRV (10/74), SLJ (5/73). 583.47
How can you tell a cactus from other types of plants? Do all cacti look alike? Why can cactus plants live in the desert? These and many other questions are explored in this unusual film. Close-up and time-lapse photography capture seldom seen views of cacti in their natural environment.

CALCULATING MACHINES

COMPUTERS: FROM PEBBLES TO PRO-
GRAMS (Filmstrip—Sound). *See* Computers

INTRODUCING THE ELECTRONIC CAL-
CULATOR (Filmstrip—Sound). BFA Educational Media, 1975. 2 color, sound filmstrips; 2 cassettes or discs; Teacher's Guide.
Cassettes #VGB000 ($36), Discs #VGA000
($36). Gr. 4–8. MTE (5/77). 681.14
Contents: 1. A Boxful of Magic. 2. Electronic Wizard.
An overview to help students understand
the capabilities of the calculator and to
teach them to use it to solve mathematical
problems.

MATH ON DISPLAY (Kit). *See* Mathematics

CALDECOTT MEDAL BOOKS

ARROW TO THE SUN (Motion Picture—
16mm—Sound). *See* Indians of North America—Legends

SAM, BANGS, AND MOONSHINE (Motion
Picture—16mm—Sound). *See* Imagination—
Fiction

A STORY A STORY (Filmstrip—Sound). *See*
Folklore—Africa

SYLVESTER AND THE MAGIC PEBBLE
PUPPET (Kit). *See* Magic—Fiction

WHY MOSQUITOES BUZZ IN PEOPLE'S
EARS (Kit). *See* Animals—Fiction

CALENDARS

CALENDAR STUDIES (Filmstrip—Sound).
Educational Direction/Learning Tree Filmstrips, 1974. 4 color, sound filmstrips, av.
60 fr. ea.; 2 cassettes, av. 5 min. ea.; Teacher's
Guide. #LT436 ($52). Gr. 2–5. BKL
(9/75), LGB (1974), 574.5
Contents: 1. Calendars. 2. Time.
Stories are used to introduce the concepts
of days, weeks, months, the year, and
seasons.

IT'S ABOUT TIME (Filmstrip—Sound).
January Productions, 1976. 4 color, sound
filmstrips, av. 47 fr. ea.; 4 cassettes, av. 7
min. ea.; Teacher's Guide. Set ($58), Indi-
vidual ($14.95). Gr. K–2. BKL (11/1/76),
PRV (12/1/76). 529
Contents: 1. The Town without Clocks.
2. The Unhappy Clock. 3. A Helping Second Hand. 4. Calendar Talk.
The first 3 filmstrips simplify the task of
learning to tell the hours, quarter hours,
and half hours, and the roles of seconds and
minutes; the fourth filmstrip teaches the
days of the week and familiarizes students
with the calendar.

CAMPING

CAMPING (Filmstrip—Sound). Great American Film Factory, 1975. 1 color, sound
filmstrip, 72 fr,; 1 cassette, 19:30 min.
#FS-3 ($35). Gr. 5–A. BKL (2/1/76),
PRV (1/77), PVD (4/77). 796.54
Supplies information about camping, emphasizing the idea of taking nothing from
the wilderness to leave an unspoiled site for
those who follow. Comparative data about
site choices, cooking, and tents; provides
rules and helpful hints.

SUMMER CAMP (Motion Picture—16mm—
Sound). McGraw-Hill Films, 1976. 16mm
color, sound film, 13 min.; Guide. #106868-
6 ($195). Gr. K–3. PRV (11/1/76). 796.54
Originally a television production and now
available for the classroom, the film presents
Bill Cosby's famous Fat Albert and the
Cosby Kids with some live action footage of
Cosby himself. The problems of summer
camp and the miseries of home sickness, in
addition to the necessity of getting along
with newcomers to the group—one a mean,
trick-playing bully—confront the Cosby
Kids at camp. Their experiences are amusing
and provide lessons in dealing with other people. The film also will help prepare children
for the more pleasant adventures awaiting
them at summer camp.

CANADA

CANADA (Filmstrip—Sound). National Geographic, 1976. 5 color, sound filmstrips; 5
cassettes or discs, 12–14 min.; (also available
in French-English). Discs #03782 ($74.50),
Cassettes #03783 ($74.50). Gr. 5–12. M&M
(4/77). 917.1
Contents: 1. The Atlantic Provinces. 2. Quebec. 3. Ontario. 4. The Prairie Provinces
and Northwest Territories. 5. British Columbia and the Yukon Territory.
Canada's national life and breathtaking geography are presented in this set, along with
its abundance of resources and industries.

CANADA: LAND OF NEW WEALTH (Filmstrip—Sound). EBEC, 1976. 5 color, sound
filmstrips, av. 77 fr. ea.; 5 discs or cassettes,
10 min. ea.; Teacher's Guide. Discs #6946
($72.50), Cassettes #6946K ($72.50). Gr.
4–12. ESL (1977), MDU (4/77). 917.1
Contents: 1. The Physical Base. 2. Natural
Resources. 3. Food Production. 4. Industry. 5. Cities.
Following World War II, Canada's history
has been one of sudden and dramatic change
brought about by rapid industrialization.
This series examines that transition and the
factors responsible.

CANADA: NORTHERN GIANT (Filmstrip—
Sound). BFA Educational Media, 1970. 8
color, sound filmstrips; 8 cassettes or discs.

Cassettes #VH4000 ($138), Disc #VH3000 ($138). Gr. 4–8. BKL (5/15/71). 917.1

Contents: 1. A Geographic Overview. 2. An Historical and Social Overview. 3. Canadian Industry. 4. Canadian Mining. 5. Canadian Natural Resources. 6. Transportation in Canada. 7. Canadian Education. 8. Canadian Agriculture.

This set explores many facets of life in Canada—its culture, its people, and its industry.

THE CANADIANS (Filmstrip–Sound). EBEC, 1976. 5 color, sound filmstrips, av. 77 fr. ea.; 5 discs or cassettes, 11 min. ea.; Teacher's Guide. Discs #6954 ($72.50), Cassettes #6954K ($72.50). Gr. 4–9. BKL (6/15/77), MDU (4/77). 917.1

Contents: 1. The Two Founding Nations. 2. Canadian, Canadien: A Portrait of Two Families. 3. The Many Canadians. 4. Canada and the World. 5. Unity in Diversity.

Although Canada has long been a land of many cultures, its recent industrial progress has added to the problems that accompany such ethnic diversity. This series traces the early settlement patterns by the French and English, portrays some current manifestations of the dual heritage, and examines the continuing influence of the original natives—the Indians and Eskimos.

DOCUMENTARY ON CANADA (Filmstrip–Sound). Society for Visual Education, 1973. 6 color, sound filmstrips, av. 89 fr.; 3 discs or cassettes, av. 19 min.; 1 Guide. Discs #274-SAR ($83), Cassette #274-SATC ($83). Gr. K–A. BKL (4/73). 917.1

Contents: 1. The Fishermen of Nova Scotia. 2. Quebec City and the French Canadians. 3. Pinawa, Manitoba, Suburb for Atomic Energy. 4. Yellowknife: Capitol. 5. Canada's Arctic Settlements. 6. The Port of Vancouver: Canada's Pacific Gateway.

This set examines a cross section of the country of Canada in the light of modern problems. Each filmstrip describes the unique background of a particular region and focuses on people and their lives.

OUR NEIGHBORS: CANADA AND MEXICO (Filmstrip–Sound). See North America

CANADA—HISTORY

PAUL KANE GOES WEST (Motion Pictures–16 mm–Sound). See Indians of North America—Canada

CAREERS. See Occupations; Vocational Guidance; Work

CARLSON, CHESTER F.

TRAILBLAZERS OF INVENTION (Filmstrip–Sound). See Inventors

CARRADINE, JOHN

THE LEGEND OF SLEEPY HOLLOW AND ICHABOD CRANE (Motion Picture–16mm–Sound). See Legends–U.S.

CARROLL, LEWIS

ALICE IN WONDERLAND (Kit). See Fantasy–Fiction

EPISODES FROM FAMOUS STORIES (Filmstrip–Sound). See Literature–Collections

THROUGH THE LOOKING GLASS (Phonodiscs). See Fantasy–Fiction

CARVER, GEORGE WASHINGTON

TRAILBLAZERS OF INVENTION (Filmstrip–Sound). See Inventors

CATTLE

DAIRY COWS (Film Loop–8mm–Silent). Thorne Films/Prentice-Hall Media, 1972 (Barnyard Animals). 8mm color, silent film loop, approx. 4 min. #HAT 432 ($26). Gr. 1–6. EYR (10/73), INS (12/72), TEA (11/72). 636.2

Dairy cows grazing in a pasture are observed. The film follows their movements and eating habits. Many close-up scenes allow the study of the cow's physical appearance.

CAVES

THE CRYSTAL CAVERN (Filmstrip–Sound). Lyceum/Mook & Blanchard, 1974. 1 color, sound filmstrip, 61 fr.; 1 cassette or disc, 11 min.; Teacher's Guide. Cassette #LY35274C ($25), Disc #LY35274R ($19.50). Gr. 6–A. BKL (10/15/74), CPR (12/75), PRV (3/75). 796.525.

Marcia Brown, twice winner of the Caldecott Award, uses beautiful photography and imaginative prose to take us through the Crystal Cavern of Xanadu. The classic poem "Kubla Khan" by Samuel Coleridge is used as a point of departure. The objective of this filmstrip is to stimulate students' imagination through nature.

CENTRAL AMERICA

CENTRAL AMERICA: FINDING NEW WAYS (Motion Picture–16mm–Sound). EBEC, 1974. 16mm color, sound film, 17 min. #3306 ($220). Gr. 4–9. LFR (5/19/75), PRV (4/75). 917.28

Linking North and South America are 6 republics with 2 merging cultures—Spanish and Mayan. This film shows how the poor live and work, and the many programs instituted by the government to redistribute land, modernize farming, diversify crops, and develop industries.

CENTRAL EUROPE

EAST CENTRAL EUROPE, GROUP ONE
(Filmstrip—Sound). Society for Visual Education, 1972. 6 color, sound filmstrips, av.
68 fr.; 3 discs or cassettes, av. 19-3/4 min.
Discs #292 SAR ($83), Cassettes #292
SATC ($83). Gr. 4-9. BKL (2/73), PRV
(2/73). 914.3
Contents: 1. The Culture of Czechoslovakia.
2. Czech Agriculture. 3. Hungary's Collec-
tive Farms. 4. The Danube: Hungary's
"Seacoast." 5. Poland's Paradox, Religion
and Communism. 6. Poland's Educational
System.
Contemporary photos, historical maps, and
charts blend with an authoritative narration
to create a fascinating overview of 6 East
Central European countries. Viewers study
geography, culture, industry, agriculture,
religion, education, and politics of these
important nations.

CETEWAYO

FAMOUS STORIES OF GREAT COURAGE
(Filmstrip—Sound). See Heroes and Heroines

CHAGALL, MARC

PICTURES ARE FUN TO LOOK AT (Art
Prints). See Art Appreciation

CHANNING, CAROL

ROLAND, THE MINSTREL PIG AND
OTHER STORIES (Phonodisc or Cassette).
See Children's Literature—Collections

CHAPLIN, CHARLES SPENCER

CHAPLIN—A CHARACTER IS BORN
(Motion Picture—16mm—Sound). S-L Film
Productions, 1977. 16mm black/white,
sound film, 40 min. ($270). Gr. 7-A. AFF
(1977), FLN (1/2/77). 791.43
The film traces the evolution of the character created by Charlie Chaplin from his
earliest film through the high points of
his early achievements. Included are selections from many of his classic films.

CHAPMAN, JOHN—FICTION

JOHNNY APPLESEED AND PAUL BUN-
YAN (Phonodisc or Cassette). See Folklore—U.S.

CHARLES, RAY

CONTINENTAL SOLDIERS: HEROES OF
THE AMERICAN REVOLUTION, SET
ONE (Filmstrip—Sound). See U.S.—His-
tory—1775–1783—Revolution

CONTINENTAL SOLDIERS: HEROES
OF THE AMERICAN REVOLUTION,
SET TWO (Filmstrip—Sound). See U.S.—
History—1775–1783—Revolution

CHASE, RICHARD

FIRST CHOICE AUTHORS AND BOOKS
(Filmstrips—Sound). See Authors

CHEETAHS

CHEETAH (Motion Picture—16mm—Sound).
EBEC, 1971 (Silent Safari). 16mm color,
sound, nonnarrated film, 11 min.; Teacher's
Guide. #3125 ($150). Gr. 2-9. AIF
(1977), BKL (10/1/76), CGE (1977). 599.7
Shows the fleet cheetah, the fastest mammal, in action as it hunts its favorite prey,
the Thompson's gazelle. Unsuccessful, it
playfully attacks a topi and then dodges
a scavenging lion. Hunt scenes show how
the cheetah uses its tail for balance.

THE CHEETAHS OF THE SERENGETI
PLAIN (Kit). Classroom Complements/
EBEC, 1976 (Animal Life Stories). 1
color, sound filmstrip; 1 cassette; 5 identical
Storybooks; Teacher's Guide. #6974K
($27.95). Gr. K-6. TEA (11/77). 599.7
Young readers can learn how cheetahs move,
build homes, and fight for food and survival.
Scientifically accurate story describes the
lives of cheetahs in their natural habitat.
A storybook reproduces all the narration
and full-color art from the filmstrip.

CHICKENS

BIRTH AND CARE OF BABY CHICKS
(Film Loop—8mm—Captioned). BFA Educational Media, 1973. 8mm color, captioned
film loop, approx. 4 min. #481419 ($30).
Gr. 4-9. BKL (5/1/76). 636.5
Demonstrates experiments, behavior, and
characteristics of baby chicks.

CHICKENS (Film Loop—8mm—Silent).
Thorne Films/Prentice-Hall Media, 1972.
8mm color, silent film loop, approx. 4 min.
#HAT 436 ($26). Gr. 1-6. AUR (1978).
636.5
Chickens are seen in the barnyard pecking,
drinking, and walking.

EMBRYOLOGY OF THE CHICK (Film
Loop—8mm—Captioned). See Embryology

HATCHING OF A CHICK (Film Loop—
8mm—Silent). Thorne Films/Prentice-Hall
Media, 1972 (Barnyard Animals). 8mm
color, silent film loop, approx. 4 min.
#HAT 435 ($26). Gr. 1-6 EYR (10/73),
INS (12/72), TEA (11/72). 636.5
This loop shows the eggs in an incubator
followed by a chick beginning to hatch, continuing 12 hours later when the chick is actively trying to hatch out of the egg, and

finally 3 chicks are seen 16 hours after they first began pecking out of their shells.

CHILD DEVELOPMENT

AT YOUR AGE (Motion Picture—16mm—Sound). Yehuda Tarmu/FilmFair Communications, 1972. 16mm color, sound film, 10 min. #C180 ($135). Gr. K–6. BKL (11/72), LFR (4/72), PRV (9/1/73). 155.4
This film helps children express their feelings about growing up and assuming responsibilities.

EARLY LEARNING LIBRARY (Filmstrip—Sound). Miller-Brody Productions, 1972. 6 color, sound filmstrips, 40–75 fr.; 6 cassettes or discs, 7–12 min.; Teacher's Guide. Discs #8-E401/6 ($96), Cassettes #8-E 401/6-C ($96). Gr. K–2. PRV (9/72), PVB (5/73). 155.4
Contents: 1. How Do You Do. 2. The King and. . . . 3. Under the Rainbow. 4. Ooo-Loo, the Kangaroo. 5. Who Gives Us That? 6. Nimble B. Nimble.
Specific ways of developing skills in listening, knowing, thinking, and imagining are presented. The materials were derived from the Headstart Books by Shari Lewis and Jacquelyn Reinach. Shari Lewis narrates and sings in English and Rita Moreno performs in Spanish. Skills taught include knowing left from right; how to shake hands; learning name, phone number, address, colors, parts of the body; identifying objects and associating products with sources; speaking clearly and listening carefully. Available in Spanish.

HOW WE GROW (Filmstrip—Sound). BFA Educational Media, 1975. 4 color, sound filmstrips; 4 cassettes or discs. Cassette #VEY000 ($85), Discs #VEX000 ($85). Gr. 6–9. BKL (3/15/76). 612.4
Contents: 1. Physical Growth. 2. Mental Growth. 3. Emotional Growth. 4. Social Growth.
Prepares preadolescent and early adolescent students for the changes they soon will, or have already begun to, experience. Helps students develop positive attitudes to their own growth pattern and to those of others.

IDENTITY THREE (Kit). Children's Press, 1976. 4 cassettes, av. 9–12 min.; 4 books; 1 Guide. #03180-5 ($39.95). Gr. 1–3. BKL (12/15/77). 155.4
Contents: 1. Daydreams and Night. 2. I'm Not Going. 3. Tracy. 4. Why Me?
Designed to help children with everyday problems such as moving to a new locality, adapting to home and school situations as a handicapped individual, daydreaming, and coping with group pressures. Two books are complete stories and the other 2 are vignettes centered around a common problem.

IT'S GOOD TO BE ME (Filmstrip—Sound). *See* Emotions

CHILDREN AS ARTISTS

LIFE TIMES NINE (Motion Picture—16mm—Sound). *See* Life

CHILDREN AS AUTHORS

POETRY AND ME (Filmstrip—Sound). Coronet Instructional Media, 1974. 4 color, sound filmstrips, 46–51 fr.; 4 cassettes or 2 discs, 6:30–9:40 min. Cassettes #M276 ($65), Discs #S276 ($65). Gr. 1–3. BKL (2/1/75), PRV. 028.5
Contents: 1. How I Feel. 2. When I Play. 3. Places Near and Far. 4. People I See.
Photography and "poetry begins with me" feeling help children form a personal view of life and express what they see and feel about the world around them.

POETRY BY AND FOR KIDS (Kit). *See* Poetry-Collections

CHILDREN—FICTION

A HOUSEFUL OF OCEAN (Kit). Guidance Associates, 1973. 1 color, sound filmstrip, 56 fr.; 1 cassette or disc, 9 min.; 4 Read-along Books; Teacher's Guide. Disc #9A-302 545 ($34), Cassette #9A-302 552 ($34). Gr. K–3. BKL (5/76). Fic
Kathy imagines what might happen if the beach and ocean followed her home—a day of real and fantasy adventure.

THE MISSING WHISTLE (Kit). Guidance Associates, 1973. 1 color, sound filmstrip, 55 fr.; 1 cassette or disc, 8 min.; 4 Read-along Books; Teacher's Guide. Disc #9A-302 586 ($34), Cassette #9A-302 594 ($34). Gr. K–3. BKL (5/76). Fic
The search for a prized whistle reveals lots of things—but no whistle. Finally, Billy's dad gives him a clue he needs. This leads to a rewarding surprise ending.

MY BROTHER IS A PUMPKIN (Kit). Guidance Associates, 1973. 1 color, sound filmstrip, 57 fr.; 1 cassette or disc, 9 min.; 4 Read-along Books; Teacher's Guide. Disc #9A-302 560 ($34), Cassette #9A-302 578 ($34). Gr. K–3. BKL (5/76). Fic
Ellen calmly reveals that her brother is a pumpkin, which her father confirms. A final, delightful twist holds students' interest and motivates them to a read-along.

NOISY NANCY NORRIS (Filmstrip—Sound). Guidance Associates. 1 color sound filmstrip, 71 fr.; 1 cassette or disc, 13 min. #1B-301-703 ($27.75), #1B-301-729 ($27.75). Gr. K–3. AFF. Fic
From the book by Lou Ann Gaeddert, illustrated by Gioia Fiammenghi, this comedy encourages children to read while offering

CHILDREN—FICTION (cont.)

a subtle message on self-discipline and living with others.

CHILDREN IN THE U.S.

HOW CHILDREN LIVE IN AMERICA (Filmstrip—Sound). Troll Associates, 1975. 6 color, sound filmstrips, av. 69 fr.; 3 cassettes, av. 8 min. ea.; Teacher's Guide. ($78). Gr. 2–7. BKL (1/15/76), PRV (3/76). 917.3

Contents: 1. I Live on a Farm. 2. I Live on a Ranch. 3. I Live in a City. 4. I Live in a Town. 5. I Live in a Large Metropolitan Area. 6. I Live in a Rural Area.

Explores the different regions that American children call home to point out what makes each family unique and important.

CHILDREN'S LITERATURE— COLLECTIONS

HURRAY FOR CAPTAIN JANE! & OTHER LIBERATED STORIES FOR CHILDREN (Phonodisc or Cassette). Caedmon Records, 1974. 1 cassette or disc, approx. 60 min. Disc #TC1455 ($6.98), Cassette #CDL51455 ($7.95). Gr. K–3. M&M (1975). Fic

Contents: 1. Sam Reavin: Hurray for Captain Jane. 2. Lou Ann Gaeddert: Noisy and Nick. 3. Miriam Young: Jellybeans for Breakfast. 4. Sarah Evane Boyte: Jenny's Secret Place. 5. Bernard Waber: Ira Sleeps Over. 6. Phil Ressner: Dudley and Louise. 7. Joan M. Lexau: Emily and the Klunky Baby and the Next-Door Dog. 8. Barbara Danish: The Dragon and the Doctor. 9. Magrit Eichler: Martin's Father. 10. Janice May Udry: The Sunflower Garden.

These 10 stories for young children present a range of spunky and adventurous female heroines with whom to identify. Boys will enjoy Ira's triumph in Bernard Waber's story about a little boy who discovers that his best friend, like himself, cannot go to bed at night without a teddy bear.

MOTHER GOOSE RHYMES AND OTHER STORIES (Cassette). *See* Nursery Rhymes

ROLAND, THE MINSTREL PIG AND OTHER STORIES (Phonodisc or Cassette). Caedmon Records. 1 cassette or disc, approx. 55 min.; Jacket Notes. Disc #TC1305 ($6.98), Cassette #CDL51305 ($7.95). Gr. K–4. LBJ, SLJ. Fic

Contents: 1. "Roland the Minstrel Pig" by William Steig. 2. "Loudmouth" by Richard Wilbur. 3. "Tom, Sue and the Clock" by Conrad Aiken. 4. "The B Book" by Phyllis McGinley.

Carol Channing's reading and singing of these excellent children's stories adds to the enjoyment of hearing them.

SOUND FILMSTRIP SET 35 (Filmstrip— Sound). Weston Woods Studios, 1973. 4 color, sound filmstrips, 16–38 fr.; 1 disc or cassette; Text Booklet. Set 35 ($32.50). Gr. K–3. PRV (12/74), PVB (5/75). 808.8

Contents: 1. May I Bring a Friend? 2. The Rich Man and the Shoemaker. 3. Patrick. 4. Mr. Grumpy's Outing.

A set of children's stories photographically reproduced with high quality sound. The musical accompaniment adds greatly in the actual wild animal sounds and the lively violin music.

THRESHOLD FILMSTRIPS, SERIES C (Kit). Insight Media Programs/Macmillan Library Services, 1976. 12 color, sound filmstrips, av. 34–61 fr. ea.; 12 cassettes or discs, av. 3–7 min.; 12 Scripts. Cassettes set #95266 ($160), Discs #95265 ($160), Individual Titles ($14.95). Gr. 4–8. BKL (9/1/77). 808.8

Contents: 1. How the Sun Was Brought Back to the Sky. 2. Jack and Fred. 3. Miranda's Magic. 4. The Mouse and the Knitted Cat. 5. Mushroom in the Rain. 6. New Blue Shoes. 7. No School Today. 8. Rooster Brother. 9. The Silver Christmas Tree. 10. Tough Jim. 11. What Do You See? 12. The Wind Blew.

Macmillan has adapted 12 of their most popular picture books of 1973–1975 to sound filmstrips with scripts for read-aloud potential. Authors and illustrators of the selections are: Mirra Ginsburg, Jose Aruego, Ariane Dewey, Byron Barton, Antonella Bolliger-Savelli, Eve Rice, Franz Brandenberg, Aliki, Nonny Hogrogian, Pat Hutchins, Lillian Hoban, Janina Domanska, and Miriam Cohen.

CHILDREN'S SONGS

THE LEARNING PARTY, VOL. ONE (Phonodisc or Cassette). Educational Activities, 1974. 1 disc or cassette; 1 Guide. Disc #AR560 ($6.95), Cassette #AC560 ($7.95). Gr. K–3. BKL (8/77). 784.6

A party setting, but curriculum-guided approach to help children get acquainted, learn about themselves, their senses, self-concepts, families, and friends. Available in Spanish.

THE LEARNING PARTY, VOL. TWO, GOING PLACES (Phonodisc or Cassette). Educational Activities, 1974. 1 disc or cassette; 1 Guide. Disc #AR567 ($6.95), Cassette #AC567 ($7.95). Gr. K–3. BKL (8/77). 784.6

The second volume emphasizes rhyming and problem-solving, number identification, contrast between fantasy and real-

ity, and other concepts. Available in Spanish.
See also Choruses and Part Songs

CHINA

CHINA . . . A PLACE OF MYSTERY (Filmstrip–Sound). Marshfilm, 1972. 1 color, sound filmstrip, 65 fr.; 1 cassette or disc, 15 min. #1114 ($21). Gr. 2–6. INS (12/73), PRV (1/74). 915.1

This filmstrip illustrates life in China today, similarities and differences between the Chinese and American ways of life from a child's point of view.

CHINA–CIVILIZATION

CHINA: PEOPLE, PLACES AND PROGRESS (Filmstrip–Sound). Prentice-Hall Media, 1974. 6 color, sound filmstrips, 58–71 fr.; 6 cassettes or discs, 8-1/2–10 min.; Teacher's Guide. Cassettes #HAC 5410 ($99), Discs #HAR 5410 ($99). Gr. 1–7. BKL (3/15/74). 915.103

Contents: 1. Kwangchow: A River Port. 2. Shangkiu: An Industrial City. 3. Tientsen: A Suburb of the City. 4. Hong Kong: The Floating Population. 5. Peking: The Capital City. 6. Dahli Commune: A Communal Farm and Fish Nursery.

The description of working conditions, commerce, clothing, food, and recreation are presented by children featured as guides to their hometowns or native cities.

CHINA–FICTION

THE EMPEROR AND THE KITE (Filmstrip–Sound/Captioned). Listening Library, 1976 (Look, Listen and Read). 1 color, sound/captioned filmstrip, 49 fr.; 1 cassette, 12 min.; Teacher's Guide. #JFS 151 ($14.95). Gr. K–3. PRV (3/77). Fic

A Caldecott Honor Book and an ALA Notable Children's Book that poetically tells the story of the importance to an Emperor of a young girl's deed. Illustrations and narration taken verbatim from the book. Read by Corinne Orr.

CHINA–HISTORY–1949-1976

PEOPLE OF CHINA (Filmstrip–Sound). Educational Dimensions Group, 1976. 2 color, sound filmstrips, av. 40 fr.; 2 cassettes, av. 8 min.; 1 Guide. #816 ($33). Gr. 1–3. BKL (3/15/77), PRV (1/77), PVB (4/77). 951.

Makes a simple presentation of the land, historical prints, and photographs of the Chinese people. Provides the basics of the Chinese heritage, life-styles, and changes that have occurred since the 1949 revolution. Explained in simple generalizations and terms for young viewers.

CHINA–SOCIAL LIFE AND CUSTOMS

CHINESE COUNTRY CHILDREN (Filmstrip–Sound). Spoken Arts, 1977. 4 color, sound filmstrips, av. 29–43 fr.; 4 discs or cassettes, av. 5–8 min.; 8 Duplicating Masters; 1 Guide. Discs #SA-2038 ($79.95), Cassettes #SAC-2038 ($79.95). Gr. K–3. BKL (12/15/77). 915.1

Contents: 1. Little Pals. 2. I Am a Monitor. 3. Guarding the Cornfield. 4. Poems of Country Children.

Introduces the modern rural culture of the People's Republic of China by focusing on children's activities of school and chores.

CHORUSES AND PART SONGS

LET'S SING A ROUND (Phonodiscs). Bowmar Publishing. 1 disc. #214 ($6.95). Gr. 3–8. AUR (1978). 784.1

Songs are introduced in unison, then as rounds. Such songs as "Kookaburra," "Are You Sleeping?," "White Coral Bells," and others are included.

CHRISTMAS

A MISERABLE MERRY CHRISTMAS (Motion Picture–16mm–Sound). WNET/13 (Glenn Jordan) Educational Broadcasting/EBEC, 1973. 16mm color, sound film, 15 min. #3300 ($185). Gr. 1–12. BKL (12/74), LFR (12/74), PRV (2/11/75). 394.26

Based on a chapter from the *Autobiography of Lincoln Steffens*, this film tells a true story about a boy who refused to compromise. It also raises questions about the spirit and values of Christmas.

THE STORY OF CHRISTMAS (Motion Picture–16mm–Sound). National Film Board of Canada/Films, 1976. 16mm color, sound, narrationless film, 8 min. #101-0074 ($145). Gr. 6–A. BKL (6/76), FLN. 394.2

Using a medieval setting and music of the same period, this is a narrationless animated film. Paper cut-out animation and Elizabethan music re-create the Christmas story.

CHRISTMAS–FICTION

A CHRISTMAS CAROL (Phonodisc or Cassette). Listening Library, 1973. 3 discs or cassettes, 150 min. Discs #AA-3386/88 ($20.95), Cassettes #CX-386/88 ($22.95). Gr. 4–A. BKL (3/15/74), NYR, PRV. Fic

With Patrick Horgan reading the classic story by Charles Dickens, Tiny Tim and Scrooge come alive in this Christmas favorite.

A CHRISTMAS CAROL (Kit). Jabberwocky Cassette Classics, 1972. 1 cassette, 60 min.; 6 Read-along Scripts. #1121 ($15). Gr.

CHRISTMAS—FICTION (cont.)

5-A. BKL (1975), JOR (1974), PRV (11/73). Fic

A female narrator adds counterpoint to the cast of characters Dickens brought together on Christmas Eve. The dramatization is lively and faithful to the original. Sound effects enhance the mood of the tale.

CHRISTMAS IN NOISY VILLAGE (Filmstrip —Sound). Viking Press. 1 color, sound filmstrip; 1 cassette; Teacher's Guide. ($13.95). Gr. K-2. PRV (2/74), PVB (5/74). Fic

From the picture book of the same name by Astrid Lindgren, an attractive picture of a Swedish Christmas in the country.

CHRISTMAS TALES FROM MANY LANDS (Filmstrip—Sound). United Learning, 1975. 5 color, sound filmstrips, av. 50–68 fr. ea.; 5 cassettes, av. 8–14 min. ea.; Teacher's Guide. #60 ($75). Gr. 2–5. PRV (10/77). 394.2

Contents: 1. The Humblest Gift (Mexico). 2. The Legend of La Befana (Italy). 3. The Nutcracker's Happy Christmas (Germany). 4. O'Reilly's Christmas Cap (Ireland). 5. The Little Camel (Syria).

Here is a series of Christmas tales that justify themselves by their ethnic content and literary merit.

HOW THE GRINCH STOLE CHRISTMAS (Kit). See Wit and Humor

THE LITTLEST ANGEL (Phonodisc or Cassette). Caedmon Records, 1973. 1 cassette or disc, approx. 50 min. Disc #TC1384 ($6.98), Cassette #CDL51384 ($7.95). Gr. K-8. INS (1973). 394.26

Contents: 1. The Littlest Angel. 2. The Bells of Christmas.

Here are 2 of the best-loved Christmas stories of all time, read by Dame Judith Anderson. Music composed and performed by Dick Hyman.

THE TAILOR OF GLOUCESTER, A CHRISTMAS STORY (Cassette). See Mice —Fiction

CITIES AND TOWNS

BOOMSVILLE (Motion Picture—16mm— Sound). National Film Board of Canada/ Learning Corporation of America, 1970. 16mm, color, animated, sound film, 11 min. ($170). Gr. 3-A. AFF (1970), BKL (10/1/70), STE (10/71). 301.3

An animated overview of the growth of cities, showing what people have done to their environment. Re-creates human interaction with surroundings, tracing the process by which we have created a frantic, congested "boomsville."

CITIES OF AMERICA, PART ONE (Filmstrip—Sound). See U.S.—Description and Travel

CITIES OF AMERICA, PART TWO (Filmstrip—Sound). See U.S.—Description and Travel

CITY AND TOWN (Filmstrip—Sound). Educational Direction/Learning Tree Filmstrips, 1974. 4 color, sound filmstrips, av. 60 fr. ea.; 2 cassettes, av. 6 min. ea.; Teacher's Guide. #LT428 ($52). Gr. 2-8. ESL (1976); PRV (10/74). 301.3

Contents: 1. The Megalopolis. 2. The City. 3. The Town. 4. The Small Town.

The revealing full-color photographs in this set take the student to, and demonstrate the wide variety of, the places we all live in— from the megalopolis to the most remote areas.

A CRACK IN THE PAVEMENT (Motion Picture—16mm—Sound). See Natural History

FROM CAVE TO CITY (Motion Picture— 16mm—Sound). See Civilization

MY SENSES AND ME (Filmstrip—Sound). See Senses and Sensation

NIGHT PEOPLE'S DAY (Motion Picture— 16mm—Sound). Bob Kurtz/FilmFair Communications, 1971. 16mm color, sound film, 10-1/2 min. ($150). Gr. K-8. BKL (9/15/71), CGE (1973), LFR (5/71). 301.3

This film explores the city at night, with emphasis on the people who work nights and their occupations. Night people tell why they prefer to work at that time.

PLANT A SEED (Motion Picture—16mm— Sound). Phoenix Films, 1977. 16mm color, sound film, 3 min. ($75). Gr. 3-A. M&M (9/77). 301.3

This film shows what any individual can do to help bring floral beauty into the urban setting.

CITIES AND TOWNS—CHINA

CHINA: PEOPLE, PLACES AND PROGRESS (Filmstrip—Sound). See China—Civilization

CIVIL SERVICE—U.S.

SERVING THE NATION (Filmstrip—Sound). See Vocational Guidance

CIVILIZATION

COMPARATIVE CULTURES AND GEOGRAPHY, SET ONE (Filmstrip— Sound). Learning Corporation of America, 1973. 4 color, sound filmstrips, av. 150 fr.; 4 cassettes. ($94). Gr. 5-10. EGT (2/75), M&M (4/77), PRV (9/74). 901.9

Contents: 1. Two Cities: London and New York. 2. Two Factories: Japanese and American. 3. Two Towns: Gubbio, Italy and Chillicothe, Ohio. 4. Two Families: African and American.

This set of filmstrips reveals how the interplay of people and nature has evolved in our present-day world. Moving back and forth between continents, each filmstrip provides comparison of contrasting cultures within similar geographical regions.

COMPARATIVE CULTURES AND GEOGRAPHY, SET TWO (Filmstrip—Sound). Learning Corporation of America, 1973. 4 color, sound filmstrips, av. 150 fr.; 4 cassettes. ($94). Gr. 5-10. EGT (2/75), M&M (4/77), PRV (9/74). 901.9

Contents: 1. Two Deserts: Sahara and Sonora. 2. Two Farms: Hungary and Wisconsin. 3. Two Grasslands: Texas and Iran. 4. Two Mountainlands: Alps and Andes.

This set presents similarities and differences among societies in various cultural regions. Central focus is on human adaptation to natural environment with culture.

FROM CAVE TO CITY (Motion Picture—16mm—Sound). FilmFair Communications, 1973. 16mm color, sound film, 10 min. #C193 ($135). Gr. 4-A. CRA (1973), LFR (10/73), PRV (4/74). 901.9

The unique film traces human evolution from cave dweller—hunter and gatherer—to present status as members of a highly complex urban society. The emphasis is on human needs and goals, and the implicit questions raised deal with our future.

CIVILIZATION, MODERN

NEW FRIENDS FROM DISTANT LANDS: THE CULTURE WE SHARE (Filmstrip—Sound). Pathescope Educational Media, 1973. 5 color, sound filmstrips, 44-55 fr.; 5 cassettes, 12-18 min.; Teacher's Manual. #302 ($90). Gr. 4-8. BKL (3/74). 901.94

Contents: 1. Georges Breidy of Beirut, Lebanon. 2. Mary Mantinea of Athens, Greece. 3. Patrizia de Forti of Rome, Italy. 4. Ilhan Gorksun of Istanbul, Turkey. 5. Robert Stevens of London, England.

Modern children in this series talk to American children about their native lands. Against a background of history, their narratives encompass the geography and culture of their homelands.

CLASSICAL MYTHOLOGY. See Mythology, Classical

CLASSIFICATION, DEWEY DECIMAL

DEWEY DECIMAL CLASSIFICATION (Filmstrip—Sound). Library Filmstrip Center, 1976. 1 color, sound filmstrip, 50 fr.; 1 cassette or disc, 10:49 min. Disc #76-730017 ($24), Cassette #76-730017 ($26). Gr. 6-A. AFF (1977), PRV (4/78). 028.4

This filmstrip takes a step-by-step approach to the use of the card catalog. The cards and books illustrated are classified by the Dewey Decimal Classification system. The types of cards used in the card catalog are explained, with special emphasis on author, title, and subject cards. The lettering and numbering of trays, guide headings, call numbers, cross references, and how to locate a book on the shelf are explained.

CLEARY, BEVERLY

FIRST CHOICE AUTHORS AND BOOKS (Filmstrip—Sound). See Authors

CLEMENS, SAMUEL LANGHORNE. See Twain, Mark

CLIFF DWELLERS AND CLIFF DWELLINGS

AFRICAN CLIFF DWELLERS: THE DOGON PEOPLE OF MALI, PART ONE (Kit). See Africa

AFRICAN CLIFF DWELLERS: THE DOGON PEOPLE OF MALI, PART TWO (Kit). See Africa

CANYON DE CHELLY CLIFF DWELLINGS (Film Loop—8mm—Silent). Thorne Films/Prentice-Hall Media, 1972 (Southwest Indians). 8mm color, silent film loop, approx. 4 min. #HAT 270 ($26). Gr. 4-A. PRV (4/73). 970.1

Shows the cliff dwellings of the Indians of the Southwest.

INDIAN CLIFF DWELLINGS AT MESA VERDE—SLIDE SET (Slides). Donars Productions, 1973. 48 cardboard mounted, color slides in booklet of plastic storage pages; Notes. ($30). Gr. 4-8. BKL (3/1/74). 970.1

Shows in detail the structures of the cliff dwellings at Mesa Verde, Colorado, emphasizing prominent features of these structures. Also presents photographs of artifacts and a mummy found at the site, and depicts possible methods of construction and areas of present archeological interest.

MESA VERDE (Study Print). EBEC, 1975. 8 13″ X 18″ color study prints. Study Guide. #6840 ($19.50). Gr. 5-A. MDU (5/76), PRV (11/77). 970.1

Contents: 1. Cliff Palace. 2. House of Many Windows. 3. Spruce Tree House. 4. Cliff Palace in Winter. 5. Long House. 6. Plaza House of the Kivas—Spruce Tree House. 7. The Kiva Story. 8. Square Tower House.

CLIFF DWELLERS AND CLIFF DWELLERS (cont.)

Eight colorful study prints detail the land and the lives of the Anasazi, a mysterious Indian people of the American Southwest whose highly developed civilization ended abruptly around 1300 A.D.

PUYE DE CHELLY CLIFF DWELLINGS (Film Loop–8mm–Silent). Thorne Films/ Prentice-Hall Media, 1972 (Southwest Indians). 8mm color, silent film loop, approx. 4 min. #HAT 271 ($28). Gr. 4–A. AUR (1978). 970.4

This film loop shows the cliff dwellings of the Puye De Chelly Indians of the Southwest.

CLOCKS AND WATCHES

IT'S ABOUT TIME (Filmstrip–Sound). *See* Calendars

CLOCKS–FICTION

CLOCKS AND MORE CLOCKS (Filmstrip– Sound). Weston Woods Studios, 1972. 1 color, sound filmstrip, 29 fr.; 1 cassette, 5 min. #SF135C ($12.75). Gr. K–3. PRV (12/73). Fic

Based on the charming story by Pat Hutchins, quaint Mr. Higgins buys another clock to check his grandfather clock. There is a discrepancy, so he buys a third and a fourth. Still they disagree. He calls in a specialist who, with watch in hand, pronounces them all correct. Mr. Higgins promptly buys a watch. Since then, all his clocks have been right.

CLOTHING AND DRESS

THE CLOTHES WE WEAR (Filmstrip– Sound). Burt Munk/Society for Visual Education, 1976. 6 color, sound filmstrips, 37–53 fr.; 6 cassettes or discs, 6:15–10:40 min.; 1 Guide. Discs #A213-SAR ($90), Cassettes #A213-SATC ($90). Gr. 4–8. BKL (1/15/77). 646

Contents: 1. Natural Fibers. 2. Synthetic Fibers. 3. Fiber to Fabric. 4. Cloth to Clothes. 5. Shoes and How They are Made. 6. Clothing Care.

A class travels to various sources of fibers to observe the development of fibers into clothing.

CLOTHING AND DRESS–FICTION

CHARLIE NEEDS A CLOAK (Motion Picture–16mm–Sound). Weston Woods Studios, 1977. 16mm color, sound, animated film, 8 min. ($150). Gr. K–4. BKL (10/77), LGB (1977). Fic

Adapted from the book *Charlie Needs a Cloak*, Charlie is a shepherd with a cozy house, a big hat, a crook, a flock of fat sheep—and a tattered cloak. In the springtime, Charlie decides to make himself a new red cloak. He shears his sheep and fashions his new garment from the wool. This animated film, which is sparked by whimsical Italian tarantella musical score, follows the process of making woolen cloth into clothing.

COHEN, MIRIAM

THRESHOLD FILMSTRIPS, SERIES C (Kit). *See* Children's Literature–Collections

COLERIDGE, SAMUEL

THE CRYSTAL CAVERN (Filmstrip– Sound). *See* Caves

COLLAGE

HOW TO DO: SLIDE COLLAGE (Filmstrip– Sound). Educational Dimensions Group, 1977. 2 color, sound filmstrips, av. 60 fr.; 2 cassettes, av. 16–18 min. #667 ($49). Gr. 6–A. BKL (7/1/77). 745.59

A versatile art of slide collage where photographic and drawing skills are not needed. After the film is prepared, a variety of effects can be achieved with simple, inexpensive resources, i.e., felt-tip pens, tissue paper, feathers, spices, thread.

COLLECTIVE SETTLEMENTS–ISRAEL

ISRAELI BOY: LIFE ON A KIBBUTZ (Motion Picture–16mm–Sound). *See* Israel

COLLIER, JAMES LINCOLN

MY BROTHER SAM IS DEAD (Phonodisc or Cassette). *See* U.S.–History–1775–1783– Revolution–Fiction

COLLODI, CARLO

PINOCCHIO (Phonodisc or Cassette). *See* Puppets–Fiction

THE PIED PIPER AND OTHER STORIES (Phonodisc or Cassette). *See* Fairy Tales

COLOR

BASIC COLORS (Kit). Clearvue, 1976. 6 color, sound filmstrips, av. 33 fr.; 6 cassettes or 3 discs, av. 6 min. Cassettes #CL579-C ($78.50), Discs #CL579-R ($78.50). Gr. K–3. BKL (10/15/77). 701.8

Contents: 1. The Traveller: Green. 2. The Magical Forest: Yellow. 3. Mr. Blue Jeans: Orange. 4. The Magician: Red. 5. The Three Wishes: Blue. 6. The Color Full World.

Conversational crayons find colors everywhere they turn as the 5 basic colors are presented. The names of the colors are given as well as the identification of many objects of the same color.

COLOR AND ITS PERCEPTION (Filmstrip–Sound). Coronet Instructional Media, 1971. 3 color, sound filmstrips, 25–28 fr.; 3 cassettes or 2 discs, 8-1/2 min. #S217 ($50). Gr. 6–12. BKL (1972), PRV (1972). 535.6
Contents: 1, 2, and 3. Color and Its Perception.
Photographs, drawings, charts, and special camera techniques demonstrate the visual and mental effects of color.

THE DAY THE COLORS WENT AWAY (Motion Picture–16mm–Sound). Film Polski/EBEC, 1974. 16mm color, sound film, 10 min. #3344 ($150). Gr. K–4. BKL (1/15/75), LFR (1975), PRV (11/75). 535.6
What would the world be without colors? A little girl finds out when she creates a painting mess, and angers the watercolors in her paint kit. The watercolors get up and leave to play on a rainbow, taking all the colors of the world with them. The film is nonnarrated, with animation.

OBSERVING AND DESCRIBING COLOR (Kit). EBEC, 1973. 2 filmstrips; 1 cassette; Scope and Sequence Chart; Teacher's Manual; Response Cards; Activity Sheets; Transparency; Transparent Acetates. #6620 ($64.50). Gr. K–1. BKL (9/15/73), LFR (5/72), PRV (10/73). 535.6
This multimedia kit is designed to achieve specific behavioral objectives. Children learn to discriminate among and name the 9 basic colors, to associate these basic colors with innumerable values and intensities, and to group and describe by color.

COLORADO

MONUMENTS TO EROSION (Motion Picture–16mm–Sound). See Erosion

COMMUNICATION

CAN YOU DO IT? (Filmstrip–Captioned). EBEC, 1976 (Developing Language Skills). 4 color, captioned filmstrips, 45 fr ea.; Teacher's Guide. #13260 ($32.90). Gr. K–3. BKL (4/15/77), LAM (10/77), PRV (9/1/77). 372.6
Contents: 1. What Can You Do at the Beach? 2. What Can You Do in a City Park? 3. What Can You Do in the Woods? 4. What Can You Do on the Farm?
The captions both describe the scenes and ask questions to stimulate thinking and discussions. The focus is on oral language rather than reading.

IS IT ALWAYS RIGHT TO BE RIGHT? (Motion Picture–16mm–Sound). See Human Relations

MAKING WORDS WORK (Filmstrip–Sound). See Vocabulary

WHERE IS IT? (Filmstrip–Captioned). See Language Arts

COMMUNICATION–PSYCHOLOGICAL ASPECTS

BASIC COMMUNICATION SKILLS, ONE (Filmstrip–Sound). Learning Tree Filmstrips, 1977. 4 color, sound filmstrips, 50–56 fr.; 4 cassettes, 10 min. ea.; Teacher's Guide. #LT757 ($58). Gr. 4–6. PRV (4/78). 301.45
Contents: 1. Listening Better. 2. Seeing More. 3. Reading to Learn. 4. Remembering.
Each filmstrip focuses individually on skills for improving listening, seeing, reading, and remembering.

HOW DO YOU KNOW WHAT'S FAIR? (Filmstrip–Sound). See Values

COMMUNITY LIFE

FOUR FAMILIES (Filmstrip–Sound). See Family Life

ON OUR BLOCK (Filmstrip–Sound). See Puerto Ricans in the U.S.

WHAT IS A COMMUNITY? (Filmstrip–Sound). Educational Direction, 1976. 4 color, sound filmstrips, av. 59 fr. ea.; 2 cassettes, av. 8–9 min. ea.; Teacher's Guide. ($58). Gr. 1–8. ESL (1977), PRV (3/77). 301.34
Contents: 1. Communities are People. 2. People Make Laws. 3. People Help Each Other. 4. Communities Help Each Other.
The set examines the concept of a community as a nucleus of people and services presented through the eyes of a family that moves to a new town.

WHO HELPS US? (Filmstrip–Sound). BFA Educational Media, 1970. 10 color, sound filmstrips; 10 cassettes or discs. Cassettes #VM8000 ($172), Discs #V06000 ($172). Gr. K–3. BKL (5/15/71). 301.34
Contents: 1. The Fire Department. 2. The Police Department. 3. The Supermarket. 4. The Bakery. 5. The Laundry-Dry Cleaners. 6. The Service Station. 7. The Dentist. 8. The Dairy. 9. The Library. 10. The Post Office.
These filmstrips emphasize the interdependence of people, goods, and services in a community.

WHO'S RUNNING THE SHOW? (Filmstrip–Sound). See Leadership

WORKING IN U.S. COMMUNITIES, GROUP TWO (Filmstrip–Sound). See Occupations

COMMUNITY LIFE, COMPARATIVE

BUON GIORNO: GOOD MORNING TEACHER (Filmstrip—Sound). *See* Italy—Social Life and Customs

FAMILIES: ALIKE AND DIFFERENT (Motion Picture—16mm—Sound). *See* Family Life

FAMILIES AROUND THE WORLD (Filmstrip—Sound). *See* Family Life

FAMILIES OF ASIA (Filmstrip—Sound). *See* Asia

FAMILIES OF SOUTH AMERICA (Filmstrip—Sound). *See* South America

FAMILIES OF WEST AFRICA: FARMERS AND FISHERMEN (Filmstrip—Sound). *See* Africa, West

FIVE CHILDREN, UNIT 2 (Filmstrip—Sound). *See* U.S.—Social Life and Customs

FIVE FAMILIES, UNIT 1 (Filmstrip—Sound). *See* Minorities

KNOWING AMERICA (Filmstrip—Sound). *See* U.S.—Description and Travel

LIVING IN OTHER LANDS (Filmstrip—Sound). Educational Direction/Learning Tree Filmstrips, 1974. 12 color, sound filmstrips, av. 42 fr. ea.; 6 cassettes, av. 8 min. ea.; Teacher's Guide. ($156). Gr. 3-9. CHH (9/76), PRV (4/75), PVB (5/75). 901.9

Contents: 1. A/B Great Britain and the Netherlands. 2. C/D France and Spain. 3. E/F West Germany and Sweden. 4. G/H Australia and New Zealand. 5. I/J Japan and India. 6. K/L Turkey and Iran.

This set is designed to give the student insight into what life is like in countries around the world from a humanistic point of view.

MY HOME AND ME (Filmstrip—Sound). *See* U.S.—Geography

ONE WORLD (Filmstrip—Sound). Troll Associates, 1975. 8 color, sound filmstrips, av. 65 fr ea.; 4 cassettes, av. 8 min. ea.; Teacher's Guide. ($104). Gr. 3-6. PRV (4/76). 910

Contents: 1. I Live in Greece. 2. I Live in Norway. 3. I Live in France. 4. I Live in Mexico. 5. I Live in Japan. 6. I Live in Australia. 7. I Live in New Zealand. 8. I Live in Israel.

True-to-life filmstrips help students develop an awareness of other lands and other people, as well as an appreciation of themselves.

OTHER PEOPLE, PLACES AND THINGS (Filmstrip—Sound). Educational Direction/Learning Tree Filmstrips, 1974. 4 color, sound filmstrips, av. 55 fr. ea.; 2 cassettes, av. 6-7 min. ea.; Teacher's Guide. #LT431 ($52). Gr. 1-7. BKL (7/1/75), PRV (9/75), PVB (4/76). 901.9

Contents: 1. The Landscape. 2. Ways People Work. 3. Other Ways of Living. 4. All Different—All Alike.

By showing people, places, and ways of life throughout the world, this set clearly demonstrates the range of life-styles, places, and cultures that represent the different ways in which people everywhere live.

REGIONS OF AMERICA (Filmstrip—Sound). *See* U.S.—Description and Travel

WORKING IN U.S. COMMUNITIES, GROUP ONE (Filmstrip—Sound). *See* Occupations

A WORLD NEARBY: GHANA (Filmstrip—Sound/Captioned). *See* Ghana

A WORLD NEARBY: HONG KONG (Filmstrip—Sound/Captioned). *See* Hong Kong

A WORLD NEARBY: NEW ZEALAND (Filmstrip—Sound/Captioned). *See* New Zealand

WORLDVIEW UNIT ONE (Filmstrip—Sound). *See* Geography

WORLDVIEW UNIT TWO (Filmstrip—Sound). *See* Geography

COMMUNITY LIFE, COMPARATIVE—FICTION

READING FOR THE FUN OF IT—MANY LANDS (Filmstrip—Sound). *See* Literature—Study and Teaching

COMPARATIVE GOVERNMENT

JOURNEY TO DEMOCRACY (Filmstrip—Sound). *See* Political Science

COMPARISONS

BASIC GEOMETRIC SHAPES (Filmstrip—Sound). *See* Geometry

MEASUREMENT COMPARISONS (Filmstrip—Sound). *See* Size and Shape

NOSES AND TOES, PART ONE AND TWO (Filmstrip—Sound). Miller-Brody Productions, 1976. 2 color, sound filmstrips, av. 44 fr.; 2 cassettes, 4-4:45 min.; 1 Guide. Cassette #SB202C ($32), Disc #SB202 ($32). Gr. K-2. BKL (5/15/77). 153.2

Adapted from the book by Richard Hefter.

OUR VISUAL WORLD (Filmstrip—Sound). *See* Art Appreciation

POSITIONAL AND DIRECTIONAL RELATIONSHIPS (Filmstrip—Sound). *See* Orienteering

COMPUTERS

COMPUTERS: FROM PEBBLES TO PROGRAMS (Filmstrip—Sound). Guidance Associates, 1975 (Math Matters). 3 color, sound filmstrips, av. 76 fr.; 3 discs or cassettes, av. 12 min.; Teacher's Guide. Discs #1B-301-422 ($68.50), Cassettes #1B-301-414 ($68.50). Gr. 5-8. ATE. 621.3819

Outlines the history of calculation from ancient times through the 20th century. Reviews computer development, surveys current applications, and suggests future directions for computer technology.

CONCEPTS

LEARNING TO SOLVE PROBLEMS (Filmstrip—Sound). *See* Thought and Thinking

LEARNING TO USE YOUR MIND (Filmstrip—Sound). *See* Thought and Thinking

NOSES AND TOES, PART ONE AND TWO (Filmstrip—Sound). *See* Comparisons

TADPOLE, SET ONE (Filmstrip—Sound). *See* Perception

TADPOLE, SET TWO (Filmstrip—Sound). *See* Perception

CONCERTOS

CONCERTO FOR ORCHESTRA (Phonodiscs). Deutsche Grammophon. 2 discs. #2530 479 ($8.98). Gr. 4-A. PRV (12/75). 785.6

The orchestral sonorities achieved by the composer are as imaginative as the structure and expressive plan of the work itself. Rafael Kubelik conducts the Boston Symphony Orchestra.

PIANO CONCERTO NO. 3 IN D MINOR (Phonodiscs). Philips Records, 1974. 1 disc. #6500-540 ($5.50). Gr. 3-A. PRV (5/75). 785.6

Pianist Rafael Orozco with Edo de Waart conducting the Royal Philharmonic Orchestra, in this Rachmaninoff favorite.

TSCHAIKOVSKY: PIANO CONCERTO NO. ONE (Phonodiscs). RCA Educational. 1 disc. #ARL1-0751 ($6.98). Gr. 5-A. PRV (12/75). 785.6

Eugene Ormandy and the Philadelphia Orchestra have recorded and performed this work many times. The swirls of dynamics are captivating. Pianist Tedd Joselson shares his exceptional talent as he starts his career at age 23.

CONDUCT OF LIFE. *See* Human Behavior

CONFLICT, SOCIAL. *See* Social Conflict

CONREID, HANS

DOCTOR SEUSS: HAPPY BIRTHDAY TO YOU (Phonodisc or Cassette). *See* Stories in Rhyme

CONSERVATION OF NATURAL RESOURCES

ENERGY AND THE EARTH (Filmstrip—Sound). Lyceum/Mook & Blanchard, 1973. 2 color, sound filmstrips, 56–69 fr.; 2 cassettes or discs, 11–17:30 min. Cassettes #LY35373SC ($46), Discs #LY35373SR ($37). Gr. 6-A. FLN (2/3/74), IFT (1973), INS (4/74). 333

Contents: 1. Earth: The Early Years. 2. Earth: The Years of Decision.

This series develops an understanding of the fundamental energy resources of the earth and how they have been and are being expanded. Environmental effects are considered.

KEEPING OUR AIR, WATER AND EARTH CLEAN (Film Loop—8mm—Silent). *See* Pollution

PRESERVING THE ENVIRONMENT (Filmstrip—Sound). *See* Vocational Guidance

CONSONANTS

READING READINESS (Filmstrip—Sound). *See* Reading—Study and Teaching

CONSTRUCTION. *See* Building

CONSUMER EDUCATION

ALICE IN CONSUMERLAND (Filmstrip—Sound). January Productions, 1974. 5 color, sound filmstrips, av. 45 fr.; 5 cassettes, av. 5-6 min.; Teacher's Guide. Set ($72.50), Individual ($14.95). Gr. K-3. CCI (11/75), PRV (9/75), PVB (4/76). 339.42

Contents: 1. When There's a Hole in Your Pocket—Budgeting. 2. And This Little Bottle Went to Market—Distribution. 3. Fables and Labels—Comparison Shopping. 4. Catch a Commercial—TV Advertising. 5. When Things Don't Work—Complaints.

Makes children aware of the economic problems they may face.

CONCERNING YOUNG CONSUMERS (Filmstrip—Sound). Macmillan Library Services, 1974. 6 color, sound filmstrips, 65–85 fr.; 6 cassettes or discs, 8–11 min.; Teacher's Guide. ($130). Gr. 4-8. PRV (1/76). 339.42

Contents: 1. What's behind the Price Tag? 2. Are You Getting the Message? 3. Does Shopping Mean Buying? 4. How Do You Pay for It? 5. Do Consumers Have Rights? 6. When Does Value End?

Covers many facets of consumer buying. Children are used as the buyers visiting stores, etc., and learning about selling, prices, advertising, budgeting, and consumer rights.

CONSUMER EDUCATION (cont.)

CONSUMER EDUCATION: THE PRICE IS
RIGHT—OR IS IT? (Filmstrip—Sound).
Urban Media Materials, 1973. 4 color,
sound filmstrips, 73–80 fr.; 2 discs or cas-
settes, 19–20 min. Discs ($60), Cassettes
($70). Gr. 3–6. BKL (1973), PRV (11/73),
PVB (5/74). 339.42

Contents: 1. Let's Make a Deal. 2. Get
Your Money's Worth. 3. Super Snooper. 4.
Big Sister and the Lemon.

Through story characters, children become
more aware of their rights as consumers and
are shown the value of investigating and
evaluating a product before purchasing.
Photographs and drawings are used.

ECONOMICS FOR PRIMARIES (Filmstrip—
Sound). Q+ED Productions, 1973. 4 color,
sound filmstrips, 44–59 fr.; 4 discs or cassettes, 6–8 min. Discs ($76), Cassettes
($84). Gr. K–3. PRV (4/74), PVB (5/74).
339.42

Contents: 1. The Toy Store. 2. The Dog-
house. 3. The Breakfast. 4. The Garden.

The scenes describe actual situations that require the use of the child's intellectual and
financial assets and accompanying skills.
Motivates an interest and understanding, at
a primary level, of financial, economical,
and consumer affairs.

LEARNING TO BE A WISE CONSUMER
(Filmstrip—Sound). Guidance Associates,
1975. 4 color, sound filmstrips, av. 70 fr.
ea.; 4 discs or cassettes, 15 min.; Teacher's
Guide. Discs #9A-302-123 ($84.50), Cas-
settes #9A-302-131 ($84.50). Gr. 4–6.
LGB (1975), PRV (12/75), PVB (4/76).
339.42

Contents: 1. Who Is a Consumer? 2. Consumer Choices. 3. Buying Wisely. 4. The
Two R's: Rights and Responsibilities.

Students learn that families with limited
money must budget and spend with care.
They learn how advertising can influence
spending.

MARKET ECONOMY (Filmstrip—Sound).
BFA Educational Media, 1971. 6 color,
sound filmstrips; 6 discs or cassettes. Cassettes #VK1000 ($104). Discs #V29000
($104). Gr. 4–6. BKL (9/15/71). 339.42

Contents: 1. Introduction. 2. Subsistence
Farmer. 3. Craftsmen. 4. Specialized
Farmer and Specialized Vendor. 5. Travel-
ing Vendor. 6. Store Owner.

This set deals with the relationships between producers and consumers and between
environment and products in a market economy.

NICKELS, DIMES AND DOLLARS (Filmstrip—Sound). ACI Media/Paramount Communications, 1975. 4 color, sound filmstrips, 64–69 fr.; 4 cassettes, 5:00–8:30
min.; Teacher's Guide. #9116 ($78). Gr.
3–6. BKL (2/76). 339.42

Contents: 1. Earn and Save. 2. Shop with
Care. 3. Make It Yourself. 4. Fix it Yourself.

Vignettes dealing with money problems in
familiar situations and in terms a youngster
can understand. Each situation reveals that
children can use their imagination and creativity to solve the problem and even to improve the arrangement.

SOOPERGOOP (Motion Picture—16mm—
Sound). *See* Advertising

CONTINENTS

HOW OUR CONTINENT WAS MADE (Filmstrip—Sound). *See* North America

COOKERY

EDIBLE ART (Filmstrip—Sound). Paramount
Communications, 1975. 6 color, sound
filmstrips; 6 cassettes, 8–10 ea.; Teacher's
Guide; Recipes. #9106 ($98). Gr. 4–12.
BKL (7/76), PRV (10/76), PVB (1977).
641.5

Contents: 1. Modeled Cookies. 2. Candy
Clay. 3. Bread Sculpture. 4. Frosting Paint.
5. Graham Cracker Construction. 6. Fruit
and Vegetable Assemblage.

This set combines art elements—color, texture, line, and shape—with the inclination to
make foods aesthetically pleasing. It provides recipes and instructions for festive
foods for many occasions.

COONEY, BARBARA

SQUAWK TO THE MOON, LITTLE GOOSE
(Filmstrip—Sound). *See* Animals—Fiction

COOPERATION—FICTION

THE MULE WHO REFUSED TO BUDGE
(Filmstrip—Sound/Captioned). Listening
Library, 1976 (Look, Listen and Read). 1
color, captioned, sound filmstrip, 42 fr.; 1
cassette, 8 min.; Teacher's Guide. JFS
#160 ($14.95). Gr. K–3. LGB (12/77),
PRV (12/77). Fic

An uncooperative mule gets his just desserts
when neighbors band together to teach him
a lesson. Narration by the author is taken
verbatim from the book, as are the illustrations by Harold Berson.

CORRERAS DE MOTOCROS

MOTOCROSS RACING (Kit). See Spanish
Language—Reading Materials

COSGROVE, STEPHEN

SERENDIPITY CASSETTE BOOKS (Kit).
See Short Stories

COUNTING

THE CARETAKER'S DILEMMA (Motion Picture–16mm–Sound). *See* Arithmetic

DECIMAL NUMERATION SYSTEM (Filmstrip–Sound). *See* Arithmetic

LET'S LEARN THE ALPHABET (Filmstrip–Sound). *See* Alphabet

NUMBERS: FROM NOTCHES TO NUMERALS (Filmstrip–Sound). Guidance Associates, 1975 (Math Matters). 2 color, sound filmstrips, av. 61 fr.; 2 cassettes or discs, av. 11 min.; Teacher's Guide. Discs #1B-301-364 ($52.50), Cassettes #1B-301-356 ($52.50). Gr. 4–8. ATE. 513
Reviews systems used in Egyptian, Babylonian, Roman, Mayan, and other ancient cultures. Traces development of Hindu-Arabic number system, and explains the binary system used in program computers.

PRESENTANDO NUMEROS (INTRODUCING NUMBERS) (Filmstrip–Sound). BFA Educational Media, 1976. 6 color, sound filmstrips, 31–41 fr.; 6 cassettes or discs, 4:56–6:12 min.; Teacher's Guide. Disc #VGZ000 ($92), Cassette #VHA000 ($92). Gr. 1–6. PRV (4/78). 513
Contents: 1. Como Usamos Los Numeros. 2. Numeros y Numerales. 3. Valor de Lugar. 4. Inversos. 5. Igualdad y Desigualdad. 6. Conceptos Acerca de Numeros.
In this series, students see the many ways to use numbers. They learn to tell the difference between numbers and numerals, and how to relate numerals to number ideas in their own surroundings.

COURAGE

FAMOUS STORIES OF GREAT COURAGE (Filmstrip–Sound). *See* Heroes and Heroines

COURAGE–FICTION

HANS BRINKER, OR THE SILVER SKATES (Phonodisc or Cassette). *See* Netherlands–Fiction

COURTESY

BEING GOOD–BEING BAD (Filmstrip–Sound). *See* Human Behavior

BEING KIND (Filmstrip–Sound). *See* Human Behavior

COWHANDS–FICTION

FANCIFUL TALES (Filmstrip–Sound). *See* Spanish Language–Reading Materials

CREATION (LITERARY, ARTISTIC, ETC.)

ADVENTURES IN IMAGINATION SERIES (Filmstrip–Sound). *See* English Language–Composition and Exercises

DESCRIBING WHAT WE SEE (Motion Picture–16mm–Sound). *See* English Language–Composition and Exercises

THE FIRST MOVING PICTURE SHOW (Motion Picture–16mm–Sound). *See* Motion Pictures

ON LOCATION WITH COMPOSITION–LEVEL ONE, TWO AND THREE (Filmstrip–Sound). *See* English Language–Composition and Exercises

OPEN BOX: IDEAS FOR CREATIVE EXPRESSION (Kit). *See* English Language–Composition and Exercises

SELF-EXPRESSION AND CONDUCT (Filmstrip–Sound). *See* Culture

STORIES (Motion Picture–16mm–Sound). *See* English Language–Composition and Exercises

WORDS (Motion Picture–16mm–Sound). *See* English Language–Composition and Exercises

CREATIVE ABILITY

CREATIVE EXPRESSION UNIT (Motion Picture–16mm–Sound). Sutherland Learning Associates/EBEC, 1972 (Most Important Person). 6 16mm color, sound films. Also avail. 8mm film; 1 record; 6 posters; 1 Song Card; Teacher's Guide. #6734 ($345.60). Gr. K–3. BKL (7/1/74), CHT (9/10/74), CPR (1/76). 153.3
Contents: 1. This Is Me. 2. Rhythm around You. 3. Use Your Imagination. 4. Be Curious! 5. When You're Waking Up. 6. Without Saying a Word.
The most important person is a creative person in this segment of this series. Children are encouraged to use their talents and abilities in expressing themselves in a special way.

CREATIVE MOVEMENT

BODY MOVEMENT UNIT (Motion Picture–16mm–Sound). Sutherland Learning Associates/EBEC, 1972 (Most Important Person). 6 16mm color, sound films. Also avail. 8mm films; 1 record; 6 posters; 1 Song Card; Teacher's Guide. #6737 ($345.60). Gr. K–3. BKL (7/1/74, CHT (9/10/74), CPR (1/76). 152.3
Contents: 1. Watch Your Balance! 2. It Takes Muscles. 3. Follow the Leader. 4. How Big Is Big? 5. Joints Let You Bend. 6. Put Your Hands on the Top of Your Head!

CREATIVE MOVEMENT (cont.)

Here the concern is with the young child's motor development, motor skills, and coordination.

KEEP ON STEPPIN' (Phonodisc or Cassette). *See* Physical Education and Training

SENSORIMOTOR TRAINING IN THE CLASSROOM, VOL. ONE (Phonodisc or Cassette). Educational Activities, 1976. 1 disc or cassette; 1 Manual. Disc #AR532 ($7.95), Cassette #AC532 ($8.95). Gr. K-3. JLD (10/77). 152.3
This well-rounded program of carefully selected perceptual activities helps to develop body image, laterality, space, directionality, basic movement, physical fitness, ocular training, and auditory discrimination.

CRESWICK, PAUL

ADVENTURES OF ROBIN HOOD, VOL. 1: HOW ROBIN BECAME AN OUTLAW (Phonodisc or Cassette). *See* Folklore—England

ADVENTURES OF ROBIN HOOD, VOL. 2: OUTLAW BAND OF SHERWOOD FOREST (Phonodisc or Cassette). *See* Folklore—England

ADVENTURES OF ROBIN HOOD, VOL. 3: ADVENTURES WITH LITTLE JOHN (Phonodisc or Cassette). *See* Folklore—England

ADVENTURES OF ROBIN HOOD, VOL. 4: ROBIN AND HIS MERRY MEN (Phonodisc or Cassette). *See* Folklore—England

CRIME

CRIME: EVERYBODY'S PROBLEM (Filmstrip—Sound). Associated Press/Pathescope Educational Media, 1976 (Contemporary Issues). 1 color, sound filmstrip, 63 fr.; 1 cassette or disc, 7:06 min.; Teacher's Guide. #9504 ($28). Gr. 4-8. PRV (4/78). 364
Crime has grown to such a proportion that it affects all of us in some manner. A brief look at how ideas and laws change, presented in a clear and direct manner with emphasis placed on everyone's responsibility to combat crime.

PROJECT AWARE (Motion Picture—16mm—Sound). *See* Juvenile Delinquency

SHOPLIFTING, IT'S A CRIME (Motion Picture—16mm—Sound). FilmFair Communications, 1975. 16mm color, sound film, 12 min. ($165). Gr. 4-9. LFR (5/75), LNG (12/75), PRV (1275). 364
Typical shoplifting incidents are dramatized with young people of elementary and high school age. The film points out the additional cost to shoppers, the methods of ap-

prehension, the embarrassment and consequences of being caught.

CROCE, JIM

MEN BEHIND THE BRIGHT LIGHTS (Kit). *See* Musicians

CROCODILES—FICTION

LYLE, LYLE, CROCODILE AND OTHER ADVENTURES OF LYLE (Phonodisc or Cassette). Caedmon Records, 1974. 1 cassette or disc, approx. 50 min. Disc #TC1350 ($6.98), Cassette #CDL51350 ($7.95). Gr. K-3. BKL (1975), LBJ. Fic
Contents: 1. The House on East 88th Street. 2. Lyle, Lyle, Crocodile. 3. Lyle and the Birthday Party. 4. Lovable Lyle.
There is gentle humor in the Lyle books, and children relish the delightful contrast between lovable, charming Lyle and the snappish, evil-looking crocodiles they see at the zoo. This recording is read by Gwen Verdon. The Lyle stories were written by Bernard Waber.

CROWS

SAMMY THE CROW (Filmstrip—Sound). Lyceum/Mook & Blanchard, 1970. 1 color, sound filmstrip, 35 fr.; 1 cassette or disc, 5-1/2 min. Cassette #LY35170C ($25), Disc #LY35170R ($19.50). Gr. K-9. FLN (2/3/71). 598.8
This strip, based on the book *Sammy the Crow, Who Remembered* by Elizabeth Baldwin Hazelton, has been photographed by Ann Atwood. Sammy is a likable, mischievous wild crow who befriends a young boy. It is a true tale of Sammy and his friends, Timmy the cat, Salty the seagull, and the wild crows that lure him away. The set helps students appreciate and respect wild creatures through observation and understanding.

CUENTITOS DE FANTASIA

FANCIFUL TALES (Filmstrip—Sound). *See* Spanish Language—Reading Materials

CULTURE

COMPARATIVE CULTURES AND GEOGRAPHY, SET ONE (Filmstrip—Sound). *See* Civilization

COMPARATIVE CULTURES AND GEOGRAPHY, SET TWO (Filmstrip—Sound). *See* Civilization

CULTURE AND ENVIRONMENT: LIVING IN THE TROPICS (Filmstrip—Sound). *See* Tropics

OTHER PEOPLE, PLACES AND THINGS (Filmstrip—Sound). *See* Community Life, Comparative

PEOPLE OF THE FOREST: A STUDY IN
HUMAN VALUES (Kit). Society for Visual
Education, 1975 (Basic Living Skills). 6
color, sound filmstrips; 6 discs or cassettes;
Activity Cards; Games; Murals; Wax Mark-
ers; Classroom Management Guides. #CM-
61 ($175). Gr. K–6. BKL (3/76), PRV
(2/77). 301.2

This kit teaches students about the development of human values by helping them
explore the relationship of the individual to
the society. With multisensory materials,
students form an imaginary society that
existed 10,000 years ago—the Forest People
Tribe. This activity helps students gain
insight into some of the factors that make
all societies operate: basic needs, cooperation, change, and education.

SELF-EXPRESSION AND CONDUCT
(Filmstrip–Sound). HBJ Films/Harcourt
Brace Jovanovich, 1975. 3 units, 2 color,
sound filmstrips ea., 65–115 fr.; 2 discs or
cassettes, 7–19 min.; Teacher's Guide. Per
Unit ($48). Gr. 3–4. PRV (9/76), PVB
(4/77). 301.2

Contents: Box A: 1. Dreams on an Old
Trombone. 2. Folk Tales and Fairness.
Box B: 1. What We Care About. 2. Rope,
Wood, and Clay; Box C: 1. What's So
Funny. 2. We Celebrate.

Makes children aware of values. Children
learn that people in all cultures through
the ages have used the arts as a way of
expressing their values.

WHY CULTURES ARE DIFFERENT (Filmstrip–Sound). Filmstrip House/United
Learning, 1974. 6 color, sound filmstrips,
av. 55–75 fr. ea.; 3 cassettes or phonodiscs,
av. 10–13 min. ea.; Script/Guide. Cassettes
#50202 ($80), Discs #50201 ($80). Gr.
5–8. BKL (5/75), ESL (10/77), PRV
(9/75). 301.2

Contents: 1. Culture: What is It? 2. Land
and Climate. 3. Government and Economy.
4. Education and Technology. 5. History.
6. Religion.

An introduction to the concept of different
ways of life, which shows clearly the wide
variations between Eskimo and Japanese,
French and Arabian life-styles. The filmstrips present the factors contributing to
the differences, show how they developed,
and illustrate many of them.

CURIE, MARIE

CHILDHOOD OF FAMOUS WOMEN,
VOLUME THREE (Cassette). *See* Women–
Biography

TRAILBLAZERS OF INVENTION (Filmstrip–Sound). *See* Inventors

CURIOSITIES AND WONDERS

MONSTERS AND OTHER SCIENCE
MYSTERIES (Filmstrip–Sound). Bendick

Associates/Miller-Brody Productions, 1977.
8 color, sound filmstrips, av. 77–91 fr. ea.;
8 cassettes or discs, av. 18–21 min. ea.
#MSM 100 ($160). Gr. 4–9. BKL (1/78).
001.9

Contents: 1. The Mystery of the Loch Ness
Monster. 2. The Mystery of the Abomi-
nable Snowman. 3. The Mystery of the
Bermuda Triangle. 4. The Mystery of Life
on Other Worlds. 5. The Mystery of
Atlantis. 6. The Mystery of Witchcraft.
7. The Mystery of ESP. 8. The Mystery of
Astrology.

Eight questions are explored in this program, using original art, photography, maps,
old drawings, and engravings. Each filmstrip
presents the facts and theories that should
be considered.

READING QUIZZES FROM GUINNESS
WORLD RECORDS (Filmstrip–Sound/
Captioned). Society for Visual Education,
1978. 4 color, captioned, sound filmstrips;
4 cassettes; 1 Guide; 4 Score Sheets. #171-
SATC ($80). Gr. 4–9. TEA (2/78). 001.9

Contents: 1. Record Feats and Achievements. 2. Record Sizes and Weights. 3.
Record Events and Happenings. 4. Records
of Human Endurance.

The captioned filmstrips provide questions
and answers about more than 100 world
records: the largest pizza, oldest human,
greatest weight lifted, etc. The format is
the same on each filmstrip. Students read
a question about a record, guess the answer
and mark it on their scoring sheet, then read
the correct answer on the next frame. The
narration provides read-along practice plus
additional information about the record.
Available separately.

DAHL, ROALD

CHARLIE AND THE CHOCOLATE
FACTORY (Phonodisc or Cassette). *See*
Fantasy–Fiction

JAMES AND THE GIANT PEACH (Phonodisc or Cassette). *See* Fantasy–Fiction

DAIRYING

THE DAIRY FARM AND THE DAIRY
(Filmstrip–Sound). BFA Educational
Media, 1969. 4 color, sound filmstrips; 4
cassettes or discs. Cassettes #VZ9000
($62), Discs #V78000 ($62). Gr. K–3.
BKL (6/15/70). 637

Contents: 1. Raising Cows on the Farm. 2.
Growing Things on the Farm. 3. Milk and
Butter at the Dairy. 4. Making Cheese at
the Dairy.

A modern Wisconsin farm is the setting for
these filmstrips on how dairy products are
produced. The dairy farm owner is both a
farmer and businessman, and every member
of the family helps with the work.

DAIRYING (cont.)

MILK: FROM FARM TO YOU (3RD
EDITION) (Motion Picture—16mm—
Sound). EBEC, 1972. 16mm color, sound
film, 13 min.; Teacher's Guide. #3170
($185). Gr. K-6. CPR (6/73), PRV
(11/74), SLJ (3/73). 637

The story of milk, from the cow to the
carton, is presented in simple, entertaining
scenes. Common misconceptions concerning the production of milk are corrected.
A modern dairy farm is shown, a calf is
born, and a variety of dairy workers describe their tasks. Pasteurization, homogeni-
zation, and testing for butter-fat content
and bacteria are discussed. The many dairy
products made from milk are identfied.

DANCING

AMERICA DANCES (Phonodisc or Cassette).
See Folk Dancing

DE BRUNHOFF, JEAN

SIGHTS AND SOUNDS FILMSTRIPS, SET
4 (Filmstrip—Sound). *See* Reading—Study
and Teaching

DE BRUNHOFF, LAURENT

BEGINNER BOOKS FILMSTRIPS, SET
4 (Filmstrip—Sound). *See* Reading—
Study and Teaching

SIGHTS AND SOUNDS FILMSTRIPS, SET 3
(Filmstrip—Sound). *See* Reading—Study
and Teaching

DE LA MARE, WALTER

BLUEBEARD (Cassette). *See* Fairy Tales

CINDERELLA AND OTHER FAIRY TALES
(Phonodisc or Cassette). *See* Fairy Tales

LITTLE RED RIDING HOOD AND THE
DANCING PRINCESSES (Phonodisc or
Cassette). *See* Fairy Tales

DE MAUPASSANT GUY. *See* Maupassant,
Guy de

DE PAOLA, TOMIE

CHARLIE NEEDS A CLOAK (Motion Picture
—16mm—Sound). *See* Clothing and Dress
—Fiction

DE REGNIERS, BEATRICE SCHENCK

SOUND FILMSTRIP SET 35 (Filmstrip—
Sound). *See* Children's Literature—
Collections

DE VILLENEUVE, MADAME

BEAUTY AND THE BEAST AND OTHER
STORIES (Phonodisc or Cassette). *See*
Fairy Tales

LIBRARY 5 (Cassette). *See* Literature—
Collections

DEATH

DEATH: A NATURAL PART OF LIVING
(Filmstrip—Sound). Marshfilm, 1977
(Mental Health/Hygiene). 1 color, sound
filmstrip, approx. 55 fr.; 1 disc or cassette,
approx. 9 min. #1134 ($22). Gr. 5–9.
PRV (2/78), PVB (4/78). 128.5

Included are the results of recent research
on the 5 steps of death acceptance by the
dying. An interesting and factual look at
death as a natural part of the life cycle of
all living organisms; presents ancient and
foreign customs, modern trends and concerns, and practical guidance for young
people.

LIVING WITH DYING (Filmstrip—Sound).
Sunburst Communications, 1973. 2 color,
sound filmstrips, 72–78 fr.; 2 discs or
cassettes, 14–15 min.; 2 Student Activity
Cards; Teacher's Guide. ($45). Gr. 6–12.
BKL (8/73), PRV (1/74), PVB (5/74). 128.5

Contents: 1. Acceptance. 2. Immortality.

This set takes the view that children should
cope with death's inevitability. A falling
leaf, a dead bird, a young woman with a
terminal disease create the awareness of
death while offsetting the imagery; an
academic presentation of 5 stages of death
acceptance. Included are historic flashbacks to death customs of the past to the
problems of those facing death today.

WHERE IS DEAD? (Motion Picture—16mm—
Sound). EBEC, 1975. 16mm color, sound
film, 19 min. #3417 ($225). Gr. 4–A.
INS (1/77), LNG (75/76), TEA (5/6/76).
155.937

Low-keyed drama deals compassionately,
yet realistically, with a subject that young
children may be forced to face: the death
of a loved one. Six-year-old Sarah plays and
fights with her 9-year-old brother David in
a series of recognizable childhood vignettes.
David's sudden death rends the family
fabric. Sarah's parents attempt to explain
what has happened—with tenderness but
without sentimentality. Gradually, the little
girl is able to cope with her feelings of sadness, confusion and fear—and life regains
most of its earlier joys.

DECIMAL NOTATION

KING VAT (Motion Picture—16mm—Sound).
See Metric System

DECISION-MAKING

CAN YOU IMAGINE? (Filmstrip—Sound).
Educational Direction/Learning Tree Filmstrips, 1975. 4 color, sound filmstrips, av.
49 fr. ea.; 2 cassettes, av. 5 min. ea.; Teacher's Guide. #LT558 ($52). Gr. K–3. BKL
(1/15/76). 153.8
Contents: 1. How Tall Is Your Mountain.
2. How Wide Is Your Ocean. 3. How High
Is Your Sky. 4. How Deep Is Your Sea.
Real and exciting adventures—mountain
climbing, sailing, scuba diving, soaring—are
used both to intrigue the viewer and demonstrate that a broad array of human activities
exists.

CROSSROADS—STORIES ABOUT VALUES
AND DECISIONS (Filmstrip—Sound).
United Learning, 1973. 5 color, sound film-
strips, 40–52 fr.; 5 cassettes, 15–20 min.;
Teacher's Guide. #9030 ($65). Gr. 4–7.
PRV (9/74), PVB (5/75). 153.8
Contents: 1. Generosity. 2. Honesty. 3.
Guilt. 4. Hostility. 5. Integrity.
This set provides experiences that will en-
courage students to think before acting and
making important decisions that can affect
their self-worth and happiness.

DECISIONS, DECISIONS (Filmstrip—Sound).
Marshfilm, 1977 (Mental Health/Hygiene).
1 color, sound filmstrip, approx. 55 fr.; 1
disc or cassette, approx. 9 min. #1135
($21). Gr. 5–9. PRV (2/78), PVB (4/78).
153.8
Being prepared to make the right decision is
what this filmstrip is all about. Value judgment, choices, options and consequences,
awareness of alternatives, weighing pros and
cons, all are presented with cartooning and
photographs.

DIVIDED MAN, COMMITMENT OR COM-
PROMISE? (Motion Picture—16mm—
Sound). Film Polski/Bosustow Productions,
1973. 16mm color, sound, animated film,
5 min. ($120). Gr. 5–10. BKL (11/11/73),
CIF (1975), PRV (1973). 153.8
A solitary figure travels a road happily until
he comes to a fork. He hesitates; there is no
indication what may lie ahead on either
path. He makes several false starts, and returns to the original point. Because he is
struggling to make the perfect choice, he
divides and travels both paths. The 2 halves
reunite at a later crossroads, but the 2 halves
no longer fit together. They have changed
on their journeys, and they cannot be the
same man again.

DEER

AS LONG AS THE GRASS IS GREEN
(Picture—16mm—Sound). See Indians of
North America

AN INDIAN SUMMER (Motion Picture—
16mm—Sound). See Indians of North
America

DEFOE, DANIEL

EPISODES FROM FAMOUS STORIES
(Filmstrip—Sound). See Literature—
Collections

ROBINSON CRUSOE (Filmstrip—Sound).
See Shipwrecks—Fiction

DENVER, JOHN

MEN BEHIND THE BRIGHT LIGHTS (Kit).
See Musicians

DESERTS

DESERT LIFE (Filmstrip—Captioned). Jam
Handy/Prentice-Hall Media, 1972. 4 color,
captioned filmstrips, 45 fr. ea.; Teacher's
Guide. #KAC 3450 ($74). Gr. 2–5. PRV
(10/72), PVB (5/73). 551.58
Contents: 1. What Is a Desert? 2. How
Desert Plants Survive. 3. How Desert Animals Survive. 4. Balance of Life in a Desert.
The strips emphasize the relationship of
plants, animals, weather, and other factors
in the cycles of life on the desert.

THE DESERT: PROFILE OF AN ARID
LAND (Filmstrip—Sound). EBEC, 1974.
5 color, sound filmstrips, av. 101 fr. ea.;
5 discs or cassettes, 15 min. ea.; Teacher's
Guide. Discs #6497 ($72.50), Cassettes
#6497K ($72.50). Gr. 4–8. CPR (11/75),
ESL (1977), PRV (5/76). 551.58
Contents: 1. The Desert Environment: An
Overview. 2. Face of the Desert: Patterns of
Erosion. 3. Life in the Desert: Plants. 4.
Life in the Desert: Animals. 5. The Desert:
Environment in Danger.
This series shows how deep canyons are
formed by desert streams and sand dunes by
violent windstorms; how one plant survives
by growing its own shade and how a tiny
animal manufactures its own water. The
last filmstrip in the series shows how humans are changing the face of the desert and
why they pose a threat to this environment.

THE ECOLOGY OF A DESERT: DEATH
VALLEY (Filmstrip—Sound). Educational
Development, 1973. 2 color, sound filmstrips, 35–40 fr.; 2 cassettes or discs, 10:43–
11:39 min.; Manual. Discs #406-R ($30),
Cassettes #406-C ($32). Gr. 5–8. BKL
(3/15/74). 551.58
Contents: 1. Deserts. 2. Ecology.
The set describes the ways in which certain
animals have adapted to Death Valley, explains the area's geological structure, shows
towns abandoned in the late 1800s because
of drought and isolation, and examines the

DESERTS (cont.)

brief influx of gold, silver, and borax seekers.

THE WILD YOUNG DESERT SERIES (Filmstrip–Sound). Lyceum/Mook & Blanchard, 1970. 2 color, sound filmstrips, 50 fr.; 2 cassettes or discs, 10 min. Cassette #LY35570SC ($25), Disc #LY35570SR ($19.50). Gr. K–A. BKL (9/1/70), STE (2/1/71). 551.58

Contents: 1. The Making of a Desert. 2. Life Conquers the Desert.

Written and photographed by Ann Atwood, the color photography of this set brings an appreciation of the desert to those who know and love it and to those who have never experienced it. This set deepens awareness of the geological background, ecological balance, and unique beauty of the desert.

DESIGN, DECORATIVE

CHANGING THE FACE OF THINGS (Filmstrip). Visual Publications, 1972. 6 color, silent filmstrips, 22–38 fr.; Handbooks. #CFT/E ($54). Gr. 6–A. PRV (12/73), PVB (5/74). 745.4

Contents: 1. General Introduction. 2. Effects of Pattern and Color. 3. Effects of Reflection and Light. 4. Unification, Emphasis, and Division. 5. Camouflage and Displays. 6. Designs and Surface Qualities.

An exploration of the interplay between surface, form, and space using as examples buildings, boats, furniture, clothing, pottery, sculpture, posters, trick photography, face makeup, masks, shop signs, and a host of other things.

CUT-OUTS UP-TO-DATE (Filmstrip). National Film Board of Canada/Donars Productions, 1974. 1 color, silent filmstrip, 46 fr.; Teacher's Guide. ($7). Gr. 3–6. PRV (11/74). 745.4

This filmstrip shows many possible designs produced simply from using variations of the circle and the square, and includes a short commentary designed to promote discovery of other possibilities.

DESIGN IS A DANDELION (Filmstrip–Sound). BFA Educational Media, 1969. 6 color, sound filmstrips; 6 cassettes or discs. Cassettes #R6000 ($104), Discs #95000 ($104). Gr. 4–8. BKL (7/1/70). 745.4

Contents: 1. Design in Nature. 2. Design in Form. 3. Design in Texture. 4. Design in Balance. 5. Design in Rhythm. 6. Design in Contrast.

Designed to enhance sensitivity to, and appreciation of, the major elements of design as well as the beauty around us.

Adapted by George Manitzas from the book by Janice Lovoos.

DEWEY, ARIANE

THRESHOLD FILMSTRIPS, SERIES C (Kit). *See* Children's Literature–Collections

DICKENS, CHARLES

A CHRISTMAS CAROL (Phonodisc or Cassette). *See* Christmas–Fiction

A CHRISTMAS CAROL (Kit). *See* Christmas –Fiction

LIBRARY 3 (Cassette). *See* Literature–Collections

THE MAGIC FISHBONE (Filmstrip–Sound/Captioned). *See* Magic–Fiction

DIET

BEFORE YOU TAKE THAT BITE (Motion Picture–16mm–Sound). *See* Nutrition

TOO MUCH OF A GOOD THING (Filmstrip–Sound). *See* Nutrition

VITAL VITTLES WIN THE WEST (Filmstrip–Sound). *See* Nutrition

DILLON, DIANE

WHY MOSQUITOES BUZZ IN PEOPLE'S EARS (Kit). *See* Animals–Fiction

DILLON, LEO

WHY MOSQUITOES BUZZ IN PEOPLE'S EARS (Kit). *See* Animals–Fiction

DINOSAURS

ALL ABOUT DINOSAURS (Filmstrip–Sound). Eye Gate Media, 1976. 6 color, sound filmstrips; 3 cassettes; 12 Spirit Masters. #TH744 ($83.10). Gr. K–6. MDU (7/77). 568.1

Contents: 1. All about Fossils. 2. All about Prehistoric Sea Life. 3. All about the Age of Reptiles. 4. All about Prehistoric creatures of the Air. 5. All about Dinosaurs Today–A Trip to the Museum and Tar Pits. 6. All about Animals Today That Look Prehistoric.

Part of a high interest reading program, the captioned set is supported by cassettes to give students dual input as the world of dinosaurs opens up. Difficult names are presented visually so students can see as well as hear the word and can see the phonetic pronunciation. A combination of pictures of actual fossil bones and the artist's interpretation of how the animals looked in their natural habitat are presented.

DINOSAUR TALES (Filmstrip—Sound).
Coronet Instructional Media, 1976. 4 color,
sound filmstrips, 64–69 fr.; 4 cassettes or
2 discs, 15–17 min.; 1 Guide. Cassettes
#M302 ($62), Discs #S302 ($57). Gr.
K–2. BKL (12/15/76). 568.19

Contents: 1. The Monster of the Lagoon.
2. Diplodocus Meets the First Bird. 3.
Baby Horned-face and the Egg-stealer.
4.The Last of Tyrannosaurus Rex.

Make-believe stories about dinosaurs that
include biological facts and information on
the eras in which they lived. Humorous
personifications of the animals through
their voices and the unusual illustrations of
clay, paper cutout figures, and watercolors
are largely the work of Marshall Izen, a professional puppeteer.

DIRECTION SENSE. *See* Orienteering

DISABLED. *See* Physically Handicapped

DISCOVERIES (IN GEOGRAPHY)—
FICTION

THE KING'S FIFTH (Filmstrip—Sound).
Miller-Brody Productions, 1976, (Newbery Award Records). 2 color, sound filmstrips, 125–137 fr.; 2 cassettes or discs, 16–
17:30 min.; 1 Guide. Cassette #NSF-
3066C ($32), Disc #NSF-3066 ($32). Gr.
3–9. BKL (4/15/77). Fic

Scott O'Dell's 1967 Newbery Honor Book
is adapted in this abridged filmstrip version.
It is a tale of the Spanish conquistadors.

DIVORCE

DON'T YOU LOVE ME ANYMORE? (Filmstrip—Sound). Current Affairs Films, 1977
(Marriage, Separation and Divorce). 4 color,
sound filmstrips, av. 74 fr.; 4 cassettes, av.
16 min.; Teacher's Guide. YW-11 ($88).
Gr. K–6. BKL (11/15/77). 301.428

Contents: 1. It's Not Fair. 2. My Dad Lives
in Springvale. 3. Can I Ever Count on Anyone Again? 4. Could It Happen to My
Family?

A noncondescending approach to a trou-
bling topic; students are offered positive advice and comforting guidance from children
their own age who are surviving a divorce
situation.

MY PARENTS ARE GETTING A DIVORCE
(Filmstrip—Sound). Human Relations Media Center. 2 color, sound filmstrips, 71–
80 fr.; 2 discs or cassettes, 9–10 min.; 1
Guide. ($45). Gr. 6–12. BKL (11/15/76).
301.428

Contents: 1. Separation. 2. Adjusting.

Straightforward answers and mature discussions are needed when young people are
left hanging in limbo over their parents'
separation. The set offers explanations for
the unusual behavior parents may exhibit,
warns of reactions of other family members
and of emotions children may feel but not
understand.

DOCTOR DOLITTLE

DOCTOR DOLITTLE (Filmstrip—Sound).
See Animals—Fiction

DOCTOR SEUSS. *See* Seuss, Doctor

DODGE, MARY MAPES

HANS BRINKER, OR THE SILVER SKATES
(Phonodisc or Cassette). *See* Netherlands—
Fiction

DOGS—FICTION

CALL OF THE WILD (Filmstrip—Sound).
Listening Library. 2 color, sound filmstrips; 2 cassettes. ($28). Gr. 5–9. LNG
(3/76). Fic

The familiar Jack London story, adapted to
this 2-part filmstrip with cartoon illustrations. It contains all the adventure, pathos,
and vitality of the original.

HARRY THE DIRTY DOG (Filmstrip—
Sound). Miller-Brody Productions, 1977.
4 color, sound filmstrips, av. 70 fr.; 4 cassettes, av. 7–14 min. #HDD201 ($64). Gr.
4–8. BKL (12/15/78). Fic

Contents: 1. Harry the Dirty Dog. 2. Harry
by the Sea. 3. No Roses for Harry. 4.
Harry and the Lady Next Door.

Joy and good humor as characterized by
Harry, his family, and friends. Based on
the books by Gene Zion and illustrated by
Margaret Bloy Graham. Available in
Spanish.

LASSIE COME HOME (Phonodisc or Cassette). Caedmon Records, 1973. 1 cassette
or disc, 65 min. Disc #TC1389 ($6.98),
Cassette #CDL51389 ($7.95). Gr. 4–8.
BKL (2/15/74). Fic

Eric Knight's beloved story, which features
a resourceful collie whose courage and
brightness are tested in each adventurous
episode. David McCallum's beautifully
controlled reading preserves the suspense
and adventure of the story in this carefully
abridged adaptation.

DOLPHINS

BOTTLENOSE DOLPHIN (Film Loop—
8mm—Silent). Walt Disney Educational
Media, 1966. 8mm color, silent film loop,
approx. 4 min. #62-5465L ($30). Gr.
K–12. MDU (1/74). 599.53

DOLPHINS (cont.)

Presents the birth of a dolphin and shows the herd protecting it. Dolphins play and chase a turtle and shark, while the mother nurses the newborn and guides it to the surface for air.

COME SEE THE DOLPHIN (Motion Picture–16mm–Sound). Coronet Instructional Media. 16mm color, sound film, 13 min. #3480 ($189). Gr. 1–3. PRV (11/76). 599.33

A dolphin keeper at the Chicago Zoological Society tells his son about the dolphins and their unique characteristics, appearance, diet, a mammal's adaptation to aquatic life, and their means of communication.

DOMANSKA, JANINA

THRESHOLD FILMSTRIPS, SERIES C (Kit). *See* Children's Literature–Collections

DRAGONS–FICTION

THE BOOK OF DRAGONS (Phonodisc or Cassette). Caedmon Records, 1973. 1 cassette or disc. Disc #TC1427 ($6.98), Cassette #CDL51427 ($7.95). Gr. 3–6. HOB (1974), JOR, PRV (3/75). Fic

Contents: 1. The Dragon Tamers. 2. The Fiery Dragon.

Dame Judith Anderson narrates these fiery, fascinating, and enduring stories by E. Nesbit.

THE RELUCTANT DRAGON (Phonodisc or Cassette). Caedmon Records. 1 cassette or disc, approx. 55 min. Disc #TC1074 ($6.98), Cassette #CDL51074 ($7.95). Gr. 3–5. ESL, LBJ, NYR. Fic

This children's story tells how an introverted and poetic dragon makes friends with a little boy who has very much the same personality. The 2 read their poems to each other and enjoy each other's company until the day the villagers send for St. George to vanquish the dreaded beast.

DRUG ABUSE

ALCOHOL AND ALCOHOLISM: THE DRUG AND THE DISEASE (Filmstrip–Sound). *See* Alcoholism

NO, NO, PINOCCHIO (Filmstrip–Sound). Miller-Brody Productions, 1973. 2 color, sound filmstrips, 76–95 fr.; 1 disc or cassette, 9–11 min.; Teacher's Guide. Discs #7-DE-101 ($32), Cassettes #7-DE-101-C ($32). Gr. 1–6. NEF (1973), PRV (9/74), PVB (5/74). 613.8

An original version of the classic story about a little wooden puppet who gets into all kinds of drug-related troubles. A preventive drug abuse presentation.

PROJECT AWARE (Motion Picture–16mm–Sound). *See* Juvenile Delinquency

WHAT ARE YOU GOING TO DO ABOUT ALCOHOL? (Filmstrip–Sound). *See* Alcohol

DRUM

THE FIRST DRUM: HOW MUSIC FIRST BEGAN (Filmstrip–Sound). Contemporary Drama Service, 1976. 1 color, sound filmstrip, 42 fr.; 1 cassette, 6 min. #B-FS-4 ($13.50). Gr. K–5. BKL (4/15/77). 789

A story of Boy-Who-Likes-to-Listen and how he accidentally hits a drying animal skin on a stump and hears a boom similar to his enjoyable thunder.

DUBROVIN, VIVIAN

SADDLE UP! (Kit). *See* Horses–Fiction

DUCKS

IMPRINTING IN DUCKLINGS (Film Loop–8mm–Silent). BFA Educational Media, 1973 (Animal Behavior). 8mm color, silent film loop, approx. 4 min. #481418 ($30). Gr. 4–9. BKL (5/1/76). 598.4

Demonstrates experiments with ducklings, their behavior and characteristics.

DUCKS–FICTION

DUCKS (Motion Picture–8mm–Sound or Captioned). ACI Media/Paramount Communications, 1971 (Starting to Read Series). 16mm color film, captioned; 7 min.; Teacher's Guide; Song Sheets. #7059 ($125). Gr. K–2. Aff (1970), BKL (10/1/70), CFF (1970). Fic

Big and little ducks waddle about a farm eating, drinking, swimming, and quacking.

DUKAS, PAUL ABRAHAM

FUN AND FANTASY SERIES (Cassette). *See* Literature–Collections

DURDEN, KENT

TWO FOR ADVENTURE (Kit). *See* Animals–Fiction

DUTCH IN THE U.S.–FICTION

RIP VAN WINKLE (Phonodisc or Cassette). Caedmon Records. 1 cassette or disc, approx. 45 min. Disc #TC1241 ($6.98), Cassette #CDL51241 ($7.95). Gr. 2–6. EGT, LBJ. Fic

If Washington Irving did not originate the Hudson River legends, he certainly called the attention of the western world to them and to the charm of this geographic region. On this recording, Ed Begley brings out the warmth and humor that have contributed to this story's long popularity.

DUVOISIN, ROGER

THE HAPPY LION SERIES, SET ONE (Filmstrip—Sound). *See* Lions—Fiction

THE HAPPY LION SERIES, SET TWO (Filmstrip—Sound). *See* Lions—Fiction

HIDE AND SEEK FOG (Filmstrip—Sound). *See* Fog—Fiction

PETUNIA (Phonodisc or Cassette). *See* Geese—Fiction

SIGHTS AND SOUNDS FILMSTRIPS, SET 1 (Filmstrip—Sound). *See* Reading—Study and Teaching

SIGHTS AND SOUNDS FILMSTRIPS, SET 2 (Filmstrip—Sound). *See* Reading—Study and Teaching

SIGHTS AND SOUNDS FILMSTRIPS, SET 3 (Filmstrip—Sound). *See* Reading—Study and Teaching

DYES AND DYEING

CREATIVE BATIK (Filmstrip—Sound). *See* Batik

CREATIVE TIE/DYE (Filmstrip—Sound). Warner Educational Productions, 1975 (Art Craft Teaching Films). 2. color, sound filmstrips; 1 cassette, 15 min.; Teacher's Guide. ($39.50). Gr. 6-A. BKL (1/15/75). 746.6
Demonstrates the technique of this art with close-up photographs of step-by-step procedures.

EAGLES

BIRD OF FREEDOM (Motion Picture—16mm—Sound). Unit One Film Productions, 1976. 16mm color, sound film, 13-1/2 min.; Guide. ($225). Gr. 5-10. BKL (10/15/77). 598.9
The majestic spirit of the American bald eagle is shown in its physical characteristics and range of habitat as well as its symbolic image throughout U.S. history and its interpretation by various artists.

THE GOLDEN EAGLES (Kit). Classroom Complements/EBEC, 1976 (Animal Life Stories). 1 color, sound filmstrip; 1 cassette; 5 identical Storybooks; Teacher's Guide. #6967K ($27.95). Gr. K-6. TEA (11/77). 598.91
Young readers can learn how animals live, move, build homes, and fight for food and survival. A 56-page storybook reproduces

all of the narration and full-color art from the filmstrip.

EAR

HEAR BETTER: HEALTHY EARS (Motion Picture—16mm—Sound). Coronet Instructional Media, 1975. 16mm color, sound film, 12 min. #3443 ($172). Gr. 4-6. PRV (11/76). 611.85
Beginning information on the workings of the ear is shown in a 3-dimensional model. Proper care and protection of the ear are readily understandable by even younger grades than recommended.

EASTERN EUROPE

EASTERN EUROPE FROM WITHIN (Filmstrip—Sound). EBEC, 1973. 6 color, sound filmstrips, av. 103 fr. ea.; 6 discs or cassettes, 15 min. ea.; Teacher's Guide. Discs #6470 ($86.95), Cassettes #6470 ($86.95). Gr. 5-9. BKL (11/15/74), ESL (1977), PRV (4/75). 914.3
Contents: 1. Poland: My Country. 2. Czechoslovakia: My Country. 3. Hungary: My Country. 4. Yugoslavia: My Country. 5. Romania: My Country. 6. Bulgaria: My Country.
Shrouded in a veil of half-legend and half-propaganda, the small countries of Eastern Europe are difficult for outsiders to know and understand. In this series, nationals of these countries speak about life in their homelands.

EASTMAN, P. D.

BEGINNER BOOKS FILMSTRIPS, SET 2 (Filmstrip—Sound). *See* Reading—Study and Teaching

BEGINNER BOOKS FILMSTRIPS, SET 3 (Filmstrip—Sound). *See* Reading—Study and Teaching

BEGINNER BOOKS FILMSTRIPS, SET 4 (Filmstrip—Sound). *See* Reading—Study and Teaching

SIGHTS AND SOUNDS FILMSTRIPS, SET 2 (Filmstrip—Sound). *See* Reading—Study and Teaching

ECOLOGY

ABC'S OF ENVIRONMENT (Filmstrip—Sound). Pathescope Educational Media, 1975. 2 color, sound filmstrips, 50-80 fr.; 2 discs or cassettes, 13-20 min.; Student Activity Book; 24 Spirit Masters; Teacher's Manual. ($55). Gr. 3-6. BKL (12/1/75), PVB (4/77). 574.5
Demonstrates to students how they can help save the world. Not a doomsday set, but helps to create awareness of the beauty

ECOLOGY (cont.)

and problems of today's world. Ways to improve neighborhoods and communities are presented.

AESTHETICS (Filmstrip—Sound). *See* Environment

ANIMALS IN DIFFERENT COMMUNITIES (Filmstrip—Sound/Captioned). *See* Animals—Habits and Behavior

AUTUMN IN THE FOREST (Filmstrip—Sound). *See* Autumn

DESERT LIFE (Filmstrip—Captioned). *See* Deserts

DISCOVERING OUR ENVIRONMENT (Study Print). *See* Environment

ECOLOGICAL COMMUNITIES (Filmstrip—Sound). Coronet Instructional Media, 1971. 6 color, sound filmstrips, av. 53 fr.; 6 cassettes or 3 discs, av. 11 min. Cassettes #M205 ($95), Discs #S205 ($95). Gr. 5–12. BKL, PVB. 574.5

Contents: 1. The Deciduous Forest. 2. Ponds and Lakes. 3. The Streams. 4. The Meadow. 5. The Thicket. 6. The Northern Coniferous Forest.

Photography of 6 major types of ecological communites and close-up studies show the interdependence of plant and animal life and adaptations for survival.

ECOLOGY: BALANCE OF NATURE (Filmstrip—Sound). Marshfilm, 1972 (Ecology). 1 color, sound filmstrip, 45 fr.; 1 cassette or disc, 15 min.; Teacher's Guide. #1112 ($21). Gr. 4–9. BKL (4/1/73), ESL (1977), SLJ (4/72). 574.5

Everything on earth affects everything else. Interactions are seen through food chains, changes in natural communities, pyramids of plant and animal mass living in an area, disease, weather, and the cycles of chemicals.

ECOLOGY: EXPLORATION AND DISCOVERY (Filmstrip—Sound). United Learning, 1975. 6 color, sound filmstrips, av. 53 fr. ea.; 6 cassettes, av. 7 min. ea.; Guide. #48 ($85). Gr. 4–6. PRV (11/76). 574.5

Contents: 1. Organisms and Environment. 2. Food Chains. 3. Habitat. 4. Populations. 5. Plant and Animal Communities. 6. Ecosystems.

Basic concepts in ecology are developed through discussion and experiments that can be performed in the classroom. Special stop frames provide opportunities to discuss the interdependence of plants and animals on each other and on the environment.

THE ECOLOGY OF A DESERT: DEATH VALLEY (Filmstrip—Sound). *See* Deserts

THE ECOLOGY OF A TEMPERATE RAIN FOREST (Filmstrip—Sound). *See* Rain Forests

ECOLOGY: SPACESHIP EARTH (Filmstrip—Sound). Marshfilm, 1971 (Ecology). 1 color, sound filmstrip, 45 fr.; 1 cassette or disc, 15 min.; Teacher's Guide. #1111 ($21). Gr. 4–8. BKL (4/1/73), ESL (1976), SLJ (4/72). 574.5

This filmstrip emphasizes the life-support systems of earth, i.e., energy supply, food, air, water, raw materials, and the living. The problems of pollution, overpopulation, and consumption are related to the continued survival of our planet.

ECOLOGY: UNDERSTANDING THE CRISIS (Filmstrip—Sound). EBEC, 1971. 6 color, sound filmstrips, av. 82 fr. ea.; 6 cassettes or discs, 9 min. ea.; Teacher's Guide. Discs #6454 ($86.95), Cassettes #6454K ($86.95). Gr. 5–A. BKL (2/15/74), LFR (10/72), PRV (9/72). 574.5

Contents: 1. Environments and Ecosystems. 2. Man in Ecosystems. 3. Human Communities Simple and Complex. 4. Creating Imbalances. 5. Destroying the Future. 6. Creating the Future.

Ecology holds the key to understanding today's environmental crisis, an understanding vital to the survival of our planet. How the crisis has come about is shown with dramatic clarity in this series.

ENERGY AND OUR ENVIRONMENT (Filmstrip—Sound). Coronet Instructional Media, 1975. 4 color, sound filmstrips, av. 51 fr.; 4 discs or 2 cassettes, av. 10 min. Discs ($53), Cassettes ($58). Gr. 5–12. BKL (1975), PRV (1975), PVB (1976). 574.5

Contents: 1. Man and the World's Energy. 2. Waste and Pollution. 3. Our Growing Use of Energy. 4. The Future.

Increasing demands for energy require us to look for new sources and to conserve present ones. Energy alternatives and methods of conservation are discussed.

ENVIRONMENTAL DECISIONS: AN INQUIRY (Filmstrip—Captioned). BFA Educational Media, 1970. 5 color, captioned filmstrips. #VF8000 ($40). Gr. 4–6. BKL (2/15/72). 574.5

Contents: 1. Forests. 2. Air. 3. Wildlife. 4. Soil. 5. Water.

Each filmstrip asks students to consider a major ecological problem. Information is presented so that alternative solutions are obvious. No conclusions are declared right or wrong.

EXPLORING ECOLOGY (Filmstrip—Sound). National Geographic, 1974. 5 color, sound filmstrips, 60–72 fr.; 5 discs or cassettes, 12–14 min. Discs #03758 ($74.50), Cassettes #03759 ($74.50). Gr. 4–12. PRV (5/75), PVB (4/76). 574.5

Contents: 1. The Mountain. 2. The River. 3. The Woodland. 4. The Prairie. 5. The Swamp.

Explores the relationship of living things in 5 distinct environments. Adaptations of mountain plants and animals, the myriad forms of life in rivers and swamps, the seasonality in the woodlands, and the productivity of prairies are observed through the beautiful photography.

FIRE! (Motion Picture—16mm—Sound). *See* Forest Fires

FOUR BIOMES (Filmstrip—Sound). Jean-Michel Cousteau/BFA Educational Media, 1976. 4 color, sound filmstrips, av. 55–74 fr.; 4 cassettes or discs, av. 9:13–12:32 min. Cassettes #VHV000 ($70), Discs #VHU000 ($70). Gr. 6–9. BKL (7/1/77). 574.5

Contents: 1. The Temperate Forest Biome. 2. The Rain Forest Biome. 3. The Grassland Biome. 4. The Desert Biome.

Climate is the basic factor that determines which organisms live in various parts of the world. However, a host of other factors interact to create the living community.

GRASSLAND ECOLOGY—HABITATS AND CHANGE (Motion Picture—16mm—Sound). *See* Grasslands

HABITAT (Filmstrip—Captioned). *See* Animals—Habits and Behavior

LAND, WATER, SKY AND THINGS THAT GROW (Filmstrip—Sound). *See* Natural History

LET'S FIND THE POLLUTION SOLUTION (Filmstrip—Sound). January Productions, 1973. 5 color, sound filmstrips, av. 39 fr. ea.; 5 cassettes av. 5 min.; Teacher's Guide. ($72.50). Gr. K–3. BKL (9/74), TEA (5/6/74). 301.31

Contents: 1. The Cloudmaker. 2. The Day the Litter Talked. 3. A Sad Day for Mr. Bear. 4. The Stream That Lost Its Friend. 5. 21 Maple Street.

Tells a story that deals with the problems of air pollution, water pollution, litter, and conservation; shows influence of these problems on the lives of animals and people.

LIFE CYCLE OF COMMON ANIMALS, GROUP 2 (Filmstrip—Sound). *See* Sheep

NATURAL RESOURCES, OUR CHANGING ENVIRONMENT (Filmstrip—Sound). *See* Natural Resources

ONCE AROUND THE SUN (Filmstrip—Sound). *See* Seasons

PARADISE LOST (Motion Picture—16mm—Sound). *See* Man—Influence on Nature

PLANT WORLD (Filmstrip—Sound). *See* Plants

SAND DUNE SUCCESSION (Filmstrip—Sound). Imperial Educational Resources, 1975. 2 color, sound filmstrips; 2 cassettes or discs; Teacher's Notes. Discs #3RG40400 ($30), Cassette #3KG40400 ($33). Gr. 4–8. BKL (11/15/75), PRV (4/76). 574.5

Contents: 1. From Beach to Pine Forest. 2. From Pine Forest to Beech-Maple.

This set begins with the description of environmental communities and their structure, then proceeds to the processes by which these communities are changed through time. The principles of ecological succession are examined through the stages of sand dune succession.

STORIES OF ANIMALS WHICH SHARE AN ENVIRONMENT (Filmstrip—Sound). Imperial Educational Resources, 1972. 4 color, sound filmstrips; 4 cassettes or discs. Discs #3RG43800 ($56), Cassettes #3KG43800 ($62). Gr. 2–6. BKL (4/73), STE (12/72). 591.5

Contents: 1. The Fawn—The Bear. 2. The Osprey—The Trout. 3. The Swan—The Beaver. 4. The Tanager—The Dipper.

Each strip tells 2 separate stories about distinct animal species. The format clearly demonstrates that environmental systems sustain a variety of interdependent life forms.

VISITING NATURE ONE (Filmstrip—Sound). Educational Direction/Learning Tree Filmstrips, 1976. 4 color, sound filmstrips, av. 69 fr. ea.; 4 cassettes, av. 11 min. ea.; Teacher's Guide. #LT686 ($58). Gr. K–6. BKL (4/15/77), LGB (1977), PRV (10/77). 574.5

Contents: 1. Up a Mountain. 2. In a Marsh. 3. Through a Forest. 4. Across a Field.

Provides a beautiful introduction to various geographical environments.

VISITING NATURE TWO (Filmstrip—Sound). Educational Direction/Learning Tree Filmstrips, 1976. 4 color, sound filmstrips, av. 69 fr. ea.; 4 cassettes, av. 11 min. ea.; Teacher's Guide. #LT687 ($58). Gr. K–6. BKL (4/15/77), LGB (1977), PRV (10/77). 574.5

Contents: 1. In a Yard. 2. Along a Stream. 3. At a Seashore. 4. Along a Pond.

Provides a beautiful introduction to various geographical environments.

WHAT ARE ECOSYSTEMS? (Filmstrip—Sound). Troll Associates, 1975. 6 color, sound filmstrips, av. 41 fr. ea.; 3 cassettes, av. 10 min. ea.; Teacher's Guide. ($78). Gr. 4–6. BKL (7/76), PRV (4/76), TEA (2/76). 574.5

Contents: 1. The Pond Ecosystem. 2. The Stream Ecosystem. 3. The Salt Marsh and Seashore Ecosystem. 4. The Forest Ecosystem. 5. The Human Urban Ecosystem. 6. Comparing the City to Natural Ecosystems.

An ecology series focusing on 6 different ecosystems.

ECOLOGY (cont.)

WHAT IS ECOLOGY? (Film Loop—8mm—
Captioned). Troll Associates, 1974. 4 8mm
color film loops, av. 4 min. ea.; Film Notes
on container; Teacher's Guide. ($99.80).
Gr. 2-6. PRV (2/75). 574.5
Contents: 1. What Are Ecological Systems?
2. What Is a Food Chain? 3. What Is a
Balanced Ecological System? 4. What
Causes Ecological Changes?
Using nature as their laboratory, students
discover the reason why plants and animals
are interdependent upon each other and
how the sun is the source of life.

THE WILD YOUNG DESERT SERIES (Filmstrip—Sound). *See* Deserts

WINTER IN THE FOREST (Filmstrip—
Sound). *See* Winter

ECOLOGY—FICTION

THE LORAX BY DOCTOR SEUSS (Kit).
Random House, 1977. 2 color, sound filmstrips, 82-93 fr.; 2 cassettes or discs, 10-11
min.; 1 Book; 1 Teacher's Guide. Cassettes
#04653-6 ($48), Discs #04652-8 ($48).
Gr. K-5. BKL (12/15/77). Fic
A spooky story that follows the original
text. Although full of humorous nonsense,
it presents a message of the need to conserve
the environment.

ECONOMICS

HOW MONEY WORKS (Filmstrip—Sound).
See Money

MARKET PLACE IN MEXICO (Motion
Picture—16mm—Sound). *See* Mexico

MONEY: FROM BARTER TO BANKING
(Filmstrip—Sound). *See* Money

SOMETHING SPECIAL—WORK (Filmstrip—
Sound). *See* Work

EDUCATION, BILINGUAL

EARLY LEARNING LIBRARY (Filmstrip—
Sound). *See* Child Development

I CAN, UNIT ONE (Filmstrip—Sound). *See*
Self-Perception

IT'S OK FOR ME: IT'S OK FOR YOU
(Filmstrip—Sound). *See* Emotions

MEDIA: RESOURCES FOR DISCOVERY
(Filmstrip—Sound). *See* Audio-Visual
Materials

EDUCATIONAL GUIDANCE

WHY AM I STUDYING THIS? (Filmstrip—
Sound). Teaching Resources Films, 1974.
4 color, sound filmstrips, av. 53 fr.; 4 discs
or cassettes, 10-12 min.; Teacher's Guide.

Discs #410710 ($56), Cassettes #410711
($60). Gr. 4-8. PRV (4/76). 371.42
Contents: 1. Why Am I Studying English?
2. Why Am I Studying Mathematics? 3.
Why Am I Studying Science? 4. Why Am
I Studying Social Studies?
This set attempts to show the relationship
between the classroom curriculum and
students' daily lives. Portions of the strips
deal with career opportunities in each of
the fields. Cartoonlike visuals are used.

EGYPT—ANTIQUITIES

ANCIENT EGYPT: LAND/PEOPLE/ART
(Filmstrip—Sound). Educational Dimensions Group, 1976. 2 color, sound filmstrips, 58-61 fr.; 2 cassettes, 14-16 min.;
Teacher's Guide. #820 ($37). Gr. 4-12.
BKL (12/1/76), PRV (4/77), PVB (4/78).
913.32
Life in Ancient Egypt is described as photos
of artworks and artifacts are shown. An
overview of life and customs and information about how scholars learned about this
interesting land are related by the narrator.

ELECTRICITY

JUNIOR ELECTRICIAN (Filmstrip—Sound).
Filmstrip House/United Learning, 1976.
4 color, sound filmstrips, av. 65 fr. ea.; 2
cassettes or discs, av. 12 min. ea.; Script and
Guide. Cassettes #66302 ($55), Discs
#66301 ($55). Gr. 2-4. BKL (5/1/77),
PRV (2/77). 537
Contents: 1. Neg, Poz and Static Electricity. 2. Magnets—A Polar Exploration. 3.
Current Lights a Lamp. 4. Our Electrical
World.
The setting for these filmstrips is in an
electrical repair shop where Mr. Electron
teaches his son and his son's best friend
the principles of electricity. They start with
simple experiments with static electricity,
discuss magnets, batteries, lamps, and
motors. It is this gradual progression that
makes the series useful on several levels.

ELEPHANTS

ELEPHANT (Motion Picture—16mm—
Sound). EBEC, 1971 (Silent Safari). 16mm
color, sound nonnarrated film, 11 min.;
Teacher's Guide. #3121 ($150). Gr. K-9.
BKL (10/1/76). 599.6
Follow the African elephant through its
daily routine of foraging, dusting, playing,
roaming, and drinking an average of 60
gallons a day from a waterhole. Physical
characteristics of this 10- to 12-foot high
beast are graphically illustrated. Scenes of
herds, numbering up to 100 elephants,
include shots of cows and calves.

ZIGGY, THE ELEPHANT (Kit). Classroom
Complements/EBEC, 1976 (Animal Life

Stories). 1 color, sound filmstrip; 1 cassette; 5 identical Storybooks; Teacher's Guide. #6963K ($27.95). Gr. K-6. TEA (11/77). 599.6

Students can learn how elephants live, move, build homes, and fight for food and survival. A 56-page storybook reproduces all of the narration and full-color art from the filmstrip.

ELEPHANTS—FICTION

DUMBO (Kit). Walt Disney Educational Media, 1975 (Walt Disney Read-along, Set Five). 1 cassette or disc, 13:45 min.; 10 paperback booklets; 1 Guide. #66-0034 ($27). Gr. K-3. BKL (4/15/77). Fic

The appealing story about the flying elephant as narrated by Shari Lewis. One side of the disc is an introduction to the story; the other side is a word-for-word reading.

ELIZABETH I, QUEEN OF ENGLAND—FICTION

SHE WAS NICE TO MICE (Phonodisc or Cassette). Caedmon Records, 1976. 1 cassette or disc, approx. 55 min.; Jacket Notes. Disc #TC1506 ($6.98), Cassette #CKL51506 ($7.95). Gr. K-3. AUR (1978). Fic

A side of Elizabeth I never revealed before, because no historian has been a mouse before. Performed and created by Alexandra Sheedy.

ELKIN, BENJAMIN

THE PONY ENGINE AND OTHER STORIES FOR CHILDREN (Phonodisc or Cassette). *See* Short Stories

EMBRYOLOGY

EMBRYOLOGY OF THE CHICK (Film Loop—8mm—Captioned). BFA Educational Media, 1973 (Animal Behavior). 8mm color, captioned film loop, approx. 4 min. #481420 ($30). Gr. 4-9. BKL (5/1/76). 501.3

Demonstrates experiments, behavior, and characteristics of chicken embryos.

EMOTIONS

ATTITUDES UNIT (Motion Picture—16mm—Sound). *See* Attitude (Psychology)

DEALING WITH FEELINGS (Filmstrip—Sound). *See* Human Relations

FEELINGS UNIT (Motion Picture—16mm—Sound). Sutherland Learning Associates/EBEC, 1972 (Most Important Person). 3 16mm color, sound films. Also avail. 8mm film; 1 record; 3 Posters; 3 Song Cards; Teacher's Guide. #6732 ($172.80).

Gr. K-3. BKL (7/1/74), CHT (9/10/74), CPR (1/76). 152.4

Contents: 1. Feeling Good, Feeling Happy! 2. I Used to Be Afraid. 3. Different Kinds of Love.

Each lesson emphasizes feelings of happiness, love, or fear from the child's point of view.

THE HATING BOOK (Kit). Harper & Row/Guidance Associates, 1976 (Mediabook Series). 1 color, sound filmstrip, 42 fr.; 1 disc or cassette, 4 min.; 4 Student Booklets; Teacher's Guide. Disc #303501 ($32.50), Cassette #303519 ($32.50). Gr. K-4. PRV (10/76), PVB (4/77). 152.4

Designed to support reading and language arts while dealing with guidance and self-development.

HOW DO YOU FEEL? (Motion Picture—16mm—Sound). FilmFair Communications, 1971. 16mm color, sound film, 9-3/4 min. ($135). Gr. K-6. CGE (1972), LFR (10/71), NEF (1972). 152.4

A motivational film designed to encourage children to think and talk about their feelings of love, happiness, sadness, and fear. They voice their innermost feelings about the happiest times in their lives and also about their fears. Lyrical camera work and children's art help to make the points. An original folk song amplifies this evocative film.

LO IMPORTANTE QUE ERES (Filmstrip—Sound). *See* Self

IT'S GOOD TO BE ME (Filmstrip—Sound). Q+ED Productions, 1976. 5 color, sound filmstrips, 59-69 fr.; 5 cassettes or discs, 8-9 min.; 1 Guide. Cassettes #GME-10 ($99.50), Discs ($89.50). Gr. 1-4. BKL (4/1/77). 155.4

Contents: 1. Lions and Tigers and Bears. 2. Different Is O.K. 3. Once upon a Swing. 4. Birthday Bike. 5. So Big.

To help children identify, accept, and express the range of emotions they experience, familiar situations are presented involving family and peers; stressing that all people have feelings, but respond differently.

IT'S OK FOR ME: IT'S OK FOR YOU (Filmstrip—Sound). ACI Media/Paramount Communications, 1975 (ACI Media). 4 color, sound filmstrips; 4 cassettes: Teacher's Guide. #9110 ($78). Gr. 2-5. PRV (9/76). 152.4

Contents: 1. It's OK to Be Angry. 2. It's OK to Make Mistakes. 3. If It's OK for Me, It's OK for Others. 4. What Would You Do?

These filmstrips help children realize that making mistakes and feeling strong emotions are part of being human. This understanding helps youngsters show empathy with others and helps them learn to deal with anger in nondestructive ways. Available in Spanish.

EMOTIONS (cont.)

LEARNING ABOUT ME (Filmstrip—Sound). *See* Self-Perception

MY FEELINGS COUNT (Filmstrip—Captioned). EBEC, 1976 (Developing Language Skills). 4 color, captioned filmstrips, av. 46 fr. ea.; Teacher's Guide. #13265 ($32.90). Gr. K–3. BKL (4/15/77), LFR (1/2/77), PRV (1977). 152.4

Contents: 1. I Wonder. 2. The Me I Like. 3. When Things Go Wrong. 4. When I Feel Afraid.

Happy, mad, warm, lonely may be just words to a child, but they can communicate a world of feelings when the child learns what the words mean and how to use them. By focusing on true-to-life situations with which children can identify, students have an opportunity to talk about their own feelings, to share their feelings with other students, and to expand their vocabulary in an atmosphere that is free, open, and encouraging.

OF LONELINESS AND LOVE (Filmstrip—Sound). ACI Media/Paramount Communications, 1975. 4 color, sound filmstrips, 57 fr.; 4 cassettes, 7-1/2 min.; 1 Guide. #9117 ($78). Gr. 1–4. BKL (9/76). 152.4

Contents: 1. Loneliness—Friendship. 2. Success—Failure. 3. Love—Hate. 4. Sharing—Shirking.

This set helps children identify and understand the various emotions they have experienced or may encounter.

UNDERSTANDING YOUR FEELINGS (Filmstrip—Sound). Educational Direction/Learning Tree Filmstrips, 1976. 4 color, sound filmstrips, av. 43 fr. ea.; 2 cassettes, av. 7 min. ea.; Teacher's Guide. ($58). Gr. K–3. BKL (1/1/77). 152.4

Contents: 1. What Is an Emotion. 2. Emotions and Their Many Faces. 3. Everyone's Felt Like That. 4. Living with Emotions.

This set explains and demonstrates that everyone has emotions, but there are a number of ways they can be expressed.

YOU (Motion Picture—16mm—Sound). *See* Human Relations

ENDANGERED SPECIES. *See* Rare Animals; Rare Birds; Rare Plants; etc.

ENERGY. *See* Force and Energy; Power Resources

ENGLAND—FICTION

A CHRISTMAS CAROL (Kit). *See* Christmas—Fiction

MARY POPPINS (Phonodisc or Cassette). *See* Fantasy—Fiction

MARY POPPINS AND THE BANKS FAMILY (Phonodisc or Cassette). *See* Fantasy—Fiction

MARY POPPINS: BALLOONS AND BALLOONS (Phonodisc or Cassette). *See* Fantasy—Fiction

MARY POPPINS COMES BACK (Phonodisc or Cassette). *See* Fantasy—Fiction

MARY POPPINS FROM A TO Z (Phonodisc or Cassette). *See* Alphabet Books

MARY POPPINS OPENS THE DOOR (Phonodisc or Cassette). *See* Fantasy—Fiction

ENGLAND—HISTORY—FICTION

A CHRISTMAS CAROL (Phonodisc or Cassette). *See* Christmas—Fiction

WILL'S QUILL (Filmstrip—Sound). *See* Geese—Fiction

ENGLISH AS A SECOND LANGUAGE

BASIC ENGLISH FOR SPANISH-SPEAKING CHILDREN (Phonodisc or Cassette). Listening Library, 1973. 2 phonodiscs, 33-1/3 rpm or 2 cassettes, 110 min.; Teacher's Guide. Cassette ($16.95), Disc #AA3344 ($13.95). Gr. K–3. BKL (9/1/77), LTP (6/74). 372.65

Designed to help solve a language problem all too prevalent in many urban schools, these recordings introduce English to the Spanish-speaking pupil at the kindergarten and primary levels, thus helping the child overcome the language barrier.

ENGLISH LANGUAGE—COMPOSITION AND EXERCISES

ADVENTURES IN IMAGINATION SERIES (Filmstrip—Sound). McGraw-Hill Films, 1974. 4 color, sound filmstrips, av. 25 fr. ea.; 4 cassettes or discs, 4-1/2 min. ea. Teacher's Guide. ($68). Gr. 4–12. BKL (4/15/75), PRV (11/75). 372.6

Contents: 1. Being Alone. 2. Being with Others. 3. Getting Caught and Going Free. 4. Something's Going to Happen—What?

Each of the 4 sound filmstrips explores a different theme, using bold visual images and an original musical score to encourage students to draw from their own experiences and fantasies and to start ideas flowing for stories, poems, essays, and other endeavors in creative communication.

AND THEN WHAT HAPPENED? (Filmstrip—Sound). HBJ Films/Harcourt Brace Jovanovich, 1976 (Self Expression and Conduct: Humanities, Level K). 2 color, sound filmstrips, av. 76 fr. ea.; 2 cassettes or discs, 9 min. ea. Cassette #3733474 ($48), Disc #3733466 ($48). Gr. K–1. CIF (1976). 372.6

Contents: 1. Funny Faces, Sunny Spaces. 2. And Then What Happened?

Three puppet characters–Beginning, Middle, and End–sing a happy song describing the parts they play in creating a story. As they sing, the children see several picture stories. Each story is shown in sequence with a beginning, a middle, and an end. The children see 3 pictures that are out of sequence and are invited to tell how they would arrange them in their proper order. Finally, the puppets tell the beginning of a story, and End invites the children to complete the story with a middle and an end.

BASIC STUDY SKILLS 3 (Filmstrip–Sound). *See* Study, Method of

COMPOSITION POWER (Kit). *See* English Language–Study and Teaching

DESCRIBING WHAT WE SEE (Motion Picture–16mm–Sound). S-L Film Productions, 1971. 16mm color, sound film, 12 min. ($165). Gr. K–3. EGT (1972), FLN (1972). 372.6

This is a motivational film for student writing. It presents descriptive writing with examples, then gives the students 2 situations to write about after the film is finished, situations rich with descriptive details of color, sound, and shape.

ENGLISH COMPOSITION FOR CHILDREN, SET 1 (Filmstrip–Sound). *See* English Language–Study and Teaching

ENGLISH COMPOSITION FOR CHILDREN, SET 2 (Filmstrip–Sound). *See* English Language–Study and Teaching

ENGLISH COMPOSITION FOR CHILDREN, SET 3 (Filmstrip–Sound). *See* English Language–Study and Teaching

ENGLISH COMPOSITION FOR CHILDREN, SET 4 (Filmstrip–Sound). *See* English Language–Study and Teaching

ENGLISH COMPOSITION FOR CHILDREN, SET 5 (Filmstrip–Sound). *See* English Language–Study and Teaching

HEAR IT AND WRITE (Filmstrip–Sound). Guidance Associates, 1974. 2 color, sound filmstrips, av. 60 fr.; 2 discs or cassettes, av. 8 min.; Teacher's Guide. Discs #6D-300-663 ($48.50), Cassettes #6D-300-671 ($48.50). Gr. 4–6. BKL (1/75), PRV (12/75), PVB (4/76). 372.6

Part I shows Bernie and Carlos investigating the fun of using all kinds of words. Part II shows how sound creates moods, how specific letter-sounds create various effects.

ON LOCATION WITH COMPOSITION–LEVEL ONE, TWO AND THREE (Filmstrip–Sound). Harper & Row/Xerox Educational Publications, 1976. 9 color, sound filmstrips, av. 66–88 fr. (3 per level); 9 cassettes, av. 9–12 min. (3 per level); Teacher's Guide. Set #SC034 ($170), Individual Levels ($60). Gr. 3–7. BKL (12/15/77), PVB (1976). 372.6

Contents: 1. Telling a Story. 2. Writing a Description. 3. Sharing a Feeling. 4. Creating a Character. 5. Writing a Dialogue. 6. Creating a Mood. 7. Finding the Facts. 8. Organizing the Information. 9. Making a Convincing Argument.

This program outlines specific techniques for varying stories and making them more interesting. Students work with dialogue, develop characters, and organize information. Examples of writing are presented to use as models.

OPEN BOX: IDEAS FOR CREATIVE EXPRESSION (Kit). EBEC, 1977. 10 shortstrips; 3 cassettes; 54 Picture Cards; 2 Shortstrip Viewers; Teacher's Guide. #6944K ($55). Gr. 2–4. BKL (11/15/77), CHH (6/77), LAM (10/77). 372.6

This language arts program is a resourceful box full of ideas for creative expression. Children of all reading levels can participate because many ideas are presented through art and sound as well as print.

PARAGRAPH POWER (Kit). *See* English Language–Study and Teaching

SEE IT AND WRITE (Filmstrip–Sound). Guidance Associates, 1974 (Write Now Wordshop). 2 color, sound filmstrips, av. 70 fr. ea.; discs or cassettes, av. 8 min. ea.; Teacher's Guide. Discs #9A-300-622 ($52.50), Cassettes #9A-300-630 ($52.50). Gr. 4–6. BKL (1/75), PRV (12/75), PVB (4/76). 372.6

In Part I, students are invited to discover hidden shapes and pictures in photographed scenes and objects; Part II illustrates the importance of using the right words to communicate visual experiences.

SENTENCE PROBLEMS TWO (Filmstrip–Sound). Filmstrip House, 1972. 4 color, sound filmstrips, 49–55 fr.; 2 cassettes or discs, 11 min.; Script Book. ($45). Gr. 5–10. PRV (12/73), PVB (5/74). 372.61

Contents: 1. Choppy Sentences. 2. Run-on Sentences. 3. Dangling Modifiers. 4. Wordiness–Excess Baggage.

The various forms of each problem are explored in detail, then summarized. Photographs give effective visual support to ideas in example sentences.

STORIES (Motion Picture–16mm–Sound). Churchill Films, 1977 (The Joy of Writing). 16mm color, sound film, 14 min.; Study Guide. ($195). Gr. 2–4. BKL (2/15/78). 372.6

Children working with a teacher make up a round-robin collaborative story, formulate characters, illustrate how they get ideas for stories and how settings can add to stories,

ENGLISH LANGUAGE– COMPOSITION AND EXERCISES (cont.)

and talk about the importance of beginnings and endings.

WORDS (Motion Picture–16mm–Sound). Churchill Films, 1977 (The Joy of Writing). 16mm color, sound film, 14 min.; Study Guide. ($195). Gr. 2–4. BKL (2/15/78). 372.6

Children working with a teacher make letters and words with their bodies, brainstorm words for alliterative sentences, pantomime words, use words as inspirations for stories, compose cinquains, and visit a printer to have their cinquain realized in type.

WORDS WE NEED (Filmstrip–Sound). Filmstrip House/United Learning, 1973 (Language for Young Children). 4 color sound filmstrips; 2 cassettes or phonodiscs; Script/ Guide. Cassette #84602 ($55), Disc #84601 ($55). Gr. K–3. STE (3/27/75). 372.4

Contents: 1. Nouns. 2. Verbs. 3. Adjectives. 4. Adverbs.

A story featuring circus characters motivates children to explore the kinds of words needed for different functions in writing sentences.

WRITE A STORY (Filmstrip–Sound). Guidance Associates, 1974. 2 color, sound filmstrips, av. 60 fr. ea.; 2 discs or cassettes, av. 8 min. ea.; Teacher's Guide. Discs #6D 300-689 ($52.50), Cassettes #6D 300-697 ($52.50). Gr. 4–6. BKL (1/75), PRV (12/75), PVB (4/76). 372.6

Helps students to visualize 4 basic approaches to writing good stories. An imagined adventure with a friend, solving a problem, conducting a search, imagining that one aspect of life has changed drastically.

WRITE IN ORDER (Filmstrip–Sound). Guidance Associates, 1974. 2 color, sound filmstrips, av. 60 fr. ea.; 2 discs or cassettes, av. 8 min. ea.; Teacher's Guide. Discs #6D-300-762 ($52.50), Cassettes #6D-300-770 ($52.50). Gr. 4–6. BKL (1/75), PRV (12/75), PVB (4/76). 372.6

Shows the need for and suggests practical ways to provide structure description, sequence in sentences and paragraphs so they have coherence.

WRITE LIVELY LANGUAGE (Filmstrip–Sound). Guidance Associates, 1974. 2 color, sound filmstrips, av. 60 fr. ea.; 2 discs or cassettes, av. 8 min. ea.; Teacher's Guide. Discs #6D-300-721 ($52.50), Cassettes #6D-300-739 ($52.50). Gr. 4–6. BKL (1/75), PRV (12/75), PVB (4/76). 372.6

Demonstrates creative techniques of imagery, simile, hyperbole, personification, and other vivid terms for students to apply to their own writings.

ENGLISH LANGUAGE– DICTIONARIES

THE DICTIONARY (Filmstrip–Sound). Society for Visual Education, 1977. 4 color, sound filmstrips av. 52 fr. ea.; 4 cassettes or discs, av. 9 min. ea.; Teacher's Guide. #A151-SA ($70). Gr. 3–7. BKL (11/1/77). 423

Contents: 1. Introducing the Dictionary. 2. Finding Words. 3. Pronouncing Words. 4. Meanings of Words.

Humorous visuals work with an informative narration to detail the form and function of dictionaries. An interview with Robert Barnhart reveals the process through which words find their way into dictionaries.

DICTIONARY SKILL BOX (Cassette). Troll Associates, 1977. 6 cassette tapes, av. 7 min. ea.; 24 Spirit Masters; Teacher's Guide. ($56). Gr. 3–8. BKL (1/15/78). 028.7

Contents: 1. What Is a Dictionary? 2. How Do You Find It? 3. How Do You Say It? 4. What Does It Mean? 5. More about the Entry. 6. Front and Back Matter.

Introducing the middle-grade student to the dictionary, this program shows how the tool aids in spelling, definition, pronunciation, and providing other sources of information.

TROLL TALKING PICTURE DICTIONARY (Kit). Troll Associates, 1974. 16 cassettes, approx. 22 min. ea.; 64 paperback books, 4 copies of ea. title.; Teacher's Guide. ($145). Gr. 1–4. BKL (6/15/75), INS (3/75). 411

Each letter of the alphabet is demonstrated by several words beginning with that letter. Simple definitions are illustrated with animal figures. Cassettes follow the text in the books, word for word.

ENGLISH LANGUAGE–GRAMMAR

ON YOUR MARKS: PART I (Motion Picture–16mm–Sound). See Punctuation

ON YOUR MARKS: PART II (Motion Picture–16mm–Sound). See Punctuation

SENTENCE PROBLEMS TWO (Filmstrip–Sound). See English Language–Composition and Exercises

SPEAKING OF GRAMMAR (Filmstrip–Sound). Guidance Associates, 1975 (Language Skills). 2 color, sound filmstrips, 60–74 fr.; 2 cassettes or discs, 11–14 min. Cassettes #301-992 ($52.50), Discs #301-984 ($52.50). Gr. 5–8. BKL (2/15/76), LGB (1975), PRV (1975). 372.61

Contents: 1. The Parts of Speech. 2. A Language about Language.

An overview of grammatical terms and techniques, helping students define parts of speech and learn how words, phrases, and clauses combine to make sentences. Identifies simple sentence patterns as well as compound and complex sentences.

THE STRUCTURE OF LANGUAGE (Filmstrip–Sound). Multi-Media Productions, 1976. 4 color, sound filmstrips, 41–46 fr.; 4 cassettes, 7–9 min.; Available separately. #5009C ($50). Gr. 4–12. PRV (4/78). 372.61

Contents: 1. End Punctuation. 2. Sentences. 3. Capitalization and Clauses. 4. Those Crazy Hooks . . . and Friends.

This group of 4 sound filmstrips covers punctuation rules and marks, the use of capitalization, sentence structure, and clauses. Each item is defined and illustrated. Color photographs of catchy billboards frequently serve as visuals.

ENGLISH LANGUAGE–HISTORY

LANGUAGE–THE MIRROR OF MAN'S GROWTH (Filmstrip–Sound). Centron Films, 1971. 5 color, sound filmstrips; 5 discs or cassettes. Discs ($59.50), Cassettes ($69.50). Gr. 4–8. BKL (5/15/71), ELE (11/72), STE (9/72). 420.9

Contents: 1. Language and Its Mysteries. 2. What Age Has Done to English. 3. How Is It That an Englishman Speaks English? 4. Languages Are Born . . . Sometimes They Die. 5. The American Language–Or When the King's English Came to America.

These 5 artwork filmstrips trace the development of language in general and American English in particular.

ENGLISH LANGUAGE–SPELLING

SPEAKING OF SPELLING (Filmstrip–Sound). Guidance Associates, 1975 (Language Skills). 2 color, sound filmstrips, av. 61 fr.; 2 discs or cassettes, av. 11 min. #1B-301968 ($52.50), #1B-301976 ($52.50). Gr. 5–8. BKL (2/15/76), LGB (1975), PRV (1975). 421.52

Contents: 1. The System. 2. Using the System.

Illustrates "how to" tips for competent spelling: learning basic patterns, dealing with complex words, and devices to help with irregular spellings.

THE SPELLING MONSTERS: UNIT A (Filmstrip–Sound). Scholastic Book Services, 1977. 5 color, sound filmstrips, 65–97 fr.; 5 cassettes or discs, 6–10 min.; 30 Duplicating Masters; 1 Guide. Cassettes #4016 ($89.50), Discs #4015 ($89.50). Gr. 2–6. BKL (2/15/77), RTE (5/77). 372.63

Contents: 1. Land of the Monsters. 2. Land of the Rhyme Monsters. 3. Hunters. 4. Vampire Village. 5. Monster Sitters.

This kit emphasizes phonics and structural patterns as well as letter recognition and visual discrimination covering short vowels, consonant sounds, silent e, doubling consonants, rhyming, and consonant substitution. The cartoon pictures of 2 young people traveling through monster land support the concepts.

THE SPELLING MONSTERS: UNIT B (Filmstrip–Sound). Scholastic Book Services, 1977. 5 color, sound filmstrips, 65–95 fr.; 5 cassettes, 6–10 min.; Duplicating Masters; 1 Guide. Cassettes #4018 ($89.50), Discs #4017 ($89.50). Gr. 3–7. BKL (2/15/78), FLN (12/77). 372.63

Contents: 1. Valley of the Vowels. 2. TV Terrors. 3. The Wicked Wizard of Wonder. 4. Double Trouble. 5. The Monster Market.

This set deals with long vowel sounds, consonant blends, vowels followed by "R," homonyms, and consonant diagraphs.

THE SPELLING MONSTERS: UNIT C (Filmstrip–Sound). Scholastic Book Services, 1977. 5 color, sound filmstrips, 65–97 fr.; 5 cassettes or discs; 30 Ditto Masters; Teacher's Guide. ($89.50). Gr. 3–7. BKL (2/15/77), LGB (12/77), RTE (5/77). 372.63

Contents: 1. The Witches. 2. The Magic Monster. 3. The Robot's Tale. 4. Doomed. 5. In Werewolf Swamp.

This set tackles plurals, contractions, possessives, sound of oo, sounds of ow and ou.

THE SPELLING MONSTERS: UNIT D (Filmstrip–Sound). Scholastic Book Services, 1977. 5 color, sound filmstrips; 5 cassettes or discs; 30 Duplicating Masters; 1 Guide. ($89.50). Gr. 3–7. INS (9/77), LNG (6/77), RTE (5/77). 372.63

Deals with unusual consonant sounds, syllables, and the sounds of au, aw, oi, oy and k; and also with unusual consonant sounds, silent consonants, syllables, and le words.

ENGLISH LANGUAGE–STUDY AND TEACHING

COMPOSITION POWER (Kit). United Learning, 1971. 4 color, sound filmstrips; 2 cassettes or discs; 16 Spirit Masters; 1 Script/Guide. Cassette #79502 ($55), Disc #79501 ($55). Gr. 4–12. BKL (2/72). 372.6

Contents: 1. Outline Power. 2. Opening. 3. Meat of the Sandwich. 4. Closing and Revising.

Presents the fundamentals of composition and revising so that students will be able to write intelligently and clearly.

ENGLISH COMPOSITION FOR CHILDREN, SET 1 (Filmstrip–Sound). Pied Piper Productions, 1973. 4 color, sound filmstrips, 75–80 fr.; 4 discs or cassettes, av. 9–10:10 min.; Teacher's Guide. Cassettes #E010C ($68), Discs #E010R ($68). Gr. 4–6. BKL (11/1/74), PRV (11/74). 372.6

ENGLISH LANGUAGE–STUDY AND TEACHING (cont.)

Contents: 1. Kinds of Sentences. 2. Paragraphs. 3. More Than One Paragraph. 4. Outlines.

Interesting situations are used to promote understanding in these areas of composition. A county fair is used to examine the different kinds of sentences, while a day at the beach illustrates the parts of a paragraph. Contrasts between compositions of 2 sisters, one 5 and the other 10 years old, provide insight into what makes good composition. A shopping list is used to demonstrate the organization of outlines.

ENGLISH COMPOSITION FOR CHILDREN, SET 2 (Filmstrip–Sound). Pied Piper Productions, 1973. 4 color, sound filmstrips, av. 61–78 fr.; 4 cassettes or discs, av. 7–9:35 min.; Teacher's Guide. Cassettes #E020C ($68), Discs #E020R ($68). Gr. 4–6. LGB (12/74), PRV (11/74), PVB (1973-74). 372.6

Contents: 1. Picture Words. 2. Action Words. 3. Figures of Speech. 4. Sensory Descripton.

Encourages students to use better and more descriptive words in their writing. Examples are provided and motivational stimuli presented to get students to use their senses in writing.

ENGLISH COMPOSITION FOR CHILDREN, SET 3 (Filmstrip–Sound). Pied Piper Productions, 1974. 4 color, sound filmstrips, av. 75 fr.; 4 discs or cassettes, av. 10 min.; Teacher's Guide. ($65). Gr. 5–7. BKL (11/1/74), PVB (1976). 372.6

Contents: 1. Creating Fables. 2. Creating a Picture Book. 3. Being the Thing. 4. Creating Just So Stories.

Children in a realistic sixth-grade setting are shown discussing, reporting, and interviewing on a variety of topics.

ENGLISH COMPOSITION FOR CHILDREN, SET 4 (Filmstrip–Sound). Pied Piper Productions, 1975. 4 color, sound filmstrips, av. 75 fr.; 4 discs or cassettes, av. 10 min.; Teacher's Guide. Discs ($55), Cassettes ($65). Gr. 5–7. BKL (5/15/76), PVB (1976). 372.6

Contents: 1. Practical Writing–News Reporting. 2. Giving Directions. 3. Interviewing. 4. Taking a Stand.

Technically smooth productions with content useful for many grade levels and topics. Real children are shown participating.

ENGLISH COMPOSITION FOR CHILDREN, SET 5 (Filmstrip–Sound). Pied Piper Productions, 1976. 4 color, sound filmstrips, 58–70 fr.; 4 cassettes or discs, av. 11–12:30 min.; Teacher's Guide. Cassettes #E050C ($68), Discs #E050R ($68). Gr. 4–7. BKL (5/76), PRV (5/77), PVB (4/78). 372.6

Contents: 1. Creating a Beginning. 2. Developing a Character. 3. Building a Conflict. 4. Elements of a Story.

Using excerpts from several popular stories and books, this set provides guidance in narrative writing.

LANGUAGE EXPERIENCES IN READING, LEVEL 1 (Kit). EBEC, 1974. 6 filmstrips, approx. 11 fr. ea.; 14 discs or cassettes, 6 min. ea.; 72 4-page cardboard Reading Experiences; 64 Duplicating Masters; 1 Print Set; Kidbits 1 & 2; First Magazine; Teacher's Guide. Discs #66100R ($289), Cassettes #66100K ($289), Each Level ($289). Gr. K–3. BKL (6/15/75), RTE (1/76), TEA (5/6/75). 372.6

Contents: 1. M–E Spells Me. 2. Familiar Faces and Places. 3. Especially Wonderful Days. 4. Wonder in My World. 5. Growing Up Green. 6. Animals Live Here, Too.

Level One focuses upon the child's perceptions, interests, and needs, and teaches through a highly structured, multisensory approach that integrates reading, writing, listening, and speaking. Thematic units interweave a unique program of specific, sequential skill development and manipulative activities certain to intrigue the young while fostering positive self-concepts. There are 3 other levels available.

LANGUAGE EXPERIENCES IN READING: LEVEL 2 (Kit). EBEC, 1975. 6 filmstrips, approx. 11 fr.; 14 discs or cassettes, 6 min. ea.; 72 4-page cardboard Reading Experiences; 64 Duplicating Masters; Print Set; Kidbits 3; Second Magazine; Guide. Discs #66130R ($289), Cassettes #66130K ($289). Gr. K–3. CPR (4/76), RTE (1/76). 372.6

Contents: 1. Sometimes I Feel. 2. Neighborhood Voices. 3. Moose, Mice, and Other Mammals. 4. Do I Have to Eat My Spinach? 5. Buses and Bikes. 6. Get the Message.

Focuses upon the child's perceptions, interests, and needs, and teaches through a highly structured, multisensory approach that integrates reading, writing, listening, and speaking. Six thematic units interweave a program of specific, sequential skill development and manipulative activities to foster positive self-concepts.

LANGUAGE EXPERIENCES IN READING: LEVEL 3 (Kit). EBEC, 1975. 6 filmstrips, approx. 11 fr.; 14 discs or cassettes 6 min. ea.; 72 4-page cardboard Reading Experiences; 64 Duplicating Masters; 1 Print Set; Third Mag.; 7 Teacher's Guides; Resource Cards. Discs #66160R ($289), Cassettes #66160K ($289). Gr. K–3. RTE (1/76). 372.6

Contents: 1. My Senses and Me. 2. From My Front Door. 3. Things That Go Bump in the Night. 4. Calendars and Clocks. 5.

Things with Wings. 6. On Your Mark, Get Set, Go.

Focuses upon the child's perceptions, interests, and needs, and teaches through a highly structured, multisensory approach that integrates reading, writing, listening, and speaking. Six thematic units interweave a program of specific, sequential skill development and manipulative activities to foster positive self-concepts.

ON STAGE: WALLY, BERTHA, AND YOU (Kit). EBEC, 1972. 2 large Puppets; 132 Activity Cards; 16 Icebreaker Cards; 16 Story Cards; 42 Construction Cards; Teacher's Guide, including skills scope and sequence chart. #6650 ($69.95). Gr. K–3. BKL (9/15/73), EYR (9/73). 372.6

Materials in this kit build a child's self-confidence and personal awareness, as well as confidence within and before a group. Youngsters engage in creative dramatics activities to gain valuable experience in oral expression. They develop good listening skills, and they come to understand the elements of a story—plot, characterization and character analysis, and organization.

PARAGRAPH POWER (Kit). United Learning, 1971. 4 color, sound filmstrips; 4 cassettes or discs; 16 Spirit Masters; 1 Script/ Guide Book. Cassettes #79402 ($55), Discs #79401 ($55). Gr. 4–12. BKL (1/72). 372.6

Contents: 1. Thinking in Paragraphs. 2. Topic Sentence Power. 3. Paragraph Unity Power. 4. Paragraph Development.

Illustrates how to organize ideas into paragraphs for clear, logical flow, how to construct topic sentences, and how to unify sentences into paragraphs.

SO MANY WORDS TO CHOOSE FROM (Filmstrip–Sound). BFA Educational Media, 1975. 4 color, sound filmstrips, 48 fr.; 4 cassettes or discs, 6-1/2 min.; Teacher's Guide. Cassettes #VEW000 ($70), Discs #VEV000 ($70). Gr. 4–6. PRV (4/76), RTE (12/75). 372.6

Contents: 1. Antonyms. 2. Homonyms. 3. Synonyms. 4. Figures of Speech.

The filmstrips in this set introduce the learner to 130 vocabulary words and their meanings (or multiple meanings). Using a combination of real-life photographs, artwork, and captions, each filmstrip presents the word group and its definition.

THE STRUCTURE OF LANGUAGE (Filmstrip–Sound). See English Language—Grammar

WRITING: FROM ASSIGNMENT TO COMPOSITION (Filmstrip–Sound). Guidance Associates, 1974. 2 color, sound filmstrips, av. 78 fr. ea.; 2 discs or cassettes, av. 9–12 min. ea.; Teacher's Guide. Discs #4E-503-340 ($52.50), Cassettes #4E-503-357

($52.50). Gr. 4–8. BKL (1/76), PRV (12/75), PVB (4/76). 372.6

The step-by-step process for writing an interesting, coherent composition. "How to" tips for selecting a topic, organizing an outline, doing a first draft, and doing a rewrite.

ENVIRONMENT

AESTHETICS (Filmstrip–Sound). EMC, 1971 (Our Environment). 2 color, sound filmstrips, 60–78 fr.; 2 cassettes, 7–9 min.; 2 Wall Charts; 30 Activity Sheets; Teacher's Guide. #EE-103000 ($36). Gr. 1–3. BKL (6/72), STE (10/71). 301.31

Contents: 1. What Is the Problem? 2. It's Really Up to Us.

Natural beauty in our everyday surroundings is being threatened by urban sprawl, industrial technology, and a lack of general concern. All must do their part to restore and preserve essential contact with nature in the immediate environment.

DISCOVERING OUR ENVIRONMENT (Study Print). Coronet Instructional Media, 1971. 40 Photo Study Prints; Teacher's Guide; 1 "Survival Game" (units available separately). #F130 ($64). Gr. 4–6. BKL (1972), SLJ. 301.31

Contents: 1. What Is Our Environment? 2. Living Things Use the Environment. 3. Man Misuses the Environment. 4. Restoring and Conserving the Environment.

Study prints and the "survival game" help clarify complex ecological concepts and stimulate discussion. The back of each print includes information, scientific experiments, and activities stressing the concepts. *See also* Ecology; Man—Influence of Environment; Man—Influence on Nature

ERDOES, RICHARD

SUN DANCE PEOPLE: THE PLAINS INDIANS (Filmstrip–Sound). *See* Indians of North America—Plains

ERIE CANAL—SONGS

THE ERIE CANAL(Filmstrip–Sound). Weston Woods Studios, 1974. 1 color, sound filmstrip, 30 fr.; 1 cassette, 6 min.; 1 Script. #157C ($12.75). Gr. 4–9. PRV (1975). 784.756

Based on the book by Peter Spier, it tells the story of the boats that carried people and freight on the canal in the nineteenth century. Spier's colorful and accurate pictures add much to the production.

EROSION

MONUMENTS TO EROSION (Motion Picture—16mm—Sound). EBEC, 1974.

EROSION (cont.)

16mm color, sound film, 11 min. #3340
($150). Gr. 4–12. PRV (5/76), SCT
(4/76). 551.3

This film presents the red rock country
of the Colorado Plateau as it has rarely
been seen before. The camera glides over
towering stone arches and delicate spires,
revealing a unique natural mosaic of sugges-
tive shapes and colors. The narration approaches the land from several viewpoints:
as an inspiring reflection of the patterns
and rhythms of nature, as the product of
the erosional process that shaped it, and as a
brief moment in the geologic lifetime of an
ancient planet.

ESKIMOS

HOW TO BUILD AN IGLOO–SLIDE SET
(Slides). *See* Igloos

ESKIMOS–FICTION

JULIE OF THE WOLVES (Phonodisc or Cassette). Caedmon Records, 1973. 1 cassette
or disc, 39:58 min.; Jacket Notes. Disc
#TC1534 ($6.98), Cassette #CDL51534
($7.95). Gr. 4–8. BKL (5/1/74). Fic
From Jean Craighead George's Newbery
winner, Irene Worth presents this dramatization, which captures the unique and thrilling
experiences of Julie (Miyax) the Eskimo girl.

ESTES, ELEANOR

ELEANOR ESTES (Filmstrip–Sound). *See*
Authors

ESTHETICS

AESTHETICS (Filmstrip–Sound). *See*
Environment

ETHICS

WHAT DO YOU THINK? (Filmstrip–Sound).
Troll Associates, 1975. 6 color, sound filmstrips, av. 45 fr. ea.; 3 cassettes, av. 6 min.
ea.; Teacher's Guide. ($78). Gr. 2–6.
PRV (9/76). 170

Contents: 1. What Are Values? 2. Lying.
3. Cheating. 4. Stealing. 5. Promises. 6.
Thoughtfulness.

This unit encourages children to think about
situations where value judgements are required in order to help the children formulate their own values—and decide what's
best for themselves.

ETHNIC GROUPS. *See* Minorities

ETIQUETTE

THE GOOPS: A MANUAL OF MANNERS
FOR MOPPETS (Filmstrip–Sound/Cap-
tioned). Listening Library, 1976 (Look,
Listen and Read). 1 color, captioned/sound
filmstrip, 36 fr.; 1 cassette, 9 min.; Teacher's Guide. #JFS156 ($14.95). Gr. K–3.
PRV (12/77). 395

The deplorable habits of these graceless
creatures have amused generations of
readers, and in this new format will serve as
a funny manual of manners for moppets.

EUROPE

WESTERN EUROPE, GROUP ONE (Filmstrip–Sound). Society for Visual Education, 1975. 6 color, sound filmstrips, 90–
100 fr.; 3 discs or cassettes, av. 20 min.;
Teacher's Guide. Discs #293-SAR ($83),
Cassettes #293-SATC ($83). Gr. 4–10.
BKL (3/15/76), PRV (11/76). 914

Contents: 1. Benelux: A United European
Community. 2. Austria: Modern Nation,
Ancient Crafts. 3. France: The Basques in
the 20th Century. 4. Andorra and Liechten-
stein: Two Mini-Countries. 5. Monaco:
Skyward and Seaward. 6. Switzerland: The
Banking Nation.

People, places, customs, and contemporary
problems are discussed. Emphasis is placed
on the idea that each country retains its own
culture and character even though European economy is interdependent.

WESTERN EUROPE, GROUP TWO (Filmstrip–Sound). Society for Visual Education, 1975. 6 color, sound filmstrips, 90–
100 fr.; 3 discs or cassettes, av. 20 min.;
Teacher's Guide. Discs #293-SBR ($83),
Cassettes #293-SBTC ($83). Gr. 4–10.
BKL (3/15/76), PRV (11/76). 914

Contents: 1. Italy: Venice, the Modern
Atlantis. 2. Malta: Mediterranean Melting
Pot. 3. Portugal: People of the Land and
Sea. 4. San Marino: The Postage Stamp Re-
public. 5. Spain: A Nation Goes Forward.
6. The Vatican: A Nation within a City.

People, places, customs, and contemporary
problems are discussed. Emphasis is placed
on the idea that each country retains its
own culture and character even though
European economy is interdependent.

See also Central Europe; Eastern Europe

EUROPE–HISTORY–476–1492

MEDIEVAL EUROPE (Filmstrip–Sound).
See Middle Ages

EVOLUTION

LIFE LONG AGO (Filmstrip–Sound). *See*
Fossils

EXERCISE

KEEP ON STEPPIN' (Phonodisc or Cassette).
See Physical Education and Training

POSTURAL IMPROVEMENT ACTIVITIES (Phonodiscs). Educational Records/Educational Activities. 4 discs, 12 in. 78 rpm. #HVP25 ($12.95). Gr. 4–6. MDU (1978). 613.7

Contents: 1. Walking. 2. Foot Strengthening. 3. Abdominal Strengthening. 4. Stretching for Back-legs-shoulder Strengthening. 5. Chest Stretching. 6. Flexibility of Spine. 7. Improve Head Position.

These 4 records and the illustrated manual show how to evaluate the posture of students. The records and manual go into exercise for improvement in specific areas. Each record contains several exercises.

EXPLORERS

AGE OF EXPLORATION AND DISCOVERY (Filmstrip–Sound). Coronet Instructional Media, 1975. 6 color, sound filmstrips, 46–50 fr.; 6 cassettes or 3 discs, 12:45–15:00 min. ($95). Gr. 5–8. BKL (6/15/75), PRV. 910.92

Contents: 1. Marco Polo. 2. Prince Henry and the Portuguese Navigators. 3. Christopher Columbus. 4. Ferdinand Magellan. 5. Sir Francis Drake. 6. Search for the Northern Passages.

Capturing the historic significance of oceanic voyages and experiences of famous discoverers, this set traces important exploration and our increasing knowledge of our world from the thirteenth to the twentieth centuries.

EXPLORERS–FICTION

THE KING'S FIFTH (Filmstrip–Sound). *See* Discoveries (In Geography)–Fiction

EYEGLASSES

GLASSES FOR SUSAN (Motion Picture–16mm–Sound). *See* Vision

FABLES

AN AESOP ANTHOLOGY (Filmstrip–Sound). Educational Enrichment Materials, 1978. 6 color, sound filmstrips, 38–42 fr.; 6 cassettes, 5–10 min. #51021 ($108). Gr. 1–6. PRV (2/78). 398.2

Contents: 1. The Country Mouse and the City Mouse, etc. 2. The Grasshopper and the Ant, etc. 3. The Lion and the Mouse, etc. 4. The Fox and the Grapes, etc. 5. The Hare and the Tortoise, etc. 6. The Boy Who Cried Wolf, etc.

Retelling of 18 of Aesop's familiar and lesser-known fables. The tales are reduced from the original adult versions, but the illustrations are upbeat and the "lessons in life" are still valid today.

AESOP'S FABLES (Phonodisc or Cassette). Caedmon Records. 1 cassette or disc, 12 in. Disc #TC1221 ($6.98), Cassette #CDL51221 ($7.95). Gr. K–4. ESL, NYR. 398.2

With few exceptions, these fables of Aesop are short, satirical tales in which 2 or at times 3 animals talk and act like human beings. Designed to teach a lesson because of their brevity, their simplicity, and their appropriateness to any time or place, they have become classics. Included in this performance by Boris Karloff are "The Fox and the Lion," "The Old Hound," "The Fox and the Grapes," and "The Lion in Love."

BIRDS OF A FEATHER (Motion Picture–16mm–Sound). *See* Birds–Fiction

FABLES OF INDIA (Phonodisc or Cassette). Caedmon Records, 1966. 1 cassette or disc, approx. 50 min. Disc #TC1168 ($6.98), Cassette #CDL51168 ($7.95). Gr. 3–6. AUR (1978), ESL (1968), NCT. 398.2

Contents: 1. The Brahmin and the Villain. 2. The Long Eared Cat and the Vulture. 3. The Restless Pigeon and His Wife. 4. The Camel and His Neighbor. 5. The Adder and the Fox. 6. The Twin Parrots. 7. The Blue Jackal. 8. Good-speed and the Elephant King. 9. The Monkey's Heart.

This Indian fable collection is probably the closest to the original store of folklore that exists.

THE GRIZZLY AND THE GADGETS AND FURTHER FABLES FOR OUR TIME (Phonodisc or Cassette). Caedmon Records, 1972. 1 cassette or disc, approx. 55 min. Disc #TC1412 ($6.98), Cassette #CDL51412 ($7.95). Gr. 4–A. BKL (12/15/72), JOR, LBJ. 398.2

Here is the story of a grizzly bear who finds the antics of his relatives, the gadgets of the twentieth century, and the complacency of his wife intolerable, and decides to take matters into his own paws to set his world to rights. The other animal heroes of these humorous fables reveal once again James Thurber's marvelous inventiveness and magical insight into human character.

THE HOARDER (Motion Picture–16mm–Sound). National Film Board of Canada/Benchmark Films, 1971. 16mm color, sound, animated film, 6 min. ($140). Gr. 2–A. AFF (1971). 398.2

A witty story about greed and sharing. Evelyn Lambert's colorfully animated blue jay carries away and hides all it can see, including the sun.

THE OWL AND THE LEMMING (AN ESKIMO LEGEND) (Filmstrip–Sound). *See* Folklore–Eskimo

THE OWL WHO MARRIED A GOOSE (Motion Picture–16mm–Sound). *See* Folklore–Eskimo

FABLES (cont.)

ROSIE'S WALK (Motion Picture—16mm—
Sound). *See* Animals—Fiction

FAIRY TALES

ANDERSEN'S FAIRY TALES (Filmstrip—
Sound). Coronet Instructional Media,
1970. 8 color, sound filmstrips, av. 34 fr.;
8 cassettes or 4 discs, av. 8-1/2 min. Available with caption only. Cassettes #M121
($120), Discs #S121 ($120). Gr. K–3.
BKL (1971). 398.2

Contents: 1. The Emperor's New Clothes.
2. The Steadfast Tin Soldier. 3. Hans Clod-
hopper. 4. The Snow Queen. 5. The
Emperor's Nightingale. 6. The Little Match
Girl. 7. The Ugly Duckling. 8. The Wild
Swans.

Narrated fairy tales of Hans Christian
Andersen combine whimsical adventures
with loyalty, patience, and perseverance
lessons.

BEAUTY AND THE BEAST AND OTHER
STORIES (Phonodisc or Cassette). Caedmon Records. 1 12 in. disc or cassette.
Disc #TC1394 ($6.98), Cassette
#CDL51394 ($7.95). Gr. 2–6. BKL
(10/72), LBJ. 398.2

Contents: 1. "Beauty and the Beast" by
Mme. De Villeneuve. 2. "The Princess on
the Glass Hill" by Andrew Lang. 3. "The
Boy Who Kept a Secret" by Andrew Lang.

This collection of 3 fairy tales represents the
elements of fantasy as reflected in different countries. "Beauty and the Beast," a
French fairy tale, is remarkable in its tenderness; it has no villains. "The Princess on
the Glass Hill" is a combination of Norse
gloom and humor. "The Boy Who Kept a
Secret" conveys the Hungarian fairy tale
world, a place of shadows, cruelty, and
violence. It is performed by Douglas
Fairbanks, Jr.

BLUEBEARD (Cassette). Children's Classics
on Tape, 1974. 1 cassette; detailed Study
Guide. #CCT-118 ($9.50). Gr. 4–6. ESL
(10/77), PRV (9/75). 398.2

Fatima dares to look in husband Bluebeard's
secret chamber while he is away. She finds
the bodies of his former wives just as Bluebeard returns.

CHINESE FAIRY TALES (Phonodisc or
Cassette). Caedmon Records, 1973. 1 cassette or disc, 41-1/2 min.; Jacket Notes.
Disc #TC1328 ($6.98), Cassette
#CDL51328 ($7.95). Gr. K–6. BKL
(2/15/74). 398.2

Contents: 1. The Chinese Red Riding
Hood. 2. The Faithful One. 3. The Tiger's
Teacher. 4. The Sparrow and the Phoenix.
5. Teardrop Dragon. 6. The Discontented
Mason. 7. How Some Animals Become as
They Are.

Similar to the Grimm tales, these stories are
read by Siobhan McKenna.

CINDERELLA AND OTHER FAIRY TALES
(Phonodisc or Cassette). Caedmon Records,
1977. 1 12 in. LP or 1 Cassette. Disc #TC-
1330 ($6.98), Cassette #CDL-51330
($7.95). Gr. K–6. BKL, HOB, SLJ. 398.2

Contents: 1. Cinderella and the Glass
Slipper. 2. The Musicians of Bremen. 3.
Bluebird.

First published in 1927 under the title of
"Told Again" by Walter de la Mare; Claire
Bloom now performs the enchanting stories.

CLASSIC FAIRY TALES (Filmstrip—Sound).
EBEC, 1966. 10 color, sound filmstrips,
av. 45 fr.; 10 discs or cassettes, approx. 11
min.; Teacher's Guide. Disc #6409
($127.25), Cassette #6409K ($127.25).
Gr. K–3. MDU (1975). 398.2

Contents: 1. The Story of Cinderella. 2.
The Story of Little Red Riding Hood. 3.
The Story of Snow White. 4. The Story of
Aladdin. 5. The Story of Puss in Boots.
6. The Story of Little Thumb. 7. The Story
of King Midas. 8. The Story of Sinbad the
Sailor. 9. The Story of Pied Piper. 10. The
Story of Little Mermaid.

Designed to stimulate enjoyment of reading.
Colorful artwork and skillful narration aid
in the appreciation of these favorites.

DICK WHITTINGTON AND HIS CAT AND
OTHER ENGLISH TALES (Phonodisc or
Cassette). *See* Folklore—England

THE EMPEROR'S NEW CLOTHES AND
OTHER TALES (Phonodisc or Cassette).
Caedmon Records, 1958. 1 cassette or disc,
approx. 50 min. Disc #TC1073 ($6.98),
Cassette #CDL51073 ($7.95). Gr. K–6.
AUR (1978), NCT, NYR. 398.2

Contents: 1. The Tinder Box. 2. The
Emperor's New Clothes. 3. The Steadfast
Tin Soldier. 4. The Emperor's Nightingale.

This selection of fairy tales is by the Danish
writer Hans Christian Andersen. The stories
reveal many moods; for example, the hero
is largely a figure of fun in "The Emperor's
New Clothes," while the Chinese emperor in
the "Nightingale" is a figure of great
dignity.

FAIRY TALES OF THE BROTHERS
GRIMM (Kit). Society for Visual Education, 1976. 6 cassettes, 10–14 min.; 60
books (6 titles). #BC-002-S ($96), Individ-
ual ($16.95). Gr. K–3. BKL (6/15/77).
398.2

Contents: 1. King Grisly Beard. 2. The
Goose Girl. 3. The Water of Life. 4. Don-
key Lettuce. 5. The Golden Buttons. 6.
The Four Servants.

Each tale is highlighted by colorful illustrations and read-along narrations of adaptations from the Grimms collection. Musical

introductions and dramatic sound effects enhance the presentations.

FOLK STORIES AND TALES (Cassette). Troll Associates, 1972. 5 cassette tapes, av. 10 min. ea. ($27.50). Gr. K–3. BKL (12/15/73). 398.2

Contents: 1. Sailor and Crocodile. 2. Tailor and the Mouse. 3. When Froggie Went Courting. 4. The Very Scary Witch. 5. Magical Folk Tales from Ireland, Greece, Norway, Russia, Mexico, and the American Indians.

Burl Ives tells each story in this collection of folk stories and tales.

FOLKTALES OF SOUTH AMERICA (Filmstrip–Sound). *See* Folklore

THE GREAT QUILLOW (Phonodisc or Cassette). *See* Giants–Fiction

HANS CHRISTIAN ANDERSEN CASSETTE-BOOKS (Kit). Society for Visual Education, 1976. 4 cassettes, 9–15 min.; 40 books. #BC-001-S ($64), Each title ($16.75). Gr. K–3. BKL (6/15/77). 398.2

Contents: 1. The Wild Swans. 2. It's Perfectly True. 3. Hans Clodhopper. 4. The Little Mermaid.

Designed as read-along lessons for individuals or small groups, these shortened adaptations of familiar Andersen tales follow the original texts fairly closely, with few important details omitted and with only minor variations at the conclusion of some of the stories.

HANSEL AND GRETEL AND OTHER FAIRY TALES BY THE BROTHERS GRIMM (Phonodisc or Cassette). Caedmon Records, 1976. 1 cassette or disc, approx. 50 min. Disc #TC1274 ($6.98), Cassette #CDL51274 ($7.95). Gr. K–6. LBJ, NYR. 398.2

Contents: 1. Hansel and Gretel. 2. The Golden Goose. 3. Mrs. Owl. 4. Shiver and Shake.

The Grimm Brothers collected many fairy tales beloved by children all over the world. This recording contains 4 of these favorites.

THE HAPPY PRINCE AND OTHER OSCAR WILDE FAIRY TALES (Phonodisc or Cassette). Caedmon Records, 1956. 1 cassette or disc, approx. 50 min. Disc #TC1044 ($6.98), Cassette #CDL51044 ($7.95). Gr. 4–A. ESL, NCT, NYR. 398.2

Contents: 1. The Happy Prince. 2. The Selfish Giant. 3. The Nightingale and the Rose.

Among the immortal stories written for children are these 3 by Oscar Wilde and performed by Basil Rathbone. They are stamped with their creator's personal genius, and nothing he wrote is likely to be remembered longer than these.

HAROLD'S FAIRY TALE (Motion Picture–16mm–Sound). Weston Woods Studios, 1975. 16mm, color, sound, animated film, 8 min. ($150). Gr. K–3. PRV (11/75). Fic

Adapted from the book *Harold's Fairy Tale*, written and illustrated by Crockett Johnson, Harold draws an enchanted garden, only to discover that nothing can grow there because of the machinations of a Giant Witch. With the aid of his purple crayon, he defeats the Witch and makes the garden bloom again, but not before he encounters a variety of strange and wonderful experiences.

IRISH FAIRY TALES (Phonodisc or Cassette). *See* Folklore–Ireland

THE KING OF THE GOLDEN RIVER (Phonodisc or Cassette). Caedmon Records, 1976. 1 cassette or disc, approx. 48 min. Disc #TC1284 ($6.98), Cassette #CDL51284 ($7.95). Gr. 5–9. LBJ (1976), NYR (1976). 398.2

This fairy tale is an example of a children's story that should be read aloud. In this way, children catch the essential meaning and atmosphere and are challenged and delighted by the unfamiliar words, even though they may not fully understand them.

LIBRARY 5 (Cassette). *See* Literature–Collections

THE LITTLE LAME PRINCE (Phonodisc or Cassette). Caedmon Records, 1975. 1 cassette or disc, approx. 60 min. Disc #TC1293 ($6.98), Cassette #CDL51293 ($7.95). Gr. 4–8. LBJ (1975), NYR. Fic

This story tells of a little prince who escaped from the prison tower of his paralysis and on the way conquered the hearts of his countrymen. This slightly abridged version of the story by Dinah Marie Mulock is read by Cathleen Nesbitt.

THE LITTLE MATCH GIRL AND OTHER TALES (Phonodisc or Cassette). Caedmon Records, 1961. 1 cassette or disc, approx. 50 min. Disc #TC1117 ($6.98), Cassette #CDL51117 ($7.95). Gr. K–8. ESL, HOB, NYR. 398.2

Contents: 1. The Swineherd. 2. The Top and the Ball. 3. The Red Shoes. 4. Thumbelina. 5. The Little Match Girl.

Five of Hans Christian Andersen's fairy tales are presented by Boris Karloff. There is a warmth characteristic of no other writer and there is sympathy for all the world's creatures that matches that of every little child. These tales were first translated into English in 1846.

THE LITTLE MERMAID (Phonodisc or Cassette). Caedmon Records, 1967. 1 cassette or disc, approx. 55 min. Disc #TC1230 ($6.98), Cassette #CDL51230 ($7.95). Gr. K–8. ESL, HOB, LBJ. 398.2

FAIRY TALES (cont.)

The particular attraction of this fairy tale is that it offers children the opportunity to weep for themselves when they weep for the lovely little mermaid who longs for what she cannot have.

LITTLE RED RIDING HOOD AND THE DANCING PRINCESSES (Phonodisc or Cassette). Caedmon Records, 1956. 1 cassette or disc, approx. 50 min. Disc #TC1041 ($6.98), Cassette #CDL51041 ($7.95). Gr. K–6. BKL, HOB, NYR. 398.2

Contents: 1. Little Red Riding Hood. 2. The Dancing Princesses.

Fairy tales retold by Walter de la Mare are endowed with vigor and beauty. Claire Bloom adds her own gift for narration to the rendition.

THE MAGIC FISHBONE (Filmstrip–Sound/ Captioned). *See* Magic–Fiction

THE PIED PIPER AND OTHER STORIES (Phonodisc or Cassette). Caedmon Records, 1972. 1 cassette or disc, approx. 55 min. Disc #TC1397 ($6.98), Cassette #CDL51397 ($7.95). Gr. K–6. BKL (9/72), ESL, HOB. 398.2

Contents: 1. "The Pied Piper" by Andrew Lang. 2. "The Colony of Cats" and "Thumbelina" by Hans Christian Andersen.

All 3 European fairy tales heard on this recording are among the world's finest, and likely to withstand the test of time in the future as they have in the past.

PRINCE RABBIT AND OTHER STORIES (Phonodiscs). Caedmon Records, 1975. 1 LP disc or 1 cassette. Disc #TC1490 ($6.98), Cassette #CDL51490 ($7.95). Gr. K–A. PRV (4/76). 398.2

Contents: 1. The Princess Who Could Not Laugh. 2. The Princess and the Apple Tree. 3. The Magic Hill. 4. Prince Rabbit.

Here are 4 of Milne's delightful stories for children headed by an interesting rabbit who imagines that he is as smart as any human and a princess whose funny bone needs tickling. Tammy Grimes tickles all funny bones on this record.

PUSS IN BOOTS AND OTHER FAIRY TALES FROM AROUND THE WORLD (Phonodisc or Cassette). Caedmon Records. 1 cassette or disc, approx. 60 min. Disc #TC1247 ($6.98), Cassette #CDL51247 ($7.95). Gr. K–6. LBJ, NYR. 398.2

Contents: 1. Puss in Boots. 2. Saturday, Sunday, Monday. 3. The Hopi Turtle. 4. Cockie Lockie, Henny Penny and Mr. Korbes the Fox. 5. Biggoon and the Little Duck. 6. Baba Yaga.

Children love these tales, read by Cathleen Nesbitt, because they are simple and direct. One knows from the beginning who is the hero and who is the villain.

THE RELUCTANT DRAGON (Phonodisc or Cassette). *See* Dragons–Fiction

THE SHOEMAKER AND THE ELVES (Motion Picture–16mm–Sound). Films, 1972. 16mm color, sound film, 15 min. #106-0074 ($250). Gr. K–6. CFF (1973), Fic

The midnight magic of a pair of cobbler elves reverses the misfortunes of a poor shoemaker. In gratitude he and his wife leave 2 sets of new clothes on the workbench for their tiny helpers. The elves are delighted. Freeform puppetry is used for the visuals.

SNOW QUEEN (Phonodisc or Cassette). Caedmon Records. 1 disc or cassette. Disc #TC1229 ($6.98), Cassette #CDL51229 ($7.95). Gr. 4–6. LBJ. 398.2

Recorded by Cathleen Nesbitt, this is almost a novella with a small hero and heroine. This long story by Andersen ends with wisdom and happiness.

THE SNOW QUEEN (Cassette). Children's Classics on Tape, 1973. 1 cassette (2 parts); detailed Study Guide. #CCT-102,142,144. ($10.95). Gr. K–4. BKL (9/15/75), CHH (1976), PRV (1/75). 398.2

Tells of Gerda's adventures as she searches for her friend Kaj, who has been enchanted and carried off by the beautiful, mysterious Snow Queen.

SNOW WHITE AND OTHER FAIRY TALES (Phonodisc or Cassette). Caedmon Records. 1 cassette or disc, approx. 55 min. Disc #TC1266 ($6.98), Cassette #CDL51266 ($7.95). Gr. 4–6. HOB (1971), LBJ (1971), NYR. 398.2

Contents: 1. Snow White. 2. Hare and the Hedgehog. 3. The Valiant Little Tailor.

Claire Bloom performs these fairy tales from the Grimms collection; retold by Amabel Williams-Ellis.

SNOW WHITE AND ROSE RED AND OTHER ANDREW LANG FAIRY TALES (Phonodisc or Cassette). Caedmon Records, 1973. 1 disc or cassette, 52:32 min.; Jacket Notes. Disc #TC1414 ($6.98), Cassette #CDL51414 ($7.95). Gr. K–4. BKL (5/1/74), HOB (1974), PRV (10/74). 398.2

Contents: 1. Snow-White and Rose-Red. 2. The True Story of Little Golden-Hood. 3. East of the Sun and West of the Moon.

The 3 fairy tales on this album were chosen from Andrew Lang's *Blue Fairy Book* and *Red Fairy Book*. The Lang versions of these familiar stories contain some surprising elements.

THE TALE OF RUMPELSTILTSKIN (Motion Picture–16mm–Sound). *See* Folklore

TALES OF HANS CHRISTIAN ANDERSEN (Filmstrip–Sound). Society for Visual

Education, 1975. 6 color, sound filmstrips, 54–71 fr.; 3 cassettes or discs, 8–15 min.; 6 Guides. Discs #143-SAR ($83), Cassettes #143-SATC ($83). Gr. 1–8. BKL (9/15/76), PRV (5/76), PVB (4/77). 398.2

Contents: 1. The Wild Swans, Part I. 2. The Wild Swans, Part II. 3. It's Perfectly True! 4. Hans Clodhopper. 5. The Little Mermaid, Part I. 6. The Little Mermaid, Part II.

Each story captures the rhythm, humor, and personality of Andersen's characters while retaining the uniqueness and beauty of each tale. Original artwork, music, and sound effects support the stories.

THE TOMTEN AND THE FOX (Filmstrip–Sound). See Foxes–Stories

THE UGLY DUCKLING AND THE STORY OF HANS CHRISTIAN ANDERSEN (Cassette). Children's Classics on Tape, 1974. 1 cassette; Study Guide. #CCT-125 ($8.50). Gr. K–3. BKL (9/75), PRV (9/75). 398.2

An ugly duckling, teased and tormented, at last turns into a beautiful swan. Hans Christian Andersen's life is told and compared to the plight of the ugly duckling.

THE WIZARD (Motion Picture–16mm–Sound). See Magic–Fiction

YOU DECIDE/OPEN-ENDED TALES (Filmstrip–Sound). Troll Associates, 1974. 6 color, sound filmstrips, av. 42 fr. ea.; 3 cassettes. av. 12 min. ea.; Teacher's Guide. ($78). Gr. 4–6. PRV (4/75). 398.2

Contents: 1. Jack and the Beanstalk. 2. The Gallant Tailor. 3. The Golden Touch. 4. The Frog Prince. 5. The Pied Piper. 6. Emperor's New Clothes.

Traditional fairy tales with unusual endings stimulate creativity and discussion.

FALL. See Autumn

FAMILY

YOUR FAMILY (Filmstrip–Sound). Educational Direction/Learning Tree Filmstrips, 1974. 4 color, sound filmstrips, av. 49 fr. ea.; 2 cassettes, av. 6 min. ea.; Teacher's Guide. ($52). Gr. K–6. ESL (1976), PRV (11/74), PVB (5/75). 301.427

Contents: 1. From Childhood to Old Age. 2. What Family Members Do. 3. Other Ways of Meeting These Needs. 4. What Else Families Are.

In addition to structure and function, the concepts of family and the emotional needs that are fulfilled by a happy family are also explored.

FAMILY IN LITERATURE AND ART

THE FAMILY (Art Prints). Shorewood Reproductions. 12 prints, paper stock, card-board mounts or unmounted 22-1/2 in. X 28-1/2 in., color; Teacher's Guide. Mounted ($50), Unmounted ($35). Gr. K–4. PRV (4/76). 704.942

The concept of the extended family from baby to grandparents is presented in these art reproductions. Artists representative of various periods, media, and styles are included.

FAMILY LIFE

FAMILIAS NORTEAMERICANAS–AMERICAN FAMILIES (Filmstrip–Sound). Coronet Films, 1976. 6 color, sound filmstrips, av. 45 fr.; 6 cassettes, av. 10 min.; Teacher's Guide. #M507 ($95). Gr. 4–6. PRV (1/77), PVB (4/77). 301.427

Contents: 1. Los Garcia–the Garcias. 2. Los Wang–The Wangs. 3. Los De Stefano–The DeStefanos. 4. Los Taylor–The Taylors. 5. Los Jackson–The Jacksons. 6. Los Mandel–The Mandels.

Six urban American families with different national origins are viewed in their daily lives. Students get a good look at the similarities and differences in the kinds of homes, work, and interests of people from different social, religious, economic, and racial backgrounds.

FAMILIES: ALIKE AND DIFFERENT (Motion Picture–16mm–Sound). Churchill Films, 1976 (Families). 16mm color, sound film, 15 min.; Study Guide. ($210). Gr. 2–6. AAS (12/77). 301.42

This film presents families and the settings in which they live, and shows each child at home, playing in the neighborhood, and enjoying a family gathering.

FAMILIES AROUND THE WORLD (Filmstrip–Sound). Science Research Associates, 1977. 8 color, sound filmstrips; 4 cassettes; Teacher's Guide. ($165). Gr. 4–12. MDU (1977). 301.42

Contents: 1. Family in China. 2. Family in Japan. 3. Family in Bangladesh. 4. Family on the Ivory Coast. 5. Family in Israel. 6. Family in Lebanon. 7. Family in Germany. 8. Family in Mexico.

Each family is shown carrying on daily activities–working, eating, educating children, enjoying each others' company, and expressing hope for the future. They show students differences and likenesses of people around the world. Although the family structure may differ in different countries and cultures, the basic functions of the family are the same.

FAMILIES OF ASIA (Filmstrip–Sound). See Asia

FAMILIES OF SOUTH AMERICA (Filmstrip–Sound). See South America

FIVE FAMILIES, UNIT 1 (Filmstrip–Sound). See Minorities

FAMILY LIFE (cont.)

FOUR FAMILIES (Filmstrip–Sound). Educational Direction/Learning Tree Filmstrips, 1975. 4 color, sound filmstrips, av. 53 fr. ea.; 2 cassettes, av. 6 min. ea.; Teacher's Guide. #LT553 ($52). Gr. 5–8. BKL (1/76), ESL (1976), PRV (11/75). 301.34
Contents: 1. We Live in New York City. 2. We Live in Springfield. 3. We Live in Middletown. 4. We Live in Clinton Corners.
This set presents the differences caused by living in a megalopolis, an average-sized city, a town, and a farm community.

ON OUR BLOCK (Filmstrip–Sound). *See* Puerto Ricans in the U.S.

ONE WORLD (Filmstrip–Sound). *See* Community Life, Comparative

UNDERSTANDING CHANGES IN THE FAMILY (Filmstrip–Sound). Guidance Associates, 1973. 5 color, sound filmstrips, av. 27 fr. ea.; 5 discs or cassettes, av. 5-1/2 min.ea. #1B-303-246 ($87.50), #1B-303-253 ($87.50). Gr. K–3. CFF (1974), PRV (5/75), PVB (10/74). 301.42
Contents: 1. What's a Family? 2. Little Brother, Big Pest! 3. We're Adopted! 4. Not Together Any More. 5. Playing Dead.
Five separate units to stimulate discussion of family life.

WHAT IF A CRISIS HITS YOUR FAMILY? (Filmstrip–Sound). Educational Direction/Eye Gate Media, 1976. 6 color, sound filmstrips, 45–57 fr.; 3 cassettes, 6:32–8 min. #TX700 ($74.70). Gr. 1–7. BKL (3/15/77). 362.8
Contents: 1. My Parents Are Divorced. 2. Shifting Relationships: That New Baby. 3. Mom Is in the Hospital. 4. When Dad Lost His Job. 5. Since Mom Died.
This set offers the reassurance that children need when their formerly secure world is shaken and they are confused and troubled. It also prepares a child by watching a crisis in an impersonal way and helping him or her to understand the reactions that are likely to occur in anyone.

FAMILY LIFE–AFRICA

FAMILIES OF WEST AFRICA: FARMERS AND FISHERMEN (Filmstrip–Sound). *See* Africa, West

FOUR FAMILIES OF KENYA (Filmstrip–Sound). *See* Kenya

FAMILY LIFE–FICTION

FRANCES (Phonodisc or Cassette). *See* Badgers–Fiction

THE GIFT (Motion Picture–16mm–Sound). *See* Gifts–Fiction

LITTLE WOMEN (Phonodisc or Cassette). Listening Library, 1974. 2 phonodiscs or 2 cassette tapes, 105 min. Discs #AA-33110 ($12.95), Cassettes #CX-3110 ($15.90). Gr. 5–A. ESL (1977), LTP (4/75), PRV (11/75). Fic
The March girls grow up under the care and guidance of a watchful and loving mother. Two of them find happiness in marriage, and a family tragedy takes Beth. This is a story of family affection at the turn of the century and has long been a classic favorite with children.

LITTLE WOMEN (Phonodisc or Cassette). Caedmon Records, 1975. 1 cassette or disc. Cassette #CDL51470 ($7.95), Disc #TC1470 ($6.98). Gr. 4–8. PRV (4/76). Fic
Julie Harris reads 3 chapters of this popular book by Louisa May Alcott. They are "A Merry Christmas," "Gossip," and "The First Wedding." Young listeners will enjoy the reading and should be motivated to read the book.

THE PETERKIN PAPERS (Phonodisc or Cassette). Caedmon Records. 1 disc or cassette. Disc #TC1443 ($6.98), Cassette #CDL51443 ($7.95). Gr. 4–A. INS. Fic
Contents: 1. The Lady Who Puts Salt in Her Coffee. 2. About Elizabeth Eliza's Piano. 3. The Peterkins Try to Be Wise. 4. The Peterkins at Home. 5. The Peterkins Snowed-up. 6. The Peterkin's Picnic.
These delightful stories by Lucretia Hale laugh at human folly.

FAMILY LIFE–JAPAN

JAPAN: SPIRIT OF IEMOTO (Filmstrip–Sound). *See* Japan–Social Life and Customs

FAMILY LIFE–MIDDLE EAST

FAMILIES OF THE DRY MUSLIM WORLD (Filmstrip–Sound). *See* Middle East–Social Life and Customs

FANTASY

IF TREES CAN FLY (Motion Picture–16mm–Sound). *See* Imagination

THE LITTLE CIRCLE (Filmstrip–Sound). Lyceum/Mook & Blanchard, 1970. 1 color, sound filmstrip, 53 fr.; 1 cassette or disc, 12-1/2 min. Cassette #LY35870C ($25), Disc #LY35870R ($19.50). Gr. K–3. BKL (3/1/71), IFT (1970). Fic
Born as a zero, or nothing, on a blackboard, the Little Circle goes on a quest to find his identity. He finds himself as a hoop, a daisy, round ripples, and bubbles on the shore. Ann Atwood's beautiful photography stimu-

lates the imagination and awakens perception to shapes in nature through this story. Also available with the book.

FANTASY–FICTION

ALICE IN WONDERLAND (Kit). Jabberwocky Cassette Classics, 1972. 1 cassette, 60 min.; 6 Read-along Scripts. #1051 ($15). Gr. 5–A. BKL (4/74), PRV (11/73). Fic

In this combined reading and dramatization of Lewis Carroll's classic story, Alice, the White Rabbit, the Caterpillar, the Cheshire Cat, the Mad Hatter, and the Queen of Hearts are aptly characterized. This is an adaptation, not a straight reading of the story.

THE BEAST OF MONSIEUR RACINE (Motion Picture–16mm–Sound). See Monsters–Fiction

THE BORROWERS (Phonodisc or Cassette). Caedmon Records, 1975. 1 cassette or disc, 67 min.; Jacket Notes. Disc #TC1459 ($6.98), Cassette #CDL51459 ($7.95). Gr. 3–6. BKL (1/15/76). Fic

A condensation, told in the author's own words, of the tiny clock family who inhabit that miniscule but completely plausible world created by Mary Norton. Claire Bloom does the narration.

CHARLIE AND THE CHOCOLATE FACTORY (Phonodisc or Cassette). Caedmon Records, 1975. 1 cassette or disc, 31 min. Disc #TC1486 ($6.98), Cassette #CDL51486 ($7.95). Gr. 4–6. BKL (11/1/75), LBJ. Fic

Based on the book by the same name written by Roald Dahl, this favorite is an unusual fantasy in which the author blends obnoxious and loveable characters, contriving a plot with unexpected twists but amusing situations. Dahl reads his own adapted version.

CHITTY CHITTY BANG BANG (Phonodisc or Cassette). See Automobiles–Fiction

DAYDREAMS AND MAKE BELIEVE (Filmstrip–Sound). Educational Enrichment Materials, 1976. 4 color, sound filmstrips, av. 35 fr.; 4 cassettes or phonodiscs, av. 8 min. 71053 ($76). Gr. K–3. BKL (3/15/77). Fic

Contents: 1. Someday. 2. When I Have a Little Girl. 3. When I Have a Son. 4. The Three Funny Friends.

These filmstrips bring Zolotow's works an audiovisual exposure that is sure to heighten viewer interest in the books.

DUMBO (Kit). See Elephants–Fiction

THE GAMMAGE CUP (Filmstrip–Sound). Miller-Brody Productions, 1976 (Newbery Award Sound Filmstrip Library). 2 color, sound filmstrips, 131–132 fr.; 1 disc or 2

cassettes, 22–23 min.; Teacher's Guide. #NSF3073 ($32). Gr. 4–8. PRV (4/78). Fic

The Minnipins, a mountain valley society, exile a group of inhabitants for questioning the wisdom of the leading family, the Periods. The exiles establish a new home for themselves and then discover that the Minnipins's ancient enemies are preparing an attack. This fantasy-world story is based on the book by Carol Kendall.

HAROLD'S FAIRY TALE (Motion Picture–16mm–Sound). See Fairy Tales

A HOUSEFUL OF OCEAN (Kit). See Children–Fiction

JAMES AND THE GIANT PEACH (Phonodisc or Cassette). Caedmon Records, 1977. 1 cassette or disc, approx. 50 min. Disc #TC15431 ($6.98), Cassette #CDL515431 ($7.95). Gr. 4–6. AUR (1978). Fic

All the best that is Roald Dahl is captured in this story of the little boy, the mysterious seeds, unexpected results, terrible aunts, and curious creatures. Marvelous poems and the story are read by the author.

JUST SO STORIES BY RUDYARD KIPLING (Filmstrip–Sound). See Animals–Fiction

KICK ME (Motion Picture–16mm–Sound). Little Red Filmhouse, 1976. 16mm color, sound film, 8 min. ($140). Gr. 5–A. BKL (10/15/77). Fic

An outrageous tale about a pair of kicking legs. A tree, its fruit, and a baseball are victims until the ball begins to grow. The tables are turned and the legs must flee in an uproarious chase sequence. Other characters get involved and soon all are running in circles. Swarthe uses the technique of drawing animation on 35mm film frames and transferring it to 16mm format.

MARY POPPINS (Phonodisc or Cassette). Caedmon Records. 1 cassette or disc, approx. 60 min. Disc #TC1246 ($6.98), Cassette #CDL51246 ($7.95). Gr. K–6. SLJ, NYR, NYT. Fic

These stories have been selected from P. L. Travers's first book about the immortal Mary Poppins and her adventures. A large cast, led by Maggie Smith, enlivens the recording, which should have equal appeal to the young at heart of all ages. Music composed and conducted by Leslie Pearson.

MARY POPPINS AND THE BANKS FAMILY (Phonodisc or Cassette). Caedmon Records. 1 cassette or disc, approx. 49 min. Disc #TC1270 ($6.98), Cassette #CDL51270 ($7.95). Gr. K–6. NYR. Fic

The stories on this recording are taken from P. L. Travers's book, *Mary Poppins Comes Back*. Maggie Smith plays the most unusual governess, and the music is composed and conducted by Leslie Pearson.

FANTASY—FICTION (cont.)

MARY POPPINS: BALLOONS AND BAL-
LOONS (Phonodisc or Cassette). Caedmon
Records. 1 cassette or disc, approx. 50 min.
Disc #TC1348 ($6.98), Cassette
#CDL51348 ($7.95). Gr. K–6. BKL, NYR.
Fic

Contents: 1. Mary Poppins Comes Back:
Balloons and Balloons. 2. Mary Poppins
Opens the Door: Mr. Twigley's Wishes.
This recording, performed by a fine cast led
by Maggie Smith as the beloved English
nanny and Robert Stephens as the narrator,
contains excerpts from P. L. Travers's books.
Music composed and conducted by Leslie
Pearson.

MARY POPPINS COMES BACK (Phonodisc
or Cassette). Caedmon Records. 1 cassette
or disc, approx. 55 min. Disc #TC1269
($6.98), Cassette #CDL51269 ($7.95). Gr.
K–6. NYR. Fic

This recording contains stories from P. L.
Travers's original books. The delightful
governess is played by Maggie Smith. Music
is composed and conducted by Leslie Pearson.

MARY POPPINS FROM A TO Z (Phonodisc
or Cassette). See Alphabet Books

MARY POPPINS OPENS THE DOOR (Phonodisc or Cassette). Caedmon Records. 1 cassette or disc, approx. 50 min. Disc #TC1271
($6.98), Cassette #CDL51271 ($7.95). Gr.
K–6. LBJ, NYR. Fic

The stories on this recording are taken from
P. L. Travers's classic book for children.
Maggie Smith plays the lead assisted by an
able cast. Music composed and conducted
by Leslie Pearson.

MAURICE SENDAK'S REALLY ROSIE
STARRING THE NUTSHELL KIDS (Motion Picture—16mm—Sound). See Imagination—Fiction

MONSTERS AND OTHER FRIENDLY
CREATURES (Filmstrip—Sound). See
Monsters—Fiction

A PICTURE FOR HAROLD'S ROOM (Filmstrip—Sound). Weston Woods Studios,
1973. 1 color, sound filmstrip, 64 fr.; 1
cassette, 6 min. #SF133C ($12.75). Gr.
K–3. PRV (12/73). Fic

"Harold" draws a picture for his room and
then steps into it and his travels begin. This
filmstrip is true to the book written and
illustrated by Crockett Johnson.

THE PRINCE AND THE PAUPER (Phonodisc or Cassette). Caedmon Records, 1977.
1 cassette or disc, approx. 60 min. Disc
#TC1541-1 ($6.98), Cassette #CDL51541-
1 ($7.95). Gr. 5–9. AUR (1978). Fic

Mark Twain wrote this great yarn of 2 boys
in medieval England. The story has all of
Twain's love of a tale for a tale's sake. Ian

Richardson provides the many voices and
sharp characterizations.

QUEEN ZIXI OF IX, OR THE STORY OF
THE MAGIC CLOAK (Phonodisc or Cas-
sette). Caedmon Records, 1977. 1 cas-
sette or disc. Disc #TC1529-1 ($6.98),
Cassette #CDL51529-1 ($7.95). Gr. 4–6.
AUR (1978). Fic

L. Frank Baum interweaves the story of the
wish-fulfilling cloak with the story of Bud
and Meg in a tale that is at once homespun
and mysterious. In this abridgement of the
old favorite, we meet these children and, of
course, Queen Zixi. Ray Bolger is the storyteller with many voices and much hilarity.
Music by Don Heckman.

READING FOR THE FUN OF IT—FAN-
TASY (Filmstrip—Sound). See Literature—
Study and Teaching

ROOTABAGA STORIES: HOW TO TELL
CORN FAIRIES WHEN YOU SEE 'EM
(Phonodisc or Cassette). Caedmon Records. 1 cassette or disc, approx. 55 min.;
jacket notes. Disc #TC1159 ($6.98), Cas-
sette #CDL51159 ($7.95). Gr. K–6. ESL,
HOB, LBJ. Fic

Carl Sandburg reads his delightful children's
short stories.

ROOTABAGA STORIES: THE FINDING OF
THE ZIG ZAG RAILROAD (Phonodisc or
Cassette). Caedmon Records. 1 cassette or
disc, approx. 55 min.; Jacket Notes. Disc
#TC1089 ($6.98), Cassette #CDL51089
($7.95). Gr. K–6. ESL, HOB, SLJ. Fic

Some of Carl Sandburg's stories that he first
told to his own little girls; now favorites of
many children. Read by Sandburg.

ROOTABAGA STORIES: THE HAYSTACK
CRICKET (Phonodisc or Cassette). Caed-
mon Records. 1 cassette or disc, approx. 55
min.; Jacket Notes. Disc #TC1306 ($6.98),
Cassette #CDL51306 ($7.95). Gr. K–6.
ESL, HOB, SLJ. Fic

Carl Sandburg reads this charming collection of children's stories that are enjoyed as
much today as when he first told them to
his own little girls.

THE SECRET GARDEN (Phonodisc or Cassette). Caedmon Records, 1975. 1 disc or
cassette. Cassette #CDL-51463 ($7.95),
Discs #TC-1463 ($6.98). Gr. K–8. BKL
(10/15/76), PRV (11/76). Fic

An abridged version of this favorite classic
is read by Clarie Bloom.

STUART LITTLE (Filmstrip—Sound). See
Mice—Fiction

TCHOU TCHOU (Motion Picture—16mm—
Sound). National Film Board of Canada/
EBEC, 1972. 16mm color, sound film, 15
min.; Teacher's Guide. #3336 ($185). Gr.
K–A. LAM (2/76), LFR (10/74), LNG
(12/75). Fic

This imaginative, nonnarrated film shows toy blocks forming a child's city. All animation is within the confines of the 6 sides of each block. One block is a bird fluttering wings, another a ladybug moving legs. It takes 3 blocks each to form a boy and a girl, who move as though self-propelled. A chain of blocks makes a dragon that topples buildings to warning sounds in music and drumrolls. While the dragon sleeps, the children outwit him in a surprise ending.

THROUGH THE LOOKING GLASS (Phonodiscs). CMS Records. 3 discs; Complete Illustrated Text. #673/3L ($20.94). Gr. 4–A. PRV (4/76). Fic

This Lewis Carroll work is told by George Rose with Sarah Jane Gwillim as Alice. Carroll's witty writing, Rose's brilliant characterizations (he plays everyone but Alice), and Gwillim—charming, well-mannered, and awfully British—create an enjoyable rendition of this classic.

THE VELVETEEN RABBIT (Filmstrip—Sound). Miller-Brody Productions, 1976. 2 color, sound filmstrips, av. 60 fr. ea.; 2 cassettes or discs, av. 12 min. ea.; Guide. Cassettes #L-512-FC ($32), Discs #L-512-FR ($32). Gr. 1–A. BKL (1/1/77), LGB (12/76), PVB (4/78). Fic

The narration conveys the mood of the fantasy of Margery Williams's book about the lifegiving power of love in a small boy's nursery.

THE VOYAGES OF DOCTOR DOLITTLE (Filmstrip—Sound). See Animals—Fiction

THE WIND IN THE WILLOWS (Phonodisc or Cassette). See Animals—Fiction

WIZARD OF OZ (Cassette). Jabberwocky Cassette Classics, 1972. 2 cassettes, av. 60 min. #1041, #1042 ($15.96). Gr. 1–7. BKL (3/1/74), JOR (11/74). Fic

In this version of the favorite by L. Frank Baum, a female narrator introduces and carries the story. Music is used to denote the passage of time, and there are dramatizations of familiar scenes.

FARBER, NORMA

AS I WAS CROSSING BOSTON COMMON (Filmstrip—Sound/Captioned). See Animals—Fiction

FARM LIFE

FARMING (Film Loop—8mm—Captioned). See Frontier and Pioneer Life

LIVING ON A FARM (Filmstrip—Sound). Coronet Instructional Media, 1972. 6 color, sound filmstrips, 49 fr.; 3 discs or 6 cassettes, 11 min. Disc #S162 ($95), Cassette #M162 ($95). Gr. 1–4. PRV (5/73), PVB (5/74). 630.1

Contents: 1. A General Farm. 2. A Dairy Farm. 3. A Fruit Farm. 4. An Egg Farm. 5. A Cattle Ranch. 6. A Vegetable Farm. This set introduces students to modern farmers and their farms. Shows how crops are grown and harvested, products marketed, livestock raised, and farm equipment used. The necessity of migrant workers for handwork is explained.

FATIO, LOUISE

THE HAPPY LION SERIES, SET ONE (Filmstrip—Sound). See Lions—Fiction

THE HAPPY LION SERIES, SET TWO (Filmstrip—Sound). See Lions—Fiction

FICTION. See individual subject headings

FIEDLER, ARTHUR

CLASSICAL MUSIC FOR PEOPLE WHO HATE CLASSICAL MUSIC (Phonodiscs). See Orchestral Music

FIESTA DE APRENDER

THE LEARNING PARTY, VOL. ONE (Phonodisc or Cassette). See Children's Songs

THE LEARNING PARTY, VOL. TWO, GOING PLACES (Phonodisc or Cassette). See Children's Songs

FINANCE, PERSONAL. See Money

FINK, MIKE

MIKE FINK AND STORMALONG (Phonodisc or Cassette). See Folklore—U.S.

FIRE PREVENTION

ALL ABOUT FIRE (Motion Picture—16mm—Sound). Farmhouse Films, National Safety Council/Pyramid Films, 1976. 16mm color, sound film, 10 min. #0153 ($175). Gr. K–8. LNG (2/78). 614.8

Colorful animation and a cynical cat bring the message on fire prevention. Accented are the hazards in the average family home as pointed out by the fire captain.

FIRE AND THE WITCH (Motion Picture—16mm—Sound). Film Communicators, 1976. 16mm color, sound film, 11 min. ($175). Gr. K–6. BKL (6/1/77). 614.8

A comic version of Hansel and Gretel serves as the basis to review the points of fire prevention and safety in this puppet film.

FIRE SAFETY—WHAT'S THAT? (Slides). IHS Associates/Film Communicators, 1976. 40 color slides, plastic mount; 1 cassette, 9

FIRE PREVENTION (cont.)

min.; 1 Guide. ($69). Gr. 1–5. BKL (6/1/77). 614.8

Willie goes through a fire safety program at school and takes the information home to check out the fire hazards there.

TIGER, TIGER, BURNING BRIGHT (Filmstrip–Sound). Marshfilm, 1976 (Safety). 1 color, sound filmstrip, 50 fr.; 1 cassette or disc, 15 min.; Teacher's Guide. #1129 ($21). Gr. 4–8. INS (1/78), NYF (1976). 614.8

Dramatizes the benefits as well as the hazards of fire through familiar situations; shows how to prevent fires in the home and outdoors, how to get help in an emergency, and how to give first aid treatment for burns and shock.

FIRST AID

FIRST AID FOR LITTLE PEOPLE (Kit). Instructional Materials Laboratories, 1976. 1 filmstrip, 68 fr.; 1 cassette, 12 min.; 4 Duplicating Masters; 30 Student Booklets; 30 Student Awards; 1 Teacher's Guide. ($8.50). Gr. K–4. BKL (10/15/77). 614.8

Cartoon illustrations with clear, concise narration by a girl and boy provide a primary first aid course that reiterates an important message: "Be aware, be careful, and when necessary, get help!" Basic remedies for the first aid emergencies of bleeding, cessation of breathing, ingestion of poison, as well as minor injuries are discussed.

FISHER, LEONARD EVERETT

STORIES OF LATIN AMERICA, SET ONE (Filmstrip–Sound). *See* Latin America–Fiction

STORIES OF LATIN AMERICA, SET TWO (Filmstrip–Sound). *See* Latin America–Fiction

FISHES

THE BROWN TROUT (Film Loop–8mm–Captioned). *See* Trout

SALMON RUN (Film Loop–8mm–Silent). *See* Salmon

See also names of individual fish, i.e., Sharks.

FLACK, ROBERTA

THE LEGEND OF JOHN HENRY (Motion Picture–16mm–Sound). *See* Folklore–U.S.

FLAGS–U.S.

FOLK SONGS IN AMERICAN HISTORY: THE AMERICAN FLAG (Filmstrip–Sound). *See* Folk Songs–U.S.

FLEISCHMAN, SID

FIRST CHOICE AUTHORS AND BOOKS (Filmstrip–Sound). *See* Authors

FLEMING, IAN

CHITTY CHITTY BANG BANG (Phonodisc or Cassette). *See* Automobiles–Fiction

FOG–FICTION

HIDE AND SEEK FOG (Filmstrip–Sound). Weston Woods Studios, 1972. 1 color, sound filmstrip, 32 fr.; 1 cassette, 7 min. #SF136C ($12.75). Gr. K–3. PRV (12/73). Fic

Based on the book by Alvin Tresselt and illustrated by Roger Duvoisin, this is a filmstrip of a mood picture book about the fog that rolls in on an Atlantic seacoast village for 3 days.

FOLK ART, AMERICAN

AMERICAN FOLK ARTS (Filmstrip–Sound). Troll Associates, 1975. 8 color, sound filmstrips, av. 55 fr. ea.; 8 cassettes, av. 10 min. ea. Teacher's Guide. Each Title ($32), Series ($128). Gr. 4–8. BKL (12/1/75), LGB (1975-76), PRV (3/76). 745.44

Contents: 1. Weathervanes and Whirligigs. 2. Scrimshaw. 3. Sculpture. 4. Art Technique. 5. Household Crafts. 6. Pottery. 7. Oil Painting. 8. Documentary Art.

Set displays the work of weavers, sculptors, artisans, and craftspeople who, using only the most basic materials, produced a wide variety of folk art forms–the authentic art of the young United States.

FOLK DANCING

AMERICAN DANCES (Phonodisc or Cassette). Activity Records/Educational Activities. 1 disc or cassette, 30 min. Teacher's Guide. Cassette #AC57 ($8.95), Disc #AR57 ($7.95). Gr. 2–8. PRV (9/75). 793.31

Contents: 1. Hornpipe. 2. Mowrah Cawkah. 3. Cherkessia. 4. Hokey Pokey. 5. Cissy. 6. Come Dance with Me. 7. Rabbit and the Fox. 8. Bingo.

A variety of American folk dances reflecting the spirit, variety, and multicultural makeup of the United States.

AMERICAN FOLK DANCES (Phonodiscs). Bowmar Publishing. 1 disc. #114 ($6.95). Gr. 2–6. AUR (1978). 793.3

Virginia Reel, polka, Captain Junks, and other American folk dances are presented on this recording.

FOLK DANCES FROM AROUND THE WORLD (Phonodiscs). Bowmar Publishing.

1 disc. #113 ($6.95). Gr. 2-5. AUR (1978). 793.3

Bleking, Hopp Mor Annika, Guslof's Skoal, and other folk dances are on this recording.

SINGING GAMES AND FOLK DANCES (Phonodiscs). Bowmar Publishing. 1 disc. #112 ($6.95). Gr. K-3. AUR (1978). 793.3

Children's Polka, Skip to My Lou, Thread Follows the Needle, and many other favorite singing and dancing songs.

FOLK DANCING, SWISS

SONGS AND DANCES OF SWITZERLAND (Phonodiscs). Folkways Records, 1954. 1 disc, 10" 33-1/3 rpm; Guide. #6807 ($5). Gr. 6-12. MDU (1978). 793.3

Includes yodeling, Alpine horn, and the bell-tree.

FOLK SONGS

AMERICA SINGS (Phonodisc or Cassette). Activity Records/Educational Activities. 1 disc or cassette, 30 min. Disc #AR-698 ($6.95), Cassette #AR-698 ($7.95). Gr. 2-8. PRV (9/75). 784.4

Contents: 1. Blow Ye Winds. 2. Beautiful Dreamer. 3. Two Brothers. 4 Battle Hymn of the Republic. 5. Davy Crockett. 6. Erie Canal. 7. Sixteen Tons. 8. Revolutionary Tea. 9. America the Beautiful. 10. World War I. 11. World War II.

People and events in America's 200-year history come alive in these evocative, traditional songs, celebrating "Happy Birthday, America."

AMERICAN SINGS (Phonodisc or Cassette). Activity Records/Educational Activities. 1 disc or cassette, 30 min; Teacher's Guide. Disc #AR56 ($6.95), Cassette #AC56 ($7.95). Gr. 2-8. PRV (9/75). 784.4

Contents: 1. America the Beautiful. 2. Arkansas Traveler. 3. Blow Ye Winds. 4. Casey Jones. 5. Down the Stream. 6. Get Along Little Doggies. 7. Old Joe Clark. 8. Pop Goes the Weasel. 9. Yankee Doodle, etc.

A collection of American folk songs especially chosen for their animation and singability; representative of different strands of American folk music heritage.

HAYWIRE MAC (Phonodiscs). Folkways Records. 1 disc. #FD5272 ($6.98). Gr. 4-A. PRV (12/75). 784.7

An important documentary of the music of World War I, performed by Harry K. McClintock. He tells stories, sings songs, and spreads his message. Informative and entertaining, this recording is strong in musical content and sociological significance.

THE OLD HEN CACKLED AND THE ROOSTER'S GONNA CROW (Phonodiscs).

Rounder Records. 1 disc. #1003 ($6.95). Gr. 3-A. PRV (12/75). 784.4

This album contains some specimens of the old fiddle-accompanied singing style, some humorous and sad songs, and flashy pyrotechnics with Carson's Virginia Reelers backup group.

FOLK SONGS, INDIAN

AS LONG AS THE GRASS SHALL GROW (Phonodiscs). Folkways Records, 1963. 1 disc, 12 in. 33-1/3 rpm; Guide. #2532 ($5.95). Gr. 6-A. MDU (1978). 784.75

Peter La Farge sings of the Indians. A member of the Narraganset Tribe, La Farge fulfills a long dream of interpreting his people in music.

PETER LA FARGE ON THE WARPATH (Phonodiscs). Folkways Records, 1965. 1 disc, 12 in. 33-1/3 rpm; Guide. #2535 ($5.95). Gr. 6-A. MDU (1978). 784.75

These contemporary songs bridge the worlds of whites and Indians.

WAR WHOOPS AND MEDICINE SONGS (Phonodiscs). Folkways Records, 1964. 1 disc, 12 in. 33-1/3 rpm; Guide. #4381 ($8.95). Gr. 3-A. MDU (1978). 784.75

Collected at Upper Dells, Wisconsin, during the annual Stand Rock Indian Ceremonials.

FOLK SONGS—U.S.

AMERICAN FOLK SONGS FOR CHILDREN (Phonodiscs). Folkways Records, 1954. 1 disc, 10 in. #7001 ($5). Gr. K-6. MDU (1978). 784.75

This disc includes "Bought Me a Cat," "This Old Man," "Clap Your Hands," and others.

THE ERIE CANAL (Filmstrip—Sound). See Erie Canal—Songs

FOLK SONGS IN AMERICAN HISTORY, SET ONE: 1700-1864 (Filmstrip—Sound). Warren Schloat Productions/Prentice-Hall Media, 1967. 6 color, sound filmstrips; 6 cassettes or discs. Cassettes #HAC501 ($138), Discs #HAC501 ($138). Gr. 5-A. SLJ, MDU (1978). 784.75

Contents: 1. Early Colonial Days. 2. The Revolutionary War. 3. Workers of America. 4. In Search of Gold. 5. The South. 6. The Civil War.

The spirit and folklore of America's heritage reflected through traditional folk songs. Performers include Joan Baez; Peter, Paul and Mary; Pete Seeger; Burl Ives; and Josh White. The focus is on paintings, documentary photographs, and authentic illustrations.

FOLK SONGS IN AMERICAN HISTORY, SET TWO: 1865-1967 (Filmstrip—Sound). Warren Schloat Productions/Prentice-Hall

FOLK SONGS–U.S. (cont.)

Media, 1969. 6 color, sound filmstrips; 6 cassettes or discs. Cassettes #HAC503 ($138), Discs #HAR503 ($138). Gr. 5–A. MDU (1978), STE. 784.75

Contents: 1. Reconstruction and the West. 2. Immigration and Industrialization. 3. World War I. 4. 1920's and the Depression. 5. World War II. 6. The Post War Years.

America's heritage is reflected through traditional folk songs performed by such famous artists as Joan Baez; Peter, Paul and Mary; Pete Seeger; Burl Ives; and Josh White. The lyrics appear on the screen. Important period paintings, documentary photographs, and authentic illustrations are also used.

FOLK SONGS IN AMERICAN HISTORY: THE AMERICAN FLAG (Filmstrip– Sound). Warren Schloat Productions/ Prentice-Hall Media, 1970. 2 color, sound filmstrips; 2 cassettes or discs. Cassettes #HAC ($48), Discs #HAC ($48). Gr. 5–A. AFF. 784.75

This 2-part set on the American flag reflects the spirit and folklore of America's heritage through traditional folk songs performed by famous artists.

FOLK SONGS IN AMERICA'S HISTORY SINCE 1865 (Filmstrip–Sound). Globe Filmstrips/Coronet Instructional Media, 1977. 6 color, sound filmstrips; 6 cassettes. #M716 ($99). Gr. 4–9. MDU (1978). 784.75

Contents: 1. Songs of Labor. 2. Songs of Happiness. 3. Songs of Protest. 4. Songs of Sorrow. 5. Songs of Injustice. 6. Songs of Heroism.

Here is U.S. history in drawings, photographs, and song. Two of the songs included in this set are "Hallelujah, I'm a Bum" and "This Land Is Your Land."

THE FOOLISH FROG (Motion Picture– 16mm–Sound). Weston Woods Studios, 1973. 16mm color, sound, animated film, 8 min. ($150). Gr. K–6. AFF (1972), CFF (1972), MER (1/73). 784.75

Adapted from the book *The Foolish Frog*, this tells of a bullfrog who falls into the mud and a passing farmer who makes up a song about it. Soon everybody is singing about the frog. When the frog hears the song, he explodes with pride, imparting a valuable lesson to all.

MR. FROG WENT A-COURTING (Motion Picture–16mm–Sound). National Film Board of Canada/Films, 1976. 16mm color, sound, animated film, 5 min. #101-0075 ($110). Gr. K–A. AFF (1976), BKL (1/1/77), IAF (1976). 784.75

Allowing that a frog might go courting a mouse, there follows a chain of events in line with the basic law of nature–that bigger creatures prey on smaller ones. The ancient Scottish folk song is interpreted by artist/animator Evelyn Lambert with lyrics sung by Derek Lamb to lute accompaniment.

SHE'LL BE COMIN' 'ROUND THE MOUN-TAIN (Filmstrip–Sound). Weston Woods Studios, 1975. 1 color, sound filmstrip, 40 fr.; 1 cassette 7:24 min.; Teacher's Guide. #FS169C ($12.75). Gr. 2–6. PRV (11/76). 784.75

The familiar American folk song is presented in this filmstrip version of Robert Quackenbush's picture book. The script includes the tune as well as an updated melodrama.

FOLKLORE

FOLK STORIES AND TALES (Cassette). *See* Fairy Tales

FOLK TALES FROM OTHER LANDS (Filmstrip–Sound). Young World/Current Affairs Films, 1976. 6 color, sound filmstrips, 37–49 fr.; 6 cassettes, av. 16 min.; 1 Guide. ($93). Gr. K–4. BKL (11/15/76). 398.2

Contents: 1. Clever Manka (Czechoslovakia). 2. The Five Chinese Brothers (China). 3. The Goose Girl (Germany). 4. Gudbrand-on-the-Hillside (Scandinavia). 5. Pinocchio (Italy). 6. The Tinker and the Ghost (Spain).

Six popular representative folk tales from other lands are presented with unique visuals. Puppet characters dramatize the tales.

FOLKTALE CLASSICS FROM OTHER LANDS (Filmstrip–Sound). BFA Educational Media, 1976. 4 color, sound filmstrips; 4 cassettes or discs. Cassettes #VJF000 ($70), Discs #VJE000 ($70). Gr. 3–6. MDU (4/78). 398.2

Contents: 1. Clever Semiletka. 2. Anansi Plays Dead. 3. The Story of Wali Dad. 4. The Seven Brothers.

These folk tales are adaptations of stories from 4 cultures–Russian, African, Indian, and Chinese.

FOLKTALES OF SOUTH AMERICA (Filmstrip–Sound). Q+ED Productions, 1976. 6 color, sound filmstrips, 41–69 fr.; 6 cassettes or discs, 8–17 min.; 1 Guide. Cassettes #TSE-10 ($110.50), Discs #TSE-10 ($99.50). Gr. K–4. BKL (11/15/76). 398.2

Contents: 1. The Rice in the Ashes; A Tale of Argentina. 2. The Fisherman and the Monkey; A Tale of Brazil. 3. The Green Moss Prince; A Tale of Uruguay. 4. The Little Black Book of Magic; A Tale of Argentina. 5. The Pot That Cooked by Itself; A Tale of Guyana. 6. The Golden Gourd; A Tale of Brazil.

This set presents some South American folk tales with the universal folk elements represented.

THE GREAT QUILLOW (Phonodisc or Cassette). *See* Giants—Fiction

HANSEL AND GRETEL AND OTHER FAIRY TALES BY THE BROTHERS GRIMM (Phonodisc or Cassette). *See* Fairy Tales

MAGIC CHANGES, SET ONE (Filmstrip—Sound). Acorn Films, 1976. 4 color, sound filmstrips, 66–74 fr.; 4 cassettes, 7–9 min.; 1 Guide. ($65). Gr. 3–10. BKL (9/15/77). 398.2

Contents: 1. Baucis and Philemon. 2. The Clever Student. 3. Peterkin and the Rabbit. 4. The Rainbow Fish.

Favorites are gathered together in these enticing collections of magical tales. Each is resolved around a transformation from one thing to another.

MAGIC CHANGES, SET TWO (Filmstrip—Sound). Acorn Films, 1976. 4 color, sound filmstrips, 61–72 fr.; 4 cassettes, 8–13 min.; 1 Guide. ($65). Gr. 3–10. BKL (9/15/77). 398.2

Contents: 1. The Bunyip. 2. The Caliph Stork. 3. Circe the Enchantress. 4. The Simple Hearted Man.

A continuation of magical tales centered around a transformation from one thing to another.

THE PIED PIPER AND OTHER STORIES (Phonodisc or Cassette). *See* Fairy Tales

SNOW WHITE AND OTHER FAIRY TALES (Phonodisc or Cassette). *See* Fairy Tales

SNOW WHITE AND ROSE RED AND OTHER ANDREW LANG FAIRY TALES (Phonodisc or Cassette). *See* Fairy Tales

STORY-TIME FAVORITES (Filmstrip—Sound). EBEC, 1973. 4 color, sound filmstrips, av. 69 fr. ea.; 4 cassettes or phonodiscs av. 9 min. ea.; Teacher's Guide. Discs #6476 ($57.95), Cassettes #6476K ($57.95). Gr. K–4. BKL (9/1/74), LFR (12/74). 398.2

Contents: 1. The Three Little Pigs. 2. The Gingerbread Boy. 3. The Bremen Town Musicians. 4. The Emperor's New Clothes.

Each of the popular fairy tales in this set has been skillfully adapted to the filmstrip medium. Supported by various sound effects, some hilariously exaggerated, the strips are entertaining for recreational viewing and language arts and story hours.

THE TALE OF RUMPELSTILTSKIN (Motion Picture—16mm—Sound). EBEC, 1974. 16mm color, sound film, 21 min. #3302 ($290). Gr. K–4. CPR (1/76), LFR (3/75), PRV (2/75). 398.2

A live action version of the famous fairy tale of a miller's daughter who, because of her father's boasting, is ordered to spin straw into gold for the king. She completes her task with the help of the dwarf, Rumpelstiltskin, but he demands her firstborn child if she becomes queen. She agrees, and years later he returns and asks for the child. His compromise is for her to guess his name, which, luckily, is overheard by one of her messengers.

WORLD MYTHS AND FOLKTALES (Filmstrip—Sound). Coronet Instructional Media, 1974. 8 color, sound filmstrips, av. 52 fr.; 8 discs or cassettes, av. 11-1/2 min. Cassettes #M701 ($129), Discs #S701 ($129). Gr. 5–12. BKL (7/15/74). 398.2

Contents: 1. Hiawatha and the Iroquois Nation (U.S.A.). 2. Petit Jean (Canada). 3. Quetzalcoatl, Aztec God (Mexico). 4. Pele, The Fire Goddess (Hawaii). 5. The Excellent Archer (China). 6. Siegfried and the Jealous Queen (Germany). 7. Paris and the Golden Apple (Greece). 8. The Day the World Went Dark (Nigeria).

Each tale is retold in an appropriate dialect and in a suitable ethnic context.

FOLKLORE—AFRICA

ANANSI THE SPIDER (Filmstrip—Sound). Weston Woods Studios, 1974. 1 color, sound filmstrip; 1 cassette; Text Booklet. #151 ($12.75). Gr. K–6. RTE (1/76). 398.2

This strip is based on the book by Gerald McDermott. Anansi is an African folk tale.

ANANSI THE SPIDER (Motion Picture—16mm—Sound). Texture Films, 1969. 16mm color, sound film, 10 min. ($165). Gr. 1–A. BKL (10/1/76), CGE (1970), FLN (9/69). 398.2

An animated film that graphically relates the adventures of the cunning spider Anansi, trickster hero of the Ashanti people of Ghana.

THE MAGIC TREE (Motion Picture—16mm—Sound). Texture Films, 1970. 16mm color, sound film, 10 min. ($165). Gr. 4–A. BKL (5/1/73), CGE (1971), FLN (1971). 398.2

A tale from the Congo of a homely, unloved boy who leaves his family and finds a secret paradise. But he loses it all when he breaks his vow of secrecy and reveals the mystery.

A STORY A STORY (Filmstrip—Sound). Weston Woods Studios, 1973. 1 color, sound filmstrip, 40 fr.; 1 cassette, 10 min. #SF123C ($12.75). Gr. K–3. RTE (1/74). 398.2

Based on the African folk tale of the old spider man, Anansi, wanting to buy the Sky God's stories. He completes, by his cleverness, 3 seemingly impossible tasks set as the price for the golden box of stories,

FOLKLORE—AFRICA (cont.)

which he takes back to earth. This is a
reproduction and reading of the book by
Gail E. Haley.

WHY MOSQUITOES BUZZ IN PEOPLE'S
EARS (Kit). *See* Animals—Fiction

FOLKLORE, BLACK

FOLKTALES OF BLACK AMERICA (Film-
strip—Sound). International Film Bureau,
1977. 4 color, sound filmstrips, av. 56 fr.;
4 cassettes, av. 7 min. ($62.50). Gr. 5–A.
BKL (11/15/77), PRV (4/78). 398.2
Contents: 1. A Tale to Tell: Introducing
Folk Poetry. 2. The Signifyin' Monkey. 3.
Dolomite. 4. The Titanic.
Warm, relaxed, and exaggerated stories of
the streets where these tales are usually told.
Pin-the-tail-on-the donkey, jump rope songs,
cat calls, the Bermuda Triangle, and Bigfoot
are part of the "living folklore" covered.
An excellent example of the rhythm, dialect, and tone of Black oral literature is
provided by the narrator.

FOLKLORE—CHINA

CHINESE FAIRY TALES (Phonodisc or Cassette). *See* Fairy Tales

THE SUPERLATIVE HORSE (Motion Picture—16mm—Sound). Phoenix Films, 1975.
16mm color, sound film, 36 min. #0160
($450). Gr. 4–12. PRV (11/77). 398.2
Based on Jean Merrill's allegorical children's
story, a tale from Ancient China. It proves
that people should not judge things, animals, or other people by their outer appearances, but rather by their inner qualities.

FOLKLORE—ENGLAND

ADVENTURES OF ROBIN HOOD, VOL.
1: HOW ROBIN BECAME AN OUTLAW
(Phonodisc or Cassette). Caedmon Records,
1972. 1 cassette or disc, 12 in. Disc
#TC1369 ($6.98), Cassette #CDL51369
($7.95). Gr. 4–7. BKL, CHH, NYR. 398.2
In this recording about Robin Hood's adventures, the hero has the first of many
encounters with the Sheriff of Nottingham
and meets Mistress Fitzwalter, the Maid
Marian who helps him to escape. Music
composed and conducted by Don Hickman;
story retold by Paul Creswick and performed by Anthony Quayle.

ADVENTURES OF ROBIN HOOD, VOL.
2: OUTLAW BAND OF SHERWOOD
FOREST (Phonodisc or Cassette). Caed-
mon Records, 1972. 1 cassette or disc.
Disc #TC1370 ($6.98), Cassette
#CDL51370 ($7.98). Gr. 4–7. BKL, CHH,
NYR. 398.2
In this recording performed by Anthony

Quayle, Robin Hood's adventures include
fleeing to the woods where he and his com-
panions live on water, dry bread, and ber-
ries, and sleep in caves. Music composed
and conducted by Don Hickman; retold by
Paul Creswick.

ADVENTURES OF ROBIN HOOD, VOL. 3:
ADVENTURES WITH LITTLE JOHN
(Phonodisc or Cassette). Caedmon Records,
1972. 1 cassette or disc, 12 in. Disc
#TC1371 ($6.98), Cassette #CDL51371
($7.95). Gr. 4–7. BKL, CHH, NYR. 398.2
In this recording about Robin Hood's ad-
ventures, Little John appears and helps the
hero outwit the Sheriff of Nottingham.
Music composed and conducted by Don
Hickman; story retold by Paul Creswick and
performed by Anthony Quayle.

ADVENTURES OF ROBIN HOOD, VOL. 4:
ROBIN AND HIS MERRY MEN (Phonodisc or Cassette). Caedmon Records, 1972.
1 cassette or disc, 12 in. Disc #TC1372
($6.98), Cassette #CDL51372 ($7.98).
Gr. 4–7. BKL, CHH, NYR. 398.2
In this recording of Robin Hood's adventures, Friar Tuck joins the merry men in
Robin Hood's band. Robin once again
escapes the clutches of the Sheriff of Nottingham, taking with him the handmaiden
of the sheriff's daughter, Maid Marian. Music composed and conducted by Don Hickman; story retold by Paul Creswick and
performed by Anthony Quayle.

DICK WHITTINGTON AND HIS CAT AND
OTHER ENGLISH TALES (Phonodisc or
Cassette). Caedmon Records, 1975. 1 cas-
sette or disc, approx. 40 min. Disc
#TC1265 ($6.98), Cassette #CDL51265
($7.95). Gr. K–6. NYR (1976). 398.2
Contents: 1. Dick Whittington and His
Cat. 2. Tom Tit Tot. 3. Tattercoats. 4.
Simpleton Peter.
For generations, these 4 stories have been
told to grown-ups as well as children. They
are part of the cultural heritage of everyone
who uses the English language.

FOLKLORE—ESKIMO

THE OWL AND THE LEMMING (AN ES-
KIMO LEGEND) (Filmstrip—Sound).
Donars Productions, 1973. 1 color, sound
filmstrip, 60 fr.; 1 cassette, 6 min. ($15).
Gr. K–2. BKL (10/1/77), PRV (12/77).
398.2
The story of a foolish owl who becomes
distracted by flattery and loses his prey. Interpreted in sealskin characters with authentic sounds and Eskimo music.

THE OWL WHO MARRIED A GOOSE (Motion Picture—16mm—Sound). National
Film Board of Canada/Stephen Bosustow
Productions, 1975. 16mm color, sound
film, 7-1/2 min. ($145). Gr. K–A. AFF
(1977), BKL (1/1/77), LGB (1977). 398.2

In the solitude of the Arctic, a goose captures the fancy of an owl. Although the owl is hopelessly in love, he can never hope to keep up with the goose and her goslings. The owl pursues his dream of sharing her life, even though it means his destruction.

FOLKLORE—GREECE

PIGS AND PIRATES (Filmstrip—Sound). *See* Pigs—Fiction

FOLKLORE—HUNGARY

THE THREE POOR TAILORS (Filmstrip—Sound). Weston Woods Studios, 1973. 1 color, sound filmstrip, 20 fr.; 1 cassette, 4 min. #SF140C ($12.75). Gr. K-3. RTE (1/74). 398.2
Based on the Hungarian folk tale by Victor G. Ambrus, this is a delightful story retold about 3 tailors who ride to town on a goat. After getting into debt, they have to stay in prison until they mend all the townspeople's clothes. Ambrus won the "Kate Greenaway" Medal (in the United Kingdom) for the illustrations in the book, which are used in this filmstrip.

FOLKLORE—INDIA

WHAZZAT? (Motion Picture—16mm—Sound). Encyclopaedia Britannica Educational, 1975. 16mm color, sound film, 10 min. #3347 ($150). Gr. K-3. IAF (10/4/75), LAM (5/12/76), PRV (12/75). 398.2
Six clay figures create fun by jumping into and out of new shapes as they skip, crawl, stumble, and flow over one another toward an adventure with an elephant. These characters cannot see, and when they meet and touch the elephant, each thinks the animal is something else. By pooling their knowledge, they recognize the object for what it is. Based on an East Indian folk tale, this animated version is told without narration.

FOLKLORE, INDIAN

ARROW TO THE SUN (Motion Picture—16mm—Sound). *See* Indians of North America—Legends

FOLKLORE—IRELAND

IRISH FAIRY TALES (Phonodisc or Cassette). Caedmon Records, 1972. 1 cassette or disc, approx. 50 min. Disc #TC1349 ($6.98), Cassette #CDL51349 ($7.95). Gr. 4-8. LBJ. 398.2
Contents: 1. Cucullin and the Legend of Knockmany. 2. Guleesh.
These 2 fairy tales are gathered from Celtic oral literature collected during the nineteenth century from storytellers whose native language was Irish or Scottish Gaelic, performed here by Cyril Cusack.

FOLKLORE—JAPAN

REFLECTIONS: A JAPANESE FOLK TALE (Motion Picture—16mm—Sound). EBEC, 1975. 16mm color, sound film, 19 min. #3473 ($255). Gr. 4-9. BKL (12/15/75), LFR (3/4/75), LGB (1975-76). 398.2
A tale designed to probe the many faces of perception. The old Japanese story in which a son believes that he has found his dead father inside a small box in a gift shop. Unfamiliar with mirrors, he takes the reflection for that of his father. His wife, curious about the box and as unfamiliar with mirrors as her husband, is enraged when she looks in the box and thinks that he is hiding a young woman there. They take the box to a holy woman, but she discovers an old woman inside.

THE STONECUTTER (Filmstrip—Sound). Weston Woods Studios, 1976. 1 color, sound filmstrips, 33 fr.; 1 cassette, 6:53 min.; 1 Guide. #178 ($12.75). Gr. K-3. BKL (2/1/77). 398.2
Gerald McDermott interpretatively reads his version of the Japanese legend as his geometrically stylized illustrations develop the universality of the story's theme.

TALES FROM JAPAN (Filmstrip—Sound). Coronet Instructional Media, 1971. 8 color, sound filmstrips; 8 cassettes or 4 discs. Cassettes #M196 ($120), Discs #S196 ($120). Gr. 1-6. BKL (1972), INS (1972), SLJ (1972). 398.2
Contents: 1. The Moonbeam Princess. 2. The Tears of the Dragon. 3. The Rolling Rice Ball. 4. The Monkey and the Crab. 5. Inn of the Sparrows. 6. The Story of the Sunset Glow. 7. The Crane's Magic Gift. 8. The Man Who Made Trees Blossom.
The mystery and magnificence of Japanese culture are captured in this collection of stories that range from traditional fairy tales, legends, and fables, to more modern stories. Haiku introduces each story.

FOLKLORE—LATIN AMERICA

LATIN-AMERICAN FOLKTALES (Filmstrip—Sound). Coronet Instructional Media, 1974. 6 color, sound filmstrips; 6 cassettes or 3 discs. Also available in Spanish. Cassettes #M221 ($95), Discs #S221 ($95). Gr. 4-6. PRV (2/75), PVB (5/75). 398.2
Contents: 1. How Spring Was Born. 2. Why the Rabbit Has Long Ears. 3. The Bridge of the Incas. 4. How the Cactus Got Its Thorns. 5. How the Andes Mountain Came to Be. 6. How the Jaguar Got Its Spots.
Latin-American folk tales disclose how ancient Indians believed the earth evolved. Illustrations enrich legends that reveal devotion, humor, and compassion.

FOLKLORE—MEXICO

MEXICAN INDIAN LEGENDS (Motion Picture—16mm—Sound). BFA Educational Media, 1976. 16mm color, sound film, 16:15 min. #11668 ($230). Gr. 4–10. BKL (1/15/77). 398.2

Tales from the Toltec, Aztec, and Mayan cultures are retold by a narrator with a Spanish accent as actors pantomime the legends. The legend behind the founding of Mexico City and the interpretation of such natural phenomena as the sun, moon, and creation of the mountains.

FOLKLORE—PUERTO RICO

CHIQUITIN AND THE DEVIL: A PUERTO RICAN FOLKTALE (Filmstrip—Sound). Guidance Associates, 1973. 1 color, sound filmstrip; 1 disc or cassette, 15 min.; Teacher's Guide. Disc #9A-301885 ($27.75), Cassette #9A-301893 ($27.75). Gr. 3–6. BKL (8/74), PVB (3/74). 398.2

A retelling of the folk tale made popular by Pura Belpre's *Ote: A Puerto Rican Folk Tale*, in which a small boy outwits the nearsighted devil and saves the family from starvation.

FOLKLORE—RUSSIA

THE GREAT BIG ENORMOUS TURNIP (Filmstrip—Sound). Weston Woods Studios, 1973. 1 color, sound filmstrip, 24 fr.; 1 cassette, 4 min. #SF140C ($12.75). Gr. K–4. RTE (1/74). 398.2

Based on the book by Alexei Tolstoy with illustrations by Helen Oxenbury, the story is a version of the Russian folk tale about the man who grew a turnip so huge he had to get his wife, granddaughter, dog, cat, and mouse to help him pull it up.

RUSSIAN FAIRY TALES (Phonodisc or Cassette). Caedmon Records, 1975. 1 cassette or disc, approx. 55 min. Disc #TC1332 ($6.98), Cassette #CDL51332 ($7.95). Gr. K–6. BKL, NYR. 398.2

Contents: 1. The King Who Liked Fairy Tales. 2. The Chatterbox. 3. The Doctor Who Knew Everything. 4. The Town of Fools. 5. Two Brothers. 6. The Stolen Turnips.

These tales are stories of such people as the idiot, the pauper, the shrew. They are expressions of childlike dreams, in which the wicked are beaten, the poor become rich, justice triumphs, and even the stupid are shown to be wiser than the sages.

FOLKLORE—TURKEY

NEW PATCHES FOR OLD (Filmstrip—Sound). Weston Woods Studios, 1976. 1 color, sound filmstrip, 44 fr.; 1 cassette,

10:30 min.; 1 Teacher's Guide. #180 ($12.75). Gr. K–2. BKL (7/15/77). 398.2

Based on the delightful Turkish tale about Hasan the Shoemaker as told in the book by Ahmet Uysal and narrated here by Barbara Kwilker. Harold Berson's illustrations from the book are used successfully in the filmstrip.

FOLKLORE—U.S.

AMERICAN FOLKLORE (Filmstrip—Sound). Coronet Instructional Media, 1970. 6 color, sound filmstrips, av. 46 fr.; 6 cassettes or 3 discs, av. 10-1/2 min. Available captioned also. Discs #S166 ($95), Cassettes #M166 ($95). Gr. 1–6. BKL (1972), GRT, INS. 398.2

Contents: 1. Paul Bunyan. 2. Mike Fink. 3. Pecos Bill. 4. John Henry. 5. Joe Magarac. 6. Casey Jones.

Six tall tales of loggers, rivermen, cowboys, steel workers, and engineers, told with folk music and original artwork. Backgrounds of the tales are tied to American history.

DAVY CROCKETT AND PECOS BILL (Phonodisc or Cassette). Caedmon Records, 1972. 1 cassette or disc, approx. 45 min. Disc #TC1319 ($6.98), Cassette #CDL51319 ($7.95). Gr. 3–6. BKL (1972), LBJ (1973). 398.2

Partly factual, partly folklore, and partly the creation of professional writers were such names as Davy Crockett. He became the prototype of the heroic backwoodsman, conqueror of every natural obstacle. Pecos Bill was the cowboy superman, part dunce, part genius, as revealed on this recording as well as in the legends that grew up about him. Book by Adrien Stoutenburg.

FOLKTALES OF BLACK AMERICA (Filmstrip—Sound). *See* Folklore, Black

JACK AND THE ROBBER (Motion Picture—16mm—Sound). Pied Piper Productions, 1975. 16mm color, sound film, 15 min.; Guide. ($185). Gr. 2–6. BKL (11/15/75), CGE (1975), PRV (1975). 398.2

Using animation in a depiction of this folk tale, this shows how Jack's 5 adopted animals help him out in a confrontation with a band of robbers.

JOHN HENRY AND JOE MAGARAC (Phonodisc or Cassette). Caedmon Records, 1972. 1 cassette or disc, approx. 50 min. Disc #TC1318 ($6.98), Cassette #CDL51318 ($7.95). Gr. 3–8. BKL (1972), LBJ (1972), NYR. 398.2

Ed Begley reads 2 tales of legendary American heroes. Powerful, black John Henry was the hero of the rock gangs who blasted out the tunnels for the trains. Joe Magarac was the name legend makers bestowed on the man they considered the greatest steel worker of them all.

JOHNNY APPLESEED AND PAUL BUNYAN (Phonodisc or Cassette). Caedmon Records, 1972. 1 cassette or disc, approx. 60 min. Disc #TC1321 ($6.98), Cassette #CDL51321 ($7.95). Gr. 3–8. BKL, LBJ. 398.2

Prophet, fanatic, saintlike—whatever the real man was—Johnny Appleseed is a permanent part of American folk literature. Paul Bunyan, the other hero described in this fourth volume of American Tall Tales recorded by Caedmon, was not only a symbol of brawn, but of American ingenuity in overcoming obstacles.

THE LEGEND OF JOHN HENRY (Motion Picture—16mm—Sound). Bosustow Productions, 1974 (American Folktales). 16mm color, sound animated film, 11 min.; Leader's Guide. ($160). Gr. 5–A. CFF (1974), CGE (1974), WLB (6/74). 398.2

The legend of the great steel-driving man. With a deadline of tunneling through Big Ben Mountain before winter, the railroad bosses decide to replace John Henry and his crew with a steam drill. John Henry declares, "Before I give in and let the steam drill win, I'll hammer myself to death." The race pits the power of one mighty and determined human against the steady relentless machine. After days of exhausting hammering, John Henry wins the race. He beats the steam drill, but it costs him his life. Sung by Roberta Flack.

THE LEGEND OF PAUL BUNYAN (Motion Picture—16mm—Sound). Bosustow Productions, 1973 (American Folktale). 16mm color, sound, animated film, 13 min.; Leader's Guide. ($180). Gr. 2–A. BKL (1/1/74), CGE (1974), PRV (11/74). 398.2

The legend of the giant woodsman Paul Bunyan, tells of Babe the blue ox and Paul's prosperous logging business. A favorite in American folklore, Paul Bunyan was known for his gentle temperament and fair dealing as well as his size and strength. But one day, Hels Helsun, the Bull of the Woods, pushes him a little too far by giving poor Babe a dose of poison sumac. They have such a battle, the force of their blows creates the Grand Canyon, the Great Lakes, the Mississippi River, and Niagara Falls.

THE LEGEND OF SLEEPY HOLLOW (Motion Picture—16mm—Sound). *See* Legends—U.S.

THE LEGEND OF SLEEPY HOLLOW AND OTHER STORIES (Cassette). *See* Legends—U.S.

MIKE FINK AND STORMALONG (Phonodisc or Cassette). Caedmon Records, 1972. 1 cassette or disc, approx. 60 min. Disc #TC1320 ($6.98), Cassette #CDL51320 ($7.95). Gr. 3–8. BKL (1972). 398.2

Contents: 1. Mike Fink. 2. Stormalong. Mike Fink was acknowledged as the rough-

est, toughest, and most reckless of all the fierce, feared rivermen. He became a legendary symbol of his breed. Also described on this recording is Stormalong, the hero of the deepwater men in the days of the sailing ships.

PAUL BUNYAN IN STORY AND SONG (Phonodisc or Cassette). Caedmon Records. 1 cassette or disc, approx. 50 min. Disc #TC1275 ($6.98), Cassette #CDL51275 ($7.95). Gr. 3–A. LBJ, NYR, SLJ. 398.2

From the times when the axmen cut their way across the timberlands as their part in building America, we cherish a little lore, especially the stories about Paul Bunyan. Some of the favorites included in this recording are "Paul's Cradle," "Paul and the Giant Mosquito," and "The Wonderful Ox."

SOONER HOUND AND FLYING-JIB; HOSS-MACKEREL AND BASSOON BOBBY (Phonodisc or Cassette). Caedmon Records, 1970. 1 cassette or disc, av. 50 fr. Disc #TC1325 ($6.98), Cassette #CDL51325 ($7.95). Gr. 4–6. BKL (1971), HOB, LBJ. 398.2

Contents: 1. The Sooner Hound and Flying-jib. 2. The Hoss-Mackerel and Bassoon Bobby.

Adrien Stoutenburg's tales include some favorites of the American settlers during the time when telling tall stories was a cherished tradition.

FONDA, PETER

NOT SO EASY (MOTORCYCLE SAFETY) (Motion Picture—16mm—Sound). *See* Motorcycles

FOOD SUPPLY

FOOD AND US (Filmstrip—Sound). Audio Visual Associates/BFA Educational Media, 1976. 4 color, sound filmstrips, 55–62 fr.; 4 discs or cassettes, 9:46–12:34 min.; Teacher's Guide. Discs #VJL000 ($68), Cassettes #VJM000 ($68). Gr. 4–7. PRV (4/78). 338.1

Contents: 1. Our Food Needs. 2. How We Use Food. 3. Getting Our Food. 4. The Problems of Food Supply.

The focus of this set is on eating a balanced diet to gain the most nutrition from the foods we eat. It also discusses where food comes from and how it is prepared for market. A variety of diets to provide the essential nutrients for a growing population is presented.

FOODS WE EAT (Filmstrip—Sound). Society for Visual Education, 1971. 6 color, sound filmstrips, 52–66 fr.; 3 discs or cassettes; 6 Guides. Cassettes #211-SATC ($78), Discs #211-SAR ($78). Gr. K–6. BKL (6/72), PRV (10/72). 338.1

FOOD SUPPLY (cont.)

Contents: 1. How We Get Bread. 2. How We Get Milk. 3. How We Get Meat. 4. How We Get Poultry and Eggs. 5. How We Get Fruit. 6. How We Get Vegetables.

This set helps students understand the basic economics of production, distribution, and consumption of food in the United States. Students learn where food comes from, who works to bring them food, and how it gets to their tables.

THE HUNGRY PLANT (Filmstrip—Sound). *See* Plants—Nutrition

THE PEOPLE PROBLEM: FEEDING THE WORLD FAMILY (Filmstrip—Sound). Associated Press/Pathscope Educational Media, 1977 (Let's Find Out). 1 color, sound filmstrip, 63 fr.; 1 disc or cassette, 7-1/2 min.; Spirit Masters; Teacher's Guide. Disc #9510 ($25), Cassette #9510C ($25). Gr. 4–8. PRV (4/78). 338.1

Designed to give overall insight into a problem affecting the entire world.

SOYBEANS—THE MAGIC BEANSTALK (Motion Picture—16mm—Sound). *See* Soybeans

FOOTBALL

CENTER FOR A FIELD GOAL (Film Loop—8mm—Silent). Athletic Institute (Football). 8mm color, silent film loop, approx. 4 min.; Guide. #I-7 ($22.95). Gr. 3–12. AUR (1978). 796.33

A single-concept loop demonstrating the basic technique.

CENTER SNAP FOR PUNT (Film Loop—8mm—Silent). Athletic Institute (Football). 8mm color, silent film loop, approx. 4 min.; Guide. #I-6 ($22.95). Gr. 3–12. AUR (1978). 796.33

A single-concept loop demonstrating the basic technique.

CENTER TO QUARTERBACK EXCHANGE (Film Loop—8mm—Silent). Athletic Institute (Football). 8mm color, silent film loop, approx. 4 min.; Guide. #I-5 ($22.95). Gr. 3–12. AUR (1978). 796.33

A single-concept loop demonstrating the basic technique.

FIELD GOAL AND EXTRA POINTS (Film Loop—8mm—Silent). Athletic Institute (Football). 8mm color, silent film loop, approx. 4 min.; Guide. #I-9 ($22.95). Gr. 3–12. AUR (1978). 796.33

A single-concept loop demonstrating the basic technique.

FIELD GOAL AND KICKOFF (SOCCER STYLE) (Film Loop—8mm—Silent). Athletic Institute (Football). 8mm color, silent film loop, approx. 4 min.; Guide. #I-15 ($22.95). Gr. 3–12. AUR (1978). 796.33

A single-concept loop demonstrating the basic technique.

HAND OFF (Film Loop—8mm—Silent). Athletic Institute (Football). 8mm color, silent film loop, approx. 4 min.; Guide. #I-2 ($22.95). Gr. 3–12. AUR (1978). 796.33

A single-concept loop demonstrating the basic technique.

KICKOFF AND ONSIDE KICK (Film Loop—8mm—Silent). Athletic Institute (Football). 8mm color, silent film loop, approx. 4 min.; Guide. #I-14 ($22.95). Gr. 3–12. AUR (1978). 796.33

A single-concept loop demonstrating the basic technique.

MIDDLE GUARD PLAY (Film Loop—8mm—Silent). Athletic Institute (Football). 8mm color, silent film loop, approx. 4 min.; Guide. I-10 ($22.95). Gr. 3–12. AUR (1978). 796.33

A single-concept loop demonstrating the basic technique.

OFFENSIVE BACKS (Film Loop—8mm—Silent). Athletic Institute (Football). 8mm color, silent film loop, approx. 4 min.; Guide. #I-1 ($22.95). Gr. 3–12. AUR (1978). 796.33

A single-concept loop demonstrating the basic technique.

OFFENSIVE LINE BLOCKING (Film Loop—8mm—Silent). Athletic Institute (Football). 8mm color, silent film loop, approx. 4 min.; Guide. #I-12 ($22.95). Gr. 3–12. AUR (1978). 796.33

A single-concept loop demonstrating the basic technique.

PASS PROTECTION (Film Loop—8mm—Silent). Athletic Institute (Football). 8mm color, silent film loop, approx. 4 min.; Guide. #I-13 ($22.95). Gr. 3–12. AUR (1978). 796.33

A single-concept loop demonstrating the basic technique.

PASSING SKILLS, PART 1 (Film Loop—8mm—Silent). Athletic Institute (Football). 8mm color, silent film loop, approx. 4 min.; Guide. #I-3 ($22.95). Gr. 3–12. AUR (1978). 796.33

A single-concept loop demonstrating the basic technique.

PASSING SKILLS, PART 2 (Film Loop—8mm—Silent). Athletic Institute (Football). 8mm color, silent film loop, approx. 4 min.; Guide. #I-4 ($22.95). Gr. 3–12. AUR (1978). 796.33

A single-concept loop demonstrating the basic technique.

PUNTING (Film Loop—8mm—Silent). Athletic Institute (Football). 8mm color, silent film loop, approx. 4 min.; Guide. #I-8 ($22.95). Gr. 3–12. AUR (1978). 796.33

A single-concept loop demonstrating the basic technique.

FORCE AND ENERGY

FIRST IDEAS ABOUT ENERGY (Filmstrip—Sound). BFA Educational Media, 1975. 4 color, sound filmstrips; 4 cassettes or discs. Cassettes #VFV000 ($70), Discs #VFU000 ($70). Gr. 1–4. BKL (1/15/76). 531

Contents: 1. What Makes Things Move? 2. What Are the Different Kinds of Energy? 3. Where Do We Get Energy? 4. How Do We Use Energy?

Introduces students to energy in all its forms. Viewers will learn about our most important source of energy—the sun. Viewers also will become aware of our need to conserve our present sources.

FORCES MAKE FORMS (Motion Picture—16mm—Sound). FilmFair Communications, 1974. 16mm color, sound film, 12-1/2 min. #D272 ($165). Gr. 3–8. BKL (1/15/75), CFF (1975), PRV (9/75). 531

Unusual and everyday objects and events encourage critical observation and logical association between forces in operation and their resultant forms.

FORECASTING

A TIME OF CHANGES UNIT THREE (Motion Picture—16mm—Sound). See Occupations

FOREST FIRES

FIRE! (Motion Picture—16mm—Sound). Film Polski/Encyclopaedia Britannica Educational, 1977. 16mm color, sound film, 9 min. #3562 ($145). Gr. K–A. NEF (1978). 634.9

Unusual animation technique (oil painting on glass slides) is combined with dramatic music to carry this nonnarrated film. The forest is at first alive with birds singing and animals playing. Suddenly the animals and birds leave and a raging fire approaches, destroying everything in its path. Then rain falls, the fire smolders and dies. Soon a single plant and bud emerge, and the life cycle begins anew.

FORESTS AND FORESTRY

AMAZON JUNGLE (Film Loop—8mm—Silent). Walt Disney Educational Media, 1966. 8mm color, silent film loop, approx. 4 min. #62-5315L ($30). Gr. 4–12. MDU (1974). 634.9

The Amazon jungle is surveyed in this motion picture. Views of impenetrable rain forest, rivers, uncharted streams, and extraordinary vegetation, as well as some of the animal life are presented.

AUTUMN IN THE FOREST (Filmstrip—Sound). See Autumn

THE GODS WERE TALL AND GREEN (Filmstrip—Sound). Lyceum/Mook & Blanchard, 1972. 2 color, sound filmstrips, 56 fr.; 2 cassettes or discs, 13-3/4 min. Cassettes #LY35272SC ($46), Discs #LY35272SR ($46). Gr. 6–A. BKL (9/15/72), IFT (1972), PVB (5/73). 574.981

Contents: 1. Trees: An Ancient Kinship. 2. The Kingdom of the Forest.

Ann Atwood takes us on a photographic art journey into nature. She crosses the latitudes of the tropics, the temperate zone, California's redwoods, and the Olympic Rain Forest, helping us to understand the ecology of the forest.

WINTER IN THE FOREST (Filmstrip—Sound). See Winter

FORM (ART)

BASIC SHAPES (Filmstrip—Sound). Clearvue, 1976. 6 color, sound filmstrips, av. 32–42 fr.; 6 cassettes or 3 discs, av. 5 min. Cassette #CL-580-C ($78.50), Disc #CL-580-R ($78.50). Gr. K–3. BKL (10/15/77). 701.8

Contents: 1. Falling Star and the Clever Clowns. 2. Sam Shape and the Clumsy Car. 3. Shapelessville "Shapes" Up. 4. The "Star" of the Triangle Trapeze. 5. Sam Shape Meets Magic Man. 6. The Circular Circus on Parade.

Repetition is the underlying technique utilized in this set on shapes. Highly imaginative stories on the various basic shapes are explored.

FOSSILS

FOSSILS (Filmstrip—Sound). Educational Dimensions Group, 1976. 2 color, sound filmstrips, 57–60 fr.; 2 cassettes, 15–17 min.; Teacher's Guide. #520 ($37). Gr. 4–9. PRV (11/76), PVB (1977). 560

A fossil is any trace of life that lived through ancient times. The fossil record begins roughly 600 million years ago. Tracing the 12 geological periods through the 3 eras, students see ice caps and oceans ebb and flow, plants and animals briefly appear and then disappear, remaining as fossils.

LIFE LONG AGO (Filmstrip—Sound). Society for Visual Education, 1976. 6 color, sound filmstrips, 42–46 fr.; 6 cassettes or discs, 7:35–8:35 min.; 1 Guide. Cassettes #A432-SATC ($99), Discs #432-SAR ($99). Gr. 3–6. BKL (3/1/77). 560

Contents: 1. Beginnings of Life on Earth. 2. From Out of the Sea. 3. When Dinosaurs Ruled the Earth. 4. From Earliest Mammals to First Humans. 5. Evolution and Change. 6. Hunters for the Past.

FOSSILS (cont.)

Many forms of life that once existed are presented, as well as how these living things altered over millions of years. Viewers examine the reasons for evolution and study the methods scientists used to uncover the past.

FOUJITA, ISUGOHARU

PICTURES ARE FUN TO LOOK AT (Art Prints). *See* Art Appreciation

FOXES—STORIES

THE TOMTEN AND THE FOX (Filmstrip—Sound). Weston Woods Studios, 1973. 1 color, sound filmstrip; 1 cassette. #SF66C ($12.75). Gr. K–3. RTE (1/74). Fic
This filmstrip is taken from the book by Astrid Lindgren, adapted from a poem by Karl-Erik Forsslund. It is the story of Reynard the fox, who is intercepted by Tomten (the troll), guardian of all life on the farm, as he creeps toward the hen house. After eating the porridge given him by Tomten, Reynard retreats to his den.

FRANCE

SEEING FRANCE (Filmstrip—Sound). Coronet Instructional Media, 1971. 6 color, sound filmstrips, av. 51 fr.; 6 cassettes or 3 discs, av. 13 min.; Teacher's Notes. Cassettes #M197 ($95), Discs #S197 ($95). Gr. 4–6. BKL (1972), PRV (1972), PVB (1972). 914.4
Contents: 1. Land and Resources. 2. Agriculture and Fishing. 3. Industry and Commerce. 4. History and Government. 5. Its People. 6. Its Culture.
This set highlights history, romantic culture, and the people of France.

FRANCE—STORIES

MADELINE AND THE GYPSIES AND OTHER STORIES (Phonodisc or Cassette). Caedmon Records. 1 cassette or disc, approx. 55 min. Disc #TC1304 ($6.98), Cassette #CDL51304 ($7.95). Gr. K–4. LBJ, SLJ. Fic
Contents: 1. The Castle Number Nine. 2. Madeline in London. 3. Quito Express. 4. Madeline and the Gypsies.
This recording contains several of Ludwig Bemelmans' delightful Madeline stories performed by Carol Channing. Also included is the charming story of Pedro, the little Ecuadorian boy who was lost and found, and his adventures in between.

FRANK, ANNE

THE DIARY OF ANNE FRANK (Filmstrip—Sound). *See* Biography

FRANKLIN, BENJAMIN

BENJAMIN FRANKLIN—SCIENTIST, STATESMAN, SCHOLAR AND SAGE (Motion Picture—16mm—Sound). Handel Film, 1970 (Americana Series #5). 16mm color, sound film, 30 min.; Film Guide. ($360). Gr. 4–A. FLN (1970), LFR (2/70). 921
Traces the life of Benjamin Franklin, including his career as printer, publisher, scientist, inventor, philosopher, and statesman; his work with the development of the Constitution and the postal system, and his role in the founding of the first subscription library and the first charity hospital in America.

FREEDOM OF THE PRESS

FREE PRESS: A NEED TO KNOW THE NEWS (Filmstrip—Sound). *See* Journalism

FREEMAN, DON

WILL'S QUILL (Filmstrip—Sound). *See* Geese—Fiction

FRENCH LANGUAGE—READING MATERIALS

A. J. MILLER'S WEST: THE PLAINS INDIAN—1837—SLIDE SET (Slides). *See* Indians of North America—Paintings

FRIENDSHIP

GETTING ALONG WITH OTHERS UNIT (Motion Picture—16mm—Sound). *See* Human Relations

FRIENDSHIP—FICTION

ANGEL AND BIG JOE (Motion Picture—16mm—Sound). *See* Values—Fiction

THE BRIDGE (Filmstrip—Sound/Captioned). *See* Human Relations—Fiction

FROG AND TOAD TOGETHER (Filmstrip—Sound). Miller-Brody Productions, 1976 (Newbery Award). 5 color, sound filmstrips, av. 37–59 fr. ea.; 5 cassettes or discs, av. 5–7 min. ea.; 5 Guides. Cassettes #NSF-3084-01C-05C ($80), Discs #NSF-3084-01-05 ($80). Gr. K–3. BKL (8/15/77). Fic
Contents: 1. A List. 2. The Garden. 3. Cookies. 4. Dragons and Giants. 5. The Dream.
Five stories about 2 inseparable friends.

THE GIVING TREE (Motion Picture—16mm—Sound). Bosustow Productions, 1973. 16mm color, sound, animated film, 10 min.; Leader's Guide. ($175). Gr. 2–A. CFF (1974), INS (6/7/73), NEF (1973). Fic

This is the story of a boy and a tree. The tree unselfishly offers everything it has for the boy's comfort. He never gives anything in return, but the tree is always happy to see him and happy to offer its resources. The boy grows and his life takes him away from his beloved tree, but old age brings him back again. They enjoy a peaceful and heartening reunion. Based on the book by Shel Silverstein, who does the narration.

PHILIP HALL LIKES ME: I RECKON MAYBE (Phonodisc or Cassette). Miller-Brody Productions, 1976. 1 cassette or disc, 58 min.; Notes. Disc #NAR-3085 ($6.95), Cassette #NAC-3085 ($7.95). Gr. 6–10. BKL (9/15/77). Fic
Narrated by Ruby Dee, this recording is an abridgement of the Newbery Honor Award book by the same name. The trials of growing up plus a test of friendship arising from competition at a country fair in Arkansas are related.

FRISBEES

FLAT FLIP FLIES STRAIGHT (Motion Picture–16mm–Sound). *See* Games

FRITH, MICHAEL

SIGHTS AND SOUNDS FILMSTRIPS, SET 2 (Filmstrip–Sound). *See* Reading–Study and Teaching

FROGS

THE LITTLE TADPOLE WHO GREW (Motion Picture–16mm–Sound). Coronet Films, 1976. 16mm color, sound film, 9:30 min.; Teacher's Guide. ($150). Gr. K–3. PRV (12/77). 597
A tadpole hides in an underwater soda can, which becomes a trap when he grows. With the help of a crayfish, he is rescued.

FROGS–FICTION

FROG AND TOAD TOGETHER (Filmstrip–Sound). *See* Friendship–Fiction

FRONTIER AND PIONEER LIFE

THE BLACKSMITH (Film Loop–8mm–Captioned). Coronet Instructional Media, 1971 (Pioneer Village in the 1830's). 8mm color, captioned film loop, approx. 4 min. #T4009 ($30). Gr. 4–6. PRV (1972). SLJ (1972). 973.5
This film loop shows the blacksmith at work in a pioneer village during the 1830s.

FARMING (Film Loop–8mm–Captioned). Coronet Instructional Media, 1972 (Pioneer Village in the 1830's). 8mm color, captioned film loop, approx. 4 min. #T4009

($30). Gr. 4–6. PRV (1972), SLJ (1972). 973.5
This film loop shows primitive farming methods used in a pioneer village in the 1830s.

HOME LIFE (Film Loop–8mm–Captioned). Coronet Instructional Media, 1971 (Pioneer Village in the 1830's). 8mm color, captioned film loop, approx. 4 min. #T4009 ($30). Gr. 4–6. PRV (1972), SLJ (1972). 973.5
Documents the struggles and triumphs of pioneer living with focus on home life.

PIONEER COMMUNITY (Filmstrip–Sound). Coronet Instructional Media, 1970. 6 color, sound filmstrips, av. 47 fr.; 6 cassettes or 3 discs, av. 12 min. Cassettes #M178 ($95), Discs #S178 ($95). Gr. 4–6. SLJ. 973.5
Contents: 1. Family Life. 2. Foods. 3. Crafts. 4. Schools and Recreation. 5. Work and Trade. 6. Farm Life.
The homes, tools, shops, and craftspeople of a pioneer village reveal the interdependence of family and neighbors.

PIONEER SKILLS–SLIDE SET (Slides). National Film Board of Canada/Donars Productions, 1974. 20 cardboard mounted, color slides in plastic storage pages. ($15). Gr. 4–9. BKL (2/15/75). 973
Illustrates skills and crafts of the nineteenth century, such as spinning, weaving, making butter, candles, cheese, and bread, splitting shingles, pit sawing, making ropes, and blacksmithing.

SCHOOL (Film Loop–8mm–Captioned). Coronet Instructional Media, 1971 (Pioneer Village in the 1830's). 8mm color, captioned film loop, approx. 4 min. #T4009 ($30). Gr. 4–6. PRV (1972). 973.5
Shows the early settlers of the 1830s as they receive their schooling.

SETTLERS OF NORTH AMERICA (Filmstrip–Sound). United Learning, 1973. 5 color, sound filmstrips, av. 49–59 fr. ea.; 5 cassettes, av. 12–15 min. ea.; Teacher's Guide. #16 ($75). Gr. K–8. PRV (3/75). 973
Contents: 1. Transportation. 2. Commerce. 3. Furniture and Household Goods. 4. The Making of a Farm. 5. Community Life.
Introduces students to pioneer life with a realistic reenactment of the daily routines, difficulties, and pleasures of pioneer living.

SOCIAL LIFE (Film Loop–8mm–Captioned). Coronet Instructional Media, 1971 (Pioneer Village in the 1830's). 8mm color, captioned film loop, approx. 4 min. #T4009 ($30). Gr. 4–6. PRV (1972), SLJ (1972). 973.5
This film loop shows the social life of the early settler in a pioneer village.

FRONTIER AND PIONEER LIFE (cont.)

WOOL INTO CLOTHING (Film Loop–
8mm–Captioned). Coronet Instructional
Media, 1971 (Pioneer Village in the 1830's).
8mm color, captioned film loop, approx. 4
min. #T4009 ($30). Gr. 4–6. PRV (1972),
SLJ (1972). 973.5

Shows sheep shearing and spinning of wool
during the frontier and pioneer periods.

FUEL

ENERGY: CRISIS AND RESOLUTION
(Filmstrip–Sound). *See* Power Resources

LEARNING ABOUT HEAT: SECOND EDI-
TION (Motion Picture–16mm–Sound).
See Heat

FUTAMATA, EIGORO

SERIES SEVEN: A LITTLE LOVIN' AND A
LITTLE LAUGHIN' (Filmstrip–Sound).
See Short Stories

FUTURE. *See* Forecasting

GAEDDERT, LOU ANN

NOISY NANCY NORRIS (Filmstrip–Sound).
See Children–Fiction

GAMES

FLAT FLIP FLIES STRAIGHT (Motion
Picture–16mm–Sound). Films, 1970.
16mm color, sound film, 4 min. #296-
0001 ($120). Gr. K–12. AIF (1971),
CGE (1971). 790

A boy and his amazingly dextrous dog play
frisbee on the seashore; a good language arts
film.

GANGS. *See* Juvenile Delinquency

GARDENING

PLANT A SEED (Motion Picture–16mm–
Sound). *See* Cities and Towns

GARN, DORIS

THE PONY ENGINE AND OTHER STORIES
FOR CHILDREN (Phonodisc or Cassette).
See Short Stories

GATES, DORIS

FIRST CHOICE AUTHORS AND BOOKS
(Filmstrip–Sound). *See* Authors

GEESE–FICTION

PETUNIA (Phonodisc or Cassette). Caedmon
Records, 1975. 1 cassette or disc, 53:54
min.; Jacket Notes. Disc #TC1489 ($6.98),

Cassette #CDL51489 ($7.95). Gr. K–3.
BKL (4/1/76). Fic

Contents: 1. Petunia. 2. Petunia and the
Song. 3. Petunia, I Love You. 4. Petunia's
Christmas. 5. Petunia's Treasure.

Roger Duvoisin's beloved books for young
children as read by Julie Harris. The story
of the goose called Petunia and all her barnyard friends shows the goose as silly, at
times haughty, and frequently making mistakes.

WILL'S QUILL (Filmstrip–Sound). Viking
Press, 1976. 1 color, sound filmstrips, 44
fr.; 1 cassette, 9:48 min.; 1 Guide. ($13.95).
Gr. K–5. BKL (2/1/77), LGB (12/77). Fic

This is the story of Willoughby Waddle, the
country goose, and his desire to see more of
Merrie Olde England and the world than his
farm pond. An adaptation of Don Free-
man's book of the same title.

GEISEL, THEODOR SEUSS. *See* Seuss, Doctor

**GEOGRAPHICAL DISTRIBUTION OF ANI-
MALS AND PLANTS**

FOUR BIOMES (Filmstrip–Sound). *See*
Ecology

GEOGRAPHY

GEOGRAPHY: CONCEPTS AND SKILLS
(Filmstrip–Sound). Guidance Associates,
1976. 4 color, sound filmstrips, av. 100 fr.;
4 cassettes or discs, av. 14 min.; 1 Guide for
each. Discs #9A-304-848 ($99.50), Cas-
settes #9A-304-855 ($99.50). Gr. 3–6.
BKL (3/15/77). 910

Contents: 1. Maps. 2. Shelter. 3. Land
Use. 4. Climate

Encourages students to discover through observations the facts and generalizations that
form the basis of geography.

ONE WORLD (Filmstrip–Sound). *See* Community Life, Comparative

WORLDVIEW UNIT ONE (Filmstrip–
Sound). Scholastic Book Services, 1976
(Worldview). 5 color, sound filmstrips,
approx. 69 fr. ea.; 5 phonodiscs or cassettes,
approx. 6-3/4 min. ea.; Teacher's Guide.
Cassette #561 ($69.50), Disc #560 ($69.50).
Gr. 2–4. BKL (2/1/77), INS (4/77), TEA
(4/77). 910

Contents: 1. Bread and Rice. 2. Hats and
Shoes. 3. Homes and Families. 4. Its Wet.
5. A Joy Forever.

Each filmstrip introduces one basic social
studies concept giving the student a global
perspective. Shot in 30 countries by photo-
journalist Ken Heyman, the filmstrips show
a concept in a variety of different communities among a variety of different people
around the world.

WORLDVIEW UNIT TWO (Filmstrip—Sound). Scholastic Book Services, 1976 (Worldview). 5 color, sound filmstrips, approx. 69 fr. ea.; 5 phonodiscs or cassettes, approx. 6-3/4 min. ea. Cassettes #579 ($69.50), Discs #578 ($69.50). Gr. 2–4. BKL (2/1/77), INS (4/77), TEA (4/77). 910

Contents: 1. Cities and Villages. 2. Tools and Machines. 3. From Place to Place. 4. Think about It. 5. Just for Fun.

Follows the same format as Unit One, but introduces different social studies concepts.

GEOLOGY

DISCOVERING ROCKS AND MINERALS (Filmstrip—Sound). Coronet Instructional Media, 1970. 4 color, sound filmstrips, av. 51 fr.; 4 cassettes or 2 discs, av. 13 min. Cassettes #M140 ($65), Discs #S140 ($65). Gr. 4–6. BKL. 552

Contents: 1. Kinds of Rocks. 2. Kinds of Minerals. 3. How We Identify Them. 4. Their Values to Us.

Photographs show the beauty of rocks and tell the stories of 3 rock classes: igneous, sedimentary, and metamorphic. Explanations of where and how they are formed, their locations, how to identify them, their value to plants and animals, and uses of metallic and nonmetallic minerals are provided.

DISCOVERING THE POWERS OF NATURE (Filmstrip—Sound). *See* Natural Disasters

THE EARTH (Filmstrip—Sound). Scholastic Book Services, 1977 (Adventures in Science). 4 color, sound filmstrips, av. 53–78 fr.; 4 cassettes or discs, av. 9–14 min. Discs #8625 ($69.50), Cassettes #8626 ($69.50). Gr. 4–8. BKL (12/15/77). 551.1

Contents: 1. Continental Drift. 2. Mountain Building. 3. Earthquakes and Tsunamis. 4. Volcanoes.

This set treats geology on the basis of theories, i.e., Charles Darwin's discovery of seashells in the Andes Mountains provides the basis for theories on the formation of mountains.

EARTH AND UNIVERSE SERIES, SET 1 (Filmstrip—Sound). University Films/ McGraw-Hill Films, 1972. 3 color, sound filmstrips, 76–84 fr.; 3 cassettes, 19–20 min.; Teacher's Guide. #102694-0 ($60). Gr. 4–9. PRV (11/76). 551

Contents: 1. How the Earth's Surface Is Worn Down. 2. How the Earth's Surface Is Built Up. 3. The Air around Us.

A comprehensive study with concepts simply presented. The effects of erosion, weather, wind, plant growth, and human activity are discussed. Properties of air, such as weight, volume, and wind movement, are also presented.

EARTH AND UNIVERSE SERIES, SET 2 (Filmstrip—Sound). University Films/

McGraw-Hill Films, 1976. 3 color, sound filmstrips, av. 76 fr.; 2 cassettes, av. 14:45– 18:22 min. #10269-3 ($54). Gr. 4–8. BKL (9/15/77). 551

Contents: 1. The Oceans. 2. The Water Cycle. 3. Water and Its Properties.

Clear photographs, diagrams, and maps offer a blend of earth science and social studies to demonstrate concepts that have contributed to our transportation, recreation, food production, and mineral extraction.

EARTH SCIENCE LOOPS SERIES, SET TWO (Film Loop—8mm—Silent). McGraw-Hill Films, 1970. 7 8mm color, silent film loops, av. 3–4 min. ea.; Teacher's Guide. #101739 ($154). Gr. 7–12. PRV (2/73). 551

Contents: 1. Crustal Evolution. 2. Ocean Base Topography. 3. Ocean Currents. 4. Sedimentation and Sedimentary Rocks. 5. Stream Action. 6. Thunderstorms. 7. Wind Erosion and Deposition.

Time-lapse photography and animation are used to explain fundamental concepts and illustrate natural processes in the areas of meteorology, oceanography, and geology.

THE EARTH'S RESOURCES (Filmstrip— Captioned). *See* Natural Resources

EXPLORING THE EARTH AROUND US (Filmstrip—Sound). National Geographic, 1977. 5 color, sound filmstrips, 41–47 fr.; 5 discs or cassettes, 11–14 min.; Teacher's Guide. Discs #03241 ($74.50), Cassettes #03242 ($74.50). Gr. 2–6. PRV (2/78), PVB (4/78). 551

Contents: 1. Mountains. 2. Plains. 3. Deserts. 4. Rivers. 5. Oceans.

Explores 5 distinct physical environments and how people use them. The powerful geological forces that have shaped the earth—water, waves, wind, glaciers, volcanic eruptions—are presented.

FOSSILS (Filmstrip—Sound). *See* Fossils

HOW OUR CONTINENT WAS MADE (Filmstrip—Sound). *See* North America

MONUMENTS TO EROSION (Motion Picture—16mm—Sound). *See* Erosion

OUR CHANGING EARTH (Filmstrip— Sound). Coronet Instructional Media, 1974. 6 color, sound filmstrips, av. 50 fr.; 3 discs or 6 cassettes, av. 12:30 min. Discs #S129 ($70), Cassettes #M129 ($78). Gr. 6–12. TEA (1975), PRV (11/15/75), PVB (4/74). 551.1

Contents: 1. How We Study It. 2. Water and Its Work. 3. Wind, Weathering and Wasting. 4. Pressure and Change beneath the Earth's Surface. 5. Thermal Activity and Igneous Formations. 6. Man and His Geological Environment.

A thorough and comprehensive overview of

GEOLOGY (cont.)

the earth; photography and diagrams clearly define many complicated concepts.

ROCKS AND MINERALS (Filmstrip— Sound). Imperial Educational Resources, 1974. 4 color, sound filmstrips; 4 cassettes. #3KG41000 ($62). Gr. 4–8. INS (10/74), STE (10/74). 552

Contents: 1. Igneous Rocks. 2. Sedimentary Rocks. 3. Metamorphic Rocks. 4. Minerals.

An introduction to basic concepts about rocks and minerals. Shows the actual location on the North American continent where various kinds of rocks are located and makes clear their relationship to specific geological formations.

GEOMETRY

BASIC GEOMETRIC SHAPES (Filmstrip— Sound). January Productions, 1977 (Perceptual Development). 4 color, sound filmstrips, av. 50 fr. ea.; 4 cassettes, av. 5–6 min. ea.; Teacher's Guide. Set ($58), One Strip ($14.95). Gr. K–2. BKL (6/1/77), PRV (9/77). 152.1

Contents: 1. Circle. 2. Square. 3. Triangle. 4. Rectangle.

Children form mathematical concepts by observing and reacting to objects in their environment.

INTRODUCING GEOMETRY (Filmstrip— Sound). BFA Educational Media, 1973. 4 color, sound filmstrips; 4 cassettes or discs. Cassettes #VZ2000 ($62), Discs #VZ1000 ($62). Gr. 3–6. BKL (7/1/74). 516

Contents: 1. Thinking about Curves. 2. Planes, the Line Segments, and Points. 3. A Shadow Game. 4. Wheels and Circles.

This series of filmstrips helps create an understanding of some basic concepts of geometry.

MAGIC RECTANGLE (Motion Picture— 16mm—Sound). *See* Arithmetic

GEORGE, JEAN CRAIGHEAD

JEAN CRAIGHEAD GEORGE (Filmstrip— Sound). *See* Authors

JULIE OF THE WOLVES (Phonodisc or Cassette). *See* Eskimos—Fiction

GERGELY, TIBOR

SIGHTS AND SOUNDS FILMSTRIPS, SET 1 (Filmstrip—Sound). *See* Reading— Study and Teaching

GHANA

A WORLD NEARBY: GHANA (Filmstrip— Sound/Captioned). Guidance Associates,

1976 (Cross-Cultural Studies). 2 color, sound and 1 captioned filmstrips, av. 51– 85 fr.; 2 cassettes, av. 12 min.; 1 Guide. Cassettes #300-374 ($51.50), Discs #300- 366 ($51.50). Gr. 4–7. BKL (2/15/77). 916.67

Contents: 1. Introduction—Overview. 2. Living in the Culture. 3. Pictures to Talk About.

Explores the social tradition, economy, language, climate, and geography of other cultures.

GHOST STORIES

SCARY TALES (Filmstrip—Captioned). Leonard Peck Productions, 1976. 4 captioned filmstrips, av. 49–55 fr.; 4 Guides. ($32.95). Gr. 2–8. BKL (10/15/77). Fic

Contents: 1. The Haunted Piano. 2. Nightmare Highway. 3. Maldor, the Mad Magician. 4. The Phantom Express.

Appealing plots, descriptive visuals, and simple texts motivate and entertain reluctant readers.

STORIES OF GHOSTS AND MONSTERS (Filmstrip—Sound). *See* Reading Materials

GIANTS—FICTION

THE GREAT QUILLOW (Phonodisc or Cassette). Caedmon Records, 1972. 1 cassette or disc, 41 min.; Jacket Notes. Disc #TC1411 ($6.98), Cassette #CDL51411 ($7.95). Gr. 3–A. BKL (5/1/73), LBJ, STE (1973). Fic

James Thurber's tale of the creative toymaker who drives a giant out of his mind and out of town is related by Peter Ustinov. A modern fable set in the ageless time of folk tales.

GIFTS—FICTION

THE GIFT (Motion Picture—16mm—Sound). Barr Films, 1976. 16mm color, sound films, 11 min. #B207 ($180). Gr. 1–5. BKL (4/1/77). Fic

A dramatization portraying childhood feelings and family relationships. Carol's sister helps her with her desire to give a "larger" gift to her mother than the present from her brother—and it can only cost 75 cents.

GINSBURG, MIRRA

THRESHOLD FILMSTRIPS, SERIES C (Kit). *See* Children's Literature—Collections

GIRAFFES

GIRAFFE (Motion Picture—16mm—Sound). EBEC, 1971 (Silent Safari). 16mm color, sound nonnarrated film, 10 min.; Teacher's

Guide. #3124 ($150). Gr. K–9. BKL
(10/1/76). 599.7

The giraffe, the tallest mammal, is shown at
home in Tanzania. Close-ups examine its
unusual shape and size; the markings that
camouflage it in bush country; independent
family units follow simple daily patterns for
foraging, carrying tick birds, and drinking.

GIRLS

THERE'S A NEW YOU COMIN' FOR GIRLS
(Filmstrip–Sound). Marshfilm, 1974 (The
Human Growth). 1 color, sound filmstrip,
50 fr.; 1 cassette or disc, 15 min.; Teacher's
Guide. #1117 ($21). Gr. 5–7. ESL (1976),
PRV (12/74), PVB (5/75). 613

Tailored to the special needs of the growing
girl, including a basic study of female
anatomy and functions.

GIRLS–FICTION

GIRL STUFF (Kit). EMC 1973. 4 paperback
books; 4 read-along cassettes; Teacher's
Guide. #ELC-216000 ($55). Gr. 4–10.
INS (1/74), STE (11/73). Fic

Contents: 1. Stand Off. 2. Break In. 3.
Stray. 4. Hot Shot.

Difficult situations are dealt with in an
entertaining and resourceful way. Designed
to improve reluctant readers' abilities, comprehension, and vocabulary skills.

REALLY ME (Kit). EMC, 1974. 4 cassettes,
av. 30 min.; 4 paperback books; 1 Teacher's
Guide. ($53.10). Gr. 6–8. BKL (6/75),
CPR (2/77), SLJ (4/75). Fic

Contents: 1. Will the Real Jeannie Murphy
Please Stand Up. 2. Checkmate Julie. 3.
Everyone's Watching Tammy. 4. A Candle,
a Feather, a Wooden Spoon.

High interest, low vocabulary stories about
teenage problems of growing up.

GLIDING AND SOARING

HANG GLIDING: RIDING THE WIND (Kit).
Troll Associates, 1976 (Troll Reading
Program). 1 cassette; 10 soft cover books;
1 library edition; 4 Duplicating Masters;
1 Teacher's Guide. ($48). Gr. 4–9. BKL
(2/15/77). 797.5

The filmstrip visuals are the pictures in the
book, and the cassette is a word-for-word
reading of the text. The kit provides information about the sport of hang gliding.

GLOBES

HOW TO USE MAPS AND GLOBES (Filmstrip–Sound). *See* Maps

GOATS

DAIRY GOATS (Film Loop–8mm–Silent).
Thorne Films/Prentice-Hall Media, 1972

(Barnyard Animals). 8mm color, silent film
loop, approx. 4 min. #HAT 433 ($26).
Gr. 1–6. EYR (10/73), INS (12/72), TEA
(11/72). 636.39

Nubian and Saanen goats grazing together in
an open pasture are observed. Also included
are scenes of the adults butting, eating, and
digging in comparison with the young goats'
behavior.

GODDARD, ROBERT

TRAILBLAZERS OF INVENTION (Filmstrip
–Sound). *See* Inventors

GOLD RUSH. *See* Dogs–Fiction

THE GOLDEN TOUCH

MASTERY STORY TELLER, SET ONE
(Filmstrip–Sound). *See* Literature–
Collections

GOOD MORNING TEACHER

BUON GIORNO: GOOD MORNING
TEACHER (Filmstrip–Sound). *See* Italy–
Social Life and Customs

GORILLAS

THE MOUNTAIN GORILLA (Kit). Classroom Complements/EBEC, 1976 (Animal
Life Stories). 1 color, sound filmstrip;
1 cassette; 5 identical storybooks; Teacher's
Guide. #6963K ($27.95). Gr. K–6. TEA
(11/77). 599.88

Young readers can learn how gorillas live,
move, build homes, and fight for food and
survival. A scientifically accurate story
describes the life of animals in their natural
habitat. A storybook reproduces all the
narration and art from the filmstrip.

GOVERNMENT, COMPARATIVE. *See*
Comparative Government

GRAHAM, MARGARET BLOY

HARRY THE DIRTY DOG (Filmstrip–
Sound). *See* Dogs–Fiction

GRAHAME, KENNETH

THE RELUCTANT DRAGON (Phonodisc or
Cassette). *See* Dragons–Fiction

THE WIND IN THE WILLOWS (Phonodisc or
Cassette). *See* Animals–Fiction

GRAMATKY, HARDIE

LITTLE TOOT STORIES (Phonodisc or
Cassette). *See* Tugboats–Fiction

GRANDPARENTS–FICTION

GRANDMOTHER LUCY IN HER GARDEN
(Filmstrip–Sound/Captioned). Listening
Library, 1976 (Look, Listen and Read).
1 color, sound/captioned filmstrip, 51 fr.;
1 cassette, 11 min.; Teacher's Guide. JFS
#152 ($14.95). Gr. K–3. PRV (9/77). Fic
A young girl experiences the joys of spring
under the guidance of her sympathetic
grandmother. Illustrations and narration
taken verbatim from the book.

A PAIR OF RED CLOGS (Filmstrip–Sound/
Captioned). *See* Japan–Fiction

GRAPHIC METHODS

INTRODUCING GRAPHS (Filmstrip–
Sound). BFA Educational Media, 1975.
4 color, sound filmstrips, 60 fr.; 4 discs or
cassettes. Discs #VFD000 ($70), Cassettes
#VFE000 ($70). Gr. 4–6. PRV (4/76).
001.422
Contents: 1. Why Graphs? 2. Bar and
Pictographs. 3. Single Bar and Circle
Graphs. 4. Coordinate System.
Each kind of graph helps us organize information in an easy-to-read way. This set
shows how to select the graph style that is
best for displaying the information collected, how to construct each kind of graph,
and how to interpret information presented
in graphs.

GRASSLANDS

GRASSLAND ECOLOGY–HABITATS AND
CHANGE (Motion Picture–16mm–Sound).
Centron Films, 1970. 16mm color, sound
film, 13 min.; Leader's Guide. ($205).
Gr. 2–8. BKL (12/1/71), CGE (1971),
STE (10/71). 574.5
Taking a historical approach to the ecology
of the American prairies, unique wildlife
photography shows how bison, prairie dogs,
etc., affect our nation's grasslands. Examines the human role in changing the prairies
through agriculture, construction, and use
of chemicals.

GRAY, GENEVIEVE

GIRL STUFF (Kit). *See* Girls–Fiction

GREECE

SEEING GREECE: ANCIENT AND
MODERN (Filmstrip–Sound). Coronet
Instructional Media, 1973. 4 color, sound
filmstrips, av. 56 fr.; 4 cassettes or 2 discs,
av. 11 min. Cassettes #M265 ($65), Discs
#S265 ($65). Gr. 4–6. BKL (9/15/74),
LNG (12/74), M&M (1974). 914.95
Contents: 1. A Rocky Peninsula. 2. A Seafaring Nation. 3. Village Life. 4. Athens
and Its Heritage.

Photographs and maps capture the mood of
seafaring Greece. How geography has
affected its way of life, its history as a
farming nation, and its commerce for over
3,400 years is explored.

GREENE, BETTE

PHILIP HALL LIKES ME: I RECKON
MAYBE (Phonodisc or Cassette). *See*
Friendship–Fiction

GREENE, GRAHAM

POPULAR PICTURE BOOKS FILMSTRIPS:
SET THREE (Filmstrip–Sound). *See*
Reading Materials

GREENE, NATHANAEL

FAMOUS PATRIOTS OF THE AMERICAN
REVOLUTION (Filmstrip–Sound). *See*
U.S.–History–Biography

GRIFALCONI, ANN

THE TOY TRUMPET (Kit). *See* Toys–
Fiction

GRIMES, TAMMY

PRINCE RABBIT AND OTHER STORIES
(Phonodiscs). *See* Fairy Tales

GRIMM, JAKOB

FAIRY TALES OF THE BROTHERS
GRIMM (Kit). *See* Fairy Tales

HANSEL AND GRETEL AND OTHER
FAIRY TALES BY THE BROTHERS
GRIMM (Phonodisc or Cassette). *See*
Fairy Tales

LIBRARY 5 (Cassette). *See* Literature–
Collections

SNOW WHITE AND OTHER FAIRY
TALES (Phonodisc or Cassette). *See*
Fairy Tales

GROFE, FERDE

AMERICAN SCENES (Phonodiscs). *See*
Orchestral Music

GROOMING, PERSONAL

PERSON POWER (Filmstrip–Sound). Marshfilm, 1977 (Mental Health/Hygiene). 1
color, sound filmstrip, approx. 56 fr.; 1
cassette or disc, approx. 9-1/2 min. #1133
($21). Gr. 5–9. PRV (2/78), PVB (4/78).
646.7
The filmstrip includes the basics of good
grooming and reasons why personal hygiene
is not only pleasant but necessary.

GROWTH

ANIMALS AND HOW THEY GROW
(Filmstrip—Sound). *See* Animals

HOW WE GROW (Filmstrip—Sound). *See*
Child Development

GROWTH (PLANTS)

ANGIOSPERMS: THE LIFE CYCLE OF A
STRAWBERRY (Film Loop—8mm—
Captioned). BFA Educational Media,
1973 (Plant Behavior). 8mm color,
captioned film loop, approx. 4 min.
#481425 ($30). Gr. K–9. BKL (5/1/76).
581.3
Demonstrates experiments, phenomena,
and behavior in plants.

GUINNESS WORLD RECORDS

READING QUIZZES FROM GUINNESS
WORLD RECORDS (Filmstrip—Sound/
Captioned). *See* Curiosities and Wonders

GUMPERTZ, BOB

POPULAR PICTURE BOOKS FILMSTRIPS:
SET THREE (Filmstrip—Sound). *See*
Reading Materials

GURNEY, ERIC

BEGINNER BOOKS FILMSTRIPS, SET 3
(Filmstrip—Sound). *See* Reading—Study
and Teaching

GURNEY, NANCY

BEGINNER BOOKS FILMSTRIPS, SET 3
(Filmstrip—Sound). *See* Reading—Study
and Teaching

GWILLIM, SARAH JANE

THROUGH THE LOOKING GLASS
(Phonodiscs). *See* Fantasy—Fiction

HAIKU

HAIKU: THE HIDDEN GLIMMERING
(Filmstrip—Sound). Lyceum/Mook &
Blanchard, 1973. 1 color, sound filmstrip,
60 fr.; 1 cassette or disc, 14-1/2 min.;
Teacher's Guide. Cassettes #LY35173C
($25), Discs #LY35173R ($19.50). Gr.
5–A. BKL (6/1/73), NEA (1973), PVB
(5/74). 895.61
Ann Atwood, author/photographer, explores the lives of 3 Japanese poets—Basho,
Issa, and Buson—and discovers their world
views and values. Helps to develop an
appreciation for Haiku and Eastern cultures.

HAIKU: THE MOOD OF EARTH (Filmstrip
—Sound). Lyceum/Mook & Blanchard,
1971. 2 color, sound filmstrips, 55 fr.;
2 cassettes or discs, 14 min. Cassettes
#LY35371SC ($46), Discs #LY35371SR
($37). Gr. 6–12. EGT (12/73), M&M
(2/74), NEF (1972). 895.61
Contents: 1. The Heart of Haiku. 2. Haiku:
A Photographic Interpretation.
Through this series, Ann Atwood conveys
the concept or sense of Haiku with thought-
ful consideration of its Japanese origin.
Helps to understand, appreciate, and compose Haiku poetry. Also available with the
book.

HALE, LUCRETIA P.

THE PETERKIN PAPERS (Phonodisc or Cassette). *See* Family Life—Fiction

HALEY, GAIL E.

A STORY A STORY (Filmstrip—Sound). *See*
Folklore—Africa

HAMILTON, VIRGINIA

VIRGINIA HAMILTON (Filmstrip—Sound).
Miller-Brody Productions, 1976 (Meet the
Newbery Author). 1 color, sound filmstrip,
101 fr.; 1 disc or cassette, 15 min. Disc
#MNA-1007 ($32), Cassette #MNA-1007C
($32). Gr. 5–12. BKL (12/1/76). 921
Many relationships between the author and
her works, as well as biographical information, notes on her family life, her writing
habits, and her feelings about her occupa-
tion, are related in a conversational tone by
the voice-over narrator and by Hamilton
herself. Excerpts from Miller Brody's sound
filmstrip production of *M. C. Higgins, the
Great* are used in the early portion of this
filmstrip, as are old snaphots selected from
the author's family album. The majority
of the visuals consist of photos taken of
Hamilton with her husband and her
children.

HANDICAPPED CHILDREN

WHAT IS A HANDICAP? (Filmstrip—
Sound). BFA Educational Media, 1975.
4 color, sound filmstrips; 4 cassettes or
discs; 24 Duplicating Masters. Cassettes
#E12000 ($76.50), Discs #E11000
($76.50). Gr. 4–6. BKL (2/1/76). 362.7
Contents: 1. Mark. 2. Rosa. 3. Cindy.
4. Tony.
Gives viewers the opportunity to know 4
young people who are handicapped. The
filmstrips show these characters in everyday
situations and clearly explain the handicaps
and feelings to the viewers. The filmstrips
are open-ended.

HANDICAPPED–RECREATION

A MATTER OF INCONVENIENCE (Motion Picture–16mm–Sound). Stanfield House, 1974. 16mm color, sound film, 10 min. ($170). Gr. 5–A. BKL (11/15/74). 796.019

This film illustrates how amputee skiers negotiate the slopes using specially designed poles and how blind skiers judge distances and place turns by trusting the familiar voices of their instructors. In some on-screen interviews, some disabled skiers explain they "don't feel handicapped, just inconvenienced."

HANDICRAFT

AT YOUR FINGERTIPS (Filmstrip–Sound). ACI Media/Paramount Communications, 1973. 6 color, sound filmstrips; 6 cassettes, av. 8 min. ea. Teacher's Guide. #91026 ($98). Gr. K–6. BKL (6/74), EYR (11/76). 745.592

Contents: 1. Boxes. 2. Cylinders. 3. Floats. 4. Grasses. 5. Play Clay. 6. Sugar and Spice.

Found objects are imaginatively transformed into toys, ornaments, and free-form art objects.

EDIBLE ART (Filmstrip–Sound). *See* Cookery

FREE TO BE . . . YOU AND ME (Kit). *See* Individuality

THE HOLIDAY MAKE-IT-YOURSELF KIT (Filmstrip–Sound). *See* Holiday Decoration

JUNK ECOLOGY (Filmstrip–Sound). Troll Associates, 1975. 6 color, sound filmstrips, av. 50 fr. ea.; 3 cassettes av. 10 min. ea.; Teacher's Guide. ($78). Gr. 3–8. PRV (4/76), TEA (2/76). 745.5

Contents: 1. Recycling Paper and Cardboard/Wood and Sticks. 2. Recycling Plastic Throw-Aways. 3. Tin Cans and Bottle Caps. 4. Recycling Jars and Bottles. 5. Fix Up, Clean Up. 6. Special Crafts.

Gets students involved in crafts and ecology by showing how different types of discarded junk materials can be collected and turned into interesting and useful things.

PIONEER SKILLS–SLIDE SET (Slides). *See* Frontier and Pioneer Life

REDISCOVERY: ART MEDIA SERIES, SET 1 (Filmstrip–Sound). ACI Media/ Paramount Communications, 1974. 4 color, sound filmstrips, 37–59 fr.; 4 cassettes, 8 min. ea.; Teacher's Guide. #9561 ($78). Gr. 4–12. BKL (6/74). 745.5

Contents: 1. Leather. 2. Macrame. 3. Stitchery. 4. Weaving.

Demonstrates the creation of utilitarian and aesthetically pleasing objects.

REDISCOVERY: ART MEDIA SERIES, SET 2 (Filmstrip–Sound). ACI Media/ Paramount Communications, 1974.4 color, sound filmstrips, 57–74 fr.; 4 cassettes, 8 min.; Teacher's Guide. #9562 ($78). Gr. 4–A. BKL (6/15/74), PRV (1/75). 745.5

Contents: 1. Collage. 2. Crayon. 3. Posters. 4. Prints.

This set offers 4 techniques using very basic material–paper.

REDISCOVERY: ART MEDIA SERIES, SET 3 (Filmstrip–Sound). ACI Media/ Paramount Communications, 1974. 4 color, sound filmstrips; 4 cassettes, 8 min. ea.; Teacher's Guide. #9563 ($78). Gr. 4–12. BKL (6/15/74). 745.5

Contents: 1. Clay. 2. Paper Construction. 3. Paper Mache. 4. Puppets.

Places emphasis on the processes themselves in these 4 art media. Basic tools, raw materials, and the simple techniques are cited.

REDISCOVERY: ART MEDIA SERIES, SET 4 (Filmstrip–Sound). ACI Media/ Paramount Communications, 1974. 4 color, sound filmstrips, av. 44 fr.; 4 cassettes, 8 min. ea.; Teacher's Guide. #9564 ($78). Gr. 4–12. BKL (6/15/74), PRV (5/75). 745.5

Contents: 1. Batik. 2. Enameling. 3. Silkscreen. 4. Watercolor.

Brief overviews include techniques and show completed works.

HAPPINESS–FICTION

THE HAPPY OWLS (Motion Picture–16mm– Sound). Weston Woods Studios, 1969. 16mm color, sound, animated film, 8 min. ($150). Gr. K–3. BKL (9/15/73). Fic

Adapted from the book *The Happy Owls*, written and illustrated by Celestino Piatti, this beautiful and wise legend uses a special animation technique that retains the vibrant color of the pictures. In an old stone ruin live 2 owls who are happy all the year. One day, the quarreling barnyard fowl send a peacock to ask the reason for the owls' happiness. The owls explain that observing the change of seasons makes them rejoice and gives them peace. The fowl, not ready for such wisdom, only turn their backs and go on squabbling.

HARTILIUS, MARGARET A.

POPULAR PICTURE BOOKS FILMSTRIPS: SET THREE (Filmstrip–Sound). *See* Reading Materials

HARVEY, PHYLLIS

SQUARE PEGS–ROUND HOLES (Motion Picture–16mm–Sound). *See* Individuality

HAWAII

FIRE IN THE SEA (Motion Picture—16mm—Sound). *See* Volcanoes

HAWAII: THE FIFTIETH STATE (Filmstrip—Sound). EBEC, 1974. 4 color, sound filmstrips, av. 87 fr. ea.; 4 discs or cassettes, 16 min. ea. Discs #6493 ($66.50), Cassettes #6493K ($66.50). Gr. 5-A. PRV (4/76), PVB (5/75). 919.69

Contents: 1. Hawaii's Origins: Its First People. 2. Hawaii's History: From Kingdom to Statehood. 3. Hawaii's Economy: Growth and the Future. 4. Hawaii's People: Islands of Contrasts.

Ancient songs and legends, firsthand accounts, drawings, and artifacts help to re-create the story of our fiftieth state. The series identifies the customs and traditions of Hawaii's first society, then traces the transformation from agricultural kingdom to modern industrial state. Visits to 3 Hawaiian families representing a rich cultural mix of backgrounds and life-styles are revealing.

HAWTHORNE, NATHANIEL

KING MIDAS AND THE GOLDEN TOUCH (Cassette). *See* Mythology, Classical

MASTERY STORY TELLER, SET ONE (Filmstrip—Sound). *See* Literature—Collections

HAYWARD, LINDA

SIGHTS AND SOUNDS FILMSTRIPS, SET 3 (Filmstrip—Sound). *See* Reading—Study and Teaching

HAZELTON, ELIZABETH BALDWIN

SAMMY THE CROW (Filmstrip—Sound). *See* Crows

HEALING PROCESS (BIOLOGY)

YOUR INVISIBLE ARMY (Filmstrip—Sound). *See* Accidents

HEALTH. *See* Hygiene

HEALTH EDUCATION

FEELING FINE (Filmstrip—Sound). January Productions, 1975. 5 color, filmstrips, av. 45 fr. ea.; 5 cassettes, av. 6 min. ea.; Teacher's Guide. Set ($72.50), Each strip with Cassette and Guide ($14.95). Gr. K-3. PVB (1976). 372.37

Contents: 1. From Head to Toe, Our Bodies Go. 2. From Magic to Medicine. 3. Foods to Grow By. 4. A Clean Sweep. 5. How Happiness Became Me.

Using cartoons, these filmstrips introduce basic good health practices.

GOOD HEALTH AND YOU, PART TWO (Filmstrip—Sound). Clearvue/Nystrom, 1975. 4 color, sound filmstrips, 65-90 fr.; 2 discs or cassettes, 9:48-12 min. Cassettes #CL575-C ($52), Discs #CL575-R ($52). Gr. 1-4. BKL (7/15/76), ESL (1977), PRV (4/76). 372.7

Contents: 1. Exercise and Health. 2. Cleanliness and Health. 3. Happiness and Health. 4. Diet and Health.

This set takes youngsters on 8 exciting adventures where good nutrition, exercise, cleanliness, and attitude come to the rescue of unhealthy children. Humorous stories told with the use of cartoon characters.

HEALTH EDUCATION (Filmstrip—Sound). *See* Hygiene

A HEALTHY YOU (Filmstrip—Sound). *See* Hygiene

HEARING

HEAR BETTER: HEALTHY EARS (Motion Picture—16mm—Sound). *See* Ear

HEAT

LEARNING ABOUT HEAT: SECOND EDITION (Motion Picture—16mm—Sound). EBEC, 1974 (Introduction to Physical Science). 16mm color, sound film, 15 min. #3365 ($220). Gr. 4-9. LFR (4/75), PRV (4/19/76). 536

Any understanding of the energy crisis presupposes an understanding of the nature of heat as the basic energy force. Through laboratory demonstrations interwoven with animated episodes, this film discusses the molecular basis of heat, friction, changes of state in gases, solids, and liquids, and the movement of heat through radiation, convection, and conduction.

HEFTER, RICHARD

NOSES AND TOES, PART ONE AND TWO (Filmstrip—Sound). *See* Comparisons

HEILBRONER, JOAN

BEGINNER BOOKS FILMSTRIPS, SET 4 (Filmstrip—Sound). *See* Reading—Study and Teaching

HENRY, JOHN

THE LEGEND OF JOHN HENRY (Motion Picture—16mm—Sound). *See* Folklore—U.S.

HENRY, MARGUERITE

FIRST CHOICE AUTHORS AND BOOKS (Filmstrip—Sound). *See* Authors

HENRY, O.

MASTERY STORY TELLER, SET ONE
(Filmstrip—Sound). *See* Literature—Collections

HENRY, PATRICK

FAMOUS PATRIOTS OF THE AMERICAN
REVOLUTION (Filmstrip—Sound). *See*
U.S.—History—Biography

HERCULES

FAMOUS STORIES OF GREAT COURAGE
(Filmstrip—Sound). *See* Heroes and Heroines

HEROES AND HEROINES

FAMOUS STORIES OF GREAT COURAGE
(Filmstrip—Sound). United Learning, 1974.
6 color, sound filmstrips, av. 55–77 fr. ea.;
6 cassettes, av. 11–16 min. ea.; Teacher's
Guide. #37 ($85). Gr. 3–6. BKL (9/15/
75), PRV (3/76). 920
Contents: 1. Adventuresome Marco Polo. 2.
Good King Arthur. 3. Commanding Joan of
Arc. 4. Magnificent Cetewayo. 5. Super
Jesus. 6. Noble Hercules.
Dramatizations of 6 extraordinary historical
characters re-create episodes when individual
courage changed the course of history.

HEROIC ADVENTURES (Filmstrip—Sound).
See Legends

HIPPOPOTAMUS—FICTION

THE SECRET HIDING PLACE (Filmstrip—
Sound or Captioned). Listening Library,
1976 (Look, Listen and Read). 1 color captioned filmstrip, av. 46 fr.; 1 cassette tape,
8-1/2 min.; Teacher's Guide. #JFS154
($14.95). Gr. K–3. LNG (12/77), PRV
(4/77), PVB (4/78). Fic
This ALA Notable Children's Book is a captivating animal story about a young hippo
who learns to live with the restrictions of a
protective adult world.

HISPANIC—BIOGRAPHY

HISPANIC HEROES OF THE U.S.A. (Kit).
See Biography—Collections

HISTORICAL FICTION

READING FOR THE FUN OF IT—HISTORI-
CAL FICTION (Filmstrip—Sound). *See*
Literature—Study and Teaching

HOBAN, LILLIAN

SERIES SEVEN: A LITTLE LOVIN' AND A
LITTLE LAUGHIN' (Filmstrip—Sound).
See Short Stories

THRESHOLD FILMSTRIPS, SERIES C (Kit).
See Children's Literature—Collections

HOBAN, RUSSELL

FRANCES (Phonodisc or Cassette). *See* Badgers—Fiction

HOCKEY. *See* Ice Hockey

HOGROGIAN, NONNY

THRESHOLD FILMSTRIPS, SERIES C (Kit).
See Children's Literature—Collections

HOLIDAY DECORATION

THE HOLIDAY MAKE-IT-YOURSELF KIT
(Filmstrip—Sound). ACI Media, 1975. 4
color sound filmstrips, 4 cassettes, av. 8–10.
min. ea.; Teacher's Guide #9109 ($78). Gr.
3–6. ARA (10/76), BKL (6/76), PRV (11/
76). 394.2
Contents: 1. Halloween and Harvest. 2.
Christmas and Hanukah. 3. Valentine's Day;
Washington's Birthday; Lincoln's Birthday.
4. Easter and Spring.
Demonstrates how to make decorations,
costumes, masks, and greeting cards from
available materials for major holiday times
of the year.

HOLIDAYS

FALL BRINGS CHANGES, SECOND EDI-
TION (Motion Picture—16mm—Sound).
See Autumn

THE FOUR SEASONS (Filmstrip—Sound).
See Seasons

HOLIDAYS: HISTORIES AND LEGENDS
(Filmstrip—Sound). EBEC, 1976. 6 color,
sound filmstrips, av. 59 fr. ea.; 6 discs or
cassettes, 7 min. ea.; Teacher's Guide. Discs
#6943 ($86.95), Cassettes #6943K
($86.95). Gr. K–6. CHH (9/77), MDU
(4/77). 394.2
Contents: 1. New Year's Day. 2. St. Valentine's Day. 3. St. Patrick's Day. 4. Mother's
Day and Father's Day. 5. Halloween. 6.
Christmas.
These filmstrips tell the fascinating histories
behind popular holidays, and in doing so,
reveal insights about human needs and values.

HOLIDAYS: SET ONE (Filmstrip—Sound).
Random House, 1977. 4 color, sound film-
strips, 66–80 fr.; 4 cassettes or discs, 9–12
min.; Teacher's Guide. Discs #05072 ($72),
Cassettes #05073 ($72). Gr. K–8. LGB
(1977), PRV (2/78). 394.2
Contents: 1. Halloween. 2. Christmas/
Hanukka. 3. Easter/Passover. 4. Indepen-
dence Day.
The origins, history, and practices of major

holidays are presented in a mixture of original and archival photography and appropriate music and effects.

PATRIOTIC HOLIDAYS (Filmstrip—Sound). EBEC, 1975. 6 color, sound filmstrips, av. 56 fr.; 6 discs or cassettes, av. 8 min. ea. Discs #6912 ($86.95), Cassettes #6912K ($86.95). Gr. 3–6. MFC (2/4/77), PRV (12/76), TEA (5/6/76). 394.2

Contents: 1. Labor Day. 2. Columbus Day. 3. Thanksgiving Day. 4. Washington's Birthday. 5. Memorial Day. 6. Independence Day.

These filmstrips deal not only with the "when" of our national holidays, but also with the "why" and "how" we celebrate them. A historical and contemporary perspective shows how each is observed in different sections of the country.

HOLIDAYS—FICTION

HOLIDAY TALES CASSETTE BOOKS (Kit). Society for Visual Education, 1977. 4 cassettes, av. 15 min. ea.; 40 paperbacks (4 titles); Teacher's Guide. #BC-2800-SS ($64). Gr. 2–4. BKL (12/15/77). 394.2

Contents: 1. Winnie the Witch and the Frightened Ghost. 2. The Elves and the Shoemaker. 3. The Easter Basket Mystery. 4. The Mystery of the Missing Valentines.

Holiday stories are well narrated in these read-a-long cassette-books. Illustrations are black and white, but bright and cheerful, and help move the plots along. The musical background and tone to turn the pages are well balanced and paced.

HOLIDAYS—SONGS

HOLIDAY RHYTHMS (Phonodiscs). See Rhythms

HOLIDAY SONGS (Phonodiscs). See Songs

HOLL, ADELAIDE

SIGHTS AND SOUNDS FILMSTRIPS, SET 4 (Filmstrip—Sound). See Reading—Study and Teaching

HOMER

HEROES OF THE ILIAD (Cassette). See Mythology, Classical

HOMER, WINSLOW

PICTURES ARE FUN TO LOOK AT (Art Prints). See Art Appreciation

HONG KONG

A WORLD NEARBY: HONG KONG (Filmstrip—Sound/Captioned). Guidance Associates, 1976 (Cross-Cultural Studies). 2 color, sound and 1 captioned filmstrip, av. 58–88 fr.; 2 cassettes, 14–16 min.; 1 Guide. Cassettes #300-432 ($51.50), Discs #300-424 ($51.50). Gr. 4–7. BKL (2/15/75). 915.125

Contents: 1. Introduction—Overview. 2. Living in the Culture. 3. Pictures to Talk About.

Explores the social tradition, economy, language, climate, and geography of other cultures.

HOPI

HOPIS—GUARDIANS OF THE LAND (Motion Picture—16mm—Sound). Filmfair Communications, 1971. 16mm color, sound film, 9-3/4 min. ($135). Gr. 4–10. LFR (12/71), PRV (11/73). 970.3

This film explores the traditional Hopi way of life and the threat that hangs over them. The Hopi philosophy of unity with the land and the way their land is being threatened are presented.

HORROR—FICTION

TEN TALES OF MYSTERY AND TERROR (Cassette). See Literature—Collections

HORSES

BIRTH OF A COLT (Film Loop—8mm—Silent). Thorne Films/Prentice-Hall Media, 1972. 8mm color, silent film loop, approx. 4 min. #HAT430 ($26). Gr. 1–6. EYR (10/73), INS (12/72), TEA (11/72). 636.1

The stallion and the mare are observed prior to the birth. The mare is then seen lying down in her stall giving birth; 3 hours later the colt is seen struggling to its feet and standing. The following morning, the colt and the mare are viewed walking outdoors.

HORSES . . . TO CARE IS TO LOVE (Motion Picture—16mm—Sound). AIMS Instructional Media Service, 1976. 16mm color, sound film, 12 min. #9447 ($190). Gr. 4–10. BKL (2/15/77). 636.1

This film shows that owning a horse places continuing demands on the owner to care for it. It provides valuable detail on housing, hygiene, grooming, and feeding. How to purchase a horse is covered as well as the tremendous cost of owning one.

HORSES—FICTION

BLACK BEAUTY (Filmstrip—Sound). Teaching Resources Films/Educational Enrichment Materials, 1976. 2 color, sound filmstrips, av. 69–77 fr.; 2 cassettes or 2 33-1/3 rpm discs, av. 35 min. ea.; 1 paperback book; Teacher's Guide. #51008 ($40). Gr. 3–7. PRV (12/76). Fic

HORSES—FICTION (cont.)

Contents: 1. Part One 2. Part Two

An adaptation of the novel by Anna Sewell telling about the life of the horse, Black Beauty.

SADDLE UP! (Kit). EMC, 1975. 4 paperback books; 4 read-along cassettes; Teacher's Guide. #ELC127000 ($55). Gr. 4–9. BKL (5/76), SLJ (3/76). Fic

Contents: 1. A Better Bit and Bridle. 2. A Chance to Win. 3. Trailering Troubles. 4. Open the Gate.

These 4 books revolve around young teenage girls who meet the difficulties and demands of horses and learn some hard truths about themselves as well. The illustrations help relate the world of horses, their care and competition.

THE SUPERLATIVE HORSE (Motion Picture—16mm—Sound). *See* Folklore—China

TEN TALES OF MYSTERY AND TERROR (Cassette). *See* Literature—Collections

TWO FOR ADVENTURE (Kit). *See* Animals—Fiction

HORTICULTURE

DEBBIE GREENTHUMB (Filmstrip—Sound). Filmstrip House, 1973. 4 color, sound filmstrips, 49–73 fr.; 2 discs or cassettes, 12 min.; Teacher's Guide. ($40). Gr. 4–8. BKL (3/15/74). 635

Contents: 2. Plants, Plants Everywhere. 2. Where Plants Come From. 3. How Plants Grow. 4. Plants in Your Life.

A cross-country trip with Debbie and her greenhouse-operator mother helps show where plants live as Debbie's mother explains how climate, soil, and rainfall influence vegetation. Plant propagation, the use of light, heat, and water in relation to plant growth and the association of foods, clothing, and building materials with plant origins round out the set.

HOSPITALS

THE HOSPITAL (Motion Picture—16mm—Sound). *See* Medical Care

HOUSES—FICTION

THE LITTLE HOUSE (Filmstrip—Sound). Weston Woods Studios, 1973. 1 color, sound filmstrip, 55 fr.; 1 cassette, 13 min. #SF142C ($12.75). Gr. K-3. PRV (12/73). Fic

Based on Virginia Lee Burton's book by the same name, this story is important in showing changes in a neighborhood and in telling what happens as cities grow larger and swallow up more and more fields and orchards.

HOW THE WHALE GOT HIS THROAT

MASTERY STORY TELLER, SET ONE (Filmstrip—Sound). *See* Literature—Collections

HOWELL, RUTH

A CRACK IN THE PAVEMENT (Motion Picture—16mm—Sound). *See* Natural History

HUMAN BEHAVIOR

BEING GOOD—BEING BAD (Filmstrip—Sound). Educational Direction/Learning Tree Filmstrips, 1976. 4 color, sound filmstrips, av. 50 fr. ea.; 4 cassettes, av. 8 min. ea.; Teacher's Guide. LT677 ($66). Gr. 2–4. BKL (10/15/77), PRV (9/77), TEA (4/77). 158.2

Contents: 1. Hey, You're Good at That. 2. It's Not Bad to Be Mad. 3. The "Who" They Think Is You. 4. It Could Be Them, Not You!

The major focal point of this set is the child's self-concept. It has 2 purposes: first, to explain to children that the things they see as being bad and that cause them guilt are common to most people; and, second, that doing, saying, or feeling bad things does not mean that you are bad.

BEING KIND (Filmstrip—Sound). Educational Direction/Learning Tree Filmstrips, 1976. 4 color, sound filmstrips, av. 45 fr. ea.; 4 cassettes, av. 9 min. ea.; Teacher's Guide. ($58). Gr. K-3. PRV (10/77). 158.2

Contents: 1. Are You the Right "Kind?" 2. The Realm of the Rotten. 3. The Kingdom of the "Kind." 4. What If You Were Another "Kind?"

Students will begin to think about the concept of kindness as they observe the character of Kate, who has several experiences with both kind and unkind behavior.

DIVIDED MAN, COMMITMENT OR COMPROMISE (Motion Picture—16mm—Sound). *See* Decision Making

LIVING TOGETHER AS AMERICANS (Filmstrip—Sound). *See* Human Relations

PROJECT AWARE (Motion Picture—16mm—Sound). *See* Juvenile Delinquency

UNDERSTANDING YOUR FEELINGS (Filmstrip—Sound). *See* Emotions

WHAT DO YOU DO WHILE YOU WAIT? (Motion Picture—16mm—Sound). Encyclopaedia Britannica Educational, 1973. 16mm color, sound film, 11 min. #3201 ($150). Gr. K-6. LFR (12/73), PRV (3/75). 158.1

This film uses live-action photography to illustrate a variety of familiar situations in which children have to wait, and the restless, bored, or angry feelings they may experience. The end of the film suggests imaginative ways a child can entertain him- or herself in waiting situations. Songs and sound effects enhance the lively narration in which children describe what is happening and how they feel about it.

WHAT DO YOU THINK? (Filmstrip—Sound). *See* Ethics

WINNING AND LOSING (Filmstrip—Sound). Troll Associates, 1976. 4 color, sound filmstrips, av. 48 fr. ea.; 4 cassettes, av. 6 min. ea.; Teacher's Guide. ($56). Gr. 3–6. PRV (9/77). 175

Contents: 1. Any Number Can Play. 2. Why We Compete. 3. Winners and Losers. 4. It's Only a Game.

This set of filmstrips helps children put competition into perspective. They also learn an important secret of good sportsmanship—how to win and lose gracefully.

HUMAN BEHAVIOR—FICTION

DOROTHY AND THE NECKLACE (Motion Picture—16mm—Sound). *See* Parrots—Fiction

DOROTHY AND THE PARROT (Motion Picture—16mm—Sound). *See* Parrots—Fiction

DOROTHY AND THE POP-SINGER (Motion Picture—16mm—Sound). *See* Parrots—Fiction

DOROTHY AND THE WITCH (Motion Picture—16mm—Sound). *See* Parrots—Fiction

HUMAN ECOLOGY

ENVIRONMENTAL STUDIES SERIES (Filmstrip—Sound). *See* Pollution

ON POPULATION (Filmstrip—Sound). *See* Population

PLANT A SEED (Motion Picture—16mm—Sound). *See* Cities and Towns

HUMAN RELATIONS

DEALING WITH FEELINGS (Filmstrip—Sound). BFA Educational Media, 1977. 4 color, sound filmstrips, av. 59–74 fr.; 4 cassettes or discs, av. 5:25–8 min. Cassettes #VHG000 ($70), Discs #VHF000 ($70). Gr. K–3. PRV (2/78). 158.2

Contents: 1. How Do You Feel? 2. People Are Not for Hitting. 3. Let's Not Laugh at People. 4. Mistakes Can Help Us Grow.

Designed to create awareness of different emotions and provide moral guidelines for handling negative ones.

FREE TO BE. . .YOU AND ME (Kit). *See* Individuality

GETTING ALONG WITH OTHERS UNIT (Motion Picture—16mm—Sound). Sutherland Learning Associates/EBEC, 1972 (Most Important Person). 7 16mm color, sound films. Also Avail. 8mm films; 1 record; 7 Posters; 2 Song Cards; Teacher's Guide. #6736 ($403.20). Gr. K–3. BKL (7/1/74), CHT (9/10/74), CPR (1/76). 155.5

Contents: 1. Growing Up. 2. Doing Something Nice. 3. Thinking of Others. 4. What Is a Friend? 5. What Do You Mean? 6. Living Things Are All around Us. 7. Share It with Someone.

Cooperation, understanding, and thoughtfulness are qualities included in this study of interpersonal relationships.

HOW DO YOU KNOW WHAT'S FAIR? (Filmstrip—Sound). *See* Values

IDENTITY THREE (Kit). *See* Child Development

IS IT ALWAYS RIGHT TO BE RIGHT? (Motion Picture—16mm—Sound). Bosustow Productions, 1970 (Parables for the Present). 16mm color, sound, animated film, 8 min.; Teacher's Guide. ($150). Gr. 6–A. AFF (1971), BKL (6/1/71), NEF (1971). 158.2

This fast-moving parable interlaces live action and animation to describe a land where everyone "is always right." The resulting conflict and lack of communication lead to total cessation of activity. Finally, someone has the courage to admit "I may be wrong," to which an opposing person answers "No, you may be right." Discussion resumes, and the film ends on a note of hope and challenge. Narrated by Orson Welles.

KINDLE THREE, GETTING ALONG (Filmstrip—Sound). Insight Media Programs/Scholastic Book Services, 1973 (Kindle). 5 color, sound filmstrips, av. 59–73 fr. ea.; 5 7 in. LP discs or cassettes, 5–6 min. ea.; Teacher's Guide. Disc #6981 ($69.50), Cassette #6993 ($69.50). Gr. K–2. BKL (10/1/73), LNG (5/73), PRV (5/74). 301.45

Contents: 1. It's Mine. 2. Sticks 'n Stones. 3. Will You Be My Friend? 4. Smiles Don't Just Happen. 5. I Don't Care, Anyhow!

Introduces children to the concept of relationships and why they are important to us.

LEARNING ABOUT OTHERS (Filmstrip—Sound). ACI Media/Paramount Communications, 1975. 4 color, sound filmstrips; 4 cassettes; Teacher's Guide. #9112 ($78). Gr. 2–5. PRV (9/76). 158.2

Contents: 1. People Close to Me. 2. Boys and Girls. 3. It's a Big Country. 4. In the Whole, Wide World.

This filmstrip set helps children empathize

HUMAN RELATIONS (cont.)

with others whose behavior may differ from their own. Although each person has feelings and reactions that are unique, people are enough alike so that we can get along with one another.

LIVING TOGETHER AS AMERICANS (Filmstrip—Sound). Eye Gate Media, 1976. 6 color, sound filmstrips; 3 cassettes. #TH748 ($74.70). Gr. 4–9. MDU (4/76). 301.45

Contents: 1. Our Minorities—Just Who Is An American? 2. Indians. 3. Asian Americans. 4. Mexican Americans. 5. Blacks. 6. Middle Eastern Cultures.

The theme of this set is that a real American is a person who has learned to live together with his or her fellow Americans, respecting their customs and traditions.

PEOPLE NEED PEOPLE (Filmstrip—Sound). Educational Direction/Learning Tree Filmstrips, 1976. 4 color, sound filmstrips, av. 46 fr. ea.; 4 cassettes, av. 8 min. ea.; Teacher's Guide. ($58). Gr. 1–4. BKL (7/1/77), PRV (11/77). 301.45

Contents: 1. Our Friends. 2. Grown-Ups We Know. 3. Others We Need. 4. Growing Up.

Shows the basic dependent and interdependent relationships between people.

PEOPLE OF THE FOREST: A STUDY IN HUMAN VALUES (Kit). *See* Culture

SUMMER CAMP (Motion Picture—16mm—Sound). *See* Camping

THEY (Motion Picture—16mm—Sound). Centron Films, 1972 (Trilogy). 16mm color, sound film, 16 min.; Leader's Guide. ($250). Gr. 2–A. CFF, STE (2/74). 301.45

Through symbolism, the film examines the human society in microcosm. A young boy meets the "we" people and the "they" people. When he crosses the river to meet the "they" people, he raises questions about human relationships, which makes this film outstanding for class discussion and individual contemplation.

YOU (Motion Picture—16mm—Sound). Centron Films, 1973 (Trilogy). 16mm color, sound film, 16-1/2 min.; Leader's Guide. ($260). Gr. 2–5. BKL (12/1/73), LFR (5/74), STE (2/74). 301.45

Introducing children to the concept of empathy in human relations, this film witnesses a typical sibling argument and tells how the brothers learn to explore each other's feelings and viewpoints.

HUMAN RELATIONS—FICTION

ANGEL AND BIG JOE (Motion Picture—16mm—Sound). *See* Values—Fiction

THE BRIDGE (Filmstrip—Sound/Captioned). Listening Library, 1976 (Look, Listen and Read). 1 color, sound/captioned filmstrip, 48 fr.; 1 cassette, 11-1/2 min.; Teacher's Guide. #JFS153 ($14.95). Gr. K–3. PRV (10/77). Fic

Children make the best diplomats in this story of 2 young boys who try to bridge the gaps of mistrust and misunderstanding between their elders. Illustrations and narration are taken verbatim from the book.

HUMMINGBIRDS

CHUPAROSAS: THE HUMMINGBIRD TWINS (Filmstrip—Sound). Lyceum/Mook & Blanchard. 1 color, sound filmstrip, 42 fr.; 1 cassette or disc, 9-1/4 min. Cassette #LY351070C ($25), Disc #LY351070R ($19.50). Gr. K–12. BKL (1/1/72), FLN (12/71). 598.8

The life cycle of hummingbirds, smallest of the vertebrates, are presented. Hummingbird twins are photographed in a desert habitat, from egg to first flight.

HUMOROUS STORIES. *See* Wit and Humor

HUMPERDINCK, ENGELBERT

STORIES IN BALLET AND OPERA (Phonodiscs). *See* Music—Analysis, Appreciation

HUNT, IRENE

ACROSS FIVE APRILS (Filmstrip—Sound). *See* U.S.—History—1861–1865—Civil War—Fiction

HUTCHINS, PAT

CLOCKS AND MORE CLOCKS (Filmstrip—Sound). *See* Clocks—Fiction

ROSIE'S WALK (Motion Picture—16mm—Sound). *See* Animals—Fiction

THE SURPRISE PARTY (Filmstrip—Sound). *See* Animals—Fiction

HYGIENE

THE ADVENTURES OF SUPERNUT, SET ONE (Filmstrip—Sound). Knowledge Aid/United Learning, 1976. 6 color, sound filmstrips, av. 44–56 fr. ea.; 6 cassettes, av. 6–8 min. ea.; Poster; Teacher's Guide. #4210 ($85). Gr. 1–4. PRV (11/77). 613

Contents: 1. The Story of the Beginning: The Search for Good Health. 2. The Sugar Slugs: Proper Tooth Care. 3. The Protein Planet: Body Building Blocks. 4. Oil and Water: Not Too Much, Not Too Little. 5. The Planet Lie Around: Exercise and Rest. 6. The Secret of Good Health: Balance of Diet, Exercise, Rest, and Cleanliness.

Creative stories combined with original music score and cartoon characters will help children establish good health habits. Children will be intrigued with Supernut's encounters with the Big Cracker.

ALL ABOUT LICE (Filmstrip–Sound). *See* Lice

THE CLEAN MACHINE (Filmstrip–Sound). Marshfilm, 1977 (Mental Health/Hygiene). 1 color, sound filmstrip, approx. 55 fr.; 1 disc or cassette, approx. 9 min. ($21). Gr. K–2. PRV (2/78), PVB (4/78). 372.37

A tale of how the clean machine works its transformation on a dirty little boy in this colorful cartoon-pictured filmstrip. Introduces hygiene at the K–2 level.

FEELING FINE (Filmstrip–Sound). *See* Health Education

GOOD HEALTH AND YOU, PART TWO (Filmstrip–Sound). *See* Health Education

HABITS OF HEALTH: THE PHYSICAL EXAMINATION (Motion Picture–16mm– Sound). BFA Educational Media, 1975. 16mm color, sound film, 10 min.; Teacher's Guide. #11624 ($140). Gr. 1–6. PRV (11/76). 613

Acquaints children with doctors and the reason for a physical examination. Reference to immunization and a simple explanation of injections are discussed.

HEALTH: A NEW LOOK (Filmstrip– Sound). United Learning, 1973. 4 color, sound filmstrips, av. 38–45 fr. ea.; 4 cassettes, av. 5–8 min. ea.; Guide. #21 ($60). Gr. 1–4. PRV (4/75). 613

Contents: 1. Exercise–A New Look. 2. Teeth–A New Look. 3. Cleanliness–A New Look. 4. Nutrition–A New Look.

Good factual health care is introduced as children are photographed enjoying exciting adventures that provide the opportunity for young children to follow the rules of good health.

HEALTH AND YOUR BODY UNIT (Motion Picture–16mm–Sound). Sutherland Learning Associates/EBEC, 1972 (Most Important Person). 6 16mm color, sound films. Also avail. 8mm films; 1 record; 6 Posters; Teacher's Guide. #6738 ($345.60). Gr. K–3. BKL (7/1/74), CHT (9/10/74), CPR (1/76). 613

Contents: 1. Take Care of Your Teeth! 2. The Voice Box. 3. Where Does Food Go? 4. Tell Us How You Feel! 5. When You Get Hurt. 6. Visiting the Doctor.

This unit encourages children to be more aware of body functions and to maintain good health.

HEALTH EDUCATION (Filmstrip–Sound). BFA Educational Media, 1970. 4 color,

sound filmstrips; 4 cassettes or discs. Cassettes #VDH000 ($70), Discs #V89000 ($70). Gr. K–3. BKL (7/15/70). 372.37

Contents: 1. Dear Little Mumps Child. 2. Michael Gets the Measles. 3. Peter Gets the Chicken Pox. 4. Karen Gets a Fever.

Based on the series of books with the same titles written by Dr. Margaret Rush Lerner, these stories provide a good understanding of the causes and effects of these illnesses as well as helping relieve children's anxiety.

A HEALTHY YOU (Filmstrip–Sound). Educational Direction/Learning Tree Filmstrips, 1976. 6 color, sound filmstrips, av. 47 fr. ea.; 3 cassettes, av. 10 min. ea.; Teacher's Guide. ($78). Gr. K–3. LGB (1976), PRV (11/76). 613

Contents: 1. Your Amazing Body. 2. How Your Body Works. 3. Good Food–Good Health. 4. How to Be Healthy. 5. Others Who Help Keep You Healthy. 6. Staying Healthy.

This set is designed to create a better understanding of the human body, which will lead to the development of a greater respect for the body and an ongoing desire to stay healthy.

THERE'S A NEW YOU COMIN' FOR GIRLS (Filmstrip–Sound). *See* Girls

YOU AND ME AND OUR WORLD (Slides/ Cassettes). *See* Science

I AM SPECIAL

SONGSTORIES: I AM SPECIAL (Filmstrip– Sound). *See* Self

ICE HOCKEY

HOCKEY HEROES (Kit). *See* Athletes

IGLOOS

HOW TO BUILD AN IGLOO–SLIDE SET (Slides). National Film Board of Canada/ Donars Productions, 1971. 10 cardboard mounted, color slides in plastic storage page; Notes in English and Spanish. ($10). Gr. 4–A. PRV (12/74), PVB (5/75). 970.3

With only a saw and a knife in his possession, an Eskimo can build an igloo in less than half an hour. This slide set and the accompanying guide show you how this can be done with relative ease.

ILLUSTRATION OF BOOKS

LITERATURE FOR CHILDREN, SERIES 3 (Filmstrip–Sound). *See* Literature–Study and Teaching

IMAGINATION

ADVENTURES IN IMAGINATION SERIES (Filmstrip—Sound). *See* English Language—Composition and Exercises

A BOY CREATES (Motion Picture—16mm—Sound). *See* Sculpture

IF TREES CAN FLY (Motion Picture—16mm—Sound). Phoenix Films, 1976. 16mm color, sound film, 12 min. #0175 ($180). Gr. 5–A. BKL (4/1/77). 153.3
Scenes of seagulls, eagles, and other birds fill this production's visuals with a sense of freedom. An introspective, poetic film that captures both children's and adults' attention.

LISTEN! (Motion Picture—16mm—Sound). *See* Music—Analysis, Appreciation

OPEN BOX: IDEAS FOR CREATIVE EXPRESSION (Kit). *See* English Language—Composition and Exercises

IMAGINATION—FICTION

DAYDREAMS AND MAKE BELIEVE (Filmstrip—Sound). *See* Fantasy—Fiction

MAURICE SENDAK'S REALLY ROSIE STARRING THE NUTSHELL KIDS (Motion Picture—16mm—Sound). Weston Woods Studios, 1975. 16mm, color, animated, sound film, 26 min. ($365). Gr. K–3. AFF (1977), CGE (1976), HOB (6/77). Fic
Rosie challenges all to believe that she's a star from afar, terrific at everything, an absolutely fascinating personality. She is determined to prove that make-believe, played to the hilt, is not just a pastime but a life-style, and she sweeps the neighborhood Nutshell Kids into the beam of her private spotlight.

PRIVATE ZOO (Filmstrip—Sound). *See* Shades and Shadows—Fiction

SAM, BANGS, AND MOONSHINE (Motion Picture—16mm—Sound). BFA Educational Media, 1976. 16mm color, sound film, 15 min. #11713 ($220). Gr. K–6. BKL (5/15/77). Fic
An adaptation of Evaline Ness's picture book that won the 1967 Caldecott Medal. The story of a fisherman's daughter who learns the difference between reality and her own daydreams.

IMMIGRATION AND EMIGRATION

IMMIGRATION AND MIGRATION (Motion Picture—16mm—Sound). *See* U.S.—History

IMMORTALITY

LIVING WITH DYING (Filmstrip—Sound). *See* Death

INDIA

INDIA: TRADITION AND CHANGE (Filmstrip—Sound). Society for Visual Education, 1977. 5 color, sound filmstrips, av. 79 fr. ea.; 5 cassettes or 33-1/3 rpm discs, av. 13-1/2 min.; ea. Teacher's Guide. Cassette #A387-SATC ($85), Discs #A387-SAR ($85). Gr. 5–9. BKL (1/1/78). 915.4
Contents: 1. India's Land. 2. India's People. 3. Patterns of Family Life. 4. Village Life. 5. City Life.
While presenting much basic information on India's geography and culture, the filmstrips highlight some of the key problems and challenges facing the nation's people and provide a balanced perspective on India's cultural heritage and development goals.

PEOPLE OF INDIA (Filmstrip—Sound). Educational Dimensions Group, 1976. 2 color, sound filmstrips, av. 40 fr.; 2 cassettes, av. 8 min.; 1 Guide. #815 ($33). Gr. 1–3. BKL (3/15/77). 915.4
Describes and explains the sights of India for primary grade viewers. A bare outline of the social structure, religion, and history is provided.

SOUTH ASIA: REGION IN TRANSITION (Filmstrip—Sound). *See* Asia

SOUTH ASIA: THE INDIAN SUBCONTINENT (Filmstrip—Sound). EBEC, 1976. 5 color, sound filmstrips, av. 81 fr. ea.; 5 discs or cassettes, av. 9 min. ea.; Teacher's Guide. Discs #6923 ($72.50), Cassettes #6923K ($72.50). Gr. 5–12. ESL (1977), PRV (12/77). 915.4
Contents: 1. The Physical Base. 2. The Economic Base. 3. Religions and Cultures. 4. The Villages. 5. The Cities.
Presents a pictorial investigation of India and the small countries surrounding it. Although characterized by great diversity of culture, language, and religious tradition, these 6 basically agricultural economies share the common burdens of overpopulation, inadequate food supply, and lack of capital.

INDIA—FICTION

THE CAT THAT WALKED BY HIMSELF AND OTHER JUST SO STORIES (Phonodisc or Cassette). *See* Animals—Fiction

KIM (Phonodisc or Cassette). Caedmon Records, 1976. 1 disc 12 in. or 1 cassette, 60 min. Disc #TC1480 ($6.98), Cassette #CDL51480 ($7.95). Gr. 6–8. BKL (12/15/77). Fic
Excerpts are from the first, third, and fourth chapters of Kipling's tale in which Kim, an English boy who is brought up as a native of colonial India, meets the Lama with whom he will travel over the Indian countryside. Anthony Quale's reading of

this masterpiece gives it color, power, and life.

MOWGLI AND THE WOLVES (Cassette). *See* Animals—Fiction

RED DOG BY RUDYARD KIPLING (Phonodisc or Cassette). *See* Animals—Fiction

RIKKI TIKKI TAVI (Cassette). *See* Mongooses—Fiction

RIKKI TIKKI TAVI AND WEE WILLIE WINKIE (Phonodisc or Cassette). *See* Animals—Fiction

THE WORLD OF JUST SO STORIES, SET ONE (Kit). *See* Animals—Fiction

INDIANS

CIVILIZATIONS OF EARLY AMERICA (Filmstrip—Sound). Coronet Instructional Media, 1971. 6 color, sound filmstrips, av. 51 fr.; 6 cassettes or 3 discs, av. 13 min. Cassettes #M180 ($95), Discs #S180 ($95). Gr. 4-6. BKL (1972), ESL (1972), SLJ. 970.1

Contents: 1. The Olmecs. 2. Teotihuacan to Toltec. 3. The Mayas. 4. The Aztecs. 5. Chavin to Inca. 6. The Incas.

Photographic studies of standing ruins, archeological digs, and artifacts depict the history and life of middle and South American Indian civilization before the Spanish Conquistadores.

INDIANS OF CENTRAL AMERICA

CIVILIZATIONS OF EARLY AMERICA (Filmstrip—Sound). *See* Indians

CULTURE AND ENVIRONMENT: LIVING IN THE TROPICS (Filmstrip—Sound). *See* Tropics

INDIANS OF NORTH AMERICA

ADOBE OVEN BUILDING (Film Loop—8mm—Silent). Thorne Films/Prentice-Hall Media, 1972 (Southwest Indians). 8mm color, silent film loop, approx. 4 min. #HAT290 ($28). Gr. 4-A. AUR (1978). 970.1

Indians of the Southwest are shown building an adobe oven.

AMERICAN INDIANS OF THE NORTH PACIFIC COAST (Filmstrip—Sound). Coronet Instructional Media, 1971. 6 color, sound filmstrips, av. 51 fr.; 6 cassettes or 3 discs, av. 12 min. Cassettes #M194 ($95), Discs #S194 ($95). Gr. 4-8. PRV (3/73), PVB (5/73), SLJ (1973). 970.1

Contents: 1. Lands and Tribes. 2. How They Lived. 3. Arts and Crafts. 4. Myths and Ceremonies. 5. How They Changed. 6. Their Life Today.

Indians' dependence on land and nature

and their culture were disrupted by the white settlers. Modern photographs, as well as rare historic photographs from the Oregon Historical Society, add depth to this history lesson.

AMERICAN INDIANS OF THE NORTH-EAST (Filmstrip—Sound). Coro..et Instructional Media, 1971. 6 color, sound filmstrips, av. 48 fr.; 6 cassettes or discs, av. 11-1/2 min. Cassettes #M214 ($95), Disc #S214 ($95). Gr. 4-8. BKL (12/15/76), INS. 970.1

Contents: 1. Who They Are. 2. Their History. 3. How They Lived. 4. Their Religions. 5. Their Handicrafts. 6. Their Life Today.

These filmstrips study the rise and fall of the Algonquin and Iroquois Indian empires, migrants from Asia to the northeastern United States and southern Canada. Their life today in a modern society is explained through photography, original artwork, and period drawings. The set traces ancient history, culture, and Indian reliance on nature and religious ceremonies.

AMERICAN INDIANS OF THE SOUTH-EAST (Filmstrip—Sound). Coronet Instructional Media, 1972. 6 color, sound filmstrips, 43–51 fr.; 6 cassettes or 3 discs, 10–16 min. Cassettes #M233 ($95), Discs #S233 ($95). Gr. 4-6. BKL (4/15/73), ESL (1973), PRV (1973). 970.1

Contents: 1. Who They Are. 2. Their History. 3. How They Lived. 4. Their Handicrafts. 5. Their Religions. 6. Their Life Today.

A Cherokee Indian explains Cherokee history and life today. Historical photographs, artifacts, drawings, and maps reveal the life of the Southeastern Indian tribes from prehistoric times to the present.

AROUND INDIAN CAMPFIRES (Cassette). Troll Associates, 1972. 10 cassette tapes, av. 10 min. ea. ($55). Gr. 3-6. BKL (7/15/74), PRV. 970.1

Contents: 1. Indian Homes. 2. Indian Tools. 3. Indian Hunting. 4. Indian Farming. 5. Indian Customs. 6. Indian Weapons. 7. Indian Music. 8. Indian Legends. 9. Indian Family Life. 10. Indian Celebrations.

Describes everyday life, customs, and traditions that are part of the Indian heritage.

AS LONG AS THE GRASS IS GREEN (Motion Picture—16mm—Sound). Atlantis Productions, 1973. 16mm color, sound film, 11 min.; Teacher's Guide. ($165). Gr. K-5. CFF (1973), CGE (1973). 970.1

A nonnarrative film of a summer experience shared by 4 North American Indian children; shows their relationship with a fawn, which illustrates the Indian's love for and closeness to his or her environment.

INDIANS OF NORTH AMERICA (cont.)

CANYON DE CHELLY CLIFF DWELLINGS (Film Loop—8mm—Silent). *See* Cliff Dwellers and Cliff Dwellings

CHIEFS AND LEADERS (Cassette). Troll Associates, 1972. 8 cassette tapes, av. 10 min. ea. ($44). Gr. 3–6. BKL (7/15/74). 970.1

Contents: 1. Squanto. 2. Pocahontas. 3. Sacagawea. 4. Osceola. 5. Pontiac. 6. Sequoyah. 7. Tecumseh. 8. Sitting Bull.

The personal stories of famous Indians— those who helped the first New World settlers and those who braved the loss of their own lands.

THE DAWN HORSE (Motion Picture— 16mm—Sound). Stanton Films, 1972. 16mm color, sound film, 18 min. ($230). Gr. 2–A. CGE (1973), JEH (7/8/72). 970.1

Imparts traditional American Indian attitudes toward nature. It captures the beauty of our native earth as expressed in Indian poetry, art, and music.

THE FIRST AMERICAN: CULTURE PATTERNS (Filmstrip—Sound). Prentice-Hall Media, 1974. 4 color, sound filmstrips, 84–114 fr.; 4 cassettes or discs, 15–19 min.; Teacher's Guide. ($76). Gr. 6–A. PRV (5/75), PVB (4/76). 970.1

Contents: 1. The Paleo—Indians. 2. The Arctic. 3. The Southwest. 4. The Mound Builders.

The primary purpose of this series is to expel the myth that the Pilgrims/Puritans from England were "the first Americans," and to acquaint students with the ancient history of the western hemisphere. Many of the color photographs were provided by American museums.

HORIZONTAL BELT LOOM (Film Loop— 8mm—Silent). *See* Looms

INDIAN LIFE IN NORTH AMERICA (Filmstrip—Sound). Imperial Educational Resources, 1973. 4 color, sound filmstrips, 4 cassettes or discs. Discs #3RG50200 ($56), Cassette #3KG50200 ($62). Gr. 4–8. STE (2/74). 970.1

Contents: 1. The Havasupai of the Grand Canyon—Part I. 2. The Havasupai of the Grand Canyon—Part II. 3. The Pueblo Indians of the Southwest—Part I. 4. The Pueblo Indians of the Southwest—Part II.

This set will help children to understand contemporary Indian life, its cultural heritage, and the challenges it faces.

AN INDIAN SUMMER (Motion Picture— 16mm—Sound). Atlantis Productions, 1977. 16mm color, sound film, 11 min.; Teacher's Guide. ($165). Gr. K–5. CIF (1977). 970.1

The film presents the story of 4 Woodland Indian children and their relationship with a fawn. Conveys a respect for American Indians and an appreciation for their love of nature.

INDIAN TRIBES (Cassette). Troll Associates, 1972. 10 cassette tapes, av. 10 min. ea. ($55). Gr. 3–6. BKL (7/15/74). 970.3

Contents: 1. Iroquois. 2. Cherokee. 3. Seminole. 4. Sioux. 5. Shoshoni. 6. Choctaw. 7. Pawnee. 8. Crow. 9. Hopi—Pueblo. 10. Tlingit.

Story of regional tribes in America; how they differed, how they lived in harmony with the land and its creatures, and how they reacted to the coming of the white settlers.

INDIANS OF NORTH AMERICA (Filmstrip—Sound). Society for Visual Education, 1976. 6 color, sound filmstrips, 36–47 fr.; 6 cassettes or discs, 8:20–10:50 min. Cassette #A477-SATC ($90), Discs #A477-SAR ($90). Gr. 4–8. BKL (5/1/77). 970.1

Contents: 1. Indians of the Northeast. 2. Indians of the Southeast. 3. Indians of the Plains. 4. Indians of the Northwest Coast. 5. Indians of the Southwest. 6. Indians of the Far North.

The life-styles and cultures of North American Indians in 6 geographic areas are presented, including diet, dress, ceremonies, artifacts, spiritual beliefs, social structure, and intertribal relationships.

THE INDIANS OF NORTH AMERICA (Filmstrip—Sound). National Geographic, 1973. 5 color, sound filmstrips, 55–61 fr.; 5 discs or cassettes, 13–14 min.; Teacher's Guide. Discs #03736 ($74.50), Cassettes #03737 ($74.50). Gr. 5–12. PRV (5/75), PVB (5/75). 970.1

Contents: 1. The First American. 2. The Eastern Woodlands. 3. The Plains. 4. West of the Shining Mountains. 5. Indians Today.

The subject content is authentic, noncontroversial, unbiased, and up to date. Excellent photography of current personalities adds to the set.

MESA VERDE (Study Print). *See* Cliff Dwellers and Cliff Dwellings

NATIVE AMERICAN HERITAGE (Filmstrip—Sound). EBEC, 1977. 5 color, sound filmstrips, av. 92 fr. ea.; 5 discs or cassettes; Teacher's Guide. Discs #6961 ($72.50), Cassettes #6961K ($72.50). Gr. 5–12. INS (1/78). 970.1

Contents: 1. The Old Ways. 2. Art: Reflections of a Culture. 3. The Fight for Survival. 4. Beliefs and Ceremonies. 5. The New Ways.

Contrary to popular myths, many American Indians never saw a buffalo and would not have known what to do with a teepee. This series uses artwork and photography backed by illuminating narration to banish stereotypes as it traces a richly diverse culture from pre-Columbian days to the present.

POTTERY DECORATION (Film Loop—8mm—Silent). *See* Pottery, Indian

POTTERY FIRING (Film Loop—8mm—Silent). *See* Pottery, Indian

POTTERY MAKING (Film Loop—8mm—Silent). *See* Pottery, Indian.

PUYE COMMUNITY HOUSES (Film Loop—8mm—Silent). Thorne Films/Prentice-Hall Media, 1972 (Southwest Indians). 8mm color, silent film loop, approx. 4 min. #HAT 272 ($26). Gr. 4–A. AUR (1978). 970.4

This loop illustrates the community houses used by the Southwest Indians.

PUYE DE CHELLY CLIFF DWELLINGS (Film Loop—8mm—Silent). *See* Cliff Dwellers and Cliff Dwellings

SHEEPHERDING (Film Loop—8mm—Silent). Thorne Films/Prentice-Hall Media, 1972 (Southwest Indians). 8mm color, silent film loop, approx. 4 min. #HAT 283 ($28). Gr. 4–A. AUR (1978). 970.1

This loop demonstrates the herding of sheep by the Southwest Indians.

SIX NATIVE AMERICAN FAMILIES (Filmstrip—Sound). Society for Visual Education, 1976. 6 color, sound filmstrips, av. 95 fr.; 6 cassettes, av. 12 min. Discs #478-SAR ($99), Cassette #478-SATC ($99). Gr. K–6. MDU (4/78), PRV (4/76). 970.1

Contents: 1. The Life of a Mohawk Family. 2. The Life of a Sioux Family. 3. The Life of a Seminole Family. 4. The Life of a Navajo Family. 5. The Life of a Pueblo Family. 6. The Life of a Kwakiutl Family.

This series focuses on the life-styles of 6 modern-day Native American tribes, with special emphasis on their relationship to their natural environment.

SPINNING WOOL (Film Loop—8mm—Silent). Thorne Films/Prentice-Hall Media, 1972 (Southwest Indians). 8mm color, silent film loop, approx. 4 min. #HAT 284 ($28). Gr. 4–A. AUR (1978). 970.1

This film loop illustrates the spinning of wool by the Indians of the Southwest.

UPRIGHT LOOM (Film Loop—8mm—Silent). *See* Looms

WINTER ON AN INDIAN RESERVATION (Motion Picture—16mm—Sound). Atlantis Productions, 1973. 16mm color, sound film, 11 min.; Teacher's Guide. ($165). Gr. 1–5. CFF (1973), CGE (1973), PRV (10/74). 970.1

A narrationless film about Indian children living on a forest reservation. Portrays the Indian's way of life, communicating dependence on, and harmony with, the environment.

INDIANS OF NORTH AMERICA—ART

NAVAJO SAND PAINTING CEREMONY (Film Loop—8mm—Silent). Thorne Films/Prentice-Hall Media, 1972 (Southwest Indians). 8mm color, silent film loop, approx. 4 min. #HAT 291 ($26). Gr. 4–A. MDU (1978). 709.01

The Navajo sand painting ceremony is demonstrated by the Southwest Indians.

PETROGLYPHS: ANCIENT ART OF THE MOJAVE (Filmstrip—Sound). Lyceum/Mook & Blanchard, 1971. 1 color, sound filmstrip, 51 fr.; 1 cassette or disc, 11-1/2 min. Cassette #LY351270C ($25), Disc #LY351270R ($19.50). Gr. 4–12. BKL (3/15/72). 709.01

This filmstrip explores petroglyphs and their possible meanings. It stimulates interest in the Indians, their history, and culture. These petroglyphs pictured the Indian's life; hunting with spear and bow, ceremonies attendant to the hunt, and animals that provided food, shelter, and clothing.

INDIANS OF NORTH AMERICA—CANADA

PAUL KANE GOES WEST (Motion Picture—16mm—Sound). National Film Board of Canada/Encyclopaedia Britannica Educational, 1972. 16mm color, sound film, 15 min. #3337 ($220). Gr. 4–12. BKL (10/74), CFF (10/75), PRV (5/75). 970.1

In the mid-nineteenth century, when the Indians of the Canadian West were proud and powerful, when the scenery was magnificent and natural, artist Paul Kane traveled thousands of miles between Canada's east and west. This film, accompanied by a narration from his diary, is a vivid record of Kane's adventures as seen through his forceful sketches and paintings.

INDIANS OF NORTH AMERICA—FICTION

THE LIGHT IN THE FOREST (Phonodisc or Cassette). Caedmon Records, 1974. 1 cassette or disc. Disc #TC1428 ($6.98), Cassette #CDL51428 ($7.95). Gr. 5–A. BKL (5/15/74), JOR (1974). Fic

A skillfully abridged recording of Conrad Richter's novel by the same name. Read by E. G. Marshall and others, it presents the masterful story of True Son, adopted son of Cuyloga, an Indian chief, but really John Butler, captured 11 years earlier by the Indians. When a treaty is made, True Son is returned to his real family, and he experiences a confrontation between the 2 cultures as he matures and must choose between them.

INDIANS OF NORTH AMERICA—FICTION (cont.)

SING DOWN THE MOON (Filmstrip—Sound). *See* Navajo—Fiction

INDIANS OF NORTH AMERICA—LEGENDS

ARROW TO THE SUN (Motion Picture— 16mm—Sound). Texture Films, 1973. 16mm color, sound film, 12 min. ($180). Gr. 1–A. CGE (1974), FLN (1974), PRV (4/75). 398.2

Animation is used to tell the tale of the Acoma Pueblo Indians. This legend is about a boy's search for his father, entailing his voyage on an arrow to the sun, the trials he undergoes in the sky village until he is recognized by his father the Lord of the Sun, and his return to earth to spread the sun's warm delights.

HOW BEAVER STOLE FIRE (Motion Picture—16mm—Sound). Paramount Communications, 1972. 16mm color film, 12 min.; Teacher's Guide. #7117 ($210). Gr. K–A. CGE (1972), FLN (12/73), MER (4/73). 398.2

Caroline Leaf's special sand animation technique re-creates an American Indian myth on the origin of fire.

INDIAN LEGENDS (Filmstrip—Sound). United Learning. 6 color, sound filmstrips; 6 cassettes; 1 Guide. #ML14 ($85). Gr. K–6. BKL (4/1/74), TEA (11/74). 398.2

Contents: 1. Glooskap Brings Summer. 2. The One-Horned Mountain Goat. 3. The Sun Dance of the Plains Indians. 4. The Festivals of the Seals. 5. How It All Began. 6. The Medicine That Restores Life.

Myths and legends of Indians passed down through the ages are portrayed in these filmstrips. They will aid in an understanding of the native people of North America as well as encourage thought about the ever-changing environment.

MOON BASKET: AN INDIAN LEGEND (Filmstrip—Sound). Multi-Media Productions, 1974. 1 color, sound filmstrip, 52 fr.; 1 cassette or disc, 6 min.; Teacher's Guide. Cassettes #6042C ($11.95), Discs #6042R ($11.95). Gr. 3–6. MDU (5/75), PRV (5/75), PVB (4/76). 398.2

Contents: 1. Basket Making.

The Moon Basket legend is told to the Devil's Claw plant by an old weaver. The story line connects the photographs of basket designs and relates them to the legend and to nature, whose themes and objects the artists used to create their designs.

READ ALONG AMERICAN INDIAN LEGENDS (Filmstrip—Sound). Coronet Instructional Media, 1977. 6 color, sound filmstrips, av. 47 fr.; 6 cassettes, av. 10 min.; Teacher's Guide. #M337 ($95). Gr. 3–8. PRV (4/78). 398.2

Contents: 1. How Summer Came to the Northland. 2. How the Indians Learn from the Animals. 3. The Suns of Cloud. 4. Great Rabbit and the Moon Man. 5. How Raven Brought the Sun. 6. Legend of Star-Boy.

Six native American folk tales of varying tribes, in picture book style, on filmstrips with read-along tapes are presented. These are stories told to children in almost all cultures. The words are printed at the bottom of each frame as on the page of a picture book, and a narrator reads the story along on the tape.

A VISIT TO THE FATHER (Filmstrip—Sound). Centron Films, 1972. 4 color, sound filmstrips; 4 discs or cassettes. Discs ($59.50), Cassettes ($67.50). Gr. K–12. ESL (1973), FLN (11/12/75). 398.2

Contents: 1. The Twins Set Out. 2. The Journey to Sun Bearer's House. 3. At the Home of Sun Bearer. 4. Killing the Monster Giant.

Authentic Navajo legend of origins in filmstrip episodes, translated and illustrated by Navajo artist Auska Kee.

INDIANS OF NORTH AMERICA—PAINTINGS

A. J. MILLER'S WEST: THE PLAINS INDIAN—1837—SLIDE SET (Slides). National Film Board of Canada/Donars Productions, 1975. 40 cardboard mounted, color slides in a plastic storage page; Teacher's Guide ($30). Gr. 5–A. PRV (9/76), PVB (4/77). 759.13

Photographs of A. J. Miller's paintings of the Plains Indians. The drawings for these paintings were made in the wild west region that now comprises the states of Kansas, Nebraska, Missouri, and Wyoming. The script, in English and French, was written by the artist.

INDIANS OF NORTH AMERICA—PLAINS

SUN DANCE PEOPLE: THE PLAINS INDIANS (Filmstrip—Sound). Random House, 1973 (Indians: the Southwest & the Plains Indians, Part 2). 2 color, sound filmstrips, 80–85 fr.; 2 cassettes or discs, 15–20 min.; Discussion Guide. Cassettes #12622-X ($39), Discs #12621-1 ($39). Gr. 5–A. BKL (4/1/74), PRV (4/74), PVB (5/1/74). 970.4

This set describes the North American Plains Indians life-style; from blanket courting to horse racing, revealing important facets of the culture. The visuals include paintings, drawings, and historical and contemporary photographs.

INDIANS OF NORTH AMERICA—POETRY

AMERICAN INDIAN POETRY (Filmstrip—Sound). Educational Dimensions Group,

1976. 4 color, sound filmstrips; 4 cassettes, 15–18 min. #737 ($74). Gr. 4–9. MDU (4/77), PRV (10/76). 897

Contents: 1. Eastern Indian Poetry. 2. Great Plains Indians. 3. Southwestern Indians. 4. Eskimo and Pacific Northwestern Indians.

This material increases the awareness and understanding of the Native American people. "I feel this material would help the Native American Indian identify with and be proud of his/her heritage" (Ron Hatch).

INDIANS OF NORTH AMERICA—SOCIAL LIFE AND CUSTOMS

BLESSINGWAY: TALES OF A NAVAJO FAMILY (Kit). *See* Navajo

HOPIS—GUARDIANS OF THE LAND (Motion Picture—16mm—Sound). *See* Hopi

INDIANS OF SOUTH AMERICA

CIVILIZATIONS OF EARLY AMERICA (Filmstrip—Sound). *See* Indians

INDIANS OF SOUTH AMERICA—LEGENDS

LATIN-AMERICAN FOLKTALES (Filmstrip—Sound). *See* Folklore—Latin America

INDIVIDUALITY

CHILDREN EVERYWHERE (Filmstrip—Sound). Educational Direction/Learning Tree Filmstrips, 1976. 4 color, sound filmstrips, av. 45 fr. ea.; 4 cassettes, av. 6–7 min. ea.; Teacher's Guide. ($58). Gr. 2–5. BKL (7/15/77), PRV (11/77). 155.2

Contents: 1. Just Like Me. 2. Not Like Me. 3. Are "They" Different? 4. What a Great World!

Introduces universal childhood experiences by examining the various things all children have in common, helping children to understand and appreciate the differences between individuals.

EXPLORING MY IDENTITY, UNIT ONE (Filmstrip—Sound). Scholastic Book Services, 1975 (Becoming Yourself). 4 color, sound filmstrips; 4 phonodiscs or cassettes; Teacher's Guide. Disc #3642 ($59.50), Cassette #3652 ($59.50). Gr. 4–6. BKL (4/75), PRV (4/75), TEA (5/75). 155.2

Contents: 1. Learning Yourself, One. 2. Learning Yourself, Two. 3. Feeling Your Feelings. 4. Things You Like; Things You Don't Like.

Unit One encourages each student to explore him- or herself—an activity every student is automatically ready for.

EXPRESSING MYSELF, UNIT TWO (Filmstrip—Sound). Scholastic Book Services, 1975 (Becoming Yourself). 4 color, sound filmstrips; 4 phonodiscs or cassettes; Teach-

er's Guide. Discs #3657 ($59.50), Cassettes #3667 ($59.50). Gr. 4–6. BKL (4/75), PRV (4/75), TEA (5/75). 155.2

Contents: 1. Liking Who You Are. 2. Speaking Up. 3. Becoming Yourself, One. 4. Becoming Yourself, Two.

Unit Two moves students on to the idea of expressing themselves to others and listening back, communicating, and making decisions.

FREE TO BE . . . YOU AND ME (Kit). McGraw-Hill Films, 1975. 6 color, sound filmstrips, av. 85 fr. ea.; 6 cassettes, 7 min. ea.; 1 Book; 3 Games; 1 Poster, Teacher's Guide. ($160). Gr. K–4. BKL (5/76), PRV (11/76). 155.2

A spirited adaptation of the award-winning record, book, TV special, and film of *Free to Be. . .You and Me*, this module teaches important concepts about independence, friendship, cooperation, and self-fulfillment. Art, photography, music, games to play, mazes to solve, things to make are all part of this learning module.

JUST LIKE YOU/JUST LIKE ME (Kit). *See* Self-Perception

MYSELF AND ME (Filmstrip—Sound). *See* Self

SONGSTORIES: I AM SPECIAL (Filmstrip—Sound). *See* Self

SONGSTORIES: WHAT MAKES ME THE ONLY ME? (Filmstrip—Sound). *See* Self

SQUARE PEGS—ROUND HOLES (Motion Picture—16mm—Sound). FilmFair Communications, 1974. 16mm color, sound film, 7-1/2 min. ($100). Gr. 5–12. BKL (5/75), EFL (1974), LFR (9/74). 155.2

This animated film begins with the birth of a cube. As it grows, it finds it just is not like its fellow shapes, the cones, spheres, etc., who easily fall into grooves made for them. The influences on the cube to fit neatly into a hole are to no avail. It tries to fit, but all the holes are filled. It finally realizes that each is unique and digs its own hole, then jumps in. Based on the original story by Phyllis Harvey.

UNDERSTANDING MYSELF AND OTHERS, UNIT THREE (Filmstrip—Sound). Scholastic Book Services, 1975 (Becoming Yourself). 4 color, sound filmstrips; 4 phonodiscs or cassettes; Teacher's Guide. Discs #3672 ($59.50), Cassettes #3682 ($59.50). Gr. 4–6. BKL (4/75), PRV (4/75), TEA (5/75). 155.2

Contents: 1. Alone. 2. Behaving in Groups. 3. Seeing Differences. 4. Understanding Differences.

Unit Three students are ready for a deeper understanding—not only of themselves, but of each other and of all the individuals they meet in school and daily life.

INDIVIDUALITY (cont.)

YOU'RE THE ONLY YOU (Filmstrip–
Sound). Educational Direction/Learning
Tree Filmstrips, 1974. 4 color, sound filmstrips, av. 51 fr. ea.; 2 cassettes, av. 5 min.
ea.; Teacher's Guide. ($52). Gr. K–2. BKL
(1/1/75), ESL (1976). 155.2

Contents: 1. Earth and the Universe. 2.
Throughout the Wide World. 3. Your Coun-
try, City, Neighborhood and Family. 4. The
One and Only You.

This set operating at the comprehension
level of the child, displays a complete "in-
verse expanding environment" concept. It
gives insights into the balance between human finiteness in the universe and each human's unique individuality.

INDIVIDUALITY–FICTION

THE BAT POET (Phonodisc or Cassette).
Caedmon Records, 1971. 1 12 in. disc or
cassette. Disc #TC1364 ($6.98), Cassette
#CDL51364 ($7.95). Gr. 3–A. HOB,
LBJ, NYR. Fic

The Bat Poet, according to Jarrell, was a
story "half for children and half for grown-
ups." It is about the personal world one
finds and how one is treated by the conven-
tional world when one is different.

INJURIES. *See* Accidents; First Aid

INSECTS

BACKYARD SCIENCE SERIES ONE: ANTS,
BEES, BEETLES, CRICKETS (Filmstrip–
Sound). *See* Natural History

THE HONEY BEE (Film Loop–8mm–Captioned). *See* Bees

INSECT COMMUNITIES (Film Loop–8mm–
Silent). Troll Associates. 4 8mm color, silent film loops, approx. 4 min.; Available
separately. ($99.80). Gr. K–8. AUR
(1978). 595.7

Contents: 1. Ants. 2. Bees. 3. Wasps. 4.
Termites.

These loops record in detail the lives and
habits of insects whose lives are spent in a
"community" arrangement.

LIFE OF A WORKER BEE (Film Loop–
8mm–Silent). *See* Bees

INTRODUCING MEASURING

PRESENTANDO MEDIDAS (INTRODUC-
ING MEASURING) (Filmstrip–Sound).
See Measurement

INTRODUCING NUMBERS

PRESENTANDO NUMEROS (INTRODUC-
ING NUMBERS (Filmstrip–Sound). *See*
Counting

INVENTORS

TRAILBLAZERS OF INVENTION (Filmstrip–Sound). Knowledge Aid/United
Learning, 1974. 5 color, sound filmstrips,
av. 83–86 fr. ea.; 5 cassettes, av. 12–20 min.
ea.; Teacher's Guide. #1830 ($75). Gr. 4–
7. PRV (1/75). 920

Contents: 1. Master of the Telegraph–
Samuel F. Morse. 2. Log Cabin Scientist–
George Washington Carver. 3. First Lady of
Science–Marie Curie. 4. Rocket Pioneer–
Robert H. Goddard. 5. Copying Genius–
Chester F. Carlson.

Blue Crystal is the name of a time travel
ship belonging to a scientist who takes 2
teenagers to witness history in the making.
The strips concentrate on the one major
accomplishment of each individual.

IRAN–ANTIQUITIES

ART OF PERSEPOLIS (Slides). Educational
Dimensions, 1977. 3 units with 20 slides
ea., cardboard mounts; Teacher's Guide;
Units available separately. #664 ($75). Gr.
4–A. PRV (4/78). 935

Contents: 1. Its Architecture. 2. Architec-
tural Detail. 3. The Stairways.

Through photography, this set demonstrates
how the lives of the earliest Persians affected their arts–paintings, sculpture, crafts,
and architecture.

IRAN–FICTION

FLOWER STORM (Motion Picture–16mm–
Sound). ACI Media/Paramount Communications, 1974. 16mm color, sound film, 12
min.; Teacher's Guide. ($175). Gr. K–A.
CFF (1975), PRV (11/76). Fic

An animated film from Iran, in the style of
Persian miniatures. Two emirs quarrel over
which one shot a bird during a hunt. They
decide on war, but the younger citizens,
who don't want a war, rig the cannon balls
to release birds for the one side and flowers
for the other. The war is called off.

IRELAND

THE BRITISH ISLES: SCOTLAND AND
IRELAND (Filmstrip–Sound). *See* Scotland

EUROPEAN GEOGRAPHY, SET FOUR
(Filmstrip–Sound). *See* Scotland

IRVING, WASHINGTON

EPISODES FROM FAMOUS STORIES (Filmstrip–Sound). *See* Literature–Collections

THE LEGEND OF SLEEPY HOLLOW
(Motion Picture–16mm–Sound). *See*
Legends–U.S.

THE LEGEND OF SLEEPY HOLLOW AND
ICHABOD CRANE (Phonodisc or Cassette).
See Legends–U.S.

RIP VAN WINKLE (Phonodisc or Cassette).
See Dutch in the U.S.–Fiction

ISRAEL

ISRAELI BOY: LIFE ON A KIBBUTZ
(Motion Picture–16mm–Sound). EBEC,
1973. 16mm color, sound film, 17 min.
#3178 ($240). Gr. 3–9. LNG (5/6/74),
PRV (3/75), TEA (5/6/74). 915.694

Israeli society is viewed through the eyes of
Nir, a young boy born and raised on a kibbutz. Scenes of milking, farming, schooling,
and socializing illustrate the busy goings-on
of communal life, and show why the kub-
butz succeeds as a unique social, political,
and economic entity.

ISRAEL–ANTIQUITIES

THE BIG DIG (Motion Picture–16mm–
Sound). Tele-Visual Productions/EBEC,
1973. 16mm color, sound film, 22 min.
#3363 ($290). Gr. 4–A. BKL (7/15/75),
LFR (9/10/75), PRV (1/76). 913.33

A huge mound in the Israeli desert is all
that remains of Gezer, a city that saw more
than 140 successive generations of inhabitants. This film records some of the events
in a season of excavation there, as an international team of archeologists probes
through strata of earth to uncover traces
of an ancient civilization. Students are
shown the meticulous care and backbreak-
ing labor of professional archeologists, and
are introduced to the specialized techniques
and equipment required for excavation.

ITALY–SOCIAL LIFE AND CUSTOMS

BUON GIORNO: GOOD MORNING
TEACHER (Filmstrip–Sound). Lyceum/
Mook & Blanchard, 1971. 1 color, sound
filmstrip, 63 fr.; 1 cassette or disc, 11 min.
Cassette #LY351170C ($25), Discs
#LY351170R ($19.50). Gr. 4–7. BKL
(12/15/71), PRV (2/73). 914.5

A visit to elementary and secondary schools
in Italy to bring insight into the daily lives
of Italian children.

IVES, BURL

FOLK SONGS IN AMERICAN HISTORY,
SET ONE: 1700–1864 (Filmstrip–Sound).
See Folk Songs–U.S.

FOLK SONGS IN AMERICAN HISTORY,
SET TWO: 1865–1967 (Filmstrip–Sound).
See Folk Songs–U.S.

FOLK STORIES AND TALES (Cassette).
See Fairy Tales

IZEN, MARSHALL

DINOSAUR TALES (Filmstrip–Sound). *See*
Dinosaurs

JACOBS, LINDA

REALLY ME (Kit). *See* Girls–Fiction

WOMEN WHO WIN, SET 1 (Kit). *See*
Athletes

WOMEN WHO WIN, SET 2 (Kit). *See*
Athletes

WOMEN WHO WIN, SET 3 (Kit). *See*
Athletes

WOMEN WHO WIN, SET 4 (Kit). *See*
Athletes

JAGR, MILOSLAV

THE FOOLISH FROG (Motion Picture–
16mm–Sound). *See* Folk Songs–U.S.

JAGUARS

JAGUAR: MOTHER AND CUBS (Film Loop
–8mm–Silent). Walt Disney Educational
Media, 1966. 8mm color, silent film loop,
approx. 4 min. #62-5307L ($30). Gr.
K–12. MDU (1974). 599.7

The female's gentleness and patience with
her kittens are demonstrated. The jaguar's
fine ability to swim is also presented.

JAPAN

JAPAN: ECONOMIC MIRACLE (Filmstrip–
Sound). EBEC, 1974. 5 color, sound filmstrips, av. 77 fr. ea.; 5 cassettes or discs,
8 min. ea.; Teacher's Guide. Discs #6907
($72.50), Cassettes #6907K ($72.50). Gr.
5–10. ESL (1976–77). 915.2

Contents: 1. The Physical Base. 2. Revolu-
tion in Food Supply. 3. The Industrial
Revolution. 4. Industry and Trade. 5. The
Urban Explosion.

The miracle that is modern Japan is explored through its geography, history, and
the temperament and character of its
people.

THE NEW JAPAN (Filmstrip–Sound).
Society for Visual Education, 1973. 6
color, sound filmstrips, 94–101 fr.; 3 discs
or cassettes, av. 19 1/2 min. Disc #298-
SAR ($83), Cassette #298-SATC ($83).
Gr. 4–9. BKL (1/74), PRV (4/74). 915.2

Contents: 1. Tokyo: World's Largest City.
2. A Traditional Japanese Family. 3.
Japan's Life from the Sea. 4. Silk Farming
at Takatoya. 5. Nagasaki and Her Ship-
builders. 6. Okinawa: Keystone of the
Pacific.

Photography, instructional maps, authentic
art and music, along with the narration,
picture Japanese people as they live and
work in an organized and complex society.
Japan is portrayed as both an industrial,
progressive urban society and as a simple
agricultural country deeply committed to
tradition.

JAPAN—FICTION

JAPANESE STORIES OF MAGIC (Filmstrip
—Sound). *See* Magic—Fiction

A PAIR OF RED CLOGS (Filmstrip—Sound/
Captioned). Listening Library, 1976 (Look,
Listen and Read). 1 color, sound/captioned
filmstrip, 46 fr.; 1 cassette, 13 min.;
Teacher's Guide. #JFS 150 ($14.95). Gr.
K–3. PRV (9/77). Fic
This simple story portrays the perennial joys
and mischiefs of childhood, contrasted and
complemented by the wisdom of a Japanese
grandmother. Illustrations and narration are
taken verbatim from the book.

JAPAN—SOCIAL LIFE AND CUSTOMS

JAPAN: SPIRIT OF IEMOTO (Filmstrip—
Sound). EBEC, 1974. 5 color, sound filmstrips, av. 79 fr. ea.; 5 discs or cassettes, 11
min. ea. Discs #6908 ($72.50), Cassettes
#6908K ($72.50). Gr. 5–10. ESL (1976–
77). 915.2
Contents: 1. The Spirit of Japan. 2.
Iemoto. 3. The Japanese Family. 4. The
Japanese at Work. 5. The Japanese at Play.
The unique blend of personality traits, temperament, and respect for tradition typified
by the word "Japanese" and the life-style
it evokes are the subjects of these filmstrips.
The series illustrates the many seeming con-
tradictions in the Japanese character and
unearths a few constants—a love of nature,
respect for elders, and subordination of the
individual to the welfare of the group.

JARRELL, RANDALL

THE BAT POET (Phonodisc or Cassette). *See*
Individuality—Fiction

THE GINGERBREAD RABBIT (Phonodisc
or Cassette). *See* Rabbits—Fiction

JAZZ MUSIC

ART OF DAVE BRUBECK: THE FANTASY
YEARS (Phonodiscs). Atlantic Records. 2
discs. #SD2-317 ($7.98). Gr. 3–A. PRV
(10/75). 785.42
These recordings come from 2 early con-
certs; all pretime signature improvisation.
The 11 selections include "Laura," "Star-
dust," and "Lullaby in Rhythm."

JEFFERSON, THOMAS

THE PICTORIAL LIFE-STORY OF
THOMAS JEFFERSON (Kit). Davco
Publishers, 1977 (Life Stories of Great
Presidents). 4 color, sound filmstrips, av.
68 fr.; 4 cassettes, av. 13 min.; 1 Book; 1
Teacher's Guide. ($89). Gr. 5–11. BKL
(12/15/77). 921
The filmstrips begin with the American
Revolution and an effective reading of the
Declaration of Independence. Jefferson's
life is outlined through flashbacks.

THOMAS JEFFERSON (Motion Picture—
16mm—Sound). Handel Film, 1966
(Americana Series Number Three). 16mm
color, sound film, 28 min.; Film Guide.
($360). Gr. 4–A. LAA (1967), LFR
(3/67), FLN (1967). 921
Covers Jefferson as farmer, student, scientist, inventor, architect, politician, and
president; highlights the accomplishments
and versatility of this great American leader.

JENNINGS, BLANCHE

MORE SILVER PENNIES (Phonodisc or
Cassette). *See* Poetry—Collections

JESUS

FAMOUS STORIES OF GREAT COURAGE
(Filmstrip—Sound). *See* Heroes and
Heroines

JEWS—BIOGRAPHY

THE DIARY OF ANNE FRANK (Filmstrip—
Sound). *See* Biography

JOAN OF ARC

FAMOUS STORIES OF GREAT COURAGE
(Filmstrip—Sound). *See* Heroes and
Heroines

JOE MAGARAC

JOHN HENRY AND JOE MAGARAC
(Phonodisc or Cassette). *See* Folklore—U.S.

JOHN, ELTON

MEN BEHIND THE BRIGHT LIGHTS (Kit).
See Musicians

JOHNNY APPLESEED. *See* Folklore—U.S.

JOHNSON, ANNABEL

THE GRIZZLY (Kit). *See* Bears—Fiction

JOHNSON, CROCKETT

HAROLD'S FAIRY TALE (Motion Picture—
16mm—Sound). *See* Fairy Tales

A PICTURE FOR HAROLD'S ROOM (Filmstrip—Sound). *See* Fantasy—Fiction

JOHNSON, EDGAR

THE GRIZZLY (Kit). *See* Bears—Fiction

JOHNSTON, JOHANNA

A BIRTHDAY FOR GENERAL WASHING-
TON (Kit). *See* U.S.—History—1775–1783
—Revolution—Fiction

JONES, JOHN PAUL

FAMOUS PATRIOTS OF THE AMERICAN
REVOLUTION (Filmstrip—Sound). *See*
U.S.—History—Biography

JOURNALISM

FREE PRESS: A NEED TO KNOW THE
NEWS (Filmstrip—Sound). Pathescope
Educational Media, 1977 (Let's Find Out).
1 color, sound filmstrip, 62 fr.; 1 cassette,
8-3/4 min.; 1 Guide; Worksheet Spirit
Master. #9514C ($25). Gr. 3–6. BKL
(12/1/77), PVB (4/78). 070
An introductory look at the news media
and their role in contemporary society.
Explores the need for a free press as well
as press limitations and responsibilities.

JUNGLE BOOK

MOWGLI AND THE WOLVES (Cassette).
See Animals—Fiction

JUST SO STORIES

JUST SO STORIES AND OTHER TALES
(Phonodisc or Cassette). *See* Animals—
Fiction

THE CAT THAT WALKED BY HIMSELF
AND OTHER JUST SO STORIES (Phonodisc or Cassette). *See* Animals—Fiction

THE WORLD OF JUST SO STORIES, SET
ONE (Kit). *See* Animals—Fiction

JUVENILE DELINQUENCY

PROJECT AWARE (Motion Picture—16mm
—Sound). See 'n Eye Productions, 1978.
16mm color, sound film, 29 min. ($555).
Gr. 4–A. AUR (1978), NEF (5/78). 364.2
This film is a powerful statement on the
prevention of juvenile delinquency. Using
dramatic slides of the harsh realities of life
inside prison walls, former convict David
Crawford illustrates the end effect of petty
thievery, bad associations, drugs, and
alcohol. Workshops (with the film included) for juveniles, parents, and adult
groups or agencies are available.

SHOPLIFTING, IT'S A CRIME (Motion
Picture—16mm—Sound). *See* Crime

KANE, PAUL

PAUL KANE GOES WEST (Motion Picture—
16mm—Sound). *See* Indians of North
America—Canada

KANGAROOS

KANGAROO (Film Loop—8mm—Silent).
Walt Disney Educational Media, 1966.
8mm color, silent film loop, approx. 4 min.
#62-5251L ($30). Gr. K–6. MDU (1974).
599.2
The film presents kangaroos feeding with
their young. Their unique method of movement is beautifully presented in slow
motion.

KARLOFF, BORIS

AESOP'S FABLES (Phonodisc or Cassette).
See Fables

KAY, HERSHY

MOTHER GOOSE (Phonodisc or Cassette).
See Nursery Rhymes

KEATS, EZRA JACK

GOGGLES (Filmstrip—Sound). *See* Boys—
Fiction

KEE, AUSKA

A VISIT TO THE FATHER (Filmstrip—
Sound). *See* Indians of North America—
Legends

KELLOGG, STEVEN

HOW A PICTURE BOOK IS MADE (Filmstrip—Sound). *See* Books

THE ISLAND OF THE SKOG (Filmstrip—
Sound). *See* Mice—Fiction

KENDALL, CAROL

THE GAMMAGE CUP (Filmstrip—Sound).
See Fantasy—Fiction

KENYA

FOUR FAMILIES OF KENYA (Filmstrip—
Sound). BFA Educational Media, 1974.
4 color, sound filmstrips; 4 cassettes or
discs. Cassettes #VZ4000 ($70), Discs
#VZ3000 ($70). Gr. 4–8. BKL (12/1/74).
916.762
Contents: 1. Traditional Farming Family.
2. Tea Estate Family. 3. Nairobi Family.
4. Swahili Coast Family.
Shows that Kenya, like the rest of Africa,
is composed of many established native
tribal cultures meeting with foreign ones
imported at various times in the past.

KIBBUTZ. *See* Israel

KIPLING, RUDYARD

THE CAT THAT WALKED BY HIMSELF AND OTHER JUST SO STORIES (Phonodisc or Cassette). *See* Animals—Fiction

JUST SO STORIES AND OTHER TALES (Phonodisc or Cassette). *See* Animals—Fiction

JUST SO STORIES BY RUDYARD KIPLING (Filmstrip—Sound). *See* Animals—Fiction

KIM (Phonodisc or Cassette). *See* India—Fiction

MASTERY STORY TELLER, SET ONE (Filmstrip—Sound). *See* Literature—Collections

MOWGLI AND THE WOLVES (Cassette). *See* Animals—Fiction

RED DOG BY RUDYARD KIPLING (Phonodisc or Cassette). *See* Animals—Fiction

RIKKI TIKKI TAVI (Cassette). *See* Mongooses—Fiction

RIKKI TIKKI TAVI AND WEE WILLIE WINKIE (Phonodisc or Cassette). *See* Animals—Fiction

THE WORLD OF JUNGLE BOOKS, SET ONE (Kit). *See* Animals—Fiction

THE WORLD OF JUST SO STORIES, SET ONE (Kit). *See* Animals—Fiction

KIRCHNER, ERNST LUDWIG

PICTURES ARE FUN TO LOOK AT (Art Prints). *See* Art Appreciation

KLEE, PAUL

PICTURES ARE FUN TO LOOK AT (Art Prints). *See* Art Appreciation

KLONDIKE GOLD FIELDS—FICTION

CALL OF THE WILD (Filmstrip—Sound). *See* Dogs—Fiction

KNIEVEL, EVEL

NOT SO EASY (MOTORCYCLE SAFETY) (Motion Picture—16mm—Sound). *See* Motorcycles

KNIGHT, ERIC

LASSIE COME HOME (Phonodisc or Cassette). *See* Dogs—Fiction

KOALA BEARS

KOALA BEAR (Film Loop—8mm—Silent). Walt Disney Educational Media, 1966. 8mm color, silent film loop, approx. 4 min.

#62-5252L ($30). Gr. K–12. MDU (1974). 599.7
These marsupials are seen climbing and swinging through eucalyptus trees. Interesting close-up shots of the animals' faces are presented.

KRAUSS, ROBERT

WHOSE MOUSE ARE YOU? (Filmstrip—Sound). *See* Mice—Fiction

KURALT, CHARLES

AN AMERICAN SAMPLER (Filmstrip—Sound). *See* U.S.—Social Life and Customs

LA FARGE, PETER

AS LONG AS THE GRASS SHALL GROW (Phonodiscs). *See* Folk Songs, Indian

LA FONTAINE, JEAN DE

SOUND FILMSTRIP SET 35 (Filmstrip—Sound). *See* Children's Literature—Collections

LAMBERT, EVELYN

THE HOARDER (Motion Picture—16mm—Sound). *See* Fables

PARADISE LOST (Motion Picture—16mm—Sound). *See* Man—Influence on Nature

LANG, ANDREW

BEAUTY AND THE BEAST AND OTHER STORIES (Phonodisc or Cassette). *See* Fairy Tales

THE PIED PIPER AND OTHER STORIES (Phonodisc or Cassette). *See* Fairy Tales

SNOW WHITE AND ROSE RED AND OTHER ANDREW LANG FAIRY TALES (Phonodisc or Cassette). *See* Fairy Tales

LANGUAGE AND LANGUAGES

LANGUAGE—THE MIRROR OF MAN'S GROWTH (Filmstrip—Sound). *See* English Language—History

SPEAKING OF LANGUAGE (Filmstrip—Sound). Guidance Associates, 1971 (Language Skills Series). 2 color, sound filmstrips, 75–85 fr.; 2 cassettes or discs, 12–13 min. Discs #512-275 ($52.50), Cassettes #512-283 ($52.50). Gr. 5–8. BKL (2/15/76), PRV (9/72), PVB (5/73). 401
Contents: 1. What Is It? 2. How Does It Work?
This program builds a conceptual grasp of linguistics by examining the universality of speech, the history of language, components

of grammar, and relationship of language to thought.

LANGUAGE ARTS

ANIMALS OF AFRICA (Motion Picture—16mm—Sound). *See* Animals—Africa

FIRE! (Motion Picture—16mm—Sound). *See* Forest Fires

FIRE MOUNTAIN (Motion Picture—16mm—Sound). *See* Volcanoes

WHERE IS IT? (Filmstrip—Captioned). EBEC, 1974 (Developing Basic Skills). 4 color, captioned filmstrips, av. 49 fr.; Teacher's Guide. #13070 ($32.90). Gr. K–3. CPR (4/77), PRV (4/1/76). 372.6

Contents: 1. Where Are We Hiding? 2. Where Did We Find It? 3. Where Am I? 4. Where Are My Animal Friends?

These filmstrips encourage the use of proper words to describe location. A guessing game with hidden objects teaches young viewers to use correctly such words as "under," "over," "behind," and "between." In other sequences, children find things and thus learn to tell what was found where.

See also Creation (Literary, artistic, etc.), English Language, and various divisions of Literature, and its forms, i.e., Poetry, Reading

LARRECQ, JOHN M.

SERIES SEVEN: A LITTLE LOVIN' AND A LITTLE LAUGHIN' (Filmstrip—Sound). *See* Short Stories

LATIN AMERICA—FICTION

STORIES OF LATIN AMERICA, SET ONE (Filmstrip—Sound). Random House, 1977. 4 color, sound filmstrips, 50–57 fr.; 4 cassettes or discs, 10–14 min.; Teacher's Guide. Discs #05074 ($72), Cassettes #05075 ($72). Gr. 2–6. PRV (1/78). Fic

Contents: 1. Lora, Lorita. 2. Monsieur Jolicoeur's Umbrella. 3. A Jungle Jumble. 4. Hill of Fire.

The first 3 titles are based on books by Anico Surany, illustrated by Leonard Everett Fisher. The last is by Thomas P. Lewis with pictures by Joan Sandin. Each of these filmstrips takes place in a different Latin American setting (Colombia, Haiti, Costa Rica, Mexico), providing insights into the ways of our neighbors to the south.

STORIES OF LATIN AMERICA, SET TWO (Filmstrip—Sound). Random House, 1977. 4 color, sound filmstrips, 45–50 fr.; 4 cassettes or discs, 10–13 min.; Teacher's Guide. Cassettes #05077-0 ($72), Discs #05076-2 ($72). Gr. 2–6. PRV (1/78). Fic

Contents: 1. The Musical Palm Tree. 2. Ride

the Cold Wind. 3. The Golden Frog. 4. The Burning Mountain.

The first title is based on the book by Robert Barry, the last 3 are by Anico Surany, illustrated by Leonard Everett Fisher. Each filmstrip is set in a different Latin American location (Puerto Rico, Peru, Panama, El Salvador), providing insights into the ways of our neighbors to the south.

LAW

LAW AND JUSTICE (Filmstrip—Sound). Pathescope Educational Media, 1973. 3 color, sound filmstrips; 3 cassettes; Teacher's Manual. #308 ($60). Gr. 4–8. STE (4/5/74). 340.1

Contents: 1. The Case of the Blue and White Whistle. 2. The Case of the Stolen Hub Cap. 3. The Case of the Boss's Son

This set presents law as ideals, values, and fair play rather than a collection of rules, and involves students emotionally and intellectually in making value decisions.

LEADERSHIP

WHO'S RUNNING THE SHOW? (Filmstrip—Sound). Lyceum/Mook & Blanchard, 1973. 1 color, sound filmstrips, 51 fr.; 1 cassette or disc, 6-1/2 min.; Teacher's Guide. Cassette #LY35572C ($25), Disc #LY35572R ($19.50). Gr. 6–9. FLN (1973). 158

The importance of good leadership qualities is stressed; presents examples of what society might be like if there were no leaders to make decisions and think ahead. Among the leaders cited are judges, parents, and student council presidents.

LEAF, CAROLINE

HOW BEAVER STOLE FIRE (Motion Picture—16mm—Sound). *See* Indians of North America—Legends

LEAVES

LEAF FUNCTIONS (Filmstrip—Captioned). BFA Educational Media, 1970. 5 color, captioned filmstrips. #VD8000 ($40). Gr. 4–6. BKL (1/1/71). 581.1

Contents: 1. What Do Leaves Do? 2. Transpiration. 3. Oxygen. 4. Carbon Dioxide. 5. Review of Leaf Functions.

This set of filmstrips shows how leaves serve plants as controls for water content and for the discharge of oxygen and intake of carbon dioxide.

LEGENDS

BARON MUNCHAUSEN TRULY TALL TALES (Phonodisc or Cassette). Caedmon Records, 1972. 1 12 in. disc or cassette. Disc #TC1409 ($6.98), Cassette

LEGENDS (cont.)

#CDL51409 ($7.95). Gr. 2-6. BKL (3/
15/73), HOB, LBJ. 398.2

The world's champion liar was unquestion-
ably Baron Munchausen. Like Swift's Gul-
liver, he dealt in scathing social comment.
Peter Ustinov is a perfect Baron. Included
in this collection are "My Favorite Dog,"
"What to Do if Caught between a Lion and a
Crocodile," and "Trees Flying through the
Sky and Other Amazing Results of a Storm."

HEROIC ADVENTURES (Filmstrip—Sound).
Acorn Films, 1976. 4 color, sound filmstrips, 51-75 fr.; 4 cassettes, 9-13 min.; 1
guide. ($65). Gr. 3-8. BKL (4/15/77).
398.2

Contents: 1. Gilgamesh and the Monster in
the Woods. 2. Hercules and the Golden Apple. 3. Arthur and the Magic Sword. 4.
Robin Hood and the Poor Knight.

Exciting excerpts from the adventures of
4 legendary world heroes.

READ ALONG AMERICAN INDIAN LEG-
ENDS (Filmstrip—Sound). *See* Indians of
North America—Legends

LEGENDS—GREAT BRITAIN

BEOWULF AND THE MONSTERS (Cassette). *See* Beowulf

LEGENDS—U.S.

THE LEGEND OF SLEEPY HOLLOW (Motion Picture—16mm—Sound). Bosustow
Productions, 1972 (American Folktales).
16mm color, sound animated film, 14 min.;
Leader's Guide. ($180). Gr. 4-A. BKL (7/
1/72), NEF (1973), PRV (10/72). 398.2

The legend of Ichabod Crane and his courtship of Katrina Van Tassel, the only daughter of a prosperous Dutch farmer. Ichabod's
rival Brom Bones exploits Ichabod's belief
in ghosts. Returning from a gala at the
farmer's home, Ichabod encounters the
dreaded Headless Horseman. In a wild chase,
the ghostly rider hurls his head at poor Ichabod, who mysteriously disappears and is
never seen again in Sleepy Hollow. Narrated
by John Carradine.

THE LEGEND OF SLEEPY HOLLOW AND
ICHABOD CRANE (Phonodisc or Cassette).
Caedmon Records, 1967. 1 cassette or disc,
approx. 60 min. Disc #TC1242 ($6.98),
Cassette #CDL51242 ($7.95). Gr. 5-A.
EGT, NYR, SLJ. Fic

Contents: 1. The Legend of Sleepy Hollow.
2. Ichabod Crane and the Headless Horseman.

The Legend of Sleepy Hollow by Washington Irving is his attempt to receive some de-
gree of comfort and delight from his youth-
ful scenes. This story is a combination of

Dutch folklore and personal boyhood experiences and remembrances; narrated by
Ed Begley.

LEGEND OF SLEEPY HOLLOW AND
OTHER STORIES (Cassette). Jabberwocky
Cassette Classics, 1972. 1 cassette, 60 min.
#1111 ($7.98). Gr. 5-12. BKL (3/15/74),
JOR (11/74). 398.2

Contents: 1. Legend of Sleepy Hollow. 2.
Celebrated Jumping Frog. 3. The Bride
Comes to Yellow Sky.

This dramatization faithfully captures the
spirit of a trio of famous American short
stories. Without changing the structure or
quality of the original story, each has been
condensed. Sound effects and brief musical
interludes add to the dramatization.

LEGISLATION

AMERICA ROCK (Filmstrip—Sound). *See*
U.S.—History

LEMMINGS

LEMMING MIGRATION (Film Loop—8mm—
Silent). Walt Disney Educational Media,
1966. 8mm color, silent film loop, approx.
4 min. #62-5367L ($30). Gr. K-12. MDU
(1974). 599.3

Thousands of lemmings are observed during
their doomed migration toward the sea,
which is climaxed as the lemmings cast
themselves over the edge of a cliff.

LERNER, MARGARET RUSH

HEALTH EDUCATION (Filmstrip—Sound).
See Hygiene

LESIEG, THEO

BEGINNER BOOKS FILMSTRIPS, SET 1
(Filmstrip—Sound). *See* Reading—Study
and Teaching

BEGINNER BOOKS FILMSTRIPS, SET 2
(Filmstrip—Sound). *See* Reading—Study and
Teaching

LEWIS, SHARI

EARLY LEARNING LIBRARY (Filmstrip—
Sound). *See* Child Development

LEWIS, THOMAS P.

STORIES OF LATIN AMERICA, SET ONE
(Filmstrip—Sound). *See* Latin America—
Fiction

LIBRARY SKILLS

BASIC STUDY SKILLS 1 (Filmstrip—Sound).
See Study, Method of

BASIC STUDY SKILLS 2 (Filmstrip—Sound).
See Study, Method of

DEWEY DECIMAL CLASSIFICATION
(Filmstrip—Sound). *See* Classification,
Dewey Decimal

LEARNING THE LIBRARY (Filmstrip—
Sound). Educational Activities, 1975. 4
color, sound filmstrips; 4 cassettes or discs;
3 Dittos; Decimal System Poster; 4 manuals;
1 Guide. Cassettes #FSC461 ($59), Discs
#FSR461 ($55). Gr. 3–6. BKL (6/76).
028.7
Contents: 1. Let's Go to the Library. 2. Open
Sesame. 3. Getting Around in the Media
Center. 4. Let's Look It Up.
Step-by-step teaching of library skills. Direct student involvement in responding to
and actively working with each filmstrip is a
unique feature. Games at the end of each
make testing the knowledge gained fun for
the student.

LIBRARY SKILL BOX (Cassette). Troll As-
sociates, 1975. 10 cassette tapes, av. 13 min.
ea.; 50 Spirit Masters; Teacher's Guide.
($96). Gr. 4–10. BKL (9/76). 028.7
Contents: 1. How to Use Your Library. 2.
What Is a Book? 3. How to find Reference
Material. 4. How to Use a Dictionary. 5.
How to Use an Encyclopedia. 6. How to
Use an Atlas. 7. How to Use Magazines
and Newspapers. 8. How to Research and
Write a Report. 9. How to Study. 10. How
to Give a Report.
Tapes especially valuable for individual
student use, this set covers all facets of using
the library. The duplicating masters are for
reviewing the tapes and expanding the student's awareness through visual reinforcement of supplementary information.

LITERATURE FOR CHILDREN, SERIES 3
(Filmstrip—Sound). *See* Literature—Study
and Teaching

LOOK IT UP: HOW TO GET INFORMATION
(Filmstrip—Sound). Troll Associates, 1973.
4 color, sound filmstrips, av. 46 fr. ea.; 2
cassettes, av. 12 min. ea.; Teacher's Guide.
($52). Gr. 4–6. PRV (5/75). 028.7
Contents: 1. How to Use Dictionaries. 2.
How to Use Atlases and Almanacs. 3. How
to Use Encyclopedias. 4. How to Use the
Card Catalog.
Provides an informative and imaginative approach to learning about reference materials
and other library sources.

MEDIA: RESOURCES FOR DISCOVERY
(Filmstrip—Sound). *See* Audio-Visual
Materials

YOUR LIBRARY—HOW TO USE IT (Filmstrip—Sound). United Learning, 1974. 5
color, sound filmstrips, av. 51 fr. ea.; 5
cassettes, av. 8 min. ea.; Teacher's Guide.
#47 ($75). Gr. 4–6. BKL (1/76). 027.8
Contents: 1. Discovering Your Library. 2.

Where Do I Go from Here? 3. Using Audio-
Visual Resources. 4. Doing a Project. 5.
How Do You Share Your Library?
This program will develop all essential library skills necessary to enjoy the full benefits of the library. The filmstrips are designed for self-discovery.

LICE

ALL ABOUT LICE (Filmstrip—Sound). Norcliff Thayer, 1976. 1 color, sound filmstrip,
63 fr.; 1 cassette or disc, 6 min.; 1 Spirit
Master; 1 Guide. ($6). Gr. K–6. BKL (4/
1/77), PRV (4/78). 614.432
Lice—where they live, how they spread, and
how they can be eliminated—presented
through the cartoon characters of Lotty and
Leo Louse.

LIFE

LIFE TIMES NINE (Motion Picture—16mm—
Sound). Insight Media Programs/Pyramid
Films, 1974. 16mm color, sound film, 15
min. ($225). Gr. 5–A. AFF (1974), BKL
(7/1/74). 128
A compilation of brief "commercials for
life" made by 9 youngsters between the ages
of 11 and 16. The directional control of
each "commercial" was assumed by the
author who created each idea. Two profes-
sionals assisted the productions, but final
responsibility belonged to the individual
youngsters.

LIFE (BIOLOGY)

HOW CAN YOU TELL IT'S LIVING (Filmstrip—Sound). Multi-Media Productions,
1976. 1 color, sound filmstrip, 53 fr.; 1
cassette, 9 min. #6067C ($14.50). Gr.
3–5. PRV (4/78). 577
When Salvador brings a clay turtle to class
on Special Science Day, the teacher has an
opportunity to review the characteristics of
living things—reproduction, the need to eat,
and the need for a special place to live. Both
plants and animals are used as examples.

LIGHT

LEARNING ABOUT LIGHT: SECOND EDI-
TION (Motion Picture—16mm—Sound).
EBEC, 1976 (Introduction to Physical Science). 16mm color, sound film, 15 min.
#3385 ($220). Gr. 4–9. BKL (12/1/76),
INS (12/77), LFR (9/10/76). 538
A series of engrossing demonstrations reveals properties of light that account for our
ability to harness it to our needs. Students
discover how light travels, why light rays
bend, and why the same primary colors pro-
duce white when light waves are mixed, but
near black when paint pigments are blended.

LINDGREN, ASTRID

CHRISTMAS IN NOISY VILLAGE (Film-strip—Sound). *See* Christmas—Fiction

PIPPI LONGSTOCKING (Phonodisc or Cassette). *See* Sweden—Fiction

THE TOMTEN AND THE FOX (Filmstrip—Sound). *See* Foxes—Stories

LINDNER, RICHARD

PICTURES ARE FUN TO LOOK AT (Art Prints). *See* Art Appreciation

LINGUISTICS. *See* Language and Languages

LIONNI, LEO

SIGHTS AND SOUNDS FILMSTRIPS, SET 1 (Filmstrip—Sound). *See* Reading—Study and Teaching

SIGHTS AND SOUNDS FILMSTRIPS, SET 2 (Filmstrip—Sound). *See* Reading—Study and Teaching

SIGHTS AND SOUNDS FILMSTRIPS, SET 3 (Filmstrip—Sound). *See* Reading—Study and Teaching

SIGHTS AND SOUNDS FILMSTRIPS, SET 4 (Filmstrip—Sound). *See* Reading—Study and Teaching

LIONS

LION (Motion Picture—16mm—Sound). EBEC, 1971 (Silent Safari Series). 16mm color, sound, nonnarrated film, 11 min.; Teacher's Guide. #3123 ($150). Gr. 2-9. BKL (10/1/76). 599.7

Close-up photography shows the lion eating, sleeping, and playing, and female and cubs in their natural habitat.

LION: MOTHER AND CUBS (Film Loop—8mm—Silent). Walt Disney Educational Media, 1966. 8mm color, silent film loop, approx. 4 min. #62-5202L ($30). Gr. K–12. MDU (1974). 599.7

The lion cubs are shown nursing, playing, and being carried about by their mother. Close-up of mother carrying cub by the scruff of the neck, and cubs viewed in mock battles, are included.

PRIDE OF LIONS (Film Loop—8mm—Silent). Walt Disney Educational Media, 1966. 8mm color, silent film loop, approx. 4 min. #62-5201L ($30). Gr. K–12. MDU (1974). 599.7

An African lion family is shown as it actually lives in its natural habitat. Close-up view of lions climbing trees, yawning, scratching, and relaxing in the shade.

LIONS—FICTION

THE HAPPY LION SERIES, SET ONE (Filmstrip—Sound). University Films/McGraw-Hill Films, 1971. 4 color, sound filmstrips, av. 40 fr. ea.; 4 cassettes or discs, 11 min. ea.; Teacher's Guide. Cassettes #102180 ($65), Discs #103058 ($65). Gr. 3-A. PRV (11/1/73). Fic

Contents: 1. The Happy Lion. 2. The Happy Lion's Vacation. 3. The Happy Lion in Africa. 4. The Happy Lion Roars.

Roger Duvoisin's illustrations bring to life the adventures of the enchanting French lion. Narrated by Charles Duval, based on the series of stories by Louise Fatio.

THE HAPPY LION SERIES, SET TWO (Filmstrip—Sound). University Films/McGraw-Hill Films, 1971. 4 color, sound filmstrips, av. 40 fr. ea.; 4 discs or cassettes, 11 min. ea.; Teacher's Guide. Discs #103067 ($65), Cassettes #102185 ($65). Gr. 3-A. BKL (11/1/73), PRV (9/10/73). Fic

Contents: 1. The Happy Lion's Quest. 2. The Three Happy Lions. 3. The Happy Lion and the Bear. 4. The Happy Lion's Treasure.

Roger Duvoisin's illustrations bring to life the adventures of the enchanting French lion. Narrated by Charles Duval, based on the series of stories by Louise Fatio.

LIPPMAN, PETER

SIGHTS AND SOUNDS FILMSTRIPS, SET 1 (Filmstrip—Sound). *See* Reading—Study and Teaching

LISTENING

BASIC COMMUNICATION SKILLS, ONE (Filmstrip—Sound). *See* Communication—Pyschological Aspects

FOLLOW THROUGH WITH SIGHTS AND SOUNDS (Filmstrip—Sound). *See* Perception

GUESS WHAT? (Filmstrip—Sound). Concept Media. 5 color, silent filmstrips; 5 cassettes or discs; Teacher's Idea Book; Supplementary Material. ($130). Gr. K-4. LGB (12/77). 152.1

Develops perception, imagination, and expression. The filmstrips show close-up "clues" to everyday objects. The cassettes or discs play a similar listening game with everyday sounds.

LISTENING IS COMMUNICATING (Film-strip—Sound). Imperial Educational Resources, 1975. 4 color, sound filmstrips; 4 discs or cassettes; Teacher's Notes. Discs #3RG90600 ($56), Cassettes #3KG90600 ($62). Gr. K-6. CPR (3/75), PVB (4/75). 152.1

Contents: 1. Listening to Sounds. 2. Listening to Nature. 3. Listening to Things. 4. Listening to People.

Through awareness of the qualities and significance of different sounds, children discover how much people, nature, and things around us have to say.

LITTLE GREY RABBIT'S CHRISTMAS & LITTLE GREY RABBIT GOES TO SEA (Phonodisc or Cassette). *See* Rabbits–Fiction

ON STAGE: WALLY, BERTHA, AND YOU (Kit). *See* English Language–Study and Teaching

SUPER THINK PROGRAM (Cassette). *See* Sports–Biography

LITERATURE– COLLECTIONS

EPISODES FROM FAMOUS STORIES (Filmstrip–Sound). EBEC, 1973. 6 color, sound filmstrips, av. 72 fr. ea.; 6 discs or cassettes, 13 min. ea.; Teacher's Guide. Discs #6477 ($86.95), Cassettes #6477K ($86.95). Gr. 3-10. PRV (9/74). 803.83

Contents: 1. Highlights from "Robinson Crusoe." 2. Highlights from "The Adventures of Tom Sawyer." 3. Highlights from "Treasure Island." 4. Highlights from "The Legend of Sleepy Hollow." 5. Highlights from "Heidi." 6. Highlights from "Alice's Adventures in Wonderland."

Colorful illustrations, faithful-to-original-text narrations, near-perfect voice characterizations, and exciting sound effects introduce children and young teenagers to the high points in the plots of 6 classics in literature.

FUN AND FANTASY SERIES (Cassette). Troll Associates, 1972. 8 cassette tapes, av. 10 min. ea. ($44). Gr. K-6. BKL (12/15/73). 808.83

Contents: 1. Drummer Hoff. 2. The Elephant's Child. 3. Finnerty Flynn and the Singing City. 4. The Lollipop Tree. 5. Mighty Miko. 6. Peter and the Wolf. 7. The Sorcerer's Apprentice. 8. The World's Worst Wisher.

Leonard Bernstein conducts the New York Philharmonic Orchestra in performances of Prokofiev's "Peter and the Wolf" and Dukas's "The Sorcerer's Apprentice."

LIBRARY 3 (Cassette). Jabberwocky Cassette Classics, 1975. 6 cassettes; 6 Scripts; 1 Guide. #1003C ($60). Gr. 3-8. BKL (10/15/75), PRV (9/75), TEA (5/6/75). 808.83

Contents: 1. *Aladdin; or The Wonderful Lamp.* 2. *Heidi* by Johanna Spyri. 3. *The Merry Adventures of Robin Hood* by Howard Pyle. 4. *Oliver Twist* by Charles Dickens.

Adaptations of original stories are acted out as dramas with a full cast of characters, music, and sound effects.

LIBRARY 5 (Cassette). Jabberwocky Cassette Classics, 1975. 12 cassettes, av. 20 min. ea.; 12 Scripts, 1 Workbook; Teacher's Guide. #1005C ($100). Gr. 1-8. BKL (3/15/77). 808.83

Contents: 1. *Hansel and Gretel* by Grimm. 2. *The Fisherman and His Wife* by Grimm. 3. *Pied Piper of Hamelin* by Robert Browning. 4. *Beauty and the Beast* by Mme. de Villeneuve. 5. *The Tinder Box* by H. C. Andersen. 6. *The Swineherd* by H. C. Andersen. 7. *Cinderella* by Charles Perrault. 8. *Sleeping Beauty* by Charles Perrault. 9. *The Happy Prince* by Oscar Wilde. 10. *The Nightingale and the Rose* by Oscar Wilde. 11. *Rumpelstiltskin* by Grimm. 12. *Snow White and The Seven Dwarfs* by Grimm.

Dramatic presentations of old favorites. The excellent voice variations, dialects, sound effects, and music combine to create an enjoyable listening experience.

MASTERY STORY TELLER, SET ONE (Filmstrip–Sound). Random House, 1977. 4 color, sound filmstrips, 42–56 fr.; 4 cassettes or discs, 7:45–12:59 min. Disc #05060 ($72), Cassette #05061 ($72). Gr. 4-6. PRV (4/78). 808.83

Contents: 1. *Golden Touch* by Nathaniel Hawthorne. 2. *How the Whale Got His Throat* by Rudyard Kipling. 3. *The Necklace* by Guy de Maupassant. 4. *Two Thanksgiving Day Gentlemen* by O. Henry.

These classic stories have been spellbinders for generations. Each provides the basis for introspective thought.

TEN TALES OF MYSTERY AND TERROR (Cassette). Troll Associates, 1973. 10 cassette tapes. ($65). Gr. 5-12. PRV (1/76). 808.83

Contents: 1. Fall of the House of Usher. 2. Dr. Jekyll and Mr. Hyde. 3. Hound of the Baskervilles. 4. Journey to the Center of the Earth. 5. Lost World. 6. Mysterious Island. 7. The Pit and the Pendulum. 8. Time Machine. 9. 20,000 Leagues under the Sea. 10. War of the Worlds.

These cassettes paraphrase rather than actually condense, retaining the mood and plot of Poe, Verne, and Doyle, but necessarily changing the language. They should stimulate interest in reading the originals.

LITERATURE–STUDY AND TEACHING

LITERATURE FOR CHILDREN, SERIES 1 (Filmstrip–Sound). Pied Piper Productions, 1970. 4 color, sound filmstrips, 24–58 fr.; 4 cassettes or discs. Cassette #L010C ($65), Disc #L010R ($65). Gr. 4-6. BKL (5/15/72), FLN (1973), INS (5/72). 807

Contents: 1. Story of a Book. 2. Biography. 3. Tall Tales. 4. Fantasy.

LITERATURE—STUDY AND TEACHING (cont.)

The first strip tells how *Pagoo* by Holling C. Holling was conceived and written. The second tells of biography as a special type of literature. Tall Tales gives samples as motivation to writing. Fantasy gives the basic qualities, recommends 3 authors, and tells how to locate them in the library.

LITERATURE FOR CHILDREN, SERIES 2 (Filmstrip—Sound). Pied Piper Productions, 1960. 4 color, sound filmstrips, 59–70 fr.; 4 cassettes or discs, av. 8–12 min.; Teacher's Guide. Cassette #L020C ($65), Disc #L020R ($65). Gr. 4–6. BKL (5/15/72), FLN (1973), INS (5/72). 807

Contents: 1. Animals. 2. Distant Land. 3. Fairy Tales. 4. Humor.

This set includes book talks on the topics listed with some "meet-the-authors," dramatized episodes, puppets, and occasional brief detours into library skills.

LITERATURE FOR CHILDREN, SERIES 3 (Filmstrip—Sound). Pied Piper Productions, 1971. 4 color, sound filmstrips; 4 cassettes or discs; Teacher's Guide. Cassettes #L030C ($65), Discs #L030R ($65). Gr. 4–6. BKL (5/15/72), FLN (1973), INS (5/72). 807

Contents: 1. Enjoying Illustrations. 2. Historical Fiction. 3. Myths. 4. Adventure.

Reviews modern styles of more than 40 outstanding artists as well as presenting 3 main categories of literature—historical fiction, myths, and adventure. Library skills are offered in 2 of the filmstrips.

LITERATURE FOR CHILDREN, SERIES 4 (Filmstrip—Sound). Pied Piper Productions, 1972. 4 color, sound filmstrips, 43–56 fr.; 4 discs or cassettes, av. 11–12 min.; Teacher's Guide; Worksheet Master; Bibliography. Cassettes #L040C ($65), Discs #L040R ($65). Gr. 4–6. BKL (6/1/75), INS (1973), PRV (4/1/73). 807

Contents: 1. Haiku. 2. Descriptive Words and Figures of Speech. 3. Sounds of Poetry. 4. Humorous Verse.

Stresses poetry for enjoyment as well as motivation for creative writing. A Japanese garden provides a beautiful setting for the haiku. Poems by well-loved authors and samples by children are presented, and the relationship between words and rhythm is explored.

READING FOR THE FUN OF IT— ADVENTURE (Filmstrip—Sound). Guidance Associates, 1976. 1 color, sound filmstrip; 1 disc or cassette, approx. 15 min. Disc #9A-303-147 ($27.75), Cassette #9A-303-154 ($27.75). Gr. 4–9. PRV (4/78). 807

Students can sample the adventure and physical action, exploration and inner struggles found in some books. A sampling of authors in this filmstrip includes Paula Fox, Theodore Cay, Scott O'Dell, Mark Twain, and Jean C. George.

READING FOR THE FUN OF IT— FANTASY (Filmstrip—Sound). Guidance Associates, 1976. 1 color, sound filmstrip; 1 disc or cassette, approx. 15 min. Disc #9A-303-261 ($27.75), Cassette #9A-303-279 ($27.75). Gr. 4–9. PRV (4/78). 807

Helps students explore the wonderful world of "what if." Part of a motivational series designed to help students discover books that they will enjoy. Some of the books reviewed are by such favorites as C. S. Lewis, Astrid Lindgren, E. B. White, Mary Norton, and Lloyd Alexander.

READING FOR THE FUN OF IT— HISTORICAL FICTION (Filmstrip— Sound). Guidance Associates, 1976. 1 color, sound filmstrip; 1 disc or cassette, approx. 15 min. Disc #9A-303-188 ($27.75), Cassette #9A-303-196 ($27.75). Gr. 4–9. PRV (4/78). 807

Past attitudes, beliefs, customs, and events are brought to life through the eyes and writings of Robert Lawson, William Steele, Laura Ingalls Wilder, Katherine Paterson, and others.

READING FOR THE FUN OF IT—MANY LANDS (Filmstrip—Sound). Guidance Associates, 1976. 1 color, sound filmstrip; 1 cassette or disc, approx. 15 min. Disc #9A-303-204 ($27.75), Cassette #9A-303-212 ($27.75). Gr. 4–9. PRV (4/78). 807

Helps students appreciate literature as a means of exploring customs, values, and life around the world. Authors who do this so well include Pearl Buck, Joseph Krumgold, and Scott O'Dell.

READING FOR THE FUN OF IT— MYSTERY (Filmstrip—Sound). Guidance Associates, 1976. 1 color, sound filmstrip; 1 disc or cassette, approx. 15 min. Disc #9A-303-121 ($27.75), Cassette #9A-303-139 ($27.75). Gr. 4–9. PRV (4/78). 807

Students can feel the tension and satisfaction built into psychological, criminal, and supernatural mysteries by such authors as Frank Bonham, John Billairs, Alfred Hitchcock, and Joan Aiken.

READING FOR THE FUN OF IT— REALISTIC FICTION (Filmstrip—Sound). Guidance Associates, 1976. 1 color, sound filmstrip; 1 cassette or disc, approx. 15 min. Disc #9A-303 105 ($27.75), Cassette #9A-303 113 ($27.75). Gr. 4–9. PRV (4/78). 807

Helps students identify with carefully detailed, down-to-earth stories and characters. Some of the books reviewed are by such authors as Betsy Byars, Judy Blume, Virginia Hamilton, Julia Cunningham, and Beverly Cleary.

READING FOR THE FUN OF IT—SCIENCE
FICTION (Filmstrip—Sound). Guidance
Associates, 1976. 1 color, sound filmstrip;
1 disc or cassette, approx. 15 min. Disc
#9A-303-162 ($27.75), Cassette #9A-303-
170 ($27.75). Gr. 4-9. PRV (4/78). 807
Helps students find their favorite themes:
the future of humanity, technology, special
powers of mind and spirit, creatures from
other worlds as presented by Arthur C.
Clarke, Madeleine L'Engle, Jules Verne,
Eleanor Cameron, and others.

LITTLE GREY RABBIT GOES TO SEA

LITTLE GREY RABBIT'S CHRISTMAS &
LITTLE GREY RABBIT GOES TO SEA
(Phonodisc or Cassette). *See* Rabbits—
Fiction

**A LITTLE LOVIN' AND A LITTLE
LAUGHIN'**

SERIES SEVEN: A LITTLE LOVIN' AND A
LITTLE LAUGHIN' (Filmstrip—Sound).
See Short Stories

LOBEL, ARNOLD

AS I WAS CROSSING BOSTON COMMON
(Filmstrip—Sound/Captioned). *See* Animals—Fiction

FROG AND TOAD TOGETHER (Filmstrip—
Sound). *See* Friendship—Fiction

LOFTING, HUGH

DOCTOR DOLITTLE (Filmstrip—Sound).
See Animals—Fiction

THE VOYAGES OF DOCTOR DOLITTLE
(Filmstrip—Sound). *See* Animals—Fiction

LOGIC

LET'S LOOK AT LOGIC (Filmstrip—Sound).
Guidance Associates, 1977. 2 color, sound
filmstrips, 60-78 fr.; 2 cassettes or discs,
av. 15 min. ea.; Teacher's Guide; Activity
Cards. Discs #1B-304-665 ($59.50), Cas-
sette #1B-304-673 ($59.50). Gr. 4-8.
PRV (1/78), PVB (4/78). 130
Introduces simple aspects of formal logic
and relates commonsense problem-solving
techniques to all elementary subjects. A
trip to "Logicland" sets the stage for
learning about Venn diagrams; helps discover precise meanings of "true," "valid,"
"possible," "any," "some," "all," and
"follow from."

LONDON, JACK

CALL OF THE WILD (Filmstrip—Sound).
See Dogs—Fiction

JACK LONDON CASSETTE LIBRARY
(Cassette). *See* Short Stories

LONGFELLOW, HENRY WADSWORTH

PAUL REVERE'S RIDE AND HIS OWN
STORY (Cassette). *See* American Poetry

LOOMS

HORIZONTAL BELT LOOM (Film Loop—
8mm—Silent). Thorne Films/Prentice-Hall
Media, 1972 (Southwest Indians). 8mm
color, silent film loop, approx. 4 min.
#HAT 286 ($26). Gr. 4-A. MDU (1978).
746.1
The horizontal belt loom used by Southwest
Indians is demonstrated.

UPRIGHT LOOM (Film Loop—8mm—Silent).
Thorne Films/Prentice-Hall Media (Southwest Indians). 8mm color, silent film loop,
approx. 4 min. #HAT 285 ($28). Gr. 4-A.
AUR (1978). 746.1
This film loop illustrates the use of the
upright loom by Indians of the Southwest.

LOPSHIRE, ROBERT

BEGINNER BOOKS FILMSTRIPS, SET 1
(Filmstrip—Sound). *See* Reading—Study
and Teaching

LOVOOS, JANICE

DESIGN IS A DANDELION (Filmstrip—
Sound). *See* Design, Decorative

LUNAR PROBES

BEYOND THIS EARTH (Filmstrip—Sound).
Marshfilm, 1972. 1 color, sound filmstrip,
50 fr.; 1 cassette or disc, 15 min.; Teacher's
Guide. ($21). Gr. 1-5. BKL (10/15/73),
ESL (1976), SLJ (5/73). 629.4
Actual NASA color photographs of the
Apollo 16 moon mission illustrate a discus-
sion of our ambition to explore space.

MACCLINTOCK, HARRY K. *See*
McClintock, Harry K.

MACHINERY

DISCOVERING SIMPLE MACHINES (Film-
strip—Sound). Filmstrip House/United
Learning, 1975. 4 color, sound filmstrips,
av. 45 fr. ea.; 2 cassettes or discs, av. 12
min. ea. Cassettes #65602 ($55), Discs
#65601 ($55). Gr. 4-6. BKL (10/75),
PRV (3/76). 521
Contents: 1. Levers. 2. Wheels. 3. Inclined
Plane. 4. Screw.
Through photography we see children dis-
cover principles about levers, wheels, the

MACHINERY (cont.)

inclined plane, and the screw. Everyday examples readily found in the environment are used for observing and generalizing.

SIMPLE MACHINES (Filmstrip—Sound). Society for Visual Education, 1976. 6 color, sound filmstrips, 40–47 fr.; 6 discs or cassettes. Discs #A413-SAR ($90), Cassette #A413-SATC ($90). Gr. 4–7. BKL (11/1/76). 621

Contents: 1. The Work of Simple Machines. 2. The Lever. 3. The Pulley. 4. The Wheel and Axle. 5. The Inclined Plane, Screw and Wedge.

Simple machines are presented in this strip with cartoonlike illustrations and photographs. The jobs performed by the various machines, the physics of their operation, and examples of the tools are presented.

MACRAME

CREATIVE MACRAME (Filmstrip—Sound). Warner Educational Productions, 1975 (Art Craft Teaching Films). 2 color, sound filmstrips; 1 cassette, 15 min.; Teacher's Guide. ($39.50). Gr. 6–A. BKL (1/15/75). 746.43

Demonstrates the technique of this art with close-up photographs of step-by-step procedures.

MAGIC—FICTION

JAPANESE STORIES OF MAGIC (Filmstrip —Sound). Gakken, Tokyo/Coronet Instructional Media, 1976. 6 color, sound filmstrips, av. 30 fr.; 3 discs or 6 cassettes, av. 7 min. Discs #S237 ($75), Cassettes #M237 ($83). Gr. 1–6. PRV (3/77), PVB (4/78). Fic

Contents: 1. The Red Soup Bowl. 2. Goblin's Invisible Cloak. 3. The Old Woman of the Mountain. 4. Song of a Snow Girl. 5. A Doctor for a Wooden Horse. 6. The Land of the Ogres.

Stories of magical adventures are narrated in simple language. A variety of art styles are used in the visuals.

THE MAGIC FISHBONE (Filmstrip—Sound/ Captioned). Listening Library, 1977 (Look, Listen and Read). 1 color, captioned/sound filmstrip, 66 fr.; 1 cassette, 14 min; Teacher's Guide. ($14.95). Gr. K–4. LGB (12/77). Fic

An adaptation of Dickens's delightfully nonsensical story which will charm young viewers. Through her magic talisman, Princess Alicia saves the royal family from poverty and marries the Prince. Original illustrations and narration adapted from the story.

SYLVESTER AND THE MAGIC PEBBLE PUPPET (Kit). Society for Visual Educa-

tion, 1976. 1 cassette; 2 Hand Puppets; 1 Poster; Teacher's Guide. #MK-2601 ($35). Gr. K–3. BKL (10/77). Fic

The kit is based on the Caldecott Medal book by the same title. It was designed to supplement language arts and social studies, and develop thinking and verbalization skills.

THE WIZARD (Motion Picture—16mm— Sound). Films, 1974. 16mm color, animated, sound film, 8 min. #307-0004 ($145). Gr. 1–6. BKL (4/1/75), WLB (5/75). Fic

The Wizard is an animated tale about imagination, a story of a wizard who misapplies his magical powers by casting spells on his neighbors. He learns that negative use of imagination and artistic energy leads to rejection and loneliness. Finally, he learns that by channeling his imagination to creative ends, he can be both fulfilled and admired.

MAGNETISM

LEARNING ABOUT MAGNETISM: SECOND EDITION (Motion Picture—16mm —Sound). EBEC, 1975 (Introduction to Physical Science). 16mm color, sound film, 14 min. #3396 ($220). Gr. 4–9. BKL (2/76), PRV (1/76). 538

Magnetism, its mysteries, and its practical applications are clearly explored. The subject of magnetic fields is dramatized with scenes of an 83-ton electromagnet and a magnetic field so huge that its entire expanse can be viewed only from a helicopter.

MAMMALS

BATS (Film Loop—8mm—Silent). See Bats

ELEMENTARY NATURAL SCIENCE— SMALL PREDATORY MAMMAL (Motion Picture—16mm—Sound). Centron Films, 1973 (Elementary Natural Science). 16mm color, sound film, 12-1/2 min.; Leader's Guide. ($200). Gr. 4–8. BKL (11/1/73), ENE (9/75), LFR (5/74). 599

Examines several familiar small predators (weasel, raccoon, gray fox) to illustrate prey—predator relationship, balance of nature, and other concepts.

THE GREAT TIGERS OF INDIA (Kit). See Tigers

MAMMALS (Film Loop—8mm—Captioned). See Animals—Infancy

THE MOUNTAIN GORILLA (Kit). See Gorillas

POLAR BEAR: MOTHER AND CUBS (Film Loop—8mm—Silent). See Bears

THE POLAR BEARS AND THE SEALS (Kit). Classroom Complement/EBEC,

1976 (Animal Life Stories). 1 color, sound filmstrip; 1 cassette; 5 identical Storybooks; Teacher's Guide. #6965K ($27.95). Gr. K–6. TEA (11/77). 599.7

How animals live, move, build homes, and fight for food and survival are presented scientifically in accurate stories describing the lives of animals in their natural habitat. A storybook reproduces all the narration and art from the filmstrip.

THE PORPOISES AND THE SAILOR (Kit). *See* Porpoises

PORTRAIT OF A WHALE (Motion Picture–16mm–Sound). *See* Whales

THE PRAIRIE DOG TOWN (Kit). *See* Prairie Dogs

WHALES SURFACING (Film Loop–8mm–Silent). *See* Whales

WOLF FAMILY (Film Loop–8mm–Silent). *See* Wolves

THE WOLVES OF ISLE ROYALE (Kit). *See* Wolves

ZEBRA (Motion Picture–16mm–Sound). *See* Zebras

ZIGGY, THE ELEPHANT (Kit). *See* Elephants

See also names of Mammals such as Pandas, Tigers

MAN

FROM CAVE TO CITY (Motion Picture–16mm–Sound). *See* Civilization

MAN–INFLUENCE OF ENVIRONMENT

CULTURE AND ENVIRONMENT: LIVING IN THE TROPICS (Filmstrip–Sound). *See* Tropics

WINTER ON AN INDIAN RESERVATION (Motion Picture–16mm–Sound). *See* Indians of North America

MAN–INFLUENCE ON NATURE

ABC'S OF ENVIRONMENT (Filmstrip–Sound). *See* Ecology

BIRDS OF PREY (Filmstrip–Sound). *See* Birds of Prey

BOOMSVILLE (Motion Picture–16mm–Sound). *See* Cities and Towns

THE DESERT: PROFILE OF AN ARID LAND (Filmstrip–Sound). *See* Deserts

DISCOVERING OUR ENVIRONMENT (Study Print). *See* Environment

ECOLOGY AND THE ROLE OF MAN (Filmstrip–Sound). *See* Wildlife Conservation

ECOLOGY: UNDERSTANDING THE CRISIS (Filmstrip–Sound). *See* Ecology

MAN AND HIS ENVIRONMENT (Film Loop–8mm–Silent). Troll Associates, 1974. 4 super 8mm color, film loops, approx. 4 min. ea.; Teacher's Guide; Film Notes on Containers. ($99.80). Gr. 2–6. PRV (2/75). 574.5

Contents: 1. Plant and Animal Ecology. 2. Man's Own Ecological System. 3. Can Man Change the Balance of Life? 4. What is Conservation?

Students discover that as the world of technology becomes increasingly complex, people change their environment in many ways and influence plant and animal life.

PARADISE LOST (Motion Picture–16mm–Sound). National Film Board of Canada/Benchmark Films. 16mm color, animated film, 4 min. ($95). Gr. 3–A. LBJ, NEF 574.5

Evelyn Lambert's colorful animation symbolizes the threat to all living creatures posed by the great despoiler–the human. Into the natural ecological balance in the fields and forests drift man-made pesticides, and birds and butterflies succumb.

MANUFACTURERS

WHERE DOES IT COME FROM? (Filmstrip–Sound). Imperial Educational Resources, 1974. 4 color, sound filmstrips; 4 cassettes or discs. Discs #3RG68500 ($56), Cassettes #3KG68500 ($62). Gr. 2–6. BKL (6/1/74), PRV (3/75). 670

Contents: 1. Where Do We Get Our Textiles? 2. Where Do We Get Our Meat? 3. Where Do We Get Our Iron? 4. Where Do We Get Our Seaweed?

A different and fascinating story is told as students see what happens between raw materials and finished items.

MAP DRAWING

EXPLORING THE WORLD OF MAPS (Filmstrip–Sound). *See* Maps

MAPS

EXPLORING THE WORLD OF MAPS (Filmstrip–Sound). National Geographic, 1973. 5 color, sound filmstrips; 5 discs or cassettes, 11–14 min. Discs #03734 ($74.50), Cassettes #03735 ($74.50). Gr. 5–12. PRV (11/74), PVB (5/75). 912

Contents: 1. The Message of Maps. 2. Using Maps. 3. The Round Earth on Flat Paper. 4. Surveying the Earth. 5. The Making of Maps.

The graphics of mapmaking is shown from the beginning sketches to the final product. Students discover what can be learned from maps and how to read the different kinds of maps.

MAPS (cont.)

GHOST OF CAPTAIN PEALE (Motion Picture—16mm—Sound). *See* Metric System

HOW TO USE MAPS AND GLOBES (Filmstrip—Sound). Troll Associates, 1974. 6 color, sound filmstrips, av. 43 fr. ea.; 3 cassettes, 16 min. ea.; Teacher's Guide. ($78). Gr. 4–8. INS (2/75). 912

Contents: 1. What Is a Map? 2. What Is a Globe? 3. How to Read a Map. 4. Latitude and Longitude. 5. Latitude and Climate. 6. Longitude and Time Zone.

Stimulates development of map reading skills, and helps students understand scale, symbols, direction, and distance.

MARCEAU, MARCEL

BIP AS A SKATER (Motion Picture—16mm—Sound). *See* Pantomimes

THE PAINTER (Motion Picture—16mm—Sound). *See* Pantomimes

PANTOMIME: THE LANGUAGE OF THE HEART (Motion Picture—16mm—Sound). *See* Pantomimes

THE SIDE SHOW (Motion Picture—16mm—Sound). *See* Pantomimes

MARCHES (MUSIC)

MARCHES (Phonodiscs). Bowmar Publishing. 1 disc; Lesson Guide; Theme Charts. #067 ($10). Gr. 2–8. AUR (1978). 785.1

Some of the marches on this disc include "Entrance of the Little Fawns" by Pierne, "March Militaire" by Schubert, "The March of the Siamese Children" by Rodgers.

SOUSA MARCHES (Phonodiscs). Bowmar Publishing. 1 disc. #127 ($6.95). Gr. K–6. AUR (1978). 785.1

Includes the "Star Spangled Banner" in the key of A for easier singing, plus 5 famous bugle calls. Also on the disc are "Semper Fidelis," "Stars and Stripes," and other famous marches.

WORLD OF MARCHES (Phonodiscs). Bowmar Publishing. 1 disc. #130 ($6.95). Gr. K–6. AUR (1978). 785.1

"National Emblem" (U.S.A.), "Aguero" (Spain), "Entry of the Gladiators" (Germany), "Yacatecas" (Mexico), and many others are collected in this recording.

MARCO POLO

FAMOUS STORIES OF GREAT COURAGE (Filmstrip—Sound). *See* Heroes and Heroines

MARINE ANIMALS

OCTOPUS (Film Loop—8mm—Silent). *See* Octopus

THE UNDERWATER ENVIRONMENT, GROUP ONE (Filmstrip—Sound). Imperial Educational Resources, 1971. 4 color, sound filmstrips; 4 discs or cassettes; Teacher's Notes. Discs #3RG44700 ($56), Cassettes #3KG44700 ($62). Gr. 5–12. BKL (5/15/71), TEA (9/71). 574.92

Contents: 1. Living Corals. 2. Spiny-Skinned Animals. 3. Fish in Their Environment. 4. Shellfish and Tubeworms.

Four major classes of underwater life are shown through vivid underwater photography in this set of filmstrips. Many different members of each class are identified and described, and their relationship with the underwater environment is examined.

MARINE BIOLOGY

LIFE IN THE SEA (Filmstrip—Sound). Jean-Michel Cousteau/BFA Educational Media, 1977. 4 color, sound filmstrips, av. 55 fr.; 4 cassettes or discs, av. 8 min. Cassettes #VJP00 ($70), Discs #VJN00 ($70). Gr. 5–8. BKL (11/15/77), PRV (2/78), PVB (4/78). 591.92

Contents: 1. Plants and Simple Sea Animals. 2. Sea Animals without Backbones. 3. Armored and Spiny-skinned Sea Animals. 4. Sea Animals with Backbones.

Taking the most important groups of marine plants and animals, various forms of life are introduced with bold lettering and lots of examples. Ascending the evolutionary ladder, the set examines the most primitive plants and animals and then progresses to the most complex through detailed close-up, captioned frames, and verbal descriptions.

NIGHTLIFE (Motion Picture—16mm—Sound). *See* Ocean

SEA HORSE (Film Loop—8mm—Silent). *See* Sea Horses

THE UNDERWATER ENVIRONMENT, GROUP ONE (Filmstrip—Sound). *See* Marine Animals

THE UNDERWATER ENVIRONMENT, GROUP TWO (Filmstrip—Sound). *See* Marine Plants

MARINE PLANTS

THE UNDERWATER ENVIRONMENT, GROUP TWO (Filmstrip—Sound). Imperial Educational Resources, 1972. 2 color, sound filmstrips; 2 cassettes; Teacher's Notes. Disc #3RG 44800 ($30), Cassette #3KG 44800 ($33). Gr. 5–12. BKL (10/15/72), NST. 574.92

Contents: 1. Part I—Marine Vegetation. 2. Part II—Marine Vegetation

The larger forms of marine vegetation are studied in this set of filmstrips. Both underwater and shoreline photography show a variety of specimens in natural environments that range from cold, northern waters to the subtropics.

MARINE RESOURCES

THE OCEANS: A KEY TO OUR FUTURE (Filmstrip—Sound). *See* Oceanography

MARSUPIALS

KANGAROO (Film Loop—8mm—Silent). *See* Kangaroos

KOALA BEAR (Film Loop—8mm—Silent). *See* Koala Bears

POUCHED ANIMALS AND THEIR YOUNG (Film Loop—8mm—Silent). *See* Animals

MARTIN, BILL

REACH OUT (Motion Picture—16mm—Sound). *See* Values

MASKS (FACIAL)

THE MASK (Filmstrip—Sound). Educational Dimensions Group, 1972. 1 color, sound filmstrip, 85 fr.; 1 cassette, 15 min.; Teacher's Guide. #699 ($24.50). Gr. 5–A. BKL (2/1/73), PRV (3/73), PVB (5/73). 391
A comprehensive history of the mask from the powerful and delightful designs created by primitive cultures to today's protective masks for sports and industry.

MASS MEDIA

FREE PRESS: A NEED TO KNOW THE NEWS (Filmstrip—Sound). *See* Journalism

HOW TO WATCH TV (Filmstrip—Sound). Educational Direction/Xerox Educational Publications, 1977. 4 color, sound filmstrips, 47–55 fr.; 4 cassettes, 7–8 min.; Teacher's Guide. #SC02900 ($69). Gr. 5–9. PRV (3/78), PVB (4/78). 301.16
Contents: 1. News and Documentaries. 2. Drama and Comedy. 3. Advertising. 4. Learning from Television.
An introduction to serious television viewing that motivates students to watch critically.

WORDS, MEDIA AND YOU (Filmstrip—Sound). Globe Filmstrips/Coronet Instructional Media, 1974. 6 color, sound filmstrips, av. 73 fr.; 6 discs or cassettes, av. 11:30 min.; Teacher's Guide. Discs #S702 ($99), Cassettes #M702 ($99). Gr. 5–12 BKL (1975), PVB (4/76). 301.16
Contents: 1. Mass Media—Servant or Master? 2. Words in Advertising. 3. Words in News. 4. Words in Politics. 5. Words in Entertainment. 6. Words in Literature.
Stresses the way media affects our culture. Specific individuals in various occupations explain how they choose words carefully to control emotions.

MATHEMATICS

DONALD IN MATHMAGIC LAND (Filmstrip—Sound). Walt Disney Educational Media, 1976. 4 color, sound filmstrips; 4 discs or cassettes, av. 7 min. ea.; Teacher's Guide. #63-8034L ($81). Gr. 4–8. MDU (4/77), MTE (9/77). 511
Contents: 1. Math in Music. 2. The Secret of the Pentagram. 3. Who's Keeping the Score? 4. The Shape of Things.
Based on the award-winning animated classic film. Youngsters learn how mathematical principles influence architecture, science, art, music, and sports.

INTRODUCING THE ELECTRONIC CALCULATOR (Filmstrip—Sound). *See* Calculating Machines

MATH ON DISPLAY (Kit). EBEC, 1977. 5 color, sound filmstrips, 96 fr.; 5 cassettes; 100 Task Cards; Teacher's Guide; 16mm teacher training films available. #6950K ($110). Gr. 4–8. MDU (7/77). 651.82
Contents: 1. Checking Computations on the Calculator. 2. Decimals. 3. Percentages. 4. Proportions (Equivalent Ratios). 5. Number Patterns.
Students learn how useful and usable the hand-held calculator is through these 5 presentations. Each strip employs a cartoon situation to make its point. One hundred task cards further the learning with calculator follow-up activities.

MATSUNO, MASAKO

A PAIR OF RED CLOGS (Filmstrip—Sound/Captioned). *See* Japan—Fiction

MATTER

SHAPES AND STRUCTURES IN NATURE (Filmstrip—Captioned). BFA Educational Media, 1974. 4 captioned filmstrips. #VV1000 ($32). Gr. 6–9. BKL (5/1/75), PRV. 530.4
Contents: 1. The Shape of Things. 2. What Are Things Made Of? 3. Forces, Shapes and Changes. 4. Shapes and Structures around Us.
Introduces the structure of matter; develops concepts of atomic and molecular structure and relates molecular arrangements to the properties of natural and man-make shapes and structures.

TIME, SPACE AND MATTER (Filmstrip—Sound). BFA Educational Media, 1975. 6 color, sound filmstrips; 6 cassettes or discs. Cassettes #VFG000 ($104), Discs #VFF000 ($104). Gr. 4–6. BKL (12/1/75), PRV (3/76), PVB (4/77). 530.11

MATTER (cont.)

Contents: 1. What Is Time? 2. Years, Months, Weeks, and Days. 3. Dividing the Days. 4. What Are Space and Matter? 5. Measuring Space and Matter. 6. Time, Space and Matter: How Are They Related?

Time, space, and matter are ideas used to help us describe our world. None of these ideas will appear the same in all situations and for all people. When we examine these ideas closely, we can see that time, matter, and space are related.

MAUPASSANT, GUY DE

MASTERY STORY TELLER, SET ONE (Filmstrip—Sound). *See* Literature—Collections

MAY I BRING A FRIEND?

SOUND FILMSTRIP SET 35 (Filmstrip—Sound). *See* Children's Literature—Collections

MAY, JULIAN

SPORTS CLOSE-UPS 1 (Kit). *See* Athletes

SPORTS CLOSE-UPS 3 (Kit). *See* Athletes

SPORTS CLOSE-UPS 4 (Kit). *See* Athletes

MCCLINTOCK, HARRY K.

HAYWIRE MAC (Phonodiscs). *See* Folk Songs

MCDERMOTT, GERALD

ANANSI THE SPIDER (Motion Picture—16mm—Sound). *See* Folklore—Africa

ANANSI THE SPIDER BY GERALD MCDERMOTT (Filmstrip—Sound). *See* Folklore—Africa

ARROW TO THE SUN (Motion Picture—16mm—Sound). *See* Indians of North American—Legends

THE MAGIC TREE (Motion Picture—16mm—Sound). *See* Folklore—Africa

THE STONECUTTER (Filmstrip—Sound). *See* Folklore—Japan

MCHARGUE, GEORGESS

PRIVATE ZOO (Filmstrip—Sound). *See* Shades and Shadows—Fiction

MCLEOD, EMILIE WARREN

THE BEAR'S BICYCLE (Filmstrip—Sound). *See* Bicycles and Bicycling—Fiction

MCPHAIL, DAVID

SERIES SEVEN: A LITTLE LOVIN' AND A LITTLE LAUGHIN' (Filmstrip—Sound). *See* Short Stories

MEASUREMENT

GHOST OF CAPTAIN PEALE (Motion Picture—16mm—Sound). *See* Metric System

MEASURE IT (Filmstrip—Sound). Educational Direction/Learning Tree Filmstrips, 1975. 4 color, sound filmstrips, av. 60 fr. ea.; 2 cassettes, av. 7–8 min. ea.; Teacher's Guide. #LT556 ($52). Gr. 2–4. INS (1/76), LGB (1975), PRV (1/76). 389

Contents: 1. Measure? What For? 2. The Long and Short of It. 3. Is There Enough of It? 4. Measure Today and Tomorrow.

This set has been developed to foster an awareness of both the concepts of, and the everyday need for, measurement.

MEASUREMENT COMPARISONS (Filmstrip—Sound). *See* Size and Shape

MEASUREMENT: FROM CUBITS TO CENTIMETERS (Filmstrip—Sound). Guidance Associates, 1975 (Math Matters). 2 color, sound filmstrips, av. 65 fr.; 2 discs or cassettes, av. 11 min.; Teacher's Guide. Cassettes #1/8B-301 489 ($52.50), Discs #1B 301 497 ($52.50). Gr. 4–8. ATE. 389.152

Traces the evolution of measurements from ancient times through the nineteenth century. Explains how the metric system spread throughout the world.

PRESENTANDO MEDIDAS (INTRODUCING MEASURING) (Filmstrip—Sound). BFA Educational Media, 1976. 6 color, sound filmstrips, av. 31–42 fr.; 6 cassettes or discs, av. 6:22–9:23 min.; Teacher's Guide. Cassettes #VGY000 ($92), Discs #VGX000 ($92). Gr. 4–9. PRV (11/77). 389

Contents: 1. Comparando. 2. Unidades Fijas. 3. Perimetro y Area. 4. Volumen. 5. Presando Acerca de Escalas. 6. Conceptos Acerca de Medidas: Repaso.

This set shows what measuring is and how it helps find length, perimeter, area, and volume. Why numbers are important and how to use standard units of measure to solve simple problems are presented.

MEDICAL CARE

GOING BACK UNIT THREE (Motion Picture—16mm—Sound). *See* Occupations

HABITS OF HEALTH: THE PHYSICAL EXAMINATION (Motion Picture—16mm—Sound). *See* Hygiene

THE HOSPITAL (Motion Picture—16mm—Sound). McGraw-Hill Films, 1972. 16mm

color, sound film, 12 min.; Guide. #106872-4 ($195). Gr. K–3. BKL (11/1/76). 362.1
Bill Cosby and his younger brother Russell are lured to the hospital by that old standby—the promise of all the ice cream they can eat—after their tonsils are removed! The rest of the kids hearing about the promise devise some schemes so they can reap the rewards of surgery, yet keep their tonsils. In spite of Bill Cosby's confession that the visit won't be all fun and there will be some pain involved, the film is a painless way of introducing the subject of hospitals.

MENNONITES

THE AMISH: A PEOPLE OF PRESERVATION (Motion Picture—16mm—Sound). *See* Amish

MENOTTI, GIAN CARLO

STORIES IN BALLET AND OPERA (Phonodiscs). *See* Music—Analysis, Appreciation

MERRILL, JEAN

THE SUPERLATIVE HORSE (Motion Picture—16mm—Sound). *See* Folklore—China

MERRITT, A.

SCIENCE FICTION (Filmstrip—Sound/Captioned). *See* Science Fiction

MESA VERDE NATIONAL PARK

INDIAN CLIFF DWELLINGS AT MESA VERDE—SLIDE SET (Slides). *See* Cliff Dwellers and Cliff Dwellings

METAMORPHOSIS

BUTTERFLY: THE MONARCH'S LIFE CYCLE (Motion Picture—16mm—Sound). *See* Butterflies

DON'T (Motion Picture—16mm—Sound). *See* Butterflies

LIFE CYCLE OF COMMON ANIMALS, GROUP 3 (Filmstrip—Sound). *See* Butterflies

METAMORPHOSIS (Motion Picture—16mm—Sound). *See* Butterflies

MONARCH: STORY OF A BUTTERFLY (Film Loop—8mm—Silent). *See* Butterflies

MOTHS—SLIDE SET (Slides). *See* Moths

METEOROLOGY

INQUIRING INTO WEATHER (Filmstrip—Sound). *See* Weather Forecasting

STORMS: THE RESTLESS ATMOSPHERE (Motion Picture—16mm—Sound). *See* Storms

WEATHER FORECASTING (Motion Picture—16mm—Sound). *See* Weather Forecasting

WEATHER, SEASONS AND CLIMATE (Filmstrip—Sound). BFA Educational Media, 1977. 4 color, sound filmstrips, 49–52 fr.; 4 discs or cassettes, 5:47–6:24 min.; Teacher's Guide. Disc #VJR000 ($56), Cassettes #VJS000 ($68). Gr. 4–8. PRV (4/78). 551.6
Contents: 1. What Causes Weather. 2. Our Sun and Time and Seasons. 3. The Earth's Climate. 4. Storms and Clouds.
Introduces weather, storms, seasons, and times, their causes and variations, the need for time zones, the reasons for day and night, seasons, and climates

METRIC SYSTEM

GHOST OF CAPTAIN PEALE (Motion Picture—16mm—Sound). EBEC, 1975 (Math That Counts). 16mm color, sound film, 11 min. #3471 ($150). Gr. 4–8. ATE (4/77), LFR (9/11/76), TEA (3/76). 389.152
Two important concepts—metric measurement and interpreting map scale—are introduced in this whimsical tale of a treasure map, an incompetent ghost, and a clever little girl.

KING VAT (Motion Picture—16mm—Sound). EBEC, 1975 (Math That Counts). 16mm color, sound film, 13 min. #3470 ($185). Gr. 4–8. ATE (4/77), LFR (1/2/77). 389.152
The metric system and decimal notation are visualized in this humorous story about the Land of Containers. To keep big King Vat (a kilo-liter) filled with golden elixir, his subjects operate a bucket brigade. Through clever pictorial devices, the characters figure out place value for sub-one units, so that they can add the new decimal numbers.

MEASUREMENT: FROM CUBITS TO CENTIMETERS (Filmstrip—Sound). *See* Measurement

METRIC MEETS THE INCHWORM (Motion Picture—16mm—Sound). Bosustow Productions, 1974. 16mm color, sound, animated film, 10 min.; Leader's Guide. ($175). Gr. 2–A. ATE (4/76), CIF (1975), MTE (4/76). 389.152
Fred Inchworm is understandably depressed with the new metric system. He decides he will go to work somewhere where they've never heard of metric. Poor Fred, suffering from "Metric-phobia," finds that will not be too easy. Almost all other countries of the world use the metric system. Fred's only hope is outer space, but when he joins a NASA space mission, he finds they've been using the metric system for years. Forced

METRIC SYSTEM (cont.)

to accept the change, he finds that the metric system is not so mysterious and terrifying.

METRIC SYSTEM (Filmstrip—Sound). Educational Dimensions Group, 1976. 2 color, sound filmstrips, 60 fr.; 2 cassettes, 15–17 min.; Teacher's Guide. #527 ($37). Gr. 4–8. PRV (12/76), PVB (4/77). 389.152

These filmstrips show first a comparison of the 2 systems (the metric and the English), then go on to discuss the use of the metric system, generally as easy as counting by tens.

THE METRIC SYSTEM FOR THE INTERMEDIATE GRADES, SET ONE (Filmstrip—Sound). Pathescope Educational Media, 1973. 4 color, sound filmstrips; 4 cassettes; Teacher's Manual. #306 ($70). Gr. 4–6. LGB (5/74). 389.152

Contents: 1. Units of Length Shorter than a Meter. 2. Units of Length Longer than a Meter. 3. Metric Units of Area. 4. Metric Units of Volume.

Introduces students to the meter, the basic unit in the metric system. The children are guided by Mr. Metro, the friendly decimal computer who helps them understand the relationship of metric system units to the place value in our system of numeration.

THE METRIC SYSTEM FOR THE INTERMEDIATE GRADES, SET TWO (Filmstrip—Sound). Pathescope Educational Media, 1973. 3 color, sound filmstrips; 3 cassettes; Teacher's Manual. #307 ($55). Gr. 4–6. LGB (5/74). 389.152

Contents: 1. Metric Units of Capacity. 2. Metric Units of Mass or Weight. 3. Relating Length, Capacity and Mass.

Introduces students to the meter, the basic unit in the metric system. The children are guided by Mr. Metro, the friendly decimal computer who helps them understand the relationship of metric system units to the place value in our system of numeration.

METRIC SYSTEM OF MEASUREMENT (Filmstrip—Sound). Library Filmstrip Center, 1975. 1 color, sound filmstrip, 56 fr.; 1 cassette or disc, 14 min. Cassettes ($26), Discs ($24). Gr. 4–12. PRV (11/76). 389.152

Gives a brief history of man's use of measurement. It explains the base unit for length and mass.

THE METRIC SYSTEM OF MEASUREMENT (Filmstrip—Sound). Educational Development/Imperial Educational Resources, 1975. 4 color, sound filmstrips, 50–55 fr.; 4 cassettes or discs, 10–12 min. Discs #3RG 10200 ($56), Cassettes #3KG 10200 ($62). Gr. 2–9. PRV (12/75), PVB (4/76). 389.152

Contents: 1. History of Measurement. 2. Measuring Length. 3. Measuring Weight. 4. Measuring Volume.

An introduction to the actual use of metric units, not complicated conversion formulas. Concepts of measurement are treated from an historical point, showing that many standards have been devised and improved throughout history. Fundamental methods of measuring length, weight, and volume, and applying these methods using metric units are also presented.

THE METRIC SYSTEM: UNIT 1 (Study Print). Aesop Films/EBEC, 1976. 10 13 in. X 18 in. color study prints. Study Guide. #18050 ($21.95). Gr. 2–6. MDU (1/77), PRV (9/77). 389.152

Contents: 1. SI—International System of Units. 2. Base Unit—Length. 3. Base Unit—Mass. 4. Base Unit—Time. 5. Base Unit—Temperature. 6. Prefix Kilo. 7. Prefixes Hecto and Deka. 8. Prefix Deci. 9. Prefix Centi. 10. Prefix Milli.

Unit 1 introduces base units and prefixes. Cartoon drawings with easy-to-read captions are used on the prints.

THE METRIC SYSTEM: UNIT 2 (Study Print). Aesop Films/EBEC, 1976. 10 13 in. X 18 in. color study prints. Study Guide. #18070 ($21.95). Gr. 2–6. MDU (1/77), PRV (9/77). 389.152

Contents: 1. Meter. 2. Decimeter. 3. Centimeter. 4. Millimeter. 5. Kilometer. 6. Square Meter. 7. Square Decimeter. 8. Square Centimeter. 9. Square Millimeter. 10. Hectare.

Unit 2 deals with length and area. Cartoon drawings with easy-to-read captions are used on these prints.

THE METRIC SYSTEM: UNIT 3 (Study Print). Aesop Films/EBEC, 1976. 10 13 in. X 18 in. color study prints. Study Guide. #18090 ($21.95). Gr. 2–6. MDU (1/77), PRV (9/77). 389.152

Contents: 1. Liter. 2. Milliliter. 3. Kiloliter. 4. Mass. 5. Kilogram. 6. Gram. 7. Milligram. 8. Metric Ton. 9. Freezing and Boiling Points. 10. Room Temperature.

Unit 3 surveys volume, capacity, mass, and temperature. Cartoon drawings with easy-to-read captions are used on these prints.

THE METRIC VILLAGE MEASURING KIT: TEMPERATURE (Kit). Coronet Instructional Media, 1976. 1 color, sound filmstrip; 1 cassette; 12 Activity Cards, 4 Worksheets; 3 Celsius Thermometer's; Teacher's Guide. #N120 ($70). Gr. 1–4. MDU (1977). 389.152

This kit contains a sound filmstrip to be enjoyed with the elf Mischief and the measuring problems solved by the people of Metric Village. The other materials in the kit are suitable for classroom use.

THINK METRIC (Filmstrip—Captioned). Filmstrip House/United Learning, 1975. 6 color, captioned filmstrips, av. 44–48 fr. ea.;

Guide. #60000 ($45). Gr. 3–6. PRV
(5/76). 389.152

Contents: 1. Introduction to Units of Measure. 2. Linear Measure. 3. Volume Measure. 4. Weight. 5. Area. 6. Comparison.

The series assumes no background in either the English or metric system. Using animated youngsters and Professor Metricat, the series begins with discovering the need for a standard unit of measure. Only the most common metric prefixes are used throughout, which simplifies this introduction for younger children.

MEXICAN AMERICANS. *See* Biography—
Collections

MEXICO

MARKET PLACE IN MEXICO (Motion Picture—16mm—Sound). Filmfair Communications, 1975. 16mm color, sound film, 12-1/2 min. ($165). Gr. 2–5. BKL (10/15/75), LFR (9/10/75). 917.2

A serape maker, a potter, and a rope maker in a small Mexican village are used to show how people are dependent on one another's skills to meet their basic needs. The film also tells something of the ancient Aztec marketplace and points out that although many things have changed in the 500 years since the days of the Aztecs, people's dependence for their basic needs on each other's skills has not.

MEXICO: IMAGES AND EMPIRES (Filmstrip—Sound). Lyceum/Mook & Blanchard, 1974. 1 color, sound filmstrip, 52 fr.; 1 cassette or disc, 8-1/2 min. Cassette #LY35473C ($25), Disc #LY35473R ($19.50). Gr. 5–A. FLN (4/5/74), PVB (5/75). 917.2

Perceptive portrait of Mexico by author/photographers Ron and Marcia Atwood promotes an understanding of Mexican history and culture.

MEXICO IN THE TWENTIETH CENTURY (Filmstrip—Sound). BFA Educational Media, 1970. 6 color, sound filmstrips; 6 cassettes or discs. Cassettes #VS3000 ($92), Discs #VE2000 ($92). Gr. 4–8. BKL (1/15/71). 917.2

Contents: 1. Mexico's Physical Heritage. 2. Mexico's History. 3. Mexicans at Work. 4. Mexicans at Play. 5. Mexican Art, Architecture, and Education. 6. Mexicans on the Move.

Studies similarities and differences between the students' own culture and environment and that of contemporary Mexico.

OUR NEIGHBORS: CANADA AND MEXICO (Filmstrip—Sound). *See* North America

MEXICO—DESCRIPTION AND TRAVEL

PASSPORT TO MEXICO (Filmstrip—Sound). EMC, 1976. 5 color, sound filmstrips, 104–113 fr.; 5 cassettes, 21–30 min.; Teacher's Guide. #SP-115000 ($96). Gr. 4–A. PRV (4/78). 917.2

Contents: 1. Preparation and Trip. 2. Renting a Car, at the Bank, at the Post Office, etc. 3. In the Restaurant, at the Grocery Store, at the Market. 4. Taking a Taxi, at the Bakery, at the Department Store, etc. 5. Hair Care, Overcoming the Measurement Problem.

This program will acquaint students with the day-to-day experiences of traveling in Mexico, reflecting cultural subtleties of Mexican society.

MICE—FICTION

THE ISLAND OF THE SKOG (Filmstrip—Sound). Weston Woods Studios, 1976. 1 color, sound filmstrip, 49 fr.; 1 cassette, 11:15 min.; 1 Guide. ($12.75). Gr. 4–A. BKL (1/15/77). Fic

Based on Steven Kellogg's book, the mice have an exciting adventure while learning the importance of diplomacy, comradeship, and the necessity of communicating.

SHE WAS NICE TO MICE (Phonodisc or Cassette). *See* Elizabeth I, Queen of England—Fiction

STUART LITTLE (Filmstrip—Sound). Stephen Bosustow Productions, 1976. 12 color, sound filmstrips; 12 discs or cassettes; Teacher's Guide. ($150). Gr. K–6. LGB (12/19/76). Fic

The classic E. B. White children's story about Stuart Little's adventures is presented in a 12-filmstrip set.

THE TAILOR OF GLOUCESTER, A CHRISTMAS STORY (Cassette). Children's Classics on Tape, 1974. 1 cassette; detailed Study Guide. ($9.50). Gr. K–3. BKL (11/75), PRV (9/75). Fic

A poor old tailor is making a fine coat for the mayor of Gloucester. When the tailor frees some mice his cat Simpkin has captured, the vengeful cat hides the tailor's thread. The grateful little mice help the tailor finish the coat.

WHOSE MOUSE ARE YOU? (Filmstrip—Sound). Weston Woods Studios, 1972. 1 color, sound filmstrip, 26 fr.; 1 cassette, 4 min. #SF-148C ($12.75). Gr. K–3. PRV (12/73). Fic

Based on the book by Robert Kraus, the illustrations of Jose Aruego are reproduced in this filmstrip, making it an authentic reproduction. In this story in rhyme, the little mouse mentally imagines each member of this family in a hazardous situation from which he rescues them. Having felt unloved, he is then restored to their affection.

MIDDLE AGES

MEDIEVAL EUROPE (Filmstrip—Sound).
Society for Visual Education, 1977. 4
color, sound filmstrips, av. 40–48 fr.; 4
cassettes or discs, av. 7:40–9:45 min. Cassettes #A380-SCTC ($70), Discs #A380-
SCR ($70). Gr. 4–8. BKL (10/15/77).
940.1

Contents: 1. Peopie and Migration. 2.
Society. 3. Religion. 4. Towns and Cities.

The migration of various peoples and tribes
helped determine the character of medieval
Europe. The nature of feudal society, the
participation in the crusades, the role of
religion in preserving cultural achievements,
the appearance of cities and towns are some
of the facets of medieval life that are presented.

MIDDLE AGES—FICTION

THE PRINCE AND THE PAUPER (Phonodisc or Cassette). *See* Fantasy—Fiction

MIDDLE EAST

LEARNING ABOUT THE MID-EAST RE-
GION (Filmstrip—Sound). United Learning, 1976. 6 color, sound filmstrips, 61–79
fr.; 6 cassettes, 10:31–21 min.; 1 Guide.
#2255 ($85). Gr. 5–8. BKL (6/1/77).
915.6

Contents: 1. Lands of an Awakening
Giant. 2. Birthplace of Religions. 3. His-
tory of Contributions and Conflict. 5. City
Life. 6. Economy.

History, geography, civilization, and current events are combined in this study of
the Middle East. Countries included are
Egypt, Iran, Israel, Lebanon, Saudi Arabia,
and Turkey.

THE MIDDLE EAST: FACING A NEW
WORLD ROLE (Filmstrip—Sound). Society
for Visual Education, 1976. 6 color, sound
filmstrips, av. 68 fr.; 6 discs or cassettes, av.
14 min.; 1 Guide. Disc #256-SAR ($105),
Cassette #256-SATC ($105). Gr. 4–9. BKL
(6/77), PRV (4/76). 915.6

Contents: 1. Egypt: Balancing Its Past and
Future. 2. Cairo: Restless Center in the
Arab World. 3. Jordan: A New Nation in
an Ancient Land. 4. Jordan River Valley
Project: Planning the Future. 5. Saudi
Arabia: Custodian of Tradition and Oil.
6. Saudi Arabia: Petro Power.

This set examines the daily lives of a cross
section of citizens of Jordan, Egypt, and
Saudi Arabia. The photographs, narration,
and authentic music introduce the changing
world of the Arab Middle East. Viewers
study attempts by Jordan to establish a new
settlement in the Jordan River Valley,
visit Cairo and the Suez Canal, see how oil
is changing the lives of the Saudis, and review the Arab-Israeli conflict.

MIDDLE EAST—SOCIAL LIFE AND CUSTOMS

FAMILIES OF THE DRY MUSLIM WORLD
(Filmstrip—Sound). EBEC, 1973. 5 color,
sound filmstrips, av. 70 fr. ea.; 5 cassettes
or phonodiscs, av. 6 min. ea.; Teacher's
Guide. Discs #6488 ($72.50), Cassettes
#6488K ($72.50), Each Filmstrip ($17).
Gr. 5–9. BKL (12/15/74), PRV (3/74),
PVB (5/75). 915.6

Contents: 1. Village Life in Pakistan. 2.
Oil Worker of Kuwait. 3. Cooperative
Farming in Iran. 4. A Berber Village in
Morocco. 5. Nomads of Morocco.

The differing life-styles of peoples of the
Muslim world are depicted in this series.
Through unposed photographs and narration, you become well acquainted with 5
families. Observing the differences, you also
discover similarities among these areas.

MIDDLE WEST

FOCUS ON AMERICA, THE MIDWEST
(Filmstrip—Sound). *See* U.S.—Economic
Conditions

MIGRANT LABOR

LIVING ON A FARM (Filmstrip—Sound).
See Farm Life

MILK

MILK: FROM FARM TO YOU (3RD EDI-
TION) (Motion Picture—16mm—Sound).
See Dairying

MILLAY, EDNA ST. VINCENT

CHILDHOOD OF FAMOUS WOMEN, VOL-
UME THREE (Cassette). *See* Women—
Biography

MILLER, ALFRED JACOB

A. J. MILLER'S WEST: THE PLAINS IN-
DIAN—1837—SLIDE SET (Slides). *See*
Indians of North America—Paintings

MILNE, A. A.

PRINCE RABBIT AND OTHER STORIES
(Phonodiscs). *See* Fairy Tales

WINNIE THE POOH (Phonodiscs). *See* Animals—Fiction

MINARIK, ELSE HOLMELUND

A KISS FOR LITTLE BEAR (Filmstrip—
Sound). *See* Bears—Fiction

MINERALOGY

DISCOVERING ROCKS AND MINERALS
(Filmstrip—Sound). *See* Geology

ROCKS AND MINERALS (Filmstrip—
Sound). *See* Geology

MINORITIES

AMERICA'S ETHNIC HERITAGE—
GROWTH AND EXPANSION (Filmstrip—
Sound). BFA Educational Media, 1976. 4
color, sound filmstrips; 4 cassettes or discs.
Disc #VJH000 ($68), Cassette #VJG000
($80). Gr. 4–8. PRV (4/78). 301.45
Contents: 1. Growth and Expansion. 2.
Scandinavians. 3. Irish. 4. Chinese and
Japanese.
This series chronicles America's growth
and development from 1800–1880 and the
contributions of America's ethnic groups.

FAMILIAS NORTEAMERICANAS—AMERI-
CAN FAMILIES (Filmstrip—Sound). *See*
Family Life

FIVE FAMILIES, UNIT 1 (Filmstrip—
Sound). Scholastic Book Services, 1972
(Five Children and Five Families). 5 color,
sound filmstrips, av. 60 fr. ea.; 5 7 in. LP
discs or cassettes; Teacher's Guide; Wall
Poster. Cassette #6835 ($69.50), Disc
#6815 ($69.50). Gr. K–4. BKL (5/1/73),
LNG (10/73), PRV (5/73). 301.45
Contents: 1. Chinatown. 2. Pinata. 3.
Together. 4. Ya-Ta-Hey. 5. Circus Family.
Introduces children to 5 families in the
United States, each from a particular ethnic
or cultural group. Children are encouraged
to think about their own families and are
asked to begin to examine the purpose of
families. They are also asked how families
differ from one to another. Available in
Spanish.

HERITAGE STORIES (Filmstrip—Sound).
Knowledge Aid/United Learning, 1975. 5
color, sound filmstrips, av. 50–65 fr. ea.; 5
cassettes, av. 7–10 min. ea.; Teacher's
Guide. #3210 ($75). Gr. 5–8. ESL
(10/77), PRV (12/76). 301.45
Contents: 1. La Raza—the Chicano Experience. 2. We People—the Native American
Experience. 3. Talking to the Soul—the
Puerto Rican Experience. 4. Strangers in a
Strange Land—the Chinese Experience. 5.
Moving On—the Black Experience.
An adequate presentation of the contributions and problems of different ethnic
groups as they each strive to better themselves in American society. Difficulties arise
with language, color, and other barriers that
these groups are attempting to overcome
and still retain a sense of pride in themselves, their people, and their country.

LIVING TOGETHER AS AMERICANS
(Filmstrip—Sound). *See* Human Relations

THE MANY AMERICANS, UNIT ONE (Filmstrip—Sound). *See* Biculturalism

THE MANY AMERICANS, UNIT TWO
(Filmstrip—Sound). *See* Biculturalism

MINORITIES—USA (Filmstrip—Sound).
Globe Filmstrips/Coronet Instructional
Media, 1975. 8 color, sound filmstrips,
60–78 fr.; 8 discs or cassettes, 9–15 min.;
Teacher's Guide. Cassettes #M703 ($118),
Discs #S703 ($118). Gr. 6–12. BKL
(12/15/75), PRV (10/76), PVB (4/77).
301.45
Contents: 1. The American Dilemma.
2. Who Am I? (Native Americans). 3.
A Piece of the Pie (Black Americans). 4.
La Causa (Mexican Americans). 5. Exec-
utive Order 9066 (Asian Americans). 6.
Two Different Worlds (Puerto Rican Americans). 7. You Breathe Free (Religious
Minorities). 8. Bringing About Change.
Candid case studies, documentary interviews, poetry, and photography develop the
key concepts of prejudice, discrimination,
and scapegoating. The presentation stimulates thinking about the conflict between
the American creed and how minorities are
treated.

MISTER GRUMPY'S OUTING

SOUND FILMSTRIP SET 35 (Filmstrip—
Sound). *See* Children's Literature—Collections

MOBYEDDIN, ZIA

FABLES OF INDIA (Phonodisc or Cassette).
See Fables

MOHAVE (INDIAN TRIBE)

PETROGLYPHS: ANCIENT ART OF THE
MOJAVE (Filmstrip—Sound). *See* Indians
of North America—Art

MOILLET, LOUIS

PICTURES ARE FUN TO LOOK AT (Art
Prints). *See* Art Appreciation

MONEY

ALICE IN CONSUMERLAND (Filmstrip—
Sound). *See* Consumer Education

CONCERNING YOUNG CONSUMERS
(Filmstrip—Sound). *See* Consumer Education

CONSUMER EDUCATION: THE PRICE IS
RIGHT—OR IS IT? (Filmstrip—Sound).
See Consumer Education

ECONOMICS FOR PRIMARIES (Filmstrip—
Sound). *See* Consumer Education

HOW MONEY WORKS (Filmstrip—Sound).
Educational Direction/Learning Tree Filmstrips, 1974. 4 color, sound filmstrips, av.

MONEY (cont.)

61 fr. ea.; 2 cassettes, av. 8 min. ea.; Teacher's Guide. #LT435 ($52). Gr. 2–8. ATE (5/77), LGB (1974), PRV (5/75). 332.4

Contents: 1. The Value of Things. 2. Money–What It Is. 3. Other Types of Money. 4. Getting Value.

The set is designed to explain the key concepts of money and the general pricing and value of things. It ends with a discussion of how to become a wise buyer.

LEARNING ABOUT MONEY (Filmstrip–Sound). United Learning, 1973. 4 color, sound filmstrips, av. 36–60 fr. ea.; 4 cassettes, av. 5–8 min. ea.; Guide. #22 ($60). Gr. 2–6. PRV (3/75), PVB (1975). 332.024

Contents: 1 Money–What Is It? 2. Money–Planning a Budget. 3. Money–How to Spend It. 4. Money–How Much Do You Need?

Designed to teach intermediate children about money and how to take care of it. The series, which is usable in areas of consumer education, guidance, social studies, and mathematics, should help to make children aware of today's inflation problems.

LEARNING TO BE A WISE CONSUMER Filmstrip–Sound). See Consumer Education

MONEY AND TIME: ADVENTURES OF THE LOLLIPOP DRAGON (Filmstrip–Sound). See Arithmetic

MONEY: FROM BARTER TO BANKING (Filmstrip–Sound). Guidance Associates, 1975 (Math Matters). 2 color, sound filmstrips, av. 69 fr.; 2 discs or cassettes, av. 9 min.; Teacher's Guide. Discs #1B-301-406 ($52.50), Cassettes #1B-301-398 ($52.50). Gr. 4–8. ATE. 332.4

Traces the use of barter, commodity, object, and metal money in early civilizations. Discusses development of coinage, paper money, and personal credit.

NICKELS, DIMES AND DOLLARS (Filmstrip–Sound). See Consumer Education

MONGOOSES–FICTION

RIKKI TIKKI TAVI (Cassette). Children's Classics on Tape, 1974. 1 cassette; detailed Study Guide. ($9.50). Gr. K–8. PRV (9/75). Fic

Teddy and his family adopt Rikki Tikki Tavi, an orphaned mongoose. Rikki saves Teddy from the deadly cobras Nag and Nagaina.

MONKEYS–FICTION

CURIOUS GEORGE AND OTHER STORIES ABOUT CURIOUS GEORGE

(Phonodisc or Cassette). Caedmon Records, 1972. 1 cassette or disc, 40:21 min.; Jacket Notes. Disc #TC1420 ($6.98), Cassette #CDL51420 ($7.95). Gr. K–3. BKL (2/15/73), PRV (1973), STE. Fic

Contents: 1. Curious George. 2. Curious George Takes a Job. 3. Curious George Rides a Bike. 4. Curious George Gets a Medal.

Julie Harris reads these 4 stories about a favorite character developed by H. A. Rey.

MONSTERS–FICTION

THE BEAST OF MONSIEUR RACINE (Motion Picture–16mm–Sound). Weston Woods Studios, 1975. 16mm color, sound, animated film, 9 min. 16mm ($150), Super 8 ($150). Gr. K–3. AFF (1976), BKL (11/15/75), HOB (12/75). Fic

Someone is stealing Monsieur Racine's prize pears. He lays a trap and catches the marauder, a strange but harmless-looking beast. The 2 become great friends. Monsieur Racine is perplexed by his companion's odd appearance, so he writes to the Academy of Science and is invited to Paris to present his discovery. What happens there throws Paris into an uproar and leaves Monsieur Racine a changed man. Adapted from the book of the same title.

MONSTERS AND OTHER FRIENDLY CREATURES (Filmstrip–Sound). Encyclopaedia Britannica Educational, 1974. 5 color, sound filmstrips, av. 58 fr.; 5 cassettes or discs, av. 6 min. ea.; Teacher's Guide. Discs #6495 ($72.50), Cassettes #6495K ($72.50). Gr. K–6. BKL (10/15/74), ESL, LNG (9/10/75). Fic

Contents: 1. Monsters in the Closet. 2. Emil, The Tap Dancing Frog. 3. Monster Seeds. 4. Charlie and the Caterpillar. 5. Andrew and the Strawberry Monsters.

The monsters in these 5 lively filmstrips are funny, sad, friendly, scary, ugly, and lovable. They hold noisy late-night parties in a closet, and spring full-grown from "monster seeds."

STORIES OF GHOSTS AND MONSTERS (Filmstrip–Sound). See Reading Materials

MORENO, RITA

EARLY LEARNING LIBRARY (Filmstrip–Sound). See Child Development

MORSE, SAMUEL F. B.

TRAILBLAZERS OF INVENTION (Filmstrip–Sound). See Inventors

MOSAICS

THE ART OF MOSAICS (Filmstrip–Sound). Educational Audio Visual, 1977 (Art History and Techniques). 2 color, sound filmstrips, 89–101 fr.; 2 discs or cassettes, 12–16 min. Teacher's Guide. Discs #7RF0044 ($40), Cassettes #7KF0044 ($44). Gr. 5–12. PRV (1/78), PVB (4/78). 729

Contents: 1. Techniques. 2. History.

Designed to develop interest in the making of mosaics in the past and present. These filmstrips also present a step-by-step procedure for mosaic making and show examples of completed mosaics. They trace the materials used, the styles, and the subject of mosaics.

MOTHERS

WHY MOTHERS WORK (Motion Picture–16mm–Sound). *See* Women–Employment

MOTHS

MOTHS–SLIDE SET (Slides). National Film Board of Canada/Donars Productions, 1972. 10 cardboard mounted, color slides in a plastic storage page; Script in English and French. ($10). Gr. 4–A. BKL (2/1/73). 595.781

Presents the life cycle of the moth through its 4 typical stages: egg, larva, pupa, and adult.

MOTION PICTURES

THE FIRST MOVING PICTURE SHOW (Motion Picture–16mm–Sound). Phoenix Films, 1973. 16mm color, sound film, 7 min. #73-702740 ($125). Gr. K-8. PRV (11/74). 791.43

Uses an animated clay caveman as a technique to present the story of the development of the motion picture.

MOTION PICTURES, ANIMATED

FIRE! (Motion Picture–16mm–Sound). *See* Forest Fires

THE GIVING TREE (Motion Picture–16mm–Sound). *See* Friendship–Fiction

HOW BEAVER STOLE FIRE (Motion Picture–16mm–Sound). *See* Indians of North America–Legends

KICK ME (Motion Picture–16mm–Sound). *See* Fantasy–Fiction

THE STORY OF CHRISTMAS (Motion Picture–16mm–Sound). *See* Christmas

WHAZZAT? (Motion Picture–16mm–Sound). *See* Folklore–India

MOTION PICTURES–HISTORY AND CRITICISM

CHAPLIN–A CHARACTER IS BORN (Motion Picture–16mm–Sound). *See* Chaplin, Charles Spencer

MOTOR COORDINATION. *See* Creative Movement

MOTORCYCLE RACING

MOTOCROSS RACING (Kit). *See* Spanish Language–Reading Materials

RACING NUMBERS (Kit). *See* Automobile Racing

MOTORCYCLES

MOTORCYCLE SAFETY (Filmstrip–Sound). Cal Industries/Pathescope Educational Media, 1975. 3 color, sound filmstrips, 57–91 fr.; 3 cassettes, 7:14–11:18 min.; 10 Spirit Masters; 1 Guide. #204C ($75). Gr. 6–A. BKL (3/1/77). 796.75

Contents: 1. Rider Protection and Motorcycle Maintenance. 2. Hazards of the Road. 3. The Motorcyclist in Traffic.

This set offers vital and practical safety tips. It tells riders how to take care of themselves and their bikes and how to avoid danger. It also explains the reasons behind this advice.

NOT SO EASY (MOTORCYCLE SAFETY) (Motion Picture–16mm–Sound). FilmFair Communications, 1973. 16mm color, sound film, 17-1/4 min. ($225). Gr. 4–A. CFF (1973), JEH (5/6/75), LFR (11/73). 796.75

Narrated by Peter Fonda and featuring Evel Knievel, this film demonstrates the essential safety rules of motorcycle riding. Commonsense reasons are given for wearing leather clothing, boots, a helmet, and face covering. Checking out a bike new to the rider and what to check are shown, as well as safety tips for street and highway riding.

MOWGLI'S BROTHERS

THE WORLD OF JUNGLE BOOKS, SET ONE (Kit). *See* Animals–Fiction

MULOCK, DINAH MARIE

THE LITTLE LAME PRINCE (Phonodisc or Cassette). *See* Fairy Tales

MUSEUMS

MUSEUMS AND MAN (Filmstrip–Sound). EBEC, 1974. 5 color, sound filmstrips, av. 89 fr. ea.; 5 discs or cassettes, av. 13 min. ea.; Teacher's Guide. Discs #6905 ($82.95), Cassettes #6905K ($82.95). Gr. 5–12. CPR (10/76), LFR (12/75), PRV (4/76). 069

Contents: 1. What Is a Museum? 2. An Exhibit: Behind the Scenes. 3. Museum Conservation: Preserving Our Heritage. 4. The Zoo: A Living Collection. 5. Museums: New Directions.

MUSEUMS (cont.)

Using the Smithsonian as the focus, this series depicts the modern museum as a place to "do" as well as to look. Students glimpse the museum's role as a restorer of precious and sometimes fragile objects.

MUSIC—ANALYSIS, APPRECIATION

DESIGN IN MUSIC (Phonodiscs). Bowmar Publishing. 1 disc; Overhead Transparencies. #495 ($9.45). Gr. 4–8. AUR (1978). 780.1

A collection of compositions that present the ABA form, theme and variations, rondo, and the symphony. Teaching notes help to explain musical form.

LISTEN! (Motion Picture—16mm—Sound). FilmFair Communications, 1972. 16mm color, sound film, 10 min. ($135). Gr. 1–6. BKL (9/72), LFR (9/72). 780.1

A film to stimulate the imagination and encourage children to concentrate on not only listening, but also seeing and expressing their feelings about musical sounds.

STORIES IN BALLET AND OPERA (Phonodiscs). Bowmar Publishing. 1 disc; Lesson Guides; Theme Chart. #071 ($10). Gr. 2–8. AUR (1978). 780.1

This disc presents samples from ballets and opera such as the Suite from *Amahl and the Night Visitors* by Menotti, *Hansel and Gretel* Overture by Humperdinck, the *Nutcracker Suite* by Tchaikovsky and others.

MUSIC—FICTION

PATRICK (Motion Picture—16mm—Sound). Weston Woods Studios, 1973. 16mm color, sound, animated film, 7 min. ($150). Gr. K–3. BKL (9/73), PRV (5/75), TEA (5/6/74). Fic

Patrick sets out for the town marketplace in search of a fiddle, which he buys from a junkman. With his joyous music, the lanky fiddler imbues every leaf and creature in the countryside with vibrant color and vigorous movement. Sound and sight are analogous in the lyrical portrait of music and its effect on the spirit.

MUSIC—HISTORY AND CRITICISM

THE FIRST DRUM: HOW MUSIC FIRST BEGAN (Filmstrip—Sound). *See* Drum

MUSIC, POPULAR

JAZZ, ROCK, FOLK, COUNTRY (Filmstrip—Sound). Troll Associates, 1976 (Troll Jam Sessions). Each of 4 modules contains one cassette tape, av. 12 min.; 1 color sound filmstrip, av. 34 fr.; 10 illus. soft-cover Books; 4 Duplicating Masters;

Teacher's Guide. ($42.95). Gr. 5–8. BKL (1/15/77), PRV (10/77), TEA (12/77). 785.4

Contents: 1. Jazz. 2. Rock. 3. Folk. 4. Country.

Multimedia supplementary reading program based on the topics of jazz, rock, folk, and country music, their beginnings, development, and stars. The tape follows the text in the read-along book.

MUSIC—STUDY AND TEACHING

HELLO, I'M MUSIC (Kit). EMC, 1969. 6 color, sound filmstrips; 6 cassettes or discs; Teacher's Guide; Student Worksheets on Spirit Masters. #MU-101000 ($99). Gr. 1–6. FLN (9/71), INS (9/69), STE (2/70). 781.2

Contents: 1. Orientation. 2. Melody. 3. Rhythm. 4. Harmony. 5. Form. 6. Tone Color.

An introduction to the basic elements of music using animated cartoon filmstrips and sound recordings.

THERE'S MUSIC ALL AROUND YOU (Filmstrip—Sound). Educational Direction/ Learning Tree Filmstrips, 1975. 4 color, sound filmstrips, av. 50 fr. ea.; 2 cassettes, av. 6–7 min. ea.; Teacher's Guide. #LT555 ($52). Gr. 2–6. BKL (12/75), LGB (1976), MEJ (9/76). 780.7

Contents: 1. It's Everywhere. 2. It's a Language. 3. How the Language Works. 4. Around the World.

This set stimulates the child to develop an awareness of the language of music. The child is made aware of his or her opportunities for enjoying sound and making music.

MUSICIANS

MEN BEHIND THE BRIGHT LIGHTS (Kit). EMC, 1976. 4 cassettes, 22–27 min.; 4 paperback books; 1 Teacher's Guide. #ELC-231000 ($54). Gr. 4–8. BKL (2/15/77). 920

Contents: 1. Jim Croce. 2. Stevie Wonder. 3. John Denver. 4. Elton John

The cassettes contain the text from paperbacks that focus on incidents from the lives of 4 successful and familiar musicians.

See also names of individuals, such as Baez, Brubeck, Schubert

MYSTERY AND DETECTIVE STORIES

MYSTERY IN DRACULA'S CASTLE (Cassette). Walt Disney Educational Media, 1977. 2 color, sound filmstrips; 1 cassette; 6 movie scripts; Teacher's Guide. #67-3003 ($39). Gr. 5–8. MDU (1978). Fic

A sound filmstrip adapted from a Disney

film with 6 scripts and a second silent filmstrip so students can become the actors as they read along with the visuals. Good for reading motivation.

MYSTERY STORY (Filmstrip—Sound). BFA Educational Media, 1976. 4 color, sound filmstrips, 68–75 fr.; 4 discs or cassettes, 11–14 min.; Teacher's Guide. Cassettes #VFL000 ($70), Discs #VFK000 ($70). Gr. 1–3. PRV (11/76). Fic
Contents: 1. The Case of the Hungry Stranger. 2. The Case of the Cat's Meow. 3. The Case of the Dumb Bells. 4. The Case of the Scaredy Cats.
This set uses the original artwork and texts of Crosby Bonsall's "I Can Read" mystery books adapted by Wanda Sykes. Introduces primary children to the connection between reading and mystery stories.

NO SUCH THING . . . ? (Kit). EMC, 1976. 4 paperback books; 4 read-along cassettes; Student Activities; Teacher's Guide. #ELC-130000 ($55). Gr. 4–9. CPR (5/77), INS (5/77). Fic
Contents: 1. The Ghost. 2. The Demon. 3. The Creature of Cranberry Cove. 4. The Tongue of the Ocean.
Haunting, suspenseful, and close-to-real stories that are ghostly but not grisly. These 4 easy reading mystery books with accompanying cassettes are high interest, low reading ability materials.

READING FOR THE FUN OF IT—MYSTERY (Filmstrip—Sound). *See* Literature—Study and Teaching

THE SEA WOLF MYSTERIES (Kit). EMC, 1975. 4 paperback books; 4 read-along cassettes; Teacher's Guide. #ELC122000 ($55). Gr. 3–9. SLJ (5/75). Fic
Contents: 1. Mystery of Totem Pole Inlet. 2. Treasure of Raven Hill. 3. Mystery of Tanglefoot Island. 4. Ghost Town Monster.
The Sea Wolf, a less than tip-top fishing boat, provides suspense and adventure for some young teenagers. The action takes place on a remote island off the coast of British Columbia. Explanation of Indian ways and legends adds a special touch to these easy reading mysteries.

STORIES OF MYSTERY AND SUSPENSE (Filmstrip—Sound). *See* Reading Materials

TEN TALES OF MYSTERY AND TERROR (Cassette). *See* Literature—Collections

MYTHOLOGY

HEROIC ADVENTURES (Filmstrip—Sound). *See* Legends

MYTHOLOGY, CLASSICAL

GREAT MYTHS OF GREECE (Filmstrip—Sound). EBEC, 1972. 4 color, sound film-strips, av. 60 fr. ea.; 4 discs or cassettes, 8 min. ea.; Teacher's Guide. Discs #6462 ($57.95), Cassettes #6462K ($57.95). Gr. 4–8. BKL (5/1/73), PRV (2/74). 292
Contents: 1. An Introduction to Greek Mythology and the Myth of Narcissus. 2. Demeter and Persephone. 3. Phaethon. 4. Orpheus and Eurydice.
Themes as new as today shine through the enchanting stories of these famous myths. The filmstrips will be enjoyed and of benefit on many levels.

HEROES OF THE ILIAD (Cassette). Children's Classics on Tape, 1973. 2 cassettes (4 parts); detailed Study Guide. #CCT-143 ($21.95). Gr. 4–8. BKL (4/1/75), PRV (9/75). 292
Subjects covered are: Part 1—how the Greek and Trojan war began and the quarrel between Achilles and Agamemnon; Part 2—Hector's men storming a Greek camp and Achilles' refusal to help Agamemnon; Part 3—death of Patroclus and Hector and Achilles in battle. Part 4—Hector's funeral, the Trojan horse, and the fall of Troy.

KING MIDAS AND THE GOLDEN TOUCH (Cassette). Children's Classics on Tape, 1974. 1 cassette; Study Guide. #CCT-132 ($8.50). Gr. 4–6. BKL (10/75), PRV (9/75). 292
Greedy King Midas asks a mysterious visitor to give him the power of turning everything he touches to gold. His wish is granted, with disastrous results.

MAGIC CHANGES, SET ONE (Filmstrip—Sound). *See* Folklore

MAGIC CHANGES, SET TWO (Filmstrip—Sound). *See* Folklore

THE TALE OF KING MIDAS (Motion Picture—16mm—Sound). EBEC, 1974. 16mm color, sound film, 18 min. #3308 ($255). Gr. K–4 CPR (1975), LFR (2/75). 292
This film version of the well-known legend from Greek mythology contains a sequel in which Midas gets into even more trouble with the gods. Chosen to judge a music contest between Pan and Apollo, Midas blunders and is rewarded with donkey's ears. The barber is the only person who knows of the King's disfigurement, but, being human, he is eventually compelled to share the secret with a hole in the ground. As with most secrets, it is eventually carried about by the wind. Spanish version available.

NATIONAL HOLIDAYS. *See* Holidays

NATIONAL PARKS AND RESERVES—U.S.

OUR NATIONAL PARKS (Filmstrip—Sound). Troll Associates, 1977. 6 color, sound filmstrips, av. 42 fr. ea.; 6 cassettes,

NATIONAL PARKS AND RESERVES—U.S. (cont.)

av. 7 min. ea.; Teacher's Guide. ($84). Gr. 3–7. BKL (11/1/77). 917.3

Contents: 1. Acadia National Park. 2. Carlsbad Caverns National Park. 3. Everglades National Park. 4. Grand Canyon National Park. 5. Mammoth Cave National Park. 6. Sequoia National Park.

Describes the historical significance of each national park, and how the National Park System preserves our landmarks.

NATIONAL SONGS, AMERICAN

THE STAR-SPANGLED BANNER (Filmstrip—Sound). Weston Woods Studios. 1 color, sound filmstrip, 43 fr.; 1 cassette, 8 min.; Teacher's Guide. #SF166C ($12.75). Gr. K–4. PRV (10/76), PVB (4/77). 784.71

Based on the book by Peter Spier and the 16mm film by Weston Woods, this filmstrip describes how the U.S. national anthem was officially accepted on a national basis in 1931, following President Wilson's proclamation in 1916 that the song become the national anthem for only the U.S. armed forces.

NATURAL DISASTERS

DISCOVERING THE POWERS OF NATURE (Filmstrip—Sound). National Geographic, 1977. 3 color, sound filmstrips; 3 cassettes, 11–14 min. #03237 ($50). Gr. 1–5. PRV (4/78). 904

Contents: 1. Weather and People. 2. Forest Fires and Floods. 3. Earthquakes and Volcanoes.

Scientists strive to understand the powerful natural forces such as storms, floods, fires, eruptions, and earthquakes. This set also shows people preparing for their effects.

NATURAL HISTORY

ALONG NATURE TRAILS (Film Loop—8mm—Silent). Troll Associates. 6 8mm color, silent film loops, approx. 4 min. ea.; Available separately. ($149.70). Gr. K–8. AUR (1978). 574.5

Contents: 1. A Nature Walk. 2. Pattern and Design in Nature. 3. Life in a Pond. 4. Fireflies and Other Night Insects. 5. Importance of Weeds. 6. Nature Homebuilders.

These loops allow the observer to witness fascinating activities in nature's hidden world. Close-ups reveal the lives and habits of insects and other creatures.

BACKYARD SCIENCE SERIES ONE: ANTS, BEES, BEETLES, CRICKETS (Filmstrip—Sound). BFA Educational Media, 1974. 4 color, sound filmstrips; 4 cassettes or discs. Cassettes #VES000 ($70), Discs #VER000 ($70). Gr. K–3. BKL (6/1/75). 574.5

Contents: 1. Ants. 2. Bees. 3. Beetles. 4. Crickets.

Close-up photography in these filmstrips helps students understand the relationships and differences among insects and animals. The variety within a particular species is described. Acquaints students with the structure of each animal, traces development in each life cycle, and shows the social organization of each insect and animal group.

BACKYARD SCIENCE SERIES TWO: SPIDERS, SNAILS, FISH, REPTILES (Filmstrip—Sound). BFA Educational Media, 1975. 4 color, sound filmstrips; 4 cassettes or discs. Cassettes #VFC000 ($70), Discs #VFB000 ($70). Gr. K–3. BKL (11/15/75). 574.5

Contents: 1. Spiders. 2. Snails. 3. Fish. 4. Reptiles.

The filmstrips describe the variety within a particular species, acquaint students with the structure of each animal, trace the pattern of development in each life cycle, and show the social orgainzation of each animal group.

BEAR COUNTRY AND BEAVER VALLEY (Filmstrip—Sound). Walt Disney Educational Media, 1975. 2 color, sound filmstrips; 2 cassettes. #63-0212L ($81). Gr. 5–9. PRV (11/76). 574.5

Contents: 1. Beaver Valley. 2. Bear Country.

Adapted from films of the same names, this set takes students on a field trip to see the black bears and beavers. It shows the interrelationship of a variety of animals from the bear's and beaver's environment.

CHANGING SEASONS: THE STORY OF A YEAR (Film Loop—8mm—Silent). *See* Seasons

A CRACK IN THE PAVEMENT (Motion Picture—16mm—Sound). FilmFair Communications, 1972. 16mm color, sound film, 8 min. #C182 ($115). Gr. K–6. LFR (2/73), PRV (10/73), STE (9/73). 574.5

This film creates an awareness of the "life force" and the beauty found in seemingly unlikely places such as the city. Based on the book by Ruth Howell and Arline Strong.

ENVIRONMENTAL AWARENESS (Filmstrip—Sound). Centron Films, 1972. 5 color, sound filmstrips; 5 discs or cassettes. Discs ($59.50), Cassettes ($60.50). Gr. 1–4. BKL (5/1/72), CRA (1973). 574.5

Contents: 1. Colors in Nature. 2. Textures in Nature. 3. Patterns in Nature. 4. Awareness in Forest and Field. 5. Awareness in the City.

Five startlingly beautiful filmstrips promoting visual awareness of nature.

LAND, WATER, SKY AND THINGS THAT
GROW (Filmstrip–Sound). Educational
Direction/Learning Tree Filmstrips, 1974. 4
color, sound filmstrips, av. 60 fr. ea.; 2 cas-
settes, av. 5 min. ea.; Teacher's Guide.
#LT436 ($52). Gr. 2-5. BKL (9/75),
LGB (1974). 574.5

Contents: 1. The Land. 2. The Water. 3.
The Sky. 4. Things That Grow.

Created to enrich the mind of any viewer as
well as introduce and summarize these 4
areas: land, water, sky, and growing things.
A wide range of both macro and celestial
photography is featured.

LOOKING AND LISTENING (Filmstrip–
Sound). BFA Educational Media, 1972. 6
color, sound filmstrips; 6 cassettes or discs.
Cassettes #VY7000 ($104), Discs #VY6000
($104). Gr. 4-6. BKL (11/15/74). 574.5

Contents: 1. North Woods. 2. Marsh. 3.
Oak Woodland. 4. Desert. 5. Mountain
Stream. 6. Seashore.

Miniature field trips invite viewers to look,
listen, and imagine. Each filmstrip is a
journey through an area of great natural
beauty with an opportunity to see plants
and animals in their own habitats and to
listen to the sounds of animals, wind, and
water.

NATURALLY SPEAKING (Filmstrip–
Sound). Prima Education Products, 1973.
4 color, sound filmstrips, 42–51 fr.; 4 discs
or cassettes, 8:30–9:30 min.; Spanish/En-
glish available, Teacher's Guide. Discs
#2030 ($64), Cassettes #2030 ($68). Gr.
2-9. BKL (12/1/73), PRV (10/74), PVB (5/
75). 574.5

Contents: 1. Feelings in a Forest. 2. Water
Brook Songs. 3. The Working Sea, Wind
and Sand. 4. Sounds of Silence at a Pond.

These focus on the unadorned pleasures of
nature, and their original, conscientious
ecological message offers hope about the
beauty of the outdoors.

NATURE ALL AROUND US (Filmstrip–
Sound). Educational Audio Visual/Imperial
Educational Resources, 1976. 5 color,
sound filmstrips, 5 cassettes or discs, Teacher's Guide. Discs #3RF88000 ($90), Cas-
settes #3KF88000 ($100). Gr. K-6. BKL
(4/77). 574.5

Contents: 1. The World of Nature. 2.
Spring and Summer. 3. Fall and Winter. 4.
Wonder and Surprise. 5. Near Home.

A close look at nature, which shows it not
as something separate from ourselves, but
as a whole of which we are a part. The interdependence of all of nature is stressed.

NATURE WALKS (Filmstrip–Captioned).
EBEC, 1976 (Developing Language Skills).
4 color, captioned filmstrips, 55 fr.; Teacher's Guide. #13645 ($32.90). Gr. K-3.
BKL (4/15/77), LAM (10/77), PRV (9/1/
77). 574.5

Contents: 1. Watching at the Pond. 2. Walking along the Seashore. 3. Exploring the
Desert. 4. Visiting the Forest.

These filmstrips introduce some of the
places where different and often strange
plants and animals live. Students are asked
to be observers and to talk about what they
think a desert or a forest is. Captions help
with basic concepts and provide names for
some things that live in different areas.

PLANTS (Filmstrip–Sound). *See* Plants

SEA, SAND AND SHORE (Filmstrip–Sound).
See Ocean

SPACESHIP EARTH (Filmstrip–Sound).
Hawkhill Associates, 1973. 6 color, sound
filmstrips, 78–92 fr.; 6 cassettes or discs,
13–20 min.; Teacher's Guide. ($135). Gr.
5-9. BKL (6/74), PRV (5/74), PVB (5/75).
574.5

Contents: 1. The Universe. 2. The Bio-
sphere. 3. Living Things. 4. Cells. 5. Atoms
and Molecules. 6. Awareness.

Stresses the unity and harmony of nature by
combining scientific facts and philosophy
with the arts of photography, poetry, and
music. Introduces students to current
scientific knowledge in astronomy, ecology,
biology, chemistry, and physics, and their
interdependence on each other.

THE TREE, SECOND EDITION (Motion
Picture–16mm–Sound). *See* Trees

VISITING NATURE ONE (Filmstrip–
Sound). *See* Ecology

VISITING NATURE TWO (Filmstrip–
Sound). *See* Ecology

WHAT ARE ECOSYSTEMS? (Filmstrip–
Sound). *See* Ecology

WHAT IS ECOLOGY? (Film Loop–8mm–
Silent). *See* Ecology

WILDLIFE STORIES (Filmstrip–Sound).
See Animals

NATURAL HISTORY–COLLECTIONS

DAYBREAK (Motion Picture–16mm–
Sound). *See* Poetry–Collections

NATURAL RESOURCES

THE EARTH'S RESOURCES (Filmstrip–
Captioned). Multi-Media Productions/
McGraw-Hill Films, 1970. 6 color, captioned
filmstrips, av. 40 fr. ea.; Teacher's Guide.
#619020 ($49). Gr. 4-8. PRV (1/73),
PVB (5/73). 551

Contents: 1. Ocean Resources. 2. Fresh
Water Resources. 3. Rock Resources. 4.
Fuel Resources. 5. Soil Resources. 6.
Atmospheric Resources.

These filmstrips present earth science concepts associated with some of the earth's

NATURAL RESOURCES (cont.)

natural resources; they emphasize the methods that allow scientists to formulate these concepts; and they show the importance of these resources to the environment.

ENERGY AND OUR ENVIRONMENT (Filmstrip—Sound). *See* Ecology

NATURAL RESOURCES, OUR CHANGING ENVIRONMENT (Filmstrip—Sound). Troll Associates, 1975. 6 color, sound filmstrips, av. 42 fr. ea.; 3 cassettes, av. 10 min. ea.; Teacher's Guide. ($78). Gr. 5–8. TEA (2/76). 574.5

Contents: 1. What Are Natural Resources. 2. Who Needs Natural Resources. 3. Using Up Natural Resources. 4. Pollution of Natural Resources. 5. Effects of Pollution. 6. Conserving Our Natural Resources.

Fosters understanding of the relationship between humans, their natural and man-made surroundings.

NATURE, EFFECT OF MAN ON. *See* Man—Influence on Nature

NATURE IN ORNAMENT. *See* Design, Decorative

NATURE IN POETRY

THE CRYSTAL CAVERN (Filmstrip—Sound). *See* Caves

NATURE STUDY

NATURE ALL AROUND US: A CLOSE-UP VIEW (Filmstrip—Sound). Educational Audio Visual, 1976. 5 color, sound filmstrips, 58–69 fr.; 5 cassettes or discs, 5:27–9:46 min.; 1 Guide. Cassette #7KF-028 ($45), Disc #7RF-028 ($40). Gr. 1–6. BKL (4/15/77). 574.5

Contents: 1. The World of Nature. 2. Spring and Summer. 3. Fall and Winter. 4. Wonder and Surprise. 5. Near Home.

A positive approach to the needs, habits, and characteristics of the creatures in the world.

NATURE STUDY—FICTION

THE BEAR'S NATURE GUIDE (Kit). Random House, 1976. 4 color, sound filmstrips, 65–102 fr.; 4 cassettes or discs, 6–10 min.; 12 Duplicating Masters; 1 Book; Teacher's Guide. Cassette #04160 ($90), Disc #04148 ($90). Gr. K–3. BKL (2/15/77), LNG, TEA. Fic

Stan and Jan Berenstain have produced material that is accurate, rhymed, and written in a controlled vocabulary. The 4 filmstrips are a faithful reproduction of their text and drawings. Biological and geological concepts

are included, which provide reading in a content area capability.

NAVAJO

BLESSINGWAY: TALES OF A NAVAJO FAMILY (Kit). EMC, 1976. 4 cassettes, av. 21 min.; 4 paperback books; 1 Teacher's Guide. #ELC-129000 ($52). Gr. 3–8. BKL (4/15/77). 970.3

Contents: 1. The Spiderweb Stone. 2. Tall Singer. 3. The Secret of the Mask. 4. The Magic Bear.

Stories of contemporary Navajos showing some of the problems as they move to non-Indian communities. The beliefs of the Navajos are treated respectfully and told from their standpoint.

NAVAJO SAND PAINTING CEREMONY (Film Loop—8mm—Silent). *See* Indians of North America—Art

NAVAJO—FICTION

SING DOWN THE MOON (Filmstrip—Sound). Miller-Brody Productions, 1975 (Newbery Filmstrips). 2 color, sound filmstrips, av. 98–103 fr. ea.; 1 cassette or disc, av. 18 min. Phonodisc ($24), Cassette ($28). Gr. 4–8. BKL (9/15/75). PVB (4/78). Fic

With ruggedly bold illustrations whose strokes are as strong as the spirit of the Navajo people they portray, this set capsulizes and dramatically presents Scott O'Dell's award-winning historical novel.

NAVAJO—LEGENDS

A VISIT TO THE FATHER (Filmstrip—Sound). *See* Indians of North America—Legends

NEAR EAST. *See* Middle East

THE NECKLACE

MASTERY STORY TELLER, SET ONE (Filmstrip—Sound). *See* Literature—Collections

NEGROES. *See* Blacks—Fiction

NESBIT, E.

THE BOOK OF DRAGONS (Phonodisc or Cassette). *See* Dragons—Fiction

NESS, EVALINE

SAM, BANGS, AND MOONSHINE (Motion Picture—16mm—Sound). *See* Imagination—Fiction

NETHERLANDS—FICTION

HANS BRINKER, OR THE SILVER SKATES (Phonodisc or Cassette). Caedmon Records,

1976. 1 disc or cassette, 60 min. Disc #TC1493 ($6.98), Cassette #CDL51493 ($7.95). Gr. 4–6. BKL (11/15/77). Fic

Mary Mapes Dodge's classic story of a Dutch family overcoming misfortune and poverty by hard work and faith is narrated by Claire Bloom in this greatly abridged text. Omitted are the lengthy chapters on Dutch geography and history.

NEW YORK (STATE)—FICTION

RIP VAN WINKLE (Phonodisc or Cassette). *See* Dutch in the U.S.—Fiction

NEW ZEALAND

AUSTRALIA AND NEW ZEALAND (Filmstrip—Sound). *See* Australia

A WORLD NEARBY: NEW ZEALAND (Filmstrip—Sound/Captioned). Guidance Associates, 1976 (Cross-Cultural Studies). 2 color, sound and 1 captioned filmstrips, av. 59–82 fr.; 2 cassettes, 16 min. ea.; 1 Guide. Cassette #300-457 ($51.50), Disc #300-440 ($51.50). Gr. 4–7. BKL (2/15/77). 919.31

Contents: 1. Introduction—Overview. 2. Living in the Culture. 3. Pictures to Talk About.

Explores the social tradition, economy, language, climate, and geography of other cultures.

NEWBERY MEDAL BOOKS

JULIE OF THE WOLVES (Phonodisc or Cassette). *See* Eskimos—Fiction

THE VOYAGES OF DOCTOR DOLITTLE (Filmstrip—Sound). *See* Animals—Fiction

NEWBERY MEDAL BOOKS— BIOGRAPHY

ELEANOR ESTES (Filmstrip—Sound). *See* Authors

ISAAC BASHEVIS SINGER (Filmstrip— Sound). *See* Singer, Isaac Bashevis

JEAN CRAIGHEAD GEORGE (Filmstrip—Sound). *See* Authors

LLOYD ALEXANDER (Filmstrip— Sound). *See* Authors

VIRGINIA HAMILTON (Filmstrip— Sound). *See* Hamilton, Virginia

WILLIAM H. ARMSTRONG (Filmstrip— Sound). *See* Armstrong, William

NOISE POLLUTION

WHO STOLE THE QUIET DAY? (Motion Picture—16mm—Sound). Alfred Higgins Productions, 1975. 16mm color, sound film, 15-1/2 min. ($225). Gr. 1–A. AAS (5/75), CFF (1975), PRV (3/75). 614.7

This film shows how loud noises and high frequencies destroy nerve cells within the ear—at any age. It points out that hearing loss is often not the result of aging, but a process that begins through thoughtless exposure to loud noises. Suggestions are made on how to protect hearing.

NORTH AMERICA

HOW OUR CONTINENT WAS MADE (Filmstrip—Sound). Educational Dimensions Group, 1976. 2 color, sound filmstrips, av. 60 fr.; 2 cassettes, 18 min. ea.; 1 Guide. #531 ($39). Gr. 6–10. BKL (6/1/77). 551.4

Contents: 1. Part 1: The East. 2. Part 2: The West.

A geological history of our continent and analysis of those forces that build it up and wear it down—change and reform it. Aerial photographs, satellite photographs, stylized maps, split-frame comparisons, and diagrams are used in the visuals.

OUR NEIGHBORS: CANADA AND MEXICO (Filmstrip—Sound). Educational Direction/Learning Tree Filmstrips, 1975. 4 color, sound filmstrips, av. 49 fr. ea.; 2 cassettes, av. 6–7 min. ea.; Teacher's Guide. #LT557 ($52). Gr. 4–7. BKL (5/15/76). 917

Contents: 1. Knowing Canada. 2. Living in Canada. 3. Knowing Mexico. 4. Living in Mexico.

Each country is covered in 2 filmstrips— the first deals with where and what the country is; the second shows what living in the country means.

NORTON, MARY

THE BORROWERS (Phonodisc or Cassette). *See* Fantasy—Fiction

NUCLEAR PHYSICS

MATTER (Filmstrip—Sound). Scholastic Book Services, 1977 (Adventures in Science). 4 color, sound filmstrips, av. 63–76 fr.; 4 discs or cassettes, 11–15 min. Discs #8627 ($69.50), Cassettes #8628 ($69.50). Gr. 4–8. BKL (12/15/77). 539.7

Contents: 1. Atoms: Their Origin. 2. Atoms: Their Order. 3. Atoms: Reacting. 4. Atoms: The Nucleus.

From the hypothetical answers to queries on the origin of the stars to an explanation of Einstein's theory of the inter-

NUCLEAR PHYSICS (cont.)

changeability of mass and energy; clarifies the subject of nuclear fission.

NUMBERS. *See* Counting

NURSERY RHYMES

MOTHER GOOSE (Phonodisc or Cassette).
Caedmon Records. 1 cassette or disc,
approx. 50 min. Disc #TC1091 ($6.98),
Cassette #CDL51091 ($7.95). Gr. K–A.
ESL, NCT, NYR. 398.8
Many of the Mother Goose rhymes as
composed by Hershy Kay and performed
by Cyril Ritchard, Celeste Holm, and
Boris Karloff.

THE MOTHER GOOSE BOOK (Kit).
Random House, 1977. 6 color, sound
filmstrips, av. 56 fr.; 6 cassettes or discs,
av. 5 min.; 1 Book; 1 Poster; 6 Activity
Sheets; Teacher's Guide. Cassettes
#04619 ($93), Discs #04618 ($93).
Gr. K–1. BKL (1/78). 398.8
Based on the oversized Alice and Martin
Provensen book, which contains both
the familiar and less well-known rhymes.

MOTHER GOOSE RHYMES AND
OTHER STORIES (Cassette). Clearvue,
1976. 8 cassettes, av. 18 min.; 16 Duplicating Masters. #CL830 ($58.50). Gr.
K–2. MDU (1978). 398.8
Contents: 1. Mother Goose Rhymes,
Part I. 2. Mother Goose Rhymes, Part
II. 3. The Three Bears. 4. The Straw Ox.
5. The Three Billy Goats Gruff. 6. The
Cock, the Mouse and the Little Red Hen.
7. The Three Little Pigs. 8. The Bremen
Town Musicians.
Enchanting rhymes and favorite stories
of childhood.

SONGS IN MOTION: ACTIVITY SONGS
AND NURSERY RHYMES (Phonodisc
or Cassette). *See* Rhythms

NUTRITION

THE ADVENTURES OF SUPERNUT,
SET ONE (Filmstrip–Sound). *See* Hygiene

BEFORE YOU TAKE THAT BITE (Motion Picture–16mm–Sound). Filmfair
Communications, 1974. 16mm color,
sound film, 14 min. #C249 ($185).
Gr. 4–12. LFR (3/75), PRV (10/75).
613.2
An overweight teenager begins her day
by missing breakfast and later has quick,
sweet junk foods. At lunch she chooses
desserts over foods with nutritional value
and later at a basketball game again
snacks on nutritionally empty foods. Besides weight problems, other conse-

quences of an unbalanced diet are illustrated—skin problems, tooth decay, etc.
The film provides information on the
relative nutritional values of certain
foods and encourages a balanced diet as a
primary step to good physical and emotional health. Finally, the film advises
viewers to "read the label," and thus
use their nutrition knowledge.

FOOD AND US (Filmstrip–Sound). *See*
Food Supply

FOOD FOR THOUGHT (Filmstrip–Sound).
Marshfilm, 1975. 1 color, sound filmstrip,
50 fr.; 1 disc or cassette, 15 min.; Teacher's
Guide. #1119 ($21). Gr. K–6. PRV
(9/75). 641.1
Deals with the choices made every day, and
the options available, as we select the foods
we consume. The traditional "three-
squares" may be replaced with several small
meals or snacks, as long as they contribute
to a daily food consumption goal.

HABITS OF HEALTH: FOOD TO LIVE AND
GROW (Motion Picture–16mm–Sound).
BFA Educational Media, 1975. 16mm
color, sound film, 13:30 min. #11636
($225). Gr. 2–9. PRV (11/76). 613.2
The food groups necessary for a balanced
diet are explained, and an experiment is
performed over a 3-week period with rats.
The obvious effect is achieved with the laboratory rats fed a diet deficient in these
nutrients compared with rats on a balanced
diet. Scenes in the school lunchroom are
shown where one boy regularly discards
cooked vegetables, then stuffs his mouth
with cake and soft drinks.

NUTRITION FOR YOUNG PEOPLE (Filmstrip–Sound). Guidance Associates, 1976.
4 color, sound filmstrip, 37–52 fr. ea.; 4
cassettes, 5:30–7:30 min. ea.; Discussion
Guide. Discs #6L-303-907 ($94.50), Cassettes #6L-303-915 ($94.50). Gr. 5–8.
BKL (12/1/76). 641.1
Contents: 1. Why People Eat What They
Do. 2. How Food Becomes Part of You.
3. What Foods People Need. 4. What is
Food?
An overview of nutritional concepts, it
treats seriously and thoroughly the various
aspects of nutrition for middle-school
students. Each strip approaches its subject
a little differently, all combine live action
photos, paper cut-out graphics, and voice-
over commentary to explore the importance
of human nutrition.

NUTRITION UNIT (Motion Picture–16mm–
Sound). Sutherland Learning Associates/
EBEC, 1972 (Most Important Person).
4 16mm color, sound films, av. 4 min. ea.;
avail. in 8mm; 1 record; 4 Posters; Song
Cards; Teacher's Guide. Set #6735
($230.40), Each film ($64). Gr. K–3.

BKL (7/1/74), CHT (9/10/74), CPR (1/76). 641.1

Contents: 1. Tasting Party. 2. Foods around Us. 3. What's for Breakfast? 4. Have a Snack!.

Emphasizes the importance of maintaining health and energy through proper eating habits, and introduces the great diversity of foods available.

THE SNACKING MOUSE (Filmstrip—Sound). The Polished Apple, 1977. 1 color, sound filmstrip, 41 fr.; 1 cassette, 5 min.; 1 Guide. ($19.75). Gr. K–2. BKL (7/15/77). 613.2

Sterling Holloway narrates this story about a mouse addicted to sweet snacks to the detriment of regularly eaten meals and his trim figure. The subtle message is that snacks are not the problem, but rather what you eat when you snack.

TOO MUCH OF A GOOD THING (Filmstrip—Sound). Marshfilm, 1 color, sound filmstrip, 50 fr.; 1 discs or cassette, 15 min.; Teacher's Guide. #1118 ($21). Gr. 4–9. AIF (1975), PRV (3/75), PVB. 613.25

Indirectly attacking the problem of obesity in the young, parallels are noted between the national energy crisis and a human energy crisis, comparing the body to a power plant.

VITAL VITTLES WIN THE WEST (Filmstrip—Sound). Marshfilm, 1975. 1 color, sound filmstrip, 50 fr.; 1 disc or cassette, 15 min.; Teacher's Guide. #1120 ($21). Gr. K–3. PRV (9/75). 641.1

Three-dimensional artwork and peppy characters bring to life the facts of good nutrition and teach the basic food groups.

OBEDIENCE

MATCHES (Motion Picture—16mm—Sound). *See* Safety Education

OBLIGADO, LILIAN

SIGHTS AND SOUNDS FILMSTRIPS, SET 3 (Filmstrip—Sound). *See* Reading—Study and Teaching

OCCUPATIONS

ADVENTURES IN THE WORLD OF WORK, SET ONE (Kit). *See* Vocational Guidance

ADVENTURES IN THE WORLD OF WORK, SET TWO (Kit). *See* Vocational Guidance

AUTO RACING: SOMETHING FOR EVERYONE (Kit). *See* Automobile Racing

BANKING AND INSURANCE (Filmstrip—Sound). *See* Vocational Guidance

BECAUSE IT'S JUST ME UNIT TWO (Motion Picture—16mm—Sound). WNVT

(Northern Virginia Educational TV)/ EBEC, 1973 (Watcha Gonna Do?). 16mm color, sound film, 15 min.; Teacher's Manual. #3352 ($200). Gr. 5–9. BKL (5/15/75), CPR (11/74), LFR (4/12/74). 331.702

Students are encouraged to take a self-inventory and to think about how their present abilities, interests, and hobbies might extend into career roles or to future leisure-time activities. Three individuals discuss artistic avocations as an actor, puppeteer, or a musician.

BEGINNING CONCEPTS: PEOPLE WHO WORK, UNIT ONE (Kit). *See* Vocational Guidance

BEGINNING CONCEPTS: PEOPLE WHO WORK, UNIT TWO (Kit). *See* Vocational Guidance

CAN YOU IMAGINE? (Filmstrip—Sound). *See* Decision Making

CAREER EDUCATION FOR PRIMARY GRADES (Filmstrip—Sound). EMC, 1975. 4 color, sound filmstrips, 44–95 fr.; 4 cassettes, 8–15 min.; Teacher's Guide. #CA 101000 ($81). Gr. K–3. PRV (5/76), PVB (4/77). 331.7

Contents: 1. People Make a School Go. 2. Teamwork in a Toy Factory. 3. Working for an Airline. 4. Look Out, World, Here I Come.

This set helps children relate their work to the adult career world. It emphasizes the importance and value of work and cooperation on the job.

CAREER KALEIDOSCOPE (Filmstrip—Sound). January Productions, 1973. 5 color, sound filmstrips, 49–55 fr.; 5 cassettes, 5–6 min.; Teacher's Guide. ($72.50). Gr. 2–5. PRV (9/74), PVB (5/75). 331.7

Contents: 1. All around the Shopping Mall. 2. Check In, Check Up. 3. In TV You Could Be. 4. One for All at City Hall. 5. Up, Up, and Away.

A set that focuses on the many jobs related to retailing, health, television, city government, and air transportation.

FARMING (Filmstrip—Sound). *See* Vocational Guidance

FOODS WE EAT (Filmstrip—Sound). *See* Food Supply

GETTING READY UNIT ONE (Motion Picture—16mm—Sound). WNVT (Northern Virginia Educational TV)/EBEC, 1973 (Watcha Gonna Do?). 16mm color, sound film, 15 min.; Teacher's Manual. #3358 ($200). Gr. 5–9. BKL (5/15/75), CPR (11/74), LFR (12/74). 331.702

Careers require preparation and planning. This film introduces a gymnast, an archeologist, and a policewoman, and shows how each of them goes about preparing for his or her career.

OCCUPATIONS (cont.)

GOING BACK UNIT THREE (Motion Picture—16mm—Sound). WNVT (Northern Virginia Educational TV)/EBEC, 1973 (Watcha Gonna Do?). 16mm color, sound film, 15 min.; #3355 ($200). Gr. 5–A. BKL (5/15/75), LFR (12/74), PRV (10/76). 331.702

This film focuses on how one's environment (family, peers, culture, and geography) plays a role in career decisions.

HELPING PEOPLE LOOK THEIR BEST (Filmstrip—Sound). *See* Vocational Guidance

HELPING PEOPLE SOLVE PROBLEMS (Filmstrip—Sound). *See* Vocational Guidance

IT ALL DEPENDS ON YOU (Motion Picture—16mm—Sound). *See* Vocational Guidance

JOBS IN THE CITY—WOMEN AT WORK (Motion Picture—16mm—Sound). *See* Women—Employment

MANY PEOPLE, MANY CAREERS (Filmstrip—Sound). *See* Vocational Guidance

NEW HORIZONS FOR WOMEN (Filmstrip—Sound). *See* Women—Employment

NIGHT PEOPLE'S DAY (Motion Picture—16mm—Sound). *See* Cities and Towns

PARTNERS, UNIT 3 (Motion Picture—16mm—Sound). WNVT (Northern Virginia Educational TV)/EBEC, 1973 (Watcha Gonna Do?). 16mm color, sound film, 15 min.; Teacher's Manual. #3356 ($200). Gr. 5–A. BKL (5/15/75), CGE (1974), LFR (12/74). 331.702

Some people want to be their own bosses and look for ways to create their own jobs. Many small businesses have been started through the imagination of one or 2 people. This film introduces students to how a business is run; it also shows them how, with imagination and some risk, one can carve out a job for oneself that does not already exist.

PEOPLE AT WORK, SET 2 (Filmstrip—Sound). *See* Vocational Guidance

PRESERVING THE ENVIRONMENT (Filmstrip—Sound). *See* Vocational Guidance

PUTTING ELECTRICITY TO WORK (Filmstrip—Sound). *See* Vocational Guidance

RICHARD SCARRY'S WHAT DO PEOPLE DO ALL DAY (Kit). Random House, 1976. 6 color, sound filmstrips, 50–82 fr.; 6 discs or cassettes, 8–11 min.; 1 book; Teacher's Guide; 17 Duplicating Masters; Discussion Guide. Discs #04101-1 ($99), Cassettes #40102-X ($99). Gr. K–2. PRV (2/77), PVB (4/77). 371.425

Contents: 1. Welcome to Busytown; Everyone is a Worker; Building a New House. 2. Mailing a Letter; A Voyage on a Ship. 3. Sergeant Murphy of the Busytown Police Dept.; A Visit to the Hospital; Fireman to the Rescue. 4. A Train Trip; The Story of Seeds and How they Grow; The Airplane Ride. 5. Wood and How We Use It; Digging Coal to Make Electricity; Building a New Road. 6. Cotton and How We Use It; Where Bread Comes From; Water.

Everyone does something in "Busytown" and students will see how different occupations interrelate and how the work that is done affects everyone's daily life.

SERVING THE NATION (Filmstrip—Sound). *See* Vocational Guidance

A TIME OF CHANGES UNIT THREE (Motion Picture—16mm—Sound). WNVT (Northern Virginia Educational TV)/EBEC, 1973 (Watcha Gonna Do?). 16mm color, sound film, 15 min.; Teacher's Guide. #3359 ($200). Gr. 5–A. AIF (1974), CPR (11/74), LFR (12/74). 331.702

How technological changes can affect career decisions is clearly emphasized in this film. Technology has made some working roles obsolete, but has created others. The student's imagination will be spurred to consider jobs that do not exist today, but might exist in the future.

TRAFFIC WATCHER (Motion Picture—16mm—Sound). *See* Safety Education

TRANSPORTATION OF PEOPLE AND GOODS (Filmstrip—Sound). *See* Transportation

VOCATIONAL SKILLS FOR TOMORROW (Filmstrip—Sound). *See* Vocational Guidance

WEATHER FORECASTING (Motion Picture—16mm—Sound). *See* Weather Forecasting

WHAT DO YOU THINK? UNIT ONE (Motion Picture—16mm—Sound). WNVT (Northern Virginia Educational TV)/EBEC, 1973 (Watcha Gonna Do?). 16mm color, sound film, 15 min.; Teacher's Guide. #3351 ($200). Gr. 5–A. CPR (11/74), LFR (1974), PRV (12/74). 331.702

Career choice is presented as a developmental process, a continuous series of decisions about one's self and what one wants to be. An important underlying theme is that each person is presented with choices that give him or her some control in shaping the future.

WHAT'S THE LIMIT? UNIT TWO (Motion Picture—16mm—Sound). WNVT (Northern Virginia Educational TV)/EBEC, 1973 (Watcha Gonna Do?). 16mm color, sound film, 15 min.; Teacher's Manual. #3357 ($200). Gr. 5–A. BKL (5/15/75), CPR (11/74), LFR (12/74). 331.702

All of us have limitations, and part of growing up is accepting and learning to deal with them. In this film, the students will observe 2 individuals who did not become what they had wanted to be. However, they have overcome disappointment and are happy in other occupations better suited to their abilities.

WHEN I GROW UP I CAN BE (Filmstrip—Sound). *See* Vocational Guidance

WHERE PEOPLE WORK (Filmstrip—Sound). Troll Associates, 1975. 4 color, sound filmstrips, av. 48 fr. ea.; 2 cassettes, av. 7 min. ea.; Teacher's Guide. ($52). Gr. 1–5. TEA (1/76). 331.7
Contents: 1. What Is an Office. 2. What Is a Factory. 3. What is a Bank. 4. What Is a Store.
Introduces children to the world outside their classroom with close-up looks at where some people work, showing the special services that each provides.

WHO HELPS US? (Filmstrip—Sound). *See* Community Life

WHO WORKS FOR YOU? (Kit). *See* Vocational Guidance

WHO'S WHO IN THE ZOO? (Motion Picture—16mm—Sound). *See* Zoological Gardens

WHY MOTHERS WORK (Motion Picture—16mm—Sound). *See* Women—Employment

WORKING IN THE OFFICE (Filmstrip—Sound). *See* Vocational Guidance

WORKING IN U.S. COMMUNITIES, GROUP ONE (Filmstrip—Sound). Society for Visual Education, 1970. 4 color, sound filmstrips, 43–54 fr.; 2 cassettes or discs, 9–12:30 min.; 4 Guides. Discs #201-SAR ($54), Cassettes #201-SATC ($54). Gr. 3–8. BKL (12/72). 331.7
Contents: 1. Old Sturbridge and Mystic Seaport: Historic Communities. 2. Douglas, Wyoming: Ranch Community. 3. Rockland, Maine: Coastal Community. 4. Flagstaff, Arizona: Service Community.
These filmstrips emphasize elementary economics. On-location photography shows students the diversity of business and industry both large and small, and how they meet people's needs.

WORKING IN U.S. COMMUNITIES, GROUP TWO (Filmstrip—Sound). Society for Visual Education. 4 color, sound filmstrips, 52–57 fr.; 4 cassettes or discs, 13–16 min. Disc #201-SBR ($54), Cassette #201-SBTC ($54). Gr. K–6. BKL (2/71), PRV (4/1/72). 331.7
Contents: 1. New Orleans: Marketing Community. 2. San Francisco: Financial Community. 3. Detroit: Manufacturing Community. 4. Chicago: Transportation Community.

On-location photography shows students the diversity of business and industry. Stresses people engaged in the everyday activities of making a living, how the history and geography of an area effect business, and who profits by business activities.

WORKING WITH ANIMALS (Filmstrip—Sound). *See* Animals—Treatment

THE WORLD OF WORK (Cassette). *See* Vocational Guidance

OCEAN

EARTH AND UNIVERSE SERIES, SET 2 (Filmstrip—Sound). *See* Geology

NIGHTLIFE (Motion Picture—16mm—Sound). Phoenix Films, 1976. 16mm color, sound film, 12 min. ($250). Gr. 3–A. AFF (1977). 574.5
Exploration of the wonders that exist in the depths of the silent, mysterious oceans. See underwater life at close range, and experience the quiet, shadowy world these intriguing sea creatures inhabit.

THE OCEAN IS MANY THINGS (Filmstrip—Captioned). Imperial Educational Resources, 1970. 6 color, captioned filmstrips. #3FG-14000 ($48). Gr. K–4. BKL (4/1/70), TEA (1/72). 551.46
Contents: 1. The Ocean Is Jobs for People. 2. The Ocean Is Transportation. 3. The Ocean Is a Home for Plants and Animals. 4. The Ocean Is Fun. 5. Learning about the World beneath the Waves. 6. Looking at the Ocean.
An introduction to ocean life.

SEA, SAND AND SHORE (Filmstrip—Sound). Lyceum/Mook & Blanchard, 1969. 3 color, sound filmstrips, 44–48 fr.; 3 cassettes or discs, 6–11 min. Cassettes #LY35469SC ($71), Disc #LY35469SR ($56). Gr. 3–12. BKL (9/1/69), FLN (10/69), INS (11/69). 551.46
Contents: 1. Sea, Sand and Shore. 2. Signatures in the Sand. 3. The Art of the Sea.
This set tells of the working of the sea on the shore, recounting endless pounding, carving, and smoothing of the land's edges. Written and photographed by Ann Atwood.

OCEAN LIFE. *See* Marine Biology

OCEANOGRAPHY

THE NEW OCEANS (Filmstrip—Sound). Educational Dimensions Group, 1976. 4 color, sound filmstrips, av. 60 fr. ea.; 4 cassettes, av. 16 min. ea.; 1 Guide. #526 ($74). Gr. 6–8. BKL (1/15/77), PVB (1976-77). 551.46
This set explores the role of the ocean in

OCEANOGRAPHY (cont.)

the earth's energy cycle, the ocean as a physical environment, and humanity's exploration of the ocean today for tomorrow.

THE OCEANS: A KEY TO OUR FUTURE (Filmstrip—Sound). United Learning, 1977. 5 color, sound filmstrips, av. 59–80 fr. ea.; 5 cassettes, av. 16–20 min. ea.; Teacher's Guide. #4510 ($75). Gr. 5–8. BKL (1/1/78), PRV (10/77). 551.46

Contents: 1. The Oceans: Past, Present and Future. 2. The Oceans: A Storehouse of Food. 3. The Oceans: A Storehouse of Raw Materials. 4. The Oceans: A Storehouse of Power. 5. Changing the Oceans.

Designed to relate basic earth and life science concepts to the world's oceans, this program portrays the oceans as a major resource for the future development of human society and economics. The human interrelationship with the sea is examined in historical and present-day perspectives, with emphasis on sensible and ecologically sound methods of utilizing the potential of the sea.

THE WORLD OF INNERSPACE (Filmstrip—Sound). Lyceum/Mook & Blanchard, 1973. 2 color, sound filmstrips, av. 53–58 fr.; 2 cassettes or discs. Cassettes #LY35773SC ($46), Discs #LY35773SR ($37). Gr. 5–A. BKL (7/15/74), PRV (10/74), PVB (5/75). 551.46

Contents: 1. From Aquapedes to Aquanauts. 2. Windows in the Sea.

Presents an illuminating voyage in the ocean depths aboard the newest undersea research vessel and discusses the possibilities of developing the sea riches.

OCTOPUS

OCTOPUS (Film Loop—8mm—Silent). Walt Disney Educational Media, 1966. 8mm color, silent film loop, approx. 4 min. #62-5455L ($30). Gr. K–12. MDU (1974). 594.5

Shows a female octopus caring for her nest of eggs and the hatching of the eggs, as well as the octopus hunting.

O'DELL, SCOTT

THE KING'S FIFTH (Filmstrip—Sound). See Discoveries (In Geography)—Fiction

SING DOWN THE MOON (Filmstrip—Sound). See Navajo—Fiction

OPTICAL ILLUSIONS

SENSES AND PERCEPTION: LINKS TO THE OUTSIDE WORLD (Motion Picture—16mm—Sound). See Senses and Sensation

ORCHESTRAL MUSIC

AMERICAN SCENES (Phonodiscs). Bowmar Publishing, 1965. 1 disc; 6 in. X 36 in.; Theme Charts. #074 ($10). Gr. 3–8. AUR (1978). 785.8

Contents: 1. *Grand Canyon* Suite by Grofe. 2. *Mississippi* Suite by Grofe.

Scenes of the Grand Canyon and the Mississippi are presented in dramatic music. Teaching suggestions are designed to aid students in understanding musical notation and concepts of melody, rhythm, and form.

CHILDREN'S RHYTHMS IN SYMPHONY (Phonodiscs). *See* Rhythms

CLASSICAL MUSIC FOR PEOPLE WHO HATE CLASSICAL MUSIC (Phonodiscs). Listening Library. 1 disc, 12 in. 33-1/3 rpm. #AM 20 R ($6.95). Gr. 4–A. MDU (1978). 785

Arthur Fiedler conducts the Boston Pops Orchestra in excerpts from concert favorites including such pieces as Schubert's Unfinished Symphony and Chopin's *Les Sylphides*.

STRAVINSKI GREETING PRELUDE, ETC. (Phonodiscs). Columbia Records (Special Products). 1 disc, 33-1/3 rpm. #M-31729 ($6.98). Gr. 4–A. PRV (9/75). 785

Contents: 1. Greeting Prelude. 2. Dumbarton Oaks Concerto. 3. Circus Polka. 4. Eight Instrumental Miniatures for 15 Players. 5. Four Etudes for Orchestra. 6. Two Suites for Small Orchestra.

The Canadian Broadcasting Orchestra, Columbia Symphony Orchestra, and the Columbia Chamber Orchestra, with Igor Stravinski conducting, present this enjoyable disc.

ORGEL, DORIS

BARON MUNCHAUSEN TRULY TALL TALES (Phonodisc or Cassette). *See* Legends

ORIENTEERING

POSITIONAL AND DIRECTIONAL RELATIONSHIPS (Filmstrip—Sound). January Productions, 1977 (Perceptual Development). 4 color, sound filmstrips, av. 51 fr. ea.; 4 cassettes, av. 5–6 min. ea.; Teacher's Guide. Set ($58), Each Unit ($14.95). Gr. K–2. BKL (10/15/77), PRV (9/77). 152.1

Contents: 1. Left and Right. 2. First, Next and Last. 3. Over, Under and Through. 4. Inside and Outside.

Promotes the understanding of positional and directional concepts.

ORMONDROYD, EDWARD

SERIES SEVEN: A LITTLE LOVIN' AND A LITTLE LAUGHIN' (Filmstrip—Sound). *See* Short Stories

OROZCO, RAFAEL

PIANO CONCERTO NO. 3 IN D MINOR (Phonodiscs). *See* Concertos

OSCEOLA

CHIEFS AND LEADERS (Cassette). *See* Indians of North America

OTTERS

TEEKA THE OTTER (Filmstrip—Sound). Lyceum/Mook & Blanchard, 1972. 1 color, sound filmstrip, 59 fr.; 1 cassette or disc, 10-3/4 min. Cassettes #LY351370C ($25), Discs #LY351370R ($19.50). Gr. K-6. BKL (1/1/72), STE (10/72). 599.7
This strip helps the student appreciate the delight of owning a young and unusual pet, and awakens the student to the responsibility of providing for the special needs of his or her pets.

OUTDOOR LIFE

LIFE IN RURAL AMERICA (Filmstrip— Sound). *See* U.S.—Social Life and Customs

OUTER SPACE—EXPLORATION

BEYOND THIS EARTH (Filmstrip—Sound). *See* Lunar Probes

OWLS—FICTION

LA LECHUZA—CUENTOS DE MI BARRIO (Cassette). Educational Activities. 1 cassette; Text. #BC-148 ($12.90). Gr. 5-8. PRV (11/76). 468.6
Four short stories in Spanish of mystery and suspense concerning the owl. No English translation.

OXENBURY, HELEN

THE GREAT BIG ENORMOUS TURNIP (Filmstrip—Sound). *See* Folklore—Russia

PACIFIC STATES

FOCUS ON AMERICA, ALASKA AND HAWAII (Filmstrip—Sound). *See* U.S.— Economic Conditions

PAINTING

PAINTING FROM NATURE (Motion Picture—16mm—Sound). *See* Art—Technique

PAINTING, AMERICAN

AUDUBON'S SHORE BIRDS (Motion Picture—16mm—Sound). *See* Water Birds

PAINTINGS, AMERICAN

A. J. MILLER'S WEST: THE PLAINS INDIAN—1837—SLIDE SET (Slides). *See* Indians of North America—Paintings

PAINTINGS—COLLECTIONS

PICTURES ARE FUN TO LOOK AT (Art Prints). *See* Art Appreciation

PAKISTAN

SOUTH ASIA: REGION IN TRANSITION (Filmstrip—Sound). *See* Asia

PALEONTOLOGY. *See* Fossils

PANDAS

PANDAS: A GIFT FROM CHINA (Motion Picture—16mm—Sound). EBEC, 1974. 16mm color, sound film, 14 min. #3361 ($185). Gr. 1-6. EFL (12/76), LFR (12/74), PRV (2/75). 599.74
Two rare giant pandas were presented as a gift to the United States in 1972 by the People's Republic of China. The camera records the playful cagefuls in their home at the National Zoological Park in Washington, D.C. The film also reveals the people and jobs that are important to the efficient and humane operation of zoos.

PLAYFUL PANDAS (Motion Picture— 16mm—Sound). Coronet Instructional Media, 1975. 16mm color, sound film, 10 min.; Teacher's Guide. ($170). Gr. K-3. LNG (5/6/77), TEA (9/77). 599.74
Two new tenants join Washington's National Zoo and demonstrate their playful nature in a rhymed story.

PANTOMIMES

BIP AS A SKATER (Motion Picture— 16mm—Sound). EBEC, 1975 (The Art of Silence: Pantomimes with Marcel Marceau). 16mm color, sound film, 8 min.; Teacher's Guide. #47803 ($135). Gr. 1-A. BKL (11/75), LFR (3/4/76), PRV (1/76). 792.3
Marceau created Bip as his "silent alter ego." In this Bip pantomime, we see Bip stumble, fight for balance, and joyously strive to become a great skater—on illusionary ice.

THE PAINTER (Motion Picture—16mm— Sound). EBEC, 1975 (Art of Silence: Pantomimes with Marcel Marceau). 16mm color, sound film, 8 min.; Teacher's Guide.

PANTOMIMES (cont.)

#47804 ($135). Gr. 1-12. BKL (11/1/75), FLN (3/4/77), PRV (1/76). 792.3

"Mime makes the invisible, visible and the visible, invisible." Marceau's sometimes comical, always graceful interpretation of "The Painter" in Central Park, allows the viewer to "see" objects that are not there.

PANTOMIME: THE LANGUAGE OF THE HEART (Motion Picture—16mm—Sound). EBEC, 1975 (The Art of Silence: Pantomimes with Marcel Marceau). 16mm color, sound film, 10 min.; Teacher's Guide. #47813 ($150). Gr. 1-A. BKL (11/75), FLN (3/4/77), PRV (3/76). 792.3

In this film, Marceau talks about mime—how body movement and gestures communicate attitudes and emotions. He calls pantomime the language of the heart. Brief clips from many of the pantomimes in the series vividly illustrate his words.

THE SIDE SHOW (Motion Picture—16mm—Sound). EBEC, 1975 (The Art of Silence: Pantomimes with Marcel Marceau). 16mm color, sound film, 9 min. #47810 ($140). Gr. 1-A. BKL (11/1/77), FLN (3/4/77), PRV (1/76). 792.3

In this pantomime, Marceau shows circus performers demonstrating their skills—a juggler, an acrobat, clowns pulling ropes without ropes. The major performer is a tightrope walker. Why is it more frightening to see Marceau walk a tightrope on the floor than a real tightrope many feet in the air? The answer is in Marceau's introductory remarks ". . . Illusion is stronger than reality sometimes."

PARENT AND CHILD

MY PARENTS ARE GETTING A DIVORCE (Filmstrip—Sound). *See* Divorce

PARENT AND CHILD—FICTION

THE GRIZZLY (Kit). *See* Bears—Fiction

PARROTS—FICTION

DOROTHY AND THE NECKLACE (Motion Picture—16mm—Sound). Phoenix Films, 1976 (Dorothy Series). 16mm color, sound film, 8 min. #20037 ($150). Gr. K-5. PRV (1/77). Fic

Dorothy is a little girl with a pet parrot named Coco, who is her alter ego. In this episode, Dorothy has a new necklace, which she gives to Coco. A mischievous crow steals the necklace, and a vigorous chase follows. Coco and Dorothy are constantly thwarted by the crow's many disguises until the crow encounters a hive of bees.

DOROTHY AND THE PARROT (Motion Picture—16mm—Sound). Phoenix Films, 1976 (Dorothy Series). 16mm color, sound film, 6 min. #20036 ($125). Gr. K-5. PRV (1/77). Fic

Coco the parrot is showing off, trying to impress Dorothy with his superior knowledge and ability. Anything she attempts to do, Coco can do better. The 2 friends quarrel, but they soon resolve their differences, and peace and friendship return.

DOROTHY AND THE POP-SINGER (Motion Picture—16mm—Sound). Phoenix Films, 1974 (Dorothy Series). 16mm color, sound film, 9 min. #20035 ($150). Gr. K-5. FLN (1977), PRV (12/75). Fic

Coco adores Dorothy and is jealous of the attention that she pays to a pop-singing star and one of his recordings. The parrot does everything possible to reclaim Dorothy's attention.

DOROTHY AND THE WITCH (Motion Picture—16mm—Sound). Phoenix Films, 1976 (Dorothy Series). 16mm color, sound film, 7 min. #20038 ($135). Gr. K-5. FLN (1977). Fic

In this episode, Dorothy discovers a gingerbread house—a sweetshop. Coco the parrot rescues her from the witch and an even bigger problem—obesity.

PATRICK

SOUND FILMSTRIP SET 35 (Filmstrip—Sound). *See* Children's Literature—Collections

PATRIOTISM

THE PLEDGE OF ALLEGIANCE (Filmstrip—Sound). Marshfilm, 1969. 1 color, sound filmstrip, 41 fr.; 1 cassette or disc, 15 min.; Teacher's Guide. #1102 ($21). Gr. K-3. BKL (3/1/70). 172.1

This filmstrip brings meaning to the language of the Pledge of Allegiance.

PECOS BILL

DAVY CROCKETT AND PECOS BILL (Phonodisc or Cassette). *See* Folklore—U.S.

PELICANS

PELICANS (Film Loop—8mm—Silent). Walt Disney Educational Media, 1966. 8mm color, silent film loop, approx. 4 min. #62-5407L ($30). Gr. K-12. MDU (1974). 598.4

Both species of American pelicans are examined flying, diving, brooding, and feeding their young. The nest is shown and the young observed.

PENGUINS

ANTARCTIC PENGUINS (Film Loop—
8mm—Silent). Walt Disney Educational
Media, 1966. 8mm color, silent film loop,
approx. 4 min. #62-5370L ($30). Gr.
K–12. MDU (1974). 598.4

Penguins are viewed on land and as they
swim and play in the icy water. Close-ups
of penguins and their young are shown.

PENMANSHIP

LET'S WRITE THE ALPHABET (Filmstrip—Sound). *See* Alphabet

PEOPLE'S REPUBLIC OF CHINA. *See*
China

PERCEPTION

BASIC GEOMETRIC SHAPES (Filmstrip—
Sound). *See* Geometry

**EXPERIENCES IN PERCEPTUAL
GROWTH** (Filmstrip—Sound). EBEC,
1976. 3 color, sound filmstrips, av. 68
fr. ea.; 3 discs or cassettes, 11 min. ea.
Discs #6920 ($43.50), Cassettes #6920K
($43.50). Gr. K–2. MDU (1/77), PRV
(11/77). 152.4

Contents: 1. Texture: Squish and Prickles.
2. Sounds: Lions Don't Always Roar.
3. Numbers: Peep Counts Sheep.

A group of friendly cartoon characters
takes viewers on a whimsical quest with a
serious purpose: finding the elusive words
to describe textures, sounds, and quantities.

**FOLLOW THROUGH WITH SIGHTS AND
SOUNDS** (Filmstrip—Sound). Knowledge
Aid/United Learning, 1975. 4 color, sound
filmstrips; 4 cassettes; Teacher's Guide.
#1050 ($60). Gr. K–3. PRV 9/76). 151.1

Contents: 1. There Is No School on Satur-
day. 2. Monday Is a School Day. 3. A
Rainy Day at Home. 4. Looking and
Listening Games.

This program will involve young children
in learning experiences that develop auditory-visual discrimination and association
skills. Many activities are designed to help
children follow verbal and visual instructions and recognize warning sights and
sounds.

GUESS WHAT? (Filmstrip—Sound). *See*
Listening

LET'S FIND OUT ABOUT (Cassette).
Troll Associates, 1972. 7 cassette tapes,
av. 10 min. ea. ($38.50). Gr. K–2. BKL
(12/15/73). 152

Contents: 1. Traffic Octopus. 2. Love Is
a Hug. 3. Lick a Pickle. 4. Little Red
Bird. 5. Instruments of the Orchestra.
6. Furry Gets Ready. 7. Uproar at the

Zoo. 8. The Sardine Can. 9. Shy Trunky.
10. I Found a Sound.

Entertaining stories teach very young children about colors, tastes, sounds, emotions,
traffic safety, and 11 other important
concepts.

MEASUREMENT COMPARISONS (Filmstrip—Sound). *See* Size and Shape

MY SENSES AND ME (Filmstrip—Sound).
See Senses and Sensation

**NOSES AND TOES, PART ONE AND
TWO** (Filmstrip—Sound). *See* Comparisons

OUR VISUAL WORLD (Filmstrip—Sound).
See Art Appreciation

**POSITIONAL AND DIRECTIONAL
RELATIONSHIPS** (Filmstrip—Sound).
See Orienteering

**SENSES AND PERCEPTION: LINKS TO
THE OUTSIDE WORLD** (Motion Picture—
16mm—Sound). *See* Senses and Sensation

TADPOLE, SET ONE (Filmstrip—Sound).
Insight Media Programs/Denoyer-Geppert,
1971. 5 color, sound filmstrips, 53–63 fr.;
5 cassettes or discs, 4–5:22 min.; Teacher's
Guide. #600551 ($87). Gr. K–3. PRV
(11/72), PVB (5/73). 152.1

Contents: 1. Round Is the Way Things Go.
2. Nothing Stays the Same. 3. A Doughnut
Is a Hole with Something to Eat All around
It. 4. Who Needs Pointy Shapes? 5. Yipes!
Stripes!

Teaches young children observation, discrimination, and appreciation of the world
about them. Photographs with a minimum
of narration present such concepts as round-
ness, motion, change, and patterns.

TADPOLE, SET TWO (Filmstrip—Sound).
Insight Media Programs/Denoyer-Geppert,
1973. 5 color, sound filmstrips, 53–63 fr.;
5 cassettes or discs, 4–5:22 min.; Teacher's
Guide. #600611 ($87). Gr. 3–6. BKL
(1/15/74), PRV (11/72), PVB (5/73).
152.1

Contents: 1. Up to Here. 2. Far Away.
3. How Do You Get Up There? 4. Finding Your Way. 5. Can You See the Empty?

Teaches young children observation, discrimination, and appreciation of the world
about them. Photographs with a minimum
of narration present such concepts as measurement and size relationships, means of
locomotion, and direction.

WHAT DO YOU SEE? (Filmstrip—
Captioned). *See* Senses and Sensation

WHAT IS IT? (Filmstrip—Captioned).
EBEC, 1975 (Developing Basic Skills).
4 color, captioned filmstrips, 47 fr.;
Teacher's Guide. #13060 ($32.90). Gr.
K–2. CPR (4/77), PRV (9/75). 152.1

PERCEPTION (cont.)

Contents: 1. Let's Guess: What Animal Is It? 2. Let's Guess: What Plant Is It? 3. Let's Guess: What Food Is It? 4. Let's Guess: What Person Is It?

These 4 filmstrips invite children to play a question and answer game that will sharpen their powers of observation. Each sequence illustrates part of something. Then the whole object is shown in a group with others of its class, and the student is asked to pick the correct one. Each filmstrip repeats the pattern. Close examination of color, size, shape, and texture, as well as the ability to relate parts to the whole, are the skills developed.

WHAZZAT? (Motion Picture—16mm—Sound). *See* Folklore—India

PERCUSSION INSTRUMENTS

THE BANGERS (Cassette). Contemporary Drama Service, 1976. 1 cassette, 16 min. #C-53 ($5.95). Gr. 1–5. BKL (6/15/77). 789

This covers the whole range of percussion instruments, giving some history about each, including why it is named what it is. Also described is the sound of each, as well as the material from which it is made.

PERFORMING ARTS

BECAUSE IT'S JUST ME UNIT TWO (Motion Picture—16mm—Sound). *See* Occupations

PERKINS, AL

BEGINNER BOOKS FILMSTRIPS, SET 1 (Filmstrip—Sound). *See* Reading—Study and Teaching

PERRAULT, CHARLES

LIBRARY 5 (Cassette). *See* Literature—Collections

PERSIA. *See* Iran—Antiquities; Iran—Fiction

PETER, PAUL, AND MARY

FOLK SONGS IN AMERICAN HISTORY, SET ONE: 1700-1864 (Filmstrip—Sound). *See* Folk Songs—U.S.

FOLK SONGS IN AMERICAN HISTORY, SET TWO: 1865-1967 (Filmstrip—Sound). *See* Folk Songs—U.S.

PETROGLYPHS. *See* Indians of North America—Art

PETS

ANIMAL PETS (Filmstrip—Sound). Coronet Instructional Media, 1973. 6 color, sound filmstrips, 47–58 fr.; 6 cassettes or 3 discs, 8–11:20 min. Cassettes #M171 ($95), Discs #S171 ($95). Gr. 1–3. BKL (2/1/74), PRV (2/1/74). 636.08

Contents: 1. Sunshine, the Colt. 2. Whiskers Adopts a Kitten. 3. A New Puppy for Davy. 4. Bird Talk. 5. Joan Finds a Bunny. 6. Bob's Friend, the Fawn.

This set gives good advice about animal care and hygiene, behavior, and emotional responses people have to pets.

ANIMALS AROUND YOU (Filmstrip—Sound). *See* Animals—Habits and Behavior

ANIMALS WE SEE AROUND US (Filmstrip—Captioned). *See* Animals—Habits and Behavior

PET STORIES (Filmstrip—Sound). EBEC, 1976. 6 color, sound filmstrips, 59–62 fr.; 6 cassettes or discs, 5–7:40 min.; 1 Guide. Discs #6919 ($86.95), Cassettes #6919K ($86.95). Gr. K–3. BKL (12/15/76). 591.5

Contents: 1. Bassets Aren't People. 2. Cat on a Leash? 3. The Hamster Who Hid. 4. The Boy Who Was Afraid of Horses. 5. The Parakeet Who Panicked. 6. Trout in Goldfish Bowls.

Helps children understand animal needs and the care required when keeping pets.

PETE AND PENNY'S PET CARE (Filmstrip—Sound). ACI Media/Paramount Communications, 1975. 4 color, sound filmstrips; 4 cassettes av. 8–10 min. ea.; Teacher's Guide. #9120 ($78). Gr. K–4. BKL (12/15/75), PRV (19/76), PVB (1977). 636.08

Contents: 1. Healthy Dogs and Happy Cats. 2. Bright Fish and Singing Birds. 3. Turtles, Rabbits and Others. 4. Pets You Can Find.

Pete and Penny work after school in a pet shop. Their activities cover virtually every pet species. They learn how and why to take care of their pets.

PLAYING IT SAFE WITH ANIMALS (Filmstrip—Sound). *See* Animals—Habits and Behavior

TEEKA THE OTTER (Filmstrip—Sound). *See* Otters

WE LOVE ANIMALS (Kit). Pied Piper Productions, 1976. 4 color, sound filmstrips, 71–81 fr.; 4 cassettes or discs, av. 7–8 min.; 12 Study Prints 9 in. X 12 in.; 4 Worksheets; 18 Task Cards; Teacher's Guide. Cassettes #WO-10-C ($69.50), Discs #WO-10-R ($69.50). Gr. K–5. BKL (9/77), LGB (77/78), PRV (9/77). 636.08

Contents: 1. Get My Goat. 2. A Dream.
3. Mo and Me. 4. Petunia Loves Jill.

Four filmstrips about 4 children who each
have a special relationship to one animal—
a horse, a dog, a goat, and an elephant.
The narration consists of the spontaneous
commentary of the children shown in the
filmstrip.

PHILLIPS, LYNN

DEVELOPING CHILDREN'S ATTITUDES
TOWARD SEX ROLES (Filmstrip—
Sound). *See* Sex Role

PHONETICS

THE ABC'S OF PHONICS, PROGRAM
ONE (Kit). Q+ED Productions, 1975.
3 filmstrips, av. 20 fr. ea.; 3 discs/cassettes
av. 9 min.; 1 Student Activity Book; Spirit
Masters; 1 Teacher's Guide. Cassettes
#ABE-10 ($70), Discs #ABE-10 ($65).
Gr. 1–3. BKL (2/15/77). 372.4

This kit is designed to help primary grade
children learn letter-sound relationships
of 9 initial consonants. The basic lesson
plan for each consonant is the same in all
filmstrips: Letter in upper and lower case,
key-word beginning with the letter, brief
"characterized" story introducing the
letter's sound, and visual and auditory
reinforcement of the sound. Cartoon
characters portray the story.

THE ABC'S OF PHONICS, PROGRAM
TWO: CONSONANT LETTERS M–Z
(Kit). Q+ED Productions, 1975. 4 color,
sound filmstrips, av. 20 fr.; 4 cassettes or
discs, av. 9 min.; 1 Student Activity Book;
Spirit Masters; 1 Teacher's Guide. Cassettes #ABE-20 ($90), Discs #ABE-20
($85). Gr. 4–8. BKL (12/15/76). 372.4

This kit teaches by using the key-word
concept. The visuals are cartoon figures
and are related to the script.

READING READINESS (Filmstrip—Sound).
See Reading—Study and Teaching

READING SKILLS (Kit). *See* Reading—
Study and Teaching

THE SPELLING MONSTERS: UNIT A
(Filmstrip—Sound). *See* English Language—Spelling

THE SPELLING MONSTERS: UNIT B
(Filmstrip—Sound). *See* English Language—
Spelling

THE SPELLING MONSTERS: UNIT C
(Filmstrip—Sound). *See* English Language—
Spelling

THE SPELLING MONSTERS: UNIT D
(Filmstrip—Sound). *See* English Language—
Spelling

PHOTOGRAPHY

BASIC PHOTOGRAPHY (Filmstrip—Sound).
Coronet Instructional Media, 1975. 6 color,
sound filmstrips, 58–66 fr.; 6 cassettes or 3
discs, 9:40–13:50 min. Cassettes #M304
($95), Discs #S304 ($95). Gr. 4–A. BKL
(10/15/75), PRV. 770.28

Contents: 1. Which Camera for You?
2. You're in Control. 3. Making Film Work.
4. Adding Light. 5. Darkroom Skills.
6. Taking Better Pictures.

Detailed photographs introduce students to
many types of cameras, use of their controls, and the reasons for choosing different
kinds of cameras and darkroom equipment.

PHOTOGRAPHY FOR KIDS (Filmstrip—
Sound). Media Research and Development,
1977. 6 color, sound filmstrips, av. 50 fr.;
6 cassettes, av. 4–11 min.; Teaching Materials. ($95). Gr. 4–8. BKL (11/15/77).
770.28

Contents: 1. Your Camera: The Not-So-
Magic Box. 2. Making a Pinhole Camera.
3. Using Your Camera. 4. Learning to See.
5. Developing Your Own Point-of-View.

Introduces photography, including pinhole,
110, 126, and self-processing cameras. Offers a program within the school budget and
student capabilities.

SEEING . . . THROUGH A LENS (Filmstrip—
Sound). ACI Media/Paramount Communications, 1975. 4 color, sound filmstrips;
4 cassettes, av. 8 min. ea.; Teacher's Guide.
#9124 ($78). Gr. 4–8. BKL (4/75), PVB
(1977), TEA (5/6/76). 770

Contents: 1. Click—The Fun of Photography. 2. The Process—How It Works. 3. The
Art—Light and Composition. 4. Variations
and Applications.

This set explains the process and the art of
photography and at the same time develops
the basic ability to see creatively and with
discrimination.

PHOTOTROPISM

ISOLATION AND FUNCTION OF AUXIN
(Film Loop—8mm—Silent. BFA Educational
Media, 1973 (Plant Behavior). 8mm color,
silent film loop, approx. 4 min. #481414
($30). Gr. 4–9. BKL (5/1/76). 581.18

Demonstrates experiments, phenomena, and
behavior in plants.

MECHANICS OF PHOTOTROPISM (Film
Loop—8mm—Captioned). BFA Educational
Media, 1973 (Plant Behavior). 8mm color,
captioned film loop, aprox. 4 min. #481423
($30). Gr. 4–9. BKL (5/1/76). 581.18

Demonstrates experiments, phenomena, and
behavior in plants.

THE NATURE OF PHOTOTROPISM (Film
Loop—8mm—Captioned). BFA Educational Media, 1973 (Plant Behavior). 8mm

PHOTOTROPISM (cont.)

color, captioned film loop, approx. 4 min.
#481422 ($30). Gr. 4-9. BKL (5/1/76).
581.18
Demonstrates experiments, phenomena, and
behavior in plants.

PHYSICAL EDUCATION AND TRAINING

KEEP ON STEPPIN' (Phonodisc or Cassette).
Activity Records/Educational Activities.
1 disc or cassette, 30 min.; Teacher's Guide.
Disc #AR58 ($7.95), Cassette #AC58
($8.95). Gr. 4-6. PRV (9/75). 613.7
Contents: 1. Living for the City. 2. Super-
stition. 3. Cherie Amour. 4. You Haven't
Done Nothin'. 5. High Ground.
Today's music with lyrics that give directions as part of the songs. Movements build
and stretch the major muscle groups. On
the reverse side, a fuller instrumental version, which can be used for movement exploration, creative routines, dancing, and
drama.

POSTURAL IMPROVEMENT ACTIVITIES
(Phonodiscs). *See* Exercise

**PHYSICALLY HANDICAPPED—
BIOGRAPHY**

LEO BEUERMAN (Motion Picture—16mm—
Sound). *See* Beuerman, Leo

PHYSICALLY HANDICAPPED—FICTION

THE LITTLE LAME PRINCE (Phonodisc or
Cassette). *See* Fairy Tales

PHYSIOLOGY

THE BODY (Filmstrip—Sound). Scholastic
Book Services, 1977 (Adventures in Science).
4 color, sound filmstrips, av. 54–70 fr.;
4 cassettes or discs, av. 10–12.; Teacher's
Guide. Discs #8623 ($69.50), Cassettes
#8624 ($69.50). Gr. 4-8. BKL (12/15/77).
612
Contents: 1. Circulation and Respiration.
2. Genetics and Blood. 3. Digestion and
Hunger. 4. Muscles and Nerves.
Respiratory problems suffered by some
athletes in the 1968 Mexico City Olympics
leads into the study of the circulation and
respiration of the body. The discovery of
sickle-cell anemia and the resulting research
in genetics and blood are relived. Students
learn that experiments uncovered the origins
of hunger sensation, while curiosity over the
paralyzing effects of curare led to the discovery of medicinal uses for that lethal
substance.

THE HUMAN BODY (Filmstrip—Sound).
See Anatomy

HUMAN BODY AND HOW IT WORKS
(Filmstrip—Sound). *See* Anatomy

THE HUMAN BODY, SET ONE (Filmstrip—
Sound). *See* Anatomy

THE HUMAN BODY, SET TWO (Filmstrip—
Sound). *See* Anatomy

PIATTI, CELESTINO

THE HAPPY OWLS (Motion Picture—
16mm—Sound). *See* Happiness—Fiction

PICASSO, PABLO (RUIZ)

PICTURES ARE FUN TO LOOK AT (Art
Prints). *See* Art Appreciation

PICKETT, JOSEPH

PICTURES ARE FUN TO LOOK AT (Art
Prints). *See* Art Appreciation

PICTURE WRITING

PETROGLYPHS: ANCIENT ART OF THE
MOJAVE (Filmstrip—Sound). *See* Indians
of North America—Art

PIERNE, (HENRI CONSTANT) GABRIEL

MARCHES (Phonodiscs). *See* Marches
(Music)

PIGS

PIGS (Film Loop—8mm—Silent). Thorne
Films/Prentice-Hall Media, 1972 (Barnyard
Animals). 8mm color, silent film loop,
approx. 4 min. #HAT 434 ($26). Gr. 1-6.
AUR (1978). 636.4
Adult and young pigs are seen inside the
barn and running in the open yard.

PIGS—FICTION

PIGS AND PIRATES (Filmstrip—Sound).
Weston Woods Studios, 1973. 1 color,
sound filmstrip, 48 fr.; 1 cassette, 12 min.
#SF130C ($12.75). Gr. K-3. RTE (1/74).
Fic
A Greek folk tale.

PINES, MARK

DEPUTY MARV (Filmstrip—Sound). *See*
Police

THE HUNGRY PLANT (Filmstrip—Sound).
See Plants—Nutrition

PIONEER LIFE. *See* Frontier and Pioneer
Life

PIPER, WATTY

THE LITTLE ENGINE THAT COULD:
GOLDEN ANNIVERSARY (Filmstrip—
Sound). *See* Railroads—Fiction

PIRATES—FICTION

PIGS AND PIRATES (Filmstrip—Sound).
See Pigs—Fiction

TREASURE ISLAND (Cassette). Jabberwocky Cassette Classics, 1972. 2 cassettes,
120 min. #1011–1021 ($15.96). Gr. 6–9.
BKL (3/15/74), JOR (11/74), PRV (11/73).
Fic
Stevenson's favorite tale of the search for
hidden treasure is narrated by a boy who
portrays the character of Jim Hawkins. He
relates the happenings on the voyage with
Long John Silver as the few sound effects
add to the telling of this tale.

TREASURE ISLAND (Filmstrip—Sound).
Listening Library, 1977 (Visu-Literature).
2 color, sound filmstrips, av. 85 fr.; 2 cassettes, av. 23 min. ea.; Teacher's Guide.
($29.95). Gr. 6–8. LGB (1977). Fic
Young Jim Hawkins and his friends find
themselves with blood-thirsty pirates in a
race for buried treasure. Narration adapted
from the novel.

PITCHER, MOLLY

FAMOUS PATRIOTS OF THE AMERICAN
REVOLUTION (Filmstrip—Sound). *See*
U.S.—History—Biography

PLANT PHYSIOLOGY

ANGIOSPERMS: THE LIFE CYCLE OF A
STRAWBERRY (Film Loop—8mm—
Captioned). *See* Growth (Plants)

ISOLATION AND FUNCTION OF AUXIN
(Film Loop—8mm—Silent). *See* Phot-
tropism

LEAF FUNCTIONS (Filmstrip—Captioned).
See Leaves

MECHANICS OF PHOTOTROPISM (Film
Loop—8mm—Captioned). *See* Phototropism

THE NATURE OF PHOTOTROPISM (Film
Loop—8mm—Captioned). *See* Phototropism

PLANT PROPAGATION

HOW FLOWERS REPRODUCE: THE
CALIFORNIA POPPY (Study Print).
Kenneth E. Clouse, 1974. 12 heavy stock
cardboard prints, unmounted, color 11 in ×
14 in. ($14). Gr. 5–9. PRV (10/75). 581.16
The photographs show reproduction of flowers by seed formation, using the California
poppy. Text and a labeled drawing of the

photograph are adjacent to the colored
photograph on the same side of the print,
so the entire process can be followed in
detail.

SEED DISPERSAL (Film Loop—8mm—
Silent). *See* Seeds

SEEDS SPROUTING (Film Loop—8mm—
Silent). *See* Seeds

SELF-PLANTING SEEDS (Film Loop—
8mm—Silent). *See* Seeds

PLANTS

BEGINNING SCIENCE: PLANTS
LEARNING MODULE (Kit). *See* Botany

PLANT WORLD (Filmstrip—Sound). Uni-
versity Films/McGraw-Hill Films, 1975.
6 color, sound filmstrips, av. 57 fr.; 6 cassettes or discs, 15 min.; Teacher's Guide.
Cassette #102554-5 ($109), Discs
#103921-X ($109). Gr. 3–5. PRV
(5/76). 581. 5
Contents: 1. The Wondrous Variety of
Plants: An Introduction to Plants. 2. Parts
of Plants and Their Functions. 3. From
One Generation to the Next: Where Plants
Come from and How They Are Dispersed.
4. Plants—The Foodmaker: What Plants
Need to Live and Grow. 5. Jack and the
Bean Seeds: How Plants Grow. 6. Plants
and Their Uses.
The filmstrips show the amazing variety of
plants and the many kinds of environments
in which they exist. The principles of plant
growth and development are demonstrated
in simple, easy-to-follow experiments, and
the relationship of plants to the total environment is explained.

PLANTS (Filmstrip—Sound). Clearvue,
1976 (Basic Science Program, Group One).
6 color, sound filmstrips, 55 fr.; 6 cassettes
or discs, 10–12 min.; Teacher's Guide. Disc
#CL442R ($81.50), Cassette #CL442C
($81.50). Gr. K–3. PRV (4/78). 581.5
Contents: 1. Plants. 2. Plant Food. 3. Flowers. 4. Trees. 5. Unfamiliar Plants. 6. Nature Tamed.
This set focuses on the web of interrelationships in the environment. Mother Nature,
with the help of a rather large and intelligent
bee, explores plants and their natural environment. Special mention is made of plants
that can be grown at home and school.

PLANTS—NUTRITION

THE HUNGRY PLANT (Filmstrip—Sound).
Lyceum, 1972. 1 filmstrip, 50 fr.; 1 cassette, 12:30 min. LY 35770C ($25),
LY 35770R ($19.50). Gr. 4–9. PRV
(9/72), STE (10/72). 631.5
This filmstrip explores the reasons why
some plants are healthy and others stunted.

PLANTS—NUTRITION (cont.)

It investigates how soil chemistry affects plant growth. Students are shown experimenting with growing corn and controlling nutrient, nitrogen, phosphorous, and potassium content of the soil. Soil is tested to determine which nutrients it needs and what proportions.

SOIL IS SOIL . . . ISN'T IT? (Filmstrip—Sound). *See* Soils

PLAY

FLAT FLIP FLIES STRAIGHT (Motion Picture—16mm—Sound). *See* Games

POCAHONTAS

CHIEFS AND LEADERS (Cassette). *See* Indians of North America

POETRY—COLLECTIONS

AMERICAN INDIAN POETRY (Filmstrip—Sound). *See* Indians of North America—Poetry

DAYBREAK (Motion Picture—16mm—Sound). EBEC, 1977. 16mm color, sound film, 9 min; Guide. #3392 ($115). Gr. 3–A. BKL (11/1/77). 808.81
The dawn is captured by panning the horizon of the southwestern United States. The sights, impressions, and reflections are seen through sensitive cinematography. Brief poems of Carl Sandburg and the Pima and Navajo Indians complement the vivid images.

LITERATURE FOR CHILDREN, SERIES 4 (Filmstrip—Sound). *See* Literature—Study and Teaching

MORE SILVER PENNIES (Phonodisc or Cassette). Caedmon Records, 1976. 1 cassette or disc, 32 min. Disc #TC-1511 ($6.98), Cassette #CDL-51560 ($7.95). Gr. K–A. BKL (11/17/77). 808.81
A follow-up anthology of Blanche Jenning's *Silver Pennies*. Its selections feature poets who became famous, as well as lesser knowns. The short poems are alternately read by Claire Bloom and Cyril Ritchard.

A POCKETFUL OF POETRY (Filmstrip—Sound). Guidance Associates, 1975. 2 color, sound filmstrips, av. 61–76 fr. ea.; 2 discs or cassettes, av. 11 min.; Teacher's Guide. Discs #9A-301-307 ($52.50), Cassettes #9A-301-315 ($52.50). Gr. 4–6. LGB (1975), PVB (1976). 808.81
An introduction to the techniques of rhythm, rhyme, and word selection. Demonstrates the poet's role as a storyteller.

POETRY AND ME (Filmstrip—Sound). *See* Children as Authors

POETRY BY AND FOR KIDS (Kit). Society for Visual Education, 1975. 1 color, sound filmstrip, 54 fr.; 1 cassette, 9-1/4 min.; Posters; 4 Booklets; Idea Cards; Teacher's Manual. #MK-2700 ($80). Gr. 3–6. BKL (9/76), PRV (4/76). 808.81
Contents: 1. Anything Can Happen in a Poem (filmstrip). 2. Booklets: "Comparisons," "I Used to Think," "Make a Wish," "Where I Live."
The examples in this kit help youngsters realize that logic, rhyme, and meter are not always necessary in poetry—that the direction an idea can take in a poem is limitless.

POETRY OF THE SEASONS (Filmstrip—Sound). *See* Seasons—Poetry

SEASONS OF POETRY (Filmstrip—Sound). Society for Visual Education, 1976. 4 color, sound w/partial captions filmstrips, av. 35 fr. ea.; 4 cassettes or discs, av. 8 min. ea.; Teacher's Guide. #A445-SAR/SATC ($99), Each Filmstrip with Guide ($11), Each Record or Cassette ($7.50). Gr. 2–5. BKL (1/1/77), PRV (11/77). 808.81
Contents: 1. Poems of the Fall Season. 2. Poems of the Winter Season. 3. Poems of the Spring Season. 4. Poems of the Summer Season.
The overall objective is to get children to write their own poetry. The Teacher's Guide gives suggestions for getting writing started. At the end of each filmstrip, each poem appears in print with a corresponding visual to get the mood for interpretation of the poem. A variety of poetry—haiku, American Indian verse, and the writings of distinguished poets as well as children—is included.

POETS, JAPANESE

HAIKU: THE HIDDEN GLIMMERING (Filmstrip—Sound). *See* Haiku

POLICE

DEPUTY MARV (Filmstrip—Sound). Lyceum/Mook & Blanchard, 1972. 1 color, sound filmstrip, 65 fr.; 1 cassette or disc, 10-1/2 min. Cassettes #LY35671C ($25), Discs #LY35671R ($19.50), Gr. K–3. FLN (6/72), PRV (9/72), STE (5/73). 363.2
Deputy Sheriff Marv visits the class to discuss safety rules with the children. Together they discover how to avoid trouble and how the sheriff and police officers aid and protect them. A number of vignettes of sheriffs' deputies in action are shown.

THE POLICE AND THE COMMUNITY (Filmstrip—Sound. Associated Press/Pathescope Educational Media, 1976 (Let's Find Out). 1 color, sound filmstrip, 60 fr.; 1 cassette or disc, 6:38 min.; 6 Spirit Masters; Teacher's Guide. Disc #9503 ($25), Cas-

sette #9503C ($25). Gr. 4–6. PRV (4/78).
363.2

This filmstrip covers the role of the police,
the courts, and correction agencies, and
stimulates critical thinking about problems
and possible solutions related to crime.

POLITICAL SCIENCE

JOURNEY TO DEMOCRACY (Filmstrip–
Sound). Macmillan Library Services, 1975.
4 color, sound filmstrips, av. 65 fr.; 4 discs
or cassettes, 8–10 min.; Teacher's Guide/
Script. Cassettes #48800 ($90), Discs
#48804 ($90). Gr. 4–8. BKL (12/1/75),
PRV (11/76). 351

Contents: 1. Anarchy. 2. Totalitarianism.
3. Aristocratic Privilege. 4. Democrary.

Introduces alternative governments via 2
cartoon youngsters traveling to make-believe
lands. Exaggerated situations in societies
based on the principles of anarchy, totalitarianism, and aristocratic privilege give the
viewer a simplified picture of the weakness
inherent in these forms. The final strip involves the forming of democracy in the
United States.

POLLUTION

ABC'S OF ENVIRONMENT (Filmstrip–
Sound). See Ecology

ENERGY AND OUR ENVIRONMENT
(Filmstrip–Sound). See Ecology

ENVIRONMENTAL STUDIES SERIES
(Filmstrip–Sound). Centron Films, 1972.
6 color, sound filmstrips; 6 discs or cassettes. Discs ($72.50), Cassettes ($84.50).
Gr. 4–8. BKL (10/15/72). 301.31

Contents: 1. The Rivers Must Not Die.
2. Solid Wastes. 3. Noise: The Latest Pollution. 4. The Land and the Soil. 5. Air
Pollution. 6. Pests, Pesticides and People.

Scrutinizes major environmental problems
and possible solutions.

KEEPING OUR AIR, WATER AND EARTH
CLEAN (Film Loop–8mm–Silent). Troll
Associates, 1974. 4 super 8mm color, film
loops, approx. 4 min. ea.; Teacher's Guide.
($99.80). Gr. 2–6. PRV (9/75). 333.7

Contents: 1. What Is Air Pollution. 2. How
You Can Fight Pollution. 3. What Pollutes
the Land and Water. 4. Making Our Air
Clean.

Students learn to identify and correct some
of the causes of pollution.

LET NO MAN REGRET (Motion Picture–
16mm–Sound). Alfred Higgins Productions, 1973. 16mm color, sound film, 11
min. ($150). Gr. 4–A. AFF (1974), BKL
(3/1/74), CFF (1974). 301.3

This film points out our personal responsibility to preserve the natural beauty of our
recreational areas.

LET'S FIND THE POLLUTION SOLUTION
(Filmstrip–Sound). See Ecology

See also Man–Influence on Nature

PONTIAC

CHIEFS AND LEADERS (Cassette). See
Indians of North America

PONY EXPRESS

HURRYING HOOF BEATS: THE STORY
OF THE PONY EXPRESS (Filmstrip–
Sound). Perfection Form, 1976. 1 color,
sound filmstrip, 104 fr.; 1 cassette or disc,
14 min. Disc #KH95260 ($21.45), Cas-
sette #KH95261 ($22.95). Gr. 1–A. BKL
(7/1/77). 383

Photos and artwork describe the pony express that operated briefly from 1860–1861.
Stirring music and an excellent narration
capture the spirit of this brief chapter in
American history.

POPULATION

ON POPULATION (Filmstrip–Sound). Walt
Disney Educational Media, 1976. 6 color,
sound filmstrips, av. 38–53 fr.; 6 cassettes
or discs, av. 6–10 min.; 1 Guide. #63-8037
($105). Gr. 4–8. BKL (12/1/77), M&M
(4/77). 301.32

Contents: 1. Exploding Numbers. 2. Increasing Harvests. 3. Dwindling Resources.
4. Struggling Economics. 5. Deteriorating
Environment. 6. Achieving Stability.

Key issues are gathered in this set that will
inform students about the dilemma we face
with increasing population and decreasing
resources.

PORPOISES

THE PORPOISES AND THE SAILOR (Kit).
Classroom Complements/EBEC, 1976
(Animal Life Stories). 1 color, sound film-
strip; 1 cassette; 5 identical Storybooks;
Teacher's Guide. #6971K ($27.95).
Gr. K–6. TEA (11/77). 599.53

Young readers can learn how porpoises live,
move, build homes, and fight for food and
survival. A 56-page storybook reproduces
all of the narration and full-color art from
the filmstrip.

POSTAGE STAMPS

AMERICAN HISTORY ON STAMPS (Kit).
TransMedia International, 1976. 4 color,
sound filmstrips, 54–69 fr.; 4 cassettes,
6–10 min.; 1 Game; 1 Guide. ($45).
Gr. 5–9 BKL (11/15/76). 383

This kit uses commemorative postage
stamps from the Smithsonian Institution
and a private collection to skim the nation's

POSTAGE STAMPS (cont.)

history. Many accurate facts and details about personalities related to historic events are included. The game "Moving the Mails" consists of a large U.S. wall map on which students "move" by offering postage stamps.

POSTAL SERVICE–U.S.

AMERICAN HISTORY ON STAMPS (Kit).
See Postage Stamps

HURRYING HOOF BEATS: THE STORY OF THE PONY EXPRESS (Filmstrip– Sound). *See* Pony Express

POSTURE

POSTURAL IMPROVEMENT ACTIVITIES (Phonodiscs). *See* Exercise

POTTER, BEATRIX

THE TAILOR OF GLOUCESTER, A CHRISTMAS STORY (Cassette). *See* Mice–Fiction

THE TALE OF PETER RABBIT (Filmstrip– Sound or Captioned). *See* Rabbits–Fiction

TREASURY OF BEATRIX POTTER STORIES (Filmstrip–Sound). *See* Animals–Fiction

POTTERY, INDIAN

POTTERY DECORATION (Film Loop– 8mm–Silent). Thorne Films/Prentice-Hall Media, 1972 (Southwest Indians). 8mm color, silent film loop, approx. 4 min. #HAT 288 ($26). Gr. 4–A. AUR (1978). 738.1
This loop demonstrates the decorations used on the pottery of Southwest Indians.

POTTERY FIRING (Film Loop–8mm– Silent). Thorne Films/Prentice-Hall Media, 1972 (Southwest Indians). 8mm color, silent film loop, approx. 4 min. #HAT 289 ($26). Gr. 4–A. AUR (1978). 738.1
This loop demonstrates the firing of pottery by Southwest Indians.

POTTERY MAKING (Film Loop–8mm– Silent). Thorne Films/Prentice-Hall Media, 1972 (Southwest Indians). 8mm color, silent film loop, approx. 4 min. #HAT 287 ($26). Gr. 4–A. AUR (1978). 738.1
This film loop demonstrates the making of pottery by the Southwest Indians.

POWER RESOURCES

ENERGY AND THE EARTH (Filmstrip– Sound). *See* Conservation of Natural Resources

ENERGY: CRISIS AND RESOLUTION (Filmstrip–Sound). United Learning, 1974. 6 color, sound filmstrips, av. 47–63 fr. ea.; 6 cassettes, av. 11–14 min. ea.; Guide. #46 ($85). Gr. 6–10. PRV (2/76). 333.7
Contents: 1. Introduction to Energy. 2. Fossil Fuels–Coal. 3. Fossil Fuels– Oil and Natural Gas. 4. Electrical Energy. 5. Nuclear Energy. 6. Alternatives for the Future.
A historical perspective of the world's energy sources, past and present, enhances these introductory filmstrips dealing with energy issues and with future solutions to the crisis.

ENERGY FOR THE FUTURE (Motion Picture–16mm–Sound). EBEC, 1974. 16mm color, sound film, 17 min. #3348 ($220). Gr. 4–A. BKL (5/15/75), LFR (4/75), PRV (10/75). 333.7
Constantly growing energy needs, dwindling reserves of fossil fuels, recent fuel shortages, and increasing fuel costs–such conditions have established a need for new energy sources. This film explicitly examines energy alternatives for the future, including processed coal, shale oil, geothermal heat, nuclear fission and fusion, wind, and solar heat.

PRAIRIE DOGS

THE PRAIRIE DOG TOWN (Kit). Classroom Complements/EBEC, 1976. (Animal Life Stories). 1 color, sound filmstrip; 1 cassette; 5 identical Storybooks; Teacher's Guide. #6972K ($27.50). Gr. K–6. TEA (11/77). 599.3
Young readers can learn how animals live, move, build homes, and fight for food and survival. A 56-page storybook reproduces all of the narration and full-color art from the filmstrip.

PREHISTORIC ANIMALS. *See* Fossils

PREJUDICES AND ANTIPATHIES

BALABLOK (Motion Picture–16mm– Sound). National Film Board of Canada/ EBEC, 1972. 16mm color, sound film, 8 min. Spanish version available. #3338 ($115). Gr. 4–A. AFF (6/75), LFR (10/74), PRV (3/75). 301.6
What starts a fight? Differences between people with various cultures, religions, races, and attitudes. This nonnarrated film reduces human conflict to simple forms. Animated blocks squeak friendly greetings as they walk past each other. Startled by a different shape (a ball), they taunt it, and the ball responds. Both sides call up reserves. Physical violence develops.

They batter each other until all are hexagonal and then friendly.

PRESIDENTS—U.S.

THE PICTORIAL LIFE-STORY OF GEORGE WASHINGTON (Kit). *See* Washington, George

THE PICTORIAL LIFE-STORY OF THOMAS JEFFERSON (Kit). *See* Jefferson, Thomas

PRISONS

PROJECT AWARE (Motion Picture—16mm— Sound). *See* Juvenile Delinquency

PROBLEM-SOLVING

DECISIONS, DECISIONS (Filmstrip— Sound). *See* Decision-Making

LEARNING TO SOLVE PROBLEMS (Filmstrip—Sound). *See* Thought and Thinking

LEARNING TO USE YOUR MIND (Filmstrip—Sound). *See* Thought and Thinking

LET'S LOOK AT LOGIC (Filmstrip—Sound). *See* Logic

YOU AND ME AND OUR WORLD (Slides/ Cassettes). *See* Science

PROBLEM-SOLVING—FICTION

GIRL STUFF (Kit). *See* Girls—Fiction

PROKOFIEV, SERGEI SERGEEVICH

FUN AND FANTASY SERIES (Cassette). *See* Literature—Collections

SIGHTS AND SOUNDS FILMSTRIPS, SET 2 (Filmstrip—Sound). *See* Reading—Study and Teaching

PROVENSEN, ALICE

THE MOTHER GOOSE BOOK (Kit). *See* Nursery Rhymes

SIGHTS AND SOUNDS FILMSTRIPS, SET 2 (Filmstrips—Sound). *See* Reading—Study and Teaching

PROVENSEN, MARTIN

THE MOTHER GOOSE BOOK (Kit). *See* Nursery Rhymes

SIGHTS AND SOUNDS FILMSTRIPS, SET 2 (Filmstrip—Sound). *See* Reading—Study and Teaching

PSYCHOLOGY, APPLIED

WHAT DO YOU DO WHILE YOU WAIT? (Motion Picture—16mm—Sound). *See* Human Behavior

PUBLISHERS AND PUBLISHING

HOW A PICTURE BOOK IS MADE (Filmstrip—Sound). *See* Books

PUERTO RICANS IN THE U.S.

ON OUR BLOCK (Filmstrip—Sound). McGraw-Hill Films, 1970. 6 color, sound filmstrips, av. 60 fr. ea.; 6 discs or cassettes, av. 10 min. ea.; Teacher's Guide. Discs #103076 ($97), Cassettes #102173 ($97). Gr. K-6. LFR (9/10/73), PRV (2/73), PVB (5/73). 301.45

Contents: 1. Ramon Runs Away. 2. Paulo the Boss. 3. The Ghost Upstairs. 4. The New Kid. 5. The Three Gifts. 6. The New Father.

Six stories of family and neighborhood living give children practice in differentiating between real and imagined events, drawing conclusions, and understanding how their own actions affect others.

PUERTO RICO—FICTION

CHIQUITIN AND THE DEVIL: A PUERTO RICAN FOLKTALE (Filmstrip—Sound). *See* Folklore—Puerto Rico

PUNCTUATION

ON YOUR MARKS: PART I (Motion Picture—16mm—Sound). Communications Group West, 1971. 16mm color, sound, animated film, 7 min; Also avail. in videotape format. Gr. 4-A. LFR (12/71). 421

Animation is used to show the proper usage of punctuation, as verse narration explains what each mark does.

ON YOUR MARKS: PART II (Motion Picture—16mm—Sound). Communications Group West, 1971. 16mm color, sound, animated film, 7 min.; Also avail. in videotape format. Gr. 4-A. LFR (12/71). 421

Animation is used to demonstrate how to use punctuation marks and how the punctuation marks affect the meaning of sentences.

THE STRUCTURE OF LANGUAGE (Filmstrip—Sound). *See* English Language—Grammar

PUPPETS AND PUPPET PLAYS

SYLVESTER AND THE MAGIC PEBBLE PUPPET (Kit). *See* Magic—Fiction

PUPPETS–FICTION

PINOCCHIO (Phonodisc or Cassette).
Caedmon Records, 1968. 1 cassette or disc,
approx. 60 min. Disc #TC1262 ($6.98),
Cassette #CDL51262 ($7.95). Gr. 3–6.
NYR. Fic
There are few stories so childlike in concept, so universal in appeal, that each reader
or listener feels that this story was made
especially for him or her. The performance
is by Cyril Ritchard; music composed and
conducted by Don Heckman.

PYLE, HOWARD

LIBRARY 3 (Cassette). See Literature–
Collections

QUACKENBUSH, ROBERT

SHE'LL BE COMIN' 'ROUND THE
MOUNTAIN (Filmstrip–Sound). See Folk
Songs–U.S.

QUESTIONS AND ANSWERS

READING QUIZZES FROM GUINNESS
WORLD RECORDS (Filmstrip–Sound/
Captioned). See Curiosities and Wonders

RABBITS–FICTION

THE GINGERBREAD RABBIT (Phonodisc
or Cassette). Caedmon Records, 1977.
1 cassette or disc, approx. 55 min. Disc
#TC1381 ($6.98), Cassette #CDL51381
($7.95). Gr. 4–6. AUR (1978), NYR. Fic
Of the 4 children's books written by Randall
Jarrell, this is the one most expressly for
children. It is told with the directness of
Aesop and concerns some learning experiences in a day of one of the most helpless,
most trusting, most fortunate heroes in
children's literature.

LITTLE GREY RABBIT'S CHRISTMAS &
LITTLE GREY RABBIT GOES TO SEA
(Phonodisc or Cassette). Caedmon Records,
1976. 1 disc or cassette, 60 min. Disc
#TC1510 ($6.98), Cassette #CDL51510
($7.95). Gr. 1–4. BKL (11/15/77). Fic
Tammy Grimes narrates 2 stories about
Grey Rabbit. Jacket notes include ques-
tions for teachers to use in developing
listening skills.

THE TALE OF PETER RABBIT (Filmstrip–
Sound or Captioned). Listening Library,
1976. (Look, Listen & Read). 1 color,
captioned filmstrip, 41 fr.; 1 cassette.
Teacher's Guide. #JFS158 ($14.95).
Gr. K–3. PRV (1/78). Fic
This all-time children's favorite becomes
even more fascinating as we watch Peter's
adventures in Mr. McGregor's garden through
the original Potter illustrations.

RACHMANINOFF, SERGEI WASSILIEVITCH

PIANO CONCERTO NO. 3 IN D MINOR
(Phonodiscs). See Concertos

RACING. See types of racing: Automobile;
Motorcycle

RADLAUER, ED

BOBSLEDDING: DOWN THE CHUTE
(Kit). See Winter Sports

RAILROADS–FICTION

THE LITTLE ENGINE THAT COULD:
GOLDEN ANNIVERSARY (Filmstrip–
Sound). Society for Visual Education,
1976. 1 color, sound filmstrip, 59 fr.;
1 cassette, 11 min. #A145-STC ($20).
Gr. K–2. PRV (12/77). Fic
Taken directly from the original artwork
for the book, this film introduces primary
children to an American classic.

RAILROADS–HISTORY

RAILROADS WEST (Filmstrip–Sound).
See U.S.–History–1865–1898

RAIN AND RAINFALL

WHAT MAKES RAIN? (Motion Picture–
16mm–Sound). EBEC, 1975. 16mm color,
sound film, 22 min.; Teacher's Guide. #3474
($290). Gr. 4–12. BKL (1/76), INS (2/77),
PRV (9/76). 551.5
The phenomenon of rain still holds
mysteries–even for scientists. Through
a blend of animation and live action, students learn to view clouds as physicists do:
massed drops of moisture clinging to minute
solid particles. From there, simple logical
steps reveal what makes the moisture fall
as rain, as well as other related forms of
precipitation, and how industrial pollution
is increasingly affecting weather.

RAIN FORESTS

AMAZON JUNGLE (Film Loop–8mm–
Silent). See Forests and Forestry

THE ECOLOGY OF A TEMPERATE
RAIN FOREST (Filmstrip–Sound).
Imperial Educational Resources, 1973.
2 color, sound filmstrips, 36 fr.; 2 discs or
cassettes, 11:20–12 min.; Teacher's Guide.
Disc #3RG44200 ($56), Cassette
#3KG44200 ($62). Gr. 4–12. BKL
(3/1/74), PRV (1/75), PVB (5/75).
634.9
Contents: 1. Olympic Rain Forest–Part
One. 2. Olympic Rain Forest–Part Two.
A perceptive study of rain forest ecology

that demonstrates how all life forms within this environmental system work together to sustain the cycle of forest life.

RARE AMPHIBIANS

ENDANGERED SPECIES: REPTILES AND AMPHIBIANS (Study Print). *See* Rare Reptiles

RARE ANIMALS

ECOLOGY AND THE ROLE OF MAN (Filmstrip—Sound). *See* Wildlife Conservation

ENDANGERED SPECIES: MAMMALS (Study Print). EBEC, 1976. 8 study prints, 13 in. × 18 in. unmounted in heavy vinyl pouch; Study Guide. #18040 ($19.50). Gr. 4-12. MDU (4/77). 591
Contents: 1. Timber Wolf. 2. Rocky Mountain Bighorn Sheep. 3. Siberian Tiger. 4. Cheetah. 5. Square-lipped Rhinoceros. 6. Grizzly Bear. 7. Orangutan. 8. Mountain Gorilla.

The series explores the reasons why these animals have been an endangered species by discussing the ecological niches, importance of nature's food chain, factors relating to the perpetuation of species, and the possibilities of preservation.

RARE BIRDS

ECOLOGY AND THE ROLE OF MAN (Filmstrip—Sound). *See* Wildlife Conservation

ENDANGERED SPECIES: BIRDS (Study Print). EBEC, 1976. 8 study prints, 13 in. × 18 in. unmounted, in heavy vinyl pouch; Study Guide. #6890 ($19.50). Gr. 4-A. MDU (4/77). 598.2
Contents: 1. American Peregrine Falcon. 2. Bald Eagle. 3. Brown Pelican. 4. California Condor. 5. Hawaiian Goose (Nene). 6. Kirtland's Warbler. 7. Mississippi Sandhill Crane. 8. Whooping Crane.

Basic facts about the life cycle, physical characteristics, behavior, and status of 8 American birds are presented. It is designed to create awareness of progressive destruction of the animal's habitat and the use of chemical pollutants.

RARE PLANTS

ECOLOGY AND THE ROLE OF MAN (Filmstrip—Sound). *See* Wildlife Conservation

RARE REPTILES

ENDANGERED SPECIES: REPTILES AND AMPHIBIANS (Study Print). EBEC, 1976. 8 study prints, 13 in. × 18 in. unmounted in heavy vinyl pouch; Study Guide. #18120 ($19.50). Gr. 4-12. MDU (1977). 598.1
Contents: 1. American Crocodile. 2. San Francisco Garter Snake. 3. Giant Galapagos Tortoise. 4. Hawksvill Turtle. 5. Gila Monster. 6. Tuatara. 7. Houston Toad. 8. Santa Cruz Long-toed Salamander.

These prints are backed by text, range maps, and illustrations presenting 8 reptiles and amphibians. The study prints explain how the animals' decline has resulted from their inability to adapt to fundamental changes in their living conditions. Also described are the animals' feeding habits, physical appearance, reproductive processes, and special habitats.

RASPE, RUDOLPH ERICH

BARON MUNCHAUSEN TRULY TALL TALES (Phonodisc or Cassette). *See* Legends

READING

THE HATING BOOK (Kit). *See* Emotions

PRS, THE PRE-READING SKILLS PROGRAM (Kit). Univ. of Wisconsin Research and Development Center/EBEC, 1974. 1 disc; Teacher's File; Activity Cards; Student Records; Grouping Card; Schedule Book; Sound and Visual Games; Skills Tests Book; Class Charts; Dittomasters; Flannel Board; Teacher's Guide. #66200 ($445). Gr. K-3. CPR (9/74), EYR (11/74), INS (10/75). 028
Contents: 1. Visual Skills. 2. Sound Skills.

PRS teaches youngsters 5 skills necessary for later reading success—letter order, letter orientation, word detail, sound matching, and sound blending.

READING MATERIALS

AUTO RACING: SOMETHING FOR EVERYONE (Kit). *See* Automobile Racing

MODEL AIRPLANES (Kit). *See* Airplanes—Models

MYSTERY STORY (Filmstrip—Sound). *See* Mystery and Detective Stories

NO SUCH THING. . .? (Kit). *See* Mystery and Detective Stories

POPULAR PICTURE BOOKS FILMSTRIPS: SET THREE (Filmstrip—Sound). Random House, 1977. 4 color, sound filmstrips; 4 cassettes or discs; Discussion Guide. Cassettes #05055X ($72), Discs #05054-1 ($72). Gr. K-3. LGB (12/77). Fic
Contents: 1. *The Princess and Froggie* by Harve and Kaethe Zemach, illustrated by Margot Zemach. 2. *The Little Steamroller* by Graham Greene, illustrated by Edward Ardizzone. 3. *Professor Twill's Travels* by

READING MATERIALS (cont.)

Bob Gumpertz. 4. *The Chicken's Child* by Margaret A. Hartilius.

Presents 4 story adaptations–each very different in content.

READ ALONG AMERICAN INDIAN LEGENDS (Filmstrip–Sound). *See* Indians of North America–Legends

READING FOR THE FUN OF IT–ADVENTURE (Filmstrip–Sound). *See* Literature–Study and Teaching

READING FOR THE FUN OF IT–FANTASY (Filmstrip–Sound). *See* Literature–Study and Teaching

READING FOR THE FUN OF IT–HISTORICAL FICTION (Filmstrip–Sound. *See* Literature–Study and Teaching

READING FOR THE FUN OF IT–MANY LANDS (Filmstrip–Sound). See Literature–Study and Teaching

READING FOR THE FUN OF IT–MYSTERY (Filmstrip–Sound). *See* Literature–Study and Teaching

READING FOR THE FUN OF IT–REALISTIC FICTION (Filmstrip–Sound). *See* Literature–Study and Teaching

READING FOR THE FUN OF IT–SCIENCE FICTION (Filmstrip–Sound). *See* Literature–Study and Teaching

READING QUIZZES FROM GUINNESS WORLD RECORDS (Filmstrip–Sound/ Captioned). *See* Curiosities and Wonders

SCARY TALES (Filmstrip–Captioned). *See* Ghost Stories

SERENDIPITY CASSETTE BOOKS (Kit). *See* Short Stories

STORIES OF ADVENTURE AND HEROISM (Filmstrip–Sound). Educational Direction/ Learning Tree Filmstrips, 1976 (Let's Read). 4 color, sound filmstrips, av. 58 fr. ea.; 2 cassettes, av. 9 min. ea.; Teacher's Guide. ($58). Gr. 3–8. BKL (11/1/76), PRV (2/77), RTE (5/77). 372.4

Contents: 1. The Day I Was Invisible. 2. The Girl Who Could Fly. 3. The Runaway. 4. The Spinning Wheel.

Four stimulating stories deal with the major components involved in learning to read: sight vocabulary, silent reading practice, listening practice, comprehension, and oral reading.

STORIES OF GHOSTS AND MONSTERS (Filmstrip–Sound). Educational Direction/ Learning Tree Filmstrips, 1976. (Let's Read). 4 color, sound filmstrips, av. 60 fr. ea.; 2 cassettes, av. 8 min. ea.; Teacher's Guide. ($58). Gr. 3–8. CHH (1977), PRV (3/77), TEA (3/77). 372.4

Contents: 1. The Greenhouse Horror.

2. Something's in the Attic! 3. A Visitor from Space. 4. The Birthday Secret.

Each strip begins with an audiovisual introduction designed to stimulate the viewer. Vocabulary words are introduced. The story is presented twice, first as a silent reading exercise and then as a fully illustrated sound filmstrip.

STORIES OF MYSTERY AND SUSPENSE (Filmstrip–Sound). Educational Direction/ Learning Tree Filmstrips, 1976 (Let's Read). 4 color, sound filmstrips, av. 58 fr. ea.; 2 cassettes, av. 7–9 min. ea.; Teacher's Guide. ($58). Gr. 3–8. BKL (11/1/76), TEA (3/77). 372.4

Contents: 1. The Toy Shop Mystery. 2. Buried Treasure. 3. The Secret of the Stone Tower. 4. The Lost Locket.

Each strip begins with an audiovisual introduction designed to stimulate the viewer. Vocabulary words are introduced. The story is presented twice, first as a silent reading exercise and then as a fully illustrated sound filmstrip.

TWO FOR ADVENTURE (Kit). *See* Animals–Fiction

READING–STUDY AND TEACHING

THE ABC'S OF PHONICS, PROGRAM ONE (Kit). *See* Phonetics

THE ABC'S OF PHONICS, PROGRAM TWO: CONSONANT LETTERS M–Z (Kit). *See* Phonetics

BASIC COMMUNICATION SKILLS, ONE (Filmstrip–Sound). *See* Communication–Psychological Aspects

BEGINNER BOOKS FILMSTRIPS, SET 1 (Filmstrip–Sound). Random House, 1974. 6 color, sound filmstrips, 36–70 fr.; 6 cassettes or discs, 3:35–6:07 min.; 6 Discussion Guides. Cassettes #12358-1 ($93), Disc #12354-9 ($93). Gr. K–3. BKL (11/1/74), EYR (1975), PRV (1975). Fic

Contents: 1. *Green Eggs and Ham* by Dr. Seuss. 2. *The Eye Book* by Theo LeSieg. 3. *The Nose Book* by Al Perkins. 4. *The Foot Book* by Dr. Seuss. 5. *Put Me in the Zoo* by Robert Lopshire. 6. *The Ear Book* by Al Perkins.

Based on the original books, these sound filmstrips provide rhythmic reading, percussive sound effects, and appropriate noises.

BEGINNER BOOKS FILMSTRIPS, SET 2 (Filmstrip–Sound). Random House, 1974. 6 color, sound filmstrips; 6 cassettes or discs; 6 Discussion Guides. Cassettes #12359-X ($93), Disc #12355-7 ($93). Gr. K–3. BKL (11/1/74), EYR (1975), PRV (1975). Fic

Contents: 1. *The Cat in the Hat* by Dr.

Seuss. 2. *Hop on Pop* by Dr. Seuss. 3. *Ten Apples Up on Top* by Theo LeSieg. 4. *The Bear's Picnic* by Stan and Jan Berenstain. 5. *Are You My Mother?* by P. D. Eastman. 6. *The Bear Scouts* by Stan and Jan Berenstain.

Based on the original books, these sound filmstrips provide rhythmic reading, percussive sound effects, and appropriate noises.

BEGINNER BOOKS FILMSTRIPS, SET 3 (Filmstrip–Sound). Random House, 1975. 6 color, sound filmstrips, av. 70 fr.; 6 cassettes or discs, av. 4:30 min.; 6 Discussion Guides. Cassettes #03723-5 ($93), Discs #03722-7 ($93). Gr. K–3. BKL (1975), PRV (11/75), PVB (4/76). Fic

Contents: 1. *Dr. Seuss's ABC* by Dr. Seuss. 2. *One Fish, Two Fish, Red Fish, Blue Fish* by Dr. Seuss. 3. *The Bear's Vacation* by Stan and Jan Berenstain. 4. *Bears in the Night* by Stan and Jan Berenstain. 5. *Go, Dog, Go!* by P. D. Eastman. 6. *The King, the Mice and the Cheese* by Nancy and Eric Gurney.

Based on the original books, these sound filmstrips provide rhythmic reading, good sound effects, and appropriate noises.

BEGINNER BOOKS FILMSTRIPS, SET 4 (Filmstrip–Sound). Random House, 1975. 6 color, sound filmstrips, 78–99 fr.; 6 discs or cassettes, 8:15–11:10 min.; 6 Discussion Guides. Cassettes #03763-4 ($93), Discs #03762-6 ($93). Gr. K–3. BKL (1975), PRV (10/75), PVB (4/76). Fic

Contents: 1. *The Cat in the Hat Comes Back* by Dr. Seuss. 2. *Mr. Brown Can Moo! Can You?* by Dr. Seuss. 3. *Fox in Socks* by Dr. Seuss. 4. *Babar Loses His Crown* by Laurent de Brunhoff. 5. *Robert the Rose Horse* by Joan Heilbroner. 6. *Sam and the Firefly* by P. D. Eastman.

Based on the original, well-known children's books, these filmstrips provide rhythmic reading.

BOXING (Kit). *See* Boxing

THE DOCTOR SEUSS READ ALONG SET ONE (Kit). Random House, 1976. 6 cassettes, 4–9 min.; 18 books (6 titles); 1 Discussion Guide. Cassettes only #04804 ($42), Set #04141 ($96). Gr. K–2. BKL (10/15/77). 372.4

Contents: 1. Cat in the Hat. 2. Foot Book. 3. Fox in Socks. 4. Hop on Pop. 5. Mister Brown Can Moo, Can You? 6. There's a Wocket in My Pocket.

Six Dr. Seuss titles are dramatized on cassette and accompanied with 3 read-along books for each title. Concepts such as understanding, comprehension, recalling details, and contrasting parts of a story are developed from both the stories and the activity pages.

THE DOCTOR SEUSS READ ALONG SET TWO (Kit). Random House, 1977. 6 cassettes, 5:16–12 min.; 3 copies ea. of 6 books; Teacher's Guide. Two Cassette Album #02067-7 ($42), Kit #02066-9 ($99). Gr. K–3. PRV (2/78). Fic

Contents: 1. Green Eggs and Ham. 2. Dr. Seuss's ABC. 3. One Fish, Two Fish, Red Fish, Blue Fish. 4. Marvin K. Mooney, Will You Please Go Now! 5. The Cat in the Hat Comes Back. 6. Oh! The Thinks You Can Think!

Dramatizations include multiple voices and sound effects of these favorite Dr. Seuss tales.

FUNNY BONE READING STATION (Kit). Troll Associates, 1977. 12 cassette tapes, av. 11 min. ea., 72 soft cover books (6 each of 12 titles); Spirit Masters; Teacher's Guides. ($139.50). Gr. 1–3. BKL (1/15/78). 372.4

Contents: 1. Arty the Smarty. 2. Boy, Cat and the Magic Fiddle. 3. Boy Who Fooled the Giant. 4. Fraidy Cat. 5. I Made a Line. 6. Let Papa Sleep. 7. Little Grey Mouse and the Train. 8. Secret Cat. 9. Surprise in the Storybook. 10. Surprising Pets of Billy Brown. 11. What's the Matter with That Dog. 12. More Jokes and Riddles.

The titles in this cassette-book package are from Wonder Books' Easy Reader series.

JAZZ, ROCK, FOLK, COUNTRY (Filmstrip–Sound). *See* Music, Popular

LANGUAGE EXPERIENCES IN READING, LEVEL 1 (Kit). *See* English Language–Study and Teaching

LANGUAGE EXPERIENCES IN READING: LEVEL 2 (Kit). *See* English Language–Study and Teaching

LANGUAGE EXPERIENCES IN READING: LEVEL 3 (Kit). *See* English Language–Study and Teaching

LOOK, LISTEN AND READ, SET 1 (Kit). ACI Media/Paramount Communications, 1973. 4 color, sound filmstrips, 8–10 min.; Pre-viewing and Post-viewing Tests; Word Games; Flash Cards; Poster; Media Guide; Teacher's Guide. #9531 ($80). Gr. K–2. BKL (7/74), EYR (9/75). 372.4

Contents: 1. Ducks. 2. Safety as We Play. 3. Sun. 4. Wind.

A multimedia package can be used with the language experience approach to reading instruction or as a supplement to any reading program. Helps develop vocabulary and comprehension. This set is a good introduction to units on animals, farms, ecology, the role and effects of the sun on our world, the basic concepts of weather, and safety habits.

LOOK, LISTEN AND READ, SET 2 (Kit). ACI Media/Paramount Communications, 1973. 4 color, sound filmstrips; 4 cas-

READING–STUDY AND TEACHING (cont.)

settes, 8–10 min.; Pre-viewing and Post-viewing Tests; Word Games; Flash Cards; Poster; Media Guide; Teacher's Guide. #9532 ($80). Gr. K–2. BKL (7/74), EYR (9/75). 372.4

Contents: 1. In, Out, Up, Down, Under, Over, Upside Down. 2. My Friend the Policeman. 3. Rain. 4. Z Is for Zoo.

A multimedia package can be used with the language experience approach to reading instruction or as a supplement to any reading program. Helps develop vocabulary and comprehension. This set explores the world about us, our environment, in, out, up, down, the areas of a policeman's responsibility, and the zoo.

LOOK, LISTEN AND READ, SET 3 (Kit). ACI Media/Paramount Communications, 1973. 4 color, sound filmstrips; 4 cassettes, 8–10 min.; Pre-viewing and Post-viewing Tests; Word Games; Flash Cards; Poster; Media Guide; Teacher's Guide. #9533 ($80). Gr. K–2. BKL (7/74), EYR (9/75). 372.4

Contents: 1. A Wheel Is Round. 2. County Fair. 3. Picnic. 4. Playground.

A multimedia package can be used with the language experience approach to reading instruction or as a supplement to any reading program. Helps develop vocabulary and comprehension. This set centers on places and activities that provide children with fun. It includes places where they participate in rides, games, and contests. Also presented are materials on nature study, nutrition, recreation, transportation, and shapes.

LOOK, LISTEN AND READ, SET 4 (Kit). ACI Media/Paramount Communications, 1975. 4 color, sound filmstrips; 4 cassettes, 8–10 min.; Pre-viewing and Post-viewing Tests; Word Games; Flash Cards; Poster; Media Guide; Teacher's Guide. #9534 ($80). Gr. K–2. BKL (7/74), EYR (9/75). 372.4

Contents: 1. Signs along the Highway. 2. Signs around the School. 3. Signs in the Shopping Center. 4. Traffic Signs.

A multimedia package can be used with the language experience approach to reading instruction or as a supplement to any reading program. Helps develop vocabulary and comprehension. This set explores signs—all sizes, shapes, colors, and messages.

MEN BEHIND THE BRIGHT LIGHTS (Kit). *See* Musicians

THE MIGHTY MIDGETS (Kit). *See* Automobile Racing

PRS, THE PRE-READING SKILLS PROGRAM (Kit). *See* Reading

READING ADVENTURES IN EVERYDAY SCIENCE, SERIES A (Filmstrip—Sound). *See* Science—Study and Teaching

READING ADVENTURES IN EVERYDAY SCIENCE, SERIES B (Filmstrip—Sound). *See* Science—Study and Teaching

READING READINESS (Filmstrip—Sound). United Learning, 1975. 6 color, sound filmstrips, av. 42–63 fr. ea.; 6 cassettes, av. 6–11 min. ea.; Teacher's Guide. #52 ($85). Gr. K–3. PRV (5/76), PVB (1977). 372.4

Contents: 1. The Puffer. 2. The Ticker. 3. The Doodler. 4. The Gobbler. 5. The Bungler. 6. The Cowboy.

The series is designed to develop a strong auditory-visual awareness of 6 symbols: p, t, d, g, b, and c. One symbol is presented in story context within each sound filmstrip. The program provides excellent preparation for phonetic word analysis skills required in beginning reading.

READING SKILLS (Kit). BFA Educational Media (The Reading Child). 6 color captioned and sound filmstrips, 49–73 fr.; 6 cassettes or discs, 6–11 min.; 24 Duplicating Masters; Teacher's Guide. Cassettes #EDE000 ($94), Discs #EDD000 ($94). Gr. K–3. PRV (11/76). 372.4

Contents: 1. What Are Letters For: Initial Consonants? 2. What Are Letters For: Vowels? 3. The Elephant Eats, the Penguin Eats: Nouns. 4. Monkey See, Monkey Do: Verbs. 5. Frogs Are Funny, Frogs Are Fat: Adjectives. 6. Squirrels Are Up, Squirrels Are Down: Adverbials of Place.

High interest visuals of animals and children are used to involve youngsters in language and reading experiences. Words are presented orally and visually in the carefully designed superimposition of words over pictures.

ROCK (Kit). *See* Rock Music—History

SIGHTS AND SOUNDS FILMSTRIPS, SET 1 (Filmstrip—Sound). Spectra Films/Random House, 1974. 6 color, sound filmstrips, 38–117 fr.; 6 cassettes or discs, 4:41–7:50 min.; 6 Discussion Guides. Cassettes #12360-3 ($93), Discs #12356-5 ($93). Gr. K–4. BKL (11/1/74), EYR (1975), PRV (1975). Fic

Contents: 1. *Frederick* by Leo Lionni. 2. *Theodore and the Talking Mushroom* by Leo Lionni. 3. *The Winter Picnic* by Robert Welber. 4. *Our Veronica Goes to Petunia's Farm* by Roger Duvoisin. 5. *Busy Wheels* by Peter Lippman. 6. *Busy Day, Busy People* by Tibor Gergely.

Listening skills along with obvious reading instruction can be learned in an enjoyable fashion with this collections of titles adapted to sound filmstrips.

SIGHTS AND SOUNDS FILMSTRIPS, SET 2 (Filmstrip—Sound). Spectra Films/

Random House, 1974. 6 color, sound film-strips, 30–99 fr.; 6 cassettes or discs, 3:19–10:06 min.; 6 Discussion Guides. Cassettes #12361-1 ($93), Discs #12357-3 ($93). Gr. K–4. BKL (11/1/74), EYR (1975), PRV (1975). Fic

Contents: 1. *Big Dog . . . Little Dog* by P. D. Eastman. 2. *Roses Are Red. Are Violets Blue?* by Alice and Martin Provensen. 3. *Swimmy* by Leo Lionni. 4. *Jasmine* by Rober Duvoisin. 5. *Peter and the Wolf* by Serge Prokofiev. 6. *I'll Teach My Dog 100 Words* by Michael Frith.

Listening skills along with obvious reading instruction can be learned in an enjoyable fashion with this collection of titles adapted to sound filmstrips.

SIGHTS AND SOUNDS FILMSTRIPS, SET 3 (Filmstrip–Sound). Spectra Films/Random House, 1975. 6 color, sound filmstrips; 6 cassettes or discs; 6 Discussion Guides. Cassettes #03725-1 ($93), Discs #03724-3 ($93). Gr. K–4. BKL (1976), PRV (1976). Fic

Contents: 1. *Fish is Fish* by Leo Lionni. 2. *Petunia, Beware!* by Roger Duvoisin. 3. *Petunia Takes a Trip* by Roger Duvoisin. 4. *Meet Babar and His Family* by Laurent de Brunhoff. 5. *Hansel and Gretel* illustrated by Sheilah Beckett, retold by Linda Hayward. 6. *Three Little Kittens* illustrated by Lilian Obligado.

Listening skills along with obvious reading instruction can be learned in an enjoyable fashion with this collection of titles adapted to sound filmstrips.

SIGHTS AND SOUNDS FILMSTRIPS, SET 4 (Filmstrip–Sound). Spectra Films/Random House, 1974. 6 color, sound filmstrips, 72–130 fr.; 6 discs or cassettes, 6–12 min.; 6 Discussion Guides. Cassettes #03917-3 ($93), Discs #03916-5 ($93). Gr. K–3. BKL (11/1/74), EYR (1975), PVB (4/77). Fic

Contents: 1. *The Story of Babar* by Jean de Brunhoff. 2. *The Travels of Babar* by Jean de Brunhoff. 3. *In the Rabbit Garden* by Leo Lionni. 4. *The Queen Who Couldn't Bake Gingerbread* by Dorothy van Woerkom. 5. *The Greentail Mouse* by Leo Lionni. 6. *Moon Mouse* by Adelaide Holl, illustrated by Cyndy Szekeres.

Listening skills can be learned as students listen to this enjoyable collection of titles adapted to sound filmstrips.

THE SPELLING MONSTERS: UNIT A (Filmstrip–Sound). *See* English Language–Spelling

THE SPELLING MONSTERS: UNIT B (Filmstrip–Sound). *See* English Language–Spelling

THE SPELLING MONSTERS: UNIT C (Filmstrip–Sound). *See* English Language–Spelling

THE SPELLING MONSTERS: UNIT D (Filmstrip–Sound). *See* English Language–Spelling

WORDS TO WORK WITH–I (Filmstrip–Sound). *See* Vocabulary

WORDS TO WORK WITH–II (Filmstrip–Sound). *See* Vocabulary

WORDS TO WORK WITH–III (Filmstrip–Sound). *See* Vocabulary

RECYCLING (WASTE, ETC.)

JUNK ECOLOGY (Filmstrip–Sound). *See* Handicraft

REDUCING

THE SNACKING MOUSE (Filmstrip–Sound). *See* Nutrition

REEVES, JAMES

DICK WHITTINGTON AND HIS CAT AND OTHER ENGLISH TALES (Phonodisc or Cassette). *See* Folklore–England

REFERENCE BOOKS

LOOK IT UP: HOW TO GET INFORMATION (Filmstrip–Sound). *See* Library Skills

REINACH, JACQUELYN

EARLY LEARNING LIBRARY (Filmstrip–Sound). *See* Child Development

RENOIR, PIERRE AUGUSTE

PICTURES ARE FUN TO LOOK AT (Art Prints). *See* Art Appreciation

REPRODUCTION

BIRTH AND CARE OF BABY CHICKS (Film Loop–8mm–Captioned). *See* Chickens

THE BROWN TROUT (Film Loop–8mm–Captioned). *See* Trout

REPTILES

BIG GATOR OF THE EVERGLADES (Kit). *See* Alligators

RATTLESNAKE (Film Loop–8mm–Silent). *See* Snakes

SNAKES OF THE AMAZON (Film Loop–8mm–Silent). *See* Snakes

REPTILES AND AMPHIBIANS

ENDANGERED SPECIES: REPTILES AND AMPHIBIANS (Study Print). *See* Rare Reptiles

REPTILES, FOSSIL

DINOSAUR TALES (Filmstrip—Sound).
See Dinosaurs

RESEARCH

LOOK IT UP: HOW TO GET INFORMA-
TION (Filmstrip—Sound). *See* Library
Skills

RESPIRATION

LUNGS AND THE RESPIRATORY
SYSTEM (Motion Picture—16mm—Sound).
EBEC, 1975. 16mm color, sound film.
17 min. #3395 ($240). Gr. 6–9. INS
(3/77), LFR (11/12/75), PRV (4/76).
612
This film uses diagrams, demonstrations,
and microphotography to show how
oxygen—the vital element in air—gets
from lungs to blood to each and every
tiny body cell. It reveals the body's in-
tricate system for filtering and purifying
the air we breathe, and how smoking and
breathing industrial air pollutants can
break down that marvelous system.

REVERE, PAUL

PAUL REVERE'S RIDE AND HIS OWN
STORY (Cassette). *See* American Poetry

REY, H. A.

CURIOUS GEORGE AND OTHER
STORIES ABOUT CURIOUS GEORGE
(Phonodisc or Cassette). *See* Monkeys—
Fiction

RHYTHMS

CHILDREN'S RHYTHMS IN SYMPHONY
(Phonodisc). Bowmar Publishing. 1 Disc.
#027 ($6.95). Gr. K–3. AUR (1978).
793.3
Basic and combination rhythms (as found
in "Intermezzo," "Village Dance and
March," and others) and interpretive
rhythms (as found in the "Sword Dance,"
"Wild Horsemen," "Creatures of the Garden," and others) are collected on this
recording.

FUN WITH MUSIC (Phonodiscs). Bowmar
Publishing. 1 disc. #026 ($6.95). Gr.
K–2. AUR (1978). 793.3
"Cricket," "Sleighride," "Yo-Yo," "Fly-
ing Birds," and other rhythmic response
tunes.

HOLIDAY RHYTHMS (Phonodiscs). Bowmar Publishing. 1 disc. #025 ($6.95).
Gr. K–3. AUR (1978). 793.3
Halloween, Thanksgiving, birthdays, May-
pole dance, and other holiday tunes.

THE RAINY DAY RECORD (Phonodiscs).
Bowmar Publishing. 1 disc. #138 ($6.95).
Gr. K–2. AUR (1978). 793.3
"Rain is Falling," "Tiptoe Music," "Looby
Lou," "Eency Weency Spider," and other
fun songs for a rainy day.

RHYTHM TIME: RECORD ONE (Phonodiscs). Bowmar Publishing. 1 disc. #023
($6.95). Gr. K–3. AUR (1978). 793.3
Basic rhythms, combinations, and mechan-
ical rhythms are on this disc.

SONGS IN MOTION: ACTIVITY SONGS
AND NURSERY RHYMES (Phonodisc or
Cassette). Educational Activities. 5 cassettes or discs; Descriptive Manual. Cassettes #AC-690-AC-694 ($38), Discs
#AR-690-AR-694 ($33). Gr. K–3. PRV
(4/75). 793.3
Contents: 1. Fine Motor Skills. 2. Gross
Motor Skills. 3. Songs for Language Development. 4. Songs for Round the Year.
5. Activity Songs Nursery Rhymes.
Recorded simply, clearly, and slowly,
with piano accompaniment to encourage
active participation by children.

RICE, EVE

THRESHOLD FILMSTRIPS, SERIES C
(Kit). *See* Children's Literature—Collections

THE RICH MAN AND THE SHOEMAKER

SOUND FILMSTRIP SET 35 (Filmstrip—
Sound). *See* Children's Literature—Collections

RICHARDS, DOROTHY

MY FORTY YEARS WITH BEAVERS
(Filmstrip—Sound). *See* Beavers

RICHTER, CONRAD

THE LIGHT IN THE FOREST (Phonodisc
or Cassette). *See* Indians of North America—Fiction

RIEGER, SHAY

THE BRONZE ZOO (Motion Picture—
16mm—Sound). *See* Sculpture

RIKKI TIKKI TAVI

THE WORLD OF JUNGLE BOOKS, SET
ONE (Kit). *See* Animals—Fiction

RIVERS

ALL ABOUT RIVERS (Filmstrip—Sound).
EBEC, 1974. 5 color, sound filmstrips,
av. 64 fr. ea.; 5 discs or cassettes, 8 min.

ea. Teacher's Guide. Discs #6494
($72.50), Cassettes #6494K ($72.50).
Gr. 4–8. BKL (12/15/74), ESL (1977),
PRV (11/75,76). 551.4

Contents: 1. What Is a River? 2. Rivers
Work for Us. 3. Rivers Are Highways.
4. Rivers Work against Us. 5. Rivers Need
Our Help.

This series helps children explore; how
rivers benefit people as suppliers of water,
power, and recreation becomes vividly clear.
Children also learn that rivers can be destructive and, conversely, that people can
destroy rivers.

ROBBERS AND OUTLAWS–FICTION

THE THREE ROBBERS (Motion Picture–
16mm–Sound). Weston Woods Studios,
1972. 16mm color, sound, animated
film, 6 min. ($150). Gr. K–3. AFF (1973),
NEF (1973), PRV (3/73). Fic

Adapted from the book *The Three Robbers*,
by Tomi Ungerer. Three fierce robbers
went about hidden under large black capes
and tall black hats. With a blunderbuss,
a pepper-blower, and a huge red axe, they
plundered and terrified everyone until one
day they came upon a little girl named
Tiffany. She inspired her captors to use
their trunks full of loot for a good cause.

ROBIN HOOD

ADVENTURES OF ROBIN HOOD, VOL. 1:
HOW ROBIN BECAME AN OUTLAW
(Phonodisc or Cassette). *See* Folklore–
England

ADVENTURES OF ROBIN HOOD, VOL. 2:
OUTLAW BAND OF SHERWOOD
FOREST (Phonodisc or Cassette). *See*
Folklore–England

ADVENTURES OF ROBIN HOOD, VOL. 3:
ADVENTURES WITH LITTLE JOHN
(Phonodisc or Cassette). *See* Folklore–
England

ADVENTURES OF ROBIN HOOD, VOL. 4:
ROBIN AND HIS MERRY MEN (Phonodisc or Cassette). *See* Folklore–England

ROCK MUSIC–BIOGRAPHY

MEN BEHIND THE BRIGHT LIGHTS
(Kit). *See* Musicians

ROCK MUSIC–HISTORY

ROCK (Kit). Troll Associates, 1976 (Troll
Jam Sessions). 1 color, sound filmstrip, 34
fr.; 1 cassette, 14 min.; 10 books; 4 Duplicating Masters; 1 Teacher's Guide.
($42.95). Gr. 5–8. BKL (1/15/77). 781.5
This kit covers the development of rock
music from its beginnings in the early

1950s to its present forms, emphasizing
that rock music is constantly changing.
Rock music provides the background for
the narration, and photos of different rock
performers are used in the visuals. A high
interest/low reading ability kit.

ROCKS

DISCOVERING ROCKS AND MINERALS
(Filmstrip–Sound). *See* Geology

RODGERS, RICHARD

MARCHES (Phonodiscs). *See* Marches
(Music)

ROSE, GEORGE

THROUGH THE LOOKING GLASS (Phonodiscs). *See* Fantasy–Fiction

ROUSSEAU, HENRI JULIEN

PICTURES ARE FUN TO LOOK AT (Art
Prints). *See* Art Appreciation

RURAL LIFE. *See* Farm Life; U.S.–Social
Life and Customs

RUSKIN, JOHN

THE KING OF THE GOLDEN RIVER
(Phonodisc or Cassette). *See* Fairy Tales

SACAGAWEA

CHIEFS AND LEADERS (Cassette). *See*
Indians of North America

SAFETY EDUCATION

ALL ABOUT FIRE (Motion Picture–16mm–
Sound). *See* Fire Prevention

BASIC BICYCLING SERIES (Filmstrip–
Sound). *See* Bicycles and Bicycling

THE BEAR'S BICYCLE (Filmstrip–Sound).
See Bicycles and Bicycling–Fiction

BICYCLE SAFELY (Motion Picture–16mm–
Sound). *See* Bicycles and Bicycling

BICYCLING ON THE SAFE SIDE (Motion
Picture–16mm–Sound). *See* Bicycles and
Bicycling

BIKE SAFETY: MAKING THE RIGHT
MOVES (Motion Picture–16mm–Sound).
EBEC, 1976. 16mm color, sound film,
15 min. #3386 ($205). Gr. 1–5. LFR
(1/2/77), EFL (10/77), PRV (3/77).
371.77
Live-action photography and a miniature
street model demonstrate many aspects of
careful, courteous bicycle driving. The film

SAFETY EDUCATION (cont.)

teaches proper bike fit, rules for street driving (including proper signaling), traffic hazards to watch for, and locking and registering bikes. An entertaining sequence on the history of cycling emphasizes the trend toward safer bikes and roads.

DEPUTY MARV (Filmstrip—Sound). *See* Police

FIRE AND THE WITCH (Motion Picture—16mm—Sound). *See* Fire Prevention

FIRE SAFETY—WHAT'S THAT?(Slides). *See* Fire Prevention

FIRST AID FOR LITTLE PEOPLE (Kit). *See* First Aid

MATCHES (Motion Picture—16mm—Sound). Dave Bell Associates/FilmFair Communications, 1971. 16mm color, sound film, 9 min. ($125). Gr. 1–6. LFR (11/73), PRV (3/74). 614.8
The need for safety rules and the value of a sense of responsibility are demonstrated using young children as the characters in the story.

MOTORCYCLE SAFETY (Filmstrip—Sound). *See* Motorcycles

NOT SO EASY (MOTORCYCLE SAFETY) (Motion Picture—16mm—Sound). *See* Motorcycles

PLAYING IT SAFE (Filmstrip—Sound). Current Affairs Films, 1977. 2 color, sound filmstrips, 74 fr.; 2 cassettes, 16 min.; Teacher's Guide. #576-581 ($48). Gr. 5–12. PRV (4/78). 614.8
Contents: Part I. 1. In the Home. 2. En Route. 3. In the Water. Part II. 1. Babysitting/Child Care. 2. With Food. 3. In School.
The safety needs of 6 areas of everyday life are depicted with emphasis on preventing problems and handling emergencies.

PLAYING SAFE (Filmstrip—Captioned). Filmstrip House/United Learning, 1976. 4 color, captioned filmstrips; Script Guide. #90000 ($30). Gr. 1–3. BKL (12/1/76). 371.77
Contents: 1. Playing Safe at Home. 2. Playing Safe on Streets and Sidewalks. 3. Playing Safe at School. 4. Playing Safe in Parks and Playgrounds.
Uncomplicated cartoon drawings illustrate the elementary safety rules clearly stated in the simple captions, which place positive emphasis on how children conduct themselves safely around home and school, in parks and playgrounds, and on streets and sidewalks.

SAFE IN RECREATION (Motion Picture—16mm—Sound). FilmFair Communications,

1974. 16mm color, sound film, 14-1/2 min. ($190). Gr. 1–7. LFR (3/75). 614.8
This film dramatizes typical accidents that can happen. Situations involve electricity, poisonous substances, kite flying, playground behavior on equipment and while playing baseball, hiking in the woods and along railroad tracks, picnic fires, poisonous plants, use of sharp tools, good sense with a fishing pole, and other sources of possible danger. Carelessness is demonstrated; film then shows common sense precautions and correct techniques and behavior.

SAFETY AWARENESS (Filmstrip—Sound). Imperial Educational Resources, 1975. 4 color, sound filmstrips, 42–54 fr.; 4 cassettes or discs, 4:43–6:30 min. Discs #3RG-16000 ($56), Cassettes #3KG-16000 ($62). Gr. K–3. PRV (10/75), PVB (4/76). 371.77
Contents: 1. Bicycle Safety. 2. School Bus Safety. 3. Walking to and from School. 4. Safety on the Playground and in the Cafeteria.
This set helps the young viewer to become aware of situations that affect his or her safety. Color photographic shots of multiracial children stress alertness, common sense, courtesy, and a positive attitude toward safety.

SAFETY ON TWO WHEELS (Filmstrip—Sound). *See* Bicycles and Bicycling

SAFETY ON WHEELS (Filmstrip—Sound). *See* Bicycles and Bicycling

THE SAFETY SET (Filmstrip—Sound). ACI Media/Paramount Communications, 1974. 4 color, sound filmstrips; 4 cassettes, av. 8–10 min. ea.; Teacher's Guide; Bicycle Safety Guide. #9123 ($78). Gr. K–6. BKL (4/75), PRV (3/75), PVB (5/75). 371.77
Contents: 1. Bicycle Safety. 2. Home Safety. 3. Playground Safety. 4. School Bus Safety.
Shows safety hazards in everyday situations and demonstrates the basic precautions to observe in the home, at school, on the playground, and while bike riding.

SKATEBOARD SAFETY (Motion Picture—16mm—Sound). *See* Skateboards

STORIES ABOUT SAFETY (Filmstrip—Sound). BFA Educational Media, 1975. 6 color, sound filmstrips, av. 45 fr.; 3 discs or 6 cassettes, av. 9-1/2 min.; Teacher's Guide. Discs #S286 ($80), Cassettes #M286 ($88). Gr. 1–3. PRV (4/76). 371.77
Contents: 1. The Falling Down Prince. 2. Kitchen—Handle with Care! 3. Harry in a Hurry. 4. The Turnabout School Bus. 5. Car Coming—Beep! Beep! 6. Sally Finds Help.
Puppet characters and animals are used to demonstrate safety practices. The safety

stories discuss attitudes and practices at home, at school, on the street, on a school bus, in public places, and in emergency situations.

TRAFFIC WATCHER (Motion Picture— 16mm—Sound). Flight Plan I/Encyclo- paedia Britannica Education, 1972. 16mm color, sound film, 15 min. #3334 ($185). Gr. 1–4. INS (12/75), LFR (9/74). 371.77

Captain Dan is traffic announcer for a radio station in Washington, D.C. He operates his own helicopter, manuvering it over congested streets and highways in the area. Often he visits elementary schools, landing his helicopter on the premises before the assembled children, to talk about traffic safety. By giving close attention to traffic lights and rules, each pupil can become a "traffic watcher" like Captain Dan.

WATCH OUT (Filmstrip—Sound). Educa- tional Direction/Learning Filmstrips, 1975. 4 color, sound filmstrips, av. 39 fr. ea.; 2 cassettes, av. 4–5 min. ea.; Teacher's Guide. #LT554 ($52). Gr. 2–6. PRV (1/76), PVB (4/76). 371.77

Contents: 1. Dangerous Things. 2. Danger- ous Places. 3. Poisons, Drugs and Tobacco. 4. All the Time.

The filmstrip helps the child develop an awareness of possible dangers in the imme- diate environment, and, in turn, to adopt a positive strategy of general safety.

WHATEVER HAPPENED TO LINDA? (Filmstrip—Sound). Marshfilm, 1975. 1 color, sound filmstrip, 50 fr.; 1 cassette or disc; Teacher's Guide. #1131 ($21). Gr. 4–8. INS (1978), NYF (1976). 371.77

Dramatizes potentially dangerous situations that students face in everyday life. Action moves from how to avoid trouble to what to say and do in response to unusual de- mands made by strangers, friends, or rela- tives.

WHO'S AFRAID OF THE BIG BAD WOLF? (Filmstrip—Sound). Marshfilm, 1976 (Safety). 1 color, sound filmstrip, 50 fr.; 1 cassette or disc; Teacher's Guide. #1130 ($21). Gr. K–3. EYR (9/77), INS (1976), NYF (1976). 371.77

Illustrates ways to avoid trouble; shows students who find themselves in danger how to protect themselves and what to say and do when approached by strangers. Teaches safety precautions without being alarming and reinforces students self- reliance and value judgment.

THE YELLOW SCHOOL BUS (Motion Picture—16mm—Sound). FilmFair Com- munications, 1975. 16mm color, sound film, 10-1/4 min. ($135). Gr. K–2. LFR (11/75). 614.8

Demonstrates safety practices and consid- erate behavior while riding a school bus. Safety Sheriff Joe Higgins demonstrates

emergency exit techniques and stresses the need for calmness. Points covered in the film include: promptness, safe waiting by the street, danger and nuisance of rowdy behavior, use of safety belts when available, consideration of others and of the driver, need for quiet, orderly exit on arrival.

SALMON

SALMON RUN (Film Loop—8mm—Silent). Walt Disney Educational Media, 1966. 8mm color, silent film loop, approx. 4 min. #62-5020L ($30). Gr. K–12. MDU (1974). 597.5

Follows salmon on their spawning run through rapids and falls, and as they lay eggs.

SALOMON, HAYM

FAMOUS PATRIOTS OF THE AMERICAN REVOLUTION (Filmstrip—Sound). *See* U.S.—History—Biography

SALT

THE STORY OF SALT (Filmstrip—Sound). BFA Educational Media, 1975. 4 color, sound filmstrips, 69–105 fr.; 4 cassettes or discs, 9:30–15:00 min.; Guide. Cassettes #VFJ000 ($70), Discs #VFH000 ($70). Gr. 4–6. BKL (5/1/76). 661

Contents: 1. Salt: How We Use It. 2. Salt: Its Story. 3. Salt: How We Make It. 4. Salt Ponds: Good Neighbors.

This is a presentation of the salt industry from an historical, economical, ecological, and scientific point of view. It is illustrated with lithographs, simple drawings, old black- and-white and modern color photographs.

SALVAGE (WASTE, ETC.)

A BOY CREATES (Motion Picture—16mm— Sound). *See* Sculpture

SAMPSON, DEBORAH

DEBORAH SAMPSON: A WOMAN IN THE REVOLUTION (Motion Picture—16mm— Sound). BFA Educational Media, 1975. 16mm color, sound film, 15-1/4 min. #11639 ($225). Gr. 4–A. PRV (11/76). 921

Deborah Sampson was committed to the causes of the American Revolution and un- willing to adopt one of the traditional female roles. She served in Washington's army disguised as a man, taking an active part in the battles of Tarrytown and York- town. The film shows reenactments of battles, ambushes, and dramatic encounters.

SAND PAINTING

NAVAJO SAND PAINTING CEREMONY
(Film Loop—8mm—Silent). *See* Indians of
North America—Art

SANDBURG, CARL

DAYBREAK (Motion Picture—16mm—
Sound). *See* Poetry—Collections

ROOTABAGA STORIES: HOW TO TELL
CORN FAIRIES WHEN YOU SEE 'EM
(Phonodisc or Cassette). *See* Fantasy—
Fiction

ROOTABAGA STORIES: THE FINDING
OF THE ZIG ZAG RAILROAD (Phonodisc or Cassette). *See* Fantasy—Fiction

ROOTABAGA STORIES: THE HAYSTACK
CRICKET (Phonodisc or Cassette). *See*
Fantasy—Fiction

SANDIN, JOAN

STORIES OF LATIN AMERICA, SET ONE
(Filmstrip—Sound). *See* Latin America—
Fiction

SCARRY, RICHARD

RICHARD SCARRY'S WHAT DO PEOPLE
DO ALL DAY (Kit). *See* Occupations

SCHLIEMANN, HEINRICH

HEROES OF THE ILIAD (Cassette). *See*
Mythology, Classical

SCHOOL CHILDREN—TRANSPORTATION

THE YELLOW SCHOOL BUS (Motion Picture—16mm—Sound). *See* Safety Education

SCHOOLS

SCHOOL (Motion Picture—16mm—Sound).
Communications Group West, 1970. 16mm
color, sound film, 12 min. Available in
Spanish ($165). Gr. K-A. CGE (1972),
LFR (12/71). 371
A unique documentary orientation of a
child's first school year. This film helps to
overcome the child's fears and anxieties while
encouraging positive attitudes and behavior.

STARTING SCHOOL (Motion Picture—
16mm—Sound). EBEC, 1973. 16mm color,
sound film, 14 min. #3206 ($185). Gr.
K-1. LFR (1/74), MMT (5/74), PRV
(1/75). 371
Answers the question: what is kindergarten like? Shows children engaged in lesson activity. Aimed primarily at a young
audience, would be useful to parents and
student teachers.

SCHUBERT, FRANZ

MARCHES (Phonodiscs). *See* Marches
(Music)

SCIENCE

YOU AND ME AND OUR WORLD (Slides/
Cassettes). Miller-Brody Productions, 1976.
20 color slides; 3 cassettes or discs, 15–20
min. ea.; 1 Teacher's Guide. Cassettes
#PSI-72621-C ($34), Discs #PSI-72621
($31). Gr. K-2. BKL (1/15/77). 500
Contents: 1. You. 2. The World of Plants.
3. The World of Animals. 4. The World
We Live In. 5. Alike but Different. 6. What
Makes Things Change.
Learning and science become an adventure
in listening, looking, thinking, imagining,
acting, and moving. Original songs and 2
sound puzzles are accompanied by color
slides. The Teacher's Guide provides background materials and gives ways of using
and interchanging sound and visuals for
additional options.

SCIENCE FICTION

THE FOG HORN (Filmstrip—Sound). Listening Library, 1976. 1 color, sound filmstrip;
1 cassette. #SS155 CFX ($19.95). Gr. 6–9.
LGB (12/76). Fic
This Ray Bradbury story explores the
themes of love and loneliness in an unusual
way. Not so much a scary story as a
thought-provoking one.

THE ILLUSTRATED MAN (Filmstrip—
Sound). Listening Library, 1976. 1 color,
sound filmstrip, 1 cassette. #SS156 CFX
($19.95). Gr. 5–10. LGB (12/76), PRV
(1976). Fic
One of Ray Bradbury's most memorable
short stories has been adapted into a sound
filmstrip production. It explores the theme
of reality versus illusion. The tattoos on a
man's body come to life, revealing the
future.

THE MARTIAN CHRONICLES (Phono-
disc). Caedmon Records. 1 disc or cassette.
Cassette #CDL51466 ($7.95), Disc
#TC1466 ($6.98). Gr. 5–9. PRV (4/76).
Fic
Contents: 1. There Will Come Soft Rains.
2. Usher II.
These are chilling masterpieces of science
fiction by Ray Bradbury, read by Leonard
Nimoy, Mr. Spock of "Star Trek."

READING FOR THE FUN OF IT—SCIENCE
FICTION (Filmstrip—Sound). *See* Literature—Study and Teaching

SCIENCE FICTION (Filmstrip—Sound/
Captioned). Society for Visual Education,
1977. 4 color, captioned, sound filmstrips,
av. 55–62 fr. ea.; 4 cassettes or discs, av.

8–10 min. Discs #Y454-SAR ($80), Cassettes #Y454-SATC ($80), Individual Titles ($20). Gr. 4–12. BKL (12/15/78). Fic

Contents: 1. Off on a Comet. 2. The People of the Pit. 3. The Time Traveler. 4. The Mortal Immortal.

Science fiction classics adapted to captioned sound filmstrips by Jules Verne, H. G. Wells, Mary Shelley, and A. Merritt. Four main themes of science fiction writing are represented: man's journey through space, the future vision, the battle of human against technology, and the alien world saga.

THE VELDT (Filmstrip–Sound). Listening Library, 1976. 1 color, sound filmstrip; 1 cassette. #SS159 CFX ($19.95). Gr. 5–10. LGB (1976). Fic

Relationships between parents and children are considered in this Ray Bradbury story. Set in a nursery, the children's needs are met by futuristic, mechanized contraptions.

SCIENCE–STUDY AND TEACHING

READING ADVENTURES IN EVERYDAY SCIENCE, SERIES A (Filmstrip–Sound). Bendick Associates/Miller-Brody Productions, 1974. 4 color, sound filmstrips, 70–80 fr.; 4 cassettes, 11–13 min.; 1 Worksheets; 1 Guide. #E-410/13 ($70). Gr. K–3. BKL (1/15/77). 372.3

Contents: 1. Bigfoot in the Meadow. 2. The Raft That Junk Built. 3. On the Little Island. 4. Where's Fred?

Science material is used to promote reading skills. An adventure is made out of everyday experiences of real children. Science concepts and vocabulary are reinforced with picture songs and the repetition of reading words on later frames.

READING ADVENTURES IN EVERYDAY SCIENCE, SERIES B (Filmstrip–Sound). Bendick Associates/Miller-Brody Productions, 1974. 4 color, sound filmstrips, 77–107 fr.; 4 cassettes, 13–18 min.; 4 Worksheets; 1 Guide. #E-414/417 ($70). Gr. K–3. BKL (1/15/77). 372.3

Contents: 1. Adventures of a Ball. 2. It's Hot on Our Block. 3. What's Alive? 4. A Lot Like Us.

The same focus and approach as Series A.

SCOFIELD, PENROD

THE MAGIC FISHBONE (Filmstrip–Sound/Captioned). *See* Magic–Fiction

SCOTLAND

THE BRITISH ISLES: SCOTLAND AND IRELAND (Filmstrip–Sound). University Films/McGraw-Hill Films, 1972 (European Geography, Set Four). 4 color, sound film-strips, av. 65 fr. ea.; 4 cassettes or discs, 14 min. ea.; Teacher's Guide. Cassette #102419-0 ($65), Discs #103519-2 ($65). Gr. 5–9. BKL (1973), PRV (5/73). 914.1

Contents: 1. Scotland: The Highlands. 2. Scotland: Central Lowlands and Southern Uplands. 3. Ireland: The Land. 4. Ireland: Past and Present.

The series explores the history, geography, and culture of Ireland and Scotland through photographs, maps, and some reproductions. Discussion questions are included at the end of each filmstrip.

EUROPEAN GEOGRAPHY, SET FOUR (Filmstrip–Sound). McGraw-Hill Films, 1972. 4 color, sound filmstrips, 55–70 fr.; 4 cassettes or discs, 12–15 min.; Teacher's Guide. Discs #103519-2 ($65), Cassettes #102419-0 ($65). Gr. 6–10. BKL (9/1/73), PRV (1/73), PVB (5/73). 914.1

Contents: 1. Ireland: The Land. 2. Ireland: Past and Present. 3. Scotland: The Central Lowlands and the Southern Uplands. 4. Scotland: The Highlands.

These filmstrips explore the beautiful and rugged environments of Scotland and Ireland, emphasizing how geography and climate have shaped living conditions in the various regions.

SCULPTURE

A BOY CREATES (Motion Picture–16mm–Sound). EBEC, 1971. 16mm color, sound film, 10 min. #3053 ($115). Gr. K–6. AVI (12/19/75), BKL (10/1/72), CGE (1972). 731

Demonstrates a boy's imagination in transforming "junk" into meaningful art forms. He uses lifeless figures in a deserted amusement park. From discarded bottles, plastic objects, cast-off wood, and metal, he fashions a figure and places it on a log. His "found art" sculpture becomes a person in a roadster that soars airborne on a magical journey.

THE BRONZE ZOO (Motion Picture–16mm–Sound). Texture Films, 1974. 16mm color, sound film, 16 min.; Guide. ($225). Gr. 6–A. BKL (11/15/74). 731

The film shows Shay Rieger sketching a yak, constructing the armature of chicken wire and plumbing pipes, molding with plaster of paris, and finally watching foundry workers cast it in bronze by the "lost wax" process. The narration is by Shay Rieger.

SCULPTURE WITH STRING (Filmstrip–Sound). Warner Educational Productions. 2 color, sound filmstrips, 65–72 fr.; 1 cassette, 14–15 min.; Teacher's Guide. #720 ($39.50). Gr. 3–9. PRV (11/76), PVB (4/77). 731

The presentation leads in with finished examples; then many designs are shown be-

SCULPTURE (cont.)

ing constructed with easy-to-follow instructions for each step.

SEA HORSES

SEA HORSE (Film Loop–8mm–Silent).
Walt Disney Educational Media, 1966.
8mm color, silent film loop, approx. 4 min.
#62-5456L ($30). Gr. K–12. MDU (1974).
597.53

Male sea horse is shown ejecting the young
from his pouch. The young congregate on
a nearby plant while the exhausted father
rests on the sea floor.

SEAFARING LIFE

THERE SHE BLOWS (Filmstrip–Sound).
Hawkhill Associates, 1977. 1 color, sound
filmstrip, 123 fr.; 1 cassette, 22 min.; 1
Guide. ($22.50). Gr. 3–A. BKL (7/15/
77). 639.28

Old recordings of whaling folksongs provide
background for the information narration
and the dramatic readings of life at sea
aboard a whaler 150 years ago. Drawings,
photographs, and classical paintings are
used in the presentation of details of the
daily life of whaling.

SEALS

THE POLAR BEARS AND THE SEALS
(Kit). *See* Mammals

SEASHORE

SEA, SAND AND SHORE (Filmstrip–
Sound). *See* Ocean

SEASONS

CHANGING SEASONS: THE STORY OF A
YEAR (Film Loop–8mm–Silent). Troll
Associates. 4 8mm color, silent film loops,
approx. 4 min.; Available separately.
($99.80). Gr. 1–8. AUR (1978). 525
Contents: 1. Spring. 2. Summer. 3. Fall. 4.
Winter.

Focusing on the same scene through the 4
seasons, these color film loops provide a
visual record of the recurring cycles of
nature.

ENJOYING THE SEASONS (Film Loop–
8mm–Captioned). Coronet Instructional
Media. 4 8mm, captioned film loops, 4
min. ea.; Teacher's Guide. #T123 ($110).
Gr. K–3. PRV (9/75). 525
Contents: 1. Spring. 2. Summer. 3. Autum. 4. Winter.

The relationship between seasons in the life
cycle of plants and animals. These loops
express moods of the seasons by showing
work and play activities.

EXPLORING THE SEASONS (Filmstrip–
Sound). Imperial Educational Resources,
1969. 4 color, sound filmstrips; 4 cassettes
or discs. Discs #3RG43600 ($56), Cas-
sette #3KG43600 ($62). Gr. 4–6. BKL
(2/70), TEA (9/70). 525
Contents: 1. Spring. 2. Summer. 3. Autumn. 4. Winter.

A detailed and sensitive portrait of seasonal
change that examines the interaction of
climate, environment, and living organisms.

THE FOUR SEASONS (Filmstrip–Sound).
Troll Associates, 1974. 4 color, sound filmstrips, av. 60 fr. ea.; 2 cassettes, av. 6 min.
ea.; Teacher's Guide. ($52). Gr. K–3. PRV
(9/76). 574
Contents: 1. Fall. 2. Winter. 3. Spring. 4.
Summer.

Full-color photography and narration present the story of the seasons, showing their
changing effect on plants, trees, animals,
and human beings. Appropriate holidays
are included.

LOOKING AT THE SEASONS (Film Loop–
8mm–Captioned). Coronet Instructional
Media. 4 8mm captioned film loops, 4
min. ea.; Teacher's Guide; Loops avail.
separately. #T122 ($110). Gr. 1–6. PRV
(9/75). 525
Contents: 1. Spring. 2. Summer. 3. Autumn. 4. Winter.

The relationship between the seasons and
living things are combined with the demands
and possibilities of each season. An abundance of photographed plant and animal
life in natural settings is shown.

NATURALLY SPEAKING (Filmstrip–
Sound). *See* Natural History

NATURE ALL AROUND US (Filmstrip–
Sound). *See* Natural History

ONCE AROUND THE SUN (Filmstrip–
Sound). Knowledge Aid/United Learning,
1976. 4 color, sound filmstrips, av. 45 fr.
ea.; 4 cassettes, approx. 6–8 min. ea.; Teacher's Guide; Student Activities. #4010
($60). Gr. 2–4. BKL (11/15/76), ESL (10/
77). 525
Contents: 1. Spring. 2. Summer. 3. Autumn. 4. Winter.

An explanation of why seasonal changes
occur, what those seasons are, and the effect they have on all forms of life is interwoven into the tale of a wolf pack's seasonal
migrations between mountain and valley.

THE SEASONS (Filmstrip–Captioned).
EBEC, 1976 (Developing Language Skills).
4 color, captioned filmstrips, 65 fr.; Teach-
er's Guide. #13550 ($32.90). Gr. K–3.
BKL (4/15/77), LAM (10/77), PRV (9/1/
77). 525
Contents: 1. What Can You Do and See in
Spring? 2. What Can You Do and See in
Summer? 3. What Can You Do and See in

Autumn? 4. What Can You Do and See in Winter?

Fascination with nature and the excitement of seasonal activities provide a strong basis for talking and learning about the outdoors. Students observe changes in seasons and are asked to talk about what they see, as a means of building their vocabulary.

SEEING THE SEASONS CHANGE (Filmstrip–Sound). Educational Direction/Learning Tree Filmstrips, 1974. 4 color, sound filmstrips, av. 49 fr. ea.; 2 cassettes, av. 7 min. ea. #LT437 ($52). Gr. 2–5. EYR (2/76), STE (9/74). 525

Contents: 1. Summer. 2. Fall. 3. Winter. 4. Spring.

The set is designed to give the young learner an impressionistic view of each of the 4 seasons, while introducing the concept of seasons flowing into each other in a never-ending cycle.

WEATHER, SEASONS AND CLIMATE (Filmstrip–Sound). *See* Meteorology

SEASONS–FICTION

GRANDMOTHER LUCY IN HER GARDEN (Filmstrip–Sound/Captioned). *See* Grandparents–Fiction

SEASONS–POETRY

POETRY OF THE SEASONS (Filmstrip–Sound). Centron Films, 1972. 4 color, sound filmstrips; 4 discs or cassettes. Discs ($52.50), Cassettes ($60.50). Gr. K–A. FLN (2/3/74), INS (4/74), NST (2/74). 808.81

Contents: 1. Spring. 2. Summer. 3. Autumn. 4. Winter.

Four filmstrips that capture the visual splendor of the seasons. Sparse narrative consists of blank verse poetry.

SEASONS OF POETRY (Filmstrip–Sound). *See* Poetry–Collections

SEEDS

HOW FLOWERS REPRODUCE: THE CALIFORNIA POPPY (Study Print). *See* Plant Propagation

SEED DISPERSAL (Film Loop–8mm–Silent). Walt Disney Educational Media, 1966. 8mm color, silent film loop, approx. 4 min. #62-5501L ($30). Gr. K–12. MDU (1974). 582

Shows the various manners by which seeds are dispersed–wind, pods bursting, cones dropping, and shooting pods.

SEEDS SPROUTING (Film Loop–8mm–Silent). Walt Disney Educational Media, 1966. 8mm color, silent film loop, approx.

4 min. #62-5503L ($30). Gr. K–12. MDU (1974). 582

Time-lapse photography shows the germination of seeds from the sprouting roots to the growth of stems and leaves.

SELF-PLANTING SEEDS (Film Loop–8mm–Silent). Walt Disney Educational Media, 1966. 8mm color, silent film loop, approx. 4 min. #62-5502L ($30). Gr. K–12. MDU (1974). 582

Shows the way that seeds are released from the plant and move across the ground in search of a suitable bit of soil.

SEEGER, PETE

FOLK SONGS IN AMERICAN HISTORY, SET ONE: 1700–1864 (Filmstrip–Sound). *See* Folk Songs–U.S.

FOLK SONGS IN AMERICAN HISTORY, SET TWO: 1865–1967 (Filmstrip–Sound). *See* Folk Songs–U.S.

THE FOOLISH FROG (Motion Picture–16mm–Sound). *See* Folk Songs–U.S.

SELF

AT YOUR AGE (Motion Picture–16mm–Sound). *See* Child Development

DIVIDED MAN, COMMITMENT OR COMPROMISE? (Motion Picture–16mm–Sound). *See* Decision-Making

EXPLORING MY IDENTITY, UNIT ONE (Filmstrip–Sound). *See* Individuality

EXPRESSING MYSELF, UNIT TWO (Filmstrip–Sound). *See* Individuality

LO IMPORTANTE QUE ERES (Filmstrip–Sound). BFA Educational Media, 1971. 4 color, sound filmstrips; 4 cassettes or discs. Cassettes in Spanish #VGW00 ($70), Discs in Spanish #VGV00 ($70), English #VN7000 ($70). Gr. K–3. BKL (6/15/72), PRV (4/78). 155.2

Contents: 1. You Are Somebody Special. 2. Who's in Your Family? 3. Who Are Your Friends? 4. Your Feelings.

Shows youngsters how they are like other people and different from them–but, above all, are special. Provides positive lessons on dealing with family, friends, and handling emotions. Available in English.

MYSELF AND ME (Filmstrip–Sound). EBEC, 1973. 5 color, sound filmstrips. av. 95 fr. ea.; 5 cassettes or discs, 7 min. ea.; Teacher's Guide. Discs #6461 ($72.50), Cassettes #6461K ($72.50). Gr. K–3. BKL (1/1/74), CPR (2/74), FLN (1/2/75). 155.2

Contents: 1. What Do I Look Like? 2. Who Do I Like to Be With? 3. How Do I Feel? 4. What Do I Like to Do? 5. What Do I Dream About?

SELF (cont.)

A child who feels good about him- or herself has a head start on successful learning—and living. Through captivating filmstrips, teachers can start every member of a group thinking and talking about him- or herself. Students relate to the lively youngsters as they discuss their appearances, their friends, their feelings and interests, their wishes and dreams. At the end of each filmstrip, frames for discussion invite viewers to join the conversation.

REACH OUT (Motion Picture—16mm—Sound). *See* Values

SONGSTORIES: I AM SPECIAL (Filmstrip—Sound). EBEC, 1976. 4 color, sound filmstrips, av. 65 fr.; 4 discs or cassettes, 6 min. ea.; Teacher's Guide. Discs #6918, ($57.95), Cassettes #6918K ($57.95). Gr. K–3. CPR (1/77), MDU (1/77), PRV (3/77). 155.2

Contents: 1. Katy—Something Different. 2. Murphy the Grump. 3. Martin the Artist. 4. Freda and Her Flowers.

These filmstrips (2 photographed, 2 in whimsical art) are stories told in song, and they are about the "specialness" of each person. As young viewers empathize with Katy, Murphy, Martin, and Freda, they will be reminded of their own special feelings and experiences. The songs are catchy and the choruses are reprinted in the Teacher's Guide.

SONGSTORIES: WHAT MAKES ME THE ONLY ME? (Filmstrip—Sound). EBEC, 1975. 4 color, sound filmstrips, av. 84 fr. ea.; 4 discs or cassettes, 7 min. ea.; Teacher's Guide. Discs #6915 ($57.95), Cassettes #6915K ($57.95). Gr. K–3. BKL (3/15/77), ESL (1977). 155.2

Contents: 1. What Makes Me the Only Me? 2. People I Know. 3. My Favorite Place. 4. A Holiday Is a Special Day.

Through filmstrips paced to a series of lively songs, children are invited to discover themselves and the people and things that inhabit their special, private world. The songs tell of self-discovery, familiar faces, fun places to hide or dream, and special days so important that they are even better then Christmas.

SQUARE PEGS—ROUND HOLES (Motion Picture—16mm—Sound). *See* Individuality

UNDERSTANDING MYSELF AND OTHERS, UNIT THREE (Filmstrip—Sound). *See* Individuality

SELF-CONCEPT. *See* Self-Perception

SELF—FICTION

REALLY ME (Kit). *See* Girls—Fiction

SELF-PERCEPTION

CHILDREN EVERYWHERE (Filmstrip—Sound). *See* Individuality

HELP, I'M SHRINKING (Motion Picture—16mm—Sound). *See* Self-Realization

I CAN, UNIT ONE (Filmstrip—Sound). Scholastic Book Services, 1973 (I Can). 4 color, sound filmstrips; 4 phonodiscs or cassettes; 4 Posters; Teacher's Guide. Disc #4749 ($59.50), Cassette #4764 ($59.50). Gr. K–3. INS (12/73), LNG (10/74), PRV (10/74). 155.2

Contents: 1. I Can Sing, Dance and Play Instruments. 2. I Can Cook. 3. I Can Make Something Beautiful. 4. I Can Fasten.

The aim of the "I Can" series is to help young children experience a sense of accomplishment. It is designed to develop self-awareness, self-esteem, and a positive self-concept. In I Can, Unit One, children explore creative activities in dancing and singing, cooking, making and giving gifts, and fastening things together. Bilingual edition available.

I CAN, UNIT TWO (Filmstrip—Sound). Scholastic Book Service, 1973 (I Can). 4 color, sound filmstrips; 4 phonodiscs or cassettes; Teacher's Guide; 4 Posters. Disc #4765 ($59.50), Cassette #4780 ($59.50). Gr. K–3. INS (12/73), LNG (10/74), PRV (10/74). 155.2

Contents: 1. I Can Build. 2. I Can Take Care of Myself. 3. I Can Care for People, Plants and Animals. 4. I Can Communicate with Others.

I Can, Unit Two develop's children's accomplishments in building, taking care of themselves and others, and communicating.

IDENTITY UNIT (Motion Picture—16mm—Sound). Sutherland Learning Associates/EBEC, 1972 (Most Important Person). 6 16mm color, sound films, approx. 4 min. ea.; avail. 8mm.; avail. Spanish.; 1 Record; 6 Posters; 4 Song Cards; Teacher's Guide. Set #6739 ($345.60), Each film ($64). Gr. K–3. BKL (7/1/74), CHT (10/74), CPR (1/76). 155.2

Contents: 1. I'm the Only Me! 2. Where Are You in Your Family? 3. How Do We Look? 4. What Do You Think You Want to Be? 5. Every Family Is Special. 6. The Most Important Person.

Who am I? What am I like? What is my family like? These are some of the questions encountered in this unit, which aims to develop a strong sense of self-awareness and self-importance in the young child.

JUST LIKE YOU/JUST LIKE ME (Kit). EMC, 1973. 4 paperback books; 4 read-along cassettes; Student Activities on Spirit Masters; Teacher's Guide. #ELC-005000 ($55). Gr. 2–5. BKL (3/74). 155.2

Contents: 1. Max-I-Fish. 2. On a Tight Rope. 3. Forward Roll. 4. Lost and Found.

Four books about young people who pursue their own interests and who end up feeling good about themselves. The read-along cassettes have scripts identical to the books.

LEARNING ABOUT ME (Filmstrip—Sound). ACI Media/Paramount Communications, 1975. 4 color, sound filmstrips; 4 cassettes; Teacher's Guide. #9111 ($78). Gr. 2-5. PRV (9/76). 152.4

Contents: 1. How I Know. 2. How I Feel. 3. Why I Do What I Do. 4. What Kind of Me Do I Want to Be?

An educational goal is to help the child to understand and get along in our social environment. Actions are motivated by knowledge, emotions, or both, and a child can learn to distinguish between them. These filmstrips will start children thinking and talking about their actions. Available in Spanish.

LEARNING ABOUT ME: DEVELOPING SELF-CONCEPT (Filmstrip—Sound). Q+ED Productions, 1972. 5 color, sound filmstrips, 36–48 fr.; 5 discs or cassettes, 5–6 min.; Teacher's Guide. Cassettes #LME10 ($102.50), Discs ($92.50). Gr. 4-6. IFT (1972), NEF (1972), PVB (5/73). 155.2

Contents: 1. Different Shapes. 2. First Step. 3. I'm New Here. 4. Borrowed Friendship. 5. I'm the Boss.

This set stimulates students in the exploration of a more positive self-concept. Illustrated in a contemporary, graphic art form, the series presents problem situations in an open-ended mode.

LEARNING ABOUT OTHERS (Filmstrip—Sound). See Human Relations

ON STAGE: WALLY, BERTHA, AND YOU (Kit). See English Language—Study and Teaching

UNDERSTANDING YOUR FEELINGS (Filmstrip—Sound). See Emotions

WHO ARE YOU? (Filmstrip—Sound). Troll Associates, 1975. 6 color, sound filmstrips, 40–45 fr.; 3 cassettes, 8 min. ($78). Gr. K-3. PRV (4/76). 155.2

Contents: 1. Who Am I Anyway? 2. How Your Parents See You. 3. How Your Brothers and Sisters See You. 4. How Your Friends See You. 5. How Grown-Ups See You. 6. Who I Really Am!

Here's a fascinating unit of 6 sound filmstrips that explore the relationship between family, teachers, and friends. By understanding viewpoints of others, children can better realize where they fit in at home, in the classroom, and in many other everyday situations.

WHO ARE YOU? (Motion Picture—16mm—Sound). Films, 1976. 16mm color, sound film, 9 min. #379-0001 ($150). Gr. K-6. AFF (1977). 155.2

Nero is a puppy not sure of who he is. He wanders about the farmyard asking the other animals, "Who are you?" As they reply, Nero tries to copy their features—the peacock's beautiful tail, the duck's webbed feet, etc. Nero is a comic figure as he attaches a fan to his tail, flippers to his feet, etc. But when a fox attacks the chickens, Nero shakes off his costume and chases the fox away. He realizes who he really is.

YOU'RE THE ONLY YOU (Filmstrip—Sound). See Individuality

SELF-REALIZATION

THE BEST I CAN (Motion Picture—16mm—Sound). Films, 1976 (Best of Zoom). 16mm color, sound film, 12 min. #393-0019 ($200). Gr. 4-12. AFF (1978). 155.2

Demonstrating the importance of "trying again" after failure rather than giving up are a gymnast and a diver. Marcie, during the Junior Olympics competitions, slips from the balance beam, but gets up and continues. Diver Laura has a similar experience.

HELP, I'M SHRINKING (Motion Picture—16mm—Sound). Films, 1975. 16mm color, sound film, 12 min. #315-001 ($200). Gr. K-6. AAS (5/76), FLQ, IFF. 155.2

Every time Carrie says "I can't," she shrinks until she becomes small enough to ride on the butterfly's back! Encouraged by the butterfly, she learns to say "I can," and begins to grow until her developing self-confidence restores her to her natural size.

SENDAK, MAURICE

A KISS FOR LITTLE BEAR (Filmstrip—Sound). See Bears—Fiction

MAURICE SENDAK'S REALLY ROSIE STARRING THE NUTSHELL KIDS (Motion Picture—16mm—Sound). See Imagination—Fiction

SENSES AND SENSATION

CAN YOU DESCRIBE IT? (Filmstrip—Captioned). EBEC, 1976 (Developing Language skills). 4 color, captioned filmstrips, 46 fr.; Teacher's Guide. #13155 ($32.90). Gr. K-3. BKL (4/15/77), LAM (10/77), PRV (9/1/77). 152.1

Contents: 1. What Can You Hear? 2. What Can You See? 3. What Can You Touch and Feel? 4. What Can You Taste and Smell?

A vocabulary of the senses is an important part of learning. These filmstrips will help organize and expand it.

SENSES AND SENSATION (cont.)

FACES (Motion Picture—16mm—Sound). Schloat/Prentice-Hall Media, 1973. 16mm color, sound film, 5 min. #HA 172 ($75). Gr. K-3. CFF (1973), LGB (1974), STE (1973). 152.1

Based on the book of the same title by George Ancona and Barbara Brenner, this film prompts an awareness and appreciation of our senses. Young Max shows different ways we use our perceptions to develop self-awareness.

LET'S FIND OUT ABOUT (Cassette). *See* Perception

MY SENSES AND ME (Filmstrip—Sound). EBEC, 1971. 4 color, sound filmstrips, av. 84 fr. ea.; 4 discs or cassettes, 7 min. ea.; Teacher's Guide. Discs #6449 ($57.95), Cassettes #6449K ($57.95). Gr. K-2. BKL (4/15/73), LFR (11/73), PRV (2/73). 152.1

Contents: 1. What Do I See When I Look? 2. What Do I Hear When I Listen? 3. What Do I Feel When I Touch? 4. What Do I Smell and Taste?

This series explores the rich variety of sensory experiences available to city children. Photographs of familiar activities and songs are designed to capture student interest and focus attention on the kinds of information perceived by each of the senses. Opportunities are provided for students to exercise and expand their descriptive vocabulary skills.

A SENSE OF YOURSELF (Filmstrip—Sound). ACI Media/Paramount Communications, 1975. 4 color, sound filmstrips, 49–61 fr.; 4 cassettes, 6–9 min.; Teacher's Guide. #9125 ($78). Gr. 3-6. IFP (1976), PRV (11/76). 152.1

Contents: 1. A Living Camera—Sight. 2. Listen to Learn—Hearing. 3. Special Feeling—Touch. 4. Perfect Partners—Taste and Smell.

A photo essay of sights and sounds, and our relationships with them increases awareness of the 5 senses in our daily lives.

SENSES AND PERCEPTION: LINKS TO THE OUTSIDE WORLD (Motion Picture— 16mm—Sound). EBEC, 1975. 16mm color, sound film, 18 min. #3475 ($255). Gr. 6-9. AAS (12/76), LFR (3/4/76), NST (1/77). 152.1

This film explores the world of the 5 senses, among both humans and animals, with emphasis on the role of the human eye and brain. Optical illusions help students appreciate the role of the brain in sorting sensory messages.

SENSES UNIT (Motion Picture—16mm— Sound). Sutherland Learning Associates/ EBEC, 1972 (Most Important Person). 6 16mm color, sound films. Also avail. 8mm

film; 1 record; 6 Posters; 1 Song Card; Teacher's Guide. #6733 ($345.60). Gr. K-3. BKL (7/1/74), CHT (9/10/74), CPR (1/76). 152.1

Contents: 1. The Five Senses. 2. Seeing. 3. Hearing. 4. Tasting. 5. Smelling. 6. Touching.

What amazing powers our senses have for providing us with information! The lessons encourage children to explore ways to heighten sensory awareness.

WHAT DO YOU SEE? (Filmstrip—Captioned). EBEC, 1975 (Developing Basic Skills). 4 color, captioned filmstrips, av. 48 fr.; Teacher's Guide. #13075 ($32.90). Gr. K-2. CPR (4/77, MDU (1976), PRV (3/76). 152.1

Contents: 1. What Do You See in the Snow? 2. What Do You See in the Water? 3. What Do You See in the Wind? 4. What Do You See in Light and Shadow?

These 4 filmstrips lead the young viewer to look carefully and then answer questions. Called into play is visual discrimination ability when children confront the effects of snow and water, wind and light.

YOUR SENSES AND HOW THEY HELP YOU (Filmstrip—Sound). National Geographic, 1977. 2 color, sound filmstrips; 2 cassettes or discs, 11–14 min.; 2 Teacher's Guides. ($35). Gr. K-4. CPR (10/77). 152.1

Contents: 1. Seeing and Hearing. 2. Tasting, Touching, Smelling, and Other Senses. An introduction to understanding the importance of the senses that expands children's awareness of the senses in making discoveries about their environment. Simple illustrations that show where messages from the eyes and ears are sent in the brain and which areas of the tongue pick up certain tastes; also discusses the relationships among the senses.

SEQUOYAH

CHIEFS AND LEADERS (Cassette). *See* Indians of North America

SEUSS, DOCTOR

BEGINNER BOOKS FILMSTRIPS, SET 1 (Filmstrip—Sound). *See* Reading—Study and Teaching

BEGINNER BOOKS FILMSTRIPS, SET 2 (Filmstrip—Sound). *See* Reading—Study and Teaching

BEGINNER BOOKS FILMSTRIPS, SET 3 (Filmstrip—Sound). *See* Reading—Study and Teaching

BEGINNER BOOKS FILMSTRIPS, SET 4 (Filmstrip—Sound). *See* Reading—Study and Teaching

DOCTOR SEUSS: HAPPY BIRTHDAY TO
YOU (Phonodisc or Cassette). *See* Stories
in Rhyme

THE DOCTOR SEUSS READ ALONG SET
ONE (Kit). *See* Reading–Study and
Teaching

THE DOCTOR SEUSS READ ALONG SET
TWO (Kit). *See* Reading–Study and
Teaching

HORTON HEARS A WHO! AND HORTON
HATCHES THE EGG (Kit). *See* Wit and
Humor

HOW THE GRINCH STOLE CHRISTMAS
(Kit). *See* Wit and Humor

THE LORAX BY DOCTOR SEUSS (Kit).
See Ecology–Fiction

THE SNEETCHES AND OTHER STORIES
(Kit). *See* Stories in Rhyme

YERTLE THE TURTLE AND OTHER
STORIES (Kit). *See* Wit and Humor

SEWELL, ANNA

BLACK BEAUTY (Filmstrip–Sound). *See*
Horses–Fiction

SEX INSTRUCTION

THERE'S A NEW YOU COMIN' FOR GIRLS
(Filmstrip–Sound). *See* Girls

SEX ROLE

DEVELOPING CHILDREN'S ATTITUDES
TOWARD SEX ROLES (Filmstrip–Sound).
Miller-Brody Productions, 1976. 2 color,
sound filmstrips, 36–38 fr.; 2 cassettes, 3–4
min.; 1 Guide. #SA101/102 ($32). Gr.
1–4. BKL (10/1/77). 301.41
Contents: 1. A Boy Like Me. 2. A Girl
Like Me.
Based on Lynn Phillips's 2 original stories
and sketches, these productions allow
children to see the alternative attitudes,
interests, activities, avocations, and career
choices that have traditionally been rele-
gated to stereotyped sex roles.

SHADES AND SHADOWS–FICTION

PRIVATE ZOO (Filmstrip–Sound). Viking
Press, 1976. 1 color, sound filmstrip, 38
fr.; 1 cassette, 5:54 min.; 1 Guide. #670-
90534-8 ($13.95). Gr. K–3. BKL
(3/15/77), LGB (12/77), LNG (2/77). Fic
From the book by Georgess McHargue, this
adaptation sets the mood for Lewis Harvey's
visit to his private zoo. Here his family's
and friends' shadows seem to resemble animals such as rabbits and monkeys, with help
from Lewis's imagination.

SHANNON, TERRY

THE WORLD OF INNERSPACE (Filmstrip–
Sound). *See* Oceanography

SHAPE

OBSERVING AND DESCRIBING SHAPE
(Kit). EBEC, 1973. 2 filmstrips; 1 cassette;
Teacher's Manual; Response Cards; Guess-
What Bags; Transparent Sheets; Activity
Sheets; Punch-out Shapes; Scope and Sequence Chart. #6660 ($67.50). Gr. K–1.
LFR (5/74), PRV (10/73), TEA (5/6/74).
535.6
This multimedia kit is designed both to
develop cognitive skills and to foster a
positive self-image in the young child. By
learning to observe, identify, describe and
classify by shape, the child is also acquiring
widely applicable learning skills.

See also Size and Shape

SHARKS

THE BLUE SHARK (Kit). Classroom Com-
plements/EBEC, 1976 (Animal Life
Stories). 1 color, sound filmstrip; 1 cassette; 5 identical Storybooks; Teacher's
Guide. #6975K ($27.95). Gr. K–6. TEA
(11/77). 597.3
Young readers can learn how the blue sharks
move, build homes, and fight for food and
survival. This scientifically accurate story
describes the lives of blue sharks in their
natural habitat. A storybook reproduces all
of the narration and full-color art from the
filmstrip.

SHEEDY, ALEXANDRA ELIZABETH

SHE WAS NICE TO MICE (Phonodisc or
Cassette). *See* Elizabeth I, Queen of
England–Fiction

SHEEP

LIFE CYCLE OF COMMON ANIMALS,
GROUP 2 (Filmstrip–Sound). Imperial
Educational Resources, 1973. 2 color,
sound filmstrips, av. 37 fr.; 2 cassettes or
discs, av. 10 min. Discs #3RG 44400 ($30),
Cassettes #3KG 44400 ($33). Gr. 4–9.
TEA (2/73). 591.5
Contents: 1. The Life Cycle of a Bighorn
Sheep, Part One. 2. The Life Cycle of a
Bighorn Sheep, Part Two.
These strips trace the evolution of the big-
horn's habitat, showing how it came to
depend on a special grassland environment.

SHEEP (Film Loop–8mm–Silent). Thorne
Films/Prentice-Hall Media, 1972. 8mm
color, silent film loop, approx. 4 min.
#HAT 431 ($28). Gr. 1–6. INS (12/72),
PRV (3/73), TEA (11/72). 636.3

SHEEP (cont.)

Sheep and their young are shown grazing in an open pasture. Observations are made on their grazing habits and movements.

SHELLEY, MARY WOLLSTONECRAFT

SCIENCE FICTION (Filmstrip—Sound/ Captioned). *See* Science Fiction

SHIPWRECKS—FICTION

ROBINSON CRUSOE (Filmstrip—Sound). Educational Enrichment Materials, 1976. 2 color, sound filmstrips, av. 68–72 fr. ea.; 2 cassettes or 33-1/3 phonodiscs; 1 paperback book; Teacher's Guide. Part I ($20), Part II ($20). Gr. 4–6. LGB (1977). Fic

This 2-part filmstrip set relates the familiar story of the shipwrecked Crusoe, his resourcefulness, and his relationship to the native Friday.

SHORT STORIES

DOCTOR SEUSS: HAPPY BIRTHDAY TO YOU (Phonodisc or Cassette). *See* Stories in Rhyme

FUNNY BONE READING STATION (Kit). *See* Reading—Study and Teaching

HURRAY FOR CAPTAIN JANE! & OTHER LIBERATED STORIES FOR CHILDREN (Phonodisc or Cassette). *See* Children's Literature—Collections

JACK LONDON CASSETTE LIBRARY (Cassette). Listening Library, 1976. 6 cassettes; Teacher's Guide. #CXL 517 ($44.95). Gr. 6–A. BKL (12/15/76), PRV (11/76). Fic

Contents: 1. "To Build a Fire." 2. "A Piece of Steak." 3. "Lost Face." 4. "Told in the Drooling Ward." 5. Selections from the *Call of the Wild.* 6. "The Sea Wolf." 7. "Martin Eden." 8. "The Poker Game."

Some of Jack London's best stories are included in this album as well as some lesser-known short works.

THE LEGEND OF SLEEPY HOLLOW AND ICHABOD CRANE (Phonodisc or Cassette). *See* Legends—U.S.

MASTERY STORY TELLER, SET ONE (Filmstrip—Sound). *See* Literature—Collections

THE PONY ENGINE AND OTHER STORIES FOR CHILDREN (Phonodisc or Cassette). Caedmon Records. 1 cassette or disc, approx. 60 min. Disc #TC1355 ($6.98), Cassette #CDL51355 ($7.95). Gr. K–3. NYR. Fic

Contents: 1. *The Pony Engine* by Doris Garn. 2. *The Story of Minikin and Manikin* by Louis Untermeyer. 3. *The Little Boy*

with the Long Name by Bryna Ivens Untermeyer. 4. *The Three Billy Goats Gruff.* 5. *Silly Billy.* 6. *The Old Woman and Her Pig.* 7. *Six Foolish Fishermen* by Benjamin Elkin. 8. *The Country Mouse and the Town Mouse* by Aesop.

Here are 8 short children's stories told by 3 master storytellers—Boris Karloff, Julie Harris, and David Wayne.

ROLAND, THE MINSTREL PIG AND OTHER STORIES (Phonodisc or Cassette). *See* Children's Literature—Collections

ROOTABAGA STORIES: HOW TO TELL CORN FAIRIES WHEN YOU SEE 'EM (Phonodisc or Cassette). *See* Fantasy—Fiction

ROOTABAGA STORIES: THE FINDING OF THE ZIG ZAG RAILROAD (Phonodisc or Cassette). *See* Fantasy—Fiction

ROOTABAGA STORIES: THE HAYSTACK CRICKET (Phonodisc or Cassette). *See* Fantasy—Fiction

SERENDIPITY CASSETTE BOOKS (Kit). Society for Visual Education, 1976. 14 cassettes, av. 10 min.; 140 paperback books (14 titles, 10 books per cassette). Set #BC-003-S ($224), Individual Titles ($16.75). Gr. 2–6. BKL (12/15/77). Fic

Contents: 1. In Search of the Saveopotomas. 2. The Gnome from Nome. 3. Wheedle on the Needle. 4. Serendipity. 5. The Dream Tree. 6. Hucklebug. 7. Jake O'Shawnasey. 8. Morgan and Me. 9. Creole. 10. Bangalee. 11. The Muffin Muncher. 12. Flutterby. 13. Leo the Lop. 14. Cap'n Smudge.

Read-a-long programs containing Stephen Cosgrove's delightful stories dramatically presented with music and appropriate sound effects.

SERIES SEVEN: A LITTLE LOVIN' AND A LITTLE LAUGHIN' (Filmstrip—Sound). BFA Educational Media, 1973 (Story Series). 4 color, sound filmstrips, av. 49 fr.; 4 cassettes or discs; Teacher's Manual. Cassettes #VDA000 ($70), Discs #VCZ000 ($70). Gr. K–4. BKL (11/1/74), PRV (3/76), PVB (4/77). Fic

Contents: 1. *How Not to Catch a Mouse* by Eigoro Futamata. 2. *Just Awful* by Alma Marshak Whitney, illus. by Lillian Hoban. 3. *Leave Herbert Alone* by Alma Marshak Whitney, illus. by David McPhail. 4. *Theodore* by Edward Ormondroyd, illus. by John M. Larrecq.

The illustrations and the sound tracks accompanying these favorite children's books adapted to the filmstrip format are all appropriate. The primary virtue of these strips, like their books, is in their content and in the motivational role they play in guiding primary readers to the library shelf or reading center.

SOUND FILMSTRIP SET 35 (Filmstrip—
Sound). *See* Children's Literature—
Collections

SIBELIUS, JEAN

SYMPHONIC MOVEMENTS NO. 2 (Phonodiscs). *See* Symphonies

SILVERSTEIN, SHEL

THE GIVING TREE (Motion Picture—16mm
—Sound). *See* Friendship—Fiction

SINGER, ISAAC BASHEVIS

ISAAC BASHEVIS SINGER (Filmstrip—
Sound). Miller-Brody Productions, 1976
(Meet the Newbery Author). 1 color, sound
filmstrip, 88 fr.; 1 disc or cassette, 18 min.
Disc #MNA-1008 ($32), Cassette #MNA-
1008C ($32). Gr. 3-5. BKL (10/15/76).
921

Isaac Bashevis Singer creates characters in
his books of Jewish tales and mysticism.
Singer relates his past on Warsaw's streets,
his love of animals, his daily habits, and his
love of his religion. Mrs. Singer is introduced and contributes to the conversation,
and the viewer also meets Singer's son—
another writer—who lives in Israel.

WHY NOAH CHOSE THE DOVE (Filmstrip—
Sound). *See* Bible Stories

SITTING BULL

CHIEFS AND LEADERS (Cassette). *See*
Indians of North America

THE SIX BLIND MEN AND THE ELEPHANT

WHAZZAT? (Motion Picture—16mm—
Sound). *See* Folklore—India

SIZE AND SHAPE

BASIC SHAPES (Filmstrip—Sound). *See*
Form (Art)

CUT-OUTS UP-TO-DATE (Filmstrip). *See*
Design, Decorative

THE LITTLE CIRCLE (Filmstrip—Sound).
See Fantasy

MEASUREMENT COMPARISONS (Filmstrip
—Sound). January Productions, 1977
(Perceptual Development). 4 color, sound
filmstrips, av. 48 fr.; 4 cassettes, 5 min.;
Teacher's Guide. ($58). Gr. K-2. PRV
(9/77). 516

Contents: 1. Big and Little. 2. Wide and
Narrow. 3. Heavy and Light. 4. Some and
None.

Provides visual comparisons of opposite size
and quantity concepts.

SHAPES AND STRUCTURES IN NATURE
(Filmstrip—Captioned). *See* Matter

SKATEBOARDS

SKATEBOARD MANIA (Kit). Children's
Press, 1976 (Ready, Get-Set, Go). 1 cassette; 4 paperback books; 2 Task Cards;
Ditto Masters, packaged in plastic bag.
#27275-6 ($16.95). Gr. 1-8. PRV
(9/15/77). 796.21

High interest, low reading ability material.
The cassette contains a word-for-word
reading of the book on a subject of great
interest.

SKATEBOARD SAFETY (Motion Picture—
16mm—Sound). Pyramid Films, 1976.
16mm color, sound film, 13 min. #2908
($200). Gr. 5-12. BKL (4/15/77). 796.21

This film shows the exhilaration and excitement of skateboarding while advising of its
dangers and the ways in which accidents and
injuries can be minimized.

SLIDES (PHOTOGRAPHY)

HOW TO DO: SLIDE COLLAGE (Filmstrip—
Sound). *See* Collage

SNAILS—FICTION

THE LACE SNAIL (Filmstrip—Sound).
Viking Press, 1976. 1 color, sound filmstrips, 33 fr.; 1 cassette, 9:15 min.; 1 Guide.
($13.95). Gr. 1-3. BKL (4/1/77). Fic

Based on Betsy Byars's picture book, this
adaptation maintains the quiet mood of the
original. The lace trail left by the snail in
her travels and the requests from the various
animals to adorn them with her lace are delightfully re-created in this medium.

SNAKES

RATTLESNAKE (Film Loop—8mm—Silent).
Walt Disney Educational Media, 1966.
8mm color, silent film loop, approx. 4 min.
#62-5110L ($30). Gr. K-12. MDU (1974).
598.12

The rattlesnake is shown hunting a pocket
mouse, which escapes while the snake is
diverted by a tarantula. A study is made of
the snake's fangs, tongue, and rattle.

SNAKES OF THE AMAZON (Film Loop—
8mm—Silent). Walt Disney Educational
Media, 1966. 8mm color, silent film loop,
approx. 4 min. #62-5317L ($30). Gr.
K-12. MDU (1974). 598.12

Boa constrictors as they live in the jungle.
A marmoset is seen annoying an emerald
tree boa until it is engulfed in the boa's
coils.

SNYDER, ZILPHA

FIRST CHOICE AUTHORS AND BOOKS
(Filmstrip—Sound). *See* Authors

SOAP BOX DERBIES

RACING NUMBERS (Kit). *See* Automobile
Racing

SOCCER

DRIBBLING (Film Loop—8mm—Silent).
Athletic Institute (Soccer). 8mm color,
silent film loop, approx. 4 min.; Guide.
#F-5 ($22.95). Gr. 1–12. AUR (1978).
796.33
A single-concept loop demonstrating the
basic technique.

GOAL KEEPER, CLEARING (Film Loop—
8mm—Silent). Athletic Institute (Soccer).
8mm color, silent film loop, approx. 4 min.;
Guide. #F-11 ($22.95). Gr. 1–12. AUR
(1978). 796.33
A single-concept loop demonstrating the
basic technique.

GOAL KEEPER, PART 1 (Film Loop—8mm
—Silent). Athletic Institute (Soccer). 8mm
color, silent film loop, approx. 4 min.;
Guide. #F-8 ($22.95). Gr. 1–12. AUR
(1978). 796.33
A single-concept loop demonstrating the
basic technique.

GOAL KEEPER, PART 2 (Film Loop—8mm
—Silent). Athletic Institute (Soccer). 8mm
color, silent film loop, approx. 4 min.;
Guide. #F-9 ($22.95). Gr. 1–12. AUR
(1978). 796.33
A single-concept loop demonstrating the
basic technique.

GOAL KEEPER, PART 3 (Film Loop—8mm
—Silent). Athletic Institute (Soccer). 8mm
color, silent film loop, approx. 4 min.;
Guide. #F-10 ($22.95). Gr. 1–12. AUR
(1978). 796.33
A single-concept loop demonstrating the
basic technique.

HEADING AND BACK-HEADING (Film
Loop—8mm—Silent). Athletic Institute
(Soccer). 8mm color, silent film loop,
approx. 4 min.; Guide. #F-4 ($22.95).
Gr. 1–12. AUR (1978). 796.33
A single-concept loop demonstrating the
basic technique.

KICKING (Film Loop—8mm—Silent).
Athletic Institute (Soccer). 8mm color,
silent film loop, approx. 4 min.; Guide.
#F-1 ($22.95). Gr. 1–12. AUR (1978).
796.33
A single-concept loop demonstrating the
basic technique.

TACKLING (Film Loop—8mm—Silent).
Athletic Institute (Soccer). 8mm, color,
silent film loop, approx. 4 min.; Guide.
#F-6 ($22.95). Gr. 1–12. AUR (1978).
796.33
A single-concept loop demonstrating the
basic technique.

THROW IN (Film Loop—8mm—Silent).
Athletic Institute (Soccer). 8mm, color,
silent film loop, approx. 4 min.; Guide.
#F-7 ($22.95). Gr. 1–12. AUR (1978).
796.33
A single-concept loop demonstrating the
basic technique.

TRAPPING—BALL IN AIR (Film Loop—
8mm—Silent). Athletic Institute (Soccer).
8mm, color, silent film loop, approx. 4
min.; Guide. #F-3 ($22.95). Gr. 1–12.
AUR (1978). 796.33
A single-concept loop demonstrating the
basic technique.

TRAPPING—GROUND BALL (Film Loop—
8mm—Silent). Athletic Institute (Soccer).
8mm, color, silent film loop, approx. 4
min.; Guide. #F-3 ($22.95). Gr. 1–12.
AUR (1978). 796.33
A single-concept loop demonstrating the
basic technique.

SOCIAL CHANGE

SCIENCE, TECHNOLOGY AND MODERN
MAN (Filmstrip—Sound). *See* Technology
and Civilization

TECHNOLOGY AND CHANGE (Kit). *See*
Technology and Civilization

SOCIAL CONFLICT

BALABLOK (Motion Picture—16mm—
Sound). *See* Prejudices and Antipathies

SOCIAL PROBLEMS

FIRST THINGS: VALUES (Filmstrip—
Sound). Guidance Associates, 1973. 10
color, sound filmstrips, 50–63 fr.; 5 cas-
settes or discs, 5–10 min. per side; Teacher's
Guide. Discs #1B-302 982 ($124.50), Cas-
settes #1B-302 990 ($124.50). Gr. 2–5.
PRV (10/73), PVB (5/74). 362.042
Contents: 1. That's Not Fair. 2. But It
Isn't Yours . . . . 3. The Trouble with
Truth. 4. You Promised. 5. What Do You
Do about Rules (2 filmstrips per title).
Each filmstrip presents 2 or more ethical
conflicts or dilemmas testing basic concepts
of truth, promises, fairness, rules, and
property rights.

WHAT IF A CRISIS HITS YOUR FAMILY?
(Filmstrip—Sound). *See* Family Life

SOCIAL SCIENCES

BASIC CONCEPTS IN SOCIAL STUDIES,
SET ONE (Filmstrip—Sound). Learning
Corporation of America, 1971. 4 color,
sound filmstrips; 4 cassettes, av. 6 min.;
Study Guide. ($51). Gr. 4–8. INS (4/72),
M&M (1/71), RTE (4/72). 300

Contents: 1. Why We Have Laws: Shiver,
Gobble and Snore. 2. Why We Have Taxes:
The Town That Had No Policeman. 3. Why
We Use Money: The Fisherman Who Needed
a Knife. 4. Why People Have Special Jobs:
The Man Who Made Spinning Tops.

Based on children's books, these strips give
a rapid grasp of abstract ideas that are often
difficult to master.

SOCIAL STUDIES. *See* Geography, Social
Sciences

SOFTBALL

BATTING (Film Loop—8mm—Silent). Athletic Institute (Soft Ball—Womens). 8mm
color, silent film loop, approx. 4 min.;
Guide. #SB-4 ($22.95). Gr. 4–12. AUR
(1978). 796.357

A single-concept loop demonstrating the
basic technique.

THE CATCHER (Film Loop—8mm—Silent).
Athletic Institute (Soft Ball-Womens). 8mm
color, silent film loop, approx. 4 min.;
Guide. #SB-13 ($22.95). Gr. 4–12. AUR
(1978). 796.357

A single-concept loop demonstrating the
basic technique.

CATCHING ABOVE WAIST/BELOW WAIST
(Film Loop—8mm—Silent). Athletic Institute (Soft Ball-Womens). 8mm color, silent
film loop, approx. 4 min.; Guide. #SB-2
($22.95). Gr. 4–12. AUR (1978). 796.357

A single-concept loop demonstrating the
basic technique.

DEFENSIVE RUN DOWN (Film Loop—8mm
—Silent). Athletic Institute (Soft Ball-
Womens). 8mm color, silent film loop,
approx. 4 min.; Guide. #SB-7 ($22.95).
Gr. 4–12. AUR (1978). 796.357

A single-concept loop demonstrating the
basic technique.

DOUBLE PLAY BY SHORT STOP/SECOND
BASE WOMAN (Film Loop—8mm—Silent).
Athletic Institute (Soft Ball-Womens). 8mm
color, silent film loop, approx. 4 min.;
Guide. #SB-12 ($22.95). Gr. 4–12. AUR
(1978). 796.357

A single-concept loop demonstrating the
basic technique.

FIELDING LONG HIT FLY BALL/
GROUND BALL (Film Loop—8mm—
Silent). Athletic Institute (Soft Ball-
Womens). 8mm color, silent, film loop,
approx. 4 min.; Guide. #SB-3 ($22.95).
Gr. 4–12. AUR (1978). 796.357

A single-concept loop demonstrating the
basic technique.

HOOK SLIDE/STRAIGHT IN SLIDE (Film
Loop—8mm—Silent). Athletic Institute
(Soft Ball-Womens). 8mm color, silent
film loop, approx. 4 min.; Guide. #SB-8
($22.95). Gr. 4–12. AUR (1978). 796.357

A single-concept loop demonstrating the
basic technique.

OVERHAND THROW—SIDE ARM THROW
(Film Loop—8mm—Silent). Athletic Institute (Soft Ball-Womens). 8mm color, silent
film loop, approx. 4 min.; Guide. #SB-1
($22.95). Gr. 4–12. AUR (1978). 796.357

A single-concept loop demonstrating the
basic technique.

PITCHING/WINDMILL STYLE/SLINGSHOT
STYLE (Film Loop—8mm—Silent). Athletic Institute (Soft Ball-Womens). 8mm
color, silent film loop, approx. 4 min.;
Guide. #SB-9 ($22.95). Gr. 4–12. AUR
(1978). 796.357

A single-concept loop demonstrating the
basic technique.

RUNNING TO FIRST BASE/RUNNING
EXTRA BASES/RUNNER'S HEADOFF
(Film Loop—8mm—Silent). Athletic
Institute (Soft Ball-Womens). 8mm, color,
silent film loop, approx. 4 min.; Guide.
#SB-6 ($22.95). Gr. 4–12. AUR (1978).
796.357

A single-concept loop demonstrating the
basic technique.

SACRIFICE BUNT/BUNT FOR BASE HIT
(Film Loop—8mm—Silent). Athletic Institute (Soft Ball-Womens). 8mm, color,
silent film loop, approx. 4 min.; Guide. #SB-5
($22.95). Gr. 4–12. AUR (1978). 796.357

A single-concept loop demonstrating the
basic technique.

TAG OUTS/FORCE OUTS (Film Loop—8mm
—Silent). Athletic Institute (Soft Ball-
Womens). 8mm, color, silent film loop,
approx. 4 min.; Guide. #SB-11 ($22.95).
Gr. 4–12. AUR (1978). 796.357

A single-concept loop demonstrating the
basic technique.

SOILS

SOIL IS SOIL . . . ISN'T IT? (Filmstrip—
Sound). Kenneth E. Clouse. 1 color, sound
filmstrip, 56 fr.; 1 cassette, 13 min.; Teacher's Guide. ($19.50). Gr. 4–8. PRV (3/77).
631.4

An exposition of the effect of different soils
on the success of backyard gardens. A boy
and girl, would-be gardeners, listen as earthworms explain their problems in helping
plants to grow in various kinds of soil. The

SOILS (cont.)

soil-plant-oxygen cycle is presented, and words such as "nutrients" are defined.

SOLAR SYSTEM

BEGINNING SCIENCE: EARTH AND UNIVERSE (Kit). *See* Astronomy

EARTH AND UNIVERSE SERIES, SET 3 (Filmstrip–Sound). *See* Universe

THE SUN AND THE MOON (Slides). Educational Dimensions Group, 1976. 20 slides, cardboard mount, in plastic sheet; Notes. #9129 ($25). Gr. 6-12. BKL (4/1/77). 523.2

The set identifies the sun, the moon, the earth, and various astronomical phases of these bodies.

SONGS

AMERICA SINGS (Phonodisc or Cassette). *See* Folk Songs

HOLIDAY SONGS (Phonodiscs). Bowmar Publishing. 1 disc. #168 ($6.95). Gr. 3-6. AUR (1978). 784.3

Presents a collection of holiday favorites, such as "Three Little Witches," "Will You Be My Valentine?," and "The Friendly Beasts."

SONGS IN MOTION: ACTIVITY SONGS AND NURSERY RHYMES (Phonodisc or Cassette). *See* Rhythms

SOUND

GUESS WHAT? (Filmstrip–Sound). *See* Listening

SOUND (Filmstrip–Sound). BFA Educational Media, 1976. 4 color, sound filmstrips, av. 60–72 fr.; 4 cassettes or discs, av. 8–12 min. Discs #VGT000 ($70), Cassettes #VGU000 ($70). Gr. 3-6. PRV (4/77). 534

Contents: 1. What Is Sound? 2. Sound Waves. 3. Ears and Hearing. 4. Uses of Sound.

An introduction to the physics of sound; does not deal with the scientific concepts in depth.

SOUSA, JOHN PHILIP

SOUSA MARCHES (Phonodiscs). *See* Marches (Music)

SOUTH AMERICA

THE ANDEAN LANDS (Filmstrip–Sound). EBEC, 1973. 5 color sound filmstrips, av. 81 fr.; 5 discs or cassettes, av. 8 min. ea.; Spanish-English cassettes available; Teach-

er's Guide. #6463 & #6463K ($72.50), Bilingual #6491K ($72.50). Gr. 4-9. BKL (11/73), PRV (4/75), TEA (5/6/74). 918

Contents: 1. Life in the Highlands. 2. Life in the Lowlands. 3. Venezuela: Sowing the Oil. 4. A Highland Indian Village. 5. Coffee Farmer of Colombia.

Along the Andes lies a group of countries in which striking contrasts abound. In this series students travel through these contrasts, and see the influences of geography and history on today's economic and cultural life.

FAMILIES OF SOUTH AMERICA (Filmstrip–Sound). EBEC, 1973. 6 color, sound filmstrips, av. 83 fr. ea.; 6 discs or cassettes, 8 min. ea.; Spanish-English cassettes avail.; Teacher's Guide. Discs #6453 ($86.95), Cassettes #6453K ($86.95), Bilingual #6489K ($86.95). Gr. K–6. ESL (1976), PRV (4/75), STE (4/5/74). 918

Contents: 1. Ranch Family of Brazil. 2. City Family of Argentina. 3. Family of the Amazon. 4. Indian Family of the Andes. 5. Poor Family of Lima. 6. Wealthy Family of Caracas.

Divergent cultures and life-styles within one continent are examined in this detailed look at 6 South American families. Filmstrips focus on geographical influences, work, play, education, and family interrelationships.

SOUTHERN STATES

SEEING THE SOUTH CENTRAL STATES (Filmstrip–Sound). Coronet Instructional Media, 1975. 6 color, sound filmstrips, 58–62 fr.; 3 discs or cassettes, 10:40–13:20 min.; Teacher's Guide. Discs #8291-6 ($95), Cassettes #M291-6 ($95). Gr. 4-6. PRV (11/1/76). 917.6

Contents: 1. Land and Climate. 2. Natural Resources. 3. Agriculture. 4. Industry. 5. Shipping and Commerce. 6. History and People.

On-location photography, historical prints, and visits with local residents bring the area to life. The diversity of land forms, climates, resources, and people are explored.

SOUTHWEST, NEW

CULTURE OF REGIONS: THE SOUTH-WEST (Filmstrip–Sound). Filmstrip House, 1971. 4 color, sound filmstrips, 48–59 fr.; 2 discs; Script; 16 Spirit Masters. ($45). Gr. 4-12. PRV (9/72), PVB (5/73). 917.9

Contents: 1. Early Indian Culture. 2. Spanish Heritage. 3. Early Anglo Culture. 4. The Modern Southwest.

This set on the Southwest traces the influence of traders, miners, cowboys, and farmers, as well as presenting the Indian culture and the influence of the Indian, Spanish, and Anglo on this part of the country.

SOYBEANS

SOYBEANS—THE MAGIC BEANSTALK
(Motion Picture—16mm—Sound). Centron
Films, 1975. 16mm color, sound film,
11-1/2 min.; Leader's Guide. ($185). Gr.
4–9. AAS (5/76), AFF, CGE. 633.34
History of soybeans and their use, including
how soybeans are playing a major role
in meeting world food shortages. Illustrates
planting, tending, and harvesting.

SPACE AND TIME

TIME, SPACE AND MATTER (Filmstrip—
Sound). *See* Matter

SPANISH LANGUAGE

BASIC ENGLISH FOR SPANISH-SPEAKING
CHILDREN (Phonodisc or Cassette). *See*
English as a Second Language

SPANISH LANGUAGE—READING MATERIALS

FAMILIAS NORTEAMERICANAS—AMERICAN FAMILIES (Filmstrip—Sound). *See*
Family Life

FANCIFUL TALES (Filmstrip—Sound). Educational Activities, 1975. 2 color, sound
filmstrips; 2 cassettes; Guide. #FSC149
($19). Gr. 3–6. BKL (8/15/77). 468.6
Contents: 1. Simon, the Best Cowboy in
Texas. 2. Rock That Fell Out of the Sky.
Short, humorous, brightly colored fanciful
stories with both English and Spanish versions on the same cassette. Useful for vocabulary development, story writing or telling,
and enrichment.

LA LECHUZA—CUENTOS DE MI BARRIO
(Cassette). *See* Owls—Fiction

MOTOCROSS RACING (Kit). Educational
Activities, 1973. 1 color, sound filmstrip;
1 disc or cassette; 10 paperback books;
Teacher's Guide. Kit with Disc #FSR182
($35), Kit with Cassette #FSC182 ($36).
Gr. 3–9. BKL (8/15/77). 468.6
The challenges, hazards, qualifications, and
vocabulary of motocross racing are shown in
vivid color in Spanish or English.

PASSPORT TO MEXICO (Filmstrip—Sound).
See Mexico—Description and Travel

PRESENTANDO MEDIDAS (INTRODUCING MEASURING (Filmstrip—Sound). *See*
Measurement

PRESENTANDO NUMEROS (INTRODUCING NUMBERS) (Filmstrip—Sound). *See*
Counting

THE TOY TRUMPET (Kit). *See* Toys—Fiction

SPANISH LANGUAGE—STUDY AND TEACHING

THE LEARNING PARTY, VOL. ONE
(Phonodisc or Cassette). *See* Children's
Songs

THE LEARNING PARTY, VOL. TWO, GOING PLACES (Phonodisc or Cassette). *See*
Children's Songs

SPANISH LANGUAGE MEDIA. *See* Child
Development; Counting; Measurement;
Owls—Fiction; Self; Spanish Language—
Reading Materials

SPELLING. *See* English Language—Spelling

SPIDERS

TARANTULA (Film Loop—8mm—Silent).
Walt Disney Educational Media, 1966.
8mm color, silent film loop, approx. 4 min.
#62-5117L ($30). Gr. K–12. MDU (1974).
595.4
The tarantula is seen removing soil from its
burrow and attacking several beetles. Includes views of the courtship rituals of this
spider.

SPIDERS—FICTION

CHARLOTTE'S WEB (Cassette). Bosustow
Productions/RCA Educational, 1976. 10
cassettes, av. 13:39–24:02 min.; Also available with 10 paperback books. #DEK 9-
0089 ($79.50). Gr. 3–6. BKL (5/15/77).
Fic
E. B. White reads his own book in a clear,
precise manner that indicates a comfortable
familiarity with the characters.

CHARLOTTE'S WEB (Filmstrip—Sound).
Bosustow Productions, 1974. 18 color,
sound filmstrips, 46–104 fr.; 6 discs or cassettes, 7–14 min.; Teacher's Guide; Flow
Chart; Poster. #159 ($225). Gr. K–6. PRV
(9/75), PVB (4/76). Fic
A delightful presentation of a beloved children's book, which brings the characters of
author E. B. White's story to life. The
author reads his own story in its entirety,
without abridgement or adaptation. Pastel
visuals remain faithful to the book.

SPIER, PETER

THE ERIE CANAL (Filmstrip—Sound). *See*
Erie Canal—Songs

THE STAR-SPANGLED BANNER (Filmstrip—Sound). *See* National Songs, American

SPORTS

BASIC DRIBBLE/CONTROL DRIBBLE/ SPEED (Film Loop—8mm—Silent). *See* Basketball

BATTING (Film Loop—8mm—Silent). *See* Softball

THE CATCHER (Film Loop—8mm—Silent). *See* Softball

CATCHING ABOVE WAIST/BELOW WAIST (Film Loop—8mm—Silent). *See* Softball

CENTER FOR A FIELD GOAL (Film Loop—8mm—Silent). *See* Football

CENTER SNAP FOR PUNT (Film Loop—8mm—Silent). *See* Football

CENTER TO QUARTERBACK EXCHANGE (Film Loop—8mm—Silent). *See* Football

CHEST PASS/BOUNCE PASS (Film Loop—8mm—Silent). *See* Basketball

CHEST PASS/OVERHEAD PASS (Film Loop—8mm—Silent). *See* Basketball

CROSSOVER CHANGE/REVERSE PIVOT CHANGE (Film Loop—8mm—Silent). *See* Basketball

CROSSOVER DRIBBLE/REVERSE DRIB-BLE (Film Loop—8mm—Silent). *See* Basketball

DEFENSIVE RUN DOWN (Film Loop—8mm—Silent). *See* Softball

DOUBLE PLAY BY SHORT STOP/SECOND BASE WOMAN (Film Loop—8mm—Silent). *See* Softball

DRIBBLING (Film Loop—8mm—Silent). *See* Soccer

DRIVE/CROSSOVER DRIVE (Film Loop—8mm—Silent). *See* Basketball

FIELD GOAL AND EXTRA POINTS (Film Loop—8mm—Silent). *See* Football

FIELD GOAL AND KICKOFF (SOCCER STYLE) (Film Loop—8mm—Silent). *See* Football

FIELDING LONG HIT FLY BALL/ GROUND BALL (Film Loop—8mm—Silent). *See* Softball

GOAL KEEPER, CLEARING (Film Loop—8mm—Silent). *See* Soccer

GOAL KEEPER, PART 1 (Film Loop—8mm—Silent). *See* Soccer

GOAL KEEPER, PART 2 (Film Loop—8mm—Silent). *See* Soccer

GOAL KEEPER, PART 3 (Film Loop—8mm—Silent). *See* Soccer

HAND OFF (Film Loop—8mm—Silent). *See* Football

HEADING AND BACK-HEADING (Film Loop—8mm—Silent). *See* Soccer

HOOK SLIDE/STRAIGHT IN SLIDE (Film Loop—8mm—Silent). *See* Softball

INSIDE POWER SHOT (Film Loop—8mm—Silent). *See* Basketball

JUMP SHOT (Film Loop—8mm—Silent). *See* Basketball

JUMP SHOT/ONE HAND SET SHOT/TURN-AROUND JUMP SHOT (Film Loop—8mm—Silent). *See* Basketball

KICKING (Film Loop—8mm—Silent). *See* Soccer

KICKOFF AND ONSIDE KICK (Film Loop—8mm—Silent). *See* Football

LAY UP SHOT (Film Loop—8mm—Silent). *See* Basketball

MIDDLE GUARD PLAY (Film Loop—8mm—Silent). *See* Football

OFFENSIVE BACKS (Film Loop—8mm—Silent). *See* Football

OFFENSIVE LINE BLOCKING (Film Loop—8mm—Silent). *See* Football

ONE-ON-ONE DRIVE (Film Loop—8mm—Silent). *See* Basketball

OVERARM PASS/OVERHEAD PASS/ UNDERHAND PASS (Film Loop—8mm—Silent). *See* Basketball

OVERHAND THROW—SIDE ARM THROW (Film Loop—8mm—Silent). *See* Softball

PASS PROTECTION (Film Loop—8mm—Silent). *See* Football

PASSING SKILLS, PART 1 (Film Loop—8mm—Silent). *See* Football

PASSING SKILLS, PART 2 (Film Loop—8mm—Silent). *See* Football

PITCHING/WINDMILL STYLE/SLINGSHOT STYLE (Film Loop—8mm—Silent). *See* Softball

PUNTING (Film Loop—8mm—Silent). *See* Football

REBOUNDING (Film Loop—8mm—Silent). *See* Basketball

REBOUNDING/BLOCKING OUT (Film Loop—8mm—Silent). *See* Basketball

RUNNING TO FIRST BASE/RUNNING EX-TRA BASES/RUNNER'S HEADOFF (Film Loop—8mm—Silent). *See* Softball

SACRIFICE BUNT/BUNT FOR BASE HIT (Film Loop—8mm—Silent). *See* Softball

SPEED DRIBBLE/CONTROL DRIBBLE (Film Loop—8mm—Silent). *See* Basketball

SPORTS ACTION 1 (Filmstrip—Sound). Eye Gate Media, 1976. 6 color, captioned filmstrips; 3 cassettes; 12 Spirit Masters; Available in Spanish. #H732 ($83.10). Gr. 4-9. MDU (1977). 790

Contents: 1. Skateboarding. 2. Motorcycles. 3. Bicycles and Biking. 4. Karate. 5. Surfing. 6. Rodeo.

Each filmstrip includes the correct way of doing the sport, how equipment is constructed, and how skilled performers do it. Low reading ability is considered with the captions that are used.

TACKLING (Film Loop—8mm—Silent). *See* Soccer

TAG OUTS/FORCE OUTS (Film Loop—8mm—Silent). *See* Softball

THROW IN (Film Loop—8mm—Silent). *See* Soccer

TRAPPING—BALL IN AIR (Film Loop—8mm—Silent). *See* Soccer

TRAPPING—GROUND BALL (Film Loop—8mm—Silent). *See* Soccer

TURN AROUND JUMP SHOT (Film Loop—8mm—Silent). *See* Basketball

WINNING AND LOSING (Filmstrip—Sound). *See* Human Behavior

SPORTS—BIOGRAPHY

SUPER THINK PROGRAM (Cassette). Troll Associates, 1975. 4 modules, each contains: 6 cassettes, 10 min.; 12 Duplicating Masters; Teacher's Guide. Individual Module ($48), Series ($192). Gr. 5-8. PRV (10/76), TEA (3/77). 796

Contents: 1. Football. 2. Basketball. 3. Baseball. 4. Fast Action.

A listening program dealing with notable sports figures in a variety of fields.

SPORTS—FICTION

SUMMER FUN/WINTER FUN (Kit). EMC, 1974. 4 paperback books; 4 read-along cassettes; Student Activities; Teacher's Guide. #ELC-003000 ($55). Gr. 2-6. SLJ (3/75). Fic

Contents: 1. Magic Bowling Ball. 2. Rescue on Skis. 3. Baseball Just for Fun. 4. The Track Trophy.

The lessons in these brief episodes—sportsmanship, endurance, safety—are handled well, and the inside view of sports will have an appeal for beginning readers. All 4 titles emphasize personal achievement, not being the best on the team.

SPYRI, JOHANNA

EPISODES FROM FAMOUS STORIES (Filmstrip—Sound). *See* Literature—Collections

HEIDI (Filmstrip—Sound). *See* Switzerland—Fiction

HEIDI (Phonodisc or Cassette). *See* Switzerland—Fiction

LIBRARY 3 (Cassette). *See* Literature—Collections

SQUANTO

CHIEFS AND LEADERS (Cassette). *See* Indians of North America

SQUARE DANCING

SINGING SQUARE DANCES (Phonodiscs). Bowmar Publishing. 1 disc. #233 ($6.95). Gr. 6-7. AUR (1978). 793.34

Presents "Crawdad Song," "Marianne," "Smoke on the Water," and other singing square dance tunes.

STEADMAN, RALPH

THE BRIDGE (Filmstrip—Sound/Captioned). *See* Human Relations—Fiction

STEFFENS, LINCOLN

A MISEARABLE MERRY CHRISTMAS (Motion Picture—16mm—Sound). *See* Christmas

STEIG, WILLIAM

FARMER PALMER'S WAGON RIDE (Filmstrip—Sound). *See* Animals—Fiction

SYLVESTER AND THE MAGIC PEBBLE PUPPET (Kit). *See* Magic—Fiction

STEVENSON, ROBERT LOUIS

EPISODES FROM FAMOUS STORIES (Filmstrip—Sound). *See* Literature—Collections

TREASURE ISLAND (Filmstrip—Sound). *See* Pirates—Fiction

TREASURE ISLAND (Cassette). *See* Pirates—Fiction

STORIES COLLECTIONS. *See* Short Stories

STORIES IN RHYME

AS I WAS CROSSING BOSTON COMMON (Filmstrip—Sound/Captioned). *See* Animals—Fiction

THE BEAR'S NATURE GUIDE (Kit). *See* Nature Study—Fiction

BEGINNER BOOKS FILMSTRIPS, SET 1 (Filmstrip—Sound). *See* Reading—Study and Teaching

STORIES IN RHYME (cont.)

BEGINNER BOOKS FILMSTRIPS, SET 2 (Filmstrip—Sound). *See* Reading—Study and Teaching

BEGINNER BOOKS FILMSTRIPS, SET 3 (Filmstrip—Sound). *See* Reading—Study and Teaching

BEGINNER BOOKS FILMSTRIPS, SET 4 (Filmstrip—Sound). *See* Reading—Study and Teaching

DOCTOR SEUSS: HAPPY BIRTHDAY TO YOU (Phonodisc or Cassette). Caedmon Records, 1970. 1 33-1/3 rpm disc or cassette. #CDL51287 Disc ($6.98), #CDL51287 Cassette ($7.95). Gr. K–2. BKL, LBJ. Fic
A collection of the Dr. Seuss favorites.

THE DOCTOR SEUSS READ ALONG SET ONE (Kit). *See* Reading—Study and Teaching

THE DOCTOR SEUSS READ ALONG SET TWO (Kit). *See* Reading—Study and Teaching

THE GOOPS: A MANUAL OF MANNERS FOR MOPPETS (Filmstrip—Sound/Captioned). *See* Etiquette

HORTON HEARS A WHO! AND HORTON HATCHES THE EGG (Kit). *See* Wit and Humor

HOW THE GRINCH STOLE CHRISTMAS (Kit). *See* Wit and Humor

THE LORAX BY DOCTOR SEUSS (Kit). *See* Ecology—Fiction

MADELINE AND THE GYPSIES AND OTHER STORIES (Phonodisc or Cassette). *See* France—Stories

PLAYFUL PANDAS (Motion Picture—16mm—Sound). *See* Pandas

THE SNEETCHES AND OTHER STORIES (Kit). Random House, 1976. 4 color, sound filmstrips, 21–55 fr.; 4 cassettes or discs, 2–7 min.; 1 book; 1 Poster; 1 Teacher's Guide. Cassettes #04087 ($60), Disc #04086 ($60). Gr. K–3. BKL (3/15/77). Fic
Contents: 1. The Sneetches. 2. The Yax. 3. Too Many Daves. 4. What Was I Scared of?
Like other books by Theodore Seuss Geisel, the 4 Seuss stories in this kit are familiar to children.

WHOSE MOUSE ARE YOU? (Filmstrip—Sound). *See* Mice—Fiction

YERTLE THE TURTLE AND OTHER STORIES (Kit). *See* Wit and Humor

STORIES WITHOUT WORDS

TCHOU TCHOU (Motion Picture—16mm—Sound). *See* Fantasy—Fiction

STORMALONG

MIKE FINK AND STORMALONG (Phonodisc or Cassette). *See* Folklore—U.S.

STORMS

MOUNTAIN STORM (Film Loop—8mm—Silent). *See* Weather

STORMS: THE RESTLESS ATMOSPHERE (Motion Picture—16mm—Sound). EBEC, 1974. 16mm color, sound film, 22 min. #3331 ($310). Gr. 5–A. BKL (10/15/74), LNG (1975), PRV (1/75). 551.5
In this study of thunderstorms, tornadoes, and hurricanes, the film examines the nature, structure, incidence, and consequences of these storms, then examines the elaborate systems of detection, data collection, and interpretation that meteorologists use to investigate them. Highlights include a time-lapse buildup of cumulonimbus clouds, a weather satellite's view of the eye of a hurricane, and a miniature tornado whirlwind demonstration.

STORYTELLING

AND THEN WHAT HAPPENED? (Filmstrip—Sound). *See* English Langauge—Composition and Exercises

THRESHOLD FILMSTRIPS, SERIES C (Kit). *See* Children's Literature—Collections

YOU DECIDE/OPEN-ENDED TALES (Filmstrip—Sound). *See* Fairy Tales

STOUTENBURG, ADRIEN

DAVY CROCKETT AND PECOS BILL (Phonodisc or Cassette). *See* Folklore—U.S.

JOHN HENRY AND JOE MAGARAC (Phonodisc or Cassette). *See* Folklore—U.S.

JOHNNY APPLESEED AND PAUL BUNYAN (Phonodisc or Cassette). *See* Folklore—U.S.

MIKE FINK AND STORMALONG (Phonodisc or Cassette). *See* Folklore—U.S.

SOONER HOUND AND FLYING-JIB; HOSS-MACKEREL AND BASSOON BOBBY (Phonodisc or Cassette). *See* Folklore—U.S.

STRAVINSKY, IGOR FEDOROVICH

STRAVINSKY GREETING PRELUDE, ETC. (Phonodiscs). *See* Orchestral Music

STRING ART

SCULPTURE WITH STRING (Filmstrip—
Sound). *See* Sculpture

STRONG, ARLINE

A CRACK IN THE PAVEMENT (Motion
Picture—16mm—Sound). *See* Natural
History

STUDY, METHOD OF

BASIC STUDY SKILLS 1 (Filmstrip—Sound).
Educational Direction/Learning Tree Filmstrips, 1975. 4 color, sound filmstrips, av.
47 fr. ea.; 2 cassettes, av. 7 min. ea.; Teacher's Guide. #LT559 (52). Gr. 3-7. BKL
(12/15/75), PRV (2/77), TEA (9/75).
371.302

Contents: 1. Understanding Textbooks. 2.
Outlining and Taking Notes. 3. Reading
Graphs and Charts. 4. Reviewing and Tak-
ing Tests.

Deals with effective methods of getting information from textbooks, graphs, charts,
and class notes. Tips on how to prepare for
and take exams are also included.

BASIC STUDY SKILLS 2 (Filmstrip—Sound).
Educational Direction/Learning Tree Filmstrips, 1975. 4 color, sound filmstrips, av.
49 fr. ea.; 2 cassettes, av. 7-8 min. ea.;
Teacher's Guide. #LT560 ($52). Gr. 3-7.
BKL (12/15/75), PRV (2/76), TEA (9/75).
371.302

Contents: 1. Using a Dictionary. 2. Using
An Encyclopedia. 3. Using Reference
Books. 4. Using the Card Catalog.

Covers general library and reference skills;
using a dictionary, encyclopedia, reference
books, and the card catalog.

BASIC STUDY SKILLS 3 (Filmstrip—Sound).
Educational Direction/Learning Tree Filmstrips, 1975. 4 color, sound filmstrips, av.
53 fr. ea.; 2 cassettes, av. 5-6 min. ea.;
Teacher's Guide. #LT561 ($52). Gr. 3-7.
BKL (12/15/75), PRV (5/76), TEA (9/75).
371.302

Contents: 1. Writing Compositions and Let-
ters. 2. Preparing Oral Reports. 3. Writing
Book Reports. 4. Doing Reports and
Projects.

Deals with the application of skills in writing compositions and letters, preparing oral
reports, writing book reports, doing reports
and projects.

DEVELOPING EFFECTIVE STUDY SKILLS
(Filmstrip—Sound). Knowledge Aid/United
Learning, 1976. 6 color, sound filmstrips,
av. 65-75 fr. ea.; 6 cassettes, av. 12-16
min. ea.; Teacher's Guide; Duplicating Masters. #1310 ($85). Gr. 5-8. PRV (4/77).
028.7

Contents: 1. How to Take Notes in Class.

2. Taking Notes at Home. 3. Writing Reports. 4. Following Directions—Or Else.
5. Developing Your Listening Skills. 6.
How to Remember.

The essential skills of note taking, report
writing, listening to and interpreting instructions, and aids for effective retention
of information are logically and memorably
brought together in this unit of study.

DEVELOPING STUDY SKILLS (Filmstrip—
Sound). Coronet Instructional Media, 1974.
8 color, sound filmstrips, 48-54 fr.; 4 discs
or 8 cassettes, 9-12 min.; Teacher's Guide.
Discs #S175 ($120), Cassettes #M175
($120). Gr. 4-8. BKL (1975), PRV (4/76).
028.7

Contents: 1. Why We Study. 2. Planning
Your Work. 3. Learning to Listen. 4.
Taking Notes. 5. Using a Textbook. 6.
Doing Homework. 7. How to Review. 8.
Using the Library.

This set has as its objective motivating
young people to want to study while teaching them how to study. The strength of the
series rests upon its clear, down-to-earth,
analytical approach to a task. Examples to
motivate students include an airline pilot,
football coach, TV newsperson, publisher,
and magician, who demonstrate the value
of good study habits.

THE DICTIONARY (Filmstrip—Sound). *See*
English Language—Dictionaries

DICTIONARY SKILL BOX (Cassette). *See*
English Language—Dictionaries

LET'S LEARN TO STUDY (Filmstrip—
Sound). Guidance Associates, 1974. 2
color, sound filmstrips, 66-72 fr.; 2
discs or cassettes, 9 min. ea.; Teacher's
Guide. Discs #9A-301 141 ($52.50),
Cassettes #9A-301 158 ($52.50). Gr.
4-8. PRV (2/76), PVB (4/76). 028.7

Spotlights tips for grasp and retention.
Covers organizing study time, setting objectives, ordering priorities, mastering
material, and asking questions. Suggests
ways to choose topics for independent projects, do research and present reports to
class.

LIBRARY SKILL BOX (Cassette). *See*
Library Skills

MEDIA: RESOURCES FOR DISCOVERY
(Filmstrip—Sound). *See* Audio-Visual Materials

SUCCESS

THE BEST I CAN (Motion Picture—16mm—
Sound). *See* Self-Realization

HELP, I'M SHRINKING (Motion Picture—
16mm—Sound). *See* Self-Realization

SULLIVAN, ANNE

CHILDHOOD OF FAMOUS WOMEN, VOL-
UME THREE (Cassette). *See* Women—
Biography

SURANY, ANICO

STORIES OF LATIN AMERICA, SET ONE
(Filmstrip—Sound). *See* Latin America—
Fiction

STORIES OF LATIN AMERICA, SET TWO
(Filmstrip—Sound). *See* Latin America—
Fiction

SURFING

SURFING, THE BIG WAVE (Kit). Troll
Associates, 1976 (Troll Reading Program).
1 color, sound filmstrip, 34 fr.; 1 cassette,
14 min.; 10 soft-cover books; 1 Library
Edition; 4 Duplicating Masters, 1 Teacher's
Guide. ($48). Gr. 5–9. BKL (1/15/77).
797.1
A high interest kit features an easy-to-read
book on surfing, a sound filmstrip of the
book, and practice in word building, contest clues, vocabulary, and comprehension.

SURVIVAL

SAFE IN NATURE (Motion Picture—16mm—
Sound). *See* Wilderness Survival

SURVIVAL—FICTION

ROBINSON CRUSOE (Filmstrip—Sound).
See Shipwrecks—Fiction

SWISS FAMILY ROBINSON (Phonodisc or
Cassette). *See* Adventure and Adventurers—
Fiction

SWEDEN—FICTION

CHRISTMAS IN NOISY VILLAGE (Filmstrip—Sound). *See* Christmas—Fiction

PIPPI LONGSTOCKING (Phonodisc or
Cassette). Listening Library, 1971. 3 discs
or cassettes, 150 min.; paperback book.
Discs #3311/13 ($20.95), Cassette
#3311/13 ($22.95). Gr. 3–6. LBJ
(10/15/71). Fic
The adventures of a delightful and remarkable little girl and her friends.

SWITZERLAND—FICTION

HEIDI (Filmstrip—Sound). Educational
Enrichment Materials, 1977. 3 color,
sound filmstrips, av. 60–70 fr.; 3 cassettes
or phonodiscs, 18–20 min.; 1 paperback
book; Teacher's Guide. #51009 ($60).
Gr. 2–4. PRV (3/77). Fic
The difficult task of presenting an old-
fashioned story like *Heidi* to today's chil-

dren, who are oriented to faster paced
tales, is successfully accomplished in this
series. Faithful to the book in story and
tone, this is a good addition to a collection
where there is an interest in exposing young
readers to books they might otherwise miss.

HEIDI (Phonodisc or Cassette). Caedmon
Records, 1970. 1 cassette or disc, approx.
55 min. Disc #TC1292 ($6.98), Cassette
#CDL51292 ($7.95). Gr. 3–6. NYR, SLJ.
Fic
Despite its solid writing and old-fashioned
emphasis on religion and virtue, this remains
a beloved, sought-after story. Claire Bloom
reads the abridgement with warmth and
humor.

SYMPHONIES

LEONARD BERNSTEIN CONDUCTS FOR
YOUNG PEOPLE (Phonodiscs). Columbia
Records. 1 disc, 12 in. 33-1/3 rpm.
#3ML5841 ($7.98). Gr. 4–A. MDU
(1978). 785.1
Contents: 1. Afternoon of a Fawn. 2.
Nutcracker Suite.
The New York Philharmonic plays "After-
noon of a Fawn," "The Nutcracker Suite,"
and other selections.

SYMPHONIC MOVEMENT NO. 2 (Phonodiscs). Bowmar Publishing. 1 disc; Lesson
Guides; Theme Chart. #087 ($10). Gr.
3–10. AUR (1978). 785.1
Focuses students' attention on the music,
relating the sound of music to music concepts and terminology. The music also can
be enjoyed with no follow up. Two of the
symphonic movements included are Symphony No. 5 by Beethoven and First Movement, Symphony No. 2 by Sibelius.

SZEKERES, CYNDY

SIGHTS AND SOUNDS FILMSTRIPS, SET 4
(Filmstrip—Sound). *See* Reading—Study
and Teaching

TADPOLES. *See* Frogs

TAILORS—FICTION

THE THREE POOR TAILORS (Filmstrip—
Sound). *See* Folklore—Hungary

TALE OF BENJAMIN BUNNY

TREASURY OF BEATRIX POTTER STO-
RIES (Filmstrip—Sound). *See* Animals—
Fiction

TALE OF MR. JEREMY FISHER

TREASURY OF BEATRIX POTTER STO-
RIES (Filmstrip—Sound). *See* Animals—
Fiction

TALE OF PETER RABBIT

TREASURY OF BEATRIX POTTER STO-
RIES (Filmstrip—Sound). *See* Animals—
Fiction

TALE OF SQUIRREL NUTKIN

TREASURY OF BEATRIX POTTER STO-
RIES (Filmstrip—Sound). *See* Animals—
Fiction

TALKING BOOKS

FUNNY BONE READING STATION (Kit).
See Reading—Study and Teaching

TALL TALES. *See* Folklore, Legends

TAYLOR, THEODORE

FIRST CHOICE AUTHORS AND BOOKS
(Filmstrip—Sound). *See* Authors

TAZEWELL, CHARLES

THE LITTLEST ANGEL (Phonodisc or
Cassette). *See* Christmas—Fiction

TCHAIKOVSKY, PETER ILYICH. *See*
Tschaikovsky, Peter Ilyich

TECHNOLOGY AND CIVILIZATION

SCIENCE, TECHNOLOGY AND MODERN
MAN (Filmstrip—Sound). Educational
Dimensions, 1974. 2 color, sound film-
strips, 79–83 fr.; 2 cassettes, 17 min.;
Teacher's Guide. #1034 ($49). Gr. 6–12.
PRV (4/76). 608
A survey of human development of and use
of technology from prehistoric times to the
1970s, showing that advancing technology
both solves and creates problems.

TECHNOLOGY AND CHANGE (Kit).
Nystrom, 1975 (The American Experience).
5 color, sound filmstrips, 70–90 fr,; 5 cassettes, 8–10 min.; 10 Student Readers; 1
Set Activity Sheets; 2 Teacher's Guides.
#AE3000 ($125). Gr. 6–10. BKL
(12/15/76). 608
Contents: 1. Super Grow. 2. Machines of
Plenty. 3. Interchangeable Parts. 4. Work-
ingmen's Blues. 5. Cities.
This kit shows how national growth and the
progressive mechanization of American life-
styles have resulted in tremendous waste.

TECUMSEH

CHIEFS AND LEADERS (Cassette). *See*
Indians of North America

TEENAGERS. *See* Adolescence—Fiction

TELEVISION

HOW TO WATCH TV (Filmstrip—Sound).
See Mass Media

TEXTILE DESIGN

CREATIVE BATIK (Filmstrip—Sound). *See*
Batik

CREATIVE TIE/DYE (Filmstrip—Sound).
See Dyes and Dyeing

TEXTILE INDUSTRY

THE CLOTHES WE WEAR (Filmstrip—
Sound). *See* Clothing and Dress

THOUGHT AND THINKING

LEARNING TO SOLVE PROBLEMS (Filmstrip—Sound). Guidance Associates, 1976.
3 color, sound filmstrips, 3 cassettes or
discs; 1 Guide. Cassettes #302-818
($68.50), Discs #302-800 ($68.50). Gr.
K–2. BKL (3/15/77), LGB (1976). 153.4
Contents: 1. Ernie Sleeps Out. 2. Sherlock
Hemlock's Problem-solving Service. 3. The
Monster Scouts.
Fosters the realization that there can be
more than one cause of an action, and one
action can have more than one result. It
is, therefore, necessary to think through a
problem and choose the best solution.

LEARNING TO USE YOUR MIND (Filmstrip—Sound). Guidance Associates, 1976
(Sesame Street Skills for Growing). 3 color,
sound filmstrips, 65–86 fr.; 3 cassettes or
discs, 12–15 min.; 1 Guide. Cassette
#302-834 ($68.50), Disc #302-826
($68.50). Gr. K–2. BKL (3/15/77), LGB
(1976). 153.4
Contents: 1. Going to the Beach. 2. The
Grouch Market. 3. Oscar Builds a Snake
House.
Demonstrates appropriate, systematic question asking and shows ways of evaluating
and applying information.

LET'S LOOK AT LOGIC (Filmstrip—Sound).
See Logic

THUMBELINA

THE PIED PIPER AND OTHER STORIES
(Phonodisc or Cassette). *See* Fairy Tales

THURBER, JAMES

THE GREAT QUILLOW (Phonodisc or
Cassette). *See* Giants—Fiction

THE GRIZZLY AND THE GADGETS AND
FURTHER FABLES FOR OUR TIME
(Phonodisc or Cassette). *See* Fables

TIGERS

THE GREAT TIGERS OF INDIA (Kit).
Classroom Complements/EBEC, 1976
(Animal Life Stories). 1 color, sound film-
strip; 1 cassette; 5 identical Storybooks;
Teacher's Guide. #6968K ($27.95). Gr.
K–6. TEA (11/77). 599.7
Young readers learn how animals live, move,
build homes, and fight for food and survival.
A 56-page storybook reproduces all the nar-
ration and full-color art from the sound
filmstrip.

THE WORLD OF JUNGLE BOOKS, SET
ONE (Kit). *See* Animals–Fiction

TIME

CALENDAR STUDIES (Filmstrip–Sound).
See Calendars

HOW TO TELL TIME (Filmstrip–Sound).
Troll Associates. 2 color, sound filmstrips,
av. 42 fr. ea.; 2 cassettes, av. 12 min. ea.
($26). Gr. K–4. AUR (1978). 529
Contents: 1. Lost Island of Time. 2. The
Timekeeping Frog.
Stories help young children learn important
time concepts and skills.

IT'S ABOUT TIME (Filmstrip–Sound). *See*
Calendars

MONEY AND TIME: ADVENTURES OF
THE LOLLIPOP DRAGON (Filmstrip–
Sound). *See* Arithmetic

TIME: FROM MOONS TO MICRO-
SECONDS (Filmstrip–Sound). Guidance
Associates, 1975 (Math Matters). 2 color,
sound filmstrips, av. 57 fr.; 2 discs or cassettes, av. 12 min.; Teacher's Guide. Discs
#1B-301 349 ($52.50), Cassettes #1B-301
331 ($52.50). Gr. 5–8. ATE. 529
Shows early use of natural cycles to mark
time, discusses ancient and modern calendars, traces the development of timepieces,
and explains global time zones and world
standard times.

TIME, SPACE AND MATTER (Filmstrip–
Sound). *See* Matter

TOLSTOY, ALEXEI

THE GREAT BIG ENORMOUS TURNIP
(Filmstrip–Sound). *See* Folklore–Russia

TOOMAI OF THE ELEPHANTS

THE WORLD OF JUNGLE BOOKS, SET
ONE (Kit). *See* Animals–Fiction

TOYS

AT YOUR FINGERTIPS (Filmstrip–Sound).
See Handicraft

TOYS–FICTION

THE TOY TRUMPET (Kit). Media Plus,
1972. 1 color, sound filmstrip, 50 fr.; 1
cassette or disc, 7 min.; 1 book; Teacher's
Guide. ($34). Gr. K–5. PRV (12/73),
PVB (5/74). Fic
The strip expands the book illustrations;
English version followed by Spanish. Both
are distinct, but fast paced. The book is in
English only. The guide contains the Spanish script, school activities, and a bibliography.

THE VELVETEEN RABBIT (Filmstrip–
Sound). *See* Fantasy–Fiction

WINNIE THE POOH (Phonodiscs). *See* Animals–Fiction

TOYS–HISTORY

THIS TINY WORLD (Motion Picture–
16mm–Sound). Phoenix Films, 1973.
16mm color, sound film, 15 min. #0025
($250). Gr. K–A. FLN (3/74). 649.55
Offers a glimpse into the tiny world of
toys in former days, when children were
supposed to be little grown-ups, and so their
toy-world was a meticulous copy of the
world of adults.

TRAFFIC REGULATIONS

TRAFFIC WATCHER (Motion Picture–
16mm–Sound). *See* Safety Education

TRANSPORTATION

MOVIN' ON (Motion Picture–16mm–
Sound). Films, 1977. 16mm color, sound,
animated film, 4 min. #394-0003 ($100).
Gr. 4–10. AFF (1978). 380.5
An animated history of travel on land, on
sea, and in the air points out the creative
leaps necessary between each successive
invention.

TRANSPORTATION OF PEOPLE AND
GOODS (Filmstrip–Sound). Prentice-
Hall Media, 1975. 5 color, sound film-
strips, av. 50 fr.; 5 discs or cassettes, av.
8 min. ea.; Picture Packet; Teacher's Guide.
Cassette #KAC6630 ($85), Disc #KAR6630
($85). Gr. 3–6. BKL (12/75), PRV (11/15),
PVB (4/76). 380.5
Contents: 1. By Aircraft. 2. By Train. 3.
By Bus. 4. By Truck. 5. By Ship.
Presents 5 modes of transportation; each
strip showing actual pictures and photo-
graphs with children in the main roles.
Procedures and communications involved
are shown, giving behind-the-scenes information on careers in this kind of work.

TRANSPORTATION IN LITERATURE AND ART

EARLY TRANSPORTATION (Study Print). Shorewood Reproductions. 12 prints, paper stock, cardboard mounts or unmounted 22-1/2 in. X 28-1/2 in.; Teacher's Guide. Mounted ($50), Unmounted ($35). Gr. 3–4. PRV (4/76). 704.949

Eight Currier and Ives reproductions and 4 prints by Vander Neer, Cuype, Bingham, and Winslow Homer are used to illustrate various modes of transportation in the seventeenth, eighteenth, and nineteenth centuries.

TRAVEL

AIR TRAVEL TODAY (Filmstrip–Sound). *See* Air Lines

PASSPORT TO MEXICO (Filmstrip–Sound). *See* Mexico–Description and Travel

TRAVERS, P. L.

MARY POPPINS (Phonodisc or Cassette). *See* Fantasy–Fiction

MARY POPPINS AND THE BANKS FAMILY (Phonodisc or Cassette). *See* Fantasy–Fiction

MARY POPPINS: BALLOONS AND BALLOONS (Phonodisc or Cassette). *See* Fantasy–Fiction

MARY POPPINS COMES BACK (Phonodisc or Cassette). *See* Fantasy–Fiction

MARY POPPINS FROM A TO Z (Phonodisc or Cassette). *See* Alphabet Books

MARY POPPINS OPENS THE DOOR (Phonodisc or Cassette). *See* Fantasy–Fiction

TREES

THE GODS WERE TALL AND GREEN (Filmstrip–Sound). *See* Forests and Forestry

THE TREE, SECOND EDITION (Motion Picture–16mm–Sound). Churchill Films, 1977. 16mm color, sound film, 11 min. ($175). Gr. 1–A. BKL (2/1/78). 582.16
Trees are important to sowbugs and birds, people and earthworms. A girl discovers how living things depend on each other, and the beauty and stillness of trees.

TRESSELT, ALVIN

HIDE AND SEEK FOG (Filmstrip–Sound). *See* Fog–Fiction

TROPICS

CULTURE AND ENVIRONMENT: LIVING IN THE TROPICS (Filmstrip–Sound). BFA Educational Media, 1974. 8 color, sound filmstrips, 88–120 fr.; 8 cassettes or discs, 8–10-1/2 min.; Teacher's Guide. Cassettes #VW 4000 ($138), Discs #VW 3000 ($138). Gr. 4–8. PRV (4/76), PVB (4/77). 301.3
Contents: 1. Shelter. 2. Clothing. 3. Obtaining Food. 4. Food Preparation. 5. Transportation. 6. Technology. 7. Family Life. 8. Community and Traditions.

Both the music and photography support the minimal narrative to assist in understanding the Cuna culture's fascinating transition as the Indian life-style reacts to modern practices.

TROUT

THE BROWN TROUT (Film Loop–8mm–Captioned). BFA Educational Media, 1973 (Animal Behavior). 8mm color, captioned film loop, approx. 4 min. #481417 ($30). Gr. 4–9. BKL (5/1/76). 597.55

Demonstrates experiments, behavior, and characteristics of the brown trout.

TSCHAIKOVSKY, PETER ILYICH

STORIES IN BALLET AND OPERA (Phonodiscs). *See* Music–Analysis, Appreciation

TSCHAIKOVSKY: PIANO CONCERTO NO. ONE (Phonodiscs). *See* Concertos

TUGBOATS–FICTION

LITTLE TOOT STORIES (Phonodisc or Cassette). Caedmon Records, 1977. 1 disc or cassette, 50 min. Disc #TC1528 ($6.98), Cassette #CDL5-1528 ($7.95). Gr. 1–5. BKL (10/15/77). Fic
Contents: 1. Little Toot. 2. Little Toot on the Thames. 3. Little Toot on the Grand Canal. 4. Little Toot on the Mississippi. 5. Little Toot through the Golden Gate.

Hardie Gramatky's charming stories read by Hans Conried.

TURNIPS–STORIES

THE GREAT BIG ENORMOUS TURNIP (Filmstrip–Sound). *See* Folklore–Russia

TWAIN, MARK

EPISODES FROM FAMOUS STORIES (Filmstrip–Sound). *See* Literature–Collections

TWAIN, MARK (cont.)

HUCKLEBERRY FINN (Phonodisc or Cassette). *See* U.S.—Social Life and Customs

HUCKLEBERRY FINN (Cassette). *See* U.S.—Social Life and Customs

THE PRINCE AND THE PAUPER (Phonodisc or Cassette). *See* Fantasy—Fiction

TWICE TOLD TALES

BLUEBEARD (Cassette). *See* Fairy Tales

TWO THANKSGIVING DAY GENTLEMEN

MASTERY STORY TELLER, SET ONE (Filmstrip—Sound). *See* Literature—Collections

UNGERER, TOMI

THE BEAST OF MONSIEUR RACINE (Motion Picture—16mm—Sound). *See* Monsters—Fiction

THE THREE ROBBERS (Motion Picture—16mm—Sound). *See* Robbers and Outlaws—Fiction

U.S.—ANTIQUITIES

MESA VERDE (Study Print). *See* Cliff Dwellers and Cliff Dwellings

U.S.—DESCRIPTION AND TRAVEL

AN AMERICAN SAMPLER (Filmstrip—Sound). *See* U.S.—Social Life and Customs

CITIES OF AMERICA, PART ONE (Filmstrip—Sound). Teaching Resources Films, 1972. 6 color, sound filmstrips, 53–76 fr.; 3 discs or cassettes, 5–6-1/2 min.; Teacher's Guide. ($75). Gr. 5–12. PRV (2/74), PVB (5/74). 917.3
Contents: 1. New York. 2. Chicago. 3. Boston. 4. Detroit. 5. Washington, D.C. 6. Miami/Atlanta.
A factual exploration of major American cities encompasses history, geography, landmarks, transportation, commerce, mercantile establishments, culture, education, recreation, ethnic groups, and contemporary problems.

CITIES OF AMERICA, PART TWO (Filmstrip—Sound). Teaching Resources Films, 1972. 6 color, sound filmstrips, 53–76 fr.; 3 discs or cassettes, 5–6:30 min.; Teacher's Guide. ($75). Gr. 5–12. PRV (2/74), PVB (5/74). 917.3
Contents: 1. San Francisco. 2. Denver. 3. Houston. 4. Seattle. 5. Los Angeles. 6. New Orleans/St. Louis.
A factual exploration of major American cities encompassing history, geography, landmarks, transportation, commerce, mercantile establishments, culture, education, recreation, ethnic groups, and contemporary problems.

KNOWING AMERICA (Filmstrip—Sound). Educational Direction/Learning Tree Filmstrips, 1974. 4 color, sound filmstrips, av. 59 fr. ea.; 2 cassettes, av. 9 min. ea.; Teacher's Guide. #LT429 ($52). Gr. 1–4. BKL (6/75), ESL (1976), PRV (12/74). 917.3
Contents: 1. The Landscape: By Man and Nature. 2. How We Live and Work. 3. Spending Our Time. 4. The Nation: What It Really Means.
The style of this set is impressionistic, and through superb photography carefully taken over a 2-year period, the full flavor of the many Americans that make up the United States comes through in each strip.

REGIONS OF AMERICA (Filmstrip—Sound). Educational Direction/Learning Tree Filmstrips, 1974. 12 color, sound filmstrips, av. 39 fr. ea.; 6 cassettes, av. 6–7 min. ea.; Teacher's Guide. #LT430 ($156). Gr. K–6. PRV (9/75). 917.3
Contents: 1. A/B Knowing and Living in the Northeast. 2. C/D Knowing and Living in the South. 3. E/F Knowing and Living in the Midwest. 4. G/H Knowing and Living on the Great Plains. 5. I/J Knowing and Living in the Rocky Mountain Region. 6. K/L Knowing and Living in the Pacific Region.
Each region is covered in 2 strips. The first deals with where and what the region is; the second shows what living in the region means.

TALKING ENCYCLOPEDIA OF THE NEW AMERICAN NATION (Cassette). *See* U.S.—History

U.S.—ECONOMIC CONDITIONS

FOCUS ON AMERICA, ALASKA AND HAWAII (Filmstrip—Sound). Society for Visual Education, 1973. 4 color, sound filmstrips, 71–82 fr.; 2 discs or cassettes, 15:30–18:10 min. Discs #250-SFR ($56), Cassette #250-SFTC ($56). Gr. 4–9. BKL (7/74), PRV (5/74). 917
Contents: 1. Alaska: Wealth or Wilderness? 2. Alaska: The Old Frontier Meets the New. 3. Honolulu: The Tourist Explosion. 4. Lanai: The Pineapple Island.
This set focuses on several issue-oriented, sociological studies on the chief regional problems of these 2 states. Although the issues are unrelated, they provide challenging, thought-provoking topics.

FOCUS ON AMERICA, THE MIDWEST (Filmstrip—Sound). Society for Visual

Education, 1972. 6 color, sound filmstrips, 71–87 fr.; 3 discs or cassettes,
14:45–18:20 min.; 6 Teacher's Guides.
Discs #A250SDR ($83), Cassette
#A250SDTC ($83). Gr. 5–9. BKL
(4/1/73), PRV (5/1/73), PVB (2/73).
917.7

Contents: 1. North Dakota: Are Sub-
sidies Necessary? 2. The Great Lakes:
America's "Inland Sea." 3. Howard,
Kansas: A Struggle to Survive. 4. Akron,
Ohio: The Rubber City. 5. Chicago:
The Airport Conflict. 6. Detroit: A City
Rebuilds.

The cities seem to have little in common,
yet all these places are interdependent.
The strips show some of the people in
conflicts that exist in the vast and varied
midwest region. Prints, maps, and diagrams as well as photographs are used.

FOCUS ON AMERICA, THE NEAR WEST
REGION (Filmstrip–Sound). Society for
Visual Education, 1972. 6 color, sound
filmstrips, av. 82 fr.; 3 discs or cassettes;
1 Guide. Discs #250-SBR ($83), Cas-
sette #250-SBTC ($83). Gr. 4–9. BKL
(4/73). 917.6

Contents: 1. The Cherokee Nation of
Oklahoma. 2. Texas: Land of Cattle and
Oil. 3. The Spanish Americans of New
Mexico. 4. The Mormons of Utah. 5.
Butte, Montana: City in Transition.
6. Colorado: Agriculture Technology.

Three groups of early settlers—Indians,
Spanish-Americans, and Mormons—
share their past and present and look
to the future in this set. The wealth of
this area comes from the land as portrayed in visits to oil wells and oil boom
towns in Texas, cattle feed lots in Colorado, and copper mines in Montana.

LIFE IN RURAL AMERICA (Filmstrip–
Sound). *See* U.S.–Social Life and Customs

WORKING IN U.S. COMMUNITIES,
GROUP ONE (Filmstrip–Sound). *See*
Occupations

WORKING IN U.S. COMMUNITIES,
GROUP TWO (Filmstrip–Sound). *See*
Occupations

U.S.–FOREIGN POPULATION

AMERICA'S ETHNIC HERITAGE–
GROWTH AND EXPANSION (Filmstrip–Sound). *See* Minorities

IMMIGRATION AND MIGRATION (Motion
Picture–16mm–Sound). *See* U.S.–History

U.S.–GEOGRAPHY

MY HOME AND ME (Filmstrip–Sound).
EBEC, 1971. 6 color, sound filmstrips,
av. 63 fr. ea.; 6 discs or cassettes, av. 8
min. ea.; Teacher's Guide. Discs #6452

($86.95), Cassettes #6452K ($86.95).
Gr. K–3. BKL (12/15/72), GRT (10/71),
PRV (9/72–73). 917.3

Contents: 1. My Seacoast Home. 2. My
Ranch Home. 3. My City Home. 4. My
Forest Home. 5. My Navajo Desert Home.
6. My Island Home.

Six geographical areas in the United States
are examined from the viewpoint of an 8-
year-old boy or girl living in each area.
The children describe their homes and
tell how they live, work, play, and explore in their environments.

REGIONS OF THE UNITED STATES
(Filmstrip–Sound). Troll Associates,
1977. 8 color, sound filmstrips, av. 67
fr. ea.; 8 cassettes, av. 12 min. ea.;
Teacher's Guide. ($112). Gr. 4–9.
BKL (1/15/78). 917.3

Contents: 1. New England. 2. Middle
Atlantic States. 3. Southeast. 4. Midwest. 5. North Central States. 6. South
Central States. 7. Rocky Mountain States.
8. Western and Pacific States.

Provides basic overview of U.S. regions.
Students learn about life-styles, working
conditions, geography, and resources
that have built a nation and the special
character of the American people.

SEEING THE MIDDLE ATLANTIC
STATES (Filmstrip–Sound). *See*
Atlantic States

SEEING THE SOUTH CENTRAL
STATES (Filmstrip–Sound). *See*
Southern States

U.S.–HISTORY

AMERICA ROCK (Filmstrip–Sound).
Xerox Educational Publications, 1976.
4 color, sound filmstrips, 45–53 fr.;
4 cassettes or discs, 3 min. ($60). Gr.
2–6. BKL (3/1/77). 973

Contents: 1. The Preamble. 2. Just a
Bill. 3. No More Kings. 4. Suffering
Until Suffrage.

Original pop music and cartoons provide
an innovative way to present such basic
lessons in U.S. history as the need for
colonial independence, reasons for writing
the Constitution, method by which a bill
becomes law, and the women's suffrage
movement.

AMERICAN HISTORY ON STAMPS (Kit).
See Postage Stamps

AMERICANA PLUS FIFTY (Kit). McGraw-
Hill Films, 1975. 8 modules, ea. with: 1
color sound filmstrip, av. 50 fr.; 1 cassette,
8 min.; 35 Newsletters; 10 Activity Cards;
35 Activity Sheets; 1 Poster; 1 Test; Teacher's Guide. Each Module ($35). Gr. 4–6.
BKL (10/15/76), INS (1/77), PRV (1/77).
973

U.S.–HISTORY (cont.)

Contents: 1. Exploration and Discovery. 2. Settlement of the Colonies. 3. Independence and the New Nation. 4. Early Expansion. 5. Slavery. 6. The Westward Movement. 7. Industrialization and Urbanization. 8. The United States as a World Power.

A comprehensive multimedia learning program for social studies, tracing the American story from pre-Columbus to the present. It relates our past to students' lives today and in the future. Americana Plus 50 is flexible; each module can be used independently or with a major text program.

EARLY AMERICAN HISTORY (Study Print). Society for Visual Education. 3 units with 8 prints ea. 18 in. X 13 in. unmounted cardboard stock. #PSSP2000 ($30). Gr. 3–5. PRV (4/78). 973

Contents: 1. Colonial America. 2. Family Life. 3. Moving West.

Each print illustrates some aspect of early American life. The text on the reverse gives the historical background of the situation pictured in the print and suggests related activities.

FOLK SONGS IN AMERICAN HISTORY, SET ONE: 1700-1864 (Filmstrip–Sound). *See* Folk Songs–U.S.

FOLK SONGS IN AMERICAN HISTORY, SET TWO: 1865-1967 (Filmstrip–Sound). *See* Folk Songs–U.S.

FOLK SONGS IN AMERICAN HISTORY: THE AMERICAN FLAG (Filmstrip–Sound). *See* Folk Songs–U.S.

IMMIGRATION AND MIGRATION (Motion Picture–16mm–Sound). Nystrom, 1975 (The American Experience). 5 color, sound filmstrips, 69–84 fr.; 5 cassettes, 10–12 min.; 10 Student Readers; 1 set of Activity Sheets; 2 Teacher's Programs. #AE-100 ($125). Gr. 6–11. BKL (2/15/77). 973

Contents: 1. The Golden Land. 2. The First Wave. 3. Frontiers. 4. A Flood of Peoples. 5. Strangers in the City.

Intended to present "history without politics," but with a special focus on the role of the average citizen in building and shaping America.

SETTLERS OF NORTH AMERICA (Filmstrip–Sound). *See* Frontier and Pioneer Life

TALKING ENCYCLOPEDIA OF THE NEW AMERICAN NATION (Cassette). Troll Associates, 1973. 51 cassette tapes, av. 15–20 min. ea. 8 Volumes #973-980 ($299). Gr. 5–A. PRV (5/75), TEA (12/73). 973

Contents: 1. New England. 2. Middle States. 3. Southeast. 4. Prairie States.

5. Plains States. 6. South Central. 7. Rocky Mountain States. 8. Western and Pacific.

The emphasis is on events and people that played an important part in the country's history. There is also material on geography, industry, and points of interest. Included is a cross-referenced subject guide.

WOMEN: AN AMERICAN HISTORY (Filmstrip–Sound). *See* Women–U.S.

U.S.–HISTORY–1600-1775–COLONIAL PERIOD

AMERICAN FOLK ARTS (Filmstrip–Sound). *See* Folk Art, American

JAMESTOWN ADVENTURE (Filmstrip–Sound). Troll Associates, 1975. 4 color, sound filmstrips, av. 42 fr. ea.; 2 cassettes, av. 8 min. ea.; Teacher Guide. ($52). Gr. 4–6. BKL (10/15/75). 973.2

Contents: 1. Arriving at Jamestown. 2. James Fort. 3. Struggle in the Wilderness. 4. Life in Early Jamestown.

This set shows the early history of Jamestown, tracing its development from a small outpost to a thriving colonial community.

U.S.–HISTORY–1775-1783–REVOLUTION

AMERICA IN ART: THE AMERICAN REVOLUTION (Filmstrip–Sound). Miller-Brody Productions, 1974. 2 color, sound filmstrips, 66–71 fr.; 2 cassettes or discs, av. 14-1/2 min. Cassettes #A211C ($44), Discs #A211 ($44). Gr. 6–12. BKL (12/15/74). 973.3

More about the American Revolution than about art, this set provides insight into the personalities, significant events, and the course of the struggle for independence. It features both familiar and lesser-known paintings, cartoons, and engravings of the period. The narrator includes incidental information about the artist, but the Teacher's Guide indicates the artist and year (when available) of each work used, plus information on art styles and the artists.

BECOMING A NATION (Filmstrip–Sound). Society for Visual Education, 1976. 4 color, sound filmstrips, 51–56 fr.; 4 cassettes or discs, av. 10 min. Cassettes #A314-SBTC ($64), Discs #A314-SBR ($64). Gr. 4–6. BKL (5/15/77). 973.3

Contents: 1. Becoming Americans. 2. Winning Independence. 3. Forming a Nation. 4. Life in the Colonies.

First-person narratives in this set present an appealing immediacy and interest in the historical outline of the launching of our nation.

CONTINENTAL SOLDIERS: HEROES OF THE AMERICAN REVOLUTION, SET ONE (Filmstrip—Sound). McGraw-Hill Films, 1975. 4 color, sound filmstrips, av. 51 fr.; 4 cassettes or discs, av. 3 min.; Teacher's Guide. Discs #106545-8 ($72), Cassettes #106554-7 ($72). Gr. K-6. BKL (9/1/76), PRV (5/76). 973.3

Contents: 1. John Glover. 2. Henry Knox. 3. Baron Von Steuben. 4. George Washington.

This series of biographical portraits tells of 4 men who played an important part in the American Revolution. Up-tempo framework coupled with a unique and imaginative use of inanimate objects depict key historic events, contributions, and achievements. The stories are told through original music and lyrics written by Ray Charles of the Ray Charles Singers.

CONTINENTAL SOLDIERS: HEROES OF THE AMERICAN REVOLUTION, SET TWO (Filmstrip—Sound). McGraw-Hill Films, 1975. 4 color, sound filmstrips, av. 51 fr.; 4 cassettes or discs, av. 3 min.; Teacher's Guide. Discs #102743-2 ($72), Cassettes #102748-3 ($72). Gr. K-6. PRV (5/76). 973.3

Contents: 1. Allan McLane. 2. Timothy Murphy. 3. Deborah Sampson. 4. Peter Salem.

This series of biographical portraits tells the story of 3 men and one women who played an important part in the American Revolution. Up-tempo framework coupled with a unique and imaginative use of inanimate objects depict key historic events, contributions, and achievements. The stories are told through original music and lyrics written by Ray Charles of the Ray Charles Singers.

DEBORAH SAMPSON: A WOMAN IN THE REVOLUTION (Motion Picture—16mm— Sound). *See* Sampson, Deborah

FAMOUS PATRIOTS OF THE AMERICAN REVOLUTION (Filmstrip—Sound). *See* U.S.—History—Biography

PAUL REVERE'S RIDE AND HIS OWN STORY (Cassette). *See* American Poetry

U.S.—HISTORY—1775-1783—REVOLUTION—FICTION

A BIRTHDAY FOR GENERAL WASHINGTON (Kit). Children's Press, 1976. 1 color, sound filmstrip, 59 fr.; 2 cassettes, 12-14 min.; 1 book; 2 Costume Patterns; 2 Puppet Patterns; 1 Script; 1 Teacher's Guide. ($34.95). Gr. 1-4. BKL (9/15/77). Fic

The components center around Johanna Johnston's book, a story in play form about a miller and his 2 children who

provide for Washington's starving Valley Forge troops.

MY BROTHER SAM IS DEAD (Phonodisc or Cassette). Miller-Brody Productions, 1976. 1 disc or cassette, 41 min. Disc #NAR3089 ($6.95), Cassette #NAC3089 ($7.95). Gr. 5-8. BKL (9/15/77). Fic

A dramatization based on a Newbery Honor Book by J. L. Collier. A Revolutionary War story about Sam, who volunteers for the rebel cause, leaving behind his brother who tells the story.

U.S.—HISTORY—1783-1865

HOME LIFE (Film Loop—8mm—Captioned). *See* Frontier and Pioneer Life

SCHOOL (Film Loop—8mm—Captioned). *See* Frontier and Pioneer Life

SOCIAL LIFE (Film Loop—8mm—Captioned). *See* Frontier and Pioneer Life

WOOL INTO CLOTHING (Film Loop—8mm—Captioned). *See* Frontier and Pioneer Life

U.S.—HISTORY—1861-1865—CIVIL WAR—FICTION

ACROSS FIVE APRILS (Filmstrip—Sound). Miller-Brody Productions, 1974 (Newbery Filmstrips). 2 part color, sound filmstrip, 165 fr.; cassette or disc, 38 min.; Teacher's Guide. #NAC 3034 ($32). Gr. 5-8. BKL (9/15/74), LGB (1974). Fic

Growing up is the theme of this popular story about the Civil War. The issue is the commitment of the people to a free or slave society. Based on the book by Irene Hunt.

U.S.—HISTORY—1865-1898

RAILROADS WEST (Filmstrip—Sound). Associated Press/Prentice-Hall Media, 1974 (America Comes of Age 1870-1917). 3 color, sound filmstrips, 80-94 fr.; 3 discs or cassettes, 14-20 min.; Teacher's Guide. Cassettes #KAC6850 ($72), Discs #KAR6850 ($72). Gr. 5-A. PRV (1/75), PVB (5/75). 973.8

Contents: 1. The Golden Spike. 2. The Iron Horse. 3. The End of the Wild West.

This set focuses on the nation's development and the role the railroad played. It uses a documentary approach with each strip composed of black-and-white photographs and prints. On-the-spot reports, authentic sound effects, and music bring alive this era of American history.

U.S.—HISTORY—1898-1919

RAILROADS WEST (Filmstrip—Sound). *See* U.S.—History—1865-1898

U.S.–HISTORY–1945-1953

THE DECADES: NINETEEN FIFTIES
(Cassette). Visual Education, 1975 (The
Decades). 3 cassettes, 35–65 min. #5205-
00 ($30). Gr. 5-10. BKL (7/15/77).
973.918

Contents: 1. Political Machinations of the
1950's. 2. American Society in the 1950's.
3. Technology of the 1950's.

Portrays the hopes, aspirations, dreams,
and disappointments, as well as the fears
and frustrations, of America in the period
between Korea and Vietnam, using primary sources such as news reports and
radio programs.

U.S.–HISTORY–1953-1961

THE DECADES: NINETEEN FIFTIES
(Cassette). See U.S.–History–1945–
1953

U.S.–HISTORY–BIOGRAPHY

BENJAMIN FRANKLIN–SCIENTIST,
STATESMAN, SCHOLAR AND SAGE
(Motion Picture–16mm–Sound). See
Franklin, Benjamin

CONTINENTAL SOLDIERS: HEROES OF
THE AMERICAN REVOLUTION, SET
ONE (Filmstrip–Sound). See U.S.–
History–1775–1783–Revolution

CONTINENTAL SOLDIERS: HEROES OF
THE AMERICAN REVOLUTION, SET
TWO (Filmstrip–Sound). See U.S.–
History–1775–1783–Revolution

DEBORAH SAMPSON: A WOMAN IN THE
REVOLUTION (Motion Picture–16mm–
Sound). See Sampson, Deborah

FAMOUS PATRIOTS OF THE AMERICAN
REVOLUTION (Filmstrip–Sound). Coronet Instructional Media, 1973. 6 color,
sound filmstrips, av. 45 fr.; 6 discs or cassettes, av. 11 min.; Teacher's Guide. Cassettes #M249 ($87), Discs #S249 ($79).
Gr. 4-9. BKL (1974), PRV (1974). 920

Contents: 1. Patrick Henry. 2. Crispus
Attucks. 3. Nathanael Greene. 4. Haym
Salomon. 5. Molly Pitcher. 6. John Paul
Jones.

Artist-illustrated biographies of familiar and
little-known patriots, filled with personal
and ethnic characteristics.

GEORGE WASHINGTON–THE COURAGE
THAT MADE A NATION (Motion Picture–
16mm–Sound). See Washington, George

LEADERS, DREAMERS AND HEROES
(Cassette). See Biography–Collections

THE PICTORIAL LIFE-STORY OF
GEORGE WASHINGTON (Kit). See
Washington, George

THE PICTORIAL LIFE-STORY OF
THOMAS JEFFERSON (Kit). See
Jefferson, Thomas

THOMAS JEFFERSON (Motion Picture–
16mm–Sound). See Jefferson, Thomas

WOMEN IN AMERICAN HISTORY
(Filmstrip–Sound). See Women–U.S.

U.S.–SOCIAL LIFE AND CUSTOMS

AN AMERICAN SAMPLER (Filmstrip–
Sound). Joshua Tree Productions, 1972.
6 color, sound filmstrips, 63–97 fr.; 6 discs
or cassettes, 15 min. Teacher's Guide.
Discs #1R-6900 ($95.50), Cassettes #1T-
6900 ($106.60). Gr. 6-A. PRV (9/72),
PVB (5/74). 917.3

Contents: 1. America Celebrates Tradition.
2. American Variety and Individualism.
3. America Changing and Unchanged.
4. America on the Go. 5. Americans and
Their Land. 6. America and a Job Well
Done.

An exploration of grass-roots America,
its heritage, and familiar and unfamiliar
life-styles. Based on the CBS news program
"On the Road" by Charles Kuralt, who is
the narrator.

FIVE CHILDREN, UNIT 2 (Filmstrip–
Sound). Scholastic Book Services, 1972
(Five Children and Five Families). 5 color,
sound filmstrips, av. 60 fr. ea.; 5 7 in. LP
discs or cassettes; Teacher's Guide; Wall
Poster. Cassette #6833 ($69.50), Disc
#6797 ($69.50). Gr. K-4. BKL (5/1/73),
EYR (12/72), PRV (5/73). 917.3

Contents: 1. The Cowboy. 2. A Fisherman's Son. 3. Sara's Letter. 4 Mira Mira
Marisol. 5. Happy Birthday Howard.

Illustrates the life-styles of 5 children who
live in different parts of the United States.
Youngsters are encouraged to see differences
and similarities between themselves and
others, and through this, develop a greater
awareness of themselves in relation to
others. Available in Spanish.

FOCUS ON AMERICA, ALASKA AND
HAWAII (Filmstrip–Sound). See U.S.–
Economic Conditions

FOCUS ON AMERICA, THE MIDWEST
(Filmstrip–Sound). See U.S.–Economic
Conditions

FOCUS ON AMERICA, THE NEAR WEST
REGION (Filmstrip–Sound). See U.S.–
Economic Conditions

HOW CHILDREN LIVE IN AMERICA
(Filmstrip–Sound). See Children in the U.S.

LIFE IN RURAL AMERICA (Filmstrip–
Sound). National Geographic, 1973.
5 color, sound filmstrips, av. 60 fr.; 5 cassettes or discs, 13 min. ea.; Teacher's Guide.
#03738 ($74.50), #03739 ($74.50).

Gr. 5–A. BKL (2/1/74), PRV (1/75), PVB (5/75). 917.3

Contents: 1. The Family Farm. 2. Cowboys. 3. Coal Miners of Appalachia. 4. Harvester of the Golden Plains. 5. Settlers on Alaska's Frontier.

This set discusses the programs and rewards of living on the land. It depicts the rigors and satisfaction of physical toil, the dangers and risks in producing some of our most common necessities, and the life-styles of the people involved.

U.S.–SOCIAL LIFE AND CUSTOMS– FICTION

HUCKLEBERRY FINN (Phonodisc or Cassette). Caedmon Records, 1968. 2 cassettes or discs, approx. 60 min. ea. Discs #TC2038 ($13.96), Cassettes #CDL52038 ($15.90). Gr. 5–9. LBJ. Fic

Contents: 1. "Sivilizing" Huck. 2. Huck and Pap. 3. Huck and Jim. 4. Emmeline Grangerford. 5. Life on the Raft. 5. Hamlet's Soliloquy. 7. The Shooting of Boggs. 8. Jim Gets Homesick. 9. You Can't Pray a Lie. 10. Escape Plan.

Seemingly a rambling tale for boys, this novel is in reality a subtly crafted and carefully structured masterpiece. Careful selections from various chapters carry the story line and present the flavor and excellence of Twain's writings.

HUCKLEBERRY FINN (Cassette). Jabberwocky Cassette Classics, 1972. 3 cassettes, av. 60 min. #1071-1091 ($23.94). Gr. 5–A. BKL (3/15/74), JOR (11/74). Fic

A colorful dramatization of Mark Twain's portrait of a real boy. Musical interludes indicate changes of scenes and passage of time in this novel, which has been adapted and condensed. Twain's satire and irony comes through clearly and it can be used to introduce Twain's book or to bring the novel to life after it has been read.

LITTLE WOMEN (Phonodisc or Cassette). *See* Family Life–Fiction

UNIVERSE

BEGINNING SCIENCE: EARTH AND UNIVERSE (Kit). *See* Astronomy

EARTH AND UNIVERSE SERIES, SET 3 (Filmstrip–Sound). University Films/ McGraw-Hill Films, 1976. 3 color, sound filmstrips, 76–82 fr.; 3 cassettes, 16–53 min.; 1 Guide. #102702 ($54). Gr. 4–6. BKL (9/15/77). 523

Contents: 1. Daytime, Nighttime, and the Seasons. 2. The Moon. 3. The Solar System.

Photographs, diagrams, models, and a helpful narration explore the central concepts in a succinct, thorough manner.

WHAT'S OUT THERE? (Filmstrip–Sound/ Captioned). *See* Astronomy

UNTERMEYER, BRYNA

THE PONY ENGINE AND OTHER STORIES FOR CHILDREN (Phonodisc or Cassette). *See* Short Stories

UNTERMEYER, LOUIS

THE PONY ENGINE AND OTHER STORIES FOR CHILDREN (Phonodisc or Cassette). *See* Short Stories

USTINOV, PETER

BARON MUNCHAUSEN TRULY TALL TALES (Phonodisc or Cassette). *See* Legends

UYSAL, AHMET

NEW PATCHES FOR OLD (Filmstrip– Sound). *See* Folklore--Turkey

VALUES

CAN YOU IMAGINE? (Filmstrip–Sound). *See* Decision-Making

CROSSROADS–STORIES ABOUT VALUES AND DECISIONS (Filmstrip–Sound). *See* Decision-Making

THE HATING BOOK (Kit). *See* Emotions

HOW DO YOU KNOW WHAT'S FAIR? (Filmstrip–Sound). Guidance Associates, 1975 (First Things: Social Development). 2 color, sound filmstrips, av. 60 fr.; 2 cassettes or discs, av. 6 min. ea. #1B-319-184 ($27.75), #1B-319-192 ($27.75). Gr. 2–5. LGB (1975). 301.45

Dramatizes realistic social problems that require evaluation from 2 or more points of view and helps to develop reasoning skills. In this dilemma the question is whether Keith let Jerry win at ping-pong and if so, is that fair or unfair to Jerry?

LAW AND JUSTICE (Filmstrip–Sound). *See* Law

PEOPLE OF THE FOREST: A STUDY IN HUMAN VALUES (Kit). *See* Culture

REACH OUT (Motion Picture–16mm– Sound). FilmFair Communications, 1971. 16mm color, sound film 5-1/4 min. ($85). Gr. K–3. LFR (3/71). 170

Motivates children to become aware and involved in discussing personal values and the concepts of tolerance, friendship, adaptability, and understanding one's self. Based on the book by Bill Martin, Jr.

SELF EXPRESSION AND CONDUCT (Filmstrip–Sound). *See* Culture

SQUARE PEGS–ROUND HOLES (Motion Picture–16mm–Sound). *See* Individuality

VALUES (cont.)

WHAT ARE YOU GOING TO DO ABOUT ALCOHOL (Filmstrip–Sound). *See* Alcohol

VALUES–FICTION

ANGEL AND BIG JOE (Motion Picture– 16mm–Sound). Learning Corporation of America, 1975 (Learning to Be Human). 16mm color, sound film, 27 min. ($355). Gr. 3-A. AAW (1975), BKL (6/1/77), NEF (1976). Fic

Depicts the deep friendship between Big Joe, the phone lineman, and Angel, a young migrant worker. The climax comes when Angel must choose between moving on with his family or staying and developing a business with Big Joe.

SQUAWK TO THE MOON, LITTLE GOOSE (Filmstrip–Sound). *See* Animals–Fiction

VAN WOERKOM, DOROTHY

SIGHTS AND SOUNDS FILMSTRIPS, SET 4 (Filmstrip–Sound). *See* Reading–Study and Teaching

VASARELY, VICTOR

PICTURES ARE FUN TO LOOK AT (Art Prints). *See* Art Appreciation

VERNE, JULES

SCIENCE FICTION (Filmstrip–Sound/ Captioned). *See* Science Fiction

VETERINARIANS

WORKING WITH ANIMALS (Filmstrip– Sound). *See* Animals–Treatment

VISION

GLASSES FOR SUSAN (Motion Picture– 16mm–Sound). EBEC, 1972. 16mm color, sound film, 13 min. #3166 ($185). Gr. 3-8. BKL (12/15/73). 617.7

Susan has poor vision, but she doesn't know it. Like many other youngsters who see the world out of focus, she blunders through a series of daily mishaps at school and play. This film impresses students with the importance of good vision and of wearing glasses, if needed, with a positive attitude.

VOCABULARY

ANIMALS WE SEE AROUND US (Filmstrip–Captioned). *See* Animals– Habits and Behavior

CAN YOU DESCRIBE IT? (Filmstrip– Captioned). *See* Senses and Sensation

CAN YOU DO IT? (Filmstrip–Captioned). *See* Communication

CAN YOU NAME IT? (Filmstrip–Captioned). EBEC, 1975 (Developing Language Skills). 4 color, captioned filmstrips, av. 45 fr. ea. #13115 ($32.90). Gr. K-2. BKL (7/15/76), LFR (1/2/77), PRV (9/76). 372.6

Contents: 1. What Can You Find at the Beach? 2. What Can You Find in a City Park? 3. What Can You Find in the Woods? 4. What Can You Find on the Farm?

Photographs of a woods, beach, park, and farm help children develop observational skills through the changing perspectives of the 4 locations. Children will be able to take as much time as they need to respond verbally to the printed questions.

DISCOVERING NEW WORDS (Filmstrip– Sound). Troll Associates, 1974. 6 color, sound filmstrips, av. 45 fr. ea.; 3 cassettes, av. 6 min. ea.; Teacher's Guide ($78). Gr. K-4. PRV (4/75). 428

Contents: 1. How It Moves. 2. How It Looks. 3. How It Feels. 4. How It Sounds. 5. Names of Things. 6. Kinds of People.

Helps young children discover a variety of words that describe how things look, move, sound, and feel, as well as the different kinds of people.

EXPERIENCES IN PERCEPTUAL GROWTH (Filmstrip–Sound). *See* Perception

MAKING WORDS WORK (Filmstrip–Sound). Coronet Instructional Media, 1974. 6 color, sound filmstrips, 50–58 fr.; 6 cassettes or 3 discs, 11–13 min. Cassettes #M251 ($95), Discs #S251 ($95). Gr. 5-9. BKL (5/1/75), PRV. 372.4

Contents: 1. Using Pointer Words. 2. Using Basket Words. 3. Exploring Word Meanings. 4. Using Fact and Opinion Pointers. 5. Using Figurative Language. 6. Sound and Word Order.

Combining cartoons with photography, this set describes various ways in which one can improve one's writing and speaking. TV sportcasts, conversations, lyrics, and speeches stress communication rather than grammar to show language as a tool.

MY FEELINGS COUNT (Filmstrip– Captioned). *See* Emotions

NATURE WALKS (Filmstrip–Captioned). *See* Natural History

THE SEASONS (Filmstrip–Captioned). *See* Seasons

SO MANY WORDS TO CHOOSE FROM (Filmstrip–Sound). *See* English Language– Study and Teaching

SUPER THINK PROGRAM (Cassette). *See* Sports–Biography

VOCABULARY SKILLS (Filmstrip—Sound). BFA Educational Media, 1976. 4 color, sound filmstrips, av. 84–104 fr.; 4 cassettes or discs, av. 10–14 min. Cassettes #VHT000 ($70), Discs #VHS000 ($70). Gr. 4–6. PRV (3/78). 372.4

Contents: 1. Word Wise: Compound Words. 2. Word Wise: Prefixes. 3. Word Wise: Suffixes. 4. Word Wise: Root Words.

The objective is to introduce basic vocabulary skill concepts, accomplished through a series of amusing adventures with Captain Word Wise.

WORDS, MEDIA AND YOU (Filmstrip—Sound). *See* Mass Media

WORDS TO WORK WITH–I (Filmstrip—Sound). Educational Direction/Learning Tree Filmstrips, 1976 (Words to Work With). 4 color, sound filmstrips, av. 53 fr. ea.; 4 cassettes, av. 10 min. ea.; Teacher's Guide. #LT682 ($58). Gr. 1–5. BKL (5/15/77), IFT (1977), INS (9/77). 372.4

Contents: 1. What a Day for a Picnic. 2. The Frog Princess. 3. Me and My Brothers. 4. That's a Rabbit?

Provides meaningful, humorous, and entertaining practice in word perception and decoding skills, comprehension, and vocabulary development.

WORDS TO WORK WITH–II (Filmstrip—Sound). Educational Direction/Learning Tree Filmstrips, 1976 (Words to Work With). 4 color, sound, filmstrips, av. 53 fr. ea.; 4 cassettes, av. 10 min. ea.; Teacher's Guide. #LT683 ($58). Gr. 1–5. BKL (5/15/77), IFT (1977), INS (9/77). 372.4

Contents: 1. Who Would Eat a Tuba? 2. No More Robots for Me. 3. I Had the Craziest Dream. 4. Want to Buy a Chicken?

Provides meaningful, humorous, and entertaining practice in the areas of word perception and decoding skills, comprehension, and vocabulary development.

WORDS TO WORK WITH–III (Filmstrip—Sound). Educational Direction/Learning Tree Filmstrips, 1976 (Words to Work With). 4 color, sound, filmstrips, av. 53 fr. ea.; 4 cassettes, av. 10 min. ea.; Teacher's Guide. #LT684 ($58). Gr. 1–5. BKL (5/15/77), IFT (1977), INS (9/77). 372.4

Contents: 1. Or Would You Rather Be a Pig? 2. See What's on Channel 1. 3. Monkeyshines. 4. The Six O'Clock News.

Provides meaningful, humorous, and entertaining practice in word perception and decoding skills, comprehension, and vocabulary development.

WORDS WE NEED (Filmstrip—Sound). *See* English Language—Composition and Exercises

VOCATIONAL GUIDANCE

ADVENTURES IN THE WORLD OF WORK, SET ONE (Kit). Visual Education/Random House, 1976. 6 color, sound filmstrips, 92–106 fr.; 6 cassettes or discs, 10–13 min.; 36 paperback books (6 titles); 6 Duplicating Masters; 1 Discussion Guide; 1 Teacher's Guide. Cassettes #06148-9 ($108), Disc #06149-7 ($108). Gr. 5–10. BKL (11/1/77), LGB (1976), TEA. 371.425

Contents: 1. Who Puts the Light in the Bulb? 2. Who Puts the Prints on the Page? 3. Who Puts the Ice in the Cream? 4. Who Puts the Blue in the Jeans? 5. Who Puts the Room in the House? 6. Who Puts the Grooves in the Record?

Personable, interesting tours of some basic industries not well known to the general public. Developed with the U.S. Office of Education career cluster chart.

ADVENTURES IN THE WORLD OF WORK, SET TWO (Kit). Visual Education/Random House, 1976. 6 color, sound filmstrips, 92–106 fr.; 6 cassettes or discs, 10–13 min.; 36 paperback books (6 titles); 6 Duplicating Masters; 1 Discussion Guide; 1 Teacher's Guide. Cassettes #06151-9 ($108), Discs #06150-0 ($108). Gr. 5–10. BKL (11/1/77), LGB (1976), TEA. 371.425

Contents: 1. Who Works for You? 2. Who Puts the Plane in the Air? 3. Who Puts the News on Television? 4. Who Puts the Care in Health Care? 5. Who Puts the Fun in Free Time? 6. Who Keeps America Clean?

A continuation of Set One, visiting some basic, interesting industries and occupations not often considered.

BANKING AND INSURANCE (Filmstrip—Sound). Associated Press/Pathescope Educational Media, 1975 (People at Work). 1 color, sound filmstrips, 60 fr.; 1 cassette, 11 min.; 1 Teacher's Manual; 10 Spirit Masters. #9027 ($28). Gr. 4–6. PRV (4/76). 371.425

Ann starts her first bank account, thus introducing her to the banking and insurance industries.

BEGINNING CONCEPTS: PEOPLE WHO WORK, UNIT ONE (Kit). Scholastic Book Services, 1975. 5 color, sound filmstrips, 56–63 fr.; 5 discs or cassettes, av. 7 min.; 1 Teacher's Guide/Activity Book; 5 Paper Hats; 5 Punch-out Finger Puppets. Cassettes #4218 ($79.50), Discs #4230 ($79.50). Gr. 3–8. INS (4/77), LAM (2/77), LGB (1975/76). 371.425

Contents: 1. Say, Ah! 2. Bake a Batch of Bread. 3. Pick a Pattern, Pick a Patch. 4. Park Ranger. 5. Stitch and Stuff.

This set emphasizes the variety of types of work, how kinds of work relate to the like and family of the person who performs it, some of the satisfactions and problems in working, and how the work is important.

VOCATIONAL GUIDANCE (cont.)

Unit One shows a pediatrician, a baker, a quiltmaker, a naturalist, and a toy maker.

BEGINNING CONCEPTS: PEOPLE WHO WORK, UNIT TWO (Kit). Scholastic Book Services, 1975. 5 color, sound filmstrips, 62–71 fr.; 5 cassettes or disc, av. 7 min.; 1 Teacher's Guide/Activity Book; 5 Paper Hats; 5 Punch-out Finger Puppets. Cassettes #4236 ($79.50), Discs #4248 ($79.50). Gr. 3–8. INS (4/77), LAM (2/77), LGB (1975/76). 371.425

Contents: 1. Following the Architect's Plan. 2. Click! 3. Jet Pilot. 4. Pets for Sale. 5. On Rainbow Farm.

Same focus as Unit One, presenting a farmer, a jet pilot, an architect, a photographer, and a pet store owner.

CAREER AWARENESS FIELD TRIPS (Filmstrip–Sound). Guidance Associates. 7 color, sound filmstrips, 69–84 fr.; 7 cassettes or discs, 7–10 min.; Teacher's Guide; Available separately. Discs #1B-302-883 ($174.50), Cassettes #1B-302-891 ($174.50). Gr. 3–7. BKL (7/1/74). 371.425

Contents: 1. Off We Go to the Aquarium. 2. Off We Go to the House Built in a Hurry. 3. Off We Go to the Auto Proving Ground. 4. Off We Go to the Orange Grove. 5. Off We Go to the Poster Printer. 6. Off We Go to the Bike Factory. 7. Making the Most of Your Field Trip.

In each visit, a person in the field guides the visitor through a step-by-step process, providing exceptional and often surprising detail involving the particular career.

FARMING (Filmstrip–Sound). Associated Press/Pathescope Educational Media, 1975 (People at Work). 1 color, sound filmstrip, 75 fr.; 1 cassette, 10 min.; Teacher's Manual; 10 Spirit Masters. #9010 ($28). Gr. 4–6. PRV (4/76). 371.425

Joey visits a farm and is surprised to see how many different people are involved in raising the food that he eats.

GETTING READY UNIT ONE (Motion Picture–16mm–Sound). See Occupations

HELPING PEOPLE LOOK THEIR BEST (Filmstrip–Sound). Associated Press/ Pathescope Educational Media, 1975 (People at Work). 1 color, sound filmstrip. 60 fr.; 1 cassette, 11 min.; 1 Teacher's Manual; 10 Spirit Masters. #9026 ($28). Gr. 4–6. PRV (4/76). 371.425

Marty meets a tired salesman who wants to look and feel better. He finds out about the different people who work in the fields of cosmetology and physical fitness.

HELPING PEOPLE SOLVE PROBLEMS (Filmstrip–Sound). Associated Press/ Pathescope Educational Media, 1975

(People at Work). 1 color, sound filmstrip, 60 fr.; 1 cassette, 11 min.; 1 Teacher's Manual; 10 Spirit Masters. #9021 ($28). Gr. 4–6. PRV (4/76). 371.425

Don learns all about people helpers—the various people who work in social work and the social services.

IT ALL DEPENDS ON YOU (Motion Picture –16mm–Sound). Churchill Films, 1976. 16mm color, animated, sound film, 10 min. ($160). Gr. 3–7. PRV (11/76). 371.425

An animated film to make children aware of career possibilities. The content is simple, yet profound. An introduction to career awareness.

MANY PEOPLE, MANY CAREERS (Filmstrip–Sound). EMC, 1975. 4 color, sound filmstrips, 64–112 fr.; 4 cassettes, 7–15 min.; Teaching Material. #CAC-102000 ($81). Gr. 3–7. BKL (7/76), PRV (10/76). 371.425

Contents: 1. Thinking about Tomorrow. 2. All Kinds of Careers. 3. Going to the Hospital. 4. Working with the Waltons.

Helps younger students understand the relationship of one's interests, strengths, and values to the choice of a career. The varied levels of training required for various positions are also explored. Emphasis is on the importance of all levels of work.

PEOPLE AT WORK, SET 2 (Filmstrip– Sound). Imperial Educational Resources, 1974. 4 color, sound filmstrips, 40–47 fr.; 4 discs or cassettes, 5:30–6 min.; Teacher's Notes. Discs #3RG 21100 ($56), Cassettes #3KG 21100 ($62). Gr. 1–6. PRV (10/75), PVB (4/76). 371.425

Contents: 1. At Work in Transportation. 2. At Work in Communications. 3. At Work in Offices and Factories. 4. At Work in Sports and Entertainment.

The focus is on actual people performing jobs in realistic surroundings. Nontraditional jobs, occupational levels, and backgrounds are presented as jobs often taken for granted are introduced.

PRESERVING THE ENVIRONMENT (Filmstrip–Sound). Associated Press/Pathescope Educational Media, 1975 (People at Work). 1 color, sound filmstrip, 60 fr.; 1 cassette, 11 min.; Teacher's Manual; 10 Spirit Masters. #9019 ($28). Gr. 4–6. PRV (4/76). 371.425

Jay learns about conservation of the forest, environmental protection of towns and cities, and sees how many new kinds of jobs there are in these fields.

PUTTING ELECTRICITY TO WORK (Filmstrip–Sound). Associated Press/Pathescope Educational Media, 1975 (People at Work). 1 color, sound filmstrip, 60 fr.; 1 cassette, 11 min.; Teacher's Guide; 10 Spirit Masters. #9028 ($28). Gr. 4–6. PRV (4/76). 371.425

Patrick finds out about the electronics industry and the people who design, build, install, operate, and service electronic equipment.

RICHARD SCARRY'S WHAT DO PEOPLE DO ALL DAY (Kit). *See* Occupations

SERVING THE NATION (Filmstrip—Sound). Associated Press/Pathescope Educational Media, 1975 (People at Work). 1 color, sound filmstrip, 60 fr.; 1 cassette, 11 min.; 1 Teacher's Manual; 10 Spirit Masters. #9018 ($28). Gr. 4–6. PRV (4/76). 371.425

Connie finds out that the federal government is the nation's biggest employer and that people working for it do many different jobs.

TRY OUT: UNIT ONE (Motion Picture—16mm—Sound). WNVT (Northern Virginia Educational TV)/EBEC, 1973 (Whatcha Gonna Do?). 16mm color, sound film, 15 min. #3353 ($200). Gr. 5–A. BKL (5/15/75), LFR (12/74), PRV (10/76). 371.425

This film presents children in 6 different activities that are career-related—nature studies, television broadcasting, building, tutoring, raising livestock, and a classroom manufacturing simulation. Throughout the film, children comment on their work, what they are learning about themselves, and what they might want to be. The film motivates students to reflect on how their own experiences can guide them in career choices, and take an active interest in career opportunities around them.

VOCATIONAL SKILLS FOR TOMORROW (Filmstrip—Sound). Coronet Instructional Media, 1977. 6 color, sound filmstrips, 34–54 fr.; 3 discs or 6 cassettes, 5–11 min.; Teacher's Guide. #340 ($95). Gr. 4–12. PRV (4/78). 371.425

Contents: 1. A New World of Jobs. 2. Business and Clerical Vocations. 3. Commercial and Graphic Arts. 4. Communication and Information Trades. 5. Construction and Manufacturing Trades. 6. Health and Medical Vocations.

Surveys many fields of vocational opportunity, with emphasis on the need to train for the job. Shows how rapid advances in technology create new jobs.

WHAT DO YOU THINK? UNIT ONE (Motion Picture—16mm—Sound). *See* Occupations

WHAT'S THE LIMIT? UNIT TWO (Motion Picture—16mm—Sound). *See* Occupations

WHEN I GROW UP I CAN BE (Filmstrip—Sound). ACI Media/Paramount Communications, 1974. 5 color, sound filmstrips, 5 cassettes, Teacher's Guide; Spirit Master; Study Sheet. #9131 ($88). Gr. 2–5. BKL (2/75), PRV (5/6/75). 371.425

Contents: 1. I Can Be a Builder. 2. I Can Be a Community Service Worker. 3. I Can Be a Food Production Worker. 4. I Can Be a Hospital Worker. 5. I Can Be a Mechanic.

This set explores a variety of jobs in particular career clusters and also examines well-rounded individuals, content both in their private lives and their work. Available in Spanish.

WHO WORKS FOR YOU? (Kit). Visual Education/Random House, 1976. 6 color, sound filmstrips, av. 106–126 fr.; 6 cassettes or discs, av. 11–13 min.; 36 softcover books (6 titles); 6 Duplicating Masters; Teacher's Guide. Cassettes #04754-0 ($158.16), Discs #04781-8 ($158.16). Gr. 5–8. BKL (11/15/77). 371.425

The kit covers a wide variety of service occupations. The first module explores occupations in city, state, and national governments. The second covers behind the scene work in television news. Nurses, doctors, and other health services are explored as well as careers with the airlines. Expanding leisure industries and environmental management and protection are also examined.

WORKING (Filmstrip—Sound). *See* Work

WORKING IN THE OFFICE (Filmstrip—Sound). Associated Press/Pathescope Educational Media, 1975 (People at Work). 1 color, sound filmstrip, 60 fr.; 1 cassette, 1 min.; 1 Teacher's Manual; 10 Spirit Masters. #9025 ($28). Gr. 4–6. PRV (4/76). 371.425

Rich visits a busy office and discovers what all the receptionists, secretaries, typists, accountants, and other office workers do.

THE WORLD OF WORK (Cassette). Associated Educational Materials, 1976. 12 cassettes, av. 7 min. ea.; 12 Worksheets; Teacher's Guide. #TCB-1 ($87.50). Gr. K–2. BKL (11/15/77). 371.425

Early childhood education and career awareness are combined in these cassettes. Each records the sounds of 6 workers in a career cluster and briefly discusses the activities of the workers. Areas such as transportation, home repair, road construction, and hospital service are included.

VOLCANOES

FIRE IN THE SEA (Motion Picture—16mm—Sound). EBEC, 1974. 16mm color, sound film, 10 min. #3191 ($150). Gr. 4–12. BKL (10/1/73), CGE (19/73), PRV (10/74). 551.21

When the Mt. Kilauea volcano erupted, molten lava swept through the Hawaiian countryside and into the sea. In this dangerous environment, photographers captured dramatic and rare close-up views of the awesome lava flow. The absence of nar-

VOLCANOES (cont.)

ration will inspire individual interpretation of the film.

FIRE MOUNTAIN (Motion Picture—16mm—Sound). EBEC, 1972. 16mm color, sound film, 9 min. #2991 ($115). Gr. 4–12. CGE (1973). 551.21

Rare, close-up views of the great eruption of Mt. Kilauea in Hawaii. Color, music, and natural sound enhance this narrationless film, allowing the viewer to "experience" the eruption.

VOLCANOES: EXPLORING THE REST-LESS EARTH (Motion Picture—16mm—Sound). EBEC, 1973. 16mm color, sound film, 18 min. #3208 ($225). Gr. 5–12. BKL (2/1/74), LFR (2/74), LGB (1974). 551.21

On-location photography and animated drawings illustrate volcanic phenomena in Hawaii, Mexico, Italy, and Iceland. The film distinguishes shield, cinder cone, and strato-volcano by showing how each type of volcano is formed and how each erupts.

VOLLEYBALL

SPORTS IN ACTION (Filmstrip—Sound). EBEC, 1976. 3 color, sound filmstrips, av. 77 fr.; 3 cassettes, 7 min. ea. #6942 ($43.50). Gr. 6–12. MDU (4/77). 796.32

Contents: 1. Before You Play. 2. How to Play. 3. Play to Win.

Everything players need to know about volleyball.

WABER, BERNARD

LYLE, LYLE, CROCODILE AND OTHER ADVENTURES OF LYLE (Phonodisc or Cassettes). *See* Crocodiles—Fiction

WALKER, BARBARA

PIGS AND PIRATES (Filmstrip—Sound). *See* Pigs—Fiction

WAR—FICTION

FLOWER STORM (Motion Picture—16mm—Sound). *See* Iran—Fiction

WASHINGTON, GEORGE

A BIRTHDAY FOR GENERAL WASHING-TON (Kit). *See* U.S.—History—1775-1783—Revolution—Fiction

GEORGE WASHINGTON—THE COURAGE THAT MADE A NATION (Motion Picture—16mm—Sound). Handel Film, 1968 (Americana Series #4). 16mm color, sound film, 30 min.; Film Guide. ($360), Rental 7 day ($36). Gr. 4–A. LFR (9/68). 921

Portrays the powerful personality of George Washington and some of the events that led to his decisive role in history. Describes his education, social life, military experience, and political activities against the background of the authentic locale.

THE PICTORIAL LIFE-STORY OF GEORGE WASHINGTON (Kit). Davco Publishers, 1976 (Life Stories of Great Presidents). 4 color, sound filmstrips, 68–74 fr.; 4 cassettes, av. 13 min. ea.; 1 book; 1 Teacher's Guide. ($89). Gr. 5–9. BKL (12/15/77). 921

Well-organized, accurate presentation of the myriad aspects of George Washington's life and career.

WATER

EARTH AND UNIVERSE SERIES, SET 2 (Filmstrip—Sound). *See* Geology

WATER BIRDS

AUDUBON'S SHORE BIRDS (Motion Picture—16mm—Sound). Fenwick Productions, 1977 (America's Wildlife Heritage). 16mm color, sound film, 18-1/2 min. ($225). Gr. 5–12. LGB (1977). 598.2

Re-creates what Audubon first saw and painted, using his own observations to describe ornithological adaptations and behavior. Filmed by Roy Wilcox.

WATER SUPPLY

WATER AND HOW WE USE IT (Filmstrip—Sound). Coronet Instructional Media, 1971. 6 color, sound filmstrips, av. 52 fr.; 6 cassettes or 3 discs, av. 12 min. Cassette #M209 ($95), Discs #S209 ($95). Gr. 4–6. BKL (11/15/72), ESL (1972), INS (1972). 627

Contents: 1. Power. 2. Irrigation. 3. Drinking. 4. Industry. 5. Transportation. 6. Recreation and Conservation.

Photographs show how fresh and sea water are used in different ways. Showing the misuse of water stresses the importance of conservation.

WATSON, JANE WERNER

HEROES OF THE ILIAD (Cassette). *See* Mythology, Classical

WEATHER

MOUNTAIN STORM (Film Loop—8mm—Silent). Walt Disney Educational Media, 1966. 8mm color, silent film loop, approx. 4 min. #62-5023L ($30). Gr. K–12. MDU (1974). 551.6

The spectacle of a mountain storm is viewed from start to finish. A bolt of lightning strikes a huge tree, causing it to topple.

WEATHER FORECASTING

INQUIRING INTO WEATHER (Filmstrip—
Sound). United Learning, 1974 (Moreland-
Latchford). 6 color, sound filmstrips, 40–
52 fr.; 6 cassettes, 7–9 min.; Teacher's
Guide. #43 ($85). Gr. 4–6. PRV (4/76).
551.6

Contents: 1. Starting Your Own Weather
Station. 2. A Visit to the Weather Station.
3. Using Your Own Weather Station. 4.
Weather and What Affects It. 5. Precipitation and Weather. 6. Storms, Hurricanes
and Tornados.

Through photography, students see other
students find a comprehensive definition of
weather. They visit weather stations, learn
about observation and prediction, and find
out that our main energy source, the sun, is
responsible for what we call weather.

WEATHER FORECASTING (Motion Picture—16mm—Sound). EBEC, 1975. 16mm
color, sound film, 22 min. #3372 ($290).
Gr. 4–10. CPR (3/76), LFR (9/10/75), NST
(2/77). 551.6

This film traces the development of meteorology to a sophisticated and increasingly
valuable science. Focusing on the work of
a meteorologist in an actual weather station,
the film shows how data from satellites and
reports from weather stations all over the
world and trained around-the-clock observers are combined to give the most accurate
possible prediction of a region's weather.

WEE WILLIE WINKIE

RIKKI TIKKI TAVI AND WEE WILLIE
WINKIE (Phonodisc or Cassette). *See*
Animals—Fiction

WEIGHT CONTROL. *See* Nutrition

WELBER, ROBERT

SIGHTS AND SOUNDS FILMSTRIPS, SET
1 (Filmstrip—Sound). *See* Reading—Study
and Teaching

WELLES, ORSON

IS IT ALWAYS RIGHT TO BE RIGHT?
(Motion Picture—16mm—Sound). *See*
Human Relations

WELLS, H. G.

SCIENCE FICTION (Filmstrip—Sound/
Captioned). *See* Science Fiction

THE WEST (U.S)

FOCUS ON AMERICA, THE NEAR WEST
REGION (Filmstrip—Sound). *See* U.S.–
Economic Conditions

WHALES

PORTRAIT OF A WHALE (Motion Picture—
16mm—Sound). National Geographic,
1976. 16mm color, sound film or video-
cassette, 3/4"; Teacher's Guide. Film
#06031 ($150), Videocassette #06030
($150). Gr. K–6. LFR (9/10/77), TEA
(9/77). 599.5

The subject of this film is one of the largest
and rarest of the great whales, located in the
waters off Patagonia, in southern South
America. This largest of animals on earth is
also one of the most gentle and shy. You
will learn how whales communicate and
hear the sounds whales make underwater.

WHALES SURFACING (Film Loop—8mm—
Silent). Walt Disney Educational Media,
1966. 8mm color, silent film loop, approx.
4 min. #62-5462L ($30). Gr. K–12. MDU
(1974). 599.5

Whales are shown as they surface and dive,
spouting moist air, not water, from their
lungs.

WHEELOCK, WARREN

HISPANIC HEROES OF THE U.S.A. (Kit).
See Biography—Collections

WHITE, E. B.

CHARLOTTE'S WEB (Cassette). *See* Spiders
—Fiction

CHARLOTTE'S WEB (Filmstrip—Sound).
See Spiders—Fiction

STUART LITTLE (Filmstrip—Sound). *See*
Mice—Fiction

WHITE, JOSH

FOLK SONGS IN AMERICAN HISTORY,
SET ONE: 1700–1864 (Filmstrip—Sound).
See Folk Songs—U.S.

FOLK SONGS IN AMERICAN HISTORY,
SET TWO: 1865–1967 (Filmstrip—Sound).
See Folk Songs—U.S.

WHITNEY, ALMA MARSHAK

SERIES SEVEN: A LITTLE LOVIN' AND
A LITTLE LAUGHIN' (Filmstrip—Sound).
See Short Stories

WILD ANIMALS. *See* Animals and names of
individual animals, such as Lions.

WILDE, OSCAR

THE HAPPY PRINCE AND OTHER OSCAR
WILDE FAIRY TALES (Phonodisc or
Cassette). *See* Fairy Tales

WILDE, OSCAR (cont.)

LIBRARY 5 (Cassette). *See* Literature—
Collections

WILDER, LAURA INGALLS

LAURA: LITTLE HOUSE, BIG PRAIRIE
(Filmstrip—Sound). Perfection Form,
1976. 1 color, sound filmstrip, 140 fr.;
1 cassette or disc, 18 min.; 1 Guide. Cassette #KH95267 ($22.95), Disc #KH95266
($21.45). Gr. 3-A. BKL (6/1/77). 921
Biographical facts are combined with personal impressions in this production that
intertwines the plots of the books with their
author's life.

WILDERNESS AREAS—U.S.

OUR NATIONAL PARKS (Filmstrip—
Sound). *See* National Parks and Reserves—
U.S.

WILDERNESS SURVIVAL

SAFE IN NATURE (Motion Picture—16mm—
Sound). FilmFair Communications, 1975.
16mm color, sound film, 20 min. ($265).
Gr. 3-12. BKL (12/75), LFR (5/75). 796.5
Dramatizes basic techniques of survival
when lost in wilderness areas—in the woods
and in the desert. Emphasized in detail are
3 basics: stay put, make shelter, and give
distress signals.

WILDERNESS SURVIVAL—FICTION

THE GRIZZLY (Kit). *See* Bears—Fiction

WILDLIFE CONSERVATION

ECOLOGY AND THE ROLE OF MAN (Filmstrip—Sound). EBEC, 1975. 6 color, sound
filmstrips, av. 58 fr. ea.; 6 discs or cassettes,
9 min. ea.; Teacher's Guide. Discs #6913
($86.95), Cassettes #6913K ($86.95). Gr.
5-8. ESL (1977), MFC (4/77), PRV
(11/76). 639
Contents: 1. The Passenger Pigeon: Caring
Too Late. 2. The Buffalo: Caring in Time.
3. The Bald Eagle: An Endangered Symbol.
4. The Kaibab Deer: A Lesson in Management. 5. The American Elm: A Fatal Journey. 6. The Redwood: Why Save a Tree?
Six animated filmstrips make a powerful
case for conservation by depicting the life
histories of 4 endangered species, one that
has been saved, and a sixth for which it is
too late.

WILDSMITH, BRIAN

SOUND FILMSTRIP SET 35 (Filmstrip—
Sound). *See* Children's Literature—
Collections

WILLIAMS-ELLIS, AMABEL

PUSS IN BOOTS AND OTHER FAIRY
TALES FROM AROUND THE WORLD
(Phonodisc or Cassette). *See* Fairy Tales

RUSSIAN FAIRY TALES (Phonodisc or Cassette). *See* Folklore—Russia

SNOW WHITE AND OTHER FAIRY TALES
(Phonodisc or Cassette). *See* Fairy Tales

WILLIAMS, MARGERY

THE VELVETEEN RABBIT (Filmstrip—
Sound). *See* Fantasy—Fiction

WILSON, LIONEL

THE MULE WHO REFUSED TO BUDGE
(Filmstrip—Sound/Captioned). *See*
Cooperation—Fiction

WINDOWS IN THE SEA

THE WORLD OF INNERSPACE (Filmstrip—
Sound). *See* Oceanography

WINDS

LEARNING ABOUT AIR (Motion Picture—
16mm—Sound). *See* Air

WINTER

WINTER IN THE FOREST (Filmstrip—
Sound). AIDS, 1974. 4 color, sound film-
strips, av. 50 fr. ea.; 4 cassettes or 4 discs,
av. 12 min. ea.; Teacher's Guide. ($72).
Gr. 4-10. BKL (11/74). 525
Contents: 1. Enjoying the Woodlands. 2.
Looking Closely at Forest Trees. 3. A
School and a Sawmill. 4. Sweets from the
Forest.
The inquiry method is used to take the
viewer into the forest in the winter to in-
crease awareness of problems, adventure,
concepts, and relationships in nature.

WINTER—FICTION

THE TOMTEN AND THE FOX (Filmstrip—
Sound). *See* Foxes—Stories

WINTER SPORTS

BOBSLEDDING: DOWN THE CHUTE (Kit).
Troll Associates, 1976 (Troll Reading Program). 1 color, sound filmstrip, 34 fr.; 1
cassettes, 14 min. 10 softcover books; 1
Library Edition; 4 Duplicating Masters; 1
Teacher's Guide. ($48). Gr. 4-9. BKL
(2/15/77). 796.95
This kit is based on the high interest/low
reading level of Ed Radlauer's material.
The filmstrip and cassette duplicate the text
of the book.

WIT AND HUMOR

BARON MUNCHAUSEN TRULY TALL TALES (Phonodisc or Cassette). *See* Legends

FARMER PALMER'S WAGON RIDE (Filmstrip–Sound). *See* Animals–Fiction

HARRY THE DIRTY DOG (Filmstrip–Sound). *See* Dogs–Fiction

HORTON HEARS A WHO! AND HORTON HATCHES THE EGG (Kit). Random House, 1977. 4 color, sound filmstrips, 45–86 fr.; 4 cassettes or discs, 5–10:22 min.; 2 books; Teacher's Guide. Cassette #04653-6 ($48), Discs #04652-8 ($48). Gr. K–3. BKL (9/15/77), PRV (12/77). Fic

The sets carefully follow the books on which they are based. In the first story, Horton, the elephant, hears a tiny voice that leads him to a microscopic world. In the second, Horton egg-sits for a lazy mother bird.

HOW THE GRINCH STOLE CHRISTMAS (Kit). Random House, 1976. 2 color, sound filmstrips, 42–61 fr.; 2 cassettes or discs, 7–10 min.; 1 book; 1 Poster; Teacher's Guide; 1 Catalog Card. Cassettes #04123 ($48), Discs #04122 ($48). Gr. K–3. BKL (3/15/77), PRV (9/77), PVB (4/15/78). Fic

Based on the book by Geisel (Dr. Seuss) with some added colors on the filmstrip reproduction of the illustrations in the book, this filmstrip adaptation is narrated by Zero Mostel. The moral of the story, that Christmas is not dependent on material things, is clearly conveyed.

HUCKLEBERRY FINN (Phonodisc or Cassette). *See* U.S.–Social Life and Customs

HUCKLEBERRY FINN (Cassette). *See* U.S.–Social Life and Customs

THE PETERKIN PAPERS (Phonodisc or Cassette). *See* Family Life–Fiction

PIPPI LONGSTOCKING (Phonodisc or Cassette). *See* Sweden–Fiction

THE SNEETCHES AND OTHER STORIES (Kit). *See* Stories in Rhyme

YERTLE THE TURTLE AND OTHER STORIES (Kit). Random House, 1977. 4 color, sound filmstrips, 31–71 fr.; 4 cassettes or discs; 4–9 min.; 1 book; Teacher's Guide. Cassettes #04644-7 ($78), Discs #0464505 ($78). Gr. 1–3. BKL (1/78), PRV (4/78). Fic

Contents: 1. Yertle the Turtle. 2. Gertrude McFuzz. 3. The Big Bragg.

The first Dr. Seuss favorite is about Yertle, King of the Pond, who becomes a dictator trying to rise on the backs of his turtle subjects. How he is unseated is a gentle reminder of the transient nature of power. Then Gertrude, who wanted a beautiful tail, finds that a tail can sometimes wag a bird. And bragging can reach the point where the braggart finds that even a worm is smarter than he is.

WOLVES

ONCE AROUND THE SUN (Filmstrip–Sound). *See* Seasons

WOLF FAMILY (Film Loop–8mm–Silent). Walt Disney Educational Media, 1966. 8mm color, silent film loop, approx. 4 min. #62-5356L ($30). Gr. K–12. MDU (1974). 599.74

A wolf family is studied as it hunts for food in the Arctic.

THE WOLVES OF ISLE ROYALE (Kit). Classroom Complements/EBEC, 1976 (Animal Life Stories). 1 color, sound filmstrip; 1 cassette; 5 identical Storybooks; Teacher's Guide. #6969K ($27.95). Gr. K–6. TEA (11/77). 599.74

Young readers can learn how animals live, move, build homes, and fight for food and survival. A scientifically accurate story describes the life of wolves in their natural habitat. A 56-page storybook reproduces all the narration and pictures from the filmstrip.

WOLVES–FICTION

JULIE OF THE WOLVES (Phonodisc or Cassette). *See* Eskimos–Fiction

WOMEN–BIOGRAPHY

CHILDHOOD OF FAMOUS WOMEN, VOLUME THREE (Cassette). H. Wilson, 1975. 2 cassettes; Student Response Sheets; Teacher's Guide. #S31-CT ($17.50). Gr. 4–8. PRV (11/70). 920

A collection of dramatized biographies featuring Edna St. Vincent Millay, Marie Curie, Louisa May Alcott, and Anne Sullivan. An attempt is made to describe the motivation behind the later successes of these women.

WOMEN WHO WIN, SET 1 (Kit). *See* Athletes

WOMEN WHO WIN, SET 2 (Kit). *See* Athletes

WOMEN WHO WIN, SET 3 (Kit). *See* Athletes

WOMEN WHO WIN, SET 4 (Kit). *See* Athletes

WOMEN–EMPLOYMENT

JOBS IN THE CITY–WOMEN AT WORK (Motion Picture–16mm–Sound). Centron

WOMEN—EMPLOYMENT (cont.)

Films, 1972 (Jobs in the City). 16mm color, sound film, 11 min.; Leader's Guide. ($175). Gr. 2-5. BKL (1/1/73). 331.4
Shows women at work as newspaper printers, physicians, and computer key punch operators, as well as other occupations including bank tellers, pilots, mathematicians, aircraft executives, and television commentators.

NEW HORIZONS FOR WOMEN (Filmstrip—Sound). Associated Press/Pathescope Educational Media, 1976 (People at Work). 1 color, sound filmstrip, 58 fr.; 1 cassette, 7:04 min.; Teacher's Guide; 10 Spirit Masters. #9036 ($28). Gr. 4-6. PRV (10/76). PVB (4/77). 331.4
This filmstrip presents a variety of themes concerning the transition women have made from homemakers to participants in the world of work. The history of women as workers, job discrimination that women face, the impact of day-care centers, and the effect of women on the labor market are covered.

WHY MOTHERS WORK (Motion Picture—16mm—Sound). EBEC, 1976. 16 color, sound film, 19 min. #3485 ($255). Gr. K-8. LFR (5/6/77), PRV (5/77). 331.4
Two working mothers tell why they hold jobs and reveal their hopes for the future as viewers share a long, busy day in the life of each woman.

WOMEN—SUFFRAGE

AMERICA ROCK (Filmstrip—Sound). See U.S.—History

WOMEN—U.S.

WOMEN: AN AMERICAN HISTORY (Filmstrip—Sound). EBEC, 1976. 6 color, sound filmstrips, av. 100 fr. ea.; 6 cassettes or discs, 17 min. ea.; Teacher's Guide. Discs #6916 ($86.95), Cassettes #6916K ($86.95). Gr. 5-A. LGB (75/76), LNG (12/76), MDU (1/77). 301.41
Contents: 1. Women of the New World. 2. The Mill Girl and the Lady. 3. The Fight for Equality. 4. A Combination of Work and Hope. 5. Beyond the Vote. 6. The Modern Women's Movement.
Six filmstrips trace 350 years in the history of the American woman from her paradoxical colonial role as a valued helpmate—who was legally a "nonperson"—to the many-faceted woman of the 1970s. In between, viewers see how it all came about. Throughout the series, outstanding women of history and of today's complex world come dramatically to life.

WOMEN IN AMERICAN HISTORY (Filmstrip—Sound). Activity Records/Educational Activities, 1974. 6 color, sound filmstrips, 50-65 fr.; 3 discs or cassettes, 12-15 min.; Teacher's Guide. Disc #FSR 460 ($61.95), Cassette #FSC 460 ($64.95). Gr. 5-12. PRV (10/75), PVB (4/76). 301.41
Contents: 1. The Colonies. 2. After the Revolution. 3. Slavery and Suffrage. 4. Reformers. 5. The Artists. 6. Crisis of Identity.
These strips present an accurate history of women's experiences in America. Their struggle for justice and equality and their contributions to American life are shown through memorable vignettes from the lives of outstanding women and brief excerpts from their speeches and writings. Discrimination in law, politics, religion, education, work, etc., is vividly revealed.

THE WONDER BOOK

KING MIDAS AND THE GOLDEN TOUCH (Cassette). See Mythology, Classical

WONDER, STEVIE

MEN BEHIND THE BRIGHT LIGHTS (Kit). See Musicians

WOOD, JOYCE

GRANDMOTHER LUCY IN HER GARDEN (Filmstrip—Sound/Captioned). See Grandparents—Fiction

WOOL—FICTION

CHARLIE NEEDS A CLOAK (Motion Picture—16mm—Sound). See Clothing and Dress—Fiction

WORDS. See Vocabulary

WORK

CAREER EDUCATION FOR PRIMARY GRADES (Filmstrip—Sound). See Occupations

SOMETHING SPECIAL—WORK (Filmstrip—Sound). Society for Visual Education, 1976. 6 color, sound filmstrips, av. 37-47 fr.; 6 cassettes or discs, av. 7-9 min. Discs #A231-SBR ($99), Cassettes #A231-SBTC ($99). Gr. 1-5. BKL (6/15/77). 331.1
Contents: 1. Pennies, Nickels and Dimes. 2. We Wrote Their Readers. 3. What's Your Specialty? 4. Money: One of Work's Rewards. 5. Math—Who Needs It? 6. The Joy of Giving.
This set introduces some basic economics and career-related concepts in brief story formats.

WHY WE WORK (Filmstrip—Sound). Educational Direction/Learning Tree Filmstrips, 1977. 4 color, sound filmstrips, av. 49 fr. ea.; 4 cassettes, av. 7–8 min. ea.; Teacher's Guide. ($58). Gr. 3–8. FLN (9/10/77), IFT (1977), LGB (1977). 331.1

Contents: 1. Things We Need. 2. Things We Want. 3. Liking a Job. 4. Everyone Works.

Introduction to the various aspects of work. Emphasizes different reasons to work—satisfaction of basic needs and desires, personal development, achievement, peer consideration, etc.—and discusses kinds of work we all do at different stages in our lives.

WORKING (Filmstrip—Sound). BFA Educational Media, 1974. 4 color, sound filmstrips; 4 cassettes or discs; 20 Activity Master Sheets. Cassettes #VEK000 ($74.50), Discs #VEJ000 ($74.50). Gr. 4–8. BKL (5/1/75). 331.1

Contents: 1. Why Work? 2. What You're Worth. 3. On-the-Job. 4. Forecast for the Future.

This series examines the reasons people work, the economic structure of work, the training and experience needed for different jobs, and the future of work.

WORLD WAR, 1914–1918

HAYWIRE MAC (Phonodiscs). *See* Folk Songs

WORLD WAR, 1939–1945—JEWS

THE DIARY OF ANNE FRANK (Filmstrip—Sound). *See* Biography

WRITING (AUTHORSHIP). *See* English Language—Composition and Exercises

WYSS, JOHANN

SWISS FAMILY ROBINSON (Phonodisc or Cassette). *See* Adventure and Adventurers—Fiction

YATES, ELIZABETH

ELIZABETH YATES (Filmstrip—Sound). Miller-Brody Productions, 1976 (Meet the Newbery Author). 1 color, sound filmstrip, 113 fr.; 1 cassette or disc, 19 min. Cassette #MNA-1009-C ($32), Disc #MNA-1009-R ($32). Gr. 5–12. BKL (12/15/76). 921

Intimate family photos from Elizabeth Yate's childhood and adult adventures document the life of this vibrant individual and provide an authentic note to the story of a well-known author.

YOLEN, JANE

THE EMPEROR AND THE KITE (Filmstrip—Sound/Captioned). *See* China—Fiction

YOUNG, ED

THE EMPEROR AND THE KITE (Filmstrip—Sound/Captioned). *See* China—Fiction

YOUNG, SCOTT

HOCKEY HEROES (Kit). *See* Athletes

ZEBRAS

ZEBRA (Motion Picture—16mm—Sound). EBEC, 1971 (Silent Safari). 16mm color, sound, narrationless film, 10 min.; Teacher's Guide. #3122 ($150). Gr. K–9. BKL (10/1/76). 599.7

Zebras travel in large herds, in search of edible grasses and available water. Chief among their striking physical traits are the striped markings that help camouflage them. Scenes show zebras as sociable and playful, greeting each other with conversational barking noises, enjoying running games, and grooming each other with their teeth while they depend on friendly birds to signal approaching danger.

ZEMACH, HARVE

POPULAR PICTURE BOOKS FILMSTRIPS: SET THREE (Filmstrip—Sound). *See* Reading Materials

ZEMACH, KAETHE

POPULAR PICTURE BOOKS FILMSTRIPS: SET THREE (Filmstrip—Sound). *See* Reading Materials

ZEMACH, MARGOT

POPULAR PICTURE BOOKS FILMSTRIPS: SET THREE (Filmstrip—Sound). *See* Reading Materials

ZION, GENE

HARRY THE DIRTY DOG (Filmstrip—Sound). *See* Dogs—Fiction

ZOLOTOW, CHARLOTTE

DAYDREAMS AND MAKE BELIEVE (Filmstrip—Sound). *See* Fantasy—Fiction

ZOOLOGICAL GARDENS

MUSEUMS AND MAN (Filmstrip—Sound). *See* Museums.

ZOOLOGICAL GARDENS (cont.)

PANDAS: A GIFT FROM CHINA (Motion Picture—16mm—Sound). *See* Pandas

WHO'S WHO IN THE ZOO? (Motion Picture—16mm—Sound). Centron Films, 1974. 16mm color, sound film, 12 min.; Leader's Guide. ($190). Gr. 1–6. AAS (5/76), LFR (5/75), LGB. 590.23

Introduces a number of careers involving animal care, including zoo director, curators, keepers, and zoologist. Emphasizes concepts of work specialization, division of labor, chain of command, and job satisfaction.

ZOOFARI (Filmstrip—Sound). Lyceum/ Mook & Blanchard, 1972. 2 color, sound filmstrips, av. 53 fr.; 2 cassettes or discs, 8:30–14:30 min.; Teacher's Guide. Cassettes #LY35573SC ($46), Discs #LY35573SR ($37). Gr. 3–8. FLN (2/73), PRV (9/72), PVB (5/73). 590.74

Contents: 1. New at the Zoo. 2. Safari: North American Style.

The objective of this set is to explore the varieties of animal life available in animal parks and to understand the attempts that are made to provide natural surroundings for the animals.

ZOOLOGY

ADVENTURES OF WILD ANIMALS (Filmstrip—Sound). Society for Visual Education, 1972. 6 color, sound filmstrips, 51–56 fr.; 3 cassettes or discs, 10-1/2 –
13 min.; 6 Guides. Discs #126SAR ($78), Cassettes #126SATC ($78). Gr. 3–6. BKL (9/73), PRV (5/73). 591

Contents: 1. Baleena the Blue Whale. 2. Jamboo the African Elephant. 3. Glu the Emperor Penguin. 4. Kiboko the African Hippo. 5. Marsu the Red Kangaroo. 6. Necki the African Giraffe.

The adventurous lives of 6 wild animals are realistically portrayed in these fascinating sound filmstrips. Colorful artwork and exciting narration take viewers to 3 different continents—Africa, Australia, Antarctica—where they meet and study various wild animals and their life-styles.

ANIMALS AND THEIR WORLD (Filmstrip— Sound). University Films/McGraw-Hill Films, 1975. 6 color, sound filmstrips, av. 60 fr.; 6 cassettes or discs, 12 min.; Teacher's Guide. Cassette #102590-1 ($109), Discs #103984-8 ($109). Gr. 4–6. ABT (9/76), CPR (11/75), PRV (10/76). 591

Contents: 1. Mammals. 2. Birds. 3. Reptiles. 4. Amphibians. 5. Fish. 6. Insects.

An examination of the 6 major groups of animals: mammals, birds, reptiles, amphibians, fish, and insects. Color photographs show how the animals in each group are alike, how they differ, how they develop and grow, where and how they live, and their contribution to the total ecological system. Open-ended questions throughout the filmstrips stimulate discussion.

BABOONS AND THEIR YOUNG (Film Loop—8mm—Silent). *See* Baboons

MEDIA INDEXED BY TITLE

A. J. Miller's West: The Plains Indian—1837—Slide Set (Slides) *Indians of North America—Paintings*

ABC's of Environment (Filmstrip—Sound) *Ecology*

The ABC's of Phonics, Program One (Kit) *Phonetics*

The ABC's of Phonics, Program Two: Consonant Letters M–Z (Kit) *Phonetics*

Across Five Aprils (Filmstrip—Sound) *U.S.—History—1861–1865—Civil War—Fiction*

Adobe Oven Building (Film Loop—8mm—Silent) *Indians of North America*

Adventures in Imagination Series (Filmstrip—Sound) *English Language—Composition and Exercises*

Adventures in the World of Work, Set One (Kit) *Vocational Guidance*

Adventures in the World of Work, Set Two (Kit) *Vocational Guidance*

Adventures of Robin Hood, Volume 1: How Robin Became an Outlaw (Phonodisc or Cassette) *Folklore—England*

Adventures of Robin Hood, Volume 2: Outlaw of Sherwood Forest (Phonodisc or Cassette) *Folklore—England*

Adventures of Robin Hood, Volume 3: Adventures with Little John (Phonodisc or Cassette) *Folklore—England*

Adventures of Robin Hood, Volume 4: Robin and His Merry Men (Phonodisc or Cassette) *Folklore—England*

The Adventures of Supernut, Set One (Filmstrip—Sound) *Hygiene*

Adventures of Wild Animals (Filmstrip—Sound) *Zoology*

An Aesop Anthology (Filmstrip—Sound) *Fables*

Aesop's Fables (Phonodisc or Cassette) *Fables*

Aesthetics (Filmstrip—Sound) *Environment*

Africa: Portrait of a Continent (Filmstrip—Sound) *Africa*

African Cliff Dwellers: The Dogon People of Mali, Part One (Kit) *Africa*

African Cliff Dwellers: The Dogon People of Mali, Part Two (Kit) *Africa*

Age of Exploration and Discovery (Filmstrip—Sound) *Explorers*

Air Travel Today (Filmstrip—Sound) *Air Lines*

Aircraft: Their Power and Control (Filmstrip—Sound) *Aeronautics*

Alaska: The Big Land and Its People (Filmstrip—Sound) *Alaska*

Alcohol and Alcoholism (Filmstrip—Sound) *Alcoholism*

Alcohol and Alcoholism: The Drug and the Disease (Filmstrip—Sound) *Alcoholism*

Algiers: A Step into the Future, a Step into the Past (Filmstrip—Sound) *Algeria*

Alice in Consumerland (Filmstrip—Sound) *Consumer Education*

Alice in Wonderland (Kit) *Fantasy—Fiction*

All about Dinosaurs (Filmstrip—Sound) *Dinosaurs*

All about Fire (Motion Picture—16mm—Sound) *Fire Prevention*

All about Lice (Filmstrip—Sound) *Lice*

All about Rivers (Filmstrip—Sound) *Rivers*

Alligator—Birth and Survival (Film Loop—8mm—Silent) *Alligators*

Along Nature Trails (Film Loop—8mm—Silent) *Natural History*

Amazon Jungle (Film Loop—8mm—Silent) *Forest and Forestry*

America Dances (Phonodisc or Cassette) *Folk Dancing*

America in Art: The American Revolution (Filmstrip—Sound) *U.S.—History—1775–1783—Revolution*

America Rock (Filmstrip—Sound) *U.S.—History*

America Sings (Phonodisc or Cassette) *Folk Songs*

American Folk Arts (Filmstrip—Sound) *Folk Art, American*

American Folk Dancers (Phonodisc or Cassette) *Folk Dancing*

American Folk Dances (Phonodiscs) *Folk Dancing*

American Folk Songs for Children (Phonodiscs) *Folk Songs—U.S.*

American Folklore (Filmstrip—Sound) *Folklore—U.S.*

American History: In Ballad and Song, Volume One (Phonodiscs) *Ballads, American*

American History: In Ballad and Song, Volume Two (Phonodiscs) *Ballads, American*

American History on Stamps (Kit) *Postage Stamps*

American Indian Poetry (Filmstrip—Sound) *Indians of North America—Poetry*

American Indians of the North Pacific Coast (Filmstrip—Sound) *Indians of North America*

American Indians of the Northeast (Filmstrip—Sound) *Indians of North America*

American Indians of the Southeast (Filmstrip—Sound) *Indians of North America*

American Poetry to 1900 (Phonodiscs) *American Poetry*

An American Sampler (Filmstrip—Sound) *U.S.—Social Life and Customs*

American Scenes (Phonodiscs) *Orchestral Music*

American Sings (Phonodisc or Cassette) *Folk Songs*

Americana Plus Fifty (Kit) *U.S.—History*

America's Ethnic Heritage—Growth and Expansion (Filmstrip—Sound) *Minorities*

The Amish: A People of Preservation (Motion Picture—16mm—Sound) *Amish*

Amphibians (Filmstrip—Sound) *Amphibians*

Anansi the Spider (Filmstrip—Sound) *Folklore—Africa*

Anansi the Spider (Motion Picture—16mm—Sound) *Folklore—Africa*

Ancient Egypt: Land/People/Art (Filmstrip—Sound) *Egypt—Antiquities*

And then What Happened? (Filmstrip—Sound) *English Language—Composition and Exercises*

The Andean Lands (Filmstrip—Sound) *South America*

Andersen's Fairy Tales (Filmstrip—Sound) *Fairy Tales*

Angel and Big Joe (Motion Picture—16mm—Sound) *Values—Fiction*

Angiosperms: The Life Cycle of a Strawberry (Film Loop—8mm—Captioned) *Growth (Plants)*

Animal Kingdom, Set One (Filmstrip—Sound) *Animals*

Animal Pets (Filmstrip—Sound) *Pets*

Animals and How They Grow (Filmstrip—Sound) *Animals*

Animals and Their World (Filmstrip—Sound) *Zoology*

Animals, Animals (Filmstrip—Sound) *Animals—Habits and Behavior*

Animals Around You (Filmstrip—Sound) *Animals—Habits and Behavior*

Animals in Different Communities (Filmstrip—Sound/Captioned) *Animals—Habits and Behavior*

Animals of Africa (Motion Picture—16mm—Sound) *Animals—Africa*

Animals We See Around Us (Filmstrip—Captioned) *Animals—Habits and Behavior*

Antarctic Penguins (Film Loop—8mm—Silent) *Penguins*

Antarctica: The White Continent (Filmstrip—Sound) *Antarctic Regions*

The Arab World (Kit) *Arabs*

Arithme-toons, Units One and Two (Kit) *Arithmetic*

Around Indian Campfires (Cassette) *Indians of North America*

Arrow to the Sun (Motion Picture—16mm—Sound) *Indians of North America—Legends*

Art of Dave Brubeck: The Fantasy Years (Phonodiscs) *Jazz*

The Art of Mosaics (Filmstrip—Sound) *Mosaics*

Art of Persepolis (Slides) *Iran—Antiquities*

The Art of Seeing (Filmstrip—Sound) *Art Appreciation*

The Arts of Japan—Slide Set (Slides) *Art, Japanese*

As I Was Crossing Boston Common (Filmstrip—Sound/Captioned) *Animals—Fiction*

As Long as the Grass is Green (Motion Picture—16mm—Sound) *Indians of North America*

As Long as the Grass Shall Grow (Phonodiscs) *Folk Songs, Indian*

At Your Age (Motion Picture—16mm—Sound) *Child Development*

At Your Fingertips (Filmstrip—Sound) *Handicraft*

Attitudes Unit (Motion Picture—16mm—Sound) *Attitude (Psychology)*

Audubon's Shore Birds (Motion Picture—16mm—Sound) *Water Birds*

Australia and New Zealand (Filmstrip—Sound) *Australia*

Auto Racing: Something for Everyone (Kit) *Automobile Racing*

Autumn in the Forest (Filmstrip—Sound) *Autumn*

Baboons and their Young (Film Loop—8mm—Silent) *Baboons*

Backyard Science Series One: Ants, Bees, Beetles, Crickets (Filmstrip—Sound) *Natural History*

Backyard Science Series Two: Spiders, Snails, Fish, Reptiles (Filmstrip—Sound) *Natural History*

Balablok (Motion Picture—16mm—Sound) *Prejudices and Antipathies*

The Bangers (Cassette) *Percussion Instruments*

The Book of Dragons (Phonodisc or Cassette) *Dragons—Fiction*

Books Talk Back (Filmstrip—Sound) *Books*

Boomsville (Motion Picture—16mm—Sound) *Cities and Towns*

The Borrowers (Phonodisc or Cassette) *Fantasy—Fiction*

Bottlenose Dolphin (Film Loop—8mm—Silent) *Dolphins*

Boxing (Kit) *Boxing*

A Boy Creates (Motion Picture—16mm—Sound) *Sculpture*

Brazil (Filmstrip—Sound) *Brazil*

Brian Wildsmith from A–Z (Study Print) *Alphabet*

The Bridge (Filmstrip—Sound/Captioned) *Human Relations—Fiction*

The British Isles: Scotland and Ireland (Filmstrip—Sound) *Scotland*

The Bronze Zoo (Motion Picture—16mm—Sound) *Sculpture*

The Brown Trout (Film Loop—8mm—Captioned) *Trout*

Buon Giorno: Good Morning Teacher (Filmstrip—Sound) *Italy—Social Life and Customs*

Butterfly: The Monarch's Life Cycle (Motion Picture—16mm—Sound) *Butterflies*

Cactus: Profile of a Plant (Motion Picture—16mm—Sound) *Cactus*

Calendar Studies (Filmstrip—Sound) *Calendars*

Call of the Wild (Filmstrip—Sound) *Dogs—Fiction*

Camping (Filmstrip—Sound) *Camping*

Can You Describe It? (Filmstrip—Captioned) *Senses and Sensation*

Can You Do It? (Filmstrip—Captioned) *Communication*

Can You Imagine? (Filmstrip—Sound) *Decision Making*

Can You Name It? (Filmstrip—Captioned) *Vocabulary*

Canada (Filmstrip—Sound) *Canada*

Canada: Land of New Wealth (Filmstrip—Sound) *Canada*

Canada: Northern Giant (Filmstrip—Sound) *Canada*

The Canadians (Filmstrip—Sound) *Canada*

Canyon De Chelly Dwellings (Film Loop—8mm—Silent) *Cliff Dwellers and Cliff Dwellings*

Career Awareness Field Trips (Filmstrip—Sound). *Vocational Guidance*

Career Education for Primary Grades (Filmstrip—Sound). *Occupations*

Career Kaleidoscope (Filmstrip—Sound) *Occupations*

The Caretaker's Dilemma (Motion Picture—16mm—Sound) *Arithmetic*

Carol Ryrie Brink (Filmstrip—Sound) *Brink, Carol Ryrie*

The Cat that Walked by Himself and Other Just So Stories (Phonodisc or Cassette) *Animals—Fiction*

The Catcher (Film Loop—8mm—Silent) *Softball*

Catching Above Waist/Below Waist (Film Loop—8mm—Silent) *Softball*

Center for a Field Goal (Film Loop—8mm—Silent) *Football*

Center Snap for Punt (Film Loop—8mm—Silent) *Football*

Center to Quarterback Exchange (Film Loop—8mm—Silent) *Football*

Central America: Finding New Ways (Motion Picture—16mm—Sound) *Central America*

Changing Seasons: The Story of a Year (Film Loop—8mm—Silent) *Seasons*

Changing the Face of Things (Filmstrip) *Design, Decorative*

Chaplin—A Character Is Born (Motion Picture—16mm—Sound) *Chaplin, Charles Spencer*

Charlie and the Chocolate Factory (Phonodisc or Cassette) *Fantasy—Fiction*

Charlie Needs a Cloak (Motion Picture—16mm—Sound) *Clothing and Dress—Fiction*

Charlotte's Web (Cassette) *Spiders—Fiction*

Charlotte's Web (Filmstrip—Sound) *Spiders—Fiction*

Cheetah (Motion Picture—16mm—Sound) *Cheetahs*

The Cheetahs of the Serengeti Plain (Kit) *Cheetahs*

Chest Pass/Bounce Pass (Film Loop—8mm—Silent) *Basketball*

Chest Pass/Overhead Pass (Film Loop—8mm—Silent) *Basketball*

Chickens (Film Loop—8mm—Silent) *Chickens*

Chiefs and Leaders (Cassette) *Indians of North America*

Childhood of Famous Women, Volume Three (Cassette) *Women—Biography*

Children Everywhere (Filmstrip—Sound) *Individuality*

Children's Rhythms in Symphony (Phonodiscs) *Rhythms*

China . . . a Place of Mystery (Filmstrip—Sound) *China*

China: People, Places and Progress (Filmstrip—Sound) *China—Civilization*

Chinese Country Children (Filmstrip—Sound) *China—Social Life and Customs*

Chinese Fairy Tales (Phonodisc or Cassette) *Fairy Tales*

Chiquitin and the Devil: A Puerto Rican Folktale (Filmstrip—Sound) *Folklore—Puerto Rico*

Chitty Chitty Bang Bang (Phonodisc or Cassette) *Automobiles—Fiction*

A Christmas Carol (Kit) *Christmas—Fiction*

A Christmas Carol (Phonodisc or Cassette) *Christmas—Fiction*

Developing Effective Study Skills (Filmstrip–Sound) *Study, Method of*

Developing Study Skills (Filmstrip–Sound) *Study, Method of*

Dewey Decimal Classification (Filmstrip–Sound) *Classification, Dewey Decimal*

The Diary of Anne Frank (Filmstrip–Sound) *Biography*

Dick Whittington and His Cat and Other English Tales (Phonodisc or Cassette) *Folklore–England*

The Dictionary (Filmstrip–Sound) *English Language–Dictionaries*

Dictionary Skill Box (Cassette) *English Language–Dictionaries*

Digging Up America's Past (Filmstrip–Sound) *America–Antiquities*

Dinosaur Tales (Filmstrip–Sound) *Dinosaurs*

Discovering New Words (Filmstrip–Sound) *Vocabulary*

Discovering Our Environment (Study Print) *Environment*

Discovering Rocks and Minerals (Filmstrip–Sound) *Geology*

Discovering Simple Machines (Filmstrip–Sound) *Machinery*

Discovering the Powers of Nature (Filmstrip–Sound) *Natural Disasters*

Divided Man, Commitment or Compromise? (Motion Picture–16mm–Sound) *Decision Making*

Doctor Seuss: Happy Birthday to You (Phonodisc or Cassette) *Stories in Rhyme*

The Doctor Seuss Read Along Set One (Kit) *Reading–Study and Teaching*

The Doctor Seuss Read Along Set Two (Kit) *Reading–Study and Teaching*

Documentary on Canada (Filmstrip–Sound) *Canada*

Donald in Mathmagic Land (Filmstrip–Sound) *Mathematics*

Don't (Motion Picture–16mm–Sound) *Butterflies*

Don't You Love Me Anymore? (Filmstrip–Sound) *Divorce*

Dorothy and the Necklace (Motion Picture–16mm–Sound) *Parrots–Fiction*

Dorothy and the Parrot (Motion Picture–16mm–Sound) *Parrots–Fiction*

Dorothy and the Pop-Singer (Motion Picture–16mm–Sound) *Parrots–Fiction*

Dorothy and the Witch (Motion Picture–16mm–Sound) *Parrots–Fiction*

Double Play by Short Stop/Second Base Woman (Film Loop–8mm–Silent) *Softball*

Dr. Dolittle (Filmstrip–Sound) *Animals–Fiction*

Dragstrip Challenge (Kit) *Automobile Racing*

Dribbling (Film Loop–8mm–Silent) *Soccer*

Drive/Crossover Drive (Film Loop–8mm–Silent) *Basketball*

Ducks (Motion Picture–8mm–Sound or Captioned) *Ducks–Fiction*

Dumbo (Kit) *Elephants–Fiction*

Early American History (Study Print) *U.S.–History*

Early Learning Library (Filmstrip–Sound) *Child Development*

Early Transportation (Study Print) *Transportation in Literature and Art*

The Earth (Filmstrip–Sound) *Geology*

Earth and Universe Series, Set 1 (Filmstrip–Sound) *Geology*

Earth and Universe Series, Set 2 (Filmstrip–Sound) *Geology*

Earth and Universe Series, Set 3 (Filmstrip–Sound) *Universe*

Earth Science Loops Series, Set Two (Film Loop–8mm–Silent) *Geology*

The Earth's Resources (Filmstrip–Captioned) *Natural Resources*

East Central Europe, Group One (Filmstrip–Sound) *Central Europe*

Eastern Europe from Within (Filmstrip–Sound) *Eastern Europe*

Ecological Communities (Filmstrip–Sound) *Ecology*

Ecology and the Role of Man (Filmstrip–Sound) *Wildlife Conservation*

Ecology: Balance of Nature (Filmstrip–Sound) *Ecology*

Ecology: Exploration and Discovery (Filmstrip–Sound) *Ecology*

The Ecology of a Desert: Death Valley (Filmstrip–Sound) *Deserts*

The Ecology of a Temperate Rain Forest (Filmstrip–Sound) *Rain Forests*

Ecology: Spaceship Earth (Filmstrip–Sound) *Ecology*

Ecology: Understanding the Crisis (Filmstrip–Sound) *Ecology*

Economics for Primaries (Filmstrip–Sound) *Consumer Education*

Edible Art (Filmstrip–Sound) *Cookery*

Eleanor Estes (Filmstrip–Sound) *Authors*

Elementary Natural Science–Small Predatory Mammal (Motion Picture–16mm–Sound) *Mammals*

Elementary Natural Science–Songbirds (Motion Picture–16mm–Sound) *Birds*

Elephant (Motion Picture–16mm–Sound) *Elephants*

Elizabeth Yates (Filmstrip–Sound) *Yates, Elizabeth*

Embryology of the Chick (Film Loop–8mm–Captioned) *Embryology*

The Emperer and the Kite (Filmstrip–Sound/Captioned) *China–Fiction*

The Emperor's New Clothes and Other Tales (Phonodisc or Cassette) *Fairy Tales*

Endangered Species: Birds (Study Print) *Rare Birds*

Endangered Species: Mammals (Study Print) *Rare Animals*

Endangered Species: Reptiles and Amphibians (Study Print) *Rare Reptiles*

Energy and Our Environment (Filmstrip—Sound) *Ecology*

Energy and the Earth (Filmstrip—Sound) *Conservation of Natural Resources*

Energy: Crisis and Resolution (Filmstrip—Sound) *Power Resources*

Energy for the Future (Motion Picture—16mm—Sound) *Power Resources*

English Composition for Children, Set 1 (Filmstrip—Sound) *English Language—Study and Teaching*

English Composition for Children, Set 2 (Filmstrip—Sound) *English Language—Study and Teaching*

English Composition for Children, Set 3 (Filmstrip—Sound) *English Language—Study and Teaching*

English Composition for Children, Set 4 (Filmstrip—Sound) *English Language—Study and Teaching*

English Composition for Children, Set 5 (Filmstrip—Sound) *English Language—Study and Teaching*

Enjoying the Seasons (Film Loop—8mm—Captioned) *Seasons*

Environmental Awareness (Filmstrip—Sound) *Natural History*

Environmental Decisions: An Inquiry (Filmstrip—Captioned) *Ecology*

Environmental Studies Series (Filmstrip—Sound) *Pollution*

Episodes from Famous Stories (Filmstrip—Sound) *Literature—Collections*

The Erie Canal (Filmstrip—Sound) *Erie Canal—Songs*

European Geography, Set Four (Filmstrip—Sound) *Scotland*

Experiences in Perceptual Growth (Filmstrip—Sound) *Perception*

Exploring Ecology (Filmstrip—Sound) *Ecology*

Exploring My Identity, Unit One (Filmstrip—Sound) *Individuality*

Exploring the Earth around Us (Filmstrip—Sound) *Geology*

Exploring the Seasons (Filmstrip—Sound) *Seasons*

Exploring the World of Maps (Filmstrip—Sound) *Maps*

Expressing Myself, Unit Two (Filmstrip—Sound) *Individuality*

Fables of India (Phonodisc or Cassette) *Fables*

Faces (Motion Picture—16mm—Sound) *Senses and Sensation*

Fairy Tales of the Brothers Grimm (Kit) *Fairy Tales*

Fall Brings Changes, Second Edition (Motion Picture—16mm—Sound) *Autumn*

Familias Norteamericanas—American Families (Filmstrip—Sound) *Family Life*

Families: Alike and Different (Motion Picture—16mm—Sound) *Family Life*

Families Around the World (Filmstrip—Sound) *Family Life*

Families of Asia (Filmstrip—Sound) *Asia*

Families of South America (Filmstrip—Sound) *South America*

Families of the Dry Muslim World (Filmstrip—Sound) *Middle East—Social Life and Customs*

Families of West Africa: Farmers and Fishermen (Filmstrip—Sound) *Africa, West*

The Family (Art Prints) *Family in Literature and Art*

Famous Patriots of the American Revolution (Filmstrip—Sound) *U.S.—History—Biography*

Famous Stories of Great Courage (Filmstrip—Sound) *Heroes and Heroines*

Fanciful Tales (Filmstrip—Sound) *Spanish Language—Reading Materials*

Farmer Palmer's Wagon Ride (Filmstrip—Sound) *Animals—Fiction*

Farming (Film Loop—8mm—Silent) *Frontier and Pioneer Life*

Farming (Filmstrip—Sound) *Vocational Guidance*

Fascinating Birds (Filmstrip—Sound) *Birds*

Feeling Fine (Filmstrip—Sound) *Health Education*

Feelings Unit (Motion Picture—16mm—Sound) *Emotions*

Field Goal and Extra Points (Film Loop—8mm—Silent) *Football*

Field Goal and Kickoff (Soccer Style) (Film Loop—8mm—Silent) *Football*

Fielding Long Hit Fly Ball/Ground Ball (Film Loop—8mm—Silent) *Softball*

Fire! (Motion Picture—16mm—Sound) *Forest Fires*

Fire and the Witch (Motion Picture—16mm—Sound) *Fire Prevention*

Fire in the Sea (Motion Picture—16mm—Sound) *Volcanoes*

Fire Mountain (Motion Picture—16mm—Sound) *Volcanoes*

Fire Safety—What's That? (Slides) *Fire Prevention*

First Aid for Little People (Kit) *First Aid*

The First American: Culture Patterns (Filmstrip—Sound) *Indians of North America*

First Choice Authors and Books (Filmstrip—Sound) *Authors*

The First Drum: How Music First Began (Filmstrip—Sound) *Drum*

First Ideas about Animals (Filmstrip—Sound) *Animals—Habits and Behavior*

Grassland Ecology—Habitats and Change (Motion Picture—16mm—Sound) *Grasslands*

The Great Big Enormous Turnip (Filmstrip—Sound) *Folklore—Russia*

Great Myths of Greece (Filmstrip—Sound) *Mythology, Classical*

The Great Quillow (Phonodisc or Cassette) *Giants—Fiction*

The Great Tigers of India (Kit) *Tigers*

The Grizzly (Kit) *Bears—Fiction*

The Grizzly and the Gadgets and Further Fables for Our Time (Phonodisc or Cassette) *Fables*

Guess What? (Filmstrip—Sound) *Listening*

Habitat (Filmstrip—Captioned) *Animals—Habits and Behavior*

Habits of Health: Food to Live and Grow (Motion Picture—16mm—Sound) *Nutrition*

Habits of Health: The Physical Examination (Motion Picture—16mm—Sound) *Hygiene*

Haiku: The Hidden Glimmering (Filmstrip—Sound) *Haiku*

Haiku: The Mood of Earth (Filmstrip—Sound) *Haiku*

Hand Off (Film Loop—8mm—Silent) *Football*

Hang Gliding: Riding the Wind (Kit) *Gliding and Soaring*

Hans Brinker, or the Silver Skates (Phonodisc or Cassette) *Netherlands—Fiction*

Hans Christian Andersen Cassette-Books (Kit) *Fairy Tales*

Hansel and Gretel and Other Fairy Tales by the Brothers Grimm (Phonodisc or Cassette) *Fairy Tales*

The Happy Lion Series, Set One (Filmstrip—Sound) *Lions—Fiction*

The Happy Lion Series, Set Two (Filmstrip—Sound) *Lions—Fiction*

The Happy Owls (Motion Picture—16mm—Sound) *Happiness—Fiction*

The Happy Prince and Other Oscar Wilde Fairy Tales (Phonodisc or Cassette) *Fairy Tales*

Harold's Fairy Tale (Motion Picture—16mm—Sound) *Fairy Tales*

Harry the Dirty Dog (Filmstrip—Sound) *Dogs—Fiction*

Hatching of a Chick (Film Loop—8mm—Silent) *Chickens*

The Hating Book (Kit) *Emotions*

Hawaii: The Fiftieth State (Filmstrip—Sound) *Hawaii*

Haywire Mac (Phonodiscs) *Folk Songs*

Heading and Back-Heading (Film Loop—8mm—Silent) *Soccer*

Health: A New Look (Filmstrip—Sound) *Hygiene*

Health and Your Body Unit (Motion Picture—16mm—Sound) *Hygiene*

Health Education (Filmstrip—Sound) *Hygiene*

A Healthy You (Filmstrip—Sound) *Hygiene*

Hear Better: Healthy Ears (Motion Picture—16mm—Sound) *Ear*

Hear It and Write (Filmstrip—Sound) *English Language—Composition and Exercises*

Heidi (Filmstrip—Sound) *Switzerland—Fiction*

Heidi (Phonodisc or Cassette) *Switzerland—Fiction*

Hello, I'm Music (Kit) *Music—Study and Teaching*

Help, I'm Shrinking (Motion Picture—16mm—Sound) *Self Realization*

Helping People Look their Best (Filmstrip—Sound) *Vocational Guidance*

Helping People Solve Problems (Filmstrip—Sound) *Vocational Guidance*

Heritage Stories (Filmstrip—Sound) *Minorities*

Heroes of the Iliad (Cassette) *Mythology, Classical*

Heroic Adventures (Filmstrip—Sound) *Legends*

Hide and Seek Fog (Filmstrip—Sound) *Fog—Fiction*

Hispanic Heroes of the U.S.A. (Kit) *Biography—Collections*

The Hoarder (Motion Picture—16mm—Sound) *Fables*

Hockey Heroes (Kit) *Athletes*

The Holiday Make-It-Yourself Kit (Filmstrip—Sound) *Holiday Decoration*

Holiday Rhythms (Phonodiscs) *Rhythms*

Holiday Songs (Phonodiscs) *Songs*

Holiday Tales Cassette Books (Kit) *Holidays—Fiction*

Holidays: Histories and Legends (Filmstrip—Sound) *Holidays*

Holidays: Set One (Filmstrip—Sound) *Holidays*

Home Life (Film Loop—8mm—Captioned) *Frontier and Pioneer Life*

The Honey Bee (Film Loop—8mm—Captioned) *Bees*

Hook Slide/Straight in Slide (Film Loop—8mm—Silent) *Softball*

Hopis—Guardians of the Land (Motion Picture—16mm—Sound) *Hopi*

Horizontal Belt Loom (Film Loop—8mm—Silent) *Looms*

Horses . . . to Care is to Love (Motion Picture—16mm—Sound) *Horses*

Horton Hears a Who! and Horton Hatches the Egg (Kit) *Wit and Humor*

The Hospital (Motion Picture—16mm—Sound) *Medical Care*

A Houseful of Ocean (Kit) *Children—Fiction*

How a Picture Book Is Made (Filmstrip—Sound) *Books*

How Beaver Stole Fire (Motion Picture—16mm—Sound) *Indians of North America—Legends*

How Can You Tell It's Living (Filmstrip—Sound) *Life (Biology)*

How Children Live in America (Filmstrip—Sound) *Children in the U.S.*

How Do You Feel? (Motion Picture—16mm—Sound) *Emotions*

How Do You Know What's Fair? (Filmstrip—Sound) *Values*

How Flowers Reproduce: The California Poppy (Study Print) *Plant Propagation*

How I Live in My World (Filmstrip) *Animals—Habits and Behavior*

How Money Works (Filmstrip—Sound) *Money*

How Our Continent Was Made (Filmstrip—Sound) *North America*

How the Grinch Stole Christmas (Kit) *Wit and Humor*

How to Build an Igloo—Slide Set (Slides) *Igloos*

How to Do: Slide Collage (Filmstrip—Sound) *Collage*

How to Tell Time (Filmstrip—Sound) *Time*

How to Use Maps and Globes (Filmstrip—Sound) *Maps*

How to Watch TV (Filmstrip—Sound) *Mass Media*

How We Grow (Filmstrip—Sound) *Child Development*

Huckleberry Finn (Cassette) *U.S.—Social Life and Customs*

Huckleberry Finn (Phonodisc or Cassette) *U.S.—Social Life and Customs*

The Human Body (Filmstrip—Sound) *Anatomy*

Human Body and How It Works (Filmstrip—Sound) *Anatomy*

The Human Body, Set One (Filmstrip—Sound) *Anatomy*

The Human Body, Set Two (Filmstrip—Sound) *Anatomy*

The Hungry Plant (Filmstrip—Sound) *Plants—Nutrition*

Hurray for Captain Jane! & Other Liberated Stories for Children (Phonodisc or Cassette) *Children's Literature—Collections*

Hurrying Hoof Beats: The Story of the Pony Express (Filmstrip—Sound) *Pony Express*

I Can, Unit One (Filmstrip—Sound) *Self Perception*

I Can, Unit Two (Filmstrip—Sound) *Self Perception*

Identity Three (Kit) *Child Development*

Identity Unit (Motion Picture—16mm—Sound) *Self Perception*

If Trees Can Fly (Motion Picture—16mm—Sound) *Imagination*

The Illustrated Man (Filmstrip—Sound) *Science Fiction*

Immigration and Migration (Motion Picture—16mm—Sound) *U.S.—History*

Lo Importante Que Eres (Filmstrip—Sound) *Self*

Imprinting in Ducklings (Film Loop—8mm—Silent) *Ducks*

India: Tradition and Change (Filmstrip—Sound) *India*

Indian Cliff Dwellings at Mesa Verde—Slide Set (Slides) *Cliff Dwellers and Dwellings*

Indian Legends (Filmstrip—Sound) *Indians of North America—Legends*

Indian Life in North America (Filmstrip—Sound) *Indians of North America*

An Indian Summer (Motion Picture—16mm—Sound) *Indians of North America*

Indian Tribes (Cassette) *Indians of North America*

Indians of North America (Filmstrip—Sound) *Indians of North America*

The Indians of North America (Filmstrip—Sound) *Indians of North America*

Inquiring into Weather (Filmstrip—Sound) *Weather Forecasting*

Insect Communities (Film Loop—8mm—Silent) *Insects*

An Inside Look at Animals (Study Print) *Anatomy, Comparative*

Inside Power Shot (Film Loop—8mm—Silent) *Basketball*

Introducing Geometry (Filmstrip—Sound) *Geometry*

Introducing Graphs (Filmstrip—Sound) *Graphic Methods*

Introducing the Electronic Calculator (Filmstrip—Sound) *Calculating Machines*

Investigating Birds (Filmstrip—Sound) *Birds*

Irish Fairy Tales (Phonodisc or Cassette) *Folklore—Ireland*

Is It Always Right to Be Right? (Motion Picture—16mm—Sound) *Human Relations*

Isaac Bashevis Singer (Filmstrip—Sound) *Singer, Isaac Bashevis*

The Island of the Skog (Filmstrip—Sound) *Mice—Fiction*

Isolation and Function of Auxin (Film Loop—8mm—Silent) *Phototropism*

Israeli Boy: Life on a Kibbutz (Motion Picture—16mm—Sound) *Israel*

It All Depends on You (Motion Picture—16mm—Sound) *Vocational Guidance*

It's about Time (Filmstrip—Sound) *Calendars*

It's Good to Be Me (Filmstrip—Sound) *Emotions*

It's OK for Me: It's OK for You (Filmstrip—Sound) *Emotions*

Jack and the Robber (Motion Picture—16mm—Sound) *Folklore—U.S.*

Jack London Cassette Library (Cassette) *Short Stories*

Jaguar: Mother and Cubs (Film Loop—8mm—Silent) *Jaguars*

James and the Giant Peach (Phonodisc or Cassette) *Fantasy—Fiction*

Jamestown Adventure (Filmstrip—Sound) *U.S.—History—1600–1775—Colonial Period*

Japan: Economic Miracle (Filmstrip—Sound) *Japan*

Madeline and the Gypsies and Other Stories (Phonodisc or Cassette) *France–Stories*

Magic Changes, Set One (Filmstrip–Sound) *Folklore*

Magic Changes, Set Two (Filmstrip–Sound) *Folklore*

The Magic Fishbone (Filmstrip–Sound/ Captioned) *Magic–Fiction*

Magic Rectangle (Motion Picture–16mm– Sound) *Arithmetic*

The Magic Tree (Motion Picture–16mm– Sound) *Folklore–Africa*

Making Words Work (Filmstrip–Sound) *Vocabulary*

Mammals (Film Loop–8mm–Captioned) *Animals–Infancy*

Man and His Environment (Film Loop– 8mm–Silent) *Man–Influence on Nature*

The Many Americans, Unit One (Filmstrip– Sound) *Biculturalism*

The Many Americans, Unit Two (Filmstrip– Sound) *Biculturalism*

Many People, Many Careers (Filmstrip– Sound) *Vocational Guidance*

Marches (Phonodiscs) *Marches*

Market Economy (Filmstrip–Sound) *Consumer Education*

Market Place in Mexico (Motion Picture– 16mm–Sound) *Mexico*

The Martian Chronicles (Phonodiscs) *Science Fiction*

Mary Poppins (Phonodisc or Cassette) *Fantasy–Fiction*

Mary Poppins and the Banks Family (Phonodisc or Cassette) *Fantasy–Fiction*

Mary Poppins: Balloons and Balloons (Phonodisc or Cassette) *Fantasy–Fiction*

Mary Poppins Comes Back (Phonodisc or Cassette) *Fantasy–Fiction*

Mary Poppins from A to Z (Phonodisc or Cassette) *Alphabet Books*

Mary Poppins Opens the Door (Phonodisc or Cassette) *Fantasy–Fiction*

The Mask (Filmstrip–Sound) *Masks (Facial)*

Mastery Story Teller, Set One (Filmstrip– Sound) *Literature–Collections*

Matches (Motion Picture–16mm–Sound) *Safety Education*

Math on Display (Kit) *Mathematics*

Matter (Filmstrip–Sound) *Nuclear Physics*

A Matter of Inconvenience (Motion Picture– 16mm–Sound) *Handicapped–Recreation*

Maurice Sendak's Really Rosie Starring the Nutshell Kids (Motion Picture–16mm– Sound) *Imagination–Fiction*

Measure It (Filmstrip–Sound) *Measurement*

Measurement Comparisons (Filmstrip–Sound) *Size and Shape*

Measurement: From Cubits to Centimeters (Filmstrip–Sound) *Measurement*

Mechanics of Phototropism (Film Loop– 8mm–Captioned) *Phototropism*

Media: Resources for Discovery (Filmstrip– Sound) *Audio-Visual Materials*

Medieval Europe (Filmstrip–Sound) *Middle Ages*

Meet the Builders (Filmstrip–Sound) *Building*

Men Behind the Bright Lights (Kit) *Musicians*

Mesa Verde (Study Print) *Cliff Dwellers and Cliff Dwellings*

Metamorphosis (Motion Picture–16mm– Sound) *Butterflies*

Metric Meets the Inchworm (Motion Picture– 16mm–Sound) *Metric System*

Metric System (Filmstrip–Sound) *Metric System*

The Metric System for the Intermediate Grades, Set One (Filmstrip–Sound) *Metric System*

The Metric System for the Intermediate Grades, Set Two (Filmstrip–Sound) *Metric System*

Metric System of Measurement (Filmstrip– Sound) *Metric System*

The Metric System of Measurement (Filmstrip–Sound) *Metric System*

The Metric System: Unit 1 (Study Print) *Metric System*

The Metric System: Unit 2 (Study Print) *Metric System*

The Metric System: Unit 3 (Study Print) *Metric System*

The Metric Village Measuring Kit: Temperature (Kit) *Metric System*

Mexican Indian Legends (Motion Picture– 16mm–Sound) *Folklore–Mexico*

Mexico: Images and Empires (Filmstrip– Sound) *Mexico*

Mexico in the Twentieth Century (Filmstrip– Sound) *Mexico*

The Middle East: Facing a New World Role (Filmstrip–Sound) *Middle East*

Middle Guard Play (Film Loop–8mm– Silent) *Football*

The Mighty Midgets (Kit) *Automobile Racing*

Mike Fink and Stormalong (Phonodisc or Cassette) *Folklore–U.S.*

Milk: From Farm to You (3rd Edition) (Motion Picture–16mm–Sound) *Dairying*

Minorities–USA (Filmstrip–Sound) *Minorities*

A Miserable Merry Christmas (Motion Picture–16mm–Sound) *Christmas*

The Missing Whistle (Kit) *Children–Fiction*

Model Airplanes (Kit) *Airplanes–Models*

Modern Africa: Land/People/Art (Filmstrip– Sound) *Africa*

Monarch: Story of a Butterfly (Film Loop– 8mm–Silent) *Butterflies*

Money and Time: Adventures of the Lollipop Dragon (Filmstrip–Sound) *Arithmetic*

Money: From Barter to Banking (Filmstrip–Sound) *Money*

Monsters and Other Friendly Creatures (Filmstrip–Sound) *Monsters–Fiction*

Monsters and Other Science Mysteries (Filmstrip–Sound) *Curiosities and Wonders*

Monuments to Erosion (Motion Picture–16mm–Sound) *Erosion*

Moon Basket: An Indian Legend (Filmstrip–Sound) *Indians of North America–Legends*

More Silver Pennies (Phonodisc or Cassette) *Poetry–Collections*

Mother Goose (Phonodisc or Cassette) *Nursery Rhymes*

The Mother Goose Book (Kit) *Nursery Rhymes*

Mother Goose Rhymes and Other Stories (Cassette) *Nursery Rhymes*

Moths–Slide Set (Slides) *Moths*

Motocross Racing (Kit) *Spanish Language–Reading Materials*

Motorcycle Safety (Filmstrip–Sound) *Motorcycles*

The Mountain Gorilla (Kit) *Gorillas*

Mountain Storm (Film Loop–8mm–Silent) *Weather*

Movin' On (Motion Picture–16mm–Sound) *Transportation*

Mowgli and the Wolves (Cassette) *Animals–Fiction*

Mr. Frog Went A-Courting (Motion Picture–16mm–Sound) *Folk Songs–U.S.*

The Mule Who Refused to Budge (Filmstrip–Sound/Captioned) *Cooperation–Fiction*

Museums and Man (Filmstrip–Sound) *Museums*

My Brother Is a Pumpkin (Kit) *Children–Fiction*

My Brother Sam Is Dead (Phonodisc or Cassette) *U.S.–History–1775–1783–Revolution–Fiction*

My Feelings Count (Filmstrip–Captioned) *Emotions*

My Forty Years with Beavers (Filmstrip–Sound) *Beavers*

My Home and Me (Filmstrip–Sound) *U.S.–Geography*

My Parents Are Getting a Divorce (Filmstrip–Sound) *Divorce*

My Senses and Me (Filmstrip–Sound) *Senses and Sensation*

Myself and Me (Filmstrip–Sound) *Self*

Mystery in Dracula's Castle (Cassette) *Mystery and Detective Stories*

Mystery Story (Filmstrip–Sound) *Mystery and Detective Stories*

Native American Heritage (Filmstrip–Sound) *Indians of North America*

Natural Resources, Our Changing Environment (Filmstrip–Sound) *Natural Resources*

Naturally Speaking (Filmstrip–Sound) *Natural History*

Nature All Around Us (Filmstrip–Sound) *Natural History*

Nature All Around Us: A Close-up View (Filmstrip–Sound) *Nature Study*

The Nature of Phototropism (Film Loop–8mm–Captioned) *Phototropism*

Nature Walks (Filmstrip–Captioned) *Natural History*

Navajo Sand Painting Ceremony (Film Loop–8mm–Silent) *Indians of North America–Art*

New Friends from Distant Lands: The Culture We Share (Filmstrip–Sound) *Civilization, Modern*

New Horizons for Women (Filmstrip–Sound) *Women–Employment*

The New Japan (Filmstrip–Sound) *Japan*

The New Oceans (Filmstrip–Sound) *Oceanography*

New Patches for Old (Filmstrip–Sound) *Folklore–Turkey*

Nickels, Dimes and Dollars (Filmstrip–Sound) *Consumer Education*

Night People's Day (Motion Picture–16mm–Sound) *Cities and Towns*

Nightlife (Motion Picture–16mm–Sound) *Ocean*

No, No, Pinocchio (Filmstrip–Sound) *Drug Abuse*

No Such Thing . . . ? (Kit) *Mystery and Detective Stories*

Noisy Nancy Norris (Filmstrip–Sound) *Children–Fiction*

Noses and Toes, Part One and Two (Filmstrip–Sound) *Comparisons*

Not So Easy (Motorcycle Safety) (Motion Picture–16mm–Sound) *Motorcycles*

Numbers: From Notches to Numerals (Filmstrip–Sound) *Counting*

Nutrition for Young People (Filmstrip–Sound) *Nutrition*

Nutrition Unit (Motion Picture–16mm–Sound) *Nutrition*

Observing and Describing Color (Kit) *Color*

Observing and Describing Shape (Kit) *Shape*

The Ocean Is Many Things (Filmstrip–Captioned) *Ocean*

The Oceans: A Key to Our Future (Filmstrip–Sound) *Oceanography*

Octopus (Film Loop–8mm–Silent) *Octopus*

Of Loneliness and Love (Filmstrip–Sound) *Emotions*

Offensive Backs (Film Loop–8mm–Silent) *Football*

Offensive Line Blocking (Film Loop–8mm–Silent) *Football*

The Pied Piper and Other Stories (Phonodisc or Cassette) *Fairy Tales*

Pigs (Film Loop—8mm—Silent) *Pigs*

Pigs and Pirates (Filmstrip—Sound) *Pigs—
Fiction*

Pinocchio (Phonodisc or Cassette) *Puppets—
Fiction*

Pioneer Community (Filmstrip—Sound)
Frontier and Pioneer Life

Pioneer Skills—Slide Set (Slides) *Frontier
and Pioneer Life*

Pippi Longstocking (Phonodisc or Cassette)
Sweden—Fiction

Pitching/Windmill Style/Slingshot Style
(Film Loop—8mm—Silent) *Softball*

Plant a Seed (Motion Picture—16mm—Sound)
Cities and Towns

Plant World (Filmstrip—Sound) *Plants*

Plants (Filmstrip—Sound) *Plants*

Playful Pandas (Motion Picture—16mm—
Sound) *Pandas*

Playing It Safe (Filmstrip—Sound) *Safety
Education*

Playing It Safe with Animals (Filmstrip—
Sound) *Animals—Habits and Behavior*

Playing Safe (Filmstrip—Captioned) *Safety
Education*

The Pledge of Allegiance (Filmstrip—Sound)
Patriotism

A Pocketful of Poetry (Filmstrip—Sound)
Poetry—Collections

Poetry and Me (Filmstrip—Sound) *Children
as Authors*

Poetry By and For Kids (Kit) *Poetry—Collections*

Poetry of the Seasons (Filmstrip—Sound)
Seasons—Poetry

Polar Bear: Mother and Cubs (Film Loop—
8mm—Silent) *Bears*

The Polar Bears and the Seals (Kit) *Mammals*

The Police and the Community (Filmstrip—
Sound) *Police*

The Pony Engine and Other Stories for
Children (Phonodisc or Cassette) *Short
Stories*

Popular Picture Books Filmstrips: Set Three
(Filmstrip—Sound) *Reading Materials*

The Porpoises and the Sailor (Kit) *Porpoises*

Portrait of a Whale (Motion Picture—16mm—
Sound) *Whales*

Positional and Directional Relationships
(Filmstrip—Sound) *Orienteering*

Postural Improvement Activities (Phonodiscs)
Exercise

Pottery Decoration (Film Loop—8mm—
Silent) *Pottery, Indian*

Pottery Firing (Film Loop—8mm—Silent)
Pottery, Indian

Pottery Making (Film Loop—8mm—Silent)
Pottery, Indian

Pouched Animals and their Young (Film
Loop—8mm—Silent) *Animals*

The Prairie Dog Town (Kit) *Prairie Dogs*

Presentando Medidas (Introducing Measuring)
(Filmstrip—Sound) *Measurement*

Presentando Numeros (Introducing Numbers)
(Filmstrip—Sound) *Counting*

Preserving the Environment (Filmstrip—
Sound) *Vocational Guidance*

Pride of Lions (Film Loop—8mm—Silent)
Lions

The Prince and the Pauper (Phonodisc or
Cassette) *Fantasy—Fiction*

Prince Rabbit and Other Stories (Phonodiscs)
Fairy Tales

Private Zoo (Filmstrip—Sound) *Shades and
Shadows—Fiction*

Project Aware (Motion Picture—16mm—
Sound) *Juvenile Delinquency*

PRS, The Pre-Reading Skills Program (Kit)
Reading

Punting (Film Loop—8mm—Silent) *Football*

Puss in Boots and Other Fairy Tales from
Around the World (Phonodisc or Cassette)
Fairy Tales

Putting Electricity to Work (Filmstrip—
Sound) *Vocational Guidance*

Puye Community Houses (Film Loop—8mm—
Silent) *Indians of North America*

Puye De Chelly Cliff Dwellings (Film Loop—
8mm—Silent) *Cliff Dwellers and Cliff
Dwellings*

Queen Zixi of Ix, or the Story of the Magic
Cloak (Phonodisc or Cassette) *Fantasy—
Fiction*

Racing Numbers (Kit) *Automobile Racing*

Railroads West (Filmstrip—Sound) *U.S.—
History—1865-1898*

The Rainy Day Record (Phonodiscs) *Rhythms*

Rattlesnake (Film Loop—8mm—Silent)
Snakes

Reach Out (Motion Picture—16mm—Sound)
Values

Read Along American Indian Legends (Filmstrip—Sound) *Indians of North America—
Legends*

Reading Adventures in Everyday Science,
Series A (Filmstrip—Sound) *Science—
Study and Teaching*

Reading Adventures in Everyday Science,
Series B (Filmstrip—Sound) *Science—
Study and Teaching*

Reading for the Fun of It—Adventure (Filmstrip—Sound) *Literature—Study and Teaching*

Reading for the Fun of It—Fantasy (Filmstrip—Sound) *Literature—Study and Teaching*

Reading for the Fun of It—Historical Fiction
(Filmstrip—Sound) *Literature—Study and
Teaching*

The Secret Hiding Place (Filmstrip—Sound or Captioned) *Hippopotamus—Fiction*

See It and Write (Filmstrip—Sound) *English Language—Composition and Exercises*

Seed Dispersal (Film Loop—8mm—Silent) *Seeds*

Seeds Sprouting (Film Loop—8mm—Silent) *Seeds*

Seeing Alaska (Filmstrip—Sound) *Alaska*

Seeing France (Filmstrip—Sound) *France*

Seeing Greece: Ancient and Modern (Filmstrip—Sound) *Greece*

Seeing the Middle Atlantic States (Filmstrip—Sound) *Atlantic States*

Seeing the Seasons Change (Filmstrip—Sound) *Seasons*

Seeing the South Central States (Filmstrip—Sound) *Southern States*

Seeing . . . through a Lens (Filmstrip—Sound) *Photography*

Self Expression and Conduct (Filmstrip—Sound) *Culture*

Self Planting Seeds (Film Loop—8mm—Silent) *Seeds*

A Sense of Yourself (Filmstrip—Sound) *Senses and Sensation*

Senses and Perception: Links to the Outside World (Motion Picture—16mm—Sound) *Senses and Sensation*

Senses Unit (Motion Picture—16mm—Sound) *Senses and Sensation*

Sensorimotor Training in the Classroom, Vol. One (Phonodisc or Cassette) *Creative Movement*

Sentence Problems Two (Filmstrip—Sound) *English Language—Composition and Exercises*

Serendipity Cassette Books (Kit) *Short Stories*

Series Seven: A Little Lovin' and a Little Laughin' (Filmstrip—Sound) *Short Stories*

Serving the Nation (Filmstrip—Sound) *Vocational Guidance*

Settlers of North America (Filmstrip—Sound) *Frontier and Pioneer Life*

Shapes and Structures in Nature (Filmstrip—Captioned) *Matter*

She Was Nice to Mice (Phonodisc or Cassette) *Elizabeth I, Queen of England—Fiction*

Sheep (Film Loop—8mm—Silent) *Sheep*

Sheepherding (Film Loop—8mm—Silent) *Indians of North America*

She'll Be Comin' 'Round the Mountain (Filmstrip—Sound) *Folksongs—U.S.*

The Shoemaker and the Elves (Motion Picture—16mm—Sound) *Fairy Tales*

Shoplifting, It's a Crime (Motion Picture—16mm—Sound) *Crime*

The Side Show (Motion Picture—16mm—Sound) *Pantomimes*

Sights and Sounds Filmstrips, Set 1 (Filmstrip—Sound) *Reading—Study and Teaching*

Sights and Sounds Filmstrips, Set 2 (Filmstrip—Sound) *Reading—Study and Teaching*

Sights and Sounds Filmstrips, Set 3 (Filmstrip—Sound) *Reading—Study and Teaching*

Sights and Sounds Filmstrips, Set 4 (Filmstrip—Sound) *Reading—Study and Teaching*

Signed Numbers (Filmstrip—Sound) *Arithmetic*

Simple Machines (Filmstrip—Sound) *Machinery*

Sing Down the Moon (Filmstrip—Sound) *Navajo—Fiction*

Singing Games and Folk Dances (Phonodiscs) *Folk Dancing*

Singing Square Dances (Phonodiscs) *Square Dances*

Situational Math Level Two (Filmstrip—Sound) *Arithmetic*

Six Native American Families (Filmstrip—Sound) *Indians of North America*

Skateboard Mania (Kit) *Skateboards*

Skateboard Safety (Motion Picture—16mm—Sound) *Skateboards*

The Snacking Mouse (Filmstrip—Sound) *Nutrition*

Snakes of the Amazon (Film Loop—8mm—Silent) *Snakes*

The Sneetches and Other Stories (Kit) *Stories in Rhyme*

Snow Queen (Phonodisc or Cassette) *Fairy Tales*

The Snow Queen (Cassette) *Fairy Tales*

Snow White and Other Fairy Tales (Phonodisc or Cassette) *Fairy Tales*

Snow White and Rose Red and Other Andrew Lang Fairy Tales (Phonodisc or Cassette) *Fairy Tales*

So Many Words to Choose From (Filmstrip—Sound) *English Language—Study and Teaching*

Social Life (Film Loop—8mm—Captioned) *Frontier and Pioneer Life*

Soil Is Soil . . . Isn't It? (Filmstrip—Sound) *Soils*

Something Special—Work (Filmstrip—Sound) *Work*

Songs and Dances of Switzerland (Phonodiscs) *Folk Dancing, Swiss*

Songs in Motion: Activity Songs and Nursery Rhymes (Phonodisc or Cassette) *Rhythms*

Songstories: I Am Special (Filmstrip—Sound) *Self*

Songstories: What Makes Me the Only Me? (Filmstrip—Sound) *Self*

Sooner Hound and Flying-Jib; Hoss-Mackerel and Bassoon Bobby (Phonodisc or Cassette) *Folklore—U.S.*

Soopergoop (Motion Picture—16mm—Sound) *Advertising*

Sound (Filmstrip—Sound) *Sound*

Tales of Hans Christian Andersen (Filmstrip—Sound) *Fairy Tales*

Talking Encyclopedia of the New American Nation (Cassette) *U.S.—History*

Tarantula (Film Loop—8mm—Silent) *Spiders*

Tchou Tchou (Motion Picture—16mm—Sound) *Fantasy—Fiction*

Technology and Change (Kit) *Technology and Civilization*

Teeka the Otter (Filmstrip—Sound) *Otters*

Ten Tales of Mystery and Terror (Cassette) *Literature—Collections*

There She Blows (Filmstrip—Sound) *Seafaring Life*

There's a New You Comin' for Girls (Filmstrip—Sound) *Girls*

There's Music All Around You (Filmstrip—Sound) *Music—Study and Teaching*

They (Motion Picture—16mm—Sound) *Human Relations*

Think Metric (Filmstrip—Captioned) *Metric System*

This Tiny World (Motion Picture—16mm—Sound) *Toys—History*

Thomas Jefferson (Motion Picture—16mm—Sound) *Jefferson, Thomas*

The Three Poor Tailors (Filmstrip—Sound) *Folklore—Hungary*

The Three Robbers (Motion Picture—16mm—Sound) *Robbers and Outlaws—Fiction*

Threshold Filmstrips, Series C (Kit) *Children's Literature—Collections*

Through the Looking Glass (Phonodiscs) *Fantasy—Fiction*

Throw In (Film Loop—8mm—Silent) *Soccer*

Tiger, Tiger, Burning Bright (Filmstrip—Sound) *Fire Prevention*

Time: From Moons to Microseconds (Filmstrip—Sound) *Time*

A Time of Changes Unit Three (Motion Picture—16mm—Sound) *Occupations*

Time, Space and Matter (Filmstrip—Sound) *Matter*

The Tomten and the Fox (Filmstrip—Sound) *Foxes—Stories*

Too Much of a Good Thing (Filmstrip—Sound) *Nutrition*

The Toy Trumpet (Kit) *Toys—Fiction*

Traffic Watcher (Motion Picture—16mm—Sound) *Safety Education*

Trailblazers of Invention (Filmstrip—Sound) *Inventors*

Transportation of People and Goods (Filmstrip—Sound) *Transportation*

Trapping—Ball in Air (Film Loop—8mm—Silent) *Soccer*

Trapping—Ground Ball (Film Loop—8mm—Silent) *Soccer*

Treasure Island (Cassette) *Pirates—Fiction*

Treasure Island (Filmstrip—Sound) *Pirates—Fiction*

Treasury of Beatrix Potter Stories (Filmstrip—Sound) *Animals—Fiction*

Tree of Truth (Motion Picture—16mm—Sound) *Arithmetic*

The Tree, Second Edition (Motion Picture—16mm—Sound) *Trees*

Troll Talking Picture Dictionary (Kit) *English Language—Dictionaries*

Try Out: Unit One (Motion Picture—16mm—Sound) *Vocational Guidance*

Tschaikovsky: Piano Concerto No. One (Phonodiscs) *Concertos*

Turn Around Jump Shot (Film Loop—8mm—Silent) *Basketball*

Two for Adventure (Kit) *Animals—Fiction*

The Ugly Duckling and the Story of Hans Christian Andersen (Cassette) *Fairy Tales*

Understanding and Using Decimals (Filmstrip—Sound) *Arithmetic*

Understanding and Using Percent (Filmstrip—Sound) *Arithmetic*

Understanding Changes in the Family (Filmstrip—Sound) *Family Life*

Understanding Myself and Others, Unit Three (Filmstrip—Sound) *Individuality*

Understanding Your Feelings (Filmstrip—Sound) *Emotions*

The Underwater Environment, Group One (Filmstrip—Sound) *Marine Animals*

The Underwater Environment, Group Two (Filmstrip—Sound) *Marine Plants*

Upright Loom (Film Loop—8mm—Silent) *Looms*

The Veldt (Filmstrip—Sound) *Science Fiction*

The Velveteen Rabbit (Filmstrip—Sound) *Fantasy—Fiction*

Virginia Hamilton (Filmstrip—Sound) *Hamilton, Virginia*

A Visit to the Father (Filmstrip—Sound) *Indians of North America—Legends*

Visiting Nature One (Filmstrip—Sound) *Ecology*

Visiting Nature Two (Filmstrip—Sound) *Ecology*

Vital Vittles Win the West (Filmstrip—Sound) *Nutrition*

Vocabulary Skills (Filmstrip—Sound) *Vocabulary*

Vocational Skills for Tomorrow (Filmstrip—Sound) *Vocational Guidance*

Volcanoes: Exploring the Restless Earth (Motion Picture—16mm—Sound) *Volcanoes*

The Voyages of Doctor Dolittle (Filmstrip—Sound) *Animals—Fiction*

War Whoops and Medicine Songs (Phonodiscs) *Folk Songs, Indian*

Watch Out (Filmstrip—Sound) *Safety Education*

Watching Artists at Work (Filmstrip—Sound) *Art—Technique*

Water and How We Use It (Filmstrip—Sound)
Water Supply

We Love Animals (Kit) *Pets*

Weather Forecasting (Motion Picture—
16mm—Sound) *Weather Forecasting*

Weather, Seasons and Climate (Filmstrip—
Sound) *Meteorology*

West African Artists and their Art (Filmstrip—
Sound) *Art, African*

Western Europe, Group One (Filmstrip—
Sound) *Europe*

Western Europe, Group Two (Filmstrip—
Sound) *Europe*

Whales Surfacing (Film Loop—8mm—Silent)
Whales

What Are Ecosystems? (Filmstrip—Sound)
Ecology

What Are You Going to Do about Alcohol
(Filmstrip—Sound) *Alcohol*

What Do You Do While You Wait? (Motion
Picture—16mm—Sound) *Human Behavior*

What Do You See? (Filmstrip—Captioned)
Senses and Sensations

What Do You Think? (Filmstrip—Sound)
Ethics

What Do You Think? Unit One (Motion
Picture—16mm—Sound) *Occupations*

What If a Crisis Hits Your Family? (Filmstrip—Sound) *Family Life*

What Is a Community? (Filmstrip—Sound)
Community Life

What Is a Handicap? (Filmstrip—Sound)
Handicapped Children

What Is Ecology? (Film Loop—8mm—
Captioned) *Ecology*

What Is It? (Filmstrip—Captioned) *Perception*

What Makes Rain? (Motion Picture—16mm—
Sound) *Rain and Rainfall*

Whatever Happened to Linda? (Filmstrip—
Sound) *Safety Education*

What's Out There? (Filmstrip—Captioned)
Astronomy

What's the Limit? Unit Two (Motion Picture—
16mm—Sound) *Occupations*

Whazzat? (Motion Picture—16mm—Sound)
Folklore—India

When I Grow Up I Can Be (Filmstrip—Sound)
Vocational Guidance

Where Does It Come From? (Filmstrip—
Sound) *Manufactures*

Where Is Dead? (Motion Picture—16mm—
Sound) *Death*

Where Is It? (Filmstrip—Captioned) *Language
Arts*

Where People Work (Filmstrip—Sound)
Occupations

Who Are You? (Filmstrip—Sound) *Self
Perception*

Who Are You? (Motion Picture—16mm—
Sound) *Self Perception*

Who Helps Us? (Filmstrip—Sound) *Community life*

Who Stole the Quiet Day? (Motion Picture—
16mm—Sound) *Noise Pollution*

Who Works for You? (Kit) *Vocational
Guidance*

Who's Afraid of the Big Bad Wolf? (Filmstrip—Sound) *Safety Education*

Who's Running the Show? (Filmstrip—Sound)
Leadership

Who's Who in the Zoo? (Motion Picture—
16mm—Sound) *Zoological Gardens*

Whose Mouse Are You? (Filmstrip—Sound)
Mice—Fiction

Why Am I Studying This? (Filmstrip—Sound)
Educational Guidance

Why Animals Live Where They Do (Filmstrip—Sound) *Animals—Habitations*

Why Cultures Are Different (Filmstrip—
Sound) *Culture*

Why Mosquitoes Buzz in People's Ears (Kit)
Animals—Fiction

Why Mothers Work (Motion Picture—16mm—
Sound) *Women—Employment*

Why Noah Chose the Dove (Filmstrip—Sound)
Bible Stories

Why We Work (Filmstrip—Sound) *Work*

The Wild Young Desert Series (Filmstrip—
Sound) *Deserts*

Wildlife Stories (Filmstrip—Sound) *Animals*

William H. Armstrong (Filmstrip—Sound)
Armstrong, William

Will's Quill (Filmstrip—Sound) *Geese—Fiction*

The Wind in the Willows (Phonodisc or Cassette) *Animals—Fiction*

Winnie the Pooh (Phonodiscs) *Animals—
Fiction*

Winning and Losing (Filmstrip—Sound)
Human Behavior

Winter in the Forest (Filmstrip—Sound)
Winter

Winter on an Indian Reservation (Motion
Picture—16mm—Sound) *Indians of North
America*

Wizard of Oz (Cassette) *Fantasy—Fiction*

The Wizard (Motion Picture—16mm—Sound)
Magic—Fiction

Wolf Family (Film Loop—8mm—Silent)
Wolves

The Wolves of Isle Royale (Kit) *Wolves*

Women: An American History (Filmstrip—
Sound) *Women—U.S.*

Women in American History (Filmstrip—
Sound) *Women—U.S.*

Women Who Win, Set 1 (Kit) *Athletes*

Women Who Win, Set 2 (Kit) *Athletes*

Women Who Win, Set 3 (Kit) *Athletes*

Women Who Win, Set 4 (Kit) *Athletes*

Wool into Clothing (Film Loop—8mm—
Captioned) *Frontier and Pioneer Life*

PRODUCER/ DISTRIBUTOR DIRECTORY

Where it is known that the producer differs from the distributor, both names are given in the entry. One source in the entry assumes that the producer/distributor is the same. In some cases, it was not possible to obtain addresses for producer/distributor and "no address available" is indicated.

ACI MEDIA, INC.
see Paramount Communications

AIDS
110 Old Town House Rd.
South Yarmouth, MA 02664

AIMS INSTRUCTIONAL MEDIA SERVICE
626 Justin Ave.
Glendale, CA 91201

ACORN FILMS, INC
33 Union Sq. W.
New York, NY 10003

ACTIVITY RECORDS
see Educational Activities, Inc.

ADRIAN VANCE PRODUCTIONS, INC.
Box 46456
Hollywood, CA 90046

AESOP FILMS, INC.
3701 Buchanan St.
San Francisco, CA 94123

ALFRED HIGGINS PRODUCTIONS, INC.
9100 Sunset Blvd.
Los Angeles, CA 90064

ARGO RECORDS, INC.
539 W. 25 St.
New York, NY 10001

ASSOCIATED EDUCATIONAL MA-
TERIALS COMPANY
14 Glenwood Ave.
Box 2087
Raleigh, NC 27602

ASSOCIATED PRESS
see Pathescope Educational Media, Inc.

ATHLETIC INSTITUTE
200 Castlewood Dr.
North Palm Beach, FL 33408

ATLANTIC RECORDS, INC.
(no address available)

ATLANTIS PRODUCTIONS, INC.
1252 La Granada Dr.
Thousand Oaks, CA 91360

AUDIO VISUAL ASSOCIATES, INC.
180 E. California Blvd.
Pasadena, CA 91105

AUDIOVISUAL INSTRUCTIONAL DE-
VICES INC.
see AIDS

BFA EDUCATIONAL MEDIA
Box 1795
2211 Michigan Ave.
Santa Monica, CA 90406

BAILEY FILM ASSOCIATES
see BFA Educational Media

BARR FILMS
Box 5667
Pasadena, CA 91107

BENCHMARK FILMS, INC.
145 Scarborough Rd.
Briarcliff Manor, NY 10510

BENDICK ASSOCIATES, INC.
360 Grace Church St.
Rye, NY 10580

BOSUSTOW PRODUCTIONS
Stephen Bosustow
1649 11 St.
Santa Monica, CA 90404

BOWMAR PUBLISHING CORP.
4563 Colorado Blvd.
Los Angeles, CA 90039

BURT MUNK AND COMPANY
56 E. Walton Pl.
Chicago, IL 60611

CMS RECORDS
14 Warren St.
New York, NY 10007

CAEDMON RECORDS, INC.
505 Eighth Ave.
New York, NY 10018

CAL INDUSTRIES, INC.
76 Madison Ave.
New York, NY 10016

CENTRON FILMS
1621 W. Ninth St.
Box 687
Lawrence, KS 66044

CHILDREN'S CLASSICS ON TAPE
6722 Bostwick Dr.
Springfield, VA 22151

CHILDREN'S PRESS
1224 W. Van Buren St.
Chicago, IL 60607

CHURCHILL FILMS
662 N. Robertson Blvd.
Los Angeles, CA 90069

CLEARVUE, INC.
6666 N. Oliphant
Chicago, IL 60631

KENNETH E. CLOUSE
333 Quail Hollow Rd.
Felton, CA 95018

COLUMBIA RECORDS (SPECIAL PROD-
UCTS)
51 W. 52 St.
New York, NY 10019

COMMUNICATIONS GROUP WEST
6066 Sunset Blvd.
Hollywood, CA 90028

CONCEPT MEDIA, INC.
Box 19542
Irvine, CA 92714

CONTEMPORARY DRAMA SERVICE
Box 457
Downers Grove, IL 60515

CORONET INSTRUCTIONAL MEDIA
65 E. South Water St.
Chicago, IL 60601

JEAN-MICHEL COUSTEAU
see BFA Educational Media

CURRENT AFFAIRS FILMS
24 Danbury Rd.
Wilton, CT 06897

DAVCO PUBLISHERS, INC.
8154 Ridgeway
Skokie, IL 60073

DAVE BELL ASSOCIATES, INC.
3211 Cahuenga Blvd. W.
Los Angeles, CA 90038

DENOYER-GEPPERT
5235 Ravenswood Ave.
Chicago, IL 60640

DEUTSCHE GRAMMOPHON
(no address available)

DISNEY, WALT
see Walt Disney Educational Media Co.

DONARS PRODUCTIONS
Box 24
Loveland, CO 80537

EBEC
see Encyclopaedia Britannica Educational
    Corporation

EMC CORP.
180 W. Sixth St.
St. Paul, MN 55101

EDUCATIONAL ACTIVITIES, INC.
Box 392
Freeport, NY 11520

EDUCATIONAL AUDIO VISUAL, INC.
17 Marble Ave.
Pleasantville, NY 10570

EDUCATIONAL DESIGN, INC.
47 W. 13 St.
New York, NY 10011

EDUCATIONAL DEVELOPMENT CORP.
202 Lake Miriam Dr.
Lakeland, FL 33803

EDUCATIONAL DIMENSIONS GROUP
Box 126
Stamford, CT 06904

EDUCATIONAL DIRECTION, INC.
181 W. State St.
Westport, CT 06880

EDUCATIONAL ENRICHMENT
  MATERIALS
110 S. Bedford Rd.
Mt. Kisco, NY 10549

EDUCATIONAL RECORDS, INC.
157 Chambers St.
New York, NY 10007

ENCYCLOPAEDIA BRITANNICA EDU-
CATIONAL CORPORATION
425 N. Michigan Ave.
Chicago, IL 60611

EYE GATE MEDIA
146-01 Archer Ave.
Jamaica, NY 11435

FARMHOUSE FILMS
National Safety Council
425 N. Michigan Ave.
Chicago, IL 60611

FENWICK PRODUCTIONS, INC.
134 Steele Rd.
West Hartford, CT 06119

FILM COMMUNICATORS
11136 Weddington St.
North Hollywood, CA 91601

FILM POLSKI
see Encyclopaedia Britannica Educational
Corporation

FILMFAIR COMMUNICATIONS
10820 Ventura Blvd.
Studio City, CA 91604

FILMS, INC.
1144 Wilmette Ave.
Wilmette, IL 60091

FILMSTRIP HOUSE
432 Park Ave. S.
New York, NY 10016

FLIGHT PLAN I
see Encyclopaedia Britannica Educational
Corporation

FOLKWAYS RECORDS
43 W. 63 St.
New York, NY 10023

FRANKLIN WATTS, INC.
730 Fifth Ave.
New York, NY 10019

GAKKEN CO., LTD
Tokyo, Japan

GLOBE FILMSTRIPS, INC.
175 Fifth Ave.
New York, NY 10010

GREAT AMERICAN FILM FACTORY,
INC.
Box 9195
Sacramento, CA 95816

GUIDANCE ASSOCIATES
757 Third Ave.
New York, NY 10017

HBJ FILMS
see Harcourt Brace Jovanovich, Inc.

HANDEL FILM CORPORATION
8730 Sunset Blvd.
Los Angeles, CA 90069

HARCOURT BRACE JOVANOVICH,
INC.
757 Third Ave.
New York, NY 10017

HARPER & ROW PUBLISHERS, INC.
10 E. 53 St.
New York, NY 10022

HAWKHILL ASSOCIATES, INC.
125 Gilman St.
Madison, WI 53703

HERITAGE PRODUCTIONS, INC.
1437 Central Ave.
Memphis, TN 38104

HUMAN RELATIONS MEDIA CENTER
39 Washington Ave.
Pleasantville, NY 10570

IFB
see International Film Bureau, Inc.

IHS ASSOCIATES, INC.
see Film Communicators

IMPERIAL EDUCATIONAL RESOURCES,
INC.
202 Lake Miriam Dr.
Lakeland, FL 33803

IMPERIAL INTERNATIONAL LEARNING,
INC.
Box 548
Kankakee, IL 60901

INSIGHT! INC.
100 E. Ohio St.
Chicago, IL 60611

INSIGHT MEDIA PROGRAMS, INC.
13900 Panay Way M-120
Marina del Rey, CA 90291

INSTRUCTIONAL MATERIALS LABO-
RATORIES
200 Madison Ave.
New York, NY 10016

INTERNATIONAL FILM BUREAU, INC.
332 S. Michigan Ave.
Chicago, IL 60604

JABBERWOCKY CASSETTE CLASSICS
Box 6727
San Francisco, CA 94101

JAM HANDY
see Prentice-Hall Media

JANUARY PRODUCTIONS
13-00 Plaza Rd.
Fair Lawn, NY 07410

JOSHUA TREE PRODUCTIONS
see Bosustow Productions

KNOWLEDGE AID
see United Learning

LEARNING CORPORATION OF AMERICA
1350 Ave. of the Americas
New York, NY 10019

LEARNING TREE FILMSTRIPS
Box 1590
Dept. 75
Boulder, CO 80306

LEXINGTON RECORDING COMPANY,
   INC.
29 Marble Ave.
Pleasantville, NY 10570

LIBRARY FILMSTRIP CENTER
3033 Aloma
Wichita, KS 67211

LISTENING LIBRARY, INC.
One Park Ave.
Old Greenwich, CT 06870

LITTLE RED FILMHOUSE
119 S. Kilkea Dr.
Los Angeles, CA 90048

LYCEUM
546 Hofgaarden St.
La Puente, CA 91744

MCGRAW-HILL FILMS
Dept. 423
1221 Ave. of the Americas
New York, NY 10020

MACMILLAN LIBRARY SERVICES
Div. Macmillan Pub. Co., Inc.
866 Third Ave.
New York, NY 10022

MARSHFILM, INC.
Box 8082
Shawnee Mission, KS 66208

MEDIA PLUS, INC.
60 Riverside Dr.
New York, NY 10024

MEDIA RESEARCH AND DEVELOPMENT
Arizona State University
Tempe, AZ 85281

MILLER-BRODY PRODUCTIONS, INC.
Dept. 78
342 Madison Ave.
New York, NY 10017

MOOK & BLANCHARD
546 S. Hofgaarden St.
La Puente, CA 91744

MORTON SCHINDEL
see Weston Woods Studios

MULTI-MEDIA PRODUCTIONS, INC.
Box 5097
Stanford, CA 94305

NATIONAL FILM BOARD OF CANADA
680 Fifth Ave.
New York, NY 10019

NATIONAL GEOGRAPHIC
see National Geographic Educational Services

NATIONAL GEOGRAPHIC EDUCATIONAL
   SERVICES
Dept. 77
Box 1640
Washington, DC 20013

NICK BOSUSTOW
see Bosustow Productions

NORCLIFF THAYER, INC.
One Scarsdale Rd.
Tuckahoe, NY 10707

NYSTROM
3333 Elston Ave.
Chicago, IL 60618

PARAMOUNT COMMUNICATIONS
5451 Marathon St.
Hollywood, CA 90038

PARATORE PICTURES
see Random House, Inc.

PATHESCOPE EDUCATIONAL MEDIA,
   INC.
71 Weyman Ave.
New Rochelle, NY 10802

PATHWAYS OF SOUND, INC.
102 Mt. Auburn St.
Cambridge, MA 02138

LEONARD PECK PRODUCTIONS
Box 3235
Wayne, NY 07470

PERENNIAL FILMS
477 Roger Williams
Highland Park, IL 60035

PERFECTION FORM COMPANY
1000 N. Second Ave.
Logan, IA 51546

PHILIPS RECORDS, INC.
(no address available)

PHOENIX FILMS, INC.
470 Park Ave. S.
New York, NY 10016

PIED PIPER PRODUCTIONS
Box 320
Verdugo City, CA 91406

THE POLISHED APPLE
3742 Seahorn Dr.
Malibu, CA 90265

PRENTICE-HALL MEDIA
150 White Plains Rd.
Tarrytown, NY 10591

PRIMA EDUCATION PRODUCTS, INC.
Irvington-on-Hudson
New York, NY 10533

PYRAMID FILMS
Box 1048
Santa Monica, CA 90406

Q-ED PRODUCTIONS, INC.
Box 1608
Burbank, CA 91507

RCA EDUCATIONAL DEPT.
Box RCA-1000
Indianapolis, IN 46291

RAMSGATE FILMS, INC.
704 Santa Monica Blvd.
Santa Monica, CA 90401

RANDOM HOUSE, INC.
Dept. V-8
400 Hahn Rd.
Westminster, MD 21157

ROUNDER RECORDS
(no address available)

S-L FILM PRODUCTIONS, INC.
Box 41108
Los Angeles, CA 90041

SCHLOAT
see Prentice-Hall Media

SCHOLASTIC BOOK SERVICES
904 Sylvan Ave.
Englewood Cliffs, NJ 07632

SCIENCE RESEARCH ASSOCIATES, INC.
259 Erie
Chicago, IL 60611

SCOTT EDUCATION DIVISION
see Prentice-Hall Media

SHOREWOOD REPRODUCTIONS, INC.
10 E. 53 St.
New York, NY 10020

SMALL WORLD PRODUCTIONS, INC.
Pomfret Center, CT 06259

SOCIETY FOR VISUAL EDUCATION, INC.
1345 Diversey Pkwy.
Chicago, IL 60614

SOUNDWORDS
56-11 217 St.
Bayside, NY 11364

SPECTRA FILMS
see Random House, Inc.

SPOKEN ARTS, INC.
310 N. Ave.
New Rochelle, NY 10801

STANFIELD HOUSE
900 Euclid Ave.
Santa Monica, CA 90403

STANTON FILMS, INC.
7943 Santa Monica Blvd.
Los Angeles, CA 90046

STEPHEN BOSUSTOW PRODUCTIONS
see Bosustow Productions

SUNBURST COMMUNICATIONS, INC.
Pound Ridge, NY 10576

SUTHERLAND LEARNING ASSOCIATES,
INC.
see Encyclopaedia Britannica Educational
Corporation

TEACHING RESOURCES FILMS, INC.
Station Plaza
Bedford Hills, NY 10507

TELE-VISUAL PRODUCTIONS, INC.
3377-3379 S. W. Third Ave.
Miami, FL 33143

TEXTURE FILMS, INC.
1600 Broadway
New York, NY 10019

THORNE FILMS, INC.
see Prentice-Hall Media

TRANSMEDIA INTERNATIONAL, INC.
1100 17 St. N. W.
Suite 1000
Washington, DC 20036

TROLL ASSOCIATES
320 Rte. 17
Mahwah, NJ 07430

UNIT ONE FILM PRODUCTIONS
423 W. 118 St.
New York, NY 10027

UNITED LEARNING
6633 W. Howard St.
Niles, IL 60648

UNIVERSITY FILMS
see McGraw-Hill Films

UNIVERSITY OF WISCONSIN R & D
CENTER FOR COGNITIVE DEVEL-
OPMENT
see Encyclopaedia Britannica Educational
Corporation

URBAN MEDIA MATERIALS
212 Mineola Ave.
Roselyn Heights, NY 11577

VIEWLEX EDUCATIONAL MEDIA
Broadway Ave.
Holbrook, NY 11741

VIKING PRESS
625 Madison Ave.
New York, NY 10022

VISUAL EDUCATION CORP.
Box 2321
Princeton, NJ 08540

VISUAL PUBLICATIONS
716 Center St.
Lewiston, NY 14092

WNET/13 (GLENN JORDAN) EDUCA-
TIONAL BROADCASTING
356 W. 58 St.
New York, NY 10019

WNVT (NORTHERN VIRGINIA EDUCA-
TIONAL TV)
8325 Little River Turnpike
Annandale, VA 22003

WALT DISNEY EDUCATIONAL MEDIA CO.
500 S. Buena Vista St.
Burbank, CA 91521

WARNER EDUCATIONAL PRODUCTIONS
Box 8791
Fountain Valley, CA 92708

WARREN SCHLOAT PRODUCTIONS
see Prentice-Hall Media

WATTS, FRANKLIN
see Franklin Watts, Inc.

WESTON WOODS STUDIOS
Weston, CT 06883

H. WILSON CORP.
555 W. Taft Dr.
South Holland, IL 60473

WINDMILLS LTD. PRODUCTIONS
Box 5300
Santa Monica, CA 90405

XEROX EDUCATIONAL PUBLICATIONS
1250 Fairwood Ave.
Box 444
Columbus, OH 43216